Diplomacy in a Globalizing World

Diplomacy in a Globalizing World

Theories and Practices

Edited by

PAULINE KERR
The Australian National University

GEOFFREY WISEMAN
University of Southern California

New York   Oxford
OXFORD UNIVERSITY PRESS

Oxford University Press is a department of the University of Oxford. It furthers
the University's objective of excellence in research, scholarship, and education by publishing
worldwide.

Oxford   New York
Auckland   Cape Town   Dar es Salaam   Hong Kong   Karachi
Kuala Lumpur   Madrid   Melbourne   Mexico City   Nairobi
New Delhi   Shanghai   Taipei   Toronto

With offices in
Argentina   Austria   Brazil   Chile   Czech Republic   France   Greece
Guatemala   Hungary   Italy   Japan   Poland   Portugal   Singapore
South Korea   Switzerland   Thailand   Turkey   Ukraine   Vietnam

For titles covered by Section 112 of the U.S. Higher Education Opportunity
Act, please visit www.oup.com/us/he for the latest information about
pricing and alternate formats.

Published by Oxford University Press.
198 Madison Avenue, New York, New York 10016
www.oup.com

Library of Congress Cataloging-in-Publication Data
Diplomacy in a globalizing world: theories and practices /
[edited by] Pauline Kerr, Geoffrey Wiseman.
   p. cm.
ISBN 978-0-19-976448-8 (pbk.)
1. Diplomacy.   2. Diplomats—Effect of technological innovations on.
3. Globalization.   I. Kerr, Pauline, 1945–   II. Wiseman, Geoffrey.
JZ1305.D5442 2012
327.101—dc23
                                          2012018912

With love to Jimi and Daisy, Brady and Dylan

BRIEF CONTENTS

CONTENTS

PREFACE

Like many of our colleagues, we found that when preparing our undergraduate and graduate courses on diplomacy we could not find sufficient sources that fully captured the evolutionary and contemporary nature of diplomacy. Despite many fine scholarly works, something was still missing. We needed a book that was contemporary, comprehensive, comparative, cutting-edge, and written by a diverse group of scholars from around the world. Oxford University Press in New York, and particularly Jennifer Carpenter, the Executive Editor, believed our book proposal identified that gap in the existing literature. So too did the academic reviewers of both the proposal and the first draft of the book, who enthusiastically endorsed the project and gave sage advice: Dave Benjamin, University of Bridgeport; Renato Corbetta, University of Alabama at Birmingham; Bruce Cronin, City College of New York; Bruce Gregory, George Washington University, Georgetown University, and U.S. Naval War College; Paul Webster Hare, Boston University; Vladimir Matic, Clemson University; Agnes Simon; University of Missouri; Brent Strathman, Dartmouth College; and Timothy Wedig, University of Illinois at Urbana-Champaign. The result, some two years later, is *Diplomacy in a Globalizing World: Theories and Practices*.

We think we have largely fulfilled our vision. We were fortunate. Invitations to very busy scholars were accepted in quick time, although the onerous intellectual and pedagogical tasks and the limited word length were commented upon! We asked our authors to write on their area of expertise in a way that was contemporary, comprehensive, comparative, and based on the latest research. The questions we sought their answers to were "how is diplomacy changing, why, and with what implications for future theories and practices?" They tackled the questions throughout the four parts of the book: in part I on diplomacy's historical evolution; in part II on contemporary concepts and theories; in part III on contemporary diplomacy's structures, processes, and instruments; and in part IV on today's national, regional, and international practices.

We consider that the analyses in the book's four parts, combined with the pedagogical tools, in each chapter and particularly in the extensive companion websites for students and instructors, contribute in a unique way to students' understanding the debates about the nature of diplomacy in our globalizing and electronically mediated world. Finally, the book confirms our normative belief that diplomacy should be, as Martin Wight (1979: 113) observed, "the master-institution of international relations" if our children are to live in sustainable peace and prosperity.

ACKNOWLEDGMENTS

Producing a book like this one can only succeed with a team of dedicated people working together over a long period. We had that privilege.

Jennifer Carpenter and Maegan Sherlock at Oxford University Press were unfailingly professional and engaging colleagues from start to finish. Mary-Louise Hickey, Publications Editor at the Australian National University (ANU), patiently guided us through a maze of editorial issues and prepared the manuscript for publication with splendid efficiency. The authors of each chapter inspired us with their zest for the project, their wisdom, and insights on their respective areas of research. The reviewers of both the original proposal and the first draft of the book were equally enthusiastic and also extraordinarily generous with their ideas for making the book the best available for students. The Asia-Pacific College of Diplomacy (APCD) at the ANU provided financial support for the book's production. Scot MacDonald was of great assistance in preparing the companion website, and Landry Doyle in providing research assistance. Andrea Haese from APCD was consistently supportive, as was Linda Cole at the University of Southern California's School of International Relations. Last but certainly not least, our families tolerated weekends without company and responded to our pleas for time with something akin to sainthood.

We are endlessly grateful to you all.

Pauline Kerr and Geoffrey Wiseman
The Australian National University and
University of Southern California
May 2012

ABBREVIATIONS

ABAC	APEC Business Advisory Council
ACC	Arab Cooperation Council
ADB	Asian Development Bank
ALADI	South American Integration Association
APEC	Asia-Pacific Economic Cooperation
APP	Asia-Pacific Partnership on Clean Development and Climate
ARF	ASEAN Regional Forum
ASEAN	Association of Southeast Asian Nations
ASEAN+3	ASEAN plus China, Japan, and South Korea
ASEAN-ISIS	ASEAN Institutes of Strategic and International Studies
AU	African Union
BP	British Petroleum
BRICs	Brazil, Russia, India, and China
BSEC	Black Sea Economic Cooperation
CACM	Central American Common Market
CAN	Andean Community
CARICOM	Caribbean Community
CCP	Chinese Communist Party
CDG	Chicken Dilemma Game
CEMAC	Central African Monetary and Economic Community
CEN-SAD	Community of Sahel-Saharan States
CEO	chief executive officer
CEPGL	Economic Community of the Great Lakes Countries
CIA	Central Intelligence Agency
CIS	Commonwealth of Independent States
COMESA	Common Market for Eastern and Southern Africa
COMINT	communications intelligence
COP	Conference of the Parties
CSCAP	Council for Security Cooperation in the Asia-Pacific
DDA	Doha Development Agenda

DFID	Department for International Development
DNS	Domain Name System
DPI	Department of Public Information
EABC	East Asian Business Council
EAC	East African Community
EAEC	Eurasian Economic Community
EAS	East Asia Summit
EC	European Communities
ECCAS	Economic Community of Central African States
ECO	Economic Cooperation Organisation
ECOSOC	Economic and Social Council
ECOWAS	Economic Community of West African States
EEAS	European External Action Service
EEC	European Economic Community
ELINT	electronic intelligence
ELN	National Liberation Army, Colombia
ENGO	environmental nongovernmental organization
ERIA	Economic Research Institute for ASEAN and East Asia
EU	European Union
FARC	Revolutionary Armed Forces of Colombia
FCO	Foreign and Commonwealth Office, United Kingdom
FSO	Foreign Service Officer
FTA	free trade agreement
FTAA	Free Trade Area of the Americas
G6	Group of Six
G7	Group of Seven
G8	Group of Eight
G20	Group of Twenty
GATT	General Agreement on Tariffs and Trade
GCC	Gulf Cooperation Council
GDP	gross domestic product
HUMINT	human intelligence
ICANN	Internet Corporation for Assigned Names and Numbers
ICC	International Criminal Court
ICJ	International Court of Justice
ICT	information and communication technology
IGAD	Intergovernmental Authority for Development
IGF	Internet Governance Forum
IGO	intergovernmental organization
ILO	International Labour Organization
IMF	International Monetary Fund
IP	Internet protocol
ISAF	International Security Assistance Force
ITU	International Telecommunication Union
LTTE	Liberation Tigers of Tamil Eelam
MAD	mutual assured destruction

MAI	Multilateral Agreement on Investment
MASINT	measurement and signature intelligence
MEO	mutually enticing opportunity
Mercosur	Common Market of the South
MFA	ministry of foreign affairs
MHS	mutually hurting stalemate
MOFA	Ministry of Foreign Affairs, China
NAFTA	North American Free Trade Agreement
NATO	North Atlantic Treaty Organization
NDS	national diplomatic system
NEAT	Network of East Asian Think Tanks
NGO	nongovernmental organization
NPC	National People's Congress
NPT	Nuclear Non-Proliferation Treaty
NSS	National Security Strategy
OECD	Organisation for Economic Co-operation and Development
OPEC	Organization of the Petroleum Exporting Countries
OSCE	Organization for Security and Co-operation in Europe
OSINT	open source intelligence
P5	five permanent members
PAFTAD	Pacific Trade and Development
PBEC	Pacific Basin Economic Council
PDG	Prisoners' Dilemma Game
PECC	Pacific Economic Cooperation Council
PRC	People's Republic of China
Quango	Quasi-nongovernmental organization
R2P	Responsibility to Protect
RENAMO	Mozambican National Resistance Movement
ROC	Republic of China
RUF	Revolutionary United Front, Sierra Leone
SAARC	South Asian Association for Regional Cooperation
SACU	Southern African Customs Union
SADC	Southern African Development Community
SCO	Shanghai Cooperation Organisation
SDI	Strategic Defense Initiative
SICA	Central American Integration System
SIGINT	signals intelligence
TECHINT	technical intelligence
TEMM	Tripartite Environmental Ministers' Meeting
UK	United Kingdom
UMA	Arab Maghreb Union
UN	United Nations
UNASUL	South American Community of Nations
UNHCR	UN High Commissioner for Refugees
UNITA	National Union for the Total Independence of Angola
USAID	US Agency for International Development

USIA	United States Information Agency
USIS	United States Information Service
WAEMU	Western African Economic and Monetary Union
WiFi	wireless technology
WMD	weapons of mass destruction
WO	way out
WSIS	World Summit on the Information Society
WTO	World Trade Organization

ABOUT THE CONTRIBUTORS

Bertrand Badie is Professor at Sciences Po Paris, where he is in charge of the Graduate Program in International Relations.

Soumita Basu is Assistant Professor of International Relations at the South Asian University, New Delhi.

Jozef Bátora is Associate Professor and Director at the Institute of European Studies and International Relations, Comenius University in Bratislava, Slovakia.

Raymond Cohen is Emeritus Professor of International Relations at the Hebrew University of Jerusalem.

Alan Hardacre is Lecturer in the European Decision-Making Unit at the European Institute for Public Administration in Maastricht, the Netherlands.

Alan K. Henrikson is Lee E. Dirks Professor of Diplomatic History and Director of Diplomatic Studies at the Fletcher School of Law and Diplomacy, Tufts University, and Fulbright-

Schuman Chair in US-EU Relations at the College of Europe in Bruges, Belgium (2010–11).

Brian Hocking is Emeritus Professor of International Relations, Loughborough University, UK, and Visiting Research Fellow at the Clingendael Institute, The Hague.

Pauline Kerr is Fellow and Director of Studies at the Asia-Pacific College of Diplomacy at The Australian National University, Canberra.

Jovan Kurbalija is the Founding Director of DiploFoundation, Geneva, and Visiting Professor at the College of Europe in Bruges, Belgium.

Halvard Leira is Senior Research Fellow at the Norwegian Institute of International Affairs, Oslo.

Jan Melissen is Director of Research at the Netherlands Institute of International Relations Clingendael, The Hague, and Professor of Diplomacy at the University of Antwerp, Belgium.

Iver B. Neumann is Director of Research at the Norwegian Institute of International Affairs, Oslo.

Geoffrey Allen Pigman is Fellow in the Department of Political Sciences, University of Pretoria, and Visiting Research Fellow, Centre for Global Change and Governance, Rutgers University, Newark.

Zhang Qingmin is Professor in the School of International Studies at Peking University.

Paul Sharp is Professor of Political Science at the University of Minnesota, Duluth.

Jennifer E. Sims is Visiting Professor, Security Studies Program, School of Foreign Service, Georgetown University.

Brendan Taylor is Head of the Strategic and Defence Studies Centre, College of Asia and the Pacific at The Australian National University, Canberra.

Geoffrey Wiseman is Professor of the Practice of International Relations,

and University Fellow in the Center on Public Diplomacy at the University of Southern California, Los Angeles.

Stephen Woolcock is Lecturer in International Relations at the London School of Economics and Head of the LSE's International Trade Policy Unit.

Thomas Wright is a fellow with the Managing Global Order project at the Brookings Institution, Washington, DC.

I. William Zartman is the Jacob Blaustein Professor Emeritus at the School of Advanced International Studies at the Johns Hopkins University in Washington, DC.

Suisheng Zhao is Professor and Executive Director of the Center for China-US Cooperation at the Josef Korbel School of International Studies, University of Denver.

Ye Zicheng is Professor and Chair of the Department of Diplomatic Studies in the School of International Studies at Peking University.

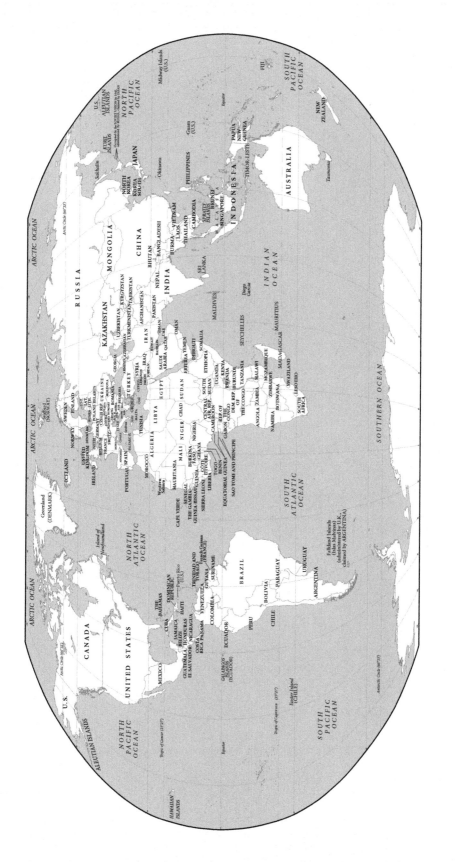

Diplomacy in a Globalizing World

INTRODUCTION

Pauline Kerr and Geoffrey Wiseman

CHAPTER CONTENTS

- The diplomacy puzzle
- Historical background, contemporary trends, and challenges for diplomacy
- The book's structure, chapter summaries, and pedagogical features

THE DIPLOMACY PUZZLE

Diplomacy is changing, that much we know. Exactly how, why, and with what implications for future theories and practices of diplomacy, is puzzling. In this book, twenty-three diplomacy scholars present their recent research to help students grapple with the "diplomacy puzzle."[1] Their arguments and findings provide fascinating insights into contemporary diplomacy and its likely future.

A good starting point for an inquiry into the changing nature of diplomacy is to reflect on how it is understood by most people. For the majority, the *Oxford English Dictionary* (1933: 385–86) definition that diplomacy is "the management of international relations by negotiation; the methods by which these relations are adjusted and managed by ambassadors and envoys" probably suffices. The release by WikiLeaks during 2010–11 of **diplomatic cables** sent from US **missions** to the US Department of State, however, would perhaps surprise those who hold images of **ambassadors** and **envoys** as unfailingly tactful and articulate professionals making the case for world peace, and with a distaste for the dark and warlike side of world politics.

Behind such popular perceptions of diplomacy and diplomats there is, however, a much more complex and fascinating story to tell about the evolution of diplomacy. A story that began thousands of years ago in Mesopotamia, now modern Iraq, which evolved over time in Europe, Asia, and the world's other regions, and which, excitingly for today's students of diplomacy, is now beginning one of its most extraordinary chapters. There are complex empirical and intellectual developments in world politics that are challenging our understandings of diplomacy. **Globalization** processes, including revolutionary means of communication and accessing information, are generating debate about the nature of contemporary diplomacy and whether or

1

not traditional understandings and practices still work for managing today's issues. It is now widely debated as to whether the centerpiece of diplomacy, the **sovereign territorial state**, is declining or adapting to the demands of the twenty-first century, and therefore whether the traditional institution of diplomacy—diplomats in **ministries of foreign affairs** (MFAs) and missions abroad, who **represent**, **report**, and **communicate** their state's interests—is also adapting or sinking into irrelevance. Similarly, it is also widely debated as to whether, under conditions of adaptation or decline, officials from other ministries as well as non-state actors, such as nongovernmental organizations (NGOs) and other **civil society groups**, and corporations are taking on roles that are changing traditional diplomatic practices.

The diplomacy puzzle that is generating this debate can be studied in many ways. Our approach is, first, to concentrate our analysis on the questions outlined earlier: How is diplomacy changing, why, and with what implications for future theories and practices? Second, we adopt a contemporary, comparative, and comprehensive approach drawing out similarities and differences, and continuities and changes in diplomacy over time and space and across different issues. For example, we compare historical and contemporary developments in diplomacy and in Western and non-Western contexts (part I); contrast theoretical and methodological understandings of diplomacy (part II); examine changes and continuities in the structures, processes, and instruments of diplomacy (part III); and outline different national, regional, and international institutional practices of diplomacy (part IV). Third, we base our analysis on recent research by scholars studying diplomacy. Research-led teaching is what students expect and deserve. In a nutshell, our approach to the diplomacy puzzle is contemporary, comparative, comprehensive, and research-driven, balancing breadth with depth.

We are convinced that our approach will provide insights about diplomacy that are needed by students, scholars, and practitioners. There are burgeoning teaching and research programs on diplomacy around the world. One example, in the United States, was the launch of the Future of Diplomacy Project by the John F. Kennedy School of Government at Harvard University in November 2010. The justification for the project, as former senior American diplomat Nicholas Burns, head of the project, rightly explains, is "the return of diplomacy as the principle vehicle for international politics today" (Future of Diplomacy Project 2010). In the same month, US president Barack Obama's secretary of state, Hillary Clinton, reminded the readers of her article in *Foreign Affairs* that she began her tenure as secretary "by stressing the need to elevate diplomacy and development alongside defense—a 'smart power' approach to solving global problems" (H. Rodham Clinton 2010: 13). Such views are behind the increasing number of diplomatic training programs that are being conducted by MFAs, as well as other government departments, and indeed by NGOs that interact with governments and civil societies around the world.

Armed with this approach, we invite you as students of diplomacy to engage critically with the analysis in this book. We hope this many-sided conversation will inspire and excite you to continue and develop the discussion toward new and better practices and theoretical propositions about diplomacy. If that happens, then we believe the world will be a much-improved place. This is our normative view about the potential for diplomacy as an important—if often misunderstood—foundation of world politics.

This introduction does two more things. First, it sketches the historical and intellectual background of diplomacy and several contemporary trends and challenges for diplomacy. Diplomacy is controversial—it has advocates and critics. That said, the main trends—globalization and interdependence, alongside regionalization, the continuing use of force, and the probable power shift in world politics—make diplomacy an imperative and perhaps the only sustainable option for managing differences between political entities, be they state or non-state actors. Second, the remainder of this introduction outlines the structure of the book, its constituent chapters, and pedagogical features.

HISTORICAL BACKGROUND, CONTEMPORARY TRENDS, AND CHALLENGES FOR DIPLOMACY

Diplomacy has a long, historical background, even if its earliest manifestations did not carry the name. As Raymond Cohen points out in the opening chapter of this book, "Since the dawn of recorded history 4,500 years ago, **sovereigns** have conducted their relations through official emissaries." Moreover, inscribed records of diplomacy that date to about 2500 BC, were "written in wedge-shaped, cuneiform script in the Sumerian language...and refer to relations between city-states." Later these records or official documents were called diplomas, a folded piece of paper, and the people who stored them in archives were called diplomats. Subsequently, the term diplomacy became associated with the practices of officials who represented their sovereigns, be they kings or states, in their exchanges with other sovereigns beyond their borders.

Over time and up to the present, countless volumes describe and analyze these exchanges. Many accounts are rich and detailed "diplomatic histories" that describe and analyze countries', and often their leaders', victories and defeats during times of war, but increasingly their international relationships on many other issues, such as trade, during periods of peace. With a few exceptions, most diplomatic histories, past and present, are a mix of a country's foreign policy and its diplomacy. There is a difference between the two activities that respected scholars of diplomacy emphasize. For Ernest Satow, "foreign policy is formulated by government, not by diplomatists," while diplomacy is to carry out foreign policy by diplomats (cited in Roberts 2011: 3). For Harold Nicolson (1946: 164–65), "foreign policy is based upon a general conception of national requirements....Diplomacy on the other hand, is not an end but a means, not a purpose but a method. It seeks, by the use of reason, conciliation and exchange of interests to prevent major conflicts between sovereign states." Even today, especially in the United States (D. Clinton 2011), the distinction is overlooked and the two types of analyses are conflated, exemplified in Henry Kissinger's tome *Diplomacy* (1994). Yet, a number of contemporary scholars insist on making the foreign policy-diplomacy distinction, so heavily emphasized by Satow and Nicolson. Renewed policy and scholarly interest in the distinction is, arguably, a minimum condition for the growth of diplomatic studies as a field.

The history of diplomacy is not only long but also controversial. Sir Henry Wootton's oft-quoted view of an ambassador as "a man of virtue sent abroad to lie for his country" was left open to at least two interpretations, one of them unfavorable.

Joseph Stalin's Machiavellian cynicism about diplomacy and diplomats was certainly not ambiguous: "A diplomat's word must have no relation to actions, otherwise what kind of diplomacy is it. Words are one thing, actions another. Good words are a mask for the concealment of bad deeds. Sincere diplomacy is no more possible than dry water and wooden iron" (Dallin 1944: 71). Some scholarly traditions in international relations thinking are also skeptical about diplomacy. In chapter 3 of this volume, Paul Sharp points to the implied place of diplomacy in the three main schools of international thought—realist, rationalist, and revolutionary: "'Classical' and 'neo-classical realists'...see diplomacy and diplomats as instruments of foreign policy and elements of state power, respectively"; for rationalists "ultimately both diplomacy and diplomats fail...because they act as servants of states"; and for revolutionary thinkers, "diplomacy and states serve established concentrations of power, no matter what the sources of this power are in any given epoch."

The authors in this book are well aware of the importance of these critical claims about diplomacy. However, they are interested in debating and analyzing contemporary diplomacy with the aim of advancing it through better, even critical, understandings. Their advocacy of diplomacy is grounded in scholarly thinking about international relations and diplomacy, perhaps amassed most astutely in the English school of international relations theory. The claim made by one of the school's original and most influential members, Martin Wight (1979: 113), that "the diplomatic system is the master-institution of international relations" supports their confidence in diplomacy as a necessary, if not sufficient, process for stabilizing world politics, and certainly one in need of constant improvement.

Among diplomacy's advocates today, there are different understandings of diplomacy and debate about the respective merit of claims being advanced. Canvassing just three of these claims, all of which are represented in this book, gives a flavor of the debate. One is that diplomacy is a state-based institution involving professional accredited diplomats from foreign ministries and embassies, who follow the **Vienna Convention on Diplomatic Relations** (1961) and the **Vienna Convention on Consular Relations** (1963); who represent, negotiate, and communicate the interests of their territorial and sovereign state with diplomats from other states; and who seek, if they deem it necessary, the views of others—perhaps officials or nonofficials—in advancing state interests. Another claim is that diplomacy is partly the state-based institution described earlier, but is more accurately conceptualized as being part of a broader "national diplomatic system" (NDS) involving many other actors who wield influence, often through **policy networks**. Yet another claim is that diplomacy is not the exclusive activity of **sovereign states**; indeed, in a globalizing world it is becoming less and less so. Rather, diplomacy is a process of communication and representation that facilitates social interaction between all human beings who have differences.

Contemporary Trends and Challenges

Five current trends make diplomacy an imperative, and yet present it with enormous challenges. The first trend is globalization and its practical effects. In the ancient past, as Cohen points out in chapter 1, borders were "divinely ordained and inviolable," a norm that continued to hold sway for centuries. In the contemporary globalization context, borders, theoretically, are neither as divine nor as inviolable as they once were. Anthony Gidden's (1990: 64) description of globalization offers one insight into why this is so: globalization is "the intensification of worldwide social relations which link distant localities in such a way that local happenings are shaped by events occurring in other parts of the world and vice versa." Different types of connections are being forged between a whole range of entities with influence or standing in world politics—states, nations, intergovernmental organizations (IGOs), NGOs, civil society groups, and individuals. Using technologies provided by the revolutions in communications (for example, emails, mobile phones, and social media), information (for example, the Internet, and cable and satellite news), and transport (for example, rapid air travel), not only are these entities becoming more numerous, but their interactions with each other are becoming more frequent. More actors, more issues, twenty-four-hour news coverage, and more bloggers make for greater complexity in world politics and put unprecedented demands on state institutions, including diplomatic ones. One conceptual challenge posed by the influence of non-state actors on states' policies is how to understand the principle of **sovereignty** that is the foundation of the institution of diplomacy. The different interests or values of many non-state actors challenge states' control over the ranking of their interests, over what is deemed to be high and low politics. Diplomats are now negotiating ways to reduce the impact of climate change partly because of continuing pressure from environmental NGOs and civil societies around the world. The public's opinion matters to diplomatic practices more than it did in the past. Exactly how much it does so is still unclear. How much it should, and over what issues, is controversial in many parts of the world.

A second challenging trend for diplomacy is how global actors will manage the shared problems of a more interdependent world. **Interdependence** may still be a contentious concept, but it accurately explains the present situation where countries depend on each other to resolve problems they have in common, such as economic instability, climate change, and, at times, pandemics. Moreover, the practical management of these shared problems shows that there are multiple interdependent stakeholders—public actors such as governments and IGOs, and private actors such as NGOs, corporations, and civil society groups. Among the challenges that interdependence poses for diplomacy is how are the collective interests of multiple stakeholders to be negotiated? Is inclusive multilateral diplomacy, for example, on climate change, an effective way of management? If not, what are the options? Are international organizations, such as the United Nations (UN), which have taken the lead on collective interests, capable of effective diplomacy? Is the new **Group of Twenty (G20)**, as a novel IGO, representing the economic collective interests of states, capable of diplomacy that reflects the economic interdependence of societies in developed and developing states? In short, will diplomats be comanagers of globalization or another of its victims?

A third challenging trend for diplomacy is how it will balance the often-competing forces of globalization and regionalization. Some regional institutions are playing a greater diplomatic role than they did in the past. The European Union (EU) is the most developed hub of regional diplomacy, and the recent appointment of a High Representative for Foreign Affairs and Security Policy and establishment of the

European External Action Service (foreign ministry) will be an interesting window into the nature and effectiveness of this type of regional diplomacy. Other regions are not as coherent as the EU, and indeed some, like the Middle East, are marked by traditional interstate diplomatic tensions, paradoxically complicated most recently by the 2011 Arab uprising. East Asia is the fastest-growing economic region, and its economic diplomacy is both regionally and globally focused. However, its regional economic diplomacy is based more on national interests than on principles of East Asian integration and an East Asian community reflecting the EU model. This tension between national and regional interests is arguably accentuated by the relationship that regional institutions have with the UN, especially with regard to diplomatic management of conflict. The main Southeast Asia institution, ASEAN, for example, had to rely on the UN for managing the 1999 crisis in East Timor, and the UN had to rely on the Australian government and the Australian Defence Force to lead the intervention into what was then an Indonesian province. Globalization has by no means ruled out considerable regional variations in the conduct of diplomacy.

A fourth challenging trend for diplomacy is that more and more global actors are demanding that diplomacy, rather than military force, be used to settle differences. There is a growing view, captured earlier by Burns, that what we are seeing is "the return of diplomacy as the principle vehicle for international politics today" (Future of Diplomacy Project 2010). However, as realists readily remind us, and as the ongoing wars in Iraq and Afghanistan demonstrate, using force remains an option frequently adopted by state and non-state actors. Moreover, the connections between the diplomat and the soldier, as Raymond Aron (1966: 5) noted many years ago, are symbolically close: "The Ambassador, in the exercise of his duties, is the political unit in whose name he speaks; the soldier on the battlefield is the political unit in whose name he kills his opposite number." Most contemporary diplomats would be reluctant to surrender their option of last resort, **coercive diplomacy**, that is to say, the threat or the limited use and demonstration of force. An entirely different perspective of the relationship between diplomacy and force is the present conundrum that diplomats confront when new (bad) non-state actors prefer to use violent means (for example, suicide bombing and improvised explosive devices) to achieve their objectives rather than to negotiate.

A fifth challenging trend for diplomacy in the contemporary global context is that the world is undergoing major power shifts, primarily from a US-centric world to a world of many powers (T. J. Christensen 2006; White 2010), and diplomats will need to figure out what role they can play in the emerging world order. The fastest-rising power is China, and following behind it are emerging economies such as India and Brazil. How China will relate to the contemporary and largely US-dominant international order of norms, law, conventions, regimes, and practices is a hotly debated question. Another is how China will relate diplomatically to its own regional neighbors, and even to distant partners in Africa, the Middle East, and Latin America. Already, many countries in East Asia justify their defense budgets, force structures, and military strategies—implicitly or explicitly—on the basis of their assessment (generally provided by diplomats) of the evolving China-US diplomatic relationship. Already claims are made that China's negotiating tactics during the 2009 Conference of the Parties to the United Nations Framework Convention on

Climate Change in Copenhagen, and its actions in the East China Sea, are indicative of a more assertive big power diplomacy. It will be important for the United States and other countries to consider if their own diplomacy differs significantly from that of China, to understand China's diplomacy, and equally important for China to appreciate the diplomatic strategies of the United States and its East Asian neighbors. More broadly, the uncertain power dynamics are highlighting the importance of understanding Asia, particularly East Asian approaches to diplomacy. Students of diplomacy will need to develop the intellectual and practical foundations to help understand and manage major structural power change.

In sum, these five trends in the global context present strong challenges for diplomacy and diplomats. Nonetheless, these developments confirm rather disconfirm the importance of diplomatic engagement and management, since most challenges can only be managed collectively. Other means, such as using force, are unlikely to be as effective. The book's premise, as stated earlier, is that the present globalizing context makes diplomacy perhaps the only sustainable option for managing differences between sociopolitical entities (Constantinou and Der Derian 2010).

KEY POINTS

- Diplomacy has a long, complex, controversial, and fascinating history, one that predates the rise of the European state system in the sixteenth and seventeenth centuries.
- Today, several empirical trends—processes of globalization and interdependence as well as regionalization, the continuing use of force, and power shifts in world politics—challenge diplomacy yet make it an imperative in world politics.

THE BOOK'S STRUCTURE, CHAPTER SUMMARIES, AND PEDAGOGICAL FEATURES

Part I

The book's four parts aim to engage students in searching for answers to the key questions we have raised. The first part explores some historical benchmarks against which we can analyze contemporary diplomacy. Chapter 1, by Raymond Cohen, begins diplomacy's story at its ancient origins some 4,500 years ago in Mesopotamia, now Iraq. When reading this chapter, students might ask such questions as: Do some of the rudimentary structures, processes, and instruments developed then and those that evolved subsequently—as part of the Western state system—have continuities with those in the present day? In what ways are the ancient and contemporary contexts different or similar? Does this long view suggest that some recent "innovations" are less revolutionary than we sometimes think?

Chapter 2, by Suisheng Zhao, establishes some more recent historical benchmarks of diplomacy in another region of great contemporary importance, East Asia. It sketches how in the nineteenth century Britain's introduction of Western state-based diplomacy, established in part on formal negotiated treaties, undermined

China's ancient tributary system of relations with regional countries. The chapter then shows how in later periods up to the end of the Cold War, the great powers in East Asia implemented their foreign policies through diplomatic practices that were connected to power politics, threats and the use of military force, and the negotiation and implementation of treaties that benefited the most powerful countries. Does diplomacy today continue to have these characteristics, or does it have different features?

Part II

Part II examines understandings of contemporary diplomacy from different theoretical and methodological perspectives. It invites readers to compare and contrast international relations theories that emphasize power politics, sociological understandings that stress relationships and norms, theories of globalization and global governance that highlight multiactor policy networks, and theories of diplomatic negotiation.

Part II begins with an analysis in chapter 3, by Paul Sharp, that canvasses how social theorists make sense of diplomacy. It examines the attractions and limitations of doing social and other types of theory. Some of the questions that this chapter pursues are: Does the sociological insight that, where people live in groups, feel separate from one another, and want to be so, mean there will be a need for good diplomacy now and in the future? If it does, can we also point to a diplomatic theory of international relations and human relations? How does this understanding of diplomacy compare with those in the realist, rationalist, and revolutionist traditions of international relations thinking? What does this comparison suggest about the theoretical evolution of diplomacy?

Chapter 4, by Geoffrey Allen Pigman, canvasses more broadly some of the principal academic debates surrounding contemporary diplomacy. It considers debates about what counts as diplomacy, how it has changed over time, and how theory relates to practice. It challenges readers to consider how such debates might be resolved, and how their resolution or lack thereof affects diplomatic practice. Do readers agree with the chapter's argument that whether as voters, investors, shareholders, members of civil society organizations, or as practicing diplomats, members of the global public are all stakeholders with an interest in effective diplomacy? If so, what does this understanding of multi-stakeholder diplomacy imply for which actors wield influence and for diplomacy's future boundaries?

Chapter 5, by Bertrand Badie, examines the contextual factors of contemporary diplomacy, globalization, and global governance, again from a sociological perspective. It focuses on new non-state social actors and what is conceptualized as their new "social routes," suggesting that this development indicates an emerging global order that incorporates a new set of relationships, or what might be called "intersocial relations," between peoples, groups, and sovereign states. If, as this chapter argues, social actors are emancipating themselves from state control and influence, then students may wish to consider not just how much influence these actors have over states today but also how this development compares with more traditional perspectives of diplomacy, for example, those established in part I and in the next chapter.

Chapter 6, by I. William Zartman, invites readers to consider a particular traditional perspective of contemporary diplomacy which argues that diplomacy is primarily about negotiation, and that negotiation is the primary business of foreign policy and international relations. To appreciate this perspective, the chapter examines different strategies of negotiation and mediation and the challenges that these processes confront in trying to resolve contemporary issues such as intrastate conflicts and problems that involve many stakeholders and require multilateral negotiation. Given these challenges, will the future of diplomacy—understood as negotiation—depend on prevention, that is, on handling conflicts before they become violent, keeping violent conflicts from escalating, and moving conflicts and problems from management to resolution? More broadly, students might compare this understanding of diplomacy-as-negotiation with some of those coming up in the next part: for example, the idea, advanced in chapter 12 that negotiation is the essential definition of economic diplomacy.

Part III

Building on the previous historical and theoretical parts of the book, part III analyzes in detail the arguments and evidence for answering the key questions about diplomacy in the twenty-first century. Each of the eight chapters in this part analyzes particular structures, processes, and instruments of contemporary diplomacy, their evolution, potential, limitations, and future.

Chapter 7, by Brian Hocking, explores the best-known and still the most significant diplomatic structure, the ministry of foreign affairs. It shows how during the evolution of state-based diplomacy, national governments developed a set of tools for interaction with their external environments and for the implementation of their international policy objectives. This development is conceptualized as the "national diplomatic system." A key question that is raised is whether the NDS is becoming more complex as a result of domestic and international factors, which are leading to paradoxical tendencies that may well challenge the MFA's capacity to adapt. Will the MFA survive, and, if so, in what form?

Chapter 8, by Jovan Kurbalija, examines the impact of a "revolutionary" instrument, the Internet, on contemporary diplomacy. It finds that information and communication technologies (ICTs), notably the Internet, are changing the environment in which diplomacy is conducted, the diplomatic agenda, and practices of diplomacy. How exactly is the Internet changing the two cornerstones of diplomacy, communications and information? Are the changes so substantively different and of such a scale that contemporary diplomacy has little in common with previous practices? Or perhaps, as chapter 1 implies, that regardless of such change, innovative developments are less revolutionary than we assume?

Chapter 9's examination of ancient consular processes and the role of consuls— protecting nationals and promoting trade—is the historical background against which contemporary practices are analyzed. Halvard Leira and Iver Neumann show that consuls perform important functions in the international system, yet their roles are not well understood and they are often seen as subordinate to diplomats. But should the functions of consuls be examined from a diplomatic perspective? Do changes toward a less sovereignty-oriented, globalizing world of commercial transactions and travel, and increasing international legal structures, indicate that the importance of consuls is being recognized at last and that the differences between them and diplomats may be increasing? If so, what does this suggest for our understanding of contemporary diplomacy?

Chapter 10, by Thomas Wright, discusses two key diplomatic processes, **bilateralism** and **multilateralism**. It compares and contrasts bilateral and multilateral diplomacy, explores different types of multilateralism, and shows how both forms are aspects of the prevailing international order. It then examines the effect of two ongoing crises on multilateral diplomacy: the long-term crisis of legitimacy and effectiveness resulting from the shifting distribution of power in the international system, and a failure to address long-term transnational threats that pose significant dangers to the international community. Will states respond to these crises by moving toward smaller, minilateral, groupings of the like-minded, and how might this impact on world politics? In comparison to earlier periods, is this possibility a new development, or are there precedents in diplomatic practice?

Chapter 11, by Jan Melissen, discusses one of the most vibrant debates in current diplomacy studies, the reemerging practice of public diplomacy. It traces the evolution of public diplomacy to its present practices and shows how, besides states, it can involve many different actors. Students might ask if such a divergence of actors and processes suggests that public diplomacy is a difficult area around which to place definitional and practical boundaries. If it is, then does this substantiate the argument that diplomatic practice is constantly in flux rather than always connecting with past processes, as some previous chapters, particularly those in part I, suggest?

Chapter 12, by Stephen Woolcock, examines economic diplomacy. The chapter stresses that the term should be understood as a process of decision making and negotiation in core issues of international economic relations. It shows that economic diplomacy has become more important as the international (or global) economy becomes increasingly multipolar and requires negotiated outcomes among states with diverse interests. The chapter asks whether there is something distinctive about economic diplomacy as opposed to general diplomacy (chapter 9 raises similar questions about consular diplomacy). Does the fact that economic diplomacy involves such a diverse range of actors, is shaped by and shapes developments in markets to such a degree that markets become "actors," and is more concerned with negotiating regimes mean it is different from general diplomacy? Students might compare the arguments in this chapter and chapter 9 and consider their implications for understanding contemporary diplomacy.

Chapter 13, by Pauline Kerr and Brendan Taylor, begins with the observation that studies of track-two diplomacy, that is, analyses of the evolving role of non-state actors (individuals or organizations) in diplomacy, challenge students because there are conflicting claims about the actors' roles, purposes, and functions. To illustrate, the chapter examines second-track institutions in East Asia and finds that their main purpose and functions revolve around provision of services to the sovereign state. What does this finding suggest about the evolution of understandings of diplomacy in East Asia?

Chapter 14, by Jennifer Sims, examines an underinvestigated instrument of diplomacy, intelligence-gathering. It suggests that, to be effective, diplomacy (at least for larger states) involves deft use of hard and soft power in appropriate mixes at the right time, and that this success often turns on the quality of the intelligence available to diplomats and other decision makers. Yet, this situation sometimes raises ethical questions, especially for democracies, about the techniques employed by the "dark arts." And, in a highly mediated world, will state-based diplomats be required to become increasingly secretive about their tactics? Does this possible trend suggest a return to previous periods when high levels of secrecy were features of diplomacy?

Part IV

The book's fourth part contains the final analysis of contemporary diplomacy. It examines three levels of diplomatic practice—the national practices of two major states, the United States and China; the diplomatic practices of several regional institutions; and the practices of the most important international institution, the UN.

Chapter 15, by Alan Henrikson, traces and assesses the conceptual foundations and progression of American diplomacy from the Cold War period to the present day through the lenses of three major US foreign policy ideas—containment, transformation, and engagement. It suggests that the United States now is diplomatically "engaged" almost everywhere, arguing that the term "engagement" has become almost a policy in itself. The chapter analyzes why this has happened and whether "engagement" has its limits, especially with large, powerful and un-like-minded states. Students might ask if diplomatic process ever substitutes for foreign policy—for actual strategy aimed at well-targeted objectives? Or must the goals of policy be well identified in order for engagement diplomacy to succeed?

Chapter 16, by Ye Zicheng and Zhang Qingmin, revisits China's diplomacy, building on the historical examination in chapter 2 and analyzing that country's contemporary practices. The chapter traces the major changes in China's diplomatic structures, processes, and instruments after 1978, when the country began to engage diplomatically with the world. What do these developments tell us about China's diplomacy in general and in comparison to that of the United States? Will China challenge American hegemony, as many realist thinkers claim?

Chapter 17, by Jozef Bátora and Alan Hardacre, gives an overview of the diplomatic structures and processes within several regional institutions to give a much-needed analysis of "regional diplomacy." It argues that there is a global trend toward increased regional diplomatic institutions and processes, inspired and catalyzed by developments in the EU, although not necessarily fully copying the European "model." One question that students may wish to ask is, if the relationship between regional institutional diplomacy and state-based diplomacy is often a tense one, then how can effective regional diplomacy be pursued?

Chapter 18, by Geoffrey Wiseman and Soumita Basu, examines the conduct of diplomacy at the United Nations. The chapter traces the evolution of diplomatic activities at the UN from its founding in 1945, including the growing significance of NGOs. Can we now understand UN diplomacy not so much from the perspective of a diplomatic corps but rather as a "diplomatic community"? The chapter considers the extent to which the norms of the UN diplomatic community are capable of transcending national interests and thereby securing more broadly conceived goals of international peace and progress.

Pedagogical Features

To further engage students and teachers, and in keeping with other volumes in the same series, the book offers several pedagogical tools. The first is a general glossary (found at the back of the book) of widely used diplomatic and international relations terms, as well as some special short glossaries of terms peculiar to the chapter topic (found within the chapters). The glossaries are important because one of the challenges of a book compiled by many authors that is comprehensive and comparative is that some key terms are used in different ways. For example, terms such as "nation-state," "sovereign state," and "statecraft" are the subject of debate among our authors, just as they are in other literatures on diplomacy and international relations. We believe that such contestation is to be encouraged and is part of the intellectual milieu that students will encounter when studying diplomacy. To help students appreciate the complexity and subtlety of such debates, we have put key terms in quotation marks where the meaning is reasonably clear from the text, and put other key terms, not fully defined in the text, in bold typeface and compiled them in the two types of glossaries.

The second set of pedagogical tools comprises a "reader's guide" (at the beginning of each chapter), "key points" (at the end of each chapter section), and "questions" (at the end of each chapter). The brief introductions found at the start of each of the four parts of the book provide a third support for students. Here students are reminded about the big questions that drive the book and how each part orientates them to find answers.

The final set of pedagogical tools is accessible online and has separate sites for students and instructors. The *companion student website* offers a range of pedagogical materials that will help students to integrate the text with lectures and test and deepen their knowledge. The resources include: further readings, websites and web-links, glossary exercises, exercises for compiling take-home messages, activities aimed at answering the book's 'big' questions, quizzes, case studies, and counterfactual reasoning exercises.

The *companion instructor website* provides a range of resource materials. There is a suggested syllabus for a fifteen-week course on diplomacy in a globalizing world. In addition each chapter in the book is organized to offer instructors some pedagogical options: first, for presenting lectures (such as outlines of the chapter's main sections and key points that are readily adaptable to PowerPoint presentations or class handouts, plus additional possible lecture topics); second, for classroom activities (such as discussion questions, test questions, Internet links, on-line video clips, student activities); and finally instructors can choose topics from a list of possible term papers.

NOTE

1. The "diplomacy puzzle" refers not to a situation that is counterintuitive or apparently contradictory but to one that is unclear and confusing.

PART I

The Historical Evolution
of Diplomacy

In this first part of the book, we provide some historical snapshots of diplomacy that will help place our contemporary examination of diplomacy in an empirical and theoretical context. We have two aims. The *first* is to offer an account of the ancient practices of diplomacy in what is now the Middle East; explain how these practices evolved into a practical institution in Europe integral to the seventeenth-century Westphalian sovereign states system; and show how these transformed practices were introduced to, and subsequently adopted by, East Asian countries in the nineteenth century. By tracing continuities and changes in diplomatic practices across historical time and geographic space, readers will be in a better position to compare and contrast how diplomatic practices have evolved in different contexts and how they are likely to evolve in future.

Our *second* aim is to provide a stronger historical basis for readers to consider the important claim that, by tracing these continuities and changes in practices across time and space, we can begin to theorize that diplomacy concerns more than sovereign states. In this view, diplomacy is a broad institution designed to communicate and represent both the interests and identities of sovereigns of all political units (tribes in the past, sovereign states today), and it is performed by a special group of individuals, or accredited representatives. These representatives can variously be located at home and abroad, adhering to agreed conventions and enjoying special immunities. The many elements built into this claim will serve as theoretical benchmarks for judging contemporary diplomacy.

CHAPTER 1

Diplomacy through the Ages

Raymond Cohen

CHAPTER CONTENTS

- Introduction
- Ancient Near Eastern diplomacy
- Classical diplomacy
- European diplomacy
- Conclusion

READER'S GUIDE

This chapter presents the "big picture," tracing the history of diplomacy from earliest times. It shows how some of the major tools of diplomacy already existed in rudimentary form thousands of years ago and evolved very gradually in response to changing needs. By taking the long view, we place modern-day diplomacy in perspective, suggesting that some recent "innovations" are less revolutionary than we sometimes think.

INTRODUCTION

Since the dawn of recorded history 4,500 years ago, **sovereigns** have conducted their relations through official emissaries. From the beginning they attached the utmost importance to relationships with other sovereigns because they considered themselves to belong to an extended family and needed things, both intangible and tangible—recognition and approval as well as goods and soldiers—from each other. Since they could hardly communicate in person, they were obliged to do this through surrogates.

This chapter seeks to track the development of diplomacy since the emergence of urban civilization long ago in ancient Mesopotamia. Clearly, the **norms**, institutions, and instruments of diplomacy have evolved over time. Diplomats rely today on digital means of communication rather than clay tablets. At the same time, diplomacy's main tools, such as **protocol**, the **note**, and the **treaty**, are marked by surprising continuity. This, then, is an exercise in political embryology: observing the progress of an organism from its first appearance to its latest manifestation in accordance with a certain consistent, internal logic.

ANCIENT NEAR EASTERN DIPLOMACY

The earliest evidence of diplomacy appears in royal inscriptions dedicated to the gods found in the ruins of the ancient cities that dot the fertile plains between the Tigris and Euphrates Rivers of southern Mesopotamia, modern Iraq. Written in wedge-shaped, cuneiform script in the Sumerian language, they date to about 2500 BC and refer to relations between city-states. Armed struggles, coalitions, border disputes, and "arbitration" awards—the settlement of a dispute by a third party—are among the subjects touched upon. Royal "envoys," or messengers, are explicitly mentioned. A king of Lagash sends his envoys to Umma, calling on the city to surrender or face annihilation. Yet for all the warfare there is a strong normative sense of order. In the rhetoric of the inscriptions, borders are divinely ordained and inviolable. Only defensive war is permissible. The kings of Lagash and Uruk agree to establish brotherhood between them (Altman 2004).

A diplomatic message from this period written on a baked clay tablet using wedge-shaped, cuneiform characters was sent from Ebla in Syria to Hamazi in Iran. The royal envoy carried it in a pouch slung around his neck on a round-trip of 2,000 kilometers. On arrival the messenger would have been received in audience, read out the message, and then expanded on it orally, answering questions. The tablet reflects basic features of early "cuneiform diplomacy": a network of city-states served by messengers traveling sometimes long distances; a working relationship between kings bound by ties of brotherhood; the obligation to reciprocity; a palace bureaucracy that dispatched (and received) envoys, and recorded and filed documents; a code of correct international custom—"protocol"—including polite forms of address; an ethic of communication and negotiation; a system of correspondence based on conventional forms and the use of an international language; and the exchange of gifts.

Underpinning the transaction is the apparatus of Mesopotamian governance: states, the brotherhood of kings, a set of norms governing royal relationships, bureaucracies, scribal schools teaching cuneiform script, not to mention far-flung land routes and extensive trade. Although the outward appearance of ancient Near Eastern diplomacy may be rudimentary, its assumptions about the world of interstate relations prefigure our own international system. It was so well adapted that it lasted for 2,000 years.

Cuneiform diplomacy entered a new phase with Sargonic hegemony, 2334–2113 BC. At its height Sargon of Akkad's dynasty governed a vast empire, from Iran to the Mediterranean. Akkadian became the international language for 2,000 years, and cuneiform diplomacy was refined and spread across the ancient Near East and beyond. The Sargonic dynasty introduced the international treaty consisting of parallel declarations made separately by both kings to each other's envoys. One treaty is believed to involve a marriage **alliance** and contains what was to become the classic formula: "your friend is my friend, your enemy is my enemy." Another contemporaneous treaty from Ebla in northern Syria contained commercial provisions, granting foreign merchants **extraterritorial rights** and dealing with taxation of foreigners, trade, and damages. The parties to the treaty were the city-states and not their kings. If this reading is correct, then this implies that states were considered legal personalities, advanced legal thinking for the time (Altman 2005).

An oath and a contingent curse strengthen the treaties' force. Archaeologists found a treaty in a ruined temple. These measures reflected the primacy assigned by the peoples of the ancient Near East to the role of the gods in interstate relations. A ruler represented the god of his city on earth, and the deities controlled human affairs. At the heart of public life was service to the gods; religion and politics were intertwined. From 2000 BC Ur there is evidence of foreign envoys regularly participating at major festivals. Because some names occur repeatedly in the records, T. M. Sharlach (2005) suggests that although not permanently resident, their regular presence may indicate the existence of an identifiable "diplomatic corps," a community of ambassadors in the one city, possibly receiving accommodation, and certainly enjoying hospitality from the palace including rations, servants, and gifts. Foreign affairs were handled by a state secretariat responsible for sending royal emissaries. It also assisted foreign ambassadors, interpreted for them, and mediated between them and other officials. The treatment of ambassadors was strictly regulated by protocol. Significantly, the same word was used for both correct international custom and proper cultic practice in the temple.

From the archives of Mari (ca. 1700–1670 BC), contemporary with the Babylonian lawgiver Hammurabi, we observe an even more advanced stage in the development of ancient Near Eastern diplomacy. Envoys are now ranked from plain messenger to "ambassador plenipotentiary," an individual who could negotiate and conclude an agreement. Important delegations may consist of hundreds of people—secretaries, guards, and servants. Some officials are explicitly called the king's "personal representatives" and receive the prostrations due to their sovereign. Bertrand Lafont (2001) argues that ambassadors enjoyed inviolability according to correct international custom. David Elgavish (2000) agrees that they were entitled to protection from harm but doubts that they possessed formal **diplomatic immunity** in the modern sense and might be detained.

An early **diplomatic passport** and **letters of accreditation** identifying their bearers were found at Mari. There was a guesthouse for visiting diplomats. The simultaneous presence of the emissaries of different kings at royal audiences again suggests the existence of a diplomatic corps. Some remained for many years at their post and were effectively resident. Besides public audiences there were also closed encounters, where secret diplomacy might be conducted. Diplomatic hints were dropped through nuances of protocol. Banquets, governed by minute etiquette, were occasions for bestowing favors, such as ceremonial garments, scented oils, and choice delicacies. Royal gifts were exchanged. Tearing a ceremonial garment expressed extreme displeasure.

Three hundred years after Hammurabi, a truly multicultural diplomatic system spanning three continents—Europe, Asia, and Africa—came into existence. The Age of the Amarna Archive (named after the village in Middle Egypt where hundreds of cuneiform tablets from the fourteenth century BC were discovered) was a period of unprecedented stability. For the duration of the system (ca. 1460–1220 BC), only one major war broke out. Six "great kings" are mentioned in the Amarna letters, each with his own language, culture, and gods. Their **vassals** were not allowed to maintain independent diplomatic relations. Small trading states also played a part.

Several factors have been credited with maintaining peace: parity between the powers, spheres of influence, and buffer zones all doubtless contributed. Contemporaries did not think in **balance of power** terms but resisted expansionist powers. There was a strong sense of brotherhood among the "great kings." The legitimacy of one strengthened the other. Their letters concern both family and politics. Dynastic marriages, visits by envoys to life-cycle events, gift giving on a grand scale, the dispatch of physicians and cultic objects, and a plentiful supply of Egyptian gold all helped to cement ties. By now there was also a body of customary law deriving from treaties, norms of conduct, and extensive precedent, regulating interstate relations and facilitating trade (Cohen 1996).

At the heart of the Amarna great peace was the **emissary**, possessing refined diplomatic skills. When he completed a mission, his counterpart accompanied him on the way home. As a negotiation proceeded, the two colleagues would travel back and forth between their respective capitals. The Amarna archive has preserved the names of such a pair of highly esteemed envoys—Mane and Keliya—negotiating a marriage alliance between Egypt and Mittani.

Ancient Near Eastern diplomacy lasted for another 600 years, although it never regained the ecumenism of the Amarna Age. With the rise of the neo-Assyrian Empire (911–612 BC) the international system shifted from one of strategic parity to imperial **hegemony**. Reciprocity remained a central ethic, but now it was protection in return for loyalty. Nevertheless, the themes of the old diplomacy remained—the brotherhood of kings, a foreign service run by the palace, the to-and-fro of messengers and emissaries, gift exchange, dynastic marriages, treaties under oath, correct international custom, and the intertwining of diplomacy and ritual.

The "great tradition" is prominently displayed in the Bible, where the diplomatic activities of the kings of Israel and Judah conform to the operating procedures of ancient Near Eastern diplomacy. King David (ca. 1040–970 BC) sends a delegation to Hanun, king of Ammon, to offer condolences on the death of his father. This is a conventional family life-cycle visit intended to initiate brotherly ties, that is, diplomatic relations, between the thrones. Ammonite officials accuse David's men of being spies and cut off half their ceremonial garments and beards, a diplomatic rebuff. They do not physically harm them. Still, war results.

Under David's son Solomon, the united kingdom of Israel and Judah is accepted as a legitimate diplomatic actor. On Solomon's accession Hiram, the king of Tyre, sends a delegation to the new king, thereby recognizing him diplomatically. They then negotiate terms for building the temple, timber delivered on site in exchange for wheat and oil. Solomon subsequently allies himself with the king of Egypt by taking his daughter's hand in marriage, another act typical of the ancient Near Eastern diplomatic tradition, although unprecedented for Pharaoh, the mighty Egyptian god-king.

There was a linguistic shift in the eighth century BC when Akkadian—old Assyrian—was displaced by Aramaic, which used a consonantal alphabet, not cuneiform. The significance of communication in the new international language is reflected in the biblical account of the Assyrian siege of Jerusalem in 701 BC. The Assyrian official Rabshakeh addresses the Jerusalem populace from outside the wall. Speaking in Judean, he attempts to persuade them to surrender with a mixture of threats and promises. This direct appeal bypassing officials is an early example of public diplomacy. King Hezekiah of Judah's officials beg Rabshakeh to address them in the diplomatic language, saying, "Please speak to your servants in Aramaic, which we understand, and not in Judean to the people on the wall." Rabshakeh declines, presumably to keep up the pressure on the palace. Assyria eventually withdrew when Hezekiah agreed to pay a huge tribute.

KEY POINTS

- Diplomatic messages and treaties have been found by archaeologists in the Middle East dating back to around 2500 BC, the period when urban civilization emerged.
- Diplomacy took the form of the exchange of letters and gifts carried by royal envoys; a body of customary law and protocol governed it.
- Kings used diplomacy to promote their personal relations and the interests of the city-states over which they ruled.

CLASSICAL DIPLOMACY

The neo-Assyrian Empire was eventually conquered by Babylonia. With the rise of Cyrus the Great (558–529 BC), Assyria and Babylonia became provinces of the vast Achaemenid Persian Empire. Darius I (522–486 BC) added Egypt and northern India to the imperial crown and invaded Greece. The substance of Persian statecraft was conquest and dominion, not negotiation with equals. Still, the forms of ancient Near Eastern diplomacy were maintained, and Darius adopted Aramaic as the official language of administration. To rule the empire, a continental network of roads was laid and a royal mail organized. Envoys traveled safely from the Persian capital Susa to Kandahar, a distance of 2,000 kilometers. Persia's attitude toward the quarrelsome Greek polities was patrician, and even the Greeks called the Persian monarch the Great King. Persia shifted its support from one polity to another and occasionally arbitrated in quarrels between them. Vassal **satraps** ruled Greek communities in Asia Minor, but supervision of mainland Greek affairs was left to the leading Greek power. Treaties of peace or alliance were made at different times, such as a series of treaties with Sparta in 412–411 BC. Their texts lack customary ancient Near Eastern formulas, such as affirmations of love and brotherhood. But there is ample evidence of Greek familiarity with the interstate treaty.

The Persians were bemused by Greek customs, such as the central role of oratory in their public life, disregard of correct international custom, and undiplomatic effrontery. Cyrus listened in astonishment to a Spartan herald's impudent speech, Herodotus tells us. When Darius I sent his emissaries to demand tribute of Athens and Sparta, they were put to death. At a later date the Spartans attributed a series of calamities to their impious act and sent volunteers to offer themselves as scapegoats in expiation of the sin. Received by Xerxes (486–465 BC), the Spartan envoys declined to prostrate themselves before the king of kings. This was not their custom, they said; they had come to make atonement with their lives. Appalled at their lack of sophistication, Xerxes refused the offer. He would not imitate Spartan ignorance of "the law of mankind" (Herodotus 1925).

At the very end, following his defeat in 333 BC by Alexander of Macedonia at the battle of Issus, and the seizure of his mother, wife, and children, Darius III finally adopted the language of diplomatic parity. Writing to Alexander as a brother Great King, he offered to renew their fathers' "ancient friendship and alliance." But Alexander now considered himself Darius's superior and contemptuously rejected a final offer of vast lands, a fortune in gold, and his daughter's hand in marriage, bringing the curtain down on 2,000 years of ancient Near Eastern diplomacy. Greek culture had supplanted that of Asia.

Diplomacy in ancient Greece was designed to handle matters among the Greek polities rather than to conduct international affairs. At one time, though, according to Hans Güterbock (1983), Achaean Greece, on the northern Peloponnese coast, belonged to the fourteenth-century BC brotherhood of Amarna states. Greek treaty terminology confirms this. The unusual Greek term for treaty, literally "bond and oath," follows Hittite legal idiom, as did the injunction "to serve or to help with all one's might and power, with all one's heart and soul." There is also the expression in intra-Greek alliance treaties and loyalty oaths, first appearing in third millennium BC treaties as noted earlier, "to be a friend to friends and an enemy to enemies" (Weinfeld 1973: 198).

Structural factors limited the scope of Greek diplomacy. There were hundreds of Greek polities preoccupied with local concerns. They did not consider diplomacy a distinct role of government, and decisions were made by public assembly, ruling out secret diplomacy. There was no system for collecting and collating intelligence or preserving records. Envoys were worthy citizens sent on single missions, rarely experienced diplomats. They were given simple, brief instructions with little scope for initiative. Returning envoys might have the fruits of their mission overturned in assembly. Classical Greek had no specialized vocabulary of statecraft and used the same word for envoy as for elder, "*presbeis*" (Osborne 2008: 218).

The practice of Greek diplomacy was quite rudimentary. Until the Hellenistic era (ca. 323–146 BC), formal letters—the hallmark of the Amarna Archive—were not sent. **Envoys**, often well-known orators, engaged in advocacy rather than in negotiation. Treaties were brief and generalized. Other major divergences from past international custom were the relative absence of protocol and formal procedure, low-key hospitality, and avoiding gifts. A shared feature, though, was the swearing of treaty-oaths and the sanctity of the herald, who was protected by the gods. He declared war, requested a truce, and opened peace talks (Osborne 2008: 217). Nevertheless, diplomats were not inviolate, and Sparta and Athens occasionally put to death each other's envoys (Adcock and Mosley 1975: 172, 229).

Compared with Persian cosmopolitanism, Greek diplomacy was provincial and unpolished. Yet it did possess forward-looking institutions. Besides the provision for dispute settlement by arbitration, there was the resident consul, or "*proxenos*," a citizen of the host state, whose job was to look after visitors from the state he represented (also see Leira and Neumann, chapter 9 in this volume). Most original was the practice of multilateral diplomacy. Invented by Sparta in the sixth century BC, multilateral alliances were meant to provide security or maintain the common peace. The Second Athenian Confederacy (378–355 BC) was set up as a defensive alliance against Sparta. Based on the principles of freedom and autonomy, Athens had a decisive voice, although the confederacy also had a common assembly in which each member state had one vote (Adcock and Mosley 1975: 239–43).

English-language historians of diplomacy begin their story with the Greeks because of familiarity with the classics and lack of acquaintance with ancient Near Eastern texts. Greek diplomacy is interesting in its own right and sometimes antici-pated modern diplomacy. Well into the modern age, authors mined the classical Greek historians for lessons and precedents. Greek diplomacy is one link between the Mesopotamian and European traditions.

Rome rose to world power through war but was ready to achieve its goals peacefully. During the Republic (509–44 BC), Rome conquered the Italian pen-insula by war interspersed by diplomacy, which was less wasteful and provided a breathing space. By 264 BC, more than 150 treaties of alliance had been concluded (B. Campbell 2001: 4). With the onset of empire, diplomacy became largely the vehi-cle for managing relations with subject peoples. Caesar Augustus (27 BC–AD 14) received numerous embassies during his reign, from provinces, client states, and even places as distant as Britain, Ethiopia, and India. But they came to pay tribute, request favors, or pay homage (Millar 1988: 349–51). The key word was *amicitia*, friendship, signifying loyalty to Rome. Foreign kings were "friends," not brothers.

Roman diplomacy borrowed from Greek practice. The Republic used Greek models, including arbitration, in its alliances with Greek states. It adopted the Greek formula "friendship for all time" in the peace of Apamea concluded with the Seleucid Empire in 188 BC (Gruen 2004: 259–60). Greek was the administrative language of the Roman Empire in the east and was the diplomatic language used in Roman official contacts with Parthia and Sassanid Persia. Roman embassies, like those of Greece, were ad hoc; high-ranking court officials and generals were chosen for important diplomatic missions. Unlike Greece, Rome had no need for the *proxenos* system of resident consuls. At any one time, imperial Rome housed numerous foreign dignitaries. These had no representative function but received a Roman education in preparation for their return home as loyal friends, imbued with Roman culture. Assemblies of the people did not receive embassies, even under the Republic. Later, the emperor received embassies in person, which could be awkward if he was on tour. Traditionally, the senate was also supposed to send and receive embassies, but this practice gradually atrophied. Provincial governors often sent dip-lomatic delegations.

Imperial Rome paid great attention to pomp and circumstance. Visiting ambas-sadors were received with meticulous protocol. They were entitled to a safe conduct, respectful treatment, and their upkeep. Rome had no time for rough-spun Greek hospitality. After Roman envoys were disrespectfully received by Corinth in 148 BC, the army sacked the city and subjected formerly autonomous Greece to Roman authority. On state occasions, foreign dignitaries were received in splendor. Gifts were exchanged to oil the wheels of a relationship.

War and peace were traditionally framed by sacred ritual. In the early days of the Republic the Fetial priesthood, which administered the rituals special to foreign relations, solemnly declared war and administered oaths accompanied by a sacrifice at the conclusion of peace. As Rome extended its empire the mutual swearing of oaths by the parties to an international treaty fell into disuse. Foreign nations, but not Rome, were expected to guarantee their promises by providing high-ranking hostages, demonstrating their subordinate status. There is no known case of such hostages ever being harmed, even when a treaty was broken (A. D. Lee 1991: 366). The momentous adoption by the emperor Constantine (306–37) of Christianity as the state religion was to transform the mission of empire but not diplomatic practice.

With the decline of Roman power in late antiquity (fourth to sixth centuries AD), diplomacy played an increasing role. In 363 the emperor Julian was killed fighting Sassanid Persia. With the empire embroiled in wars on other fronts, his successor, Jovian, was forced to conclude a humiliating peace under which he conceded territory and fortresses to the Persians and renounced Roman interests in Armenia. For the first time hostages were *exchanged* as surety (A. D. Lee 1991: 369). Payment of subsidies to the Persians and others, condemned by contemporaries as tribute and extortion, became a growing feature of Roman policy (Blockley 1985).

About this time—the mid-fourth century—the Master of the Offices, one of the key imperial officials, who controlled access to the emperor and ran the imperial courier service, acquired the responsibilities of a secretary of state. His department was now the regular channel of communication between the emperor and foreign rulers. It dealt with foreign ambassadors from their arrival to their departure and handled foreign correspondence, drawing on a pool of official interpreters (Boak 1924: 32–35). This was the turning point when diplomacy became an organized instrument of statecraft on a par with war.

The permanent division of the Roman Empire after 395 into Eastern and Western halves, then the fall of Rome to the barbarians in 476, transferred the imperial center of gravity to Constantinople, formerly Byzantium. For the next thousand years, the Byzantine Empire played a vital role in international relations, its importance magnified by its pivotal location between Europe and Asia, and its longevity. It was the conveyor belt transmitting the traditions of diplomacy from the classical to the modern worlds.

The Byzantine Empire seamlessly continued the administrative and legal practices of the undivided empire. With the loss of its Latin-speaking provinces in the late sixth century, Greek became the sole official language. Revitalized by Christianity, the empire acquired an acute sense of God-given superiority. At the same time, curving in a vast arc around the eastern Mediterranean, it faced unremitting external dangers. The great challenge was to preserve its holdings in southeast Europe, Anatolia, southwest Asia, and North Africa. Its problems and opportunities included immensely long borders (but internal supply lines), control of the trading routes from Asia to Europe, great but not limitless resources, a plethora of fractious pagan neighbors to the north, and the invariable threat of a rival empire to the east—the Persians, then the Muslim Arabs, finally the Muslim Turks.

Diplomacy was a major plank of Byzantine grand strategy, and this engendered a diplomatic machine of formidable scope and quality. The Master of the Offices emerged as one of the great ministers of the empire. In addition to his diplomatic duties, he controlled the imperial secret service and was a permanent member of the supreme advisory council. In 443 he was given oversight of the troops and fortifications of the eastern defenses (Boak 1924: 38). At his disposal was a matchless network of official and unofficial agents reporting on developments in neighboring regions, and a diplomatic service of messengers, emissaries, and interpreters able to conduct negotiations in all required languages. Not surprising, therefore, that written reports, a mainstay of European diplomacy, were a Byzantine innovation (Queller 1967: 141).

The purpose of this machine was to manage the empire's relations with its neighbors, preferably through negotiation rather than war. Byzantine goals were to thwart potential threats; coexist with its great power neighbors if possible, since it could not destroy them; strengthen and exalt the civilized Christian world centered on Constantinople; and foster the prosperity of the empire through trade (Obolensky 1963).

The first defensive goal entailed constructing a system of alliances that could deflect invasions, balance rival coalitions, and destabilize enemies. With this in mind the Byzantine Empire skillfully managed the balance of power—shifting its weight from one contending party to another to maintain equilibrium. To advance the goal of coexistence, Byzantium willingly conciliated rival great powers. In 562 Petrus, the Master of the Offices, successfully negotiated a peace treaty with the Sassanid Persians after the fall of Antioch. Neither the substance of the negotiation nor the arguments used would shame modern negotiators.

Byzantine diplomacy was indebted for its methods and ideas to Mesopotamia, Greece, Rome, and Christianity. From Mesopotamia it took the concepts of a family of kings (albeit with the emperor as their father), dynastic marriage to cement an alliance, refined protocol and hospitality, and the development of trade by merchant-ambassadors. From Greece it took the use of rhetoric in negotiation and influence over local clients through **soft power**, their admiration for Byzantine culture. From Rome it took the tactics of divide and rule, buying mercenary allies (to fight its wars) and buying off troublemakers, overawing visitors with the grandeur of the court, and providing aid to allies in the form of great civil engineering projects. From Christianity it took the conviction of its own supreme legitimacy and the mission to convert heathen peoples and win them over as allies to Constantinople.

Until the late eleventh century, the Byzantine Empire not only held its own thanks to its vast alliance system but even expanded into the Caucasus and Syria. From then on it was worn down by waves of invasions. In 1453 Ottoman Turks finally captured Constantinople, putting an end to an empire that had held its own for a thousand years, thanks not least to its adept diplomacy.

KEY POINTS

- Ancient Greek diplomatic practice influenced later European thought via the classics but was crude compared with Persian diplomacy, mostly serving parochial needs.
- Roman diplomacy at the height of empire was not concerned with negotiating agreements on an equal basis but with imposing its will and managing client states.

- As their empire declined, the Romans increasingly resorted to negotiation and conciliation. This more flexible tradition served the successor Byzantine Empire well for a thousand years, contributing to its survival.

EUROPEAN DIPLOMACY

Fifteenth-century Renaissance Italy is usually seen as the seedbed of modern European diplomacy. Yet, as Garrett Mattingly (1955: 17–25) acknowledges, Western diplomatic institutions were already highly developed by 1400, including a body of rules regulating diplomatic relations, immunities, negotiations, and treaties. During the late Middle Ages (1200–1500), the modern sovereign state, run by a central government enjoying exclusive jurisdiction within its borders, was still taking shape and had no monopoly on diplomacy.

Enveloping the medieval ruler was the feudal world of the "*respublica Christiana*," a Christian commonwealth headed by the pope, made up of overlapping jurisdictions, patchwork territories, and "countless ladders of patron-client ties." Religion was inseparable from politics (Jackson 2007: 30). Exclusive sovereignty was not considered at the time a prerequisite of diplomacy. Besides kings and popes, a variety of dignitaries and corporate bodies in the Late Middle Ages such as dukes, cardinals, cities, military orders, and trading organizations sent and received **nuncios, legates,** and **procurators**—envoys marked by fine distinctions, beginning to be dubbed **ambassadors** (Queller 1967: 68–74).

Medieval Europe was a hive of activity, and principals drew on or adapted familiar diplomatic practices to conduct their business, whether that was promoting trade, protecting merchants, performing homage, seeking allies, settling disputes, making dynastic marriages, appointing bishops, or claiming territory. Venice, which cut its diplomatic teeth negotiating trading charters with the Byzantine Empire, had by 1361 given its "baillie," the official administering the Venetian merchants' quarter in Constantinople, the functions of a resident ambassador representing the doge before the emperor (Nicol 1988: 291).

After the fall of the Byzantine Empire, Venice seamlessly maintained a diplomatic presence in Constantinople and beyond. Besides Venice, other European polities such as Aragon, Catalonia, and Genoa sent emissaries to the Muslim world under much the same ground rules as governed diplomacy among Christians. During the Crusader period there were regular diplomatic and trading relations between Christian rulers and military orders, and the Mamluks and Mongols. At least nine truces from the thirteenth century survive. With exceptions, they are of limited duration in the Muslim legal tradition, which prohibited permanent peace between a Muslim and an infidel ruler.

Throughout the period, the German Hanse, a league of trading cities in northern Europe, sent its emissaries far and wide negotiating trading access, preferential customs duties, and legal protections. It had its own lingua franca, a pidgin of Lübeck German. Anticipating modern commercial negotiating, it deployed contractual claims, financial resources, and the threat of trading sanctions to defend its members' interests (Lloyd 1991). It also arbitrated differences among them and by a treaty of 1289 became arbitrator for all conflicts between Norway and Denmark (Ralston 1929: 176–77).

When it came to peacemaking, the **papacy** was a diplomatic powerhouse, working to preserve the harmony of the *respublica Christiana* through mediation or arbitration. When mediating, it helped the parties themselves negotiate an agreed solution. When arbitrating, it rendered its own balanced judgment after hearing both sides. In 1298, the papacy arbitrated between the kings of France and England, and in 1319 between the French and the Flemings (Ralston 1929: 174–76). When arbitration became unacceptable, the popes offered their good offices as mediators. Between 1344 and 1355, they launched a series of initiatives to mediate a peace settlement between the English and French kings, and in 1454 brokered a peace between Venice and Milan.

It is sometimes erroneously believed that modern international law began with Rome. The Romans did have *ius gentium*, a law of nations. This, however, refers to the laws governing treatment of foreigners, especially provincial subjects, and not polities. It was the papacy that formatively influenced the development of international law, since the *respublica Christiana* rested on religious law. Hence the canon law of contract, the use of oaths, and the crucial assumption that promises are binding (*pacta sunt servanda*) fed through into later treaty law (Steiger 2001). The papacy, with its pivotal role, also shaped diplomatic procedures and immunities, including an early version of extraterritoriality.

Renaissance Italy did not invent diplomacy and was hardly cut off from the wider world; indeed it was a center of commerce, science, and art. But the Italian peninsula did constitute a compact regional subsystem, very much like ancient Greece, neighboring polities closely tied by culture, religion, and language. They engaged in intensive commerce, alliance making, and turbulent rivalry. For all these reasons, during the fifteenth century, Italy saw the consolidation of two of the characteristic institutions of European diplomacy: the resident ambassador and the chancery, a nascent foreign ministry.

"Resident ambassadors," envoys who stayed at their post until replaced, were introduced in the second half of the fifteenth century, most likely by Venice. Because they were on the spot, they could cultivate connections and acquire local knowledge (Berridge 1995: 3). In a world without newspapers, where information was avidly awaited back home, they became indispensable intelligence gatherers, reporting on the arrival of cargoes, the situation at court, the state of an alliance, military preparations, the atmosphere in the market, political gossip, and diplomatic to-and-fro. Mostly, ambassadors' sources were open; sometimes they used spies.

They were also good at handling routine matters such as maintaining working relations with the host government but were not ideally suited to negotiating important questions requiring high standing and close personal ties with their principal. For this a statesman or aristocrat was better suited. Notables would also be best in high-level representative roles, personifying the dignity of the ruler at life-cycle ceremonies such as weddings and funerals. On completion of their mission they returned home (Mallett 2001: 64–65).

To administer a permanent diplomatic network required an organization that could formulate foreign policy, prepare instructions, collate information, and keep records. Gian Galeazzo Visconti, first Duke of Milan (1395–1402), who was his own foreign minister, used his "chancery," originally the office producing official documents, as an embryonic foreign ministry. By the middle of the fifteenth century, all the major Italian states had chanceries capable of sustaining a coherent and continuous foreign policy and diplomatic service. With the establishment of the Most Holy League in 1454, such machinery became more important than ever. A defensive alliance set up by Florence, Venice, and Milan to bring peace to Italy, the league quickly broadened to take in all the major Italian powers (Mattingly 1955: 74, 87–88, 101). Italian technical innovations were quickly taken up by the great powers of the time, which were drawn willy-nilly into Italian affairs and spread throughout Europe. The resident ambassador quickly became the main feature distinguishing the European—meaning Christian—from the non-European practice of diplomacy. He also signified membership of an international society linked by religion and culture. Neither China nor Japan was prepared to receive resident missions until the nineteenth century (see Zhao, chapter 2 in this volume). The Ottoman Empire, however, whose armies reached the gates of Vienna in 1532, was an integral part of the European system.

Most of the major European powers had permanent missions in Constantinople by the end of the sixteenth century. Yet for 200 years, the sultans contented themselves with dispatching ad hoc missions only to Europe. J. C. Hurewitz (1961: 146–47) puts this down to Muslim introversion, lack of commercial motive, and a sense of cultural superiority. He adds that negotiations in Constantinople could be conveniently conducted in Turkish, on Ottoman terms, and on familiar ground. In 1835, a declining Ottoman Empire opened its first resident embassy in Paris, shortly followed by permanent missions in other European capitals.

The framework in place by about 1500 recognizably anticipates, in its essentials, modern diplomacy. In order to remain effective, it obviously had to develop in tune with changing needs. The forces shaping that gradual evolution were many and varied: the ever-growing power of the state; the Reformation and the replacement of the *respublica Christiana* by an international system of sovereign states; expanding trade and industry; the expansion then breakup of the European empires; the worldwide spread of diplomacy; the slow but steady expansion of political consciousness from the aristocracy to the people; system-altering wars; and a vast increase in global contacts and transactions.

Traditional forms sometimes concealed underlying changes. The kind of qualifications that fifteenth- and sixteenth-century authors required of the "ideal diplomatist" are not very different from those listed by Sir Harold Nicolson (1939: 126) in his pre–Second World War essay on diplomacy—for example, modesty, charm, tact. They read like code words for good breeding and an expensive education, evoking an age before industrialization and universal suffrage, when aristocrats still dominated diplomacy. In fact, from about the mid-nineteenth century onward, the middle classes increasingly entered the diplomatic service thanks to administrative reform, competitive entrance examinations, and more rigorous training all aimed at the "professionalization of diplomacy." Keith Hamilton and Richard Langhorne (1995: 104) note: "The composition of Europe's diplomatic services tended in the end to reflect the political structure of the societies they represented."

The nineteenth century saw the heyday of the resident ambassador, his responsibilities increasing commensurately with the expansion in foreign relations. Because of slow communications, an ambassador might have to negotiate without fresh instructions. Despite such technical innovations as the steamship and telegraph, he retained considerable discretion until 1914. After the cataclysm of the First World War, ambassadors rarely conducted negotiations independently, that task being increasingly performed in multilateral settings or by ad hoc delegations. Jet travel further restricted their role. A distinguished American statesman, George Ball, offered any embassy he desired in 1977, demurred with the comment that he did not wish to end his days "as an innkeeper for itinerant congressmen" (G. W. Ball 1982: 452).

With the rise of French power in the seventeenth century (and the use of French as the diplomatic language), growing emphasis was put on the organization directing diplomacy. In 1626 Cardinal Armand Richelieu, Louis XIII's chief minister, set up a ministry of foreign affairs to ensure the unified, harmonious administration of French foreign policy. This has been the ideal—imperfectly realized in practice—ever since. It has not been possible or advisable to keep, say, ministries of finance and defense out of foreign affairs. Richelieu was careful to cultivate public opinion and also stressed the inviolability of a state's promises, "*pacta sunt servanda*." Why else would states negotiate agreements?

The consolidation and codification of international law as a special area of law were crucial to the peaceful management of European affairs. From the sixteenth century onward, a law of nations emerged out of a patchwork of medieval laws and customs. As the *respublica Christiana* faded away, it became vital to answer certain fundamental questions, including, Who has the legal right to make war and peace, to send ambassadors, and to conclude treaties? Hugo Grotius (1583–1645), the Dutch humanist, determined that treaties between republics were always binding (as distinguished from personal treaties between rulers, which might not be) and continued to bind the successors of the original signatories (Lesaffer 2000). The 1648 Peace of Westphalia ending the Thirty Years' War marked an important stage in the evolution of an international system of sovereign states. But it was only at the Congress of Vienna in 1815 following the defeat of Napoleon that it was finally resolved that *only* sovereign states could participate in the international legal order.

By the seventeenth century theorists agreed that "ratification"—the signing and sealing of treaty documents by plenipotentiaries—constituted the treaty, not, as under canon law, the sworn oath. The concept of comprehensive diplomatic immunity steadily gained ground from Grotius onward. In 1709, the British Parliament passed legislation protecting foreign diplomats from court proceedings. The principle of inviolability eventually extended to the diplomatic mission's premises, servants, property, and mail.

Arguments over precedence and procedure dogged diplomacy throughout the seventeenth and eighteenth centuries. There were constant arguments over the placement of diplomats on official occasions. At peace conferences, enormous effort was invested in ensuring that no important ambassador was seated in an inferior position to a rival. As late as 1812, the French representative in Naples fought a government-approved duel with his Russian counterpart over precedence. At the Congress of Aix-la-Chapelle of 1818, agreement was reached on a system of ranking. Finally, the 1961 Vienna Convention on Diplomatic Relations definitively codified the rules of diplomatic practice (M. S. Anderson 1993: 56–68).

The single most significant innovation of European diplomacy was the introduction of the international conference. Under this system, national delegations assemble in a formal setting to negotiate. Peace congresses were convened at Arras in 1435 and Cateau-Cambrésis in 1559. In scope and scale, the Congress of Westphalia (1643–48) entailed a striking departure from previous diplomatic practice. Richelieu initially conceived of a congress so that France and its numerous German allies might confront the Holy Roman Empire with a united front and thereby frustrate an imperial strategy of divide and rule. "Prenegotiation," bargaining over the procedure to govern the conference, stretched over nine years because the parties were acutely aware that concessions on form had substantive implications. Sweden, seeking equality of status on the continent of Europe, insisted on equal treatment at the congress. Spain at first refused safe-conduct passes to Dutch representatives because it considered the Dutch Republic to be in a state of rebellion (Colegrove 1919). The five-year duration of the congress hints at the complexity and gravity of the issues negotiated. The system of European states was reshaped. The papacy yielded authority to secular rulers. Catholic and Protestant German states alike acquired effective independence from the Holy Roman Empire. Dutch and Swiss independence was also recognized. Rules for the peaceful settlement of disputes were formulated. With the eclipse of the papacy as a political force, international law was finally divorced from its religious background (Croxton 1999; Gross 1948).

The 1815 Congress of Vienna marked a further watershed between a world where the great powers met collectively only to make peace and one where their representatives meeting in conference managed international affairs on a continuous basis. This was the system known as the Concert of Europe. Great peace congresses continued to be held, at Paris in 1856 and Berlin in 1878. Now European ambassadors also met in conference to settle such matters as the independence of Belgium (1830–39), the carve-up of Africa (1883–84), and the settlement of Balkan questions (1912–13). The Hague Conferences of 1899 and 1907 codified the laws of war and set up the Permanent Court of Arbitration.

In January 1918, President Woodrow Wilson of the United States proclaimed a fourteen-point plan for a postwar settlement. Self-determination, diplomacy in the public view, popular consent, and a "general association of nations" were henceforth to guide international affairs. They set the parameters on twentieth-century diplomacy, no longer just European but, by the end of the century, global. English—a language spoken on four continents—eventually supplanted French as the international vernacular. Establishment of the League of Nations in 1920 institutionalized conference diplomacy within a parliamentary framework. The United Nations replaced it in 1945. After decolonization, its membership embraced the nations of the world.

Over the years a multitude of specialized international organizations were set up to deal with regional and functional issues—for example, human rights, health, trade and development, finance, children, refugees, and telecommunications. Thus legitimate international change was to be achieved by general consent, not force. Multilateral negotiation became the order of the day, empowering weak states and placing the onus on consensus building. The outcome has been a vast expansion of diplomatic activity and the emergence of a truly global society served by a global diplomacy.

KEY POINTS

- Christian Europe from the ninth century onward inherited the "great tradition" of diplomacy virtually intact.
- Major organizational innovations included the resident embassy, the diplomatic service, the foreign ministry, and the training of diplomats.
- Crucially, public international law emerged, together with the international conference and multilateral institutions.
- It was only after the dissolution of the great empires in the late twentieth century, however, that diplomacy began to overcome its old culture-bound attitudes and habits and expanded into a truly global system.

CONCLUSION

What counts in history is the long run, and diplomacy is no exception. Its story is one of evolutionary change over millennia. Some features of diplomacy display remarkable continuity; others, such as foreign ministries, had to be reinvented. There were bursts of creativity, but it is hard to find total innovations. There is nothing new about trade diplomacy, cultural diplomacy, non-state actors, multilateral alliances, and competing government agencies. In its time the Amarna system was inclusive and multicultural. Rabshakeh conducted an exercise in public diplomacy outside the walls of Jerusalem in 701 BC.

From time immemorial, emissaries were sent out by their principals to perform such tasks as conveying and receiving messages, explaining, persuading, observing, reporting, and negotiating. Obviously, ambassadors today no longer perform the range of duties that they carried out before the communications revolution. The news media cover the news now in real time, specialists conduct negotiations, and leaders regularly fly in to meet their counterparts in person. This is not to say that ambassadors do not remain extremely useful—well placed to glean high-level views not reported in the media, to express their government's position, promote their country's image, and foster good relations with their host.

They are also indispensable in a vital way. They represent, and in some sense embody, the authority and honor of their principal, whether the president, elected assembly, or people. Other agents such as private individuals, celebrities, and ex-presidents may seize the limelight and put an issue, for instance the prohibition on land mines, on the agenda. Corporate leaders may make international business deals. In the final analysis, though, arms control treaties are made by states, and governments set the rules of trade. Only states are legal personalities in international law.

Representation is an obligation that has solemn, even sacrosanct, features. Ambassadors were traditionally thought to have a quasi-sacral character. For millennia they concluded treaties within a framework hallowed by rites and oaths in the name of the divinity. That explicitly supernatural element is no longer there. Nevertheless, today ambassadors stand alongside other representative figures amid the symbols and shrines of the state as part of the paraphernalia of the civil religion with which nations solemnize their existence. Representing their sovereigns, ambassadors are there to lend their dignity to such state occasions as national days, state weddings and funerals, and inaugurations. Violation of their immunity is a sacrilegious offense against the sovereign they personify.

Finally, it is not by chance that one of the first acts of a newly independent state is to send its ambassador to the United Nations. The same social imperative that bound together the royal houses of ancient times in a brotherhood of great kings still impels modern nations to seek the approval and acceptance of their peers in the international community. The ambassador remains the symbol of peoplehood among the nations.

QUESTIONS

1. "Nothing's new under the sun." Is this true of diplomacy?
2. What have been the invariant features of diplomacy throughout history?
3. What were some limitations of historical diplomatic systems?
4. How effective is diplomacy today compared with the past?
5. Does diplomacy depend on a balance of power?
6. How have changes in communications technology throughout history affected the conduct of diplomacy?
7. What are the implications of the analysis in this chapter for your theoretical and practical understandings of contemporary diplomacy?

CHAPTER 2

Past Diplomacy in East Asia
From Tributary Relations to Cold War Rivalry
Suisheng Zhao

CHAPTER CONTENTS

- Introduction
- Collapse of the traditional East Asian order and the tributary system
- Japan's military expansion and the diplomacy of imperialism
- Cold War diplomacy in East Asia
- Diplomacy during the deterioration of the East Asian bipolar system
- Diplomacy of the strategic triangle
- Conclusion

READER'S GUIDE

This chapter briefly explores the history of diplomacy in East Asia from early times to the end of the Cold War. With the introduction of Western diplomacy and the rising power of Japan, the Chinese tributary system deteriorated during the diplomacy of imperialism. After the defeat of Japanese aggression during the Pacific War, East Asia found itself in the midst of bipolar Cold War diplomacy, in which the functional role of each state was conditioned by security alliances or blocs. The increasing diplomatic power of China in the 1970s led to the deterioration of the rigid bipolar system and created a strategic triangle in the 1980s. The tendency toward a coalition between two of the three countries (China, the USSR, and the United States) and the fear of this alliance constituted the main dynamics of triangular diplomacy.

INTRODUCTION

Compared with their Western counterparts, East Asian countries were late to the game of modern diplomacy. Prior to its defeat by Great Britain in the Opium War of 1840–42, China was a proud empire that maintained ethnocentric tributary relations for centuries. The decline of the Chinese empire gave rise to an "anarchic system" in which imperialist powers and newly emerged nation-states pursued their own interests in ways they judged best, and most often by military force if they were capable of doing so. The constant warfare left almost no room for "modern diplomacy," by which nation-states settle their disputes and defend their **sovereignty** by diplomatic bargaining and negotiations. Instead, from the late nineteenth century and for much of the twentieth century, diplomacy in East Asia can be understood, respectively, as "diplomacy of imperialism," "Cold War bloc diplomacy," and "triangular diplomacy." After analyzing the dynamics of the tributary system, this chapter traces the events that sustained these three periods of diplomacy and led to various treaties and agreements being negotiated, some to the detriment of small or weak nations.

COLLAPSE OF THE TRADITIONAL EAST ASIAN ORDER AND THE TRIBUTARY SYSTEM

The traditional East Asian order was China-centered. The Chinese emperor was a centrally recognized authority, known as *tianzhi* (the Son of Heaven). All territories arranged themselves hierarchically. China was at the center, followed by the most nearby and culturally similar tributaries, Korea, Vietnam, and the Ryukyu Islands, which were ruled by the Chinese empires on and off in history. The next tier was inner Asia, usually including Tibet and central Asia. At a farther distance over land or sea there were *wai-i* (outer barbarians), including Indochina and Southeast Asia (see figure 2.1).

China's centrality was a function of its civilization, culture, and rulers' virtue, although military means were also used to defend and expand the Chinese empire. In contrast to the Western diplomatic protocol with the emphasis on legal equality, the China-centered East Asian order was sustained by a heavy stress on ethical orthodoxy. Correct conduct according to the proper **norms** could move others by its example. Clear legal boundaries of jurisdiction and power simply did not exist. Traditional East Asian order was maintained for centuries mostly by the strength of the Chinese civilization because many societies in East Asia were developed within Chinese cultural boundaries and strongly influenced by Confucian ideas about family and social and political order. The influence of Chinese political and cultural institutions was especially strong in Korea, Japan, and Vietnam.

The traditional East Asian order was institutionalized in a "tributary system," which was primarily developed during the Ming and Qing periods. Korea, the Ryukyus, Annam (Vietnam), Burma, Laos, and Nepal sent tributary missions regularly to China (see figure 2.1). During the Ming dynasty, tributary relations were supervised by the Board of Rites Reception Department. Relations with certain tribes of aborigines along China's cultural frontiers were managed by the Department of the Board of War. After the establishment of the Qing dynasty in 1644, the Li-fan Yuan (Barbarous Affairs Department) became an integral part of the tributary system. It

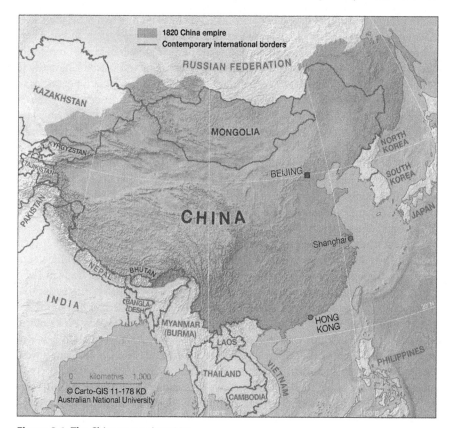

Figure 2.1 The Chinese empire 1820.

used the rites and forms of the traditional Confucian Chinese system to conduct relations with the "barbarians." The tributary relationship was always **bilateral**, never **multilateral**: one partner and China. The tributary system operated in a very ceremonial way. The tributary missions bore tribute with them and were escorted to court by the Chinese officials. Performing appropriate ceremonies at the Qing court, notably the *kowtow* (three kneeling and nine prostrating), they presented tribute memorials and a symbolic tribute of their precious native products and then were given imperial gifts in return. Usually they were also granted certain privileges of trade. Finally, Chinese missions were sent to visit in return.

The tributary system was valuable economically and politically for both the tributary states and China. For the tributary states, the presentation of tribute enabled them to conduct controlled but important trade with China and simultaneously receive validation for political power from the Chinese emperor. China also benefited from the system because China's power was substantiated through tributary nations' recognition, and China was able to trade with them for items necessary to its economy without breaking the myth of China's self-sufficiency (Y. S. Yu 1967).

China's self-sufficiency and imperial position were never seriously challenged until the nineteenth century, when European gunboats arrived and requested diplomatic recognition. When European traders and missionaries reached the shores of

China, Chinese imperial bureaucrats perceived them as no different from their East Asian neighbors who "should observe the rules of the tributary system and fit themselves into the civilized Sino-centric world order in their pursuit of foreign trade" (So and Chiu 1995: 34). The Chinese court assumed an aloof and patronizing attitude toward early European traders, keeping them confined to the southern port cities of Macao and later Guangzhou (Canton). China's rulers professed little need for Western goods and ideas. This pattern of trade relationship was known as the "Guangzhou system," in which Westerners were confined to a dozen buildings called factories outside the walls of Guangzhou city and forbidden to trade outside of these factories.

When Britain came to dominate world trade in the early nineteenth century, the constraints under the Guangzhou system became intolerable to the British, who had to find new commodities to solve the growing gap in the balance of trade payment. Opium was discovered. As the trade balance began to turn in favor of Britain and the Chinese court became aware of the devastating consequences of the opium trade for China's society and national wealth, political tensions between the British and the imperial court in Beijing mounted. An uncorrupted official, Lin Zexu, was appointed as the commissioner to oversee the Guangzhou trade in 1839. Lin's draconian measures to stop the drug trade forced the British to surrender vast stores of their opium stocks. The British government demanded an indemnity for the loss from China. After the Beijing court refused, the Opium War broke out in 1840. China was defeated and forced to sign the Treaty of Nanjing in 1842, which stipulated that China cede Hong Kong to the British; that five Chinese ports were opened to foreign trade; that foreign, rather than Chinese, laws would apply to foreigners living in the foreign "concessions" on Chinese soil; and that China was to pay Britain a huge amount of silver as compensation for the opium destroyed by Chinese officials.

The Opium War was a heavy blow to the Chinese sense of superiority. In the years following its humiliating defeat, the Chinese government was forced to sign one after another treaty with foreign powers, leading to the transition from the tributary system to a "treaty system" in which former tributary states became European colonies and the Qing court was forced to accept the Westphalian concept of diplomatic equality among **sovereign** states, shattering the fictive remnants of the ancient cultural superiority in the tributary system. Within the treaty system, China began to accept European diplomatic practices as foreign **diplomatic missions** were established in Beijing. China's recognition of the diplomatic status of other states was borne out by Emperor Xian Feng's imperial edict sanctioning the Treaty of Tianjin in 1861, as well as the compulsory acceptance of **diplomatic representation** of Western powers in Beijing and the initiation of "Zongli Yamen," a government office created to handle diplomatic relations with Western powers.

China and its former tributary states were thus brought into the Western-dominated sovereign nation-state system. By the end of the nineteenth century, nearly all East Asian countries were opened to Western trade and diplomacy, and many of them became the colonies of Western powers. A global network of economic and military outposts that was critical to Western domination of East Asia was established. China was no longer a central power but a target of European imperialist powers as they established their spheres of influence on Chinese territory.

Britain carved out a **sphere of influence** in the Yangtze Valley, France in Guangzhou, and Germany in Shandong. As a newly arrived imperial power, the United States, in September 1899, dispatched the famous Open Door Notes to major European powers and Japan, requesting that they grant traders of all countries equal treatment with respect to harbor dues and railroad charges. As a consequence, a legal provision, known as the "most-favored-nation clause," was inserted into every treaty signed by China. Concessions granted to one foreign country by China would automatically be extended to the others.

China and its East Asian tributaries no longer constituted a world unto themselves but a part of the legal and diplomatic international system dominated by the Western powers. Although China now accepted formal diplomatic equality with the other states, it was not treated equally by the victorious Western powers. The treaties that China signed with the Western powers thereafter were soon labeled in the Chinese political discourses as the "unequal treaties" because the formal diplomatic equality masked a host of provisions that disadvantaged China and set limits on its sovereignty, such as the provision of extraterritorial rights, which meant that foreign rather than Chinese laws would apply to foreigners living in China, and to place its economic interests under foreign control. By adapting to Western diplomatic practices and ceding its tributary states, China entered into the modern world under the threat of imperialism to its territorial integrity and thus became a zealous defender of its territorial integrity and sovereignty, an important underpinning of the nation-state system.

KEY POINTS

- The traditional East Asian order was China-centered, and a tributary system based on different principles than modern diplomacy was the institution of interstate relations.
- After the collapse of the China-centered East Asian order, modern diplomatic practices were introduced and accepted by China and other East Asian states.

JAPAN'S MILITARY EXPANSION AND THE DIPLOMACY OF IMPERIALISM

While China began to accept the idea of equality among nation-states and struggled to defend its sovereignty, the world had come under the domination of imperialist powers that did not treat weak nations as equals. In the age of imperialism, the status of a country was determined mostly by its military strength, and diplomacy was an instrument of imperialist expansion at the expense of small and weak nations. The great powers attempted to conquer small and weak countries by force and to trade their interest with other great powers by diplomacy.

Japan was the first East Asian country to rise to the status of a great power. The Meiji Restoration in 1868 started Japan's modernization and also set a course of Western learning, including the emulation of European-style imperialism to create Japan's own empire in East Asia. Japan's expansion began with annexing the

Ryukyu Islands in 1874, but its first major target was Korea, China's long-standing tributary state and Japan's springboard to continental Asia. Using military intimidation, Japan forced the Koreans to sign the Treaty of Kanghwa in 1876, opening two ports to Japanese trade. By recognizing Korea as an independent state, the Kanghwa Treaty ignored China's exclusive claim to suzerainty over Korea. To the Japanese, "the Western idea of sovereign statehood was a convenient tool with which to start the process of breaking the bonds uniting Korea and China" (Nelson 1945: 126). This treaty paved the way for the Sino-Japanese War in 1894. After a series of swift victories, the Japanese drove the Chinese forces out of Korea and forced China to sign the Treaty of Shimonoseki on 7 April 1895, which recognized Japan's paramount interest in Korea. China also agreed to pay an indemnity; to cede Taiwan, the Pesadores (Penghu) Islands, and the Liaodong Peninsula to Japan; and to open up a specified section of the Yangtze River to Japanese commerce and four ports to Japanese trade.

While Russia generally remained neutral during the Sino-Japanese War, it was threatened by Japan's acquisition of the Liaodong Peninsula, a strategically important foothold on the Asian mainland. On the initiative of Russia on 23 April 1895, six days after the signature of the Shimonoseki Treaty, Germany, France, and Russia sent a joint memorandum to Japan advising the restitution of Liaodong to China. Faced with what was known as the Triple Intervention, Japan was militarily too weak and diplomatically too isolated to resist and had to sign a supplementary convention on 8 November 1895, which stipulated that within three months of China's paying of a supplementary, the Japanese troops would evacuate Liaodong. The Triple Intervention helped Russia establish a stronghold in China. Russia's influence was further increased by the conclusion of the secret Li-Lobanov Agreement in 1896, by which China consented to the construction of a railway across Manchuria toward Vladivostok. The Treaty of St. Petersburg in March 1898 further empowered Russia through the right to lease Port Arthur and Dalian for twenty-five years.

Japan then turned to Great Britain, the czar's ubiquitous competitor, to find a counterweight to Russia. On 30 January 1902, the British agreed to the formal Anglo-Japanese Alliance, the first military alliance between an Asian nation and a European power, to maintain the balance of power in East Asia. With Britain on its side, Japan launched a surprise attack on the Russian fleet at Port Arthur, sinking virtually the entire Russian squadron at anchor on 8 February 1904. Two days later, Tokyo issued an official declaration of war. While the Russo-Japanese War was a veritable life-and-death struggle for the small island nation against a large European power, Japan had the advantage of fighting close to its main supply sources and had control of the sea. With Great Britain on Japan's side to deny the Russian's use of the Suez Canal, Russia's Baltic fleet had to make its way around the world to reach the Tsushima Straits, which separate Japan from Korea. The Japanese warships were already waiting there and readily demolished the Russian fleet.

The first victory of an Asian nation over a major European power, the result of the Russo-Japanese War established Japan as the peer of Western imperialist powers. With the Treaty of Portsmouth, mediated by the United States on 5 September 1905, Japan obtained Russia's recognition of its paramount interests in Korea and Manchuria by possession of the Changchun-Dalian portion of the Russian-controlled

Chinese Eastern Railway and the transfer from Russia of the Liaodong Peninsula. To protect these newly acquired rights, a Kanto (East Manchuria) army was created as the symbol of Japan's continental imperialism.

Japan's pursuit of continental expansion led to Western fears of Japanese domination in Asia. Although Great Britain took a passive attitude, the United States protested the Twenty-One Demands on the grounds that they contradicted the principles of equal opportunity and the Open Door policy. Taking advantage of the expiration of the Anglo-Japanese Alliance in November 1921, the United States called for a historic conference in Washington to restore peace and stability in East Asia. The Washington Conference produced a series of treaties signed by Japan, the United States, and major European powers and represented a multilateral diplomatic attempt to redefine East Asian international relations through a concert of powers. As a latecomer to the great power competition, however, Japan felt it was unjustly denied its rightful place because its expansion beyond Korea and Taiwan ran into opposition from the Western powers. Although Kijuro Shidehara (Japan's minister of foreign affairs, 1924–29) guided Japan's foreign policy in line with the conference agreements, senior Japanese army leaders began to pose serious challenges to the Washington Conference system when they took foreign policy into their own hands and exploited a series of events to provide a pretext for military actions against China in the early 1930s.

When Japan attacked Manchuria in 1931 in response to the Mukden Incident, the Chinese government instructed the military commander of the northeast not to retaliate but to rely on an appeal to the League of Nations, which, however, was powerless to intervene. Although the League agreed to send a committee under Britain's Lord Lytton to investigate the events in Manchuria in December 1931, the committee did not issue a report until one year later, and the league did not adopt the report until February 1933. The report rejected Japan's pretext as an unjustified intervention but fell short of calling for implementing collective security sanctions against Japan as the aggressor. Although the League of Nations did not do anything to punish the Japanese aggression, the Japanese delegation walked out and announced Japan's resignation from the League when the report was adopted. Consolidating its control over Manchuria, Japan extended its invasion to Shanghai in January 1932. Western powers, hit by the Great Depression, were too involved in their domestic problems to block Japanese aggression. Facing no meaningful resistance, Japan launched a large-scale invasion of China. An undeclared but full-fledged Sino-Japanese War started in 1937.

Without real resistance from the United States and the other great powers, the idea of moving south toward the Pacific gained currency among Japanese military leaders after the outbreak of war in Europe in the late 1930s. Japan started with a diplomatic maneuver by signing the Tripartite Mutual Defense Pact with Germany and Italy on 27 September 1940 to deter U.S. intervention in either the European war or the Sino-Japanese conflict. Japan's diplomatic offensive reached a new height when the Soviet-Japanese Neutrality Treaty was signed in Moscow on 13 April 1941. Receiving the assent of the pro-Nazi Vichy government in France, Japanese troops moved into northern Indochina and were now ready to carry out Japan's southward strategy. Japan's southward expansion set it on a collision course with the United States due to the perceived linkage between the war in Asia and the war in Europe and the Japanese striking southward to seize the mineral resources of the European empires in Southeast Asia. The United States had to take action to check the Japanese expansion in the Pacific. Washington had already placed an embargo on shipments of aircraft, arms, and other war materials to Japan in the summer of 1938, abrogated its commercial treaty with Japan in July 1939, and terminated the export of scrap iron and steel to Japan in the fall of 1940. After the Japanese attack on Indochina in July 1941, the United States froze Japanese assets and imposed an embargo on the export of oil to Japan. Great Britain, the British Commonwealth nations, and the Dutch East Indies followed suit, cutting 90 percent of Japan's oil import. This escalation of threatening economic diplomacy was intended to deter Japan from further rashness but had precisely the opposite effect because the Japanese government made a quick decision to wage war against the United States.

Without oil imports, Japan's war machine would come to a halt within a matter of months. In the choice between abandoning military expansion and a war with the United States, although a victory in the war was uncertain, the alternative of submitting to the demands of the "white imperialists" was equally hard to accept. After conclusion of the Tripartite Pact with Germany and Italy and the Russo-Japanese Neutrality Treaty, Japan launched a preemptive attack on Pearl Harbor on Sunday, 7 December 1941. Counting on the element of surprise, the Japanese plan was to force the larger and stronger America to come to the negotiating table before it could mobilize its full strength.

Until Pearl Harbor, Japan fought mostly an East Asian war. Now a genuinely Pacific-wide war started. Shocked by the surprising attack and the heavy losses of the Pacific Fleet at Pearl Harbor, the United States quickly mobilized its potential to fight back. The Pacific War was fought between Japan, which attempted to redefine the East Asian order on its own terms, and the United States, which eventually came to deter Japanese expansion in the Pacific and Asia. The final result of the war was determined primarily by the American industrial capacity to support a protracted naval strategy at long distance. The Japanese government surrendered unconditionally to the Allies after the United States dropped atomic bombs on Hiroshima and Nagasaki in 1945.

KEY POINTS

- During the age of imperialistic diplomacy in East Asia, the status of a country was determined mostly by its military strength, while diplomacy was an instrument of imperialistic expansion and often used to negotiate unfair treaties.
- Japan's victory over Russia and the resulting Treaty of Portsmouth was historically and diplomatically significant because both demonstrated the power of an Asian nation over a European country.
- Threatening forms of economic diplomacy by the United States and some other Western countries failed to deter Japan's move southward to the Pacific and consequently the start of the Pacific War.

COLD WAR DIPLOMACY IN EAST ASIA

Although the Americans and Soviets at the Yalta Conference pledged to reshape postwar peace at the end of the Pacific War, East Asia soon found itself in the midst of a global Cold War bipolar rivalry as distrust and hostility developed between these two superpowers. The United States led one pole, in which Japan, South Korea, Taiwan, the Philippines, and several Southeast Asian countries were dependent partners. On the other pole, the Soviet Union played the dominant role, with China as a junior partner and North Korea and North Vietnam as dependent partners. Due to an increased emphasis on the ideological division between the two sides, the bipolar system became tight and eventually formed rigid alliances or blocs. Cold War diplomacy was centered on the building and maintenance of the two alliances as well as the diplomatic management of crises and conflicts, most notably the limited war in Korea and the crisis across the Taiwan Strait.

The founding of the People's Republic of China (PRC) on 1 October 1949 was the starting point of Cold War diplomacy in East Asia because it had a great impact on the regional as well as the global balance of power. The Sino-Soviet alliance emerged when Mao Zedong made the historical announcement on 30 June 1949 that China would "lean to one side" in the struggle between imperialism and socialism (Mao 1969: 415). The Sino-Soviet alliance would give the communists control of the Eurasian landmass stretching from the Baltic Sea to the South China Sea.

The Moscow-Beijing alliance preceded the outbreak of the Korean War in 1950. At the end of the Second World War, the United States and the Soviet Union occupied Korea with the thirty-eighth parallel as a temporary line to fix responsibility. Once the occupation was established, however, the United States and the Soviet Union competitively set up two rival governments, and the thirty-eighth parallel was thus turned into a political line dividing Korea into two states. North Korean leader Kim Il Sung visited Moscow twice in 1949 to gain Stalin's support for a take-over of the South. Kim convinced Stalin that the war could be won quickly, before the United States had time to become involved. Mao was in Moscow in the winter of 1949–50 and approved Kim's plans, saying that the Americans would not intervene, since the war was an internal matter that the Korean people would decide for themselves (Khrushchev 1970: 367–69). With these assurances, the North launched a massive attack on 25 June 1950, advancing rapidly southward. Within six weeks, North Korean troops occupied most of the Korean peninsula.

Perceiving the North Korean move as a Soviet-sponsored attack against the free world, the United States was forced to redefine its security interests in Korea. On the US initiative, the United Nations (UN) Security Council adopted two resolutions on 25 and 27 June 1950, authorizing a UN force to restore peace in Korea. The successful amphibious landing of US Marines at Inchon on 15 September 1950 altered the entire course of the Korean War. On 20 October, the American-led UN forces captured Pyongyang, the capital city of North Korea. A week later the first American troops reached the Yalu River, the border between Korea and China. General Douglas MacArthur's "home by Christmas" dream, however, was shattered by a massive Chinese intervention in November. Pyongyang was recaptured by Chinese troops on 4 December 1950. With the Chinese intervention came a heightened danger of war, and the United States searched for a settlement through political means. On 27 July 1953, an armistice agreement was signed that restored the status quo, and Korea remained divided after the fighting was stopped.

The immediate consequence of the Korean War was the American policy adjustment to end the occupation in Japan. In September 1951, a peace conference was held in San Francisco. On the morning of 8 September, Prime Minister Shigeru Yoshida of Japan signed a peace treaty with the United States and forty-seven other countries that restored Japanese sovereignty. That same afternoon, he signed a bilateral, mutual security treaty secretly negotiated with the United States, which was designed to protect an independent but weak Japan as a countervailing force to the Sino-Soviet alliance. Although Yoshida earlier indicated his preference for a "two-China" approach in Japan's diplomatic and economic policies, he was compelled to sign a bilateral peace treaty with the Republic of China (ROC) in Taiwan on the same day that the San Francisco treaties came into effect in 1952. These arrangements, known as the "San Francisco system," symbolized the beginning of American containment policy in East Asia. Unlike the North Atlantic Treaty Organization (NATO) accord bound by the principle of reciprocal obligation, the American-Japanese security treaty stipulated Japan's unilateral and unconditional dependency upon American protection. It was just one link in the chain of bilateral treaties that the United States signed with countries in the region to contain communism. The containment system represented the recognition of Asia's strategic importance because of the demonstrated threat of the North Korean and Chinese military forces to American interests.

After the Korean War, Taiwan became a focal point of Cold War diplomacy in East Asia. One of the first decisions made by the Harry S. Truman administration after the North Korean attack on the South was to dispatch the Seventh Fleet to neutralize the Taiwan Strait. This decision forced Beijing to delay its offensive campaign against the offshore islands and Taiwan. After the Korean cease-fire agreement was reached, China began to bombard the islands of Jinmen and Mazu on 3 September 1954. In response, President Dwight Eisenhower in January 1955 submitted the Formosa (Taiwan) Resolution to Congress, which gave the president the right to order military aid for the defense of the offshore islands.

China's leadership was alarmed by possible American armed intervention. In response, Premier Zhou Enlai made a public statement on 23 April 1955, expressing that "the Chinese government is willing to sit down to discuss the question of relaxing tension in the Far East, and especially the question of relaxing tension in the Taiwan area" (Waijiaobu Yanjiushi 1960: 2250–51). Despite there being no diplomatic relations between China and the United States, on 1 August 1955, Chinese and American representatives began ambassadorial-level talks in neutral Geneva. These diplomatic negotiations, which involved seventy-three meetings, lasted for more than two years. The primary item on America's agenda was to get back American prisoners of war being held in China and to persuade the Chinese government to renounce military force in its policy toward Taiwan. The Chinese hoped to resolve essential problems in Sino-American relations, including the long-standing Taiwan issue. However, no agreement was reached at Geneva, and talks were officially terminated on 12 December 1957. The termination gravely disappointed the Chinese leaders, who decided to bombard Jinmen and Mazu for a second time in the summer of 1958. In response, President Eisenhower instructed US naval forces to implement the convoy-escort plan and amassed in the Taiwan Straits the largest single concentration of nuclear support forces in history in September of that year.

KEY POINTS

- The founding of the PRC was the beginning of Cold War diplomacy in East Asia because it had a great impact on the regional as well as the global balance of power.
- The intensified bipolar competition defined Cold War bloc diplomacy, in which the functional role of each state was conditioned by security alliances or blocs.
- Although Cold War diplomacy was characterized by incessant confrontation and recurrent crises, these crises were well controlled to avoid escalating into a general war between the two superpowers, which conducted diplomatic maneuvers rather than fought, or fought a limited war rather than a major war to pursue their interests.

DIPLOMACY DURING THE DETERIORATION OF THE EAST ASIAN BIPOLAR SYSTEM

Starting in the 1960s, the bipolar Cold War system in East Asia experienced some subtle but important changes. The first was the Sino-Soviet split. Then Japan reemerged to play a more active role in East Asian regional affairs. Finally, to pull out of Vietnam with honor, the United States accepted China as a legitimate player in East Asian power relations. These developments led to a geopolitical revolution that produced the rapprochement between the United States and China in the early 1970s.

The Sino-Soviet split, misleadingly clad in an ideological garb at the time, was fundamentally an assertion of Chinese national interests against the Soviet Union. The first serious evidence of the conflict emerged at the Twentieth Congress of the Communist Party of the Soviet Union in February 1956. Nikita Khrushchev's bitter denunciation of Stalin's cult of personality exasperated Mao, whose rule in China had many similar features (Li 1994: 118). The Soviet Union then abrogated the 1957 agreement (in which the Soviets pledged to assist China in developing nuclear weapons) in 1959 and terminated its economic and military assistance in 1960. Moreover, during the Sino-Indian border dispute in 1959–62, the Soviet Union sided with India instead of supporting the PRC. Khrushchev's policy for "peaceful coexistence" further deepened Beijing's suspicion that the **détente** between the Soviets and the West might foster the encirclement of China (Yu 1994: 18–19). These events contributed to the Sino-Soviet split, which in turn led to the emergence of China as an independent power to conduct an independent diplomacy.

The rise of Japan as an economic giant was another key factor that contributed to the deterioration of the bipolar system in East Asia. With a focus on economic development under America's military protection and nuclear umbrella, Japan quickly industrialized again. It was accepted into the Organisation for Economic

Co-operation and Development (OECD), the so-called rich nations' club, and held the Olympic Games in Tokyo in 1964. The Japanese government achieved its first diplomatic success with the conclusion of the Korea-Japan Treaty in 1965. In light of the "Asian Marshall Plan," Japan also began to be actively involved in Southeast Asia in the 1960s. In 1966, Japan played a crucial rule in the founding of the Asian Development Bank (ADB). With these advances, Japan began to assume a more active role in East Asian diplomacy.

The failure of the US intervention in Vietnam also contributed to the deterioration of the Cold War system in East Asia. The American involvement in Vietnam was formulated according to a rigid, anticommunist ideology to roll back Chinese and Soviet aggression. The Vietnam War, nevertheless, exacerbated friction between China and the Soviet Union, with Moscow counseling Hanoi to pursue a diplomatic track while Beijing advocated armed struggle. It was during the tense period of the early 1970s that a delicate Sino-American rapprochement started because Washington and Beijing were both concerned about the danger of Soviet expansionism and sought to use the other country to balance Moscow's influence.

President Richard Nixon astounded the world by announcing on 15 July 1971 that Henry Kissinger had taken a secret mission to Beijing to arrange the president's trip to China. Although Americans were uncomfortable with secret diplomacy and its association with European aristocracies, this bias toward openness had not prohibited President Nixon from adopting secret diplomacy in negotiating with China, a communist state full of secrecy in domestic as well as diplomatic practices. Following Kissinger's secret mission, which produced an "announcement that shocked the world," President Nixon arrived in Beijing on 21 February 1972 for a week of talks that "changed the world": an effort by the leaders of the world's most populous nation and the most wealthy nation to "bridge a gulf of almost 12,000 miles and 22 years of non-communication and hostility" that had riven the East Asian political landscape since the Korean War (Solomon 1981: 2). Shaking hands with Nixon at Beijing airport, Premier Zhou told his visitor that "your hands have crossed the widest ocean in the world" (Wei 1994: 85). Indeed, Nixon's visit caused a geopolitical revolution, in which the United States agreed to abandon the long-standing containment of China.

The most dramatic diplomatic consequence of the Sino-American rapprochement was the sudden normalization of Sino-Japanese relations. The announcement of Nixon's visit to Beijing was so unexpected in Japan that it was referred to as the "Nixon Shock," which was so profound that Japan reacted by starting its own rapprochement with Beijing right away to restore the nation's self-respect and international standing. The government was ready to move fast to outdistance the United States in exchanging ambassadors with China.

The Chinese were equally eager for normalization with Japan, partly because the United States proved to be a tough negotiator on the issue of diplomatic recognition. Beijing suspected that the ideologically less committed Japanese would prove more amenable to their wishes. Even with the complicated historical issues in the relationship, the Chinese leaders chose not to press Japan on the war guilt issue or demand huge reparation payments because they judged that it was a crucial time to consolidate the momentum of the Sino-US détente by adding Japan to the picture.

On 29 September 1972, five months after Nixon's China trip, a joint communiqué was signed in Beijing, declaring that Japan and China had established diplomatic relations. The normalization of Sino-Japanese relations completed the geopolitical revolution and offered China the greatest diplomatic opportunities since 1949.

KEY POINTS

- The deterioration of the rigid bipolar system in the 1970s made the US-Soviet relationship a less dominant axis of East Asian diplomacy and created conditions for some East Asian nations to play a more independent diplomatic role.
- The Sino-Soviet split led to diplomatic rapprochements between the United States and China and between China and Japan.

DIPLOMACY OF THE STRATEGIC TRIANGLE

The last decade of the Cold War in East Asia was distinguished by a significant degree of strategic interdependence among the United States, the Soviet Union, and China, known as a "strategic triangle," which meant that each bilateral relationship was contingent upon each participant's relations with the third. The triangular relationship was qualitatively different from and more vital than any other relationship in East Asia because other relationships were usually deemed as functional to the relations among the three states. For example, although Japan had a powerful economy, its strategic importance could be figured only in alliance with the United States or China. Therefore, each country was compelled to carefully assess its respective position with regard to the triangular relationship.

China was significantly less powerful than the two superpowers, and its importance in the triangle was not solely a function of its military capabilities but derived greatly from its diplomatic practice: a demonstrated and remarkable flexibility in its alignment policy. According to one account, China was the only major power to have actually switched sides in the post-1945 East-West confrontation, except for Egypt's break with the Soviet Union in 1972. China was also the only major country to have engaged in military conflicts with both superpowers, and the only major power, again excluding Egypt, to have been militarily allied with both. Again, China was the only major power to have simultaneously opposed both superpowers (Garver 1993: 32–33). Unlike France and Great Britain, whose commitment to the West eliminated any ambiguity concerning their diplomatic positions, China maintained a sufficient diplomatic flexibility so that both Moscow and Washington were not sure what diplomatic posture Beijing would take next. As a result, China assumed exaggerated diplomatic leverage.

The triangular diplomacy was formally unfolded after Nixon's historic visit to Beijing. As a counterweight to the impact of Sino-US rapprochement, the Soviet Union took dramatic actions in advancing détente with Washington by signing two arms control accords in May 1972. In response, Beijing intensified its diplomatic efforts to build an "international anti-Soviet united front" and aligned China "with the strategic objectives of the United States, Japan and Western Europe" (Lieberthal

1984: 59). The Americans were at first reluctant to convert to China's united front and sought to pursue an "evenhanded policy," hoping that American interests would be best served by seeking to improve relations with both Moscow and Beijing simultaneously (Oksenberg 1982). Yet such a policy was not successful because both China and the Soviet Union resented an American approach from which only Washington would benefit. As a result, while Beijing-Washington relations stagnated, no significant progress was achieved in Soviet-American détente either. The failure resulted in a shift from "evenhanded" diplomacy to a "balance of power" diplomacy (Oksenberg 1980: 318). After intensive negotiations, the US and China reached an agreement to establish diplomatic relations as the United States acceded to "three conditions" that Beijing had demanded since 1975: *chejun* (withdrawal of all US military forces from Taiwan), *huiyue* (termination of the US-Taiwan Mutual Security Treaty of 1954), and *duanjiao* (severance of diplomatic relations with Taiwan) (Harding 1992). Beijing also made important concessions, such as agreeing to normalize relations even though Washington would continue supplying weapons to Taiwan according to the Taiwan Relations Act enacted by the US Congress in April 1979 to preserve and promote commercial, cultural, and other relations between the people of the United States and the people of Taiwan after the United States shifted its diplomatic recognition from the ROC to the PRC. Upgrading the Chinese Liaison office in Washington and the US Liaison Office in Beijing to full embassies was followed, however, with a Sino-Vietnam War that complicated the US-China diplomatic achievements.

Although China and Vietnam were allies for many years during the US-Vietnam War, the relationship between the two countries plummeted after the Americans began withdrawing from Vietnam. While Chinese leaders felt apprehensive toward Vietnam's ambition in Indochina, Vietnam worried about Beijing's intention over Southeast Asia. Joining the Soviet-led Council for Mutual Economic Assistance and signing the Treaty of Friendship and Cooperation with the Soviet Union in November 1978, Vietnam called for the formation of a special relationship with the other two Indochinese countries of Laos and Cambodia. When the Democratic Kampuchea (Khmer Rouge) regime rejected the proposal, Vietnam invaded Cambodia on 25 December 1978. China was caught by surprise and would not tolerate the insolence of Vietnam, a tributary state in China's orbit for many centuries. Perceiving Vietnam's action as part of the Soviet southward strategy to encircle China, Deng Xiaoping ordered the People's Liberation Army troops to cross the border into Vietnam on 14 February 1979. The invasion was costly to China. It was only two weeks into the war before China was suggesting a truce and general cessation of hostilities. On 4 March, China captured the town of Long Son and subsequently claimed victory. The following day China announced a formal troop withdrawal, and all Chinese troops left Vietnamese territories on 16 March.

The outcome of the Sino-Vietnam War was a disappointment to both the Chinese and the Americans. China was disappointed in its new partner's military and diplomatic passivity within months of the euphoria of normalization. To the United States, the unilateral Chinese resort to "pedagogical war" in defense of a morally indefensible client demonstrated that Beijing could not understand or did not care much for American sensibilities. China's conduct during the invasion also showed the backwardness of China's armed forces.

At this point, the Russians began seeking an improvement in their relationship with China. At a speech in March 1982, Leonid Brezhnev said that the Soviet Union posed no threat to China's security and, unlike the United States, had consistently supported "the PRC's sovereignty over Taiwan Island." He also offered to discuss a resolution to the border dispute and to resume economic, scientific, cultural, and political relations across the Sino-Soviet frontier (Jones and Kevill 1985: 176). Although the initial Chinese response was guarded, in August 1982 General Secretary Hu Yaobang reassured Moscow that China would adopt an "independent foreign policy" and would never "attach itself to any big power or group of powers" (Hu 1982: 59), implying that China was to move away from the notion of a united front with the United States against the Soviet Union toward a peaceful coexistence with both superpowers. With a considerably more flexible and conciliatory posture, China in October resumed the bilateral negotiations that had been suspended after the Soviet invasion of Afghanistan. During the new round of talks, China repeated the three demands that Hu Yaobang had raised earlier: withdrawal of Soviet troops from Mongolia, withdrawal of Soviet troops from Afghanistan, and cessation of Soviet support for Vietnam's occupation of Cambodia.

Although the talks ended without success, Brezhnev's death in early November 1982 offered an opportunity for Sino-Soviet contacts at the highest level. A study of the "funeral diplomacy" that resulted from the rapid succession of Soviet leaders of Yuri Andropov in November 1982, Konstantin Chernenko in February 1984, and Mikhail Gorbachev in March 1985 provided interesting insights to the momentum of Sino-Soviet rapprochement. At Brezhnev's funeral, Chinese foreign minister Huang Hua held talks with his counterpart, Andrei Gromyko, but Vietnam's foreign minister, Nguyen Co Thach, met only Leonid Ilichev, a vice foreign minister. At Andropov's funeral, China was represented by Wan Li, a Politburo member and vice-premier, signaling China's positive assessment of the deceased Soviet leader as well as hopes for better relations in the future. For Chernenko's funeral, Beijing sent Vice-Premier Li Peng, who was educated in the Soviet Union and spoke Russian. Gorbachev received him twice and reaffirmed the Soviet Union's desire that Sino-Soviet relations improve in a major way (Su 1989: 112). This development intensified after Gorbachev's succession: the two sides began referring to each other as comrades, "a word suggesting that no serious ideological difficulty exists between them" (Huan 1986: 8).

Sino-Soviet relations improved drastically after Mikhail Gorbachev came to power in March 1985. In his highly publicized Vladivostok speech on 28 July 1986, Gorbachev spoke approvingly of China's reformist objectives and noted that Chinese and Soviet domestic priorities were similar. He indicated a willingness to negotiate with China a balanced and mutual reduction of the remaining forces along the Sino-Soviet border (Harding 1988). Carrying his speech on the front page of *Renmin Ribao*, Beijing welcomed Gorbachev's initiatives. In a September 1986 broadcast of the US news program *60 Minutes*, Deng offered to meet Gorbachev if the Soviet Union was willing to persuade the Vietnamese to withdraw their forces from Cambodia. Hanoi's announcement in early 1989 to withdraw all its forces in September cleared the way for a summit meeting between Deng and Gorbachev in Beijing in May 1989, the first Sino-Soviet summit in thirty years. But by the time

Gorbachev's China policy produced fruit, the collapse of Soviet power minimized its strategic significance, and the end of the Cold War eventually eliminated the triangular relationship. The strategic triangle thus became the last diplomatic drama during the Cold War years.

KEY POINTS

- The strategic triangle formed by the United States, the Soviet Union, and China shaped the diplomatic decisions of the three nations as well as all other nations in East Asia in the 1970s and 1980s. The tendency toward a coalition between two of the three countries and the fear of this alliance constituted the main dynamics.
- Although China was significantly less powerful than the two superpowers, both the United States and the Soviet Union took China very seriously because of its demonstrated diplomatic flexibility in its alignment policy during heightened Cold War competition.
- Improved Sino-Soviet relations and the end of the Cold War brought triangular diplomacy to an end.

CONCLUSION

After the downfall of the tributary system in the nineteenth century, diplomacy displayed distinctive characteristics in East Asia during different periods. One of the major diplomatic challenges during the age of imperialism was to balance the power of an anti–status quo state so that it could not create a universal empire. Therefore, diplomacy of imperialism was characterized by the constant change in balancing and counterbalancing actions. During the Cold War period, the balance of power between the two blocs was at the heart of diplomacy. Détente diplomacy emerged as a new way to protect the interests of major powers through peaceful political and diplomatic means after the deterioration of the rigid bipolar system in East Asia. This process began with the Sino-US détente. The Sino-Soviet détente coincided with the end of the Cold War and the start of a new era of post–Cold War diplomacy (see Ye and Zhang, chapter 16 in this volume).

QUESTIONS

1. With the decline of the Chinese empire came the introduction of the Western idea of the nation-state system. Where did we see the adopted idea of national and territorial sovereignty play out in the past? How is it applied in East Asia today?
2. What political, military, and diplomatic factors led to Japan's domination of East Asia from the Meiji Restoration until the end of the Pacific War?
3. Describe the key elements of imperialist diplomacy, Cold War diplomacy, and triangular diplomacy.
4. How was US containment structured in East Asia, and how was it different from the containment in Europe?

5. To what extent was the functional role of small and weak states in East Asia conditioned by supranational factors such as security alliance and super-power competition?
6. Discuss how the strategic triangle affected diplomatic decisions toward the end of the Cold War era.
7. What are the implications of the analysis in this chapter for your theoretical and practical understandings of contemporary diplomacy?

PART II

Concepts and Theories of Contemporary Diplomacy

This part of the book provides an overview of some key concepts and theories that underpin contemporary diplomacy. The four diverse yet interconnected chapters discuss how international relations and other disciplines theorize diplomacy, how these discussions galvanize and cohere into major debates, how globalization is transnationalizing diplomatic theories and practices, and how diplomacy can still be seen as being primarily about negotiation and mediation.

Our *first* aim in this part of the book is for readers to reflect more deeply on the uses and limits of theory, to consider why different disciplines take such different approaches, and to make judgments about the predictive and normative advantages of certain theories over others.

Our *second* aim is to encourage students to notice that, although most of these chapters do not explicitly examine the issue, there is nonetheless a gap between those who theorize diplomacy (scholars) and those who practice it (professional diplomats). Scholars tend to see the big picture without understanding the pressures of daily diplomatic life. Diplomatic practitioners tend to be overwhelmed by the immediate demands of the day and often unaware of the larger picture. Among other things, this part as a whole reveals the theory-practice gap, while also providing the reader with a basis for drawing one's own conclusions about it as a major problem for contemporary diplomacy.

CHAPTER 3

Diplomacy in International Relations Theory and Other Disciplinary Perspectives

Paul Sharp

READER'S GUIDE

This chapter examines how social theorists make sense of diplomacy. Social theory is concerned with explaining and understanding how people live in societies and, in this case, how those societies relate to one another. The introduction sets out the attractions and limitations of doing social theory, outlines different types of theory, and considers the uses of theory. The first section examines the place of diplomacy in three main traditions of international theory. The second section looks at sociological and anthropological studies of diplomats, what they actually do, and how they see themselves. The third section shifts the focus from theories of diplomacy to diplomatic theory, the rules and conventions that regulate professional diplomatic conduct. The final section looks at how developments in international relations have made possible a revival of interest in diplomacy to the point where diplomatic theory of international relations and human relations in general may be possible. The chapter concludes that the world is becoming more plural. Where people live in groups that feel separate from one another and want to be so, there will always be a need for good diplomacy. Thus, in the mix of global, international, regional, and local societies that appears to be emerging, good diplomatic theory of all types will be at a premium.

INTRODUCTION: THE ATTRACTIONS AND LIMITATIONS OF THEORY

Diplomats tend not to like "theory"—in the sense of formulating general, and often abstract, propositions, which help people explain and understand how they relate to one another and how they might do so. They especially do not like theorizing in this way about what diplomats do. In their experience, the quest for such general propositions invariably ends up treating things as simple that the diplomats believe are complicated (you cannot treat all states as if they were the same), and treating things as complicated that they regard as simple (what is the problem with saying that diplomats serve the national interest?). Academics, in contrast, tend to like theory, for it promises better understandings and better explanations of why the world is the way it is and what people ought to do. They also like it because theorizing offers them a way to status and power by playing to their strong suit, being clever in an intellectual sense. As some academics say when they want to frighten their undergraduates, there is no escape from theory. Every time you offer an explanation of a puzzle you find interesting or a description of how things happen, whether you know it or not, you are employing theoretical assumptions and making theoretical arguments. The only real question is whether one theorizes well or poorly. Although it may be true, the claim that one cannot escape theory is probably less important than it is made to appear. Theory is not always for someone or some purpose in a political sense, although it can always be put to good or bad use by someone else (Cox 1987: 128). Nor is it the case that if we all theorized better by making our assumptions explicit and our arguments internally consistent, the world would be a more peaceful and just place. Just look at the fights good theorists get into with each other and, more important, how the arguing does not stop and the arguments do not dry up (Bull 1966). Human beings are creatures of emotions, instincts, and egos, as well as of reason. Indeed, all four are bound up with one other. Many of our greatest life choices—for example, whether to marry, whether to have children, or whether to attack Pearl Harbor—attest to this. We jump in, and sometimes it is not clear that a systematic accounting of the factors in play and the relationships between them would provide a better way of deciding what to do. Besides, as diplomats would be among the first to remind us, the world does not stop and wait for us to complete our theoretical exercises. It goes right ahead using whatever fragments of explanation and understanding seem to fit the purpose at the time.

On the whole, however, the world is better off for having a few people who take social theorizing seriously, even if it rarely generates the sort of hard-and-fast laws of cause and effect observable in some of the natural sciences. Social theorists are useful for four reasons. First, they perform a "critical function." If theorizing is inescapable and plays a part in all our claims and arguments about what to do, then it is useful to have people who can point out inaccuracies in assumptions, fallacies in inferences drawn from them, and inconsistencies in the arguments that follow when these occur (Ashley 1989; Cox 1987; Der Derian 1987; Rosenau 1990).

Second, some theorists perform a "descriptive/explanatory function." Like their colleagues in the natural sciences, they seek to identify a world of conditions, correlations, causes, and consequences that is not always visible to those who live entirely within the terms and understandings of everyday life (Bueno de Mesquita 2003; Morgenthau 1948; Singer 1961). Thus it is possible to identify variations in the responses of different sovereign states to a similar external situation that correlate strongly with aspects of their internal organization; for example, those in which women enjoy higher social status and legal standing are less likely to respond violently to certain challenges (Hudson et al. 2008).

Third, some theorists perform a "constitutive/constructive function." Rather than identifying patterns of coexisting phenomena potentially related by causation to one another, they explore the way in which our understandings of the social world are produced by thought and action, the relationships between the different elements of our understandings, and the extent to which it is meaningful to talk of a distinction between a social world somehow "out there" and our thinking about it (Constantinou 1996; Wendt 1999). In their view, we should not be exploring the consequences of living in a world of sovereign states, and we should not accept the latter as an unambiguous given from which we proceed to reason. Instead, we should be asking how the idea that we live in a world of sovereign states is produced and circulated, how that idea gains and loses its dominance over other ways of thinking about the world, what problems thinking in these terms solves, which ones it does not address, and which ones it makes worse.

Finally, there is "normative theory" concerned with what we "ought" to be doing in a moral sense. This can engage moral questions directly. For example, are there circumstances in which it is right for diplomats to dissemble or lie? Or it can be indirect, considering the assumptions upon which certain moral principles are based, for example, diplomatic immunity, and the consequences of people maintaining such principles. In the indirect sense, it is probably more useful to see normative theory as a dimension to, or aspect of, the other forms of theorizing rather than as a form in its own right (Nardin 2009).

The distinctions between these types of theorizing are not watertight. Each has its strengths and weaknesses. Everyone likes an exposé of big claims, but no one likes a critic if all he or she does is criticize. Description leading to general causal explanation promises the most in terms of prediction, problem solving, and power. If only we could specify the economic conditions and political conduct that nearly always lead to war, for example, then surely we could avoid war more often and even get rid of it. Yet this sort of causal theorizing often assumes a hard-and-settled character for both general categories and specific instances of social constructs that invites us to beg important questions and leave important avenues unexplored. How, for example, can one advance claims about the peaceful nature of liberal states if people cannot agree on what it means to be peaceful, liberal, and a state, or whether particular states fit these categories, however one defines them? Uncovering the way social worlds are "constructed" and "constituted" seems at first glance emancipating. It allows us to escape the tramlines of conventional theoretical argument and to see our present in terms of larger and less familiar contexts. Having had the constructed character of social realities and the interdependence of the ideas that hold each social ensemble together demonstrated, however, we might still want to know why the social world is constructed in one particular way rather than another (Mearsheimer 1994/95). And we might still struggle to say much of interest or use to other people without climbing back inside the old frameworks. The idea of a rogue state rejecting international norms is a social construct, for example, and rogue states do not exist in the way they are conventionally presented. However, knowing this does not make Iran, North Korea, and their vexatious relationships with the United States disappear, and it is hard to enter the public debates over what to do about them by simply rejecting the premise—that there are rogue states—on which the debate is based (Litwak 2000; Sharp 2009).

So what use is social theory? It is not much use in instrumental terms. That is to say, it is unlikely to make you or your country more efficient or more competitive in the marketplace. Indeed, when theory becomes useful in the sense that, for example, it generates politically useful ideas like "containment" and "ideological hegemony," this is usually a sign that something has gone wrong. Indeed, one might offer the hypothesis that the more interested social theorists are in being instrumentally useful, the less useful they are likely to be as theorists. They are at their best when they uncover truths, explode "Truths," and provide new and alternative ways of looking at what seems settled and familiar. Nonetheless, it is the theorists' conceit to maintain that the unexamined life is not worth living, and that we should be dedicated to obtaining as full an understanding of our circumstances and ourselves as we can. It is perfectly possible to live a happy, successful, and valuable life without much reflection of this sort. However, most people, even diplomats, like to reflect in some way on how things are, how they might be, and their place in the scheme of things. And, given the inescapability of theorizing, most seem to benefit from being able to recognize when theorizing is more and less well done.

KEY POINTS

- Social theorizing about diplomacy is important and interesting. It helps us better understand diplomacy and the assumptions on which opinions about it are based.
- There are different types of theorizing—critical, causal, constitutive, and normative—but they all seek to generate general propositions about how diplomacy (in this case) works and why it does so.
- Social theory is not necessarily "useful" in instrumental terms, but, since most accounts of how and why the world works as it does rest on theoretical claims, it is useful in helping recognize when theorizing is more and less well done.

DIPLOMACY IN INTERNATIONAL THEORY

Until recently, diplomacy has occupied a place at the margins of international theory and social theory in general. Academics have noted the resistance of diplomacy to being theorized (Neumann 2003). Diplomats, when asked to reflect on this state of affairs, have generally expressed satisfaction with it. Nevertheless, theorizing about diplomacy and diplomats highlights important contrasts and contradictions in the

---

BOX 3-1

The Central Place of Diplomats in International Theory

In the late 1960s, the French political theorist and commentator Raymond Aron sought to develop a theory of international relations. Such a theory, he wrote, was intended "to comprehend the implicit logic of relations among politically organized collectivities" (Aron 1966: ix). In attempting to specify the subject and scope of his study at the onset, Aron claimed the following:

> Inter-state relations are expressed in and by specific actions, those of individuals whom I shall call symbolic, the *diplomat* and the *soldier*....the *ambassador*, in the exercise of his duties, *is* the political unit in whose name he speaks; the *soldier* on the battlefield *is* the political unit in whose name he kills his opposite number. (Aron 1966: 5; emphasis in original)

---

way people think about both. To demonstrate this, it is necessary to shift from characterizing theorists by the form of their approaches (critique, descriptive/explanatory, constitutive/constructive, and so on) to the content dictated by their basic assumptions. The balance of this section will examine what international theories say or imply about diplomacy (see box 3-1). The next section will look at what social theory more broadly conceived has to say about diplomats.

International theory is conventionally divided into three schools or three traditions of international thought: "realist," "rationalist," and "revolutionary" (Viotti and Kauppi 1998; Wight 1991). There are dangers in framing it this way, for to do so involves violence to facts, preempting arguments, and silencing perspectives. Awareness that this is so, however, mitigates the dangers. Treating the three traditions not as competing and mutually exclusive truth claims, but simply as ways of thinking that surface again and again when scholars and practitioners reflect on international relations, further mitigates them.

"Realist" thinkers focus on the use of power in the pursuit of interests. They do so because of the terms in which they understand human nature and the nature of any social system in which no one exercises supreme authority. In these conditions of **international anarchy**, they are generally more interested in states than any other actors because, in the world as they present it, states have the most power and pursue the highest, most inclusive interests. Diplomacy and diplomats stump realists. Are they elements of state power, instruments of foreign policy, or merely means of communicating both to others?

"Systemic" or "structural realists" plump for the latter view (Waltz 1979). Diplomacy and diplomats are concerned with communication. Communication in an international system is important insofar as someone has to undertake it, but unimportant in that variation in it cannot account for variations in important systemic outcomes. The degree of stability present in a bipolar international system, for example, will not be dependent on the degree of effectiveness with which its diplomacy is conducted. "Classical" and "neoclassical realists," in contrast, tend to see diplomacy and diplomats as instruments of foreign policy and elements of state power, respectively. For classical realists, individual statesmen and ambassadors can vary in their effectiveness with significant consequences. For neoclassical realists, the internal character of states can vary, differences in national education systems giving rise to more or less effective diplomatic services (Lobell, Ripsman, and Taliaferro 2009). Are liberal states, for example, which value tolerance and compromise, more likely to produce better diplomats (Keens Soper 1974)? Some sort of autonomous power is being ascribed to diplomats, but what sort? Is it simply intelligence and clarity of vision operating in the way that a chess player with more of both will generally beat a chess player with less? Or does it reside in their powers of persuasion and negotiation, the so-called gift of the gab? If so, then diplomacy involves far more than effectively communicating interests and the supporting promises of rewards and threats of punishment.

In communicating with one another on behalf of their states, diplomats also seem to be doing their "own thing." And as realists are quick to point out, their own thing does not always jibe well with conceptions of the state as a strategic actor whose interests are paramount. Diplomats, in their view, are far too keen on sacrificing the national interest of their own state and appeasing the interests of others in accordance with some dangerous idea of preserving peace.

"Rationalist thinkers" share with most other people a commitment to the idea that the application of reason to human relations can make existing ones work better and develop new ones by which human needs and wants may be better satisfied. In addition, however, rationalists see the world and what is important in it in terms of the tenets of "philosophical liberalism." That is, they proceed from the moral and empirical primacy of individual human beings and their interests. They stress the importance of accepting rules for protecting rights, enforcing duties, and regulating competition. And they stress the superiority of rational and representative deliberation over the exercise of power in the service of particular wills as a way of making collective decisions. Diplomats, therefore, as the builders and operators of orders, institutions, and regimes at regional, international, and global levels, are expected by rationalist thinkers to be their natural allies in bringing reason into the conduct of international relations. The emergence of the modern state system provides a compelling but incomplete story in these terms. In it, diplomats are presented as initially providing a more reliable means by which their **sovereigns** could communicate with each other than existed in the past. Then they develop a specifically diplomatic system with its own priorities and assumptions in regard to the importance of **resident embassies, diplomatic immunities**, and **continuous dialogue**, which ensures that the process of conducting relations itself does not become an unwanted source of tension.

So far, so good, but here the problems emerge. Rationalist thinkers do not constitute a homogeneous bloc. They can be distinguished from one another by the distinctively political, economic, and legal avenues of thought that they apply to making sense of international relations. These do not always fit well with one another. For example, political concerns with stability and fairness may suggest measures designed to redistribute wealth and regulate production at odds with economic concerns with maximizing efficiency and encouraging competition. And the priorities of both forms of thinking pose problems for legal reasoning's focus on the generation, interpretation, and enforcement of laws designed to specify right conduct and secure just outcomes. At a certain point, therefore, diplomacy is seen as parting company with the march of reason along these avenues. Political rationalists see diplomats as paying too much respect to illiberal forms of power like Asian dictatorships and Middle Eastern monarchies. Economic rationalists see them as having too much respect for the inefficient national economies of the political communities in which, as a result of historical accident, we happen to live. How can they, for example, ignore the law of comparative advantage in order to defend agricultural subsidies in rich countries? And by legal rationalists, diplomats are seen as having too much respect for the practice of using the law when it serves, and ignoring it when it does not on grounds of prudence. If one state is to be sanctioned for protecting terrorists, then should not every state that does so be sanctioned?

Ultimately both diplomacy and diplomats fail, according to rationalist thinkers, because they act as servants of states, a function that is becoming at once both more difficult and less important to undertake in an era when the information technologies and cultures of globalization are said to be rapidly transforming international relations.

Why are diplomats and diplomacy so tied to states? The historical record provides one sort of answer in terms of the expansion of the West and its characteristic form of political organization. Another is provided by "revolutionary thinkers" who claim that diplomacy and states serve established concentrations of power, no matter what the sources of this power are in any given epoch. Where systems of social relations involve exploitation and domination, and where centers of exploitation and domination compete with one another, diplomacy helps to cover the contradictions between the way these systems present themselves and their underlying realities, and between both of these and the universal desire of humankind for peace and justice. Who bribes the father in Joseph Conrad's *Secret Agent* (1907) into getting his simpleton son to unwittingly carry out a bomb attack in London for their own obscure purposes—the diplomats of another great power. Who thwarts the aspirations of the Iranian people for the true freedom of an Islamic republic—the "nest of spies" at the American embassy. And who reduces an environmental conference full of hope for real progress on carbon emissions into a selfish gridlock of competing demands for derogations—the diplomats. Diplomacy and revolution are, to paraphrase Martin Wight (1991), enemies. According to Leon Trotsky (1930), come the revolution, there would be no need for foreign ministries and embassies. One could simply issue a few proclamations and "shut up shop."

History was to show James Connolly's (1915) characterization of diplomacy to be just as applicable to ruthless revolutionaries, and it proved Trotsky wrong, although not in the way that people often assume (see box 3-2). To be sure, the Bolshevik revolution became a Russian state-building project (with all the attendant dangers to carrying out a social revolution of which Trotsky was well aware). As a consequence, the Soviet state required conventional **diplomatic representation**. However, like the capitalist economic and political liberal revolutions in England, France, and the Americas that preceded them, and the anticolonial revolutions in South Asia and Africa that followed, socialist revolutions (such as those in Russia

═══════════════════ BOX 3-2 ═══════════════════

James Connolly, Diplomacy as Damnation

Writing in 1915 in the midst of the First World War, the Irish revolutionary James Connolly had this to say about diplomacy, and British diplomacy in particular: "Diplomacy is the name for the business of conducting relations between governments." The language of commerce was English, and the language of diplomacy was French: "The nations, that is to say, robbed each other in English and fooled each other in French." British diplomacy, Connolly maintained, was

> hypocrisy incarnate....The diplomat holds all acts honourable which bring him success, all things are righteous which serve his ends. If cheating is necessary, he will cheat; if lying is useful, he will lie; if bribery helps, he will bribe; if murder serves, he will order murder; if burglary, seduction, arson or forgery brings success nearer, all and each of these will be done. And through it all the diplomat will remain the soul of honour—a perfect English gentleman. (Connolly 1915)

in 1917 and China in 1949) influenced the way people think about states and diplomacy. Indeed, the establishment of the modern state system in seventeenth-century Europe can be regarded as a revolution in which diplomacy was centrally involved in resolving questions about diplomatic representation and who was entitled to claim it. Diplomacy's involvement continues in the great revolutions in globalization and regionalization that the world is currently undergoing. As revolutionary thinkers are quick to point out, diplomats are often to be found representing the status quo and slowing down processes of social transformation on its behalf. However, diplomats are also to be found representing new claims to membership and standing in international society and facilitating efforts to build a global civil society of problem solvers. As the long view of history shows, in any plural society, social transformation does not drive out diplomacy. It increases the demand for it as arguments about identities and ideas are added to the ones about interests that diplomats represent and undertake in settled times.

KEY POINTS

- Diplomacy and diplomats have been resistant to theorizing by international relations scholars.
- When it is thought of in terms of traditions of thought (realist, rational, and revolutionary) rather than types of theory, we can better see what international theory has to say about diplomacy.
- Realists see diplomacy as an instrument of policy, but a suspect one given the priority diplomats accord to the interests of other states and the preservation of peace.
- Rationalists see diplomacy as an imperfect ally in their efforts to dilute nationalism, maximize prosperity, and strengthen the rule of law.
- Revolutionaries see diplomacy as the enemy, prepared to do anything that will preserve the status quo.

DIPLOMATS IN SOCIAL THEORY

International theorists try to place diplomacy in their understandings and explanations of how international relations work. Other theorists, primarily **sociologists** and anthropologists, are more likely to focus on diplomats as human beings engaged in a particular kind of social practice. One approach is to imagine early encounters between simple peoples in an anthropological fiction mirroring the use of the "state-of-nature" convention in political theory (see box 3-3).

BOX 3-3

Diplomacy in the Beginning: Prehistory and Anthropology

A favorite device of students of diplomacy is to think about how it might have started. Harold Nicolson, for example, imagines an encounter between "savages" who wish to communicate with each other but are prevented by taboos placed on having nothing to do with outsiders who wanted to talk. "The practice must therefore have become established even in the remotest times that it would be better to grant such negotiators certain privileges and immunities denied to warriors" (Nicolson 1963: 6). In a more lighthearted vein, Richard Langhorne (2004a: 7) describes this as the transition from eating envoys to inviting them for dinner. Anthropological studies like Ragnar Numelin's (1950: 13–14) also note the ubiquity of something recognizable as diplomacy at all times and all places in relations between human groups.

These approaches make it easier to imagine how standard rules for dealing with outsiders were suspended by notions of diplomatic immunity so that different groups might communicate with one another. As with the state-of-nature convention, however, there are problems with encounter narratives, not the least being the assumption of peoples living completely separate from one another with which these narratives usually begin the story of diplomacy. More empirically based and comparative anthropological studies make these shortcomings clear while, at the same time, seeking to demonstrate that wherever separate communities in relations with one another exist, there also people engaged in diplomacy will be found (see box 3-4).

This underlying concern of the anthropologists with "building up" so-called primitive societies in our understandings of them is less in evidence in how sociologists treat diplomats. In the literature on the idea of strangers, for example, diplomats are presented as a type of outsider. Other sociological approaches contrast conventional ideas of diplomacy as an esoteric and mysterious practice undertaken by quiet, sophisticated, and possibly cynical heroes with close studies of how actual diplomats see themselves and spend their working days.

There is a "tear-down" element in this to be sure. Even more than people in other professions, diplomats seem more defined and, at times, overwhelmed by the common experience of working in complex networks than by anything particular

---

BOX 3-4

Forest Diplomacy

Studies of the relations of Native American tribes with each other and with Europeans once they began to arrive suggest the existence of sophisticated systems of diplomacy to which the Europeans, on occasions, adapted their own practices. The league of the Iroquois used gatherings for condoling rituals on the death of an important person as opportunities for diplomacy. Dances were performed at the edge of encampments by the representatives of "sending" tribes in a form of prenegotiations before they were accepted by the "receiving" tribe into their village to perform a further series of pipe-smoking ceremonies. These encounters did not look like negotiations but would produce results that looked like they had been achieved by negotiations. As Michael Foster (1985) notes, wampum bead belts had messages in their patterns and were held to speak their messages directly to the receiver in much the same way as medieval envoys in Europe were seen to be their sovereigns, not merely to be acting in their stead. Europeans never learned to read the belts but learned to attach importance to their presence at talks in much the same way the Native Americans learned to attach importance to the Europeans producing documents for signature. A class of "forest negotiators" also emerged, belonging wholly to neither party but available for service when called upon.

---

to their profession. There is also, however, a "build-up" element in choosing what people actually do as diplomats, as opposed to some abstract idea of what diplomacy involves, to be the starting point for theorizing, especially in times of social transformation or uncertainty. Then the idea of practice as theory or, more prosaically, trying to establish practices rather than following established practices, becomes important as people struggle to make sense of an expanding range of hyphenated diplomacies, for example public-diplomacy, private-diplomacy, military-diplomacy, field-diplomacy, and citizen-diplomacy (see box 3-5).

KEY POINTS

- Social theorists and anthropologists have been interested in diplomacy, although not for the same reasons as international relations theorists.
- Anthropologists have been interested in the possible origins of diplomacy in encounters between simple societies and the presence of different forms of diplomacy in non-European societies past and present.
- Social theorists have examined the lived-life experiences of actual diplomats to see how personal, bureaucratic, and professional cultures operate to shape the way diplomats respond to the challenges that confront them.
- Both lines of inquiry raise questions about the conventional practice of saying that only accredited officials representing sovereign states can be properly regarded as conducting diplomacy.

BOX 3-5

Ordinary People, Rich People, and Celebrities as Diplomats

Diplomats are conventionally thought of as the **accredited represen-tatives** of states. Social theory asks why this is so and often challenges the answers given. It has always been possible to see people with-out official standing doing diplomacy, and to see them doing it on behalf of actors other than states. Now, as states are beset by many other sorts of actors in international relations like firms, humanitar-ian organizations, and even individuals, and as there is a reluctance (even on the part of states) to accept the exclusive claims of states to representation, the question asked by Langhorne (1996), "Who are the diplomats now?." becomes more important. It is not surprising, says Andrew Cooper (2008b), that one of the answers to that ques-tion is "celebrities." Looking at people like Bono, Bob Geldof, and Bill Gates, Cooper examines how, in Neumann's words, celebrities channel the public emotions invested in them toward international issues that concern them. How much good is accomplished thereby, and whether what is done is best understood as diplomacy, remain hotly contested issues.

DIPLOMATIC THEORY

Hyphenated diplomacies raise the question of what is diplomatic about the activity so identified. If one accepts that diplomacy is what diplomats do, then answering this question may not matter. It does matter, however, to diplomatic theorists, those who theorize about diplomacy in what they see as its own terms. There exists a formal body of diplomatic theory pertaining to the rights, duties, and forms of conduct of diplomats in their relations with one another and with those whom they represent. The **Vienna Convention on Diplomatic Relations** (1961) and the **Vienna Convention on Consular Relations** (1963) are the guid-ing documents in this regard. They present a set of practical understandings to facilitate the smooth operation of the diplomatic system. However, they also imply a set of claims about who and what are important in international rela-tions, what may properly be regarded as diplomacy, and, thus, who can properly be regarded as diplomats. Students of diplomatic theory like G. R. Berridge and Alan James (2001), as a consequence, reject the broader conception of diplomacy implied by its new hyphenated variants because in their view diplomats must be accredited representatives of sovereign states conducting relations between them, and because, as accredited professionals, diplomats enjoy more legitimacy and are better at conducting international relations than are other people (see box 3-6).

BOX 3-6

The Diplomatic Counterrevolution?

Until relatively recently, diplomacy has been a neglected topic in the academic study of international relations as a social science. The latter largely
accepted that whatever diplomats did was not important to explaining
what happens in international relations or understanding why international relations work the way they do. The study of diplomacy was, therefore, regarded as a specialized, esoteric, and rather old-fashioned business.
Now, however, interest in diplomacy has revived. This is partly attributable
to the end of the Cold War and the beginning of America's relative decline.
The revival also results from changes in the way international relations are
studied, notably the shift of interest to narrative and textual interpretations of what is going on in which the role of agents doing things, rather
than structures shaping things, is stressed. Despite predictions to the contrary, Berridge notes, diplomacy never went away, and, far from declining, institutions like the resident embassy only seem to have increased
in importance, even after the emergence of teleconferencing, email, and
the Internet. For "diplomatic counterrevolutionaries," diplomacy's neglect
by the academics indicates the limitations of academia, its obsession with
finding novelty, and its aversion to the necessary restating of simple, if
unpalatable, truths that ordinary people, reporters, and celebrities alike
are often unwilling to accept. As the WikiLeaks revelations show, the continuing importance of "old-fashioned" diplomacy undertaken by embassy-
based professionals has been understated in recent years. To say that not
everything has changed in the world of diplomacy, however, is not to say
that nothing of importance has changed. The challenge for theorists of
diplomacy is to get beyond such all-or-nothing claims and to make assessments of the extent to which the work of, for example, embassies, summit
conferences, public diplomacy activities, and citizen diplomats is actually
changing what we understand as diplomacy (Berridge 2011: 1–3).

Other theorists of diplomacy, like Christer Jönsson and Martin Hall (2005),
Paul Sharp (2009), and Geoffrey Wiseman (1999), regard this position as untena-
ble because the proportion of international relations conducted between states by
formally accredited diplomats relative to all international relations appears to be
shrinking. However, this creates the problem of how to make sense of the rest. Is it all
diplomacy, so that diplomacy simply serves as a synonym for international relations
as it did in the past when diplomats actually conducted most international relations?
Theorists of diplomacy have tried to answer this question in a number of ways. They
have tried to identify a distinctive activity or set of activities. Thus, Berridge and
James (2001), following Nicolson (1963), identify negotiation as the key to understanding what diplomats do (see Zartman, chapter 6 in this volume). Sharp (1999)
focuses on diplomats' roles as representatives of both the interests and the identities of those for whom they act. Philip Seib (2009) sees them as communicators

and receivers of interests and values. And Brian Hocking (1999a) presents them as catalytic coalition builders of interest groups occupying strategic nodal points in the networks of international interaction. Other theorists of diplomacy have tried to identify a distinctive problematic that captures diplomacy's essence. Jönsson and Hall (2005), for example, focus on the attempt to mediate between the self and others or the particular and the universal. The trouble with each of these is that, while they may yield important insights about diplomacy, they do not reveal what is distinctive to it. Other people negotiate, represent, report, build coalitions, and seek to reconcile particulars with universals, and selves with others without obviously being diplomats or engaging in diplomacy.

KEY POINTS

- Diplomatic theory, conventionally understood, is the formal body of conventions and understandings that regulate the conduct and specify the rights and duties of professional diplomats as set out in the Vienna conventions on diplomatic and consular relations.
- Diplomatic theory, nevertheless, engages definitional questions like What is diplomacy? and Who may be properly regarded as diplomats?
- Answers to these questions generally stress particular diplomatic functions like negotiating, representing, or reporting; the necessary qualifications for those undertaking diplomacy; or the problematic within which diplomacy operates.
- None of these are entirely satisfactory because they are not exclusive to diplomacy and are found in other kinds of human relations.

POSTPOSITIVIST DIPLOMATIC THEORY

What follows if defining what diplomacy is, who diplomats are, and what they do does not matter? **Postpositivist** theorists of diplomacy begin by relaxing the assumption that our understanding of diplomacy must be grounded in the relations of sovereign, territorial states (see box 3-7). Instead, they ask in what sort of circumstances do people start reaching for words like "diplomacy" and "diplomats," and, indeed, in what sort of circumstances were the words actually created.

"Diplomacy" and "diplomat" are terms called in when people find themselves in relations with others, or those whom they wish to declare as others, from whom they feel and wish to be separate. Post-positivist theorists of diplomacy view this "separateness" in different ways. It can be viewed as a process by which other people are made strange, and this strangeness is actively maintained, so that they can be exploited, dominated, and harmed. James Der Derian (1987) presents diplomacy and diplomats as mediating **estrangement**. They may bring people together to resolve their differences, but they do so in such a way as to make sure that the people represented by them remain estranged. Thus, even a great diplomatic coming-together like the UN General Assembly's annual opening underlines the separate and sovereign terms on which the peoples of the world come together. Separateness can also

═══════════ BOX 3-7 ═══════════

Costas Constantinou's Interpretation of Diplomacy

Costas Constantinou is interested in the way language is used to produce a social world in which people hide from the contradictions between what they say is right and wrong, on the one hand, and the consequences of how they actually live, on the other. Language is an unreliable instrument, however, because people are not always aware of what they are doing when they choose their words, and words have lives and histories of their own with all sorts of meanings and uses packed into them. Diplomacy, with its sense of mystery, ambiguity, deception, and veiled power, is one such word. To make his point about how language shapes people's understandings, Constantinou looks at the history of a famous painting, Holbein's *The Ambassadors*. The painting has a history in which the people and symbols represented contribute to contemporary understandings of diplomacy. Constantinou demonstrates that the painting has a highly ambiguous history as an unfashionable portrait, which owners and sellers may have misrepresented in their efforts to increase its value. They read diplomacy into it by declaring the key figures to be ambassadors, as people continue to read diplomacy into the painting today, and then take from the painting their sense of diplomacy reflected back to them (Constantinou 1996: 1–26).

be viewed as a condition in which people do not realize, have forgotten, or have had obscured the commonalities that unite them. David Wellman, for example, argues that the sacred writings of Christians, Muslims, and Jews share stories about how peoples should live if they are to remain in harmony with their natural environment. In this view diplomats and diplomacy, potentially at least, have a role in facilitating the (re)discovery of these commonalities (Wellman 2004).

However, separateness, if not the forms it takes, can also be seen as a permanent condition and one people should be glad is so. In this view, the task of diplomacy and diplomats is not just to handle the difficulties that arise in relations between different groups. It is also to maintain, extend, and explore the different ways of life that these groups actually and potentially embody.

Diplomatic Theory of International and Human Relations

Together these insights make possible a shift away from seeing diplomacy only as a way of conducting relations between states, that is to say, a distinctive sector of international relations with arguably wider application. Instead, our attention is directed toward the potentially diplomatic element in all international relations and, indeed, all human relations. The simple inside-outside thinking where all the relations within states are of one kind and all the relations between states are of another is replaced by a more complex understanding with potentially liberating, potentially unsettling, but fewer imposed, consequences. In this broader view of diplomacy, wherever there are groups, relations within them will differ from relations between them. People will believe themselves to be under fewer moral and legal obligations to the members of other groups than to members of their own, and they will feel less emotional attachment to others than to their own. They will likely understand them less well than they understand their own. Hence, relations between groups will be more difficult to undertake than relations within groups, especially if it is desired that misunderstanding, conflict, and violence be avoided. The successful handling of these relations will involve the elements of a "practice"—the bundle of assumptions about how the world works, what is important in it, and the techniques for achieving what is important—that are associated with diplomacy. This is true for relations between any and all of the aggregates in which people and peoples find themselves living, although whether a special class of practitioners—diplomats—is required is by no means as clear.

KEY POINTS

- Post-positivist theorists of diplomacy relax two assumptions: that diplomacy is conducted only by states, and that diplomacy needs to be precisely defined.
- They ask how and with what consequences people's ideas about diplomacy and what diplomats do are framed at different times and in different places.
- Some post-positivist theorists suggest that diplomacy is involved not in bringing people together but in marking the boundaries between them and keeping them estranged from one another.
- Others are more concerned with how conventional diplomacy supports a pattern of international life that is based on assumptions and priorities that are not environmentally sustainable. They call for a new diplomacy that creates and maintains a system of communities that are more in tune with the requirements of their environments.

CONCLUSION

Theory generally follows practice. Theorists think about problems that practical life throws in the way of people. One hundred years ago it was possible to maintain that diplomacy and international relations were synonymous. Liberal and Marxian political economists might disagree and maintain that great magnets under the chessboard of international diplomacy were regulating the moves of the major players. This was not how it seemed to most people, however. If you understood the rules of diplomacy, both formal and tacit, then you would understand what was important to know to make sense of international relations. Those who studied international relations agreed. This view was shaken by the sense of diplomacy's failure to prevent the First World War and a host of ideological arguments of political, economic, and legal provenance to the effect that international relations and the challenge of avoiding another war could not, and should not, be left to diplomacy and diplomats in the future. For the balance of the twentieth century, it was thought that peace would be better preserved by creating and sustaining the right sort of political, economic, and legal order populated by the right sort of states. This would be achieved by example where possible, and force where necessary. As a consequence, those who thought about international relations did so in terms that excluded diplomacy or took for granted what it continued to accomplish, while highlighting its shortcomings. Diplomatic theory, in particular, acquired an air of obsolescence, focused as it was on defending old forms and practices as still valuable, while the exciting bits of diplomacy like **crisis management, summitry,** and **bargaining** were hived off by subfields like foreign policy analysis and strategic studies with other priorities.

The end of the Cold War began a process of change in terms of reinstating diplomacy and raising the level of academic interest in it. It was, however, a halting recovery. Some big international disputes were unfrozen, to be sure, but the little **desecuritization**—that is, getting away from the idea that the use of force is an ever-present possibility in all international relations—of international thought that resulted was replaced by politicization and economization on the broadly liberal institutional terms associated with globalization. Paradoxically, however, a classic obstacle to diplomacy—the presence of an apparently hegemonic power that did not need to negotiate—provided a boost for diplomacy when the United States engaged in a number of wars that exposed the limits to what force could achieve alone. In the short term, the United States' rediscovery of diplomacy under Barack Obama's administration has restored interest in it in those places where most of the study of international relations is undertaken. In the short to medium term, shifts in the distribution of power that remind us of the classical balance of power and diplomacy's role in making it work may have more lasting consequences. Already scholars are beating paths to China and India to hear what they have to say about international relations in general and diplomacy in particular. When power shifts, one has to pay more attention not only to the capacities and interests of the beneficiaries but also to how they think about the world. For example, does China want to be a great power, and, if it does, how might its understanding of what it is to be a great power and of great power diplomacy differ from the American or European ones (see Zhao, chapter 2, and Ye and Zhang, chapter 16 in this volume)?

The case for insisting that we live in a single global system with a homogeneous primary membership, a single formal level of interaction, and a shared vision of how the world should be is weakening. The case for accepting the opposite—a plural world of multiple societies existing at different levels with heterogeneous memberships and many visions of the Good—is strengthening. At any given time, there are theorists who insist that the social world is not as solid as it appears, that it is produced by people as much as it produces them, and that this opens up a host of possibilities in terms of the ways we might live. In settled times, such theorists are largely ignored. They secure an audience only when the cracks are showing to everyone else. We seem to be entering such a time. A sense is growing that attempts to establish the right sort of international or global order with the right sort of membership create as many problems as they solve. If this is so, then the attempts of theorists to make sense of what diplomacy and diplomats do in accordance with their respective theoretical positions on how the world is constituted and works may become less important than they are at present. More important will be the attempts of diplomatic theorists to help develop the techniques by which the identities and interests of the inhabitants of emerging worlds can be represented as peacefully as possible and without unwanted tensions and conflict. Most important of all, however, may be the efforts of theorists of diplomacy to help wean the rest of us off the compulsion to impose an overarching order on the world—whether conceptual or actual—to help us feel more at ease with living in, and exploring ways of living in, increasingly untidy and ambiguous conditions; to help each of us, in short, to become aware of the diplomatic dimension to our lives and to become better diplomats.

KEY POINTS

- Theory seems to follow practice. Theorists examine the problems and puzzles that trouble people.
- What theorists think about things changes with time and place.
- Diplomatic theorists once assumed that all important international relations came under the rubric of diplomacy.
- From the First World War onward, the idea developed that there were many and increasingly more very important international relations, which took place outside the traditional world of diplomacy.
- Now diplomatic theory is beginning to argue that not only international relations but all human relations between plural groups may be better understood if the diplomatic dimension to them is recognized.

QUESTIONS

1. What sorts of social theory are there, and what uses do they have?
2. Why have international relations theorists been slow to examine diplomacy and the work of diplomats?
3. Why have international relations theorists become more interested in diplomacy recently?
4. How do the realist, rationalist, and revolutionary traditions of international thought make sense of diplomacy?
5. Can diplomacy be defined in terms of the essential qualifications of those who undertake it?
6. Does theory always follow practice, and does diplomatic theory always follow diplomatic practice?
7. Can diplomatic theory tell us anything about human relations in general?
8. What are the implications in this chapter for your theoretical and practical understandings of contemporary diplomacy?

CHAPTER 4

Debates about Contemporary and Future Diplomacy

Geoffrey Allen Pigman

CHAPTER CONTENTS

READER'S GUIDE

This chapter examines principal academic debates surrounding contemporary diplomacy, addressing how the debates affect diplomatic practice. The first debate involves questions of what is to be included in what scholars and practitioners consider to be diplomacy. The second debate addresses to what extent contemporary diplomacy can be considered to have changed from its historical practice, and the implications of such change for practitioners. The third debate explores how theory relates to practice in diplomacy. The chapter concludes by asking by what means academic debates over diplomacy might be resolved and how their resolution or lack thereof affects diplomatic practice. The chapter is intended to frame these debates for readers and to provide the tools that readers need to take positions in the debates for themselves.

INTRODUCTION: DEBATING DIPLOMACY

In the first decade of the twenty-first century, diplomacy came to be widely debated not only among practitioners, policy experts, and academics but also in the popular press and among the general public. One of the most significant debates concerned whether diplomacy had been or would be successful in preventing the Iraqi government of Saddam Hussein from developing and deploying weapons of mass destruction. Between 2001 and 2003, it appeared that most of the **global public** who were in a position to read a newspaper, watch television, or surf the Internet had formed an opinion, irrespective of whether they knew who was involved or how the diplomacy in question was being conducted. The US government of President George W. Bush and US allies, including the United Kingdom and Italy, were criticized by numerous other governments and **civil society organizations** for deciding on their own that multilateral diplomacy under the aegis of the United Nations (UN) had failed and hence to take military action against Iraq.

This debate about diplomacy raises a number of questions that point to underlying, scholarly debates about contemporary diplomacy that have significant implications for how diplomacy is practiced in the future. The first question is a definitional issue with **epistemological** underpinnings: What is to count as diplomacy, and what is not? That these questions are fundamental to the study of diplomacy shows that the long-standing consensus about "what we mean by diplomacy" is now breaking down. The second, overlapping debate is about the extent to which diplomacy in the contemporary period has changed and is different from, or similar to, diplomacy in the past. Key to unpacking this debate is an understanding of what constitutes continuity and change. The third debate concerns the role of theory in diplomacy: What is the relationship between theorizing and practicing diplomacy? The most intellectually challenging of the three debates, it perhaps has the most far-reaching implications for how we understand and engage in diplomacy in the contemporary environment.

That these questions engender debate rather than consensus is a result of different sorts of knowledge and understanding being apposite to different issues. Some issues have emerged because of new empirical information that challenges previously held understandings. Others have arisen as a result of competing modes of analysis of information. Yet others, such as the theory and practice debate, arise when more radically different and incompatible theoretical and epistemological approaches come into contention. The following discussions make reference to which of these causes appear relevant to each particular debate. The concluding section addresses approaches to resolving them. Understanding the debates and their main positions should help students of diplomacy to develop their own criteria for evaluating the effectiveness of diplomacy in the future.

DEBATING WHAT WE MEAN BY "DIPLOMACY"

The debate over what diplomacy means is important because it defines the bounds of what can be analyzed under the rubric of diplomatic studies: who are considered diplomats, and who are not; what are diplomatic practices, and what are not; and more broadly what counts as part of the study of diplomacy, and thus by extension what does not. In earlier times, diplomacy as a term was used much more **unreflexively** than today. Early modern usages since the seventeenth century generally referred to a process: the art of negotiation, and how to use negotiating effectively to achieve objectives of state. But over the past century, diplomacy came to be understood more broadly than as the practical art of representing the sovereign and conducting negotiations on his or her behalf. Scholars in the early twentieth century began to study diplomacy as a vehicle for understanding what was becoming known as international relations: the relationships between **nation-states** in the **international system**, and the characteristics of the international system of nation-states itself.[1] This occurred in part because of a felt need to understand the causes of the Great War (or the First World War of 1914–18) and the subsequent pitfall-strewn processes of creating international institutions, such as the League of Nations, to prevent a repeat of the war's ruinous consequences. British diplomat Sir Harold Nicolson, a founder of the modern academic discipline of diplomatic studies, in his core text *Diplomacy* (1939) endorsed the *Oxford English Dictionary* definition of diplomacy as "the management of international relations by negotiation; the method by which these relations are adjusted by ambassadors and envoys; the business or art of the diplomatist" (Nicolson 1963: 4–5).

Nicolson's definition acknowledged a broader range of diplomatic processes than only negotiations, including the range of representative and consular functions, as well as the role of the practitioners: the ambassadors, envoys, and other professional diplomats. Another British diplomat-turned-scholar, Adam Watson (1982), characterized diplomacy more generally as "the dialogue between states," a definition encapsulating the balance between diplomatic actors (the nation-state governments) and processes.

Since the end of the Cold War's overweening global focus on the balance of nuclear and conventional power between the US and Soviet superpowers, an awareness has grown among scholars and the general public that perhaps the prevailing understanding of diplomacy was still too restrictive. Latterly, as an increasing share of global economic activity is involved in cross-border flows of goods, services, capital, labor, knowledge, ideas, and culture, and as technological advances have made a growing share of global communications immediate, a wider range of actors than governments of nation-states can be seen to engage in diplomacy through a broader range of processes than those envisioned by Nicolson and Watson. For example, transnational firms such as Exxon Mobil, Deutsche Bank, and Nissan Renault represent themselves to, and negotiate with, governments of nation-states much in the way that other governments do. Multilateral institutions such as the **World Trade Organization** (WTO) have created ongoing venues and multilateral conferences for more specialized and often technical types of diplomacy, for example, the agreement and implementation of rules for international trade.

More recently, scholars such as Paul Sharp and Christer Jönsson have conceived of diplomatic actors and processes by understanding diplomacy as consisting of two core functions or activities: representation and communication (Sharp 1999; Jönsson and Hall 2003; Pigman 2010). Representation begins with the notion of the diplomatic actor, asking how the actor represents itself to others with whom it wishes to establish and maintain a relationship. Does a sovereign ruler represent him- or herself at a meeting or negotiation directly, in person? Does he or she appoint a special envoy to undertake a diplomatic mission? Does the sovereign appoint a permanent representative or ambassador to reside at the location where representation is needed? Does he or she establish regular or emergency communications channels, such as a weekly videoconference or a telephone "hotline"? How do these choices vary if the sovereign is not the head of government of a nation-state but instead the chief executive officer (CEO) of a large global firm like Microsoft, the head of a civil society organization like the International Committee of the Red Cross, or the secretary-general of an international organization like the UN (Sharp 1999)?

In order for diplomatic representation to achieve its intended purposes, authorities in the territory must understand, accept, and respect the representative's mission. Since the seventeenth century, a common understanding of the purposes and functions of diplomatic representation, at least between the governments of nation-state actors and, latterly, multilateral organizations, has emerged. Formal codification of customary international law governing the rights, protections, and responsibilities of diplomatic representatives began at the Congress of Vienna in 1815. Representatives of nation-state governments are afforded comprehensive protection under international law by the **Vienna Convention on Diplomatic Relations** (1961), a treaty negotiated under the aegis of the UN that codified the customary practices of diplomatic relations over the preceding two centuries. The convention guarantees diplomatic representatives' physical security and immunity from civil and criminal prosecution in the host jurisdiction under most circumstances. The property, archives, and documents of representative missions are also protected. By contrast, representatives engaging in diplomacy on behalf of non-state actors, such as global firms and civil society organizations, must rely for their protection upon the good faith of the receiving entity (whether a government, another firm, or organization) and the authority controlling the territory in which the receiving entity is located.

An actor's representation of itself to others also raises questions of how the actor represents itself to itself: the problem of identity. Choices about how, and to whom, to represent oneself play a direct role in who or what one is and becomes. They form part of the social construction of a diplomatic actor's identity and interests. By deciding to join the WTO in December 2001, the People's Republic of China government chose to subject itself to a set of norms of international trade favoring open markets and less government intervention, as well as to established procedures for resolving disputes and for further liberalizing trade. Joining the WTO had consequences for China's own trade policy process that the Beijing government was not necessarily able to foresee. Becoming a member of the WTO strengthened the economic position of those interests within China favoring membership, notably large exporting manufacturing firms and financial institutions, even while weakening opponents, such as heavily subsidized industries. This in turn shifted the domestic balance of political power within China on trade policy, and in so doing reconstructed a significant aspect of China's identity as a diplomatic actor on the global stage.

The other core diplomatic function or activity—communication—is distinct, although inseparable, from representation. Communication by its nature takes place not between collective entities such as nation-states, multilateral organizations, or global firms but between individuals entrusted with representing or speaking for them. The contemporary media's unparalleled power and reach have both enriched and complicated processes of communication greatly by conveying large quantities of information, accurate or not, with or without context, to huge segments of the global public. "Diplomacy is bargaining," as Thomas Schelling wrote in 1966.

"It seeks outcomes that, although not ideal for either party, are better for both than some of the alternatives" (1). The idea of communication as a core diplomatic function begins with this original understanding of diplomacy as the art of negotiation, but it recognizes that diplomacy comprises a much broader range of communications. An ambassador presenting credentials to a head of state upon arrival at a new post, a queen hosting a state dinner for a visiting president, or a commerce minister touring with the CEO of a global management consulting firm around a new technology park and export processing zone—all exemplify the maintenance of diplomatic communication no less important than a high-level negotiation over a border dispute or an economic development agreement. In the current technology-enabled age, a wider range of communication techniques has become significant for conducting public diplomacy (see Melissen, chapter 11 in this volume). A government-business partnership to promote a country as an investment destination through a multimedia website, a government-funded cultural foundation hosting an exchange of performances by local folk musicians, or an airdrop of MP3 players with prerecorded messages aimed at a population of a hostile state during a military conflict are examples of such techniques (Bull 1977; Jönsson and Hall 2003).

The power of communication, in all its guises, as a core function of diplomacy lies in its ability not only to achieve its primary objectives—resolving a conflict, maintaining a relationship, promoting socioeconomic exchange—but also in so doing to modify the interests and even the identity of the actors communicating with one another. When Egyptian president Anwar el-Sadat flew from Cairo to Jerusalem in October 1977 to meet Israeli prime minister Menachem Begin and address the Israeli Knesset, he transformed the Egypt-Israel relationship from one of enmity over thirty years since Israel's founding into one of peace and (albeit limited) commerce. In negotiating and signing a bilateral peace treaty the following year, Sadat and Begin reprioritized their respective states' major interests. Israel sacrificed its occupation and "settlement" of the Sinai Peninsula in return for peace with an Arab state. Egypt sacrificed solidarity with Arab neighbors in return for repossession of the Sinai, financial gain from reopening the Suez Canal, huge foreign aid flows from the United States, and enhanced security flowing from peace with Israel. Beyond modifying their respective interest preference orderings, however, Egypt and Israel altered their identities as nation-states. Israel abandoned its expansionist Zionist identity for that of a state willing and able to trade land for peace. At that point, Egypt gave up its identification with pan-Arabism and the destruction of Israel for the relative economic and political gains of being a state at peace with its neighbors.

Understanding what the study of diplomacy encompasses requires both a clear sense of the objects of study and a solid sense of what diplomacy is not. Of particular importance is the distinction between diplomatic studies and foreign policy analysis. The study of diplomacy differs from the study of foreign policy, in the sense that foreign policy is generally analyzed from the perspective of the state engaged in making and executing it. Those studying foreign policy ask empirical questions: What is Russia's policy toward the United States? Normative and prudential questions may be asked, for example, does the European Union (EU) have an ethical obligation, and would it be wise, to deploy troops to defend human rights in Kosovo or Darfur? Policies once executed are then evaluated: Which Chilean approaches to achieving agricultural trade liberalization in the WTO **Doha Development Round** have succeeded, which have failed, and why? Students of foreign policy may be studying the same issues and events as students of diplomacy, but the focus for diplomatic studies is different. Like foreign policy analysis (and unlike some other approaches to international relations), diplomatic studies emphasizes the link between individual agents (representatives) and the collective actors (states, multilateral organizations, and firms) that they represent or on whose behalf they make decisions. But even as they ask similar empirical and analytical or evaluative questions about these relationships, scholars of diplomacy tend to focus on the interactions (communications, negotiations, conflict resolution measures) between the actors rather than on particular actors for their own sake. How do China and the United States represent themselves to one another, through traditional approaches such as the exchange of embassies in Washington, DC, and Beijing, and through other public and private channels? How do they communicate, and how effective is their communication at achieving their respective objectives? Normative questions are also asked, both ethical and instrumental, but usually about the prevailing system and practices of diplomacy and the structure of the system of states and other actors within which diplomacy is practiced. Was the classical approach of conducting diplomatic negotiations often in secret ethically objectionable, as US president Woodrow Wilson and the first Soviet leader Vladimir Lenin both contended in the early twentieth century? Were the different modes of "open" and "revolutionary" diplomacy they advocated respectively more effective at achieving the objectives of the negotiators (Wiseman 2005)?

KEY POINTS

- The first major debate, which concerns what diplomacy means, defines the bounds of what can be analyzed under the rubric of diplomatic studies: who are considered diplomats, what are diplomatic practices, and more broadly what counts as part of the study of diplomacy.
- Diplomacy can be understood as consisting of two core functions: representation and communication.
- Diplomatic studies focuses upon interactions between actors, whereas foreign policy analysis examines and evaluates processes of policy making and implementation from the perspective of particular actors.

DEBATING CONTINUITY AND CHANGE IN CONTEMPORARY DIPLOMACY

To what extent has the nature of diplomacy changed since the early twentieth century? The significance of apparent changes in how and where diplomacy is done, as well as in who engages in diplomacy, has posed a challenge for scholars accustomed to thinking about diplomatic actors and processes and about diplomatic culture in terms of received images of nineteenth-century diplomatic practice. New actors, including multilateral institutions like the UN and the International

Monetary Fund (IMF), global firms such as Oracle and Wipro, civil society organizations like Médecins Sans Frontières and World Vision, and diplomatic venues such as the WTO, the World Economic Forum, and the UN Conferences on Women all invoke a diplomacy more diverse than ritual meetings between ambassadors of nation-states and occasional multilateral conferences. Some scholars have preferred to define interactions involving new types of diplomatic actors and newer forms of diplomatic venues as not constituting diplomacy at all (Berridge 2010). Others argue that, if the idea of diplomacy is to remain useful, the profusion of types of actor and venue implies that our understanding of what diplomacy is, and who does it, needs to be broadened accordingly (D. Lee and Hudson 2004).

The first question for debate over how much diplomacy has changed focuses on the degree of change in the range of diplomatic actors as traditionally conceived and in broadly recognized historical practices and processes. The recognition of representatives mediating **estrangement** between sovereign bodies became a defining element both of the international system and of the diplomacy that took place within it (Der Derian 1987: 116–33). The familiar traditional category of diplomatic actors, the governments of nation-states, were in effect identified and defined through recognition by their peers (Sharp 1999). Yet nation-state **sovereignty**, while still important, no longer implies functional equality for nation-states as diplomatic actors in the way it did in the eighteenth and nineteenth centuries. The number of formally recognized sovereign nation-states in the international system has increased dramatically since the end of the Second World War owing to processes of decolonization and internal collapse of multiethnic or imperial states. An equally dramatic differentiation has appeared in the size, attributes, and capacities of these nation-states (Strange 1994). Many of the more than 100 newer nation-states are small in territory and population and are impoverished. While formally equal as diplomatic actors, many of these states are unable to perform many core functions of diplomatic representation and communication to the same extent as their larger, wealthier, and older neighbors. Limited in their ability to train and pay professional diplomats, many new states send and receive far fewer permanent bilateral diplomatic missions and operate a much smaller ministry of foreign affairs with far more circumscribed capacities. The impact of this shift away from the functional equality of sovereign states has been mitigated substantially by the growing role of multilateral organizations as diplomatic venues (D. Lee and Smith 2008). Governments of smaller, less wealthy nation-states increasingly focus their limited resources on representation to, and communications with and through, major multilateral organizations, such as the UN and the WTO, and regional integration and development finance institutions.

Not only have nation-state governments as diplomatic actors become more different from one another, but they are no longer the only type of governmental actor engaging in diplomacy. Subnational regional governments such as Catalonia and supranational actors such as the EU are recognized as diplomatic actors in their own right. For example, regional governments like that of Wales maintain missions to the EU in Brussels. For its part, the EU maintains missions in major world capitals like Washington, DC (see Bátora and Hardacre, chapter 17 in this volume). Moreover, governments of large metropolitan urban areas such as London, Tokyo, Mexico City, and New York have begun to exchange representatives with other diplomatic actors and communicate over issue areas ranging from crime prevention to attracting international expositions and sporting events.

Another arguably significant change is the convergence between diplomatic actors and venues for diplomacy. Until the twentieth century, the notion of a venue for diplomacy referred primarily to the site or location where negotiation or other communications between sovereigns or their accredited representatives took place. However, with the emergence of major multilateral conferences or "congresses" for conducting ongoing diplomatic business in Europe in the nineteenth century, the notion of a venue for diplomacy began to take on a somewhat different aspect (Constantinou 1996: 31–32). The Concert of Europe, a multilateral system for maintaining the peace in Europe, was generally acknowledged as successful for the best part of the century following the 1815 Congress of Vienna. The physical location of such conferences varied, but the standing of the participants was fixed and understood in the context of the particular purpose for which the conference assembled, rather than in the context of an ongoing bilateral diplomatic relationship.

The emergence of permanent multilateral organizations for conducting diplomacy since the late nineteenth century was the next step in the evolution of the diplomatic venue. Such organizations initially were small and specific to particular issues or needs. The Brussels Sugar Convention of 1902, for example, created the Permanent Sugar Commission tasked with monitoring compliance with convention obligations by signatory countries and nonsignatories alike (Pigman 1997). After the Great War, institutional venues for multilateral diplomacy became the norm. The League of Nations was the first great multilateral experiment in entrusting some core elements that constituted traditional national sovereignty, such as protection against attack and the maintenance of peace, to a permanent institution charged with fair administration of mutually agreed rules of state behavior. Not long after the founding of the league came the establishment of the International Chamber of Commerce, the first multilateral venue for diplomacy constituted not by governments but by civil society actors, specifically international businesses. The history of the League of Nations and the raft of multilateral institutions following it—the UN, the North Atlantic Treaty Organization, the Bretton Woods "triad" of international economic organizations (the World Bank, IMF, and General Agreement on Tariffs and Trade [GATT])—showed how governments and other actors became comfortable with using multilateral venues to pursue different types of diplomatic objectives in different ways. By midcentury, multilateral venues for diplomacy had become part of diplomatic culture and international society. Multilateral institutions, as they have evolved, have taken on diverse diplomatic functions, ranging from serving as venues for communication about major global issues such as security and world peace to mediating between nation-states over much narrower economic and technical matters.

Beyond modifying traditional processes of diplomatic relations between governments, multilateral institutions have generated a more fundamental change. Although far younger than many nation-states, multilateral institutions, in developing as diplomatic venues since the mid-twentieth century, have evolved gradually toward becoming diplomatic actors in their own right. Each institution has come to take on aspects of diplomatic "actor-ness" in its own right to varying degrees. For example, League of Nations **mandates** and UN **trust territories** reflect assumption of (albeit temporary) authority by the respective institutions over the governance of territories in the process of moving toward self-government. Beginning as creatures of their founding nation-state governments or other constituents, multilateral institutions over time have developed their own identities. Managers and staff of these institutions shape, and ultimately generate, their own institutional interests and play a greater role in setting their own agendas and issue priorities, as David Mitrany (1966) foresaw in his mid-twentieth-century arguments for **functionalism**. The institutions then find themselves faced with many of the same diplomatic challenges as nation-state actors themselves. They must represent themselves to, and communicate with, other diplomatic actors: governments of nation-states and non-state actors, including other multilateral institutions. Member governments of the UN normally send a permanent representative to New York to represent their interests on an ongoing basis. Many members of the WTO now have a permanent mission to the WTO headquarters in Geneva. The World Bank and IMF often have permanent or long-term representation in the capitals of nation-states in which they are funding major projects. The EU now sends a permanent representative to the UN, who functions independently from, albeit cooperatively with, the permanent representatives to the UN of each of the EU's member states.

The qualitative nature of the change to diplomacy occasioned by the emergence of multilateral institutions' diplomatic "actor-ness" is subtle but evident nonetheless. Not only does the extent of each institution's "actor-ness" vary, but differences between institutions and other types of actors (whether governments, firms, civil society organizations, or otherwise) inevitably limit some of the ways in which diplomatic representation and communication between them take place. But the overarching significance of the evolution of multilateral institutions is that these venues that nation-states created initially to facilitate representation and communication between them have now themselves become subjects engaging in diplomatic representation and communication. The result of this addition of a new layer of diplomatic actors is that the core functions of representation and communication are becoming different rather than easier. While facilitating representation and communication, new institutions increase the number of significant diplomatic actors and add a layer of complexity.

The advent of television, video, global mobile telephony, and the Internet has changed how governments and other diplomatic actors choose to represent themselves by changing how they are able to be perceived by global publics. These new technologies have altered how diplomatic actors communicate, both by changing the available channels for communication (secure satellite links and multiple media outlets) and by increasing the speed at which communication is possible and at which choices may have to be made (**hotlines**, teleconferencing, and email). Transformation of communications technologies has also had a deeper impact upon the relationship between diplomatic actors and the constituencies that constitute and legitimate them. When voters can find out most information about their government through competing media organizations, governments that wish to remain in office must adjust how they make foreign policy, how they conduct diplomacy, and how they communicate about it to their own constituents so as to build and retain public support and legitimacy for their actions. When stockholders and consumers of global firms can learn about corporate policies and diplomacy in a similar way, managements of firms must adapt their strategies of communication to their stakeholders accordingly. Managers of large civil society organizations face a similar challenge in communicating to donors and members.

Underlying the conversation about the extent of change in diplomacy is a deeper debate over to what degree the latest developments in diplomacy are truly new rather than merely recent instantiations of long-running practices. Is the multilevel diplomacy between EU member state governments and the EU governmental institutions in Brussels a new phenomenon? Or is it more a contemporary analogue of the diplomatic relationships in the eighth and ninth centuries between the emperor Charlemagne and the provinces of his empire, which he conducted through appointed emissaries known as "missi." Is the diplomacy between firms like Citigroup and the governments of the United States and United Kingdom really a departure, or is it better understood as a more current version of the diplomacy that took place between the British and Dutch East India Companies and governments in Europe and Asia in the seventeenth century? This "metahistorical" debate over what constitutes change not only matters to scholars and students for its intrinsic interest but it is equally important for practicing diplomats. A well-grounded understanding of when circumstances have changed may suggest or even demand a real change in practice. More than a century and a half ago, Britain's Foreign Office decided to hire a night clerk following the invention of the electric telegraph. Today, as the speed of communications technology and range of channels increases rapidly, a ministry of foreign affairs seeking to respond to matters now deemed urgent in a timely and efficient manner might decide staff need to be reorganized in order to process incoming emails, voicemails, and text and video messages around the clock.

KEY POINTS

- The debate over how much diplomacy has evolved is focused on change in the range of diplomatic actors, practices, and processes.
- International institutions, such as the WTO, are evolving toward becoming diplomatic actors in their own right because they face many of the same diplomatic challenges as nation-state actors.
- Rapid communications are accelerating the speed at which diplomacy is done and causing operational changes in foreign ministries.

DEBATING THEORY AND PRACTICE IN CONTEMPORARY DIPLOMACY

Why theorize about diplomacy at all? In this primary debate over the relevance of theory, proponents argue it can serve a number of purposes: to analyze and understand better what diplomacy is and what diplomats do; to generate an understanding of best practice; and to understand the role of diplomacy in the broader range of global interactions that fall under the rubric of "international relations." Since the Second World War, two broad approaches to theorizing about diplomacy have emerged: the first a generally **positivist** approach that places diplomacy in the context of interstate security relations, and the second a **postpositivist** view of diplomacy that encompasses a broader range of actors and processes and problematizes the core diplomatic functions of representation and communication. Scholars in the first camp have played a major role in constructing our contemporary idea of diplomacy through their theorizing. Theorists of diplomacy from positivist presuppositions, from Nicolson to Watson and G. R. Berridge, have articulated a canonical understanding of diplomacy as fundamentally about relations between nation-states, concerned with matters of *"haute politique,"* or high politics, of Renaissance European lineage and possessing a transhistorical, or perhaps ahistorical, character that has persisted despite major change in the international system. Diplomacy, through this perspective, evolved along with the emergence of the nation-state and the idea of state sovereignty. The Treaties of Westphalia in 1648 were themselves both a major product of the emergence of diplomacy as we know it and a significant building block in the nation-states system that reified and reinforced diplomatic practice. Those treaties and others that followed were what diplomacy was supposed to be about: *haute politique*, the dominance of the discourse of security over other political discourses. *Haute politique* conceives of sovereignty in a particular way: as referring to territory, borders, and about populations, ultimately even conquest and colonization. *Haute politique* conceives of economic issues only within the constructs of the security discourse. Is there access to enough oil and food for the army and navy first, for the general public second? Is the power grid able to supply power to the heavy industries that can supply the armed forces? This variety of theoretical claims about diplomacy is at least in principle capable of empirical measurement and verification: warheads counted in an arms reduction treaty, barrels of oil in a strategic reserve.

Since the late 1980s, another group of scholars, including James Der Derian (1987), Costas Constantinou (1996), Brian Hocking (1999a,b), Richard Langhorne (2004b), and Donna Lee and David Hudson (2004), have argued for a more reflexive understanding of contemporary diplomatic practice. These scholars' postpositivist reading of diplomatic history finds that the canonical understanding of diplomacy downplays, marginalizes, and omits key components of the work of contemporary diplomacy. The traditional canon minimizes, when it does not omit altogether, the economic and the cultural at the expense of the security discourse at several levels. The state-centric, rationalist focus on the high politics of the Westphalia system has also privileged the position of state actors in the international system over other types of actors, for example, domestic interest groups or social classes, subnational political units, or non-state actors like firms. This focus makes only scant allowance for the role of multilateral institutions and downplays the significance of the role of non-state actors, irrespective of all the consular work, **commercial diplomacy**, export promotion, and business facilitation that most governments have always undertaken. From the Anglo-Portuguese Methuen Treaty in 1702 to the 1995 Treaty of Marrakech that created the WTO, historically many of the most important diplomatic missions, the most crucial negotiations, and the most significant bilateral and multilateral treaties have been about international trade.

The debate over theory turns in part on the question of how to model the ways in which diplomats understand their own mission. For example, scholars generally agree that in the nineteenth century and for much of the twentieth century, governments and their diplomats did not view trade and economics as constituting the core of international relations. Instead, they argue, diplomats have regarded economics as a tool to gain political advantage, or to limit threats, or to increase security. Many, if not most, traditional diplomats historically disdained commercial diplomacy, finding negotiating trade agreements degrading and beneath their usually more noble station. Historian D. C. M. Platt (1972: 374) described why diplomats at the British Foreign Office in 1870 were only too happy to abandon negotiated trade liberalization treaties in favor of a policy of unilateral free trade:

> Noblemen, bored, dispirited, and inexperienced in matters of commerce and finance, found in laissez-faire exactly the rationalization they were looking for; they could avoid a distasteful contact with the persons and problems of trade financiers, merely by referring, in good faith, to the traditions of non-intervention, Free Trade, and open competition. And it was true that *haute politique*, at their level and in the society with which they mixed, *was* far more interesting.

Diplomats in the nineteenth and early twentieth centuries perceived, often correctly, that commercial postings in the foreign ministry would be damaging to the progression of their careers. William Ewart Gladstone, one of Britain's greatest prime ministers, openly scorned the haggling and hucksterism of commercial diplomacy, which he associated with tradespeople. Yet, ironically, Gladstone must be considered one of the greatest commercial diplomats of all time for signing the Anglo-French Cobden-Chevalier Treaty of 1860, a proto-GATT of sorts that triggered a wave of bilateral commercial treaty signings that lowered tariffs across Europe more than 50 percent and changed the economic, political, and social face of Europe. Gladstone would have argued that he signed the treaty to lower military tensions building between England and France in the late 1850s (O'Brien and Pigman 1992). But while scholars may agree on how diplomats historically tended to understand their mission, the different theoretical camps diverge over whether or not this understanding has served the interests of those whom they represent.

The positivist intellectual biases and interest preferences of postwar US academics, which tended to reflect the political, economic, and cultural norms of the day, were instrumental in shaping the dominant paradigm for diplomatic studies just as they were for the broader discipline of international relations. Scholarship in diplomatic studies articulated, reinforced, and reified the traditional representations of who did diplomacy and on what they focused, foregrounding issues such as the division of Germany, the Cuban missile crisis, the Strategic Arms Limitation Talks, the struggle over how many Soviet republics and which China to seat at the UN, President Richard Nixon's visit to China, and US-Soviet détente (Kissinger 1994; Schelling 1966; Watson 1982). Research also focused on the negotiators who engaged in resolving Cold War conflicts (Kissinger 1994). Yet the global political economy was evolving, and diplomacy itself was changing functionally along with it. Throughout the Cold War period, the neorealist, bipolar security paradigm shared a bed with the ballooning neoliberal discourse of globalization. **Neorealism**, with its theoretical focus on security, and **neoliberalism**, with its focus on international cooperation, shared state-centric assumptions and a rationalist, empirical methodology. The emergence of neoliberalism in the 1970s did not so much change traditional representations as reinforce them, even if in more nuanced ways. Neoliberalism focuses on the emergence of multilateral institutions as facilitating prospects for cooperation between nation-states. Cold War era scholarship in diplomatic studies has understood these institutions as venues for diplomacy between states. Understanding such institutions as facilitating cooperation might seem a good theoretical fit for updating the ways of explaining diplomacy as representation and communication between states to mediate between interests and minimize conflict. But neoliberalism also embodies within it a particular notion of international economics that presupposes the same separation of international from domestic, public from private, politics from economics. This perspective removes from the possibility of political contestation the international economic objectives of free trade in goods and services, free flows of capital and investment across borders, and the primacy of market pricing of goods and services. Hence neoliberalism facilitates the return of the focus of nation-state diplomats, and the scholars who study them, to issues of *haute politique*. Governments of states negotiate trade agreements for politics-as-security objectives. Neoliberalism ends up marginalizing all non-state diplomatic actors, even the multilateral institutions themselves, by viewing such institutions as impartial venues in which states interact (D. Lee and Hudson 2004).

Donna Lee and David Hudson (2004) argue that the effect of the positivist, rationalist paradigm upon the theorizing of diplomacy has been to render commercial diplomacy "present-but-invisible." According to Lee and Hudson, commercial diplomacy has always been at the core of diplomatic representation and communication since long before the emergence of the Renaissance city-states in the Italian peninsula. Trade missions have been taking place since ancient times. Making arrangements for payments between polities and between different monetary systems has long been part of the core business of diplomatic relationships. Even since the emergence of modern diplomacy as understood by diplomatic studies, commercial activities have occupied the majority of the time of diplomatic missions and the ministries behind them. Lee and Hudson argue that the activity of commercial diplomacy by its nature integrates the domestic and the international, the private and the public, the economic and the political. Business leaders of global and local firms sit down with government officials to plan export promotion strategies; investment tours are organized; and foreign economic policies are debated politically between social groups with significantly different interests.

Lee and Hudson also contend that diplomacy is portrayed unreflexively as Eurocentric. The classical idea of diplomacy as a building block of the European nation-state system seats diplomacy within the frame of a particular culture and a particular historical period, even as it posits the actors, objectives, and functions of diplomacy as timeless and ahistorical. But to view diplomacy in this way excludes other cultures and the organized processes of representation and communication between cultures that have taken place across much of the world since ancient times (D. Lee and Hudson 2004). Kishan Rana's *Inside Diplomacy* (2002) offers a compelling account of contemporary diplomatic practice from an historical perspective of India's diplomacy extending back at least as far as the third century BC. The positivist approach to studying diplomacy discourages study of these interactions because, among other things, it does not recognize pre-Westphalian governments as having equivalent standing to nation-states.

Constantinou (1996: 31–62) challenges the notion that theorizing about diplomacy can be undertaken independently of diplomatic practice. Problematizing the idea of **agency**, Constantinou argues that diplomacy as a process is not only functional and structural but also by its nature **intersubjective**. Diplomatic subjects or actors do not exist prior to and independent of diplomacy but are themselves constructed socially through the mutual recognition and interaction of diplomacy. Constantinou argues that we need to ask how representative action is personified in the representative, which requires an exploration of the politics of the accreditation process that authorizes one to speak in the name of a sovereign subject. Constantinou proposes as a metaphor language itself as a kind of embassy, a diplomatic representative from the sender to the receiver, from the writer to the reader, or the speaker to the hearer. The envoy—language—brings theory from the sender to a foreign place, which makes theory both diplomatic and politicized.

Understanding diplomatic actors and the acts of representation in which they engage has direct implications for how diplomacy is practiced, according to Constantinou. French theorist Jacques Derrida, Constantinou observes, regarded philosophical discourse as acts of embassy, in which presence, or "Being," is transported. By being sent from the sender, presence or "Being" is represented to the receiver. According to Derrida, the diplomatic credentials of these linguistic envoys of theory are always subject to question because they are not the sovereign itself but only representatives of the sovereign. Hence diplomats should refuse to accredit envoys who claim the truth of their origin and the origin of their truth. When diplomats convey communications from their sovereign, the meanings of their messages are always open to interpretation. Diplomatic messages may not always be what they appear to be. Likewise, diplomats may not hear what they want to hear, so they may interpret messages in such a way as to please their own sovereign or advantage themselves. When Iraqi diplomats communicated to their US and British counterparts in 2002 that Saddam Hussein's government did not possess weapons of mass destruction, some American and British diplomats did not believe them, while others did believe the Iraqis. It became a political decision for US and UK leaders which interpretation to accept and how to act upon it. The embassy of theory can still be valid, according to Constantinou, but only if we recognize that it is a messenger possessing no sovereign authority. To be valid, diplomatic theory has to use the stratagems and discourses of diplomacy: it must persuade and convince. Theory has to become the object of diplomacy itself, always reflecting on the terms and categories that it is using. Constantinou's (1996: 31–40) logic invites us to think about diplomatic practice as always constituting diplomatic theory to the extent that practice reflects upon itself, and to the extent that neither diplomats nor scholars assert diplomatic communication as authoritative and beyond interpretation.

Ultimately the positivist and postpositivist approaches to theorizing about diplomacy differ with respect to what they prioritize regarding diplomatic actors and practice, and in terms of how they think about the role of theory itself. The traditional, positivist approach to diplomatic studies has made important contributions to our understanding of contemporary diplomacy, but perhaps only up to a point. Beyond that threshold, postpositivist theoretical approaches may be needed for making sense of the recent evolution of diplomacy and the challenges it faces in the near future.

KEY POINTS

- Theorizing about diplomacy can assist in analyzing and understanding what diplomacy is and what diplomats do, generating an understanding of best practice, and understanding the role of diplomacy in global interactions.
- Some scholars of diplomacy have embraced a positivist theoretical approach focusing on the security of nation-states in the international system, whereas others have adopted a more reflexive, postpositivist approach taking into account identity politics, non-state diplomatic actors, and the centrality of economic and social issues in diplomacy.
- Scholars such as Constantinou argue that to practice diplomacy is by definition to theorize diplomacy, in that effective diplomatic practice reflects upon itself.

CONCLUSION: HOW DEBATES ABOUT DIPLOMACY ARE, OR ARE NOT, RESOLVED

This chapter has argued that several important scholarly debates about diplomacy remain open, and that which position one takes in these debates has a significant impact upon how one understands diplomacy and, for practitioners, how one engages in it. The conclusions that practitioners draw about the outcomes of academic debates, whether they are aware of doing so or not, matter very much in terms of the outcomes of diplomatic interactions, in that the underlying assumptions about diplomacy deriving from the academic debates will affect diplomats' effectiveness in choosing and achieving objectives. For example, a government whose senior officials take a view that diplomacy has not changed to such a degree as to warrant recognizing some multilateral organizations as diplomatic actors in their own right may choose not to send as high level a permanent representative to the WTO as a government whose leadership takes the opposite view. This choice might result in significant budgetary savings for one government but substantially more efficient communications with the WTO for the other. This observation supports Constantinou's argument that to practice diplomacy *is* to theorize diplomacy.

The question then arises of whether these open-ended debates about diplomacy can ever be resolved. Academic debates admit of different methods of resolution, and debates about diplomacy are no different in that regard from other debates in the social sciences. Some of the questions debated, such as those concerning the extent and impact of change, may be able to be resolved through careful empirical observation and analysis. The turnaround time in communication between two governments using email, instant messaging, and text messages during a crisis can be measured, for example, and outcomes compared with analogous cases from earlier times when messages were sent by post or telegraph. Numbers of meetings between government diplomats and representatives of non-state diplomatic actors can be counted, compared with earlier periods, and analyzed. A more reflexive method of research for resolving questions surrounding what diplomacy is, for example, involves gathering the perceptions of diplomats through extensive interviewing and making generalizations about their shared meanings and understandings of diplomacy.

Yet to reach conclusions through research that scholars and practitioners with widely diverging theoretical and epistemological stances are likely to accept as authoritative enough to consider a debate "closed" in many cases may prove elusive. What might be more likely to resolve such debates is an effective comparative analysis of how diplomats have acted by operating on one set of assumptions, understandings, and views with how diplomats operating from an alternate position have performed. For example, have diplomats working in foreign ministries who confine their interactions to foreign ministry colleagues and counterparts of other governments' foreign ministries been less effective than those who spend time working cooperatively with colleagues from other government ministries now involved in diplomacy as well (for example, agriculture, energy, and education)? Have diplomats assigned to upgraded and enhanced public diplomacy responsibilities achieved measurable results? If the answer to these two questions is affirmative, it provides strong support for those who argue for a broader understanding of what contemporary diplomacy is, against those who favor the narrower, more classical understanding. In a recent case of diplomacy reflecting awareness of changing distributions of power in multilateral institutions, governments of the great powers, seeking to resolve the 2008 financial crisis, convened a summit meeting of the **Group of Twenty (G20)** composed of leaders of the great powers and large developing country governments in November 2008. Rather than convening a meeting of the smaller, more exclusive diplomatic club of **Group of Seven (G7)** major global financial powers, global leaders decided that effective management of a contemporary global financial crisis required not only for the G7 to continue to meet on a regular basis but also for regular meetings of the broader G20 to become part of the operational structure of economic diplomacy. Without the full and active participation of emerging economic powers such as China, India, and Brazil, the G7 alone would have found it difficult if not impossible to agree on and implement global monetary and financial measures needed to stem financial panic that can move from country to country and from bank to bank in real time.

This more indirect, two-step method could be the only potentially viable approach to resolving debates about the relationship of theory and practice in diplomacy, which, given the nature of the issue, is going to divide those from different theoretical perspectives. Thus, following Constantinou's argument, in the diplomacy of the age of a heterogeneous collection of post-Westphalian nation-states and other non-state actors, sovereignty is less important than power over outcomes. This is an argument about diplomatic effectiveness. A subnational regional government able to negotiate to bring a major investment by a global energy firm to its region with the cooperation of an international environmental organization may be deemed to be more skilled at diplomacy than the relatively ineffectual federal government that is sovereign over the territory but whose economic development ministry played no role in making the deal. As Hocking (1999a,b) argues, traditional diplomatic institutions such as foreign ministries increasingly are likely to be bypassed in the real world of diplomatic practice to the extent that foreign ministries attempt to hold on to their traditional role as gatekeepers for other government ministries that need to interact with their foreign counterparts. Only to the extent that they are willing to function as "boundary spanners" that bring together and facilitate contacts between the many organs of a government and ministries of other governments (and representatives of non-state actors) will they retain a role at the core of diplomatic practice.

Ultimately, whether or not these major debates are considered to remain open, those who study diplomacy need to decide where they position themselves with respect to each debate and act accordingly. Whether as voters, investors, shareholders, members of civil society organizations, or practicing diplomats, members of the global public are all stakeholders with an interest in effective diplomacy. Our actions, and the understandings of diplomacy that they reflect, have an impact upon all of the polities to which we belong, upon the representations and communications that constitute the diplomacy between them, and upon the peace and stability (or lack thereof) that diplomacy engenders.

QUESTIONS

1. Is it important for scholars and practitioners to agree upon a working understanding of diplomacy? Why, or why not?
2. How does the study of diplomacy differ from the study of foreign policy?
3. To what extent has diplomacy changed over the past two centuries? In what principal ways?
4. To what extent, and with what effect, have venues for diplomacy become actors in their own right?
5. To what extent have changes in technology affected diplomatic processes?
6. Can one theorize diplomacy independently of diplomatic practice?
7. How important is it for professional diplomats to understand and take positions on major contemporary debates about diplomacy?
8. What are the implications in this chapter for your theoretical and practical understandings of contemporary diplomacy?

NOTE

1. The terms "nation-state" and "nation-state system" or "nation-states system" throughout this chapter follow James Caporaso (2000). Nation-states in this context refer to the political units that have been understood to be sovereign and equal as diplomatic actors in the international system that, scholars of diplomacy argue, prevailed from the Treaties of Westphalia until sometime in the second half of the twentieth century. Thereafter, as this chapter goes on to suggest, these state actors have ceded their exclusivity as diplomatic protagonists to multilateral organizations, global firms, and other non-state actors.

CHAPTER 5

Transnationalizing Diplomacy and Global Governance

Bertrand Badie

READER'S GUIDE

Globalization is transforming world order. Sovereign states have lost their monopoly on power, and non-state actors are becoming important players in world politics, even though states are still inclined to see them as unwelcome guests and even intruders. The emerging global order incorporates a new set of relationships, or what might be called intersocial relations, between peoples, groups, and sovereign states. In these complex new relationships, social issues, such as human rights, are becoming dominant, and international social integration among the various international actors is becoming an accepted norm of diplomatic activity. Under these changing circumstances, social actors, such as private individuals and nongovernmental organizations (NGOs), are acquiring new instruments and resources for participating autonomously in diplomatic activities. In sum, they are emancipating themselves from state control and influence. Students of diplomacy need to take into account the new actors and the new social routes through which they act and which bridge the multiple sovereignties of multiple actors in the world diplomatic system, and they need to examine how traditional interstate and emerging international diplomacies interact with or confront each other. Students will also need to consider whether these developments inform processes of global governance.

INTRODUCTION

Even though expanding **globalization** and growing **transnational** relations challenge the realist's traditional theory that the sovereign state is dominant in world politics, these two challenges have not abolished diplomacy (see box 5-1). Rather, they have made international relations richer, denser, and more sophisticated. States have by no means disappeared in the global world, but they have to adapt to new roles and new activities, perhaps even reconsidering their privileges and institutional conventions, such as sovereignty.

BOX 5-1

Globalization and Global Governance

Globalization

Globalization commonly describes the process by which an integrated world market grows and mediates between national economies and the global market. However, it would be inaccurate to limit the globalization concept to the economic dimension. Globalization includes not only growing economic interdependence between national societies but also new communication technologies, by which everyone can interact rapidly with others around the world. Globalization accelerates these interdependencies at multicontinental distances, strengthens the global density, and thus undermines the political functions of distance and weakens the role of territory and borders, thus challenging traditional state theory. A globalizing world is made up of a vast and growing number of transnational relations that would be defined as relations between social actors, participating in the international arena by transgressing state sovereignty, ignoring borders, and circumventing state control, deliberately or not. These relations can be said to be transnational flows when they recur over time. Migration, international trade, information, humanitarian cooperation, and religious networks are relevant examples of these flows.

Global Governance

This concept, which was invented during the 1970s, appears as the main challenge to the Westphalian order and realist theory, since it claims that governing the world implies a close association between public and private actors, even beyond institutions as well as the sovereignty rules. As such, governance may be promoted below (involving local actors), above (through regional and international organizations), or around the state (through transnational actors, such as firms and NGOs). This association reduces any notion of hierarchical order and priorities, which are considered as poorly efficient. Governance has to be distinguished from government, which strictly refers to the sovereignty rules.

In fact, the global world is characterized by **new diplomacy**, which must be added to the traditional diplomacy associated with a world of more than 190 sovereign states. In this new diplomacy, societies (of individuals, peoples, and groups) are actively producing what I conceptualize as **intersocial diplomacy** (see box 5-5). In my understanding, new diplomacy (which may differ from other conceptualizations in this book) consists partly of state actors and partly of non-state (or transnational) actors. Importantly, it leads to a double competitive dynamic: on the one hand, between the different actors; and, on the other, between the two kinds of diplomacy, intersocial and interstate. This competition creates new roles, new functions, and new prospects for diplomatic achievements and possibly **global governance** (see box 5.1).

My sociological argument about the nature of new diplomacy obviously challenges various realist notions of international relations: notably, the "Westphalian paradigm" of the territorial, sovereign state, and the political approach to international relations grounded in **Hobbesian political theory** (see box 5-2). My argument analyzes the international arena beyond these power politics theories and moves from a political science perspective to a sociology of international relations. The sociological perspective in the discipline of international relations is mainly rooted in the "solidarist" approach that originated at the beginning of the twentieth century and is associated with French sociologist **Émile Durkheim** (see box 5-3). Political actors, such as Léon Bourgeois, Aristide Briand, and Albert Thomas, and lawyers, such as Georges Scelle, promoted this approach. They argued that states and societies were becoming increasingly dependent on each other and that this development could be conceptualized as **compenetration** (see box 5-4) (Badie 2008). In the mid-1960s, David Mitrany (1966) argued that international stability depended less on military instruments and more on the ability to satisfy human and social needs. According to this reasoning, traditional political diplomacy between states will have to coexist with a new social diplomacy promoted by an emerging and more active international public opinion. States will strive to achieve benefits from this new competition by trying to shape and control it. At the same time, states will try to restrain this new world order by opposing changes and considering new non-state actors as unwelcome guests, intruders into the international arena.

BOX 5-2

Thomas Hobbes and the Treaty of Westphalia

The great English philosopher published his major book, *Leviathan*, in 1651. Thomas Hobbes conceived of sovereignty as the most efficient way to protect individuals against the dangers they faced. Because they are sovereign and thus free from any compliance requirement, sovereigns compete in the international arena like gladiators, making wars as normal state behavior. The Treaty of Westphalia was signed in 1648, ending the Thirty Years' War. This treaty is commonly considered the starting point of the modern international system, mainly constituted by sovereign territorial states.

BOX 5-3

Émile Durkheim and the Durkheimians

Émile Durkheim (1858–1917), the most famous French sociologist, is the author of *The Division of Labor in Society* (1893) and *Suicide* (1897), among many other works. The cornerstone of his sociology is not to be found in power (contrary to Max Weber) but in social solidarity and integration that are conceived as prerequisites of social life and ways for preventing conflicts. This perspective was enlarged to international relations by French politicians Léon Bourgeois (1821–1925) and Aristide Briand (1862–1932), who were French prime ministers, founding fathers of the League of Nations, and Nobel Peace Prize winners (1920 and 1926, respectively). Albert Thomas was the creator of the International Labour Organization (ILO). International law scholars also promoted the application of this way of thinking to international relations, particularly Georges Scelle, who, with his publication of *Précis du Droit des Gens* in 1931, opened the way to a "solidarist" interpretation of international law. The adaptation of the Durkheimian sociology to international relations helps us not only understand globalization but also appreciate new forms of international conflicts that arise from social pathologies and a lack of social integration. This approach highlights the proliferation of transnational social actors. Conversely, an exclusively political approach risks blinding the social dimension of globalization and focusing only on the state dimension of the international game.

This trend toward a new social diplomacy involves enlarging the definition of diplomacy. New diplomacy incorporates the concept of **separateness**, which, as described by Paul Sharp (2009), applies to relations between states, groups, and societies (see box 5-5). Thus, diplomacy now includes separateness between societies, as well as between states. It also covers separateness of cultures, and systems of meanings, which diplomacy also has to manage. **Intersocial and intercultural** diplomacies have to mobilize new actors and new instruments for reducing social gaps in the international arena, not least because these groups generate many internal and international conflicts (see box 5-5).

BOX 5-4

Compenetration

The concept of compenetration was elaborated by Georges Scelle. The word is an amalgam of the Latin word *cum* and the word "penetration." While classical international law stressed the role of sovereignty as its cornerstone, Scelle was probably the first international lawyer who emphasized how national societies were more and more bound together and more involved in each other's affairs. He sought to adapt international law to this interpretation of transnationalization.

BOX 5-5

Separateness of Groups, and Intersocial and Intercultural Diplomacy

Separateness

Sharp has used the concept of separateness to highlight the diplomatic field's specificity. Diplomacy is a kind of social relationship that is characterized by a clear structural gap separating groups of people. The Westphalian order introduced sovereignty as the main feature of the modern international system. In contrast, as Sharp 2009: 10) argues, "the diplomatic tradition thus presents peoples as living in conditions of separateness from one another, and even when they are not physically separated, a sense of separateness remains a dimension of their relationship."

Intersocial and Intercultural Diplomacy

Intersocial diplomacy designates a form of diplomacy between state and non-state actors or among non-state actors that manages the gap separating civil societies from each other. The main issues addressed by intersocial diplomacy actors are social, not political. Transnational diplomacy can be defined as exclusively conducted by transnational actors—that is, sovereignty-free actors, such as religious players, economic players, or NGOs. Intercultural diplomacy appears as a special case of intersocial diplomacy; it manages cultural separateness and can be run by state or non-state actors.

To make this argument, the chapter first elaborates further upon the nature of intersocial diplomacy. Second, it explains the strategies that non-state actors adopt to execute intersocial diplomacy. Third, it examines the relationship between intersocial and interstate diplomacies. Fourth, it discusses the declining yet resilient state that constrains intersocial diplomacy. Finally, it sums up the argument and its implications for future diplomacy.

KEY POINTS

- Sovereign states have not disappeared in a globalizing world, but they are adjusting their roles.
- Traditional interstate diplomacy associated with sovereign states must now contend with an emerging new intersocial diplomacy involving both state and non-state actors.

FROM INTERSTATE TOWARD INTERSOCIAL DIPLOMACY

The new global world has three main properties that clearly supersede the Westphalian pattern of interstate relationships and that thicken the aspects of "globalism" that could previously affect our world (Keohane and Nye 2002). First, the new ways of communication enable people all around the world to communicate, bargain, and interact without political mediation or control by the state, as the "Arab uprising" showed in 2011. Nearly 7 billion individual actors who manage their sep-arateness more or less autonomously potentially constitute the new international arena. Second, the social needs of these individuals, or social actors, are intruding into the international arena and becoming a major issue. Third, as the global world is increasingly interdependent, security is connected less to national defense and more to global human and social needs, a central point in the United Nations Development Programme's *Human Development Report 1994* (UNDP 1994).

These new global social developments are transforming international agendas, weakening power politics, and highlighting the need for "international social inte-gration." From a Durkheimian perspective, international social integration describes how societies are merging in a global world, contributing to shape what is commonly designated as a **global civil society**. It points out how "social pathologies" (social fac-tors, such as poverty and overpopulation, that tend to inhibit personal adjustment and worsen wider social problems) in one country are more or less jeopardizing all others; it suggests that a lack of international social integration implies a high danger of conflict and instability. Thus, problems faced by Pakistan or many African societ-ies should be considered factors predisposing to war. As Durkheim observed, the higher the social density, the higher the risk of social conflict. If globalization creates an increasing social density and social inequality at the international level, it will generate conflicts. Such a large social gap inside the world system creates a new kind of social separateness that must be managed through diplomacy (Badie 2008).

The objective of international social integration must be sought through mate-rial and symbolic integration. "Material integration" is the ability of individuals to have equal access to material goods, such as food, health, and education. Hunger no longer has the same meaning it had a few decades ago. Then, victims of starvation lived in rural zones, did not protest, and were not politically mobilized. Today, star-vation is more evident in urban spaces, where it fuels protests and riots and creates conditions for conflict, which is increasingly internationalized in its consequences. Moreover, in the victims' consciousness, the international community and especially the richest countries are responsible for providing relief. "Symbolic integration" is concerned with the respect people show each other. For example, such integration was clearly absent when Western governments and public opinion hardly reacted to the 1994 genocide against the Tutsis of Rwanda, which killed nearly 1 million people. In a global world, **alterity**, the notion that all people ought to recognize each other equally, is a great source of tension (see box 5.6). Cultural gaps are a source of dangerous separateness. Bridging cultural differences is a new task for diplomacy, especially when failure to do so generates humiliation and aggressive radicalism (Cohen 2002).

International social integration requires entrepreneurs who are not limited to interstate diplomacy but do not take advantage of the lack of social integration. Some non-state actors unfortunately do this and become **violence entrepreneurs** (see box 5-6). Terrorist networks, or other such radical movements, can easily expand their membership and activities by manipulating social pathologies and using per-ceptions of humiliation to mobilize their followers. For example, radical move-ments in Palestine, Iraq, Pakistan, or Afghanistan denounce such pathologies as poverty, limited access to water, refugee flows, civilian casualties, and anti-Muslim

---

BOX 5-6

Alterity, Violence Entrepreneurs, and Social Routes

Alterity

Alterity is the notion that all people ought to recognize each other equally despite their ethnic, cultural, religious, or philosophical differences. In earlier international systems (for example, in the nineteenth century and the first half of the twentieth century), representatives of sovereign states recognized each other as diplomatic representatives, but there were no real cultural gaps between them because they all came from similar social strata. In a global world, these differences are more apparent and are likely to become greater and to be perceived as such. This new perception of difference carries risks of tensions. For these reasons, cultural hegemony by a single actor triggers conflicts and fuels humiliation by others, a perception that is nowadays a main factor of war and international violence.

Violence Entrepreneurs

From a Weberian perspective, a violence entrepreneur is an actor who invests in social pathologies to transform them into political violence that can be managed for optimizing the actor's advantages, position, and goals in the international arena, particularly for publicizing his "messages" (Richardson 2006).

Social Routes

Social routes are defined as specific new diplomatic "pathways" by which the social field (actors, resources, and issues) will be mobilized for bridging two or more states in conflict. They can be distinguished from the classical political paths, or routes, that use traditional political and military instruments.

---

behavior on the battlefield and in Western countries. Violence entrepreneurs also exploit social disasters, for example, those caused by floods (Pakistan in 2010) or earthquakes (Egypt in 1993). That is why we can postulate an international market of violence that is nowadays different from classical interstate violence. It is different because it is much more fragmented, managed, and promoted by social actors, and very poorly contained by states' classical instruments of diplomacy or use of force.

These new developments imply new diplomatic processes that we could designate as **social routes** (see box 5.6). This is a real change involving not just different actors but also different actions. Such "transnationalizing diplomacies" and "intersocial diplomacies" can be handled by states, but only by meeting three requirements: changing their current agenda, diversifying the levels of their interventions, and opening their diplomacy to new actors.

In regard to the first requirement, changing their agenda is a tough option for states because their legitimacy is built on many ceremonial and privileged conventions of diplomacy and on Hobbesian tenets. Such classical diplomacy has a code of behavior well captured by French theorist Raymond Aron's (1966) famous coupling of "the diplomat and the soldier," representing a dialectical relationship between threat of force (the diplomat) and use of force (the soldier). As such, each state considers other states its exclusive partners, and the notion of separateness is accounted for only at this political level. Today, intersocial diplomacy requires an enlargement of the classical agenda to involve a very large range of social issues, for example, human development, job security, and migrations. States usually transform these social issues into political ones, thus misinterpreting their real meaning. The challenge is to deal with social issues such as hunger, transnational health risks, and environmental pollution without reconceptualizing them as instruments of an inter-state political competition. In short, diplomacy has now two parallel agendas—the intersocial and the interstate—with two different languages, logics and principles. The challenge is to merge these two contending agendas without sublimating one to the other.

A second requirement for state diplomacy is for states to diversify their levels of intervention. The new international issues must be dealt with by using social instruments, constructing new partnerships among local actors, and moving from the state-to-state level to a multilevel game that includes the spectrum of social structures (Putnam 1988). As new international conflicts are increasingly connected to internal, or domestic, social pathologies, these conflicts can only be managed by treating them as social issues. Military instruments will not work. The conflict in Afghanistan, which also involves Pakistan, can be analyzed either through a traditional strategic approach or by analyzing the social pathologies currently afflicting Afghan and Pakistani societies. If we take into account the low redistribution of foreign aid to the Afghan people, the urban victims of starvation in Pakistan, or the youth suicide rate inside Karachi, we become aware of the social direction that diplomacy should follow. From this perspective, social treatment is a much better instrument for solving conflict than are political negotiations or military measures. Peace builders and diplomats need to wear the sociologist's clothes, embrace intersocial diplomacy, and mobilize transnational diplomacy, which is promoted by transnational actors (NGOs for the main part).

A third requirement for successful intervention in the international social field is that states open their own diplomacy to new actors. This approach to diplomacy is already promoted in many international institutions through such measures as **open multilateralism,** or **complex multilateralism** (see box 5-7). Former UN secretary-general Kofi Annan strongly supported an enhanced role for non-state actors, not least as a way of balancing the power of the states, particularly the members of the P5 (the five permanent members of the Security Council) (Knight 2000; O'Brien et al. 2000). Nowadays, more than 3,000 NGOs are accredited to the United Nation's Economic and Social Council. Most are very active in the Human Rights Council. The Arria Formula, coined by Diego Arria, the Venezuelan ambassador to the UN, even made it possible for some NGOs to participate in certain Security Council deliberations (see Wiseman and Basu, chapter 18 in this volume). At Annan's instigation, the "Delivering as One" report (United Nations 2006) opened the way for associating civil society organizations with the UN system. All these initiatives clearly include societies and social actors in the conflict-solving process. They even support a degree of social treatment of crises and, as such, are pioneering a new intersocial diplomacy.

BOX 5-7

Complex, or Open Multilateralism

Multilateralism is an interstate form of diplomacy involving more than two states, the best-known modern example being the United Nations. With increasing globalization, many actors and scholars advocate the expansion of multilateralism to include non-state actors, particularly private firms and NGOs. Former UN secretary-general Kofi Annan played an important part in promoting this "open multilateralism." Scholars such as Robert O'Brien et al. (2000) refer to a "complex" multilateralism for stressing the relevance of a multiactor approach.

The same can be said about NGOs' role in supporting and even writing international conventions. For example, Handicap International was a main author of the Convention on the Prohibition of the Use, Stockpiling, Production and Transfer of Anti-Personnel Mines and on Their Destruction. Human Rights Watch, Amnesty International, and La Fédération Internationale des Droits de l'Homme actively contributed to the Rome Statute of the International Criminal Court, adopted in 1998 and entered into force in 2002. Some UN institutions are even structured around a partnership shared by state and non-state actors, perhaps the best known being the International Labour Organization (ILO) with its tripartite membership of states, unions, and employer associations.

Multilateral diplomacy promises more avenues for participation by non-state actors than does bilateral diplomacy, which tends to give priority to state actors and considers opening the door to other actors a sign of weakness. States can also become more hospitable to non-state actors and work with them on cultural diplomacy (see Leira and Neumann, chapter 9 in this volume) and public diplomacy (see Melissen, chapter 11 in this volume), which are more open to the media, public opinion, and intellectuals. In addition, economic diplomacy (see Woolcock, chapter 12 in this volume) is increasingly more open to firms, and this too can open up the state's historically closed nature. Decentralized interactions of these kinds (see Hocking, chapter 7 in this volume) produce an important role for local actors, cities, and regional institutions (Hocking 1999b). All these emerging diplomacies are bridging separated systems by using social instruments and mobilizing social actors. They are, however, limited and even contained by the state's hierarchical and still dominant position.

KEY POINTS

- With globalization, international social integration is one of the major international challenges, including material and symbolic integration.
- There are two social routes for reaching this aim: intersocial diplomacy, promoted by states in taking social issues into account; and transnational diplomacy, conducted by non-state actors. Both are binding states and non-state actors in achieving these goals.

- Open and complex multilateralism promises new avenues in that direction.
- All these developments inform processes of global governance.

NON-STATE ACTOR PARTICIPATION IN WORLD POLITICS

Directly or not, autonomously or not, non-state actors are now in the international arena. Their participation in world politics is generally regarded with suspicion by states that fear being dispossessed and deprived of their privileges, or at least having to submit to new norms and rules that they are less able to shape to their own interests. That is why non-state actors are perceived as intruders that create uncertainty inside the international arena. This "diplomacy without diplomats" is far from being a homogeneous process. Non-state actors adopt quite different strategies from each other when they participate in world politics. We can detect four such strategies today: the diplomacy of denial, marginal diplomacy, parallel diplomacy, and non-conscious diplomacy (Hara 1999).

The "diplomacy of denial" may be seen as a non-state strategy that explicitly rejects diplomacy as a legitimate mode of international action. This strategy is highly destabilizing, creates great uncertainty, and aims to increase separateness between state and non-state political entities. Terrorist networks, warlords, militia, and private armies practice this strategy. As mentioned earlier, they act as violence entrepreneurs committed to special rules that leave no room for diplomacy. Unlike state armies, private violence entrepreneurs may even consider violence as a goal, as a way of promoting some specific aims, but not as a **Clausewitzian** instrument of state politics. Creating separateness between state and non-state actors, then, is a goal of violence entrepreneurs: separateness is not to be contained but preserved and even widened, as it is a resource for these particular non-state actors. For these reasons, violence entrepreneurs deny diplomacy and do not seek to get involved in negotiations or conflict-solving. They oppose state countermeasures, such as counterterrorist measures, and use them to fuel their fight and mobilize radical supporters.

"Marginal diplomacy" is a strategy practiced by non-state (and nonpolitical) actors in the international arena for promoting transnational interests without trying to achieve diplomatic goals. As such, they are managing different kinds of separateness relations. Religious actors, ethnic entrepreneurs, and identity group managers belong to this category. For example, religions operate beyond state borders, and religious leaders often maintain stronger authority over their believers than do state authorities. As such, these non-state actors are displaying an active transnational role that can weaken state diplomacy, in the sense that citizens are asked to be loyal to an entity, or belief, outside the state. The main activities of participants in marginal diplomacy are clearly oriented toward a nondiplomatic process of extending and strengthening their transnational influence that may have some marginal diplomatic functions, but still be within the interstate order. For example, Saudi state diplomacy is clearly backed by a powerful network of Wahabi preachers, particularly active in the Middle East and Africa. Russia can use the help of Orthodox churches, even beyond its own national territory, in the Balkans or with Orthodox **diaspora**. These functions may be positive for peace processes when religious actors are influential enough to play a mediation role. This was evident in the role of the Sant'Egidio Community in settling several conflicts, as in the Mozambique conflict, when the community's representatives participated in the October 1992 peace agreements as mediators. Interestingly, Sant'Egidio's success was attributed to its lack of hard power, and its influential role in this case illustrates the importance of social power (Nathan 2001).

However, when religious and identity actors are involved in shaping world order, there are significant risks. The clash of civilizations thesis is based on active transnational mobilization of social groupings. It redraws the social map of the world by stressing new divisions that acquire a new political meaning. This type of separateness is much tougher than interstate competition, because a religious world order is not a Westphalian one, nor is it compatible with the territorial or the coexistence principle. So, this separateness is likely to generate instability if uncontained by an institutionalized partnership that gathers religious and identity actors into a common institution, similar to the UN.

Non-state actors, particularly NGOs, promote "parallel diplomacy" that acts as a substitute for state diplomacy (Devin 2002; Fagot Aviel 2011; Hara 1999; Hocking 1999b). Parallel diplomacy is characterized by three activities: communication and fact-finding, pressure activities, and advocacy. Fact-finding is probably the core NGO function, as NGOs are open to accepting and acting on a wider range of information than are state actors. Whereas state actors must consider international conventions and diplomatic sensibilities, NGOs have the latitude, for example, to publicly criticize and stigmatize a dictator, report on human rights violations, and highlight sensitive aspects of a conflict. NGOs can promote an autonomous public diplomacy that can create new bridges and may well weaken state international action. For example, private actors often map human rights politics, whereas states often appear unwilling or unable to report them openly and to exercise their power to correct human rights abuses. NGOs denounce China's human rights record, whereas states refrain from doing so for diplomatic and geopolitical reasons. NGOs played an active role in exposing the Abu Ghraib prison abuse scandal in Iraq. And in 2010, NGOs highlighted the humanitarian situation in the Gaza Strip by commissioning a flotilla of private vessels to challenge the Israeli blockade, helping to partly reduce the goods that Israel could prevent from entering Gaza.

Such pressure activities build on the fact-finding actions of NGOs. When NGOs reveal significant human rights violations, they put pressure on public opinion and the ruling elites to create new directions and different diplomacy processes. Campaigns for bringing political criminals to justice or for abolishing the death penalty put pressure on many states' foreign policies. Increasing interdependence among all kinds of actors integrates transnational actors in the international arena with such a density that they participate increasingly in tangible processes of global governance. The Basel informal agreements between regulators on capital adequacy standards (1998 Basel capital accord, Basel II, and Basel III) grant power and autonomy to economic and financial actors and illustrate that states cannot rule exclusively by themselves, even if they had to bail out the private sector, as was the case during the 2008–9 financial crisis when business actors were integral to both the problem and its solution.

Some NGOs are also undertaking activities that states ought to be fulfilling. NGOs are now involved in writing international law. During dangerous periods of civil wars, when embassies or consulates are closed, NGOs are often the only foreign witnesses, performing functions usually carried out by state agencies. During the worst moment of the war in Chechnya, NGOs were still active. The Russian government subsequently denounced and expelled them because they became embarrassing eyewitnesses of Russia's tactics. Similar situations occurred in Afghanistan during the Russian campaign (1979–88). During the 1990s civil wars in Liberia and Sierra Leone, and, after, in Darfur, NGOs played key roles in the absence of states. NGOs often take charge of functions that states do not dare or want to perform in critical situations.

A fourth way non-state actors participate in world politics is through a strategy of "nonconscious diplomacy." Many transnational actors are performing latent diplomatic functions without necessarily being aware of it. The media are a typical example, as the Arab uprising gives evidence, when Al Jazeera (the Qatari broadcast network) played an important role in citizen mobilization and in setting up the international agenda. As transnational actors, they help to reduce separateness by filling the communication gaps in the international arena. The way they select news helps to shape the international agenda: some conflicts are left in the shadow, as was the case when the Indonesian army invaded the Portuguese colony of East Timor in 1975. It was not until a 1991 British Broadcasting Corporation team report with dramatic pictures of the Indonesian army shooting participants at a funeral in Dili that the conflict became internationalized and the international community was forced to respond. The media reshapes (consciously or not) international politics by selecting and prioritizing particular events as news.

KEY POINTS

- Non-state actors adopt different strategies for participating in world politics.
- They may act by denying or contesting the diplomatic instruments.
- They may also produce their own diplomacy, which may be described as marginal, parallel, or nonconscious.
- Such activities of non-state actors, especially NGOs, are integral to understandings of global governance.

INTERSOCIAL DIPLOMACIES VERSUS INTERSTATE DIPLOMACIES

The transformation of world order makes the two diplomacies—intersocial and interstate—compete. Intersocial diplomacy bridges societies in a decentralized and fragmented way, so no one appears as the legitimate and unique representative of a social system. This diplomacy can be identified through the issues at stake, through the concerned population, and through the actors involved. These actors are sovereignty free (Rosenau 1990), although states interfere, as previously mentioned. By contrast, state diplomacy bridges states through specialized actors (notably, professional diplomats), who can easily be identified and who strive to distinguish themselves from those they usually consider intruders in diplomacy. However, all social actors strive to influence interstate diplomacy through pressure activities, lobbying, public protests, and demonstrations (Tarrow 2005). In these ways, the two diplomacies interact.

However, in this interaction, states and state actors have a great advantage over non-state actors. From a **neoliberal institutionalist** perspective, states have a common interest in cooperation, in reaping joint benefits through international organizations, and they have an exceptional ability to build formal partnerships and participate in formal negotiations and established institutions. With this power, states can act as mediators in the intersocial arena. They may even take the upper hand in a proactive manner. However, states have so few social resources that while powerful in one sense, they are dependent and even dispossessed in another. That is, states are often circumvented by social actors that are frequently better informed and, in some cases, considered more legitimate.

States' strongest advantage is their ability to mediate among social actors. States retain the privilege to negotiate, to write, and to sign all international conventions, even those regarding social life. This privilege has some exceptions, as previously discussed, but even then, states must give their agreement, albeit at times under pressure. Some international institutions have indeed granted positions and roles to non-state actors. The ILO, which promotes regulation of labor conditions, was established because of pressure from French trade unions and employer associations. "Social forums," gatherings of NGOs in parallel with UN intergovernmental meetings, are examples of how non-state actors participate in and around state-based conferences, a good example being the 1992 Rio de Janeiro Earth Summit on the environment and development. Non-state actors participate in many summits, at least in some form, even if these are UN-held and organized.

Social forums organized around major international conferences convened by the UN demonstrate the state's mediating role. Although forums focus on social issues, they are limited to making recommendations or demands. States still make the final decisions and dominate their implementation. States are thus in a position of mediator, deciding among competing demands and interests. This mediation cannot be considered neutral: states are connecting and reinterpreting the issues at stake according to their national interest and to rulers' real interests. When facing new issues, states act to protect their dominant role in the international arena (see Kerr and Taylor, chapter 13 in this volume).

The failed 2009 Conference of the Parties to the United Nations Framework Convention on Climate Change in Copenhagen is a particularly clear instance of such a strategy. The conference dealt with an issue that put social and economic demands on the table, which could have been aggregated over time to promote global public goods for all humankind. But these issues were taken over by self-interested political actors representing competing states, and the demands for common goods were retranslated into political terms and fueled interstate competition. Other issues—national economic capabilities, competition among industrialized and rising powers, and relations between China and the United States—became more important than global warming. The conference moved from a social and technological debate to a political one. States were able to (mis)lead players in the game by rearticulating demands and interests. The Copenhagen conference shows how states achieve their goals through political containment of a transnational issue.

States are even able to gain the upper hand by instrumentalizing, or co-opting, non-state actors in the same way. States consider intersocial diplomacy an instrument of their own foreign policy. States currently use their own national firms, NGOs, and even media as a way of penetrating the international arena, to strengthen their **soft power**, promote their own diplomacy, or even to obtain new material advantages. This was demonstrated during the 1980s, when US diplomacy used soft power to balance anti-Americanism in Latin America and the Arab world. Coca-Cola and famous American television shows were used to assist US state diplomacy. During the nineteenth century, Presbyterian or evangelist missionaries were used to penetrate the Middle East, Far East, Africa, and Latin America. The same could be said about Roman Catholic missionaries who helped to expand French influence. In addition, Anglican Church missionaries helped British foreign policy in Africa, East Asia, and the Middle East. Shia and Wahabi networks helped Iran and Saudi Arabia. And Freemason lodges contributed to Western political penetration in Egypt, the Ottoman Empire, and Persia during the nineteenth century and later. However, state co-option of non-state actors does not always have welcome outcomes. The more the non-state actor is perceived to be different from the host or national state, the more the intended audience will accept the message. These actors are clearly accepted as emerging from civil society, not as political tools of the state. We can thus easily understand the success of religious networks and their ability to mobilize people around the world.

Under some circumstances, states may appear to be dependent actors. In other words, when states operate abroad, their perceived effectiveness can vary according to the support they receive from non-state actors. Taking this argument further, states could ultimately be dispossessed of their current sovereign prerogatives and roles. Thus, while sovereign in their own territory, states often lack symbolic resources and social support when they work on the international plane. Ironically, to reach foreign civil societies, the state needs to be assisted by civil, or social, actors who have their own social and transnational goals. Thus, this private diplomacy, conducted by non-state actors, may in the future transform state foreign policies such that they will ultimately become disconnected from a so-called unified national interest.

KEY POINTS

- Interstate diplomacy and intersocial diplomacy compete for influence in the international arena.
- In this competition, states have a strong advantage, as they are widely seen as retaining the rights to negotiate and to sign legal agreements such as conventions and treaties, but also to organize the basic institutional structures in the international arena.
- Successful global governance in the future will require a growing interaction between the two diplomacies.

GLOBAL GOVERNANCE AND THE DECLINING
RESILIENCE OF THE STATE

In a way, the state transformation described so far supports visions of global governance promoted at the twentieth century's close (Rosenau and Czempiel 1992). But at that time, globalization supporters had unrealistically idealistic and optimistic expectations. In reality, public and private interests are slow to converge, and states, as I have argued, are determined to maintain their prerogatives. The state's resilience is thus an important constraining parameter of transnationalizing diplomacy: it contains it, triggers new kinds of state policies, and has new ways of restraining social actors.

The interplay between the two diplomacies I am describing has nonetheless opened the way to a new game. The well-known Hobbesian gladiator fight between states has been progressively converted into a subtle triangular system in which states have to compete, deal, and sometimes make a pact not only with transnational actors but also with "identity providers," or those actors who offer various identities—cultural, ethnic, religious—that are prior to, or more important than, allegiance to a sovereign state. The last two categories of actors differ from each other, and their orientations and strategies need to be differentiated. Transnational actors are inclusive and open to a global market. Identity providers exclude those who do not share the same political, religious, or ethnic affiliation. The three actors have different commitments: states to citizenship, transnational actors to utility, and identity providers to primordial allegiance. Each has its own way of mobilization, and each competes for an individual's primary allegiance. Because in a global world none of the actors can enforce its own rule on the others, each has to deal, and compromise, with its partners. This new triangular diplomatic game is fragile and unstable and generates uncertainties. For states, it implies a real regression, as it jeopardizes their sovereignties and endangers the main principles on which they were created—institutions, centralization, national will, and violence monopoly (Badie 2001).

That is why states pursue a resilience strategy, one supported by the nature of international law, the progress of intergovernmental organizations, and the military resources of states. Promoting such strategies is a way for states to contain social pressures and keep the upper hand in the new triangular international game. This new state attempt at hegemony is not only a way of interstate competition but also a vertical instrument for containing pressures from transnational actors and identity entrepreneurs. States have, moreover, several levels of hegemony: the international (superpower), the regional (regional power), and, for some, club membership, of elite organizations like the P5, **Group of Eight (G8)**, or **Group of Twenty (G20)**. All these positions enhance the states' political resources and provide a way to claim their capacities and their hierarchical authority over transnational and identity actors. This hegemonic device is obviously much more efficient among political systems having a strong state tradition and culture, while it is less adapted to those built on a strong and powerful civil society. "Jacobine" countries like France, inspired by the French Revolution and conceptualizations of the state as an instrument of emancipation, are thus oriented toward state diplomatic overachievement, because the state is regarded as the expression of national will. By contrast, "Lockean" countries like the United

Kingdom and the United States draw mainly on the capacities of their civil society and are expected to act on their own in the international arena (Badie 2011).

State hegemony or political overachievement tragically leads to an underestimation of societies and a dangerous ignorance of their international role. In a classical realist vision, a focus on societies would have no meaning because there is a fundamental separateness between societies and domestic affairs, on the one hand, and states and international affairs, on the other. Rulers, according to realist logic, should not be concerned with social demands or social actors when handling international issues. Nowadays, such blindness to societies is one of the major sources of instability and uncertainty in the international arena—first, because international conflict is predominantly based on pathological social patterns stemming from a lack of international social integration or from insufficient national integration that weakens the state; and second, because these pathologies cannot be overcome without drastic treatment of social issues instead of a military reaction.

International society is becoming more aware of this new social orientation that is transforming the concept of security. When the United Nations Development Programme pointed out the new relevance of **human security** in its 1994 report, it noted that national securities were becoming interdependent and merging into a global security that would be less political, and less achievable through military instruments. We live in a global world, in which security has to be appreciated in social terms. Our security is threatened primarily by hunger (food security), diseases and epidemics (health security), natural disasters (environmental security), cultural tensions (cultural security), and economic crisis (economic security) (Buzan, Wæver, and de Wilde 1998; Klare and Thomas 1994). All these securities cannot be managed without close cooperation between specialized social actors and social institutions. The main danger to such cooperation comes from the traditional dilemma of states: state survival and the reproduction of rulers with power are closely bound to a political and military interpretation of international conflicts and international issues and a dismissal of conflict's social nature. Political rulers around the world accept the goal of enforcing interstate diplomacy at the expense of intersocial diplomacy. Interstate diplomacy is based on club diplomacy, which moves intersocial diplomacy to a marginal or protest position. Being on the margins, intersocial diplomacy increasingly adopts an autonomous role and operates without any rules and constraints, becoming more radicalized and triggering a world order of turbulence, or what James Rosenau (1990) describes as a complex interplay between states and non-state actors. Instead of being a regulating diplomacy, intersocial diplomacy denounces the material world order.

Nonetheless, this intersocial diplomacy is potentially functional and meets all attributes recognized in interstate diplomacy. In a globalized world, we must admit that societies not only are separated but also have a strong and dangerous desire for separateness, a point that Sharp (2009: 84) has made about states. While globalization generates increasing communication, it also highlights social contrasts, cultural gaps, and specific identities. Those who feel threatened by the evolving globalizing world use these factors as instruments of protection. In other words, cultural gaps and identity constructions are symptoms of a lack of world integration. Their management must be a priority in the new international agenda setting and must be handled through cooperation between states and social actors.

This new kind of social separateness requires measures usually associated with diplomacy: bridging particularities (Jönsson and Hall 2005), managing encounters and discoveries of others (Sharp 2009; see also Sharp, chapter 3 in this volume), and achieving international integration. But diplomats, traditionally considered credible state representatives, cannot pretend to represent their own society with the same credibility. This is because, first, the new global order grants societies an unprecedented level of autonomy. Second, we easily perceive a growing differentiation between public and private interests. And third, states face an increasing crisis of representation. These trends are evident in developing countries in the **Global South**, where failing or authoritarian states prompt citizens to seek other means of identification and mobilization. And it is occurring in developed and postindustrial societies of the **Global North**, where citizens build up multiple and often volatile identities and become increasingly involved in transnational networks.

This crisis of representation is thus jeopardizing the new intersocial diplomacy. This diplomacy weakens the state's international functions that cannot be rebuilt solely through traditional means. According to a dangerous vicious circle, the more this crisis develops, the more states strive to protect themselves by trying to recover their monopoly of power and sovereignty. The deeper the crisis, the more the political class is prompted to neglect its social dimension by translating it exclusively into political terms. These processes are more than obvious in situations of civil war, for example, in Afghanistan, or in situations of socioeconomic crisis that become internationalized, as happened, for example, in the 2010 Greek economic crisis, which was dealt with through political and intergovernmental initiatives within the European Union without consideration of the social actors that were prompted to radicalize their movement. The reluctance to admit social actors into multilateral arenas is a failure of open multilateralism, and it blocks this new way of global governance.

KEY POINTS

- Interstate and intersocial diplomacies compete with each other.
- States retain strong assets in this competition, countering early visions of the future of global governance.
- However, state resilience is decreasing, as states (particularly Lockean ones) are short on symbolic resources.
- New ways of global governance are being obstructed by states reluctant to admit social actors comprehensively to multilateral arenas.

CONCLUSION

I have argued that intersocial diplomacy is no longer an anecdote, no longer hearsay. It plays a major role in global governance in several ways. It represents active and decisive international interests, bridges social gaps that are increasingly internationally relevant, and creates new ways of transnational (and international) communication. As such, intersocial diplomacy plays an increasing role in internationalizing domestic conflicts and local issues.

I have further argued that my concept of intersocial diplomacy is based on three factors: concessions, constraints, and repression. States give concessions to non-state actors that are thus free to play a regulating role in interstate relations. Private credit rating agencies such as Standard & Poor's have the power to pressure and regulate the credit distribution to indebted states. The relevance of their function was particularly obvious during the 2010 Greek crisis. In the same way, the Basel Committee on Banking Supervision, constituted by private banking regulators from around the world, has the authority to define the banking liquidity rules that partly shape world economic growth. Constraints on intersocial diplomacy come from states that regard many non-state actors as unwelcome guests or intruders in world politics. Many states are especially suspicious of religious actors, community organizations, identity entrepreneurs, and sometimes noncompliant transnational corporations. These entities act as sovereignty-free actors and feel free of any commitment to rules. Finally, intersocial diplomacy is challenged by a strategy of state repression that aims to contain, impede, or control its advance. This desperate behavior is rarely successful. On the contrary, it fosters tensions, isolation, and even humiliation inside societies and provides an opportunity for radical initiatives.

My final argument is that the necessary convergence between interstate and intersocial diplomacy closely depends on the way these three factors evolve. The more social dynamics are repressed, the less likely the convergence. The less the non-state actor interventions can be regulated, the less relevant the diplomatic orientation of intersocial diplomacy. The future progress of transnationalizing diplomacy is thus still an imaginary balance between expected and necessary social representation and the ability to get involved in partnership and global governance. Making open multilateralism accessible to social actors is the prerequisite for a functional intersocial diplomacy.

QUESTIONS

1. Is transnational diplomacy exclusively bound to a globalized world, or is it deeply rooted in history?
2. Are non-state actors able to build up transnational relations by themselves, or do they need state help?
3. Can non-state actors ever be free from some degree of state control?
4. Do sovereignty-free non-state actors exist in authoritarian political systems?
5. How can states open up to intersocial diplomacy while maintaining their sovereign control of diplomatic institutions and processes?
6. What are social pathologies, and can the concept be used in an analysis of international conflicts?
7. What are the implications of intersocial diplomacy for understandings of global governance?
8. What are the implications in this chapter for your theoretical and practical understandings of contemporary diplomacy?

CHAPTER 6

Diplomacy as Negotiation and Mediation

I. William Zartman

CHAPTER CONTENTS

READER'S GUIDE

Diplomacy is primarily negotiation, and negotiation is the primary business of foreign policy and international relations. Negotiations take place when needed, that is, when a party (state) feels it cannot handle a problem of conflict by itself, and the problem/conflict needs handling, that is, it is troublesome and costly. Many problems/conflicts involve third parties or crutches of trust, who can carry communications between the involved parties, supply ideas and formulas for agreement, and even improve the benefits available with an agreed outcome. **Multilateral negotiations** are frequently used to set up international regimes, agreed norms, rules, principles, and expectations to handle issue areas of common concern. The biggest challenge to diplomacy is that of prevention, to handle conflicts before they become violent, keep violent conflicts from escalating, and move conflicts and problems from management to resolution.

INTRODUCTION

Diplomacy is, above all, negotiation, either direct or mediated. Harold Nicolson (1939: 4) defined it authoritatively as "the management of international relations by negotiation; the method by which these relations are adjusted and managed by ambassadors and envoys; the business or art of the diplomatist." A century and a half earlier, Fortune Barthélemy de Felice (1778/1976: 47, 48) said it more expansively:

> The term "negotiation" means the art of handling the affairs of state as they concern the respective interests of the great and supposedly independent societies interacting in a free state of nature....However, negotiation is not limited to international affairs. It takes place everywhere where there are differences to conciliate, interests to placate, men to persuade, and purposes to accomplish. Thus, all life could be regarded as a continual negotiation. We always need to win friends, overcome enemies, correct unfortunate impressions, convince others of our views, and use all appropriate means to further our projects.

Diplomacy and negotiations, alongside **communication**, **representation**, and **reporting**, are the daily practice of relations among states, taking up more time but less money than the occasional lapses of these relations into war. When those lapses do occur, negotiation and diplomacy are always present and absolutely necessary to bring them to an end (Aggestam and Jerneck 2009; Berridge 2010; Charillon 2002; de Callières 1716/2000; Jönsson and Hall 2005; Lauren 1979; Satow 1979). As noted by de Felice, diplomatic negotiation reaches beyond state-to-state relations down to domestic and up to global relations and across from (international) law to war as a means of conducting international relations. It includes conflict management but also involves the peaceful pursuit of conflict, on one level, and the constructive and constraining work of international institutions, on the other. Although it also uses official negotiators and diplomats driving on "track-one," it also increasingly involves activities of nongovernmental organizations (NGOs) on optimally parallel track-two (see Kerr and Taylor, chapter 13 in this volume). Over time, the two tracks of diplomacy have gradually come to terms with each other, official diplomacy finding that unofficial efforts could be helpful on occasion in providing the context for official actions or entering situations where official penetration could be viewed as intrusive, and unofficial practitioners recognizing that state auspices were needed to conclude binding agreements.

As democracy spreads its effects around the world, the need to take public opinion and nongovernmental interest groups into account in the conduct of diplomacy increases greatly (see Pigman, chapter 4, and Badie, chapter 5 in this volume). As a result, diplomacy and negotiation are more important to states than ever before not only as a means of conducting external relations but also as a means of pursuing domestic policies and broad notions of security. Of course, most broadly, diplomacy (particularly in its adjectival form) refers to smooth wording and good manners by anyone (a kind tribute to the officials with whom this behavior is associated); the usage here will be more specifically state-oriented, as noted.

KEY POINTS

- Diplomacy is primarily negotiation, and negotiation is the primary business of foreign policy and international relations.

- Although officially conducted by state representatives, negotiations and mediation can also be carried out by private groups and NGOs, often needing state participation at the end to become officially binding.
- Negotiations also take place vertically between state representatives and domestic groups and interests.

NEGOTIATION AND DIPLOMACY

States are **sovereign**, self-centered entities, morally responsible to their population for the defense and promotion of its security and welfare. In the evolution of the modern world, neither self-centeredness, **sovereignty**, nor security can be the absolutes that they once (if ever) were purported to be (Annan 1998; Boutros-Ghali 1995). Increasingly, states need cooperation with others to achieve their objectives, and decreasingly are they able to claim sovereignty as an indivisible value that protects their freedom to do anything with their own population without interference.

The ideal type of the process by which relations among states are carried out can be referred to as "normal diplomacy," that is, ongoing communication between formally equal parties for the purpose of maintaining relations, doing business, and preventing and handling conflicts as they may arise. Increasingly, normal diplomacy is used to help other parties out of their conflicts and to join other parties in devising cooperative agreements to solve multilateral problems. Normal diplomacy is responsible for defusing the literally innumerable conflicts that have not occurred or turned violent and for conducting the day-to-day trade, tourism, culture, and communications that take place. It is conducted by both permanent and occasional representatives in bilateral and multilateral channels (see Wright, chapter 10 in this volume). The primary charge of accredited ambassadors and their staff is the maintenance of good relations between their home and host countries; the diplomat's second task is to gain support from the host country for policy positions of importance to the home state. In dealing with internal conflicts, this situation creates obstacles to creative policy in circumstances referred to as "diplomacy as usual," for it leads the ambassador to adopt the host state's position on the rebellion and to turn a blind eye to the fact that, whatever their merits, rebellions are generally an indicator of a problem. This problem troubled US policy in the second half of the 1990s as the government of President Sese Seko Mobutu collapsed, and it continued to limit a positive US role in the subsequent phases of the succession war in Zaire.

Diplomacy is faced with two types of situations—**zero-sum** and **positive-sum**—where the parties' options are in conflict with each other (see box 6.1). In the first, a party wins at the expense of the other; in the second, a party wins in cooperation with the other(s). In a zero-sum perspective, it is better to be stalemated than to be beaten ("better dead than red," in Cold War lingo), captured in game theory by the classical "Prisoners' Dilemma Game" (PDG). In the game theory matrix (see figure 6.1), zero-sum outcomes are found in the unacceptable northeast and southwest quadrants (1/4 and 4/1), where one party holds out and the other gives in, and as a result the parties end up in the southeast quadrant in deadlock (at 2/2), unable to negotiate the second-best, cooperative outcome (at 3/3) in the northwest quadrant. Zero-sum thinking is accompanied by a perception of the stakes as **relative gains**, where a party measures its success in relation to the position of the other party (see box 6-1). Relative gains thinking in a PDG was prevalent between the superpowers during the Cold War, but it also characterizes contemporary relations between Indians and Pakistanis, Israelis and Palestinians, Francophile West Africans and Nigerians, North and South Koreans, and many other pairs of adversaries.

The problem with zero-sum encounters is that their unbalanced outcomes leave little prospect of stability and a bad impression on the loser, who looks to improve its relative gains in the next round or elsewhere. If negotiations were a one-shot affair, parties could drive the hardest bargain possible, sign, and run. But diplomacy is the business of managing ongoing relations. Even if a party feels a need to prevail in a particular diplomatic negotiation, it is preferable to do so in such a manner that the outcome does not impel the other party above all to seek revenge. "Diplomacy," said Cardinal Armand Richelieu "should aim, not at incidental or opportunistic arrangements, but at creating solid and durable relations" (Freeman 1997: 71).

Negotiation is the process of combining divergent positions into a joint decision. It takes place when the parties realize that they are blocked in their attempts to arrive at their preferred, unilateral solution to a problem or conflict and see that stalemate as the worst possible outcome, creating a situation of **ripeness** for negotiation to

---

BOX 6-1

Some Terms Associated with Game Theory

Mutually enticing opportunity (MEO): a situation where (both) conflicting parties feel that a cooperative solution is possible, are willing to work toward it, and are thereby pulled to an agreement. Also referred to as a **way out (WO)**.

Mutually hurting stalemate (MHS): a situation where (both) conflicting parties feel that they cannot escalate the conflict to a unilateral solution at an acceptable cost and that this impasse is costly to them, and are thereby pushed into considering negotiating a cooperative solution.

Nash equilibrium or determinate outcome: the point in a game theory matrix where neither party can improve its position unilaterally and hence has no incentive to move.

Positive-sum: an outcome where all parties' gains (or the total of each party's gains and losses) are positive, or where each party gains something from the outcome (although not necessarily equally, as opposed to **negative-sum**, where all lose).

Relative gains: gains that are measured in comparison to another party's gains or by interparty evaluation, in contrast to **absolute gains** measured in relation to a party's own goal or by intraparty evaluation.

Ripen: making a situation ripe by increasing the parties' perception of a MHS and WO.

Ripeness: a moment when both MHS and WO are present in the conflicting parties' perceptions.

Zero-sum: an outcome where one party's gains are equal to (and therefore balance out) the other party's losses, and vice versa.

Mr. Column

		Give in	Hold out
Ms. Row	Give in	3/3	1/4*
	Hold out	4/1*	2/2

Figure 6.1 Prisoners' Dilemma Game (ordinal form).
Note: * zero-sum outcomes; Nash equilibrium in underline.

begin (see box 6.1). They need to arrive at a joint solution with the other parties to save themselves from a continued painful deadlock. This situation is captured in the "Chicken Dilemma Game" (CDG), where no determinate outcome but two rival and mutually exclusive **Nash equilibria** (where neither party can improve its position unilaterally—see box 6.1) are present in the same northeast and southwest corners of the game theory matrix and are preferable to the worst outcome, deadlock (see figure 6.2) (Brams 1985; Druckman 2007; Goldstein 2010; Hopmann 1996; Snyder and Diesing 1977). In principle, the perceived need to escape the **mutually hurting stalemate** forces the parties to think and to try to define a **positive-sum cooperative solution** in the northwest corner (see box 6.1). If the mutually hurting stalemate of the CDG pushes the parties into negotiation, their job is to devise a **mutually enticing opportunity** to pull them into agreement (see box 6.1). However, where conflict or a problem is not ripe for immediate resolution, the challenge to third-party diplomats is to **ripen** perceptions so the parties can be brought to consider resolution rather than conflict (see box 6.1).

Positive-sum perspectives are those where both sides gain. They do not have to gain equally; the allocation of the gains is another, often distributive, matter. Positive-sum diplomacy seeks to provide something for the other party, not for goodness' sake but in order to give it an incentive to keep the agreement from which the first party also benefits. If negotiating is "giving something to get something," positive-sum attitudes reflect its basic nature: "If you can't take it, you must buy it," in a mercantilist formulation. Negotiation is the process of setting the price. Positive-sum attitudes also correspond to the perception of "absolute gains"—as opposed to relative gains—where each party finds value in the stakes that matter to it rather than in trying to beat the other party (Powell 1991).

Mr. Column

		Give in	Hold out
Ms. Row	Give in	3/3	2/4*
	Hold out	4/2*	1/1**

Figure 6.2 Chicken Dilemma Game (ordinal form).
Note: * zero-sum outcomes; ** *negative-sum outcomes*; Nash equilibrium in underline.

The challenge for diplomacy is to change PDG perspectives into CDG perspectives and then to find mutually attractive outcomes to move the preferred outcome to positive-sum cooperation (in the northwest). Parties can achieve positive sums either through "compensation" or through "construction" (reframing). Compensation refers to "giving to get," an exchange of concessions on different matters; one part "pays" for a favorable outcome in one matter by granting the other party a favorable outcome on another matter. According to "Homans' maxim," the key to successful negotiation is the situation where stakes can be put into two piles (those that are more valuable to each side and less costly to the other) and then the two piles are traded against each other (Homans 1961). A CDG situation was obtained in southwest Africa in 1988, where agreement to end the conflict in Namibia and Angola was reached by "purchasing" a withdrawal of South African troops from Namibia (and its consequent achievement of independence) with the withdrawal of Cuban troops from Angola, and vice versa, thus achieving a full realization of both parties' goals (Zartman 1989). It was also present in the early 1990s in South Africa, where the growing perception of an unacceptable stalemate enabled the parties—the ruling minority represented by the National Party and the excluded minority represented by the African National Congress—to negotiate a new and beneficial outcome (Zartman 2000). Of course, not all stakes are Homans-divisible, still leaving a distribution or zero-sum problem for those that are not. In such cases, compensations become particularly important as side payments, involving items outside the original stakes.

Construction or reframing refers to a redefinition of the stakes in such a way that both parties can find an interest in the outcome, instead of defining it distributively. It is unlikely that reframing can totally recast the stakes to the elimination of all distributive concerns (that is, stakes not open to compensation but only to a zero-sum outcome), but it can provide superordinate goals and a cooperative atmosphere that makes distribution less contentious. When the parties to what is considered the last territorial conflict in Latin America, between Peru and Ecuador, began to focus on the development of the poor and isolated region in contest rather than on the legalisms of their contending claims, they were able to reach a settlement in 1998 (Herz and Nogueira 2002; Simmons 1999).

KEY POINTS

- Normal diplomacy is the daily exercise of interstate relations that handles most problems and conflicts between/among states.
- Ripeness is required for states to turn their attention from attempts to solve/win a conflict or problem by themselves to attempts to seek a solution in cooperation with the opponent or other concerned party.
- Positive-sum outcomes are preferable to distributive or zero-sum outcomes because they tend to be more durable, since each party gets something from the agreement.
- Concession or division, compensation or exchange, and construction or reframing are the three means of arriving at an agreement over stakes at issue in a conflict or problem.

EXPANDING THE SCOPE OF DIPLOMACY

In the globalized era, the subjects of negotiation spread upward from single-state security to international security, and downward from state security to "human security". Concern for human security (the security of people, populations, and human lives) is reflected in the significant rise in importance of humanitarian conditions, emergencies, conflicts, and intervention, penetrating into the interior of the state and holding the state responsible for the plight of its citizens (HSRP 2008). Humanitarian efforts are the turf of NGOs, both as direct interveners and as advocates who seek to mold public opinion and state policy, but they are also the stuff of state actions, as they lead diplomacy into areas that were earlier considered out of bounds. States now find themselves drawn into conflicts where they have no direct interest at all but where the horror of the human condition compels a response. The 2011 intervention in Libya is a debatable example; North Atlantic Treaty Organization (NATO) states were drawn in to save lives, although some would claim they had other interests as well.

The end of the Cold War brought the monopoly and centrality of state power and authority in the economy, society, and polity into question in much of the Third World and Second World. Democracy legitimized opposition, free enterprise encouraged competition, and structural adjustment shattered a centralized economy; the end of bipolarity undercut foreign support for single-party regimes and shredded the philosophical support for democratic centralism. In addition, attempts to create a state-nation (a state that creates a new identity for its people) in the absence of a nation-state (a state based on a community of people sharing a common identity) offended traditional nations, tribes, and ethnic groups, who then reasserted themselves to contest state authority. The result has been an absolute rise in internal, often ethnic, conflicts increasing in numbers in the 1990s and again in the first decade of the twenty-first century to challenge the weakened state, foster the collapse of postindependence social contracts, and pose new problems for diplomatic negotiation (MAR 2010; UCDP 2010). At the same time, interstate war has become rare, even in some deep-seated cases such as India-Pakistan, Israel-Palestine, North and South Korea, Iran-Israel, among others, where nuclear mutual assured destruction (MAD) stalemates reminiscent of the Cold War have frozen the conflict and prevented a cataclysm from erupting.

These developments pose problems for diplomatic negotiations. Intrastate conflicts, often referred to as asymmetric, challenge the basic assumptions of formal equality and legitimacy of the parties in negotiation. They involve parties unequal in terms of both power and legitimacy: the state is the stronger sovereign, legitimate actor. This means that the rebels have to lead a triple struggle against odds—for attention, for power, and for legitimacy—with violence as their only currency with which to buy a new outcome. They claim legitimacy as spokespeople for their deprived and discriminated population and contest the legitimacy of the state as ruler of the whole political system (Montville 1990; Zartman 1995). Commitment is their equalizing source of power until their violence can balance that of the state. Unlike a state, their cause is their only cause, and they are dedicated fanatics in its pursuit. It is hard to move from the zero-sum situation of conflict to search for some positive-sum outcome.

Not only the conflict but the outcomes of intrastate negotiation differ from interstate wars. Peace between two sovereign states, whose existence is usually not challenged in the conflict, involves resolution of the issues (such as boundaries or even regimes) that started the conflict, and then the return to the states' daily business, a far cry from internal settlements that tend to involve the creation of a new political system and the readjustment of social groups' roles and practices. The economy needs rebuilding, which often involves social restructuring, ethnic inclusion, military integration, infrastructural reconstruction, and new investments. The polity and military have to be restructured to involve former excluded or contesting forces, and new institutions must be devised to fit.

There is a high tendency for such outcomes not to last (the **conflict trap**). Durability of peace agreements requires continuing third-party diplomatic attention, including international monitoring, reconstruction, and assurances of peace dividends to handle initial and conflict-driven grievances (Collier et al. 2003; Fortna 2004; Gartner and Melin 2009; Toft 2010; Walter 2002; Zartman and Kremenyuk 2005). The challenge for conflict diplomacy is to maintain attention and engagement in the conflict area long after the peace agreement is signed, a demanding requirement in the face of donor fatigue and distraction by other new or renewed conflicts. The story of Haiti is instructive, where it took a full collapse of the peace process of the mid-1990s to finally get a long-term international commitment for sustained attention in the 2000s, only to be overwhelmed by the 2009 earthquake. Similar problems of the lack of sustained commitment have weakened peace diplomacy in Palestine, Congo, Kosovo, Senegal, and Somalia, among others.

Conflict management diplomacy has produced some successes in overcoming these challenges. Mozambique and South Africa, in the early 1990s, are important instances of internal conflict management and even resolution diplomacy. Negotiations over Namibia in the late 1970s and throughout the 1980s, Eritrea in the early 1990s, East Timor and Kosovo in the late 1990s and 2000s, and Southern Sudan in the 2000s ended in independence in 1988, 1993, 2002, 2008, and 2011, respectively, although often without fully terminating the conflict. Following Zanzibar in 1964, creative negotiations in the 2000s led to various autonomy agreements short of independence in Mindanao (Philippines) in 2004 and Aceh (Indonesia) in 2005. United Nations (UN) mediation in the intrastate conflicts in El Salvador in the 1980s and Cambodia and Guatemala in the early 1990s was a new challenge both for the world organization and for the resolution of internal conflicts.

These negotiations to deal with internal conflict, with its humanitarian and strategic concerns, have carried with them new diplomatic norms. One concerns the basis of self-determination, returning to state criteria rather than human security. Since the end of the First World War, the overriding policy guideline was national self-determination, whereby new states' creation was based on the approximate territorial limits of major nationalities. Originally the application of the doctrine was restricted to the Austro-Hungarian and Ottoman empires. After the Second World War, the term "national" was given an equally limited definition, referring only to constituted colonial territories and thereby slipping into a new guideline defined as state self-determination (the creation of a new state on the basis of a former administrative unit) (Emerson 1960), locked in by the application of *uti possedetis* (possession is nine-tenths of the law) to sanctify often badly drawn colonial boundaries and launch the process of constructing a state-nation (Gordon 1971; Shehadi 1993; Starovoitova 1997; Thompson and Zartman 1975). State self-determination strengthened its hold after the Cold War, dominating the settlements over the breakup of Yugoslavia and the Soviet Union and in Africa (Eritrea, Somaliland, and—stretching it—Southern Sudan), disregarding human (ethnic) criteria contained in national self-determination. Many ethnic groups were crammed into states dominated by one majority, pieces of which were often assigned to other states. Yet, self-determination claims by Albanians in Macedonia, Serbs in Kosovo, Armenians in Azerbaijan, Indians in Chiapas, Tamils in Sri Lanka, and Diolas and others in Casamance have been rejected. Diplomacy eschewed national self-determination, which would have caused major squabbles and conflicts over the shape of the new units.

The need to deal with internal conflict and human security has also brought major reorientations in the norm of sovereignty. The doctrine of "Responsibility to Protect" (R2P)—in which sovereignty is defined as a state's responsibility to care for its own people, to help other states do the same, and to intervene if another state does not carry out its own responsibility—has been posited to replace the previous doctrine of sovereignty as protection of the state, accepted since the Peace Treaties of Westphalia of 1648 (Ban 2009; Deng et al. 1996; ICISS 2001; Zartman 2010; also see Wiseman and Basu, chapter 18 in this volume for more on R2P). Both doctrines carry great dangers. The first gives the state the right to do what it wants with its population and thus protects it from external interference, particularly by stronger states, whereas the latter gives others—particularly stronger states—the right to intervene to protect the population against its own state. The dangers are evident, to the people in the first case and to the smaller states in the second. International diplomacy has not yet worked out the limits and thresholds of the new doctrine, and the risks involved have—paradoxically— caused it to take a less prominent place in interstate politics and discussion since it was adopted by the UN Summit in 2005 (Zartman, Anstey, and Meerts 2011).

KEY POINTS

- Globalization is expanding the subjects of negotiation.
- Human security expands the concept of state security to refer to the inhabitants of the state and their safety and well-being as a concern of diplomacy and negotiation.
- Internal conflicts pose a challenge to diplomacy, since they involve one state's interference in another's internal matters.
- Self-determination criteria have shifted from the nation to the already constituted state unit, which avoids problems of drawing new boundary lines but overlooks problems of divided nationalities.
- The conflict trap is a destabilizing effect of conflict in developing nations (states) where conflict tends to perpetuate itself by weakening the state's already weak ability to handle the security of its people.
- R2P reinterprets the notion of sovereignty to protect people rather than states and to hold states responsible for the welfare of their own people, thus legitimizing other states' interference in domestic affairs.

CHALLENGING THE PROCESSES OF NEGOTIATION: MEDIATION AND MULTILATERAL DIPLOMACY

Negotiation's defining characteristics include unanimity as the decision rule, formal equality of parties, mixed motives (common and conflicting interests), and the process of exchange of offers/demands within a threefold decision choice (yes, no, continue talking) (Iklé 1964). These defining characteristics of the negotiation are under strain and often bent out of shape in an era of globalized diplomacy. The increase in internal conflict has pulled outside states great and small, and even NGOs, into mediation (any type of third-party involvement) and conflict management diplomacy (Rubin 1981; Saunders 1999). Distant events have an increasingly direct effect on great powers' and superpowers' concerns and welfare, but other states too have made mediation a vocation. The decline of superpowers' preemptive interests in distant conflicts produced a withdrawal after the Cold War similar to that which followed the end of the colonial era, liberating Third World countries from the constraints of their Cold War protectors and freeing them to pursue their own conflicts. Yet the result is unsettling to world stability and values, and external states are drawn into internal conflicts to promote negotiation among the parties. The United States is drawn into Sudan, Somalia, the Philippines, and the Sahara and Sahel by concern about globalized terrorism, and into Congo, Korea, and Burma by concern for stability in strategic and unstable neighborhoods. But other great powers and members of the UN Security Council find responsibilities for themselves in dampening the course of events in troubled areas such as Afghanistan, Cambodia, Congo, Palestine, and Sudan because of their concept of interests that goes beyond their immediate neighborhood. Striking examples are found in the first two humanitarian interventions justified by the UN in Iraqi Kurdistan in 1991 and Somalia in 1992, and in the example of Norway, which has no direct interests, enlightened or otherwise, in eastern or western Asia or Latin America but extended important efforts into the mediation of the Guatemalan, Israeli, and Sri Lankan conflicts, for purely humanitarian (and reputational) reasons.

States pursue a diplomacy of mediation in their own interest (Zartman and Touval 2007). When parties alone are unable to perceive a ripe moment, that is, a mutually hurting stalemate and potential of a way out, they need a third party to enable them to do so (see box 6.1). Parties in conflict need help; they rarely are able to negotiate their way out of the conflict by themselves. Sometimes the mediators seek an outcome favorable to themselves, but much more frequently they are motivated by a desire to end a conflict that is disturbing to them too, or to improve relations with one or both of the conflicting parties. Thus, the international mediator does not have to be neutral and unbiased (as it may in labor relations or domestic counseling) but simply to be trustworthy as a message carrier and encouraging of the parties' efforts to find a stable solution. If the mediator does have favorable ties with a party in the conflict, however, the assumption is that it will deliver that party's assent to the evolving outcome. Entry is a particular challenge for internal conflict management (Maundi et al. 2006). The intervened state generally resists mediation, since that is interference in internal affairs and implies that the state cannot handle its own problems. Mediation is generally a boost to the weaker, internal party, and it raises the question of recognition and position as equals in the negotiations, the prime goal of the rebels.

Because parties begin negotiations under the pressure of a (perceived) mutually hurting stalemate, the mediator's first challenge is to help the parties develop that perception (Touval 1982). Ripening (or heightening the parties' realization that they cannot escalate their way out of the conflict and that staying in it imposes increasingly burdensome costs) is the ticket to mediation. If this is not possible and the mediator's interests make a resolution important to it, then positioning is the best policy in order to be available when the parties become aware of their Chicken Dilemma.

Parties need help not only in formulating conflict management outcomes but also in the process of reaching them. In internal conflicts, diplomacy and negotiation are generally beyond the experience of the rebels and beyond the intentions of the state. At least initially, the rebels are a badly organized, inchoate body, with any political sense subsumed under the military demands of the struggle. They frequently are simply not organized to act and think as negotiators and need training to be able to participate in conflict management. Furthermore, as negotiations to end a conflict move toward either success or failure, paradoxically, rebel movements tend to fractionate. Success brings new splinter factions that break ranks to hold out for their own benefit or sometimes to race to an agreement before the main body. Failure brings up the tactical question between factions over more flexibility or more violence as the proper strategy (Zartman and Alfredson 2010). Proliferation was destructive to negotiations in Liberia and Darfur (Brooks 2008; Mutwol 2009; Zartman 2005). Unlike states, which generally remain intact and continue basic operations when they make peace among themselves, the parties agreeing to end an internal conflict are under deep internal strains and have to construct new relations and often enter a new political system. During a decade of armed struggle, Mozambican National Resistance Movement (RENAMO) had little idea of what it was fighting for, as opposed to what it was fighting against, and needed training and coaching to negotiate with the Mozambican government. The same problem faced the several Darfuri rebel groups in Sudan, the Revolutionary United Front (RUF) in Sierra Leone, and National Union for the Total Independence of Angola(UNITA) in Angola. Even when the goal (independence) was clear in the rebels' minds, the requirements of give-and-take in a situation where their victory was not acquired were foreign to the rebels' experience, as in the case of the Polisario in Morocco, Hamas in Palestine, the Revolutionary Armed Forces of Colombia (FARC) and National Liberation Army (ELN) in Colombia, and the Liberation Tigers of Tamil Eelam) (LTTE) in Sri Lanka. Thus, mediation is needed not only to bring the parties together on an agreeable outcome but also to train the parties how to act in looking for such an outcome.

Once mediation has begun, the mediator's job varies according to the type of obstacle that prevents the parties from seeking an agreement. If the parties are unable to hear and get messages to and from each other, they need a communicator (sometimes termed facilitator) as a mediator, serving only as a clear telephone line between the parties, as did the Vatican in the Beagle Channel dispute between Argentina and Chile. If the parties are so engrossed in their conflict that they cannot think of a way to overcome the deadlock of opposing demands in a coordinated solution, they need a formulator as a mediator, injecting ideas of its own and persuading the parties of the need and opportunity for a positive outcome. The United States has done this in its successive mediations during the Middle East peace process in 1974–91, for example. But if the obstacle to an agreement is the absence of sufficient payoffs to attract the parties away from their conflict, or the absence of sufficient equality of strength between the parties for them to come to a balanced and stable agreement, then the need is for a manipulator as a mediator, as with the huge US foreign aid promise to Egypt and Israel in 1975, making the second Sinai disengagement attractive to them. The manipulator's role may increase either the cost of the stalemate or the gain of a joint outcome; it contains the greatest degree of involvement and is also the most dangerous for the mediator.

Multilateral Diplomacy

The other direction of expansion in the practice of diplomatic negotiation concerns the higher levels of multilateral cooperation (see Wright, chapter 10 in this volume). In the area of nonmilitary security, involving economic, social, legal, and other matters, multilateral diplomacy has expanded its activity exponentially since the end of the Second World War and the creation of the UN (Kjellén 2008). States come together to enhance their security by resolving common problems and reducing transaction costs through negotiated regimes or rules, regulations, norms, and principles to govern expectations and responses in specific issue areas. Regime negotiations can be universal, such as the Law of the Sea, negotiated over twelve years and finally contained in a treaty signed in 1985, or the 1997 Kyoto Protocol to the 1992 UN Framework Convention on Climate Change. Or they can be quite limited, such as the oil pricing regime of the Organization of the Petroleum Exporting Countries (OPEC), which contains only half the oil producers but sets prices as a referent for all of them. Regime negotiations can involve an international organization, like OPEC, or merely a body of norms without even a secretariat, like the Law of the Sea or the Kyoto Protocol. And they can be expressed in **soft law**, again like the guidelines attached to the Kyoto Protocol or the UN's Guiding Principles on Internal Displacement, or in a succession of political decisions, again like the OPEC actions. Regimes are not **hard law** that pose the sharp choice of compliance or infraction as the only options but rather are recursive negotiations to examine and correct the course of the norms and regulations (Hasenclever, Mayer, and Rittberger 1997; Spector and Zartman 2003). Correction is necessary because of the shifting power and interests of the parties, the injection of new information and events, the impact of interest groups and domestic implementation within the parties, and changes in the nature of the problem itself.

Regime-building and adjustment are conducted by **multilateral negotiations,** which in important ways are quite different from the processes of bilateral diplomacy (Crump and Zartman 2003; Hampson with Hart 1995; Zartman 1994). The basic challenge of multilateral negotiation is to manage the complexity of multiple parties, multiple issues, and multiple roles to enable a consensual decision. The most frequently used mechanism for such complexity management is the formation of "coalitions" of both parties and issues. Negotiators seek to package, pair, or link several issues to simplify decision making (Sebenius 1984). Negotiators also seek to build coalitions of the whole, minimum winning coalitions, blocking coalitions, single issue-centered coalitions, as mediators between coalitions or generators of coalitions. In short, coalitions are the main method of analysis and collective decision making in multilateral negotiations.

The creation of international regimes is related to a redefinition of states' interests, moving from national interests that are qualified as "narrow" to those termed "enlightened." The first have long dominated diplomatic and realist thinking, as expressed in the doctrine of "sovereignty as protection" and PDG perceptions. Narrow national interests relate to a unilateral concern for national independence, territorial integrity, and protection of the country's way of life and standard of living (Morgenthau 1948). Enlightened interests concern the maintenance of collective agreements and reciprocal security, under the liberal or institutionalist and CDG perspectives that reciprocity (rewarding a concession with another concession—compensation) is an important element in the assurance of mutual security (Ikenberry 2001). Thus, it is important for states to cooperate in managing far-flung conflicts and to conceive of their interests in terms of mutual assurances of security and stability. Security then becomes a collective responsibility that states negotiate to promote. In a memorable statement, Ambassador Christopher Hill (2005) indicated that the purpose of the Six-Party Talks (involving China, Japan, North Korea, Russia, South Korea, and the United States) was to convince North Korea that its security would be better assured by taking its place in the international community than by unilateral measures (such as developing nuclear weapons) that only threaten the other members of that community. Managing distant conflicts and creating international regimes build on an international community with reciprocal obligations that reduce conflict and justify intervention.

Global interest has led to notable successes in conflict management, and even resolution. The Scandinavian countries have been active in East Africa in development diplomacy. The United States played the decisive role in bringing independence to Namibia and an end to the South African conflict with Angola in 1988, and was helpful in the change of regime in South African itself in 1990–94 (Crocker 1992; Lyman 2002). The United States was pulled into the conflicts in Afghanistan and Pakistan by its Cold War interests in the 1980s and by its antiterrorist interests in the 2000s, but the area, along with central Asia in general, was long beyond US interests. In fact, the attention of the Security Council members was drawn to Kosovo and Cambodia in intense diplomatic efforts at conflict management, in new extensions of their previous interests.

KEY POINTS

- The processes of negotiation are being challenged by contemporary demands for mediation and multilateral diplomacy.
- Mediation refers to any type of third-party involvement in a conflict and is usually necessary in conflicts and especially internal conflicts, since parties are too involved in their conflict to think of ways out of it.
- States are drawn into mediation for direct national interests and also for enlightened or humanitarian interests.

- Types of mediation are differentiated according to the type of obstacles it is needed to overcome: communicators when the parties cannot talk to each other, formulators when they cannot come up with resolving ideas, and manipulators when they do not see large enough benefits to outweigh costs in current resolution outcomes.
- Multilateral negotiations involve a large number of state parties in search of solutions for current international problems and are conducted by creating coalitions.
- International regimes are rules, regulations, norms, and expectations established by recursive multilateral negotiation to deal with international problems that no single state can handle.

FACING THE FUTURE OF DIPLOMATIC NEGOTIATION: PREVENTION

Normal diplomacy functions to resolve conflicts and, by extension, prevent them. It works, as testified by the literally innumerable conflicts that have not taken place or have not escalated into worse violence, and by some specific cases where negotiation was the means of prevention. The two preventive interventions in Macedonia in 1992 and 2001 are frequently cited as the model cases. Russian diplomatic intervention in the Nagorno-Karabakh conflict in 1994 brought a management of the conflict that still holds, providing a potential basis for resolution (Hopmann and Zartman 2010; Mooradian and Druckman 1999). The dissolution of the Soviet Union gave rise to some notable cases of preventive diplomacy in the Baltic States, Ukraine, and Tatarstan and Tajikistan (Hopmann 2001; Jentleson 2000).

But the focus on prevention of conflicts occurs earlier (and is now more pronounced in the post Cold War period. Prevention means keeping conflict from escalating into violence rather than the elimination of conflict per se, since conflict is the simple incompatibility of positions and quite normal in its passive state. But passive conflict may contain a potential to be activated by efforts to prevail by confrontation and violence (Zartman, Anstey, and Meerts 2011). Conflict of positions is the ground for negotiation; conflicts through violence are the object of prevention. It is necessary to examine and deal with conflicts before they become violent, in order to prevent crises but also to understand the source of the violence when it threatens or occurs. Therefore, the aim of diplomacy is to attend to conflicts before they escalate into violence, fend off conflicts that are in the violent stage, and mend conflicts that have been de-escalated from violence (Albright and Cohen 2008; Boutros-Ghali 1995; Hamburg 2008; Zartman 2010).

Conflict management refers to efforts to keep the conflict from escalating beyond the political level; conflict resolution refers to the removal of the incompatibilities that give rise to the conflict. Conflict prevention then addresses both the violent measures and the incompatible ends of conflict. UN secretary-general Dag Hammarskjöld (1953–61) was the postwar leader who pressed the notion of preventive diplomacy; his much later successor, Boutros Boutros-Ghali (1992–96), brought it back into prominence, after a Cold War interlude. At the same time, preventive diplomacy was also addressed by academic analysis and by diplomatic attention. The United States Institute of Peace and the Carnegie Corporation's Commission on Preventing Deadly Conflict undertook seminal investigations into prevention (Jentleson 2000; Lund 1996; Lute 1997; Zartman 2001). The initiative of the 2001 Swedish presidency of the European Union (EU) sought to focus and ener- gize Swedish and eventually EU policy to develop a culture of prevention (Björkdahl 2000; ISIS 1999; Swedish Foreign Ministry 1997, 1999). These various paths of attention came together in the Canadian-sponsored International Commission on Intervention and State Sovereignty, whose 2001 report declared, in bold type, that "prevention is the single most important dimension of the responsibility to protect," divided into structural or root-cause prevention and direct (operational) or conflict prevention (ICISS 2001: xii–xiii, 22–27, 47–69). These concerns then found their place, along with the R2P doctrine, in the Secretary-General's Report of the High Level Panel that was unanimously adopted by the General Assembly at the 2005 World Summit and were further elaborated by Secretary-General Ban Ki-Moon (Ban 2009).

Since then, the doctrine of prevention has run aground on the same sorts of difficulties as the doctrines of R2P and human security. As in the previous case, the shoals are both practical and conceptual. Practical difficulties concern the imple- mentation of prevention. The UN doctrine on peacekeeping, which is not written in the charter but referred to informally as "Chapter VI.5," is that peacekeeping forces are rigorously held to keeping a peace already agreed to rather than intervening in situations of violence. The Mission of the UN in Congo stretched this doctrine toward intervention when it learned that no peace had been agreed to in Eastern Congo, but possible UN prevention was dodged in 1997 in Congo-Brazzaville on the grounds that peace had not taken hold (Zartman 1998, 2000). Preventing conflicts from escalating into violence, a rising emphasis of the prevention doctrine, is even more difficult, for it amounts to telling sovereign states not to pursue their conflict with external or, more seriously, internal enemies (Zartman 2010; Zartman, Anstey, and Meerts 2011). Because intrastate conflict often arises from deprivations imposed by a narrowly based government or discriminations imposed on internal rivals, such advice and efforts to implement it are sharply resented by target states and their leaders. Governments carrying out a policy of violent conflict against an identified— and, almost necessarily, demonized—internal or external enemy are not likely to take kindly to external attempts to prevent their efforts to defend the country or regime. Even more controversial are the means to prevent a conflict or a problem that is merely on the horizon, foreseeable but lying deep within domestic conditions and state relations. Between large-scale structural prevention, such as development aid against poverty, and targeted operational prevention, such as relief deliverance to oppressed minorities, lies a large field of uncharted, unclear, and unwelcome policies of intervention.

The conceptual difficulties are similar to those of human security, and they underlie the same practical difficulties. "What to prevent when" is a major operative as well as conceptual question. Early prevention is the most difficult to justify, for the chances of the foreseen event's taking place are highly uncertain and, if prevented, can never be proved. Commentators call for early action to validate early warning, but the guarantees of a tropical storm warning turning into a tropical storm are inconclusive (Zartman and Faure 2005). Warnings and intervention—to prevent Israel from carrying out expansionist policies that arguably will take it to Masada, or Iran from carrying out nuclear policies that will assuredly feed its persecution complex—inevitably complicate attempts to cultivate better relations with the target countries. On the other hand, "early late" prevention efforts, before the conflict has reached the crisis or "too late" stage, have major obstacles of overcommitment to overcome that earlier action would have avoided.

KEY POINTS

- Prevention, referring to efforts to keep conflicts from escalating to violence, is the most difficult challenge of diplomacy and negotiation, since the pressure of ripeness is weakest and the prevention efforts are the most intrusive.
- Yet normal diplomacy and some exceptionally intense efforts in its absence have been remarkably successful and have kept conflict violence to an exceptional occurrence.

CONCLUSION

Throughout the twentieth century, under the colonial and Cold War systems of world order, great power concerns have always extended beyond their immediate neighborhood. By the end of that century and the beginning of the present one, those concerns have become enmeshed into a complex global system, without any clear notion of the particular structure or mechanism to preserve world order (Zartman 2009). Responsibility lies all around, as large states weigh their responsibilities and small states play major roles, internal conflict outpaces interstate conflict, and still immature diplomatic norms such as R2P toddle forth to slay established practices without being yet strong enough to define new ones. States and other international actors establish international regimes in an effort to coordinate rules, norms, and expectations to handle international issues based only on unenforceable and fragile consensus (Friedman 2007). The most notable effect of globalization is the rise of a multinational corporation named al-Qaeda (the Base), with a secret, mobile headquarters, a corporate culture, multinational branches and international cadres, funding from diaspora and organized criminal sources, IT and electronic communications, and state security penetration operating to attack a worldwide range of targets. This is the world in which modern diplomatic negotiation must operate, and in doing so it has the enormous advantage of flexibility, an appropriate counter to the global system's complexity. While the practice has followed a number of concepts, as presented here, that make its scope and process more understandable, they best serve as a springboard for creativity rather than as rigid restraints. The game-theoretic presentation lays out the obstacles and opportunities for negotiation, but it cannot give direction to the process or content to the northwest corner. Both normal diplomacy and diplomacy as usual contain constraints that can hinder free passage along track-one and prevent productive intersection with track-two. Yet the salient conflicts that have been managed successfully and then, once managed, have moved to resolution, nested in the infinite number of conflicts that have been prevented by the creative exercise of negotiation, testify to the importance of diplomatic negotiation in rendering violent conflict the exception rather than the rule in a globalizing world.

QUESTIONS

1. How can conflict violence be prevented and nonviolent conflicts be tended without the pressure of violence?
2. What issue areas have been the subject of international regimes, and what new issues can be usefully developed?
3. How can ripeness be induced ("ripening") into parties' perceptions in long-standing conflicts such as Israel-Palestine or India-Pakistan?
4. What can be done to exercise R2P before physical intervention into another state's affairs becomes necessary?
5. What are the advantages of state versus national self-determination?
6. How can a mediator reframe/construct a solution when exchange/compensation is not possible? Provide examples for your answer.
7. When can a mediator be only a communicator/facilitator? When does it have to be a formulator? When a manipulator?
8. What are the implications in this chapter for your theoretical and practical understandings of contemporary diplomacy?

PART III

Structures, Processes, and Instruments of Contemporary Diplomacy

In this part of the book we examine some of the key structures, processes, and instruments of contemporary diplomacy. We again have two aims. Our *first* is for you to become thoroughly familiar with each of the eight aspects of diplomacy analyzed in the chapters: the foreign ministry, modern technology, consular tasks, the bilateral-multilateral distinction, outreach to foreign publics, economics, nonofficials' activities, and intelligence. Each of the chapters allows readers to trace how these aspects have evolved over time and in different world regions, and to consider what this evolution means for future practices and theorizing about that particular aspect of diplomacy. We know that in practice there is overlap between diplomacy's structures, processes, and instruments and that debates take place about how to conceptualize them. Indeed, we emphasize these debates in each chapter. Moreover, we are keen for you to consider the extent to which globalization and the accompanying communication and information revolution shape the diplomatic world.

Our *second* aim is for you to consider the extent to which we can refer to these eight aspects collectively to make some general observations about the nature of contemporary diplomacy. That is, while each chapter is a story about an important individual diplomatic structure, process, or instrument, taken together they provide insights into the big question, What exactly is contemporary diplomacy?

CHAPTER 7

The Ministry of Foreign Affairs and the National Diplomatic System

Brian Hocking

CHAPTER CONTENTS

- Introduction
- The ministry of foreign affairs (MFA): diplomatic perspectives
- The MFA and the national diplomatic system (NDS)
- The emergence and evolution of the MFA
- The MFA and the NDS in the twenty-first century
- Conclusion

READER'S GUIDE

The ministry of foreign affairs (MFA) has come to assume a central reference point for both the study and practice of diplomacy. During the evolution of state-based diplomacy, national governments have developed a set of tools for interaction with their external environments and for the implementation of their international policy objectives. This is represented in the form of what is termed in this chapter the "national diplomatic system" (NDS). Traditionally, this system has been equated with the MFA and has often, misleadingly, been regarded as synonymous with it. But whatever form the NDS has assumed, it is increasingly apparent that it is becoming more complex as a result of domestic and international factors. This results in seemingly paradoxical tendencies. On the one hand, pressures flowing from the global environment place a premium on sound policy advice and effective overseas representation. On the other, the MFA's credentials as the logical point of interface with the international system are questioned as the constitution of "foreignness" itself seems harder to grasp in a rapidly changing and integrated world. Against this background, the chapter explores the nature and functions of the MFA and its place in the changing NDS.

INTRODUCTION

One of the consistent themes in this book is the continuing evolution of two inter-related aspects of diplomacy. First are the *processes* characterizing its essential functions such as **communication** and negotiation and their increasingly complex forms blending **bilateral** and **multilateral** diplomacy. The second facet relates to the *structures* through which such processes are carried out. At the national level, one feature of the diplomatic environment has assumed particular significance, namely, the MFA.

There are three reasons why investigating the MFA is instructive. The first is the light it sheds on how diplomacy has been studied (also see Sharp, chapter 3 in this volume). Second, debates about the MFA, its functions, and significance are one indicator of the transformation of the international environment. Third, insights into the character of what has been termed the **globalized state** can be gained by analyzing the impact of external change on its bureaucratic structures (Clark 2008), and particularly that part of the bureaucracy most associated with the "hard shell" of the **sovereign state**.

Pursuing this theme, the chapter examines the MFA and its functions in the broader context of what is termed the "national diplomatic system" or the structures that states maintain at a particular period for the management of their international environments. It is argued that MFAs are being required to redefine their role within these systems.

The chapter considers the emergence and development of the MFA, its nature and functions, and its responses to the pressures exerted on it in the context of the changing NDS.

THE MINISTRY OF FOREIGN AFFAIRS (MFA): DIPLOMATIC PERSPECTIVES

While the MFA is a common feature of national bureaucracies, there are marked differences among both academic observers and practitioners of diplomacy concerning its role and importance. At the academic level this reflects differing approaches to the nature and significance of diplomacy in contemporary world politics. Not surprisingly, state-focused narratives of diplomacy tend to assign particular importance to "state-based" agents of diplomacy, especially MFAs and their networks of overseas missions (Berridge 2010; Hocking 1999b). In contrast, "globalist" argumentation proclaimed the growing marginalization of the state and its institutions (Bisley 2007; McGrew 2008). At one level, this was a reflection of dissatisfaction with the institutions of diplomacy reflected in a growing skepticism regarding their relevance and a heightening level of introspection within MFAs concerning their role (Bátora 2008; Berridge 2010; Hocking 1999b).

What we might term "postglobalist" approaches to understanding the nature of diplomacy have identified a range of normative-analytic images of global governance architectures in which diplomacy may play varying roles (see Badie, chapter 5 in this volume). Furthermore, globalization is recognized as constituting more than a set of external systemic forces, and it can be understood from an inside-out perspective as the "globalized state" adapts its functions and structures to new realities (Clark 2008). In this light, the MFA has acquired a more ambiguous status. On the one hand, it can be seen as a significant component of a broader NDS comprising an increasingly diverse range of players. On the other, many of its working practices, norms, values, and organizational structures have attracted close scrutiny and criticism (Copeland 2009; Riordan 2003; Ross 2007).

Additional insights into MFAs have come from the application of organization theory (Bátora 2008). This helps us to understand their culture and responses to changing domestic and international environments. In large part the MFA culture reflects the accumulation of assumptions and traditions surrounding the conduct of diplomacy, its divorce from the realm of domestic policy and politics, the significance of secrecy, an emphasis on a closed community of transnational professionals working within understood codes of conduct, and the continuing legacy of a formerly aristocratic elite largely transformed into a meritocracy. As a consequence, the MFA and its foreign service are usually portrayed as having a well-defined, strong culture that is partly derived from its position at the juncture of state-focused diplomacy and the "global diplomatic system," or a common field of diplomatic action through which much—but not all—international interaction is mediated (Steiner 1982). Hence the "foreignness" of the MFA is a critical component of its culture and reflects the fact that diplomats usually serve overseas for a considerable part of their working lives (Gyngell and Wesley 2003).

But not only is the MFA linked to the outside defined in terms of the international, it is also often regarded as an outsider in its home environment, distinctive from other government departments and lacking natural domestic constituencies. These two modes of "outsideness" are reinforcing. The role of the diplomat as part of the transnational diplomatic community feeds back into headquarters whose functions are partly determined by the needs of servicing the overseas network. This helps us to understand one of the defining problems of diplomacy in general and the MFA in particular—namely, its legitimacy. Not only has the status of diplomats frequently been problematic in terms of their activities in host countries, but also their value has consistently been questioned at home. Added to this is the impact of a changing public service culture that questions the distinctiveness of the MFA, applying to it such devices as measurable performance targets (Rana 2007b).

KEY POINTS

- MFAs are characteristic features of the structures developed by governments to manage their international policy environments.
- However, alternative approaches to understanding diplomacy assign to them differing roles and significance.
- Looking at globalization from inside the state, the current condition of the foreign ministry offers a useful perspective on the organization of the "globalized state."

THE MFA AND THE NATIONAL DIPLOMATIC SYSTEM (NDS)

In one sense, MFAs represent a major bureaucratic success story, as their presence in countries large and small testifies. Nevertheless, there are differences, one of the most obvious being size and funding. As figure 7.1 demonstrates, the funding of the MFA and its diplomatic service varies hugely, reflecting the overall resources available to governments. But beyond this there are variations reflecting the obvious fact that states differ in their forms and functions as well as engagement with the international system.

A more complex security environment blending the demands imposed by globalization and regionalization, environmental issues, fragile states, transnational terrorism, and the current financial and economic crisis combined with power shifts toward the newly emerging economies has redrawn the diplomatic landscape in terms of both its processes and structures. One manifestation of this situation is the recognition that **policy networks** rather than formal, hierarchical bureaucratic structures are indispensable in managing increasingly complex international and domestic policy environments (Robinson 2008; Slaughter 2004). Consequently, despite the prevalence of MFAs, they may occupy differing positions within their discrete national settings. Furthermore, their relationship with other actors involved in the international policy processes is changing.

From this perspective, it is, as mentioned earlier, more instructive to think in terms of a set of institutions and actors, a *national diplomatic system*, configured for the management of a state's international environment (see box 7-1). The MFA is part of, but not coterminous with, this system. Indeed, it can be regarded as a sub-system within the broader NDS possessing distinctive characteristics and interacting with its other constituent actors. Even defining the MFA involves more than simply the home department identified as the "ministry" but also includes its network of **overseas posts** together with its political leadership. This points to a fluctuating

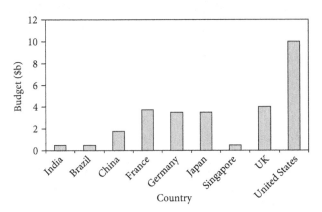

Figure 7.1 Foreign ministry budgets: a comparison.

Source: This figure originally appeared in Markey (2009: 85). Copyright © The National Bureau of Asian Research (NBR).

BOX 7-1

The Ministry of Foreign Affairs and the National Diplomatic System

MFAs—such as the Department of State in the United States, the Foreign and Commonwealth Office in the United Kingdom, the Federal Foreign Office (Auswärtiges Amt) in Germany, and the Ministry of External Relations in Brazil—are that part of the government machinery formally charged with the management of a state's foreign or external relations. Together with the network of overseas **diplomatic representation**, the MFA forms a subsystem in the national diplomatic system. This term reflects the enhanced complexity in the management of governments' international policy agendas, growing involvement of agencies outside the MFA, and a consequent degree of uncertainty as to its role and structure. Thus rather than assuming that one government department has a dominant role in managing foreign affairs, the concept of the national diplomatic system sees this as involving increasingly complex networks, recognizes the linkages between diplomacy, development, and defense, and the need to establish close working relations between a range of "domestic" government departments in specific policy areas such as the environment and global health.

---

and complex set of relationships that span the bureaucratic and political realms. Particular national requirements are likely to result in a specific configuration of tools within the NDS. Take China as an example. A recent study finds that the power of the Ministry of Foreign Affairs of the People's Republic of China has declined for two reasons: first, the changing global environment has increased the number of domestic foreign policy actors in the country, and, second, the foreign minister's power base in the Chinese Communist Party has lessened since 1998 (Jakobson and Knox 2010; see Ye and Zhang, chapter 16 in this volume).

More generally, the demands of the twenty-first-century policy environment do not match the "command and control" assumptions on which the conduct of Cold War foreign policy institutions was based. Key assumptions of that era, such as the separateness of foreign and domestic policy and the importance of secrecy, have been eroded. Consequently, the delineation of the NDS and the relationship between its component elements need to be reexamined. For example, the increasingly critical link between diplomacy and development poses questions of organizational form and the degree to which development and foreign policy should be closely linked. While most governments integrate their aid programs and their foreign ministries, in the United States and the United Kingdom (since the late 1990s), the trend has been to separate them. Thus the US Agency for International Development (USAID) is not fully integrated into the US Department of State, and the British Department for International Development (DFID) is separate from the British Foreign and Commonwealth Office (FCO) (Hyman 2010). Reinforcing the link between diplomacy and development through the strengthening of what Secretary of State Hillary Clinton has termed "civilian power" is a central theme of the Department of State's first *Quadrennial Diplomacy and Development Review* (H. Rodham Clinton 2010; US Department of State/US Agency for International Development 2010: vi–vii).

From such developments we can begin to appreciate the past and present role of the MFA in a different light. Rather than traditional preoccupations with relative dominance and decline, which have been a popular focus of attention in discussion of MFAs, the issue becomes one of the shifting character and composition of the NDS and how the MFA fits into it. The primary question is, What are the requirements for the management of international policy, and what added value can the MFA provide? Whether or not it survives in its familiar form is a secondary issue. In order to understand better the status of the MFA and its place in contemporary diplomacy, we turn to its origins and functions.

KEY POINTS

- While the MFA has emerged as a characteristic element of the structures associated with state-based diplomatic processes, it is a component of a broader bureaucratic system, the NDS.
- Interpreting the role and importance of the MFA has been associated with more general approaches to diplomacy as an institution of the international order and the ways in which states are responding to the major changes in that order.
- The purpose of the NDS is to provide a "tool kit" for national governments in their interactions with their international environments and in the pursuit of their international policy goals. Its form is conditioned by both international and domestic environmental factors and is responding to the changing demands of the post–Cold War order.

THE EMERGENCE AND EVOLUTION OF THE MFA

The characteristics of the MFA need to be viewed against its evolution as one element in the emergence of the domain of the "foreign." Thus its development as a component of the bureaucratic apparatus of the state is part of the process by which domestic and foreign policy became increasingly separated from the seventeenth century onward. As Keith Hamilton and Richard Langhorne (1995) have noted, until the early eighteenth century, it was common practice to combine both foreign and domestic policy in the same department. It was the recognition by Cardinal Richelieu, in seventeenth-century France, of the need for continuity and coordination in the management of French foreign relations in an increasingly complex system of states that led to the emergence of a separate foreign ministry. In the case of Great Britain, up until 1782, the Northern Department and Southern Department dealt with both domestic and foreign policy. However, the increased demands imposed by the international environment and the inefficiencies and frictions that two, often competing, departments could create resulted in the formation of two departments, one for home affairs and the other for foreign affairs (Tilley and Gaselee 1933).

More generally, the developing states system required an enhanced capacity at two related levels. First, the resources to communicate internationally and to project national interests through the development of networks of overseas representation were needed. Second, the ability to interact with these networks and the broader diplomatic environment and to support the shaping of international policy at home was required. During the nineteenth and early twentieth centuries, these requirements resulted in the professionalization of diplomacy through formalized recruitment processes and the introduction of examinations and training programs. It would, however, be wrong to view the MFA as the sole or even the dominant agency through which a national community interacted with the international arena. In some cases, for example, trade ministries assumed greater significance, carrying more weight in the bureaucratic hierarchy.

Allowing for such variations in the evolution of the MFA, two broad trends have marked the NDS as it evolved during the twentieth century. These can be identified as "fragmentation" and "concentration". The first term relates to a diversification of the NDS as line ministries found their responsibilities acquiring enhanced international dimensions, and transgovernmental patterns of diplomacy developed as a result. This could be seen as early as the latter part of the nineteenth century with the rise of international agencies such as the International Telegraph Union and multilateral conferences such as the International Aerial Navigation Conference of 1910 involving specialists and domestic government agencies (Hamilton and Langhorne 1995: 131).

The second trend affecting the constitution of the NDS, concentration, relates to the enhancement of the foreign policy capacity of central agencies, particularly prime ministerial and presidential offices. While this is partly a reflection of the growing significance of heads of state and government in diplomacy, it is also a recognition of the potential costs of lack of coordination in the management of international policy and the desire to minimize its costs by centralizing policy-making functions. Densely textured policy arenas such as that of the European Union (EU), with its multilayered diplomatic environment, demonstrate these developments to a high degree. Consequently, the demand for coordination at member state level is high, although the means by which this is achieved varies (Hocking and Spence 2005; Kassim, Peters, and Wright 2000).

The MFA's Functions

While MFAs are not identical from country to country in terms of their precise location and significance in a state's bureaucratic structure, by virtue of their evolution and place in diplomatic processes there are broad generic functions which MFAs perform and which can be summarized as:

- A key node in a diplomatic communications system through which information gathered from the international environment is gathered, analyzed, and disseminated.
- A policy advice function, providing expertise to politicians, to other parts of the bureaucracy, and to nongovernmental actors with interests in international policy.
- A memory bank, gathering and storing information.
- A policy transfer function through which the channels of diplomatic communication are used to exchange information and ideas on a range of issues between countries on diverse issues.

- Service functions directed at the overseas needs of specific domestic constituencies: for example, trade promotion (or commercial diplomacy) and consular services.
- Administrative functions relating to the management of the overseas diplomatic network, relationships with the resident *corps diplomatique*, and associated diplomatic protocol matters.

It is the first two of these functions that are most commonly regarded as being challenged. As a communications system, the rapid dispersal of information through the electronic media is frequently viewed as rendering the diplomatic network redundant (see Kurbalija, chapter 8 in this volume). Similarly, the emergence of rival sources of policy advice and expertise, both in other government departments and outside them, in the form of nongovernmental organizations (NGOs), for example, is seen as threatening the value of the MFA in an environment where specialist rather than generalist diplomatic expertise is valued. On the other hand, the memory bank function rarely if ever features in this debate, suggesting that observers do not value it, are unaware of its existence, or accept that it is insulated from the pressures of exogenous change. The development of the policy transfer role, which similarly tends to be ignored in discussions of the functions of contemporary diplomacy, can be interpreted as indicative of decline or adaptation to changing circumstances.

Attempting to analyze the impact of the changing policy environment on the MFA suggests a need for greater definitional clarity as to the impact of environmental factors on these various functions. The general point is that understanding the position of the contemporary MFA is helped by disaggregating and analyzing its functions rather than generalizing in broad terms about its decline.

KEY POINTS

- Historically, the emergence of the modern MFA is associated with the increased separation of domestic and international aspects of public policy.
- While MFAs vary in their precise form and function, they display a high degree of similarity.
- During the twentieth century, the management structures of international policy witnessed two linked trends—fragmentation and concentration.
- While it is not universally true that the MFA has been the sole or dominant actor in the management of international policy, its role has been increasingly challenged by the changing demands facing governments in managing international policy and, consequently, the shape and composition of the NDS.

THE MFA AND THE NDS IN THE TWENTY-FIRST CENTURY

The discussion so far moves us away from familiar arguments focusing on the relative decline of the MFA and suggests the need to examine the shifting character and composition of the NDS and how the MFA fits into this. As suggested earlier, there are two linked dimensions here: the response of the MFA as an organization seeking to ensure its survival against threats from its environment, and its adaptation as a component of the NDS.

We can gain a sense of these aspects of the MFA by taking two very different instances: the United States (Department of State) and India (Ministry of External Affairs). The MFAs in both countries have been criticized in terms of failing to respond adequately to the changing global environment and the needs that this imposes on the NDS. The MFA is portrayed as lacking key skills and training strategies appropriate to the changing international environment; a failure to develop linkages with other parts of the bureaucracy and with the private sector critical to the management of international policy; inadequate policy capacity; and a failure to absorb the implications of the importance of access to overseas domestic constituencies (Markey 2009; Metzl 2001). These are part of a broader set of issues conditioning the operation of MFAs, and it is to these that we now turn.

One key theme is the need to reconfigure the NDS, and for the MFA to build relations with other government departments, thereby enhancing the overall capabilities of national governments (hence the emphasis on the need for what is frequently termed a **whole-of-government** approach to international policy). This focuses attention on the respective roles of the MFA and other government departments with clear international responsibilities and the dangers of a country speaking with multiple voices on international issues. In this context, bureaucratic turf battles are familiar and have, in some countries, tended to grow as domestic agendas have become internationalized.

In China, the Ministry of Foreign Affairs confronts strong rivalry from key bureaucratic actors such as the Ministry of Commerce, the People's Bank of China, and the Ministry of Finance (see Ye and Zhang, chapter 16 in this volume). The consequences can be important—and not just for the country itself. Thus the highly significant position of China in the 2009 United Nations Climate Change Conference in Copenhagen has been explained in terms of bureaucratic conflict over China's stance on fixed targets for greenhouse gas emission reductions between the Ministry of Foreign Affairs and the National Development and Reform Commission (Jakobson and Knox 2010).

How these tensions play out depends on a range of domestic factors, and the situation is by no means clear-cut. Generally, for example, the United Kingdom and Australian picture is painted as more collegial than conflictual in terms of the management of international policy than is suggested by the **bureaucratic politics** model based on the US experience. On the other hand, Japan, like China, has experienced significant tensions between its Ministry of Foreign Affairs and other departments. The desire to overcome differences in Japanese policy on free trade agreements has resulted in the creation of a bureau centralizing policy making in the MFA and preventing other ministries such as the Ministry of Agriculture, Forestry and Fisheries and the Ministry of Economy, Trade and Industry from exercising an effective veto on policy in the area (Rathus 2010).

Closely associated with this aspect of the broader NDS is the impact of the changing global environment on the structure and functions of the MFA. Among the organizational issues is, first, the basic structure of the MFA. To a greater or lesser extent, all MFAs have adopted a two-pronged structure based on geographic and functional sections. Although there are clear variations in precise form, the tendency has been to favor the latter in response to an environment in which issues and areas are ever-more closely linked. The Italian Ministry of Foreign Affairs has recently announced that its structure "will no longer hinge on geographic areas but on macro-sector themes: the three pillars of security, European integration and the outward reach of the Country System" (Italian Ministry of Foreign Affairs 2010). Similarly, the Ministry of Foreign Affairs of Denmark has moved from a vertical pillar structure focusing on geographic divisions to a thematic and horizontal structure based on eleven centers as this better reflects a more complex international order and enhances policy coordination.

A second major concern is the need to strengthen policy capacity in order to cope with change. One of the most obvious ways in which this is provided for is through a policy planning unit or department, as in the US Department of State. Strengthening policy capacity, however, is increasingly understood as requiring the development of linkages with stakeholders outside the MFA. Establishing "knowledge networks" embracing not only other government departments but also business and key groups in civil society, particularly NGOs, is seen as essential to underpinning the role of the contemporary MFA. In a similar vein, bringing in outside expertise is linked to recruitment policy and advocacy of lateral recruitment: something that critics argue the Indian Ministry of External Affairs needs to undertake (Markey 2009: 78–79; Rana 2007a: 47–76).

These issues are linked in turn to the skill sets seen as necessary among modern diplomats and how these can best be developed. The most familiar expression of this problem comes in the form of the debate about diplomats as "generalists" or "specialists." While there is a strong case to be made for the continuing importance and necessity of "generalist" diplomatic skills, the broad trend during the twentieth century was toward the emphasis on specialist skills, reflecting the nature of the changing international agenda. This has posed two issues for the MFA: first, how to acquire and deploy such specialist skills; second, how to respond to the claims of specialists in functional departments to "act internationally" on behalf of their governments.

One response to this problem has been to redefine the training needs beyond the more traditional agendas common to foreign service institutes and diplomatic academies. Alongside this, MFAs have had to respond to major social and demographic change over the last fifty years, not least in terms of their gender policies. Recalling that the British FCO only started to employ women in the diplomatic service in 1946, it is indicative of the distance traveled since then that, in 2008, the first instance of a (husband and wife) job-sharing ambassadorial post occurred in the British High Commission (embassy) in Zambia (Maitland 2010).

The Public Diplomacy Imperative

One of the indicators of significant change in both domestic and international policy environments is the importance attached to public diplomacy in the shifting configuration of world politics (see Melissen, chapter 11 in this volume). In one sense, public diplomacy is a well-established facet of national diplomacy; in another, it is undergoing fundamental change. Consequently, there was a strong tendency to regard public diplomacy activity as separate from mainstream activities of the MFA and to locate it in specialist units. The end of the Cold War altered the role of public diplomacy from that of accessing closed systems to developing strategies for operating in an open system containing a multitude of voices utilizing new communications and information technologies. Fundamentally, this is altering the modalities of influence in world politics, placing increased importance on access to complex webs of transnational linkages and networks alongside traditional intergovernmental channels of diplomatic action (A. Evans and Steven 2008).

The result has been twofold. In terms of diplomatic strategies, public diplomacy is becoming integrated into international policy processes rather than being regarded as a supplementary tool outside mainstream diplomatic activity. This was one of the key themes of the 2005 Carter Review of UK public diplomacy and the subsequent creation of the Public Diplomacy Board in the FCO (Hocking 2008). Second, at an organizational level, it is being "mainstreamed" into MFA structures and human resource strategies. This goal has been a central theme in the extensive discussion of the requirements of US public diplomacy over the last decade. Here, the need to integrate the public diplomacy function overseen by the US Information Agency with Department of State geographic bureaus where policy is effectively formulated is seen as critical to integrating policy and public diplomacy (Graffy 2009).

Not surprisingly, this is an area where technological change conditions MFA activity. The rise of the Internet has led to the general development of websites regarded as having greater or lesser levels of functionality and impact. The development of **Web 2.0**, associated with web applications that facilitate interactive information-sharing and collaboration on the Word Wide Web, provides another layer of change in this area. Web 2.0 offers scope for developing interactive websites (an area where the Canadian Department of Foreign Affairs and International Trade has led the way) and the recognition of the growing significance of social networking sites is being exploited by many MFAs as they develop "digital diplomacy." Taking the FCO as one example, it runs 255 websites, which include the FCO's corporate site, country sites in multiple languages, special subject sites, and campaign sites. It has official YouTube, Flickr, and Twitter channels and in 2008 became the first UK central government department to open its blogging platform to all staff who could establish a legitimate case to blog (British Foreign and Commonwealth Office 2010). While former British foreign secretary David Milliband, a committed blogger himself, welcomed these developments as opening up the "secret garden of diplomacy" (Borger 2008), inevitably the use of social networking media such as Twitter has raised issues regarding its value and compatibility with the patterns of behavior associated with the diplomatic profession (see box 7-2).

Enhancing and redefining public diplomacy capacity is also reflected throughout the diplomatic service. It is now taken as a basic rule that diplomats in the field need to engage with a wide range of actors and interests in host countries and integrate centrally determined public diplomacy strategies into their activities. But it is not always easy. In the case of the United States, for example, a major issue for the Department of State was the rules regarding diplomats' engagement with the media in the countries in which they were serving. The need for prior clearance from the Department of State helped to generate a culture of caution and disengagement

---

BOX 7-2

Digital Diplomacy in the US Department of State

On Twitter, [Jared] Cohen, who is 28, and [Alec] Ross, who is 38, are among the most followed of anyone working for the US government, coming in third and fourth after Barack Obama and John McCain. This didn't happen by chance. Their Twitter posts have become an integral part of a new State Department effort to bring diplomacy into the digital age, by using widely available technologies to reach out to citizens, companies and other nonstate actors. Ross and Cohen's style of engagement—perhaps best described as a cross between social-networking culture and foreign-policy arcana—reflects the hybrid nature of this approach. Two of Cohen's recent posts were, in order: "Guinea holds first free election since 1958" and "Yes, the season premier [sic] of Entourage is tonight, soooo excited!" This offhand mix of pop and politics has on occasion raised eyebrows and a few hackles…yet, together, Ross and Cohen have formed an unlikely and unprecedented team in the State Department. They are the public face of a cause with an important-sounding name: 21st-century statecraft (Lichtenstein 2010).

---

rather than engagement with local media and, therefore, shaping perceptions and attitudes. These rules were changed as Karen Hughes, who held the post of under secretary of state for public diplomacy and public affairs in the George W. Bush administration, encouraged engagement and introduced structural changes that could underpin it (see box 7-3).

BOX 7-3

Changing the Public Diplomacy Culture in US Diplomatic Missions

Despite establishing the "Rules of the Road" clearance procedures, there was no pressure to make media engagement a priority. All that changed with the development of "media hubs" in Brussels, Dubai and London, which helped to generate and facilitate media appearances by senior US government officials. The European and Eurasian Bureau (EUR), under the wise counsel of the first Senior Advisor for the Media Hubs, Adam (now Ambassador) Ereli, created a "Media Matrix" which tracked who was going out on television, where and on what topic. This single-handedly changed the off-the-record default position: When the monthly chart came out showing, for example, that the consul general in Florence was doing more media than the ambassador to Spain, or that the ambassador to the Court of St. James's (UK) was more engaged than the ambassador to Italy, suddenly television interviews began to be put on the schedule (Graffy 2009).

(Colleen Graffy was the first deputy assistant secretary of state for public diplomacy to be appointed [in 2005] to the US Department of State and served in the Bureau of European and Eurasian Affairs.)

Opening up the "secret garden of diplomacy" challenges one of the principles most closely associated with the development of diplomacy—that of secrecy. The expansion and redefinition of the NDS combined with the logic of public diplomacy places a growing emphasis on the demands of transparency. But the release of US Department of State diplomatic cables by WikiLeaks starting in November 2010 poses fundamental questions concerning the norms and functions of diplomacy, as well as practical questions regarding the maintenance of secure communications in an information-rich environment. Additionally, the problems of **cybersecurity** have been underscored by reports in early 2011 that China had penetrated the FCO's internal communications systems and that a pirate Internet site replicating the official French Ministry of Foreign Affairs website was circulating bogus "official" announcements.

Adapting the Diplomatic Network

The utility of maintaining a network of overseas posts has been questioned in the light of enhanced patterns of communication and alternative, instantaneous sources of information available to policy makers. Nevertheless, despite the cost, governments maintain extensive diplomatic networks (see figure 7.2), and even small states maintain a network reflecting their core areas of interest. Having said that, most of the developments discussed so far have impacted on the overseas networks of posts.

Underpinning much of the discussion is the relationship between two core issues in the history of **diplomatic representation**: those of *access* and *presence* in the international system. Establishing access to key centers of policy activity came

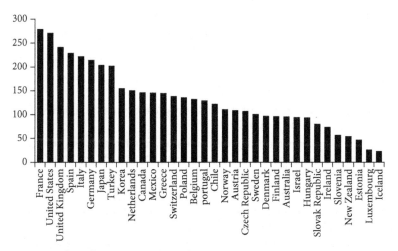

Figure 7.2 Number of missions: OECD nations.

Note: Latest available information, provided either directly by the relevant governments or from information in the public domain such as embassy websites, annual reports, and press releases. Count includes embassies, high commissions, consulates-general, consulates, and multilateral missions with separate ambassadors/heads of mission. It excludes trade and cultural offices and consular sections of embassies.

Source: Reprinted with permission from Oliver and Shearer (2011: 2).

to be associated with permanent presence, notably in the creation of networks or **resident ambassadors** in **bilateral** and **multilateral missions**. These tended to replace an older model of managing access, namely, the use of **mission diplomacy** for specific purposes.

This linkage is changing as the functions of diplomatic networks and their sheer cost have come under close examination. Increasingly, the form that diplomatic presence assumes is debated, as small, flexible, and quickly deployable posts are often better attuned to contemporary needs than the traditional embassy.

At the level of diplomatic practice as opposed to popular debate (which is strongly influenced by the image of diplomats as a privileged clique enjoying an extravagant lifestyle subsidized by hard-pressed taxpayers), significant changes are occurring at three interrelated levels:

- a redefinition of functions;
- a rebalancing of the structure of overseas posts reflecting change in the NDS outlined earlier; and
- a continuing review of the size and distribution of networks.

There is a continuing debate as to the precise functions to be served by the network and how these should respond to the broad environmental changes noted earlier (see box 7-4). A consistent theme here is the reduced importance of traditional **diplomatic reporting** as opposed to well-focused policy advice enabled by the creation of secure email systems. In some MFAs, this has brought diplomatic

---

BOX 7-4

Functions of the Diplomatic Network

According to the German Federal Foreign Office website, the essential tasks of the German missions broad include:

- collecting information
- reporting on issues that are of relevance to the various authorities of the federation and the Länder
- helping German citizens in emergencies, carrying out crisis protection measures, and assisting Germans living abroad with regard to certificates and legal documents
- issuing visas for travel to Germany
- assisting German companies with their activities in the host country and generally enhancing mutual trade
- promoting cultural exchange
- educating the host country's public about our foreign policy and also about Germany and its society and culture in general
- preparing and escorting high-level visits from Germany (German Federal Foreign Office n.d.)

---

posts more directly into central policy formulation, compensating for the reduced geographic expertise that a more functionally oriented structure might create (Rana 2007b). One of the most consistent demands in both developed and developing states is that their diplomats respond to the demands of a competitive global economy by assuming a more active role in **commercial diplomacy** (see Woolcock, chapter 12 in this volume). This is nothing new. It runs as a leitmotif in reform proposals for the British diplomatic service over the last sixty years, reemerging as a key theme of the British coalition government elected in May 2010, which proposed to appoint businesspeople as ambassadors (Barker 2010).

Another functional theme, affecting the work of both the MFA and the diplomatic service, has been the enhanced significance of consular work (see Leira and Neumann, chapter 9 in this volume). This reflects the intersection of the commercial demands on foreign services, the demands from ever-more mobile populations, and the expectations that NDSs (for this involves a range of domestic departments alongside the MFA) should actively respond to the needs of their citizens caught up in sudden natural and man-made international crises. The establishment of crisis management units at home is balanced by enhanced capacity in the field, often by means of regional "crisis hubs" linking missions in specific geographic regions.

These activities are closely related to the second dimension of change, namely, the changing structure of **diplomatic posts**, reflecting the reconfiguration of the NDS. The trend for many embassies to be staffed by members of a range of departments other than the MFA has been established for many years but in some larger posts has reached the point where professional diplomats are in a minority. This has created a somewhat paradoxical claim on the part of MFAs, which on the one hand acknowledge that overseas missions are increasingly a platform for the entire government apparatus while, on the other, frequently asserting that they constitute a key element of the "value added" afforded by the MFA in the management of international policy. However this might be viewed, a diffusion of bureaucratic interests at missions abroad poses issues of communication with central government and the conventions determining the "tasking" of posts and, ultimately, policy coordination.

The third facet of change, but by no means the least significant, is the issue of the resources available for the maintenance of the diplomatic network and how these are deployed. Around the world diplomatic services are being rationalized. Denmark, for example, announced the closure of five missions in 2010. But ,clearly, national needs differ; the size of the Indian foreign service is regarded as inadequate for a rising economic power with 669 diplomats distributed between the ministry in New Delhi and 119 missions and forty-nine consulates around the world, and is being expanded (Markey 2009). A quite different situation exists in the EU, where the creation of the European External Action Service under the Lisbon Treaty poses interesting questions regarding its impact on member state diplomatic services (see Bátora and Hardacre, chapter 17 in this volume). One feature of the emerging EU diplomatic landscape is a growing trend among member states to reduce the resources devoted to intra-EU diplomatic representation (Bátora and Hocking 2009).

Doing more with less has encouraged experiments with a range of structural reforms such as economies of scale through greater use of **multiple accreditation** of diplomats to two or more countries and assigning specific functions to regional geographic hubs. In the EU, there have been limited experiments with **colocation** of EU missions in third countries that amount to a sharing of premises. Additionally, outside the EU, greater use is being made of **nonresident ambassadors**. While by no means restricted to smaller states, these have obvious attractions for a country such as Singapore, which has used them to supplement its forty-three overseas missions. In the United States, adapting to a changing global environment combined with pressures on resources has resulted in a number of experiments, including small scale American "presence posts" first deployed in France and often staffed by one foreign service officer, **mobile diplomats** (circuit riders) operating from a mission and regularly visiting cities or regions, and "virtual presence posts" in the form of websites targeted at a geographic area and maintained from an embassy (Argyros, Grossman, and Rohatyn 2007).

Of more general significance, however, is the recognition that the redistribution of global power in the twenty-first century needs to be reflected in the distribution of scarce diplomatic resources. This theme was reflected in the "Transformational Diplomacy" initiative announced by secretary of state Condoleezza Rice in January 2006 at Georgetown University in which a major shift in the distribution of US diplomatic posts away from Europe and toward the emerging economies was proposed (Rice 2006).

The Domestic Environment

International pressures are balanced, and in some cases intensified, by domestic pressures affecting the ways in which MFAs operate. One determinant of this has already been noted in the form of a need to build relationships not only with other government departments with international responsibilities but also with a range of nongovernmental stakeholders as the NDS reshapes itself to deal with changing agendas and more complex patterns of policy making. Growing linkages and working relationships with non-state actors of various descriptions are a feature of the contemporary diplomatic environment and are therefore shaping the working environment of MFAs and their foreign services (see Pigman, chapter 4; Badie, chapter 5; and Kerr and Taylor, chapter 13 in this volume).

Related to these growing linkages and relationships is the recognition that aspects of diplomacy have become a "consumer commodity" whereby MFAs are confronted by an expanded customer base. Pressures to provide commercial services and, more recently, the public attention given to the performance of a foreign ministry in serving the needs of a more mobile traveling public through its consular functions not only are central to its work but also create standards by which it is judged. Manifestations of this are apparent from MFA websites that offer the public (as with the British FCO's LOCATE facility) the ability to register travel plans so that their location is known in case of emergency.

The other major aspect of the MFA's domestic environment relates to the impact of public sector governance demands that developed in the 1990s. Rather than being regarded as a distinctive component of government administration, the MFA has found itself increasingly subject to the demands placed on domestic departments. In general terms, this stresses the establishment of targets and the measurement of performance in quantifiable terms. The adoption of strategic plans and the publication of mission statements together with a range of documents explaining the goals of the ministry and how these are to be achieved are manifestations of this development (Christensen and Petersen 2005).

KEY POINTS

- The relevant issue for understanding the contemporary MFA is not whether it is a dominant agent of international policy or in terminal decline but how it is responding to a changing place in the NDS and what functions it performs.
- The MFA's organizational environment comprises international and domestic components.
- Public diplomacy has emerged as a major task for the MFA but assumes a more central significance demanding that it be integrated into the shaping and delivery of policy objectives.
- The network of overseas posts is a key element of the NDS and not the property of the MFA. But as with the MFA and other government departments operating internationally, it is adapting to domestic and international change.
- Increasingly, the MFA finds itself subjected to working practices originally applied to domestic bureaucratic departments. This can be seen as part of its "deforeignization."

CONCLUSION

Examining the nature and evolution of the MFA offers significant insights into both the theory and practice of diplomacy. While statist approaches to diplomacy tend to privilege these institutions and regard them as immutable aspects of the diplomatic order, alternative views have modified this image. In much of the early globalization literature, traditional forms of diplomacy came to be regarded as an obstacle rather than a solution to the management of global problems. Consequently, the institutional structures associated with diplomacy, such as the MFA, were deemed no longer fit for the purpose.

More recent interpretations of globalization cast a different light on these issues. Rather than being locked into a condition of terminal decline, the state has come to be seen as adapting to the pressures that globalization imposes. The adaptation of the "globalized state" is seen as critical to the management of pressing global issues. In terms of diplomacy, this suggests the principles of state-based diplomacy are adapting to the demands of a multiactor environment in which the construction of flexible and issue-oriented networks is critical.

The chapter has argued several points: that we can better understand these developments by recognizing that the MFA is a subsystem within a broader NDS; that the MFA as an organization is determined by its location at the point of interface between the NDS and the global diplomatic system; that the MFA, despite growing resource constraints, has at its disposal an influential and articulate transnational elite able to argue a case for the organizational status quo or, more subtly, to ensure survival through redefining and re-presenting itself; and, finally, that MFAs are likely to survive in some recognizable form because of the combined effect of inertia and uncertainty as to the value of alternative structures that seek to accommodate the complexities and interdependencies of international policy processes.

QUESTIONS

1. How do differing approaches to the study of diplomacy impact on interpretations of the status and functions of the contemporary MFA?
2. What functions do MFAs perform?
3. How are their functions affected by globalization and regionalization?
4. What is meant by the term "national diplomatic system"? How do MFAs relate to this system?
5. What changes are occurring in the structure and functions of overseas networks of diplomatic posts?
6. How helpful and relevant is the concept of the "decline" of MFAs to an understanding of their contemporary role?
7. What insights into the nature of contemporary structures and processes of diplomacy can we gain from studying the MFA?
8. Critically evaluate the main recommendations of the US Department of State's 2010 *Quadrennial Diplomacy and Development Review.*

CHAPTER 8

The Impact of the Internet and ICT on Contemporary Diplomacy

Jovan Kurbalija

CHAPTER CONTENTS

- Introduction
- Historical background: the telegraph and diplomacy
- Changing the environment for diplomacy
- A new issue on diplomatic agendas
- A new tool for diplomatic activities
- Conclusion

READER'S GUIDE

My God, this is the end of diplomacy." Such was the reported reaction of Lord Palmerston, British prime minister, on receiving the first telegraph message in the 1860s. Diplomacy has survived the telegraph as well as subsequent technological innovations, such as the radio, telephone, television, and faxes. Every new major technological device has prompted reactions similar to that of Lord Palmerston. With the introduction of cell phones and computers, and the Internet in particular, academics, diplomats, journalists, and the general public are again analyzing how these more recent technologies, many of which are the foundations of globalization, are changing diplomacy. This chapter contributes to this discussion. It argues that the Internet is changing both the environment in which diplomacy is conducted and the diplomatic agenda. It is also a new tool that is changing the practice of diplomacy. Cumulatively, the Internet is having a profound effect on the two cornerstones of diplomacy—information and communication.

INTRODUCTION

The Internet and information and communication technology (ICT) have revolutionized the way we communicate and manage information. In a matter of twenty years, our means of communication have shifted from telegraphs and faxes to using cell phones and Internet services, such as Skype. With 5 billion cell phone users and 2 billion Internet users, simple, cheap communication is now affordable for most of the world's population. Facebook and other social networks announced a new phase in the communication revolution. The digitalization process has increased access to information and knowledge. For example, with the big book-scanning projects, most English-language books will soon be available digitally. In parallel to having more information available online, sophisticated search engines, such as Google, are widely used. We not only have more information but also can access this information easily when we need it.

Given the core relevance of communication and information to diplomacy, these developments raise important issues about the influence of the Internet on diplomacy. To explore these issues, this chapter starts with a historical survey of the influence of the telegraph on diplomacy. Then it focuses on how the Internet is changing the political, social, and economic environment for diplomatic activities and the diplomatic agenda. Then follows an analysis of how the Internet is used by diplomats and how this impacts the practice of diplomacy.

HISTORICAL BACKGROUND: THE TELEGRAPH AND DIPLOMACY

The beginning of both communication and diplomacy and the links between them can be traced back to the early days of human existence. Many archaeological sources point to early forms of communication and to its role in solving conflicts peacefully. As Keith Hamilton and Richard Langhorne (1995: 7) point out, "Our predecessors realized that it was better to hear the message than to eat the messenger." The evolution of diplomacy has been closely linked to the evolution of communication technology since these early times.

The most relevant historical period for our analysis of the interplay between communication technology and diplomacy is between the Vienna Congress (1815) and the First World War (1914–18). During this period, the invention of the telegraph and radio changed both the environment in which diplomacy was conducted and methods of diplomacy in several ways (see box 8-1). First, a global communication network evolved, and diplomacy was transformed from ad hoc meetings into an organized system of diplomatic services, international organizations, and regular international gatherings. Second, the telegraph separated communications and transportation. For the first time there was no need to carry the message by car or courier. Messages could be sent much more rapidly and frequently by telegraph. Third, thanks to telegraph-facilitated communication, the world economy became increasingly integrated at the end of the nineteenth century because information could be shared, and financial and other transactions between the main stock markets became possible. Fourth, the telegraph system provided critical infrastructure with considerable political and strategic significance. With the increasing importance of underwater and land telegraphic cables, Britain and other countries started developing the so-called cable geo-strategy. By the end of the nineteenth century, Britain controlled 66 percent of all telegraphic cables around the world. Together

---

BOX 8-1

The Telegraph and Diplomatic History

The influence of technology on diplomacy can be illustrated by three leaked telegrams that influenced history: the 1870 Ems telegram (skillfully used by Otto von Bismarck to trigger the process of the unification of Germany); the Kruger telegram in 1896 (reshaped German policy in South Africa and introduced global Anglo-German antagonism); and the 1917 Zimmermann telegram (sent by German foreign minister Arthur Zimmermann to the German Mission in Mexico and intercepted by the British). This latter telegram instructed the German representative to start negotiating Mexico's entrance into the war as a German ally by offering Mexico control of the US states of New Mexico, Utah, and California after the war. The Zimmerman telegram was leaked at a time when the American public were still neutral and not ready to join the First World War. It made front-page news and prompted the United States to join the Allied forces.

The most illustrative case study of the influence of the telegraph on diplomacy was the 1914 July crisis that led to the beginning of the First World War. Telegraph messages were being sent between St. Petersburg, Berlin, Belgrade, Vienna, Paris, and other countries involved in the conflict. However, there was little awareness of how to use the telegraph properly. The Russian czar sent a conciliatory note to Germany, but the German kaiser had already sent a note that was not conciliatory at all, thus creating communication confusion and mistrust that contributed toward escalation and ultimately war. A new technology coupled with human failures led to a very unfortunate outcome.

---

with the United States, this totaled almost 80 percent. By 1892, Germany commanded 1.9 percent and later, in 1908, 7.2 percent (Headrick 1991: 94). Britain controlled all cables connecting France and its overseas territories, including Madagascar, Martinique, Morocco, Tonkin, and Tunisia. Such monopoly of cable communication gave Britain considerable economic, political, and diplomatic power. Britain's worldwide network of cables was the communication infrastructure that helped to sustain the British Empire.

In the second part of the nineteenth century, the telegraph provided the subject matter for the establishment of an early institution of global governance, the International Telegraph Union. Later renamed the International Telecommunication Union (ITU), it had a mandate to deal with global aspects of the development of other telecommunication systems, including radio and telephony.

One of the issues that existed in the early days of the telegraph, and that applies to the Internet today, is the neutrality of the telecommunications system. In the early twentieth century, the ITU negotiated a proposal to introduce the neutrality of the telegraph cable in case of war. The question of the general impartiality of Internet telecommunications infrastructure is still under discussion today. Another issue that is common to both eras is the delicate balance between *freedom* of communication and the right of states to *control* communication, especially in situations where there are concerns about national security. Both these issues will be discussed further later.

The telegraph also significantly influenced the practice of diplomacy in other ways. Diplomatic missions started communicating regularly: instead of taking weeks or even months, communications became instantaneous. The reaction of diplomats was diverse. Many diplomats in the nineteenth century did not welcome the increasing use of the telegraph in diplomacy. For example, the British ambassador to Vienna, Sir Horace Rumbold (1902), said that there was a telegraphic demoralization of those who formerly acted for themselves and now had to be content to be at the end of the wire. Diplomats lost much of their independence because they had to start acting on daily instructions newly available from the capital.

The high cost of telegrams also influenced the way in which diplomats wrote communications, forcing them to be concise. The medium (expensive telegraph) influenced the message (diplomatic language). One of the first diplomatic cables sent in 1866 from the US Department of State to its mission in France cost some $20,000. At the time, the Department of State's budget was $150,000. After this incident, the Department of State was less enthusiastic about sending telegrams, until the cost became reasonable a few decades later.

KEY POINTS

- The telegraph changed the environment in which diplomacy was conducted. The introduction of the telegraph made possible a global network that dramatically increased the speed and frequency of communications.
- As a result the telegraph changed many practices of diplomacy. Missions communicated more regularly with capitals, and diplomats abroad had less autonomy and were forced to write more concisely than they had in the past.

CHANGING THE ENVIRONMENT FOR DIPLOMACY

Diplomacy does not exist within a vacuum. It is influenced by particular social, political, and economic circumstances. Historically speaking, each epoch has its "defining technology," or its elements that determine economic, social, and political success. Control of the defining technology has usually meant control of society. The defining technology of our era is information technology and the Internet, with knowledge being of central importance. In his description of a **knowledge society**, Peter Drucker (1989: 167) observes that knowledge has become the capital of a developed economy and that knowledge workers are the group that sets society's trends.

The Internet has been the key force behind the **globalization** of the modern economy. Financial sector professionals were among the first to start intensively using the Internet. Once again, technology was both an enabler (for example, the high mobility of financial assets worldwide) and a liability (for example, the quick spillover effect after the 2008 financial crisis). The Internet also influences the production processes. For example, it supports the transfer of both labor and service activities to emerging economies, as witnessed by the thousands of programmers and other software specialists who work for the Western market while located in such places as India and other developing countries.

Finally, the Internet has also introduced a range of new actors who have a strong influence on society. Among them are hackers (for example, the underground elite of the WikiLeaks community), software companies (the institutional giants such as Google and Facebook), and open-source groups (such as developers of the Linux operating system, Wikipedia, Twitter, and Blogger). Their influence on society is founded on their technical or content-related knowledge. Many of these actors appear to have a certain sociocultural ethos more inclined to use persuasion than overt political coercion. For example, the mostly nonviolent nature of the Egyptian and Tunisian political changes during 2011 was partly inspired by some prominent members of this elite, including local bloggers and individuals such as Wael Ghonim, manager of Google Middle East (*Guardian* 2011). Such an ethos may create a more fertile ground for diplomacy and diplomatic methods in solving social and political problems (Lagon 1996).

Sovereignty

One of the major functions of diplomats is safeguarding the **sovereignty** of the state. The Internet is challenging this traditional notion of sovereignty in at least two ways. First, the Internet undermines territorial sovereignty. The idea of **cyberspace** does not correspond to the current division of the world into territorial states. Cyberspace challenges the state's claim to monopolize the governing of domestic public affairs and to establish a definitive and binding relationship between the citizen and a given territory. This tension is evident in the limited possibilities for national governments to enforce their national laws or protect rights of their citizens on the Internet. For example, national states have no mechanisms to protect privacy and data of their citizens stored on social networks such as Facebook or Twitter. Second, **nation-states** have a limited capacity to control economic transactions that involve Internet services. The intangible nature of Internet services makes it difficult for states to impose customs controls, tariff regimes, and taxation schemes. National governments are trying to regain control of Internet economic activities, particularly in areas of high fiscal importance, such as online gambling.

One of the paradoxes that diplomats now confront is that of protecting a state's sovereignty while at the same time promoting the state's participation in the processes of global and regional integration, both of which inevitably reduce the sovereignty of the state. As Carl Builder (1993: 160) points out: "For nations to be economically competitive, they must allow individual citizens access to information networks and computer technology. In doing so, they cede significant control over economic, cultural, and eventually political events in their countries." This tension was illustrated by the decision of the Egyptian government to cut national access to the Internet during the popular protests of 2011. The decision reversed the Egyptian government's previous policy of actively promoting the nation in the global Internet infrastructure.

Another issue that diplomats now face is that the state's lessening control over sovereignty is helping to increase the number of entities and actors with the capacity to participate in international political and legal issues. Individuals and groups from civil society, the business sector, and academia are learning to develop representation and negotiating capacities, which in turn boost the development of new types of diplomatic methods and procedures. One of the early examples was the use of the Internet in the campaign to ban land mines. A global civil society coalition used the web to mobilize global public opinion and motivate governments to negotiate a new treaty. It resulted in the adoption of the Convention on the Prohibition of the Use, Stockpiling, Production and Transfer of Anti-Personnel Mines and on Their Destruction in December 1997. For this achievement the International Campaign to Ban Landmines (a consortium of more than 1,000 nongovernmental organizations) was awarded the Nobel Peace Prize in 1997. This success inspired the use of the Internet by civil society in other subsequent policy processes. For example, the Internet-facilitated campaign by civil society groups blocked adoption of the 1998 Organisation for Economic Co-operation and Development Multilateral Agreement on Investment. Likewise, the use of the Internet-facilitated robust civil society participation at the 1999 World Trade Organization meeting in Seattle, which was viewed by audiences around the world. In the early part of this century, non-state actors became key players in the Internet governance negotiations during the World Summit on the Information Society (WSIS, 2002–5) and the Internet Governance Forum (IGF, 2006–10), as discussed later.

Interdependence

The Internet has considerably influenced the capacity of actors in world politics to interact with each other by providing physical technologies (easier exchange of information) and social technologies (development of common communication space with shared rules and procedures). Email, **social media**, and other services have empowered individuals and societies to communicate globally. This high-intensity communication brings more contacts and greater **interdependence**.

More interdependence most often leads to more frequent use of diplomacy as a tool for managing international relations and solving potential conflict. High levels of economic and social interdependence put considerable limitations on the use of military power and increase the importance of **soft power** and diplomacy as a way of solving international conflicts. Joseph Nye (2011) provides a detailed analysis of the role of the Internet in developing interdependence and projecting soft power.

Furthermore, growing interdependence blurs the traditional division between national and international communication spaces. As Robert Keohane and Nye demonstrate, growing interdependence is leading to an increasing number of traditionally domestic issues affecting foreign policy (Keohane and Nye 1972). The 2011 burning of the Qur'an by a Christian fundamentalist in the United States immediately triggered reactions in the Muslim world that became a foreign policy issue for US diplomacy (Harris and Gallagher 2011).

The impact of increased interdependence on diplomacy and diplomats is significant (see box 8-2). Traditionally, diplomats used different approaches to address domestic and foreign audiences. Today, diplomats, especially during times of crisis, must address both domestic audiences, who look often or typically for messages supporting national pride and determination, and foreign audiences, who look for more conciliatory signals. Modern communications blur the difference between these operating environments and reduce the room in which diplomats can maneuver. With websites, blogs, and Twitter accessible to anyone connected to the Internet,

=== **BOX 8-2** ===

The Kosovo War: The Importance and Limits of Interdependence

The Kosovo War is another example of the importance of interdependence. Serbia's Internet connection was not cut throughout the conflict. Why didn't the North Atlantic Treaty Organization (NATO) cut Internet access to Yugoslavia, which was not only technically feasible but also legally justifiable under the sanctions regime? The Internet was a very valuable source of information not only for the local population but also for NATO. NATO was able to learn about the precision of its bombing at the same time as gauging the mood of the population. Thus a mutual interest was served by leaving the Internet operational, even during the armed conflict.

diplomats can no longer target particular audiences. Diplomatic messages have to be drafted in such a way as to address all potential audiences.

KEY POINTS

- The defining technology of our time is information technology and the Internet.
- The Internet supports a range of new actors who influence society and whose technical skills and knowledge are based on persuasion rather than political coercion.
- The Internet has altered the concept of sovereignty by challenging the control that governments have over territorial space.
- Diplomats have to protect sovereignty (a core function of diplomacy) while simultaneously reducing it (by promoting countries' regional and global integration).
- As interdependence increases, the more relevant diplomacy becomes for solving conflicts.
- Growing communication interdependence blurs the distinction between national and international communication spaces and requires diplomats to target both audiences.

A NEW ISSUE ON DIPLOMATIC AGENDAS

The Internet has become an important topic in diplomatic negotiations (see Zartman, chapter 6 in this volume). Along with climate change, migration, and food security, it is one of the issues that is expanding the diplomatic agenda. As David Newsom (1989: 29) points out: "For most of the twentieth century, the international diplomatic agenda has consisted of questions of political and economic relations between nation-states—the traditional subjects of diplomacy. After the Second World War new diplomatic issues arose, spurred by the technical advances in nuclear energy and electronics."

Internet governance is the subject of intense diplomatic negotiation. Central to these negotiations is agreement among the multiple stakeholders on who exactly governs the Internet. Who are the actors likely to influence its future development? What will their policies be with regard to connectivity, commerce, content, funding, security, and other issues central to our emerging information society negotiations?

Internet governance was put on the global diplomatic agenda during the WSIS, which was organized around two main summit events: one in Geneva in 2003 and the other in Tunis in 2005. At the Tunis event, WSIS adopted the decision to establish the IGF, which is now the main global body in the field of Internet governance. The IGF is a unique global policy body because all the main stakeholders—government, business sector, and civil society—can participate on an equal basis.

Internet governance covers a wide set of issues, which can be divided into the following five areas: infrastructure and standardization; legal; development; economic; and sociocultural. This classification of Internet governance is metaphorically presented through the image of a building under construction in figure 8.1, which also reflects a formative phase of the Internet governance global regime. Some of the features of the Internet and the issues that are being negotiated to develop the regime are shown in box 8-3.

KEY POINT

- Internet governance covering a wide set of issues and involving multiple stakeholders is the subject of robust diplomatic negotiations.

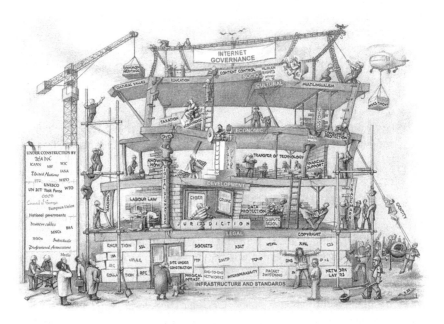

Figure 8.1 Internet governance "under construction".
SOURCE: Reproduced from Kurbalija (2010: 28).

BOX 8-3

A Summary of Internet Governance Issues

- The global regulation of the Internet occurs on three layers: tele-communication infrastructure, technical standards, and content standards.

- The most controversial issue in the current Internet governance policy is related to the Internet Corporation for Assigned Names and Numbers (ICANN)—a legal entity incorporated in California—and its link to the US government. Many countries insist that this arrangement must be changed in order to have completely international management of the Domain Name System (DNS), which handles Internet addresses (such as www.google.com) and converts them to Internet protocol (IP) numbers (see figure 8.2). Barack Obama's administration has accelerated reform of ICANN that could lead toward a new international organization managing the DNS.

- Cybersecurity and **cybercrime** are the areas of Internet governance with the most intensive diplomatic and legal coverage.

- Tension between traditional state territory and cyberspace is the basis of controversy related to legal jurisdiction in Internet issues.

- Copyright and other intellectual property rights are emerging issues but, as yet, have not been properly addressed in the field of Internet governance.

- Internet governance has an important development aspect. Closing the **digital divide** requires complex development intervention combining technological, economic, and regulatory measures, among others.

- Promotion of e-commerce was at the basis of the development of Internet governance regimes. E-commerce triggered numerous governance issues, including consumer protection and taxation.

- Content policy is one of the most controversial Internet governance issues that borders censorship and justifiable content policy (for example, blocking child pornography).

- Cloud computing shifts data from hard disks and traditional storage to the major servers (for example, gmail, hotmail, wikis), which are so called "clouds." Governments are concerned about protection of citizen data and the shift of national digital assets to facilities managed by private companies and located in other countries, mainly in the United States.

- Privacy and data protection are regulated in the policy triangle among users, state, and business (see figure 8.3). In the field of privacy and data protection, the European Union is the main player trying to set up higher levels of protection of privacy at the global level (see Sims, chapter 14 in this volume).

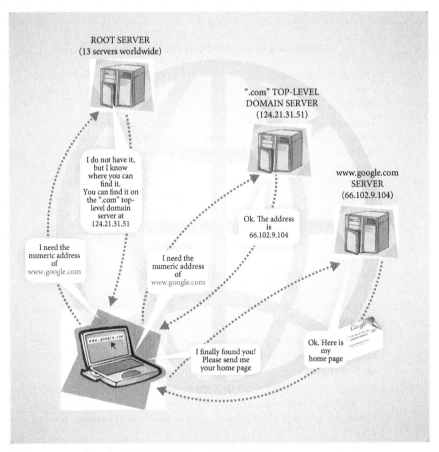

Figure 8.2 How the Domain Name System (DNS) functions.
Source: Reproduced from Kurbalija (2010: 42).

A NEW TOOL FOR DIPLOMATIC ACTIVITIES

The Internet is a practical working tool in diplomacy. Diplomats communicate intensely through emails, use search engines to find information, and use teleconferencing, social media, and other Internet services. These technologies impact the way in which modern diplomacy operates—on diplomatic meetings and negotiations, the organization of diplomatic services, access to and organization of knowledge and information, and public diplomacy.

Diplomatic Meetings and Negotiations

The first major use of computers in an international meeting was at the 1992 Earth Summit in Rio de Janiero, when mailing lists were used to follow the negotiations and engage the global community. Through mailing lists, individuals and communities worldwide received email updates about the Rio negotiations from the

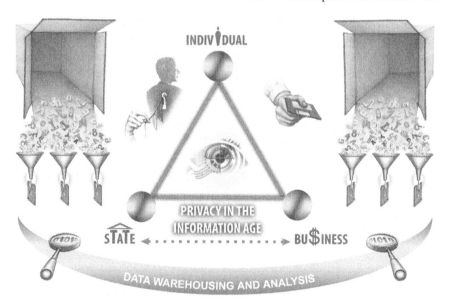

Figure 8.3 The privacy triangle.
SOURCE: Reproduced from Kurbalija (2010: 141).

ICT-empowered civil society groupings. As a result, the monopoly that diplomats had over information from this and other later global meetings was greatly
diminished. The use of mailing lists was further developed at the World Conference
on Human Rights (Vienna, 1993), the International Conference on Population
and Development (Cairo, 1994), the United Nations Fourth World Conference
on Women (Beijing, 1995), and the World Summit for Social Development
(Copenhagen, 1995).

However, the main breakthrough in the use of the Internet in such instances
came during the WSIS meetings in 2002 and 2005 and at the IGF meetings, held
annually since 2006. The WSIS and IGF meetings set new standards in e-diplomacy
and inspired the use of new e-tools in other multilateral negotiations, such as climate
change, migration, and human rights. During WSIS, the Internet entered conference
rooms through the widespread use of **wireless technology** (WiFi). At the beginning
of the WSIS process in 2002, WiFi was a relatively new technological innovation used
by participants from technically advanced countries. By 2005, WiFi had become a
mainstream service, and many delegates used it to connect their notebooks to the
Internet from the conference room.

The availability of the Internet in conference rooms introduced the possibility
of more inclusive and open international negotiations. It facilitated the participation
of an increased number of civil society and business sector representatives, including those who could not, for financial or other reasons, physically participate in
the meetings. Initially, remote participants could only follow deliberations passively,
through web broadcasting. During the 2007 IGF meeting, remote participation was

enhanced to include the possibility for remote participants to ask questions and contribute to discussions. Since 2009, remote participation in IGF meetings has been further enhanced through the introduction of "remote hubs." Remote hubs are local meetings that take place during and parallel to IGF meetings, hosted by universities, ICT centers, nongovernmental organizations, and other players who deal with Internet governance and policy issues. The organizers of these meetings project a simultaneous webcast of the IGF proceedings so that remote participants can stay informed about what is being debated. Participants can send text and video questions in real-time interventions. In addition, hubs host local panels and roundtable discussions that correlate to IGF themes. Through these activities, the local hubs enrich coordination between global and local policy processes. The 2010 IGF meeting in Vilnius was followed by thirty-two remote hubs with about 600 participants.

For diplomats at the WSIS and IGF meetings, the WiFi Internet connection provided constant contact with their ministries of foreign affairs and other government departments dealing with WSIS issues. In some cases, a WiFi network of notebooks enabled the coordination of initiatives among representatives physically present in the conference room. Electronic exchange complemented and sometimes replaced the traditional ambience of short chats between diplomats from different countries, tête-à-tête exchanges, and corridor diplomacy. Because physical movements can reveal the dynamics of negotiations or even form part of diplomatic signaling, this aspect of in situ diplomatic negotiations started changing with the use of WiFi.

The experience from WSIS and IGF meetings also shows that despite all the promises of virtual conferencing and other multimedia technologies, text remains diplomacy's central tool. Most exchanges between preparatory sessions are done via mailing lists and email. The IGF is supported by very active social media discussions, using text-intensive tools such as blogs and Twitter.

Another development that highlights the relevance of text is the emergence of "verbatim reporting" at IGF meetings. Verbatim reporting is the process whereby all verbal interventions are transcribed simultaneously by special stenographers and immediately displayed on a large screen in the conference room, as well as broadcast via the Internet. While delegates are speaking, transcripts of their speeches appear on the screen. Verbatim reporting has had an important effect on the diplomatic modus operandi. The awareness that what is said will be preserved in text transcripts, available on the Internet, makes many participants more careful in choosing the level and length of their speeches. Verbatim reporting also increases the transparency of diplomatic meetings. With further research, the implications of this development for multilateral diplomacy and negotiations will become more evident.

The Internet has potential applications also in the conversion of verbal agreements into written format; this is one of the crucial phases in the negotiation process where ambiguity and distortion may be introduced. Group editing applications enable negotiators to work collaboratively on a text by adding comments and hypertext links.

The use of new e-tools for negotiations should be approached carefully and within appropriate contexts. Diplomacy is a profession that often requires discretion. While openness is the guiding principle of good governance, many successful diplomatic deals have been done far removed from the public eye. There are many reasons why negotiations should be discreet, one of them being to protect the inter-locutor on the other side of the table. In many cases negotiators spend a lot of time finding face-saving formulas for the audience back home. Discretion usually helps to prevent effective negotiations from turning into a show for the general public. Compromise, the core of diplomacy, is not popular in many societies, especially when it conflicts with national interest, pride, and glory. Reaching a compromise and maintaining discretion in negotiations are very often closely linked. It is easy to envisage negotiations that could not be conducted efficiently in front of webcams. The decision whether to use technical tools for negotiation will probably form part of the negotiation.

The Organization of Diplomatic Services

Diplomats use e-tools intensively for internal communication and management of information. Unlike in the 1990s, when computer systems for diplomatic services were often custom-made, today many diplomatic services use tools and approaches that have been publicly tested on the Internet. For example, the success of Wikipedia and Facebook inspired the US Department of State to create similar internal ser-vices for its employees called "Diplopedia" and "Statebook" (Montalbano 2010; Rosen 2010).

The Internet is not only a tool but also an agent for organizational change (see Hocking, chapter 7 in this volume). The scope for organizational change in diplo-matic services is largely shaped by three elements of diplomatic organizational and professional culture: hierarchy, exclusivity, and secrecy. Hierarchy is a core principle within diplomatic services, and it comes in two forms: organizational and functional. In the past, organizational hierarchy was denoted by uniforms according to rank, as in the military. Today, there are no uniforms, but diplomats still have a clearly defined rank, starting from attachés and ending with ambassadors. Diplomatic ranks are used for the internal organization of diplomatic services. Diplomats progress in their career through hierarchical professional structures. Moreover, organizational hierarchy implies where responsibility and accountability for decision making can be located. Jamie Metzl (2001: 80) argues that "those functions that require the high-est levels of accountability, particularly the decision-making functions, should retain hierarchical structures."

The functional aspect of hierarchy, on the other hand, influences the way in which diplomacy is conducted. The rank of a diplomat for a specific task is usu-ally carefully chosen. Who leads delegations, welcomes foreign guests, negotiates, or attends social functions could be part of **diplomatic signaling**. The higher a diplo-mat is in the hierarchy, the more importance a particular state assigns to a particular action.

This double relevance of hierarchy—organizational and functional—shows how deeply it is entrenched in diplomatic professional and organizational cul-ture. Managing hierarchy has been one of the main challenges for diplomatic serv-ices when introducing the Internet because, as Elizabeth Smythe and Peter Smith (2002: 52) argue, "vertically organized bureaucratic structures, especially hierarchical organizations such as foreign ministries, are at a disadvantage in a networked infor-mation society." An example of how the Internet challenges the "functional hierarchy" culture of diplomatic services is that it is technically possible for junior diplomats to email the minister of foreign affairs directly, bypassing the hierarchical structure.

Most other ICT/Internet tools introduced into diplomatic services—sharing of information and automation of work processes—faced hierarchy as an important limitation. This challenge became even more apparent with the emergence of social media (blog, wiki, Twitter, and other social media tools), which further flattens the hierarchical distribution of information and may diminish the overall control that diplomatic services have over their diplomatic agendas.

Exclusivity is based in the aristocratic origins of the diplomatic profession. Today, diplomacy is no longer an elitist aristocratic profession, but exclusivity still appears to be an important aspect of diplomats' "professional ethos." Apart from diplomacy's historical origin, exclusivity has also been based on diplomats' privileged access to information. With the ICT and Internet technologies, special access to and control of information have greatly diminished. Governments are under public pressure to make more and more information available in the public domain. While the trend toward open access is strong, diplomacy needs to retain a certain level of discretion in order to perform its function, especially in delicate negotiations.

Secrecy has always been one of the core characteristics of diplomacy (see Sims, chapter 14 in this volume). The first embassies, established in Renaissance Italy in the fifteenth century, were built as a way of protecting secrets and communication. In modern times, secrecy was particularly important during the Cold War. Diplomats were on the front line of battle between the United States and the Soviet Union and their satellites. The protection of information from spies was very important. It influenced the way diplomacy was conducted and the way diplomatic services were organized. The "need to know" principle was the basis of information management. According to this principle, diplomats had access only to information of direct relevance and concern for them. Other information was not shared within the diplomatic service. This approach is exactly opposite to the principle of sharing information, facilitated by the introduction of ICT/Internet.

Since the end of the Cold War, most diplomatic services have facilitated access to a broader range of information. Yet, secrecy and the "need to know" principle still influence the decisions of diplomatic services when it comes to the use of ICT/Internet. More recently, security reasons prevailed over access to information in the decision of many diplomatic services to block the use of emerging Internet services such as Twitter, Facebook, and Skype. The shift toward more security in diplomatic services is likely to gain momentum after the WikiLeaks release of diplomatic cables. For many diplomatic services, striking the right balance between security and e-functionality will remain very challenging.

Access to Information and Knowledge

Information is one of the key elements of the diplomatic profession: information is to diplomats what money is to bankers. The old problem of finding information has, to a large extent, been replaced by the problem of managing and processing information. Abundance of information is as problematic as scarcity: important information can be lost in quantity. The fast and precise access to necessary information is *conditio sine qua non* of the proper functioning of the ministry of foreign affairs (MFA) and other participants in foreign policy.

Over the last ten years, diplomats have shifted from relying on internal resources to information available outside diplomatic services, mainly on the Internet. Sophisticated search engines, such as Google, Yahoo, Altavista, and Ask.com, made possible precise and timely access to needed information (see box 8-4). Diplomats also use new services such as Wikipedia, a web-based encyclopedia with more than 17 million articles written by contributors around the world. It is very relevant for diplomats because, in most cases, it provides complete and up-to-date coverage of main diplomatic events and policy developments. Very often, Wikipedia contains firsthand information from people on the spot. Only a few large diplomatic services can provide coverage of international events comparable to Wikipedia. Of course, like any other professionals, diplomats should check information from Wikipedia by comparing it with information from other sources.

The **blogosphere,** or blogs and their interconnections, is another highly relevant source of information and knowledge available for diplomats. Unlike anonymous Wikipedia, blogs have authors. The most important blogs are written by respected and authoritative authors. The blog as a media channel is a well-established and recognized communication tool. Blogs have been around since the 1990s. Today there

---

BOX 8-4

Diplomatic Reporting

Diplomatic reporting is one of the core information channels in diplomatic services. Matthew Anderson (1993: 23) indicates that compulsory diplomatic reporting can be traced back to Venetian diplomatic missions in the thirteenth century. In the more recent past, diplomats competed with journalists to obtain current news. In the late 1990s, a shift occurred with the so-called CNN effect—real time coverage of world events twenty-four hours a day, seven days a week, all through the year. Former Egyptian ambassador Nabil Fahmy explained this shift in the late 1990s (before the Internet revolution):

> When I came to Washington less than three years ago, I basically decided I would not compete with the media in sending information to Egypt. It was a futile attempt to get it there first. So I stopped reporting most current information. I assumed that people had the news back home because they watched CNN. (cited in Bollier 2003: 6)

Ambassador Fahmy shifted approximately 80 percent of his confidential cable traffic to open, nonsecure conduits. He figured that by the time it reached his colleagues back in Egypt, the information was fairly well known anyway. As he explained, "The only thing I actually sent confidentially is opinion—my opinion, somebody else's opinion, criticism of my own government, criticism of the US government. That's all I send confidentially" (Bollier 2003: 6). The next shift in diplomatic reporting came with the emergence of Wikipedia and blogs, which further focused diplomatic reporting on analysis and evaluation that cannot otherwise be found on the Internet.

are more than 100 million blogs with often informal, but well-established, ranking procedure. Blogs are particularly influential in specialized policy fields such as climate change, migration, and food security. They influence policy and agenda-shaping in international negotiations.

A final observation about the access of diplomatic services to multiple sources of information provided by the Internet is that because other government organizations and civil society groups also access the same sources, diplomatic services are less dependent on the MFA for information. This raises questions about the role of the MFA in contemporary diplomacy, a subject that Brian Hocking (chapter 7 in this volume) canvasses by invoking his concept of "national diplomatic systems."

Organizing Knowledge and Information

Diplomatic services preserve rich resources of knowledge and information. In the 1990s, diplomatic services started to use various knowledge management techniques to preserve and organize that knowledge and information, including databases and document management services. Today, they increasingly use social media tools, which have proved successful on the Internet. As mentioned earlier, inspired by Wikipedia, the US Department of State established Diplopedia, which has more than 12,000 articles and has become a valuable resource within the department (Rosen 2010). Articles are contributed and edited by diplomats. The Canadian diplomatic service also has an internal wiki with more than 6,000 articles. To facilitate handovers between frequently rotating staff, the US Department of State introduced "Deskipedia," a system where each diplomat provides information about his or her roles, duties, and other relevant information for the post. The system aims to facilitate easier transfer of knowledge between outgoing and incoming officials. Inspired by LinkedIn (a social network of professionals), the Canadian Department of Foreign Affairs and International Trade introduced "Connections"—a platform for collecting staff profiles and facilitating optimal use of human resources. The system aims to help identify staff with particular language skills and expertise. It can be particularly useful in a time of crisis, when the identification of the staff with right skills and knowledge is time-sensitive.

Public Diplomacy

The Internet and especially social media tools have influenced communication between diplomatic services and the public, both at home and abroad (see Melissen, chapter 11 in this volume). The main change is from traditional indirect communications between diplomatic services and the public, to direct interaction between diplomatic services and the public using such technologies as social media. Traditional media, such as the printed word and television, support one-way communication. The Internet has introduced multidirectional interactive communication by adding numerous channels for the public to voice their opinions about diplomatic activities. Today, through blogs, Twitter, Facebook, and other social media tools, the general public can share its views about any public policy issue, including foreign policy. Diplomatic services cannot ignore this development. Diplomats have to respond to comments and engage with the public more than ever before.

With video cameras built into cell phones, and web services such as YouTube, millions of citizens became potential journalists and contributors to the global information space with, in some cases, high impact on international relations. For example, the WikiLeaks film *Collateral Murder* with footage of a helicopter attack on civilians, or the horrifying photographs from Abu Ghraib prison in Iraq were disasters for the United States' image abroad.

Diplomatic services have started adjusting to this changing reality in public communication. Hardware and software are no longer major obstacles to running effective social media campaigns. Most of these services can be run from ordinary home computers. The main challenge is in shaping organizational culture and providing staff with skills and knowledge to engage with the public through websites, blogs, Twitter, Facebook, and other tools.

Websites currently provide the main presence of diplomatic services in the Internet space. There are some 150 websites of MFAs and more than 3,000 websites of diplomatic and consular missions. The main function of these websites is the dissemination of information about foreign policy. On most MFA websites it is possible to find basic foreign policy instruments, press releases, "who's who" in the MFA, travel information, information for foreigners, and more. Initially, websites were created as Internet versions of the traditional type of one-way diplomatic communication. Diplomatic services are now shifting toward more interactive communication through integration with social media tools, such as blogs and Twitter.

Blogs are now an established e-tool for diplomats engaged in public diplomacy. In the first phase of public diplomacy blogs, some pioneers experimented individually without the approval of their ministries. Some of them, such as the Croatian junior diplomat Vibor Calodjera, ended up in trouble: after a few controversial blog postings during his term in the Croatian embassy in Washington, he was suspended and recalled to Zagreb. In the current, second phase, the most advanced diplomatic services, such as the US Department of State and the British Foreign and Commonwealth Office (FCO), are encouraging diplomats to follow official guidelines and use blogs as a recognized communication tool. The main purpose is to address Internet communities in some countries. For example, Internet communities using blogs and Facebook would appear to have influenced the 2011 political protests in North Africa and the Middle East. US and British e-diplomacy is trying to address these communities. These attempts are still in the early, mainly testing, phase.

So far, the US Department of State runs the official blog "DipNote." The FCO has some fifty blogs worldwide, most of them in local languages. Some blogs are highly successful, such as the arms control blog maintained by former British ambassador for arms control and disarmament, John Duncan. However, experience shows that maintaining an attractive and engaging blog requires a lot of time and creativity and therefore extra human and financial resources. Bloggers have to identify interesting themes and to write in an informal style that will attract readers. And there are limitations: although diplomat-bloggers can write informally, they still have official regulations regarding the selection and addressing of topics.

Some diplomatic services have hired experienced bloggers to better influence debate on particular themes. The US Department of State established the Digital Outreach Team with bloggers fluent in Arabic and Farsi. Their task is to follow influential blogs in Arabic and Farsi and to enter into the debate, presenting themselves as US State Department representatives.

BOX 8-5

Social Media in Political Protests

Social media, in particular Twitter and Facebook, have been used to promote and organize political protests. The most prominent uses of Twitter in political crises include Kenya's postelection violence (winter 2007–8), the Israel-Palestine conflict in Gaza (December 2008–January 2009), and postelection crises in Moldova (August 2009) and Iran (June 2009). After the Iran crisis, Twitter received a lot of visibility in international media. It was also proposed as a candidate for the Nobel Peace Prize. Facebook has been a vital communication tool for the organization of protests in Tunisia (2010) and Egypt (2011). Facebook facilitated the rapid spread of information about the organization of protest meetings, the movement of security forces, and overall protest tactics. Following the 2011 protest in Tunisia, Egyptian authorities cut access to the Internet at the very beginning of political unrest in Cairo. These and other examples show that social media are emerging as a powerful medium for bottom-up organization of political and social movements.

Twitter provides an example of Marshal McLuhan's oft-quoted phrase "the medium is the message." Twitter is a social media platform that limits communication to short messages of no more than 140 characters ("tweets") (see box 8-5). The need for short and concise messages has influenced the way Twitter is used; for example, users both send and receive tweets on their cell phones. Initially, users mainly tweeted to update family and friends about personal daily events. However, it has gradually evolved into a tool used for professional communication. The US Department of State uses 166 Twitter feeds to provide updates on its activities and has more than 45,000 followers (twitter.com/StateDept). The FCO has 60 Twitter feeds with close to 80,000 followers.

Finally, with more than 500 million users, Facebook is a champion of public diplomacy (see box 8.5). Both the US Department of State and the British FCO use Facebook for dissemination of information. Some diplomatic Facebook accounts such as the US embassy in Jakarta, with close to 300,000 users, are highly successful. The use of Facebook in diplomacy is still in an experimental phase, and it remains to be seen how effective it will be.

Overall, the Internet has diversified communication between diplomatic services and publics and would appear to have increased engagement between the two entities. Yet, further research will need to establish whether the Internet has also distanced public diplomacy practitioners from personal contact with their audiences, if indeed social media has becomes a substitute for personal interaction.

KEY POINTS

- The use of the Internet and computers in conference rooms significantly influences the way in which international meetings are conducted.
- The Internet has significantly influenced three organizational principles for diplomatic services: hierarchy, exclusivity, and secrecy.

- The Internet has changed the way information is used. From relying predominantly on internal information gathered by diplomats, diplomatic services increasingly rely on external information available on the Internet (for example, Wikipedia, blogs).
- Diplomatic services increasingly use Internet-developed technologies for preserving and managing internal information.
- The Internet has replaced traditional one-way public diplomacy communication—from diplomats to publics—to apparent greater two-way interaction between the diplomatic services and publics. Yet, this form of engagement may come at the cost of greater personal interaction between practitioners and publics.

CONCLUSION

The Internet has substantially changed information and communication, the two cornerstones of diplomacy. Indeed, it has triggered one of the most profound changes in diplomacy. Internet-driven changes in modern society have increased both the interdependence among the major actors in world politics and the demand for diplomacy as a method of solving conflicts through negotiations and compromise. In the Internet-shaped interdependent world, diplomacy is a more practically effective way to solve conflicts.

The Internet has also changed the way in which diplomacy is organized and conducted. It supports a range of actors who can influence diplomacy, it is changing the ways in which information and knowledge are managed in diplomatic services, and it is altering how diplomatic services communicate with both domestic and foreign publics. The future of diplomacy in many respects will be shaped by these and other developments in the Internet.

QUESTIONS

1. What is a "defining technology"?
2. How did the telegraph influence the role of diplomats?
3. Why does the Internet influence diplomacy substantially?
4. How are governments limited in controlling sovereignty?
5. What is the main paradox for diplomats when it comes to changes in sovereignty?
6. What are the main elements of interdependence that are affected by the Internet in modern society?
7. What are the main Internet governance issues?
8. What are the main Internet tools used in international meetings and negotiations?
9. How does the use of computers and Internet influence hierarchical organization of diplomatic services?
10. What are the main uses of social media tools in public diplomacy?
11. What are the implications in this chapter for your theoretical and practical understandings of contemporary diplomacy?

CHAPTER 9

Consular Diplomacy

Halvard Leira and Iver B. Neumann

CHAPTER CONTENTS

- Introduction
- Definitional issues
- Emergence and development of consular tasks and offices
- The consul and the diplomat
- The consul today
- Conclusion

READER'S GUIDE

Consul-like offices have emerged in different countries and in different times in world history as a response to challenges presented, by long-distance travel and trade, to citizens of one locality traveling and trading elsewhere. Although consuls, or the persons who serve in these offices, carry out important functions in the international system—primarily protecting one's nationals and commercial interests in foreign lands—they are poorly understood and often relegated to subordinate status in the diplomatic hierarchy. This chapter argues, first, that we should focus on consular offices and tasks as they have actually existed, rather than looking at them through a diplomacy lens. The diplomat handles overall differences between groups. The consul handles the practical measures that facilitate commercial and social interactions between strangers. Second, the chapter argues that this functional interaction does not depend on the existence of sovereign states or of an international state system but rather on the existence of economic activities that involve members of more than one particular group or polity. This difference between the consul and the diplomat is likely to increase in a globalizing world.

INTRODUCTION

Consuls and their equivalents in history have handled issues of trade, law, and politics for millennia, but in a more routine and less spectacular manner than diplomats, who have generally dealt in "high politics"—treaties, intrigues, war, and peace. The consul has not depended on the existence of a network of polities with reciprocal relations among themselves; on the contrary, consuls have often emerged where diplomatic relations for some reason or other have been impossible or simply unthinkable. Diplomats are always sent from one **polity** and received in another polity, they follow and are accredited to the sovereign or government of a receiving polity, and are thus to be found in recognized capital cities or with governments in exile. Consuls, on the other hand, follow trade and people and can in principle be found anywhere. Historically, they have often existed without an explicit sending polity. Intellectual interest in consuls has peaked when their tasks have been in flux, and room for innovation the greatest. The growing interest in consular tasks and affairs among practitioners and academics alike in recent decades must necessarily be understood in light of the challenges that **globalization** presents to principles of state sovereignty, in response to which consuls seem to be more favorably positioned than many diplomats.

Still, it is hard to conceptualize consuls outside of the framework of diplomacy, and even our attempt at giving them their due is colored by the inevitable comparisons. We begin with a detailed historical presentation, including the Vienna Convention on Consular Relations (1963). We then contrast consuls and diplomats, and conclude with an overview of the increasingly lively current debate about consular work.

KEY POINTS

- The consul is commonly understood as a sideshow to the diplomat, but as an institution the consul has performed a host of different tasks and has had a varied history: it is not the same as diplomacy.
- Interest in consular tasks tends to peak in periods of perceived change in the international system.
- Being more adaptable and less tied to the sovereignty principle than diplomats, consuls might be better positioned to handle future challenges.

DEFINITIONAL ISSUES

The logic of state **sovereignty**, and in particular the gradual application of territorial law from the fifteenth to the twentieth century, changed the workings of consuls in ways that make it hard to grasp presovereign consular activities. The fusing of the consular services with diplomatic services and ministries of foreign affairs over the last 100 years has, in the eyes of most, subordinated the consul to the diplomat. This is an understandable but ahistorical reading.

As late as 1957, when doing preparatory work for the codification of consular relations in international law, the special rapporteur of the International Law

Commission, Jaroslav Zourek (1957: 81), lamented that a "complete lack of uniformity is to be noted in the generic appellations of consular representatives abroad." And even after the establishment of the Vienna Convention on Consular Relations in 1963 (discussed in detail later), no less an authority on diplomacy than Ernest Satow (1979: 211) flatly stated that "there can be no precise and at the same time universally acceptable definition of the term." On the one hand, people with the title of consul have dealt with a staggeringly wide variety of tasks; on the other, people without such a title have engaged in activities that would be easily recognizable as consular. We have chosen to look beyond the strictly technical meaning of the term, so as to enable a discussion of instances outside of the historical and geographic core of consular activity, an investigation that will in turn cast light on the consul itself. At a minimum, the historically amorphous group under study here (consuls) represent the interests of persons in one way or another foreign to those of the receiving country, or polity, and their functions are in some way related to commerce. As we discuss in the conclusion, even this definition might prove too narrow in the near future, as consular functions are once again in the process of changing. Note that our definition requires a receiving (or host) polity, but that a sending polity is not necessary.

KEY POINTS

- It is virtually impossible to provide a comprehensive and precise definition of consuls and consular offices.
- A workable definition must at minimum include functions related to commerce.

EMERGENCE AND DEVELOPMENT OF
CONSULAR TASKS AND OFFICES

The very first examples of consul-like offices can be found in the first millennium BC. At that time there were "special judges for foreigners among some of the peoples of India" (Zourek 1957: 73). Several Greek institutions warrant attention. *Proxenia* (see box 9-1) marked an extension of the guest-friendships (*xenia*) of individuals to communities or their representatives. The *proxenos* was a citizen of the host (or receiving) polity who was most often appointed by the polity that he represented. Given the lack of a legal framework for noncitizens, the *proxenos* acted as legal representative of the foreigners that he represented, as well as serving as a commercial agent. He could also be used as a messenger and as a gatherer of intelligence. *Prostatai* acted as intermediaries between the polis and foreigners living in it and were chosen by the foreigners themselves (see box 9-1).

The Roman *praetor peregrinus* was a state official who was in charge of settling cases between citizens and *peregrines* (foreigners or pilgrims), as well as between *peregrines*, adjudicating according to the appropriate law. The *prostatai* and the *praetor peregrinus* are often considered precursors to later instances of **extraterritorial jurisdiction** associated with consuls, but it should be noted that the very concept of extraterritoriality made little sense, as no clear concept of territorial sovereignty existed at that time. Rather, the principle of the **personality of laws** applied (see Box 9-1). What law applied to a case was determined by the status of the subject(s)

BOX 9-1

Some Terms Associated with Consular Diplomacy

Alderman: a consul-like head of the establishments of the Hanseatic League.

Career consul: A consul who is part of a foreign service and is a citizen of the sending state.

Consular corps: the body of consular officers resident in one city.

Consular immunity: immunity related to the consular office, covering the physical office, consular correspondence, and acts committed as a consular officer.

Diplomatic corps: the body of all diplomats resident in one capital or organization.

Honorary consul: a consul who resides permanently in the receiving state, most often also a citizen of this state.

Personality of laws: the principle that law follows the person, according to place of birth or tie of allegiance, rather than territory of residence.

Praetor peregrinus: ancient Roman office, in charge of adjudication between citizens and noncitizens.

Prostatai: ancient Greek office that acted as the intermediary between the polity and groups of noncitizens living within it.

Proxenia: ancient Greek office with clear similarities to current consular offices, concerned with enabling trade between polities.

Shabandar: consul-like office in Malacca in the fourteenth and fifteenth centuries.

Telonarii: Judges in Germanic Spain, settling cases according to the law of the sea.

Territorial law: the principle that jurisdiction follows territory, closely tied to the principle of sovereignty.

Wakil al-tujjar: Arabic office closely resembling the early consuls from the eleventh and twelfth centuries onward.

---

in question, not the territory on which they happened to reside (Liu 1925). This principle is essential for understanding the development of the consul well into the modern age, as the judicial competencies of the consuls rested on it.

The title of consul, itself a relic of republican Rome where the consul was the highest elected office, was first applied to a number of different trade-related activities in the western Mediterranean (Ulbert 2006). Gradually the terms merged, and consul became the title applied to the leader and magistrate of a colony of compatriots in a foreign polity. According to Jörg Ulbert (2006: 12), the first such usage of the term hails from the year AD 1117.

Practice predated theory. The colonies of foreigners in Constantinople had their own special magistrates from at least the ninth and tenth centuries. Italian port cities made treaties with both the Byzantine Empire and the Muslim rulers of the eastern Mediterranean. From the twelfth century onward, these magistrates were known as consuls, a title imported from the western Mediterranean. Whereas the sending polities usually elected the first consuls, as the colonies of expatriates grew, they would tend to elect their own consuls.

The European consuls of the eastern Mediterranean were gradually granted both criminal and civil jurisdiction over their compatriots, and ultimately jurisdiction also in cases where compatriots were involved in regular civil and criminal cases in the receiving polity. In the final centuries of the Ottoman Empire, consuls became virtually independent of local authorities. The practice of granting internal jurisdiction to groups of foreign merchants can be dated in Asian sources at least from the eighth century onward. In addition, in the Muslim world, the office of *wakil al-tujjar*, in existence since at least the twelfth century (see box 9-1), was quite similar to the consular office as it developed in the western Mediterranean. To the Muslim polities, the early consuls were useful in keeping the peace and settling disputes inside the trading communities. From a Muslim perspective, the privileges were granted unilaterally and could be revoked at any time (see box 9-2).

Extensive long-distance trade requires mechanisms for reducing transaction costs and information deficits, and consular offices provide just that. We find relatively similar institutions also outside of the Mediterranean, like the **shabandar** in Malacca in the fourteenth and fifteenth centuries, or the **aldermen** of the Hanseatic League in northern Europe from the thirteenth century onward (see box 9-1).

BOX 9-2

Capitulations (Ottoman-European, Seventeenth Century)

The Ottoman Turks considered the sending of envoys a mark of submission. Consequently, they followed the Islamic practice vis-à-vis tribute entities called *amān* when establishing peaceful relations not only with Islamic polities like Persia but also with European states. *Amān*, roughly "safety" or "security," meant that you were under somebody's protection. If the initial contacts went well, the next step for the Porte, as the Ottomans were often referred to, was to grant an *ahdname*. *Ahdname* (from Arabic, *ahd*, "treaty," and Persian *name*, "writ"), translated into English as "capitulations" (from Lat. *Capitula*, "chapter heading") or "covenant-letters," were granted to merchants for a year at a time by the sultans, who saw them as acts of condescension, and gave merchants the right to trade without having to pay taxes. These concessions were seen by European trading states as treaties but by the Muslim rulers as edicts. Muslim sovereigns in North Africa, Egypt, Turkey, Iran, and elsewhere granted them. These sovereigns granted capitulations to facilitate trade. Note that rights could also be granted, as when, in the 1660s, the head of the Ottoman Turks, the Sublime Porte, issued an order which stated that "the consul could not be arrested for interrogation, imprisoned, or dismissed from office; his house could not be searched or sealed up; his clothing, victuals, and other domestic supplies could be imported free of duties; lawsuits in which he was involved had to go straight to the supreme court" (S. P. Anderson 1989: 95). Capitulations were often rescinded in times of war. This made for complications, for Western powers tended to understand this as persecution of consuls, whereas to the Muslim rulers it was simply a question of taking back privileges unilaterally granted.

The autonomy of the consul, acting as the primus inter pares and judicial head of a community of merchants, came under pressure from both sending and receiving polities as states grew stronger in the seventeenth century. With a growing interest in their populations more generally in the sending states, consuls were given an increased responsibility for, and control over, compatriots in foreign ports and clearer responsibilities for the general interest of the polity. Consuls were also increasingly tasked with gathering all sorts of political and mercantile intelligence. Finally, consular positions were also attractive as positions of patronage.

The consul's emerging role as servant of the sovereign state became clearer with the publication of the first actual consular regulations, issued by Jean-Baptiste Colbert, France's secretary of state of the navy, in 1681. These regulations were soon followed by the first official instructions to French consuls in 1690. The networks of consuls also grew, fueled mainly by war and the expansion of long-distance and bulk trade. New markets were opened, and **mercantilist** states were increasingly willing to support the trade promotion and expansion of their own citizens. In states where there had been no tradition of consuls, consular and diplomatic representation was intermingled in the early years. And even where the consular and diplomatic functions were formally separated, as in Sweden, there was often no corresponding separation in representation until the middle of the eighteenth century (Müller 2004). As the rule of law was expanded to include consuls in foreign ports, a distinction was established between what anachronistically could be called "career consuls" (citizens of the sending polity dispatched by and from that polity) and "honorary consuls" (citizens of any polity but usually of the receiving one). In the latter case, consular offices tended to become semihereditary and status markers in the ports of the receiving polity.

Sending states tried to increase control over their subjects abroad through codifying the judicial powers of the consuls. Receiving states correspondingly tried to rein in the very same power to ensure their territorial sovereignty. Accordingly, during the seventeenth century, consuls lost many of the **immunities and privileges** they had enjoyed until then, and opinion against them generally grew more hostile. Nevertheless, in many instances they retained legal power over their own compatriots in the receiving state well into the nineteenth century. The move from the principle of the personality of the law (where the law followed the person, regardless of territory) to **territorial law** (associated with the sovereign state) was gradual and uneven (see box 9-1).

As the consul's judicial functions declined in importance during the seventeenth and eighteenth centuries, consuls were, in principle, supposed to take care of the commercial interests of the sending state and its merchants. Nevertheless, exceptions to this rule were relatively common. The most systematic exception can be found in the "Barbary States" (roughly present-day Morocco, Algeria, Tunisia, and Libya), where the consuls were considered to be more similar to diplomats than the run-of-the-mill consul elsewhere. These representatives could not be given the title of ambassador, given that the Barbary States were formally **vassals** of the Ottoman Empire and so not authorized to appoint or receive diplomats. That was the prerogative of courts that were considered fully sovereign. A roughly parallel situation could be found in the many nineteenth-century European capitals of **suzerain** political entities, like Belgrade, Bucharest, and Christiania. Similarly, when the expanding colonial empires desired to bestow some title on the explorers that were expanding colonial possessions, a consular one was often applied. In short, where diplomatic representation could not be established, consular representation was given political content.

These exceptions aside, the nineteenth century also saw the first establishment of actual "consular services," dedicated to the promotion of trade and the protection of the interests of compatriots abroad (Platt 1971). In many areas of the world these compatriots were first and foremost the sailors of merchant navies, but with increasing mass migration to the Americas and Australia, consuls were also involved with a number of other compatriots. The actual level and form of organization differed greatly between the states and related to where the consuls would be placed. The consuls to China and North Africa, for example, generally held higher status and received a higher salary than consuls to less remote places. Paradoxically, in a century when many diplomatic services and ministries of foreign affairs were contracting in size, the consular services were growing very rapidly. This was largely a result of the growing mobility of people and goods, but the liberal ideology of the time also mattered. To many liberals in the American revolutionary tradition and the Manchester liberals of England, diplomacy equaled nobility equaled war, while consuls equaled merchants equaled peace. When states such as the United States and Norway, both with substantial trade and shipping and strong liberal traditions, but with no prior experience of having their own diplomacy, gained independence, consular services were the preferred tools for interaction with the world. Norway, which has had one of the largest merchant marines in the world, would eventually reach a maximum of somewhere between 700 and 800 **consulates** abroad, among which roughly 25 were staffed from home, and the rest honorary, staffed mostly by nationals of the receiving states.

For the consul, the twentieth century was marked by greater standardization, in particular through the Vienna Convention on Consular Relations. Like its more well-known twin, the Vienna Convention on Diplomatic Relations (1961), it was the result of deliberations initiated within the United Nations. In the aftermath of the Second World War, the International Law Commission (ILC) started its work on the further development and codification of international law in 1949. Preparatory work was initiated in the mid-1950s. The work on diplomatic intercourse could draw on earlier codifications of diplomacy at the congresses of Vienna and Aix-la-Chapelle (in 1815 and 1818, respectively), and the discussions largely centered on proposed articles. The work on consular intercourse, on the other hand, also included a substantial discussion about its history and the varied sources of law associated with it. At roughly the time when diplomatic procedures were first being codified, British consuls in 1825 were still seen as no more than "a group of individual state servants overseas, whose only common denominator was the name of consul" (Platt 1971: 13), and the ILC thus had to establish a baseline of common understanding before any legal articles could be drafted.

As was to be expected given the relative status of diplomats and consuls, much of the work on the consular convention, particularly regarding nomenclature, was derived from the Convention on Diplomatic Relations. The rights it ascribes to consuls and honorary consuls shadow diplomatic rights, but they are not as extensive. The receiving state does not have the right to enter a consulate or interfere with its communications with the sending state. Consuls have "consular immunity," which means that, unlike diplomats, they are immune only against those acts that they have executed as part of their job as consuls. They may be tried in court cases and called as witnesses in other cases. Unlike **diplomatic immunity**, furthermore, consular immunity does not extend to family members. If the receiving state considers a consul to have misbehaved, he or she may be declared unwanted (*persona non grata*) and is expelled from the country. The convention's seventy-nine articles give a comprehensive overview of what consular work entails today (for the full text, see United Nations 2005).

In addition to the standardization provided by the Convention on Consular Relations, the subordination of consular activities to diplomacy was further formalized through the fusion of consular services, diplomatic services, and ministries of foreign affairs to unitary foreign services. Thus, the distinctiveness of professional consular services was lost, as the consulates that were staffed from home were filled with trained diplomats. Although many foreign services underwent reforms aimed at increasing the consular component of diplomacy, consular posts would tend to be viewed with disdain by career-minded diplomats. The functions of consuls were also gradually changing. The reduction of manpower needed onboard most ships reduced the need for consuls in the ports of the world. Improvements in global communications made the consuls less important as information gatherers but have increased their judicial workload, for example, where matters of custody are concerned.

KEY POINTS

- Consuls under that name emerged in the Mediterranean in the first centuries of the second millennium.
- Consul-like offices have emerged in connection with long-distance trade in a number of places.
- Consuls have helped reduce transaction costs and information deficits.
- Until the establishment of territorial jurisdiction from the seventeenth century onward, a key consular function was the meting out of justice within a community of merchants.
- With the gradual expansion and adoption of the sovereignty principle, consuls increasingly have dealt with issues of trade, but consuls have overall had a very varied set of functions.
- Unlike diplomacy, there was no common preestablished understanding of what consuls were when consular relations were to be codified.
- In the Vienna Convention on Consular Relations, consuls are given rights akin to the rights of diplomats but tied to the office, not the holder and his or her family.

THE CONSUL AND THE DIPLOMAT

Being in many ways less spectacular than the diplomats, there have never been any guides for action written specifically for consuls, like the works of François de Callières or Ernest Satow. This is not to say that consular activities have passed unnoticed, but writers have had a hard time figuring out the character of the consuls and their activities. To thinkers approaching the world through the lens of territorial sovereignty, the sometimes feudal aspects of consular practice were an anomaly. In his work on the functions of ambassadors published in 1681, Abraham de Wicquefort, diplomat and writer of one of the most influential manuals for diplomats, treated the consuls as "but merchants" and denied them extraterritorial rights, although they were still allowed to adjudicate between their compatriots. Wicquefort, however, contradicted himself by reporting that states treated acts of violence against consuls as "a breach of international law" (quoted in Zourek 1960: 3–4). Cornelius van Bynkershoek, an eighteenth-century legal theorist, best known for his work on the law of the seas and public law, followed Wicquefort, and their statements had a major influence on later court decisions. The seventeenth and early eighteenth centuries were a low tide for consular status, in international law treatises as well as in the known instances of case law. A change followed with Emerich de Vattel, one of the key eighteenth-century theorists of international law, who argued that since the consuls were appointed by a sovereign and accepted in that capacity by another sovereign, they were to some extent protected by international law. Over the course of the following centuries, this position became codified in case law as well as treaties and conventions, and finally in the Vienna Convention on Consular Relations.

Even if the juridical status of consuls was gradually established, writers still had difficulty pinning down their function and tended to view consuls through a diplomacy lens. Works on diplomacy treat consuls in one of three ways. The first is not to mention them at all—M. S. Anderson's (1993) celebrated account is a key example of this. The second way is to see them as precursors of diplomacy. Garrett Mattingly's (1955) standard account of early modern diplomacy is an example of this view: he mentions the Italian consuls in the Levant as one of the main precursors of resident embassies, and thus diplomacy as such. Also in this category, James Der Derian (1987) discusses the activities of merchants and the problems for permanent diplomacy stemming from the *droit d'aubaine* (a rule whereby the property of deceased foreigners was confiscated by the sovereign, excluding rightful heirs) under the rubric of "proto-diplomacy," but he never mentions consuls explicitly. A third approach is to see the diplomat and the consul as evolving in close parallel. Keith Hamilton and Richard Langhorne (1995) exemplify this approach. To the extent that these authors consider consuls at all, they are seen as a precursor to diplomacy. Given their perceived status as the diplomats' sidekick, consuls are also largely omitted from national histories of foreign affairs. When mentioned, attention is paid to one's national consuls overseas, not to foreign consuls residing on the polity's own soil.

While reading the history backward creates a picture of the consul as the diplomat's neglected subordinate, who is gradually integrated into a diplomacy-oriented national foreign service, as we have tried to demonstrate here, reading the history of the consul forward creates a more nuanced picture. Our argument is that consul-like offices are not logically necessarily dependent on the existence of sovereign states or on an international state system. The precondition for their emergence is not any particular form of polity but simply the existence of economic activities that involve members of more than one particular group or polity. Thus, the history of the consul, narrowly conceived, should be interpreted separately from the history of the diplomat, the exception being modern career consuls who are usually diplomats who happen to spend time at a consular post.

Whereas the diplomat handles overall differences between groups through their representatives, the consul handles the practical measures that facilitate commercial and social interactions between strangers (cf. Sharp 2009: 10). Diplomats interact over time and build up an entire **diplomatic culture**. Consuls, whose interaction is more intermittent, do not. When certain consuls in certain places at certain times have indeed been engaged in mediating cases of **estrangement,** or alienation, as were the Western consuls to the Barbary States, this happened in an ad hoc manner and did not lead to the same degree of institutionalization as in the case of the "diplomatic corps," that is, the body of all diplomats resident at one court, later also in one international organization. **Consular corps** in noncapitals exist as well, but their history is newer and their interaction not so dense (see box 9-1). When cultural differences were great, one can assume that consuls were key negotiators in making foreign practices intelligible for the sending polity. Still, when local merchants became consul for a foreign state with which they traded extensively, they usually retained their own culture, albeit with special knowledge of a different culture. Merchants who settled permanently in foreign countries or career consuls who spent their entire career in one post may be said to have become "bicultural." In either case, these cultural skills did not include mastery of an extensive and generalized set of models for how things ought to be done that added up to a specific way of "being-in-the-world" that would be instantly recognizable by other consuls. To date, no such thing as a consular culture exists, unlike, as just mentioned, a diplomatic culture identified by several writers (for example, Bull 2002; Der Derian 1996; Neumann 2010; Wiseman 2005). Consuls do not mediate in cases of estrangement beyond what is needed to be done in order to clinch the deal at hand; they have not been engaged in overcoming systemic alienation. Estrangement, however, has rarely prevented trade. When considering the wide variety of tasks in which consuls have been engaged, their overall approach could better be summarized as the mediation of distance, particularly geographic distance, but also social and cultural distance, as well as the distance created by practical complications. Whereas diplomatic activity tends to be more important for the messages it sends than for what it actually does, what consuls do is often an end in itself.

Although consuls may arguably have a longer history than do diplomats—the functions described elsewhere in this book (see Cohen, chapter 1 in this volume) pertaining to Amarna and ancient Greek interactions thousands of years ago are more reminiscent of consular than of diplomatic functions—consuls have indeed been seen as the poor cousins of ambassadors and ministers. Small wonder that one of the key works on consuls, D. C. M. Platt's (1971) study of the British consuls, carries the title *The Cinderella Service*. Nevertheless, consuls in many ways transcend diplomacy. Consular offices were established well before diplomatic services, and so their history cannot be reduced to the history of the diplomat. The multifaceted, ever-changing, and multiple functions of consuls—incorporating at various times extraterritorial jurisdiction, political intrigue in autonomous provinces, and support services for privateering—serve to undermine the once prevalent understanding of a distinct separation between domestic and foreign policy that allegedly stemmed from the peace treaties of Westphalia. It is this quality of being both inside and outside, but not dependent on sovereignty, that has led to renewed scholarly interest in consuls over the last decades. Interest in consuls and their history and functions has traditionally peaked in periods when the international society was seen to be in upheaval; when consuls could be considered agents of changes or harbingers of a time to come. As noted earlier, the first histories of the consul were written during the Napoleonic Wars. A new wave of historical interest and functional analysis took place in the interwar years of the twentieth century, when Pitman Potter (1926: 288), for example, argued that consuls might "expect to rise to heights of power not previously equaled and to rival his colleague the diplomat, if not actually to surpass him, in importance and prestige." Currently, consuls are yet again attracting some of the spotlight.

KEY POINTS

- Consuls have been poorly understood in the literature on international law and diplomacy.
- Consuls, unlike diplomats, are not dependent on sovereign states and a state system.
- There is no consular culture; the activities of consuls are functional rather than cultural.

THE CONSUL TODAY

The commercial functions of the consul have changed in recent decades, although consuls are still engaged in the promotion of trade and the provision of commercially relevant information. As new centers of manufacture and trade emerge, states, in particular small and medium-sized ones, continue to use consuls as a cost-efficient way of promoting trade and investment. This is particularly so in emerging regional hubs that are far from the capitals where embassies are located (Stringer 2011). However, consuls have increasingly also been charged with tasks of a more legal or juridical nature. Several trends have contributed to this, chief among them being the increased mobility of people and the continuing belief (at least in the Western world) that the state has a responsibility for its citizens abroad (see Hocking, chapter 7 in this volume). Ever-increasing mass tourism and travel implies that regular consular assistance (like providing safe-travel advisories and reissuing passports) takes more and more time.

Ministries of foreign affairs increasingly have to guide and aid their own citizens before, during, and after their travels abroad, while preparing for the very real possibility of mass evacuations following natural disasters, political turmoil, or war (see box 9-3). Still, consular stations and honorary consuls are often the most visible "face" of a country abroad, handling visa applications, educational and cultural exchanges, promotion of tourism, and a number of other **public diplomacy** issues. Large-scale migration of wealthy, elderly people increases the demand for consular support in countries with a stable, warm climate, while mass migration to the West in general has led to an explosion in demands for visa and other documentation services. Different forms of crime also lead to the growing need for consular assistance. Child abduction and forced marriages are examples of this, as is the steadily growing number of foreigners in the world's prisons. These trends, combined with ever-increasing media attention, have led to a partial breakdown of the boundary

---

BOX 9-3

The Floodlight of Modern Consular Problems

The earliest meaning of the word "nation" is a group of people hailing from the same place but living somewhere else. It could be a group of students, or it could be a group of merchants. Among the consular functions, taking care of compatriots has always loomed large, but it has taken different forms, depending, among other things, on who those compatriots were. In the nineteenth century, they were usually merchants, sailors, and travelers of independent means. With the explosion in the number of travelers and the introduction of the passport in the late nineteenth century, taking care of stranded emigrants and travelers took up more time. With the introduction of mass tourism in the 1960s, followed by the phenomenon of globalization, the number of people to take care of increased exponentially. Annual international tourist arrivals alone have grown from around 25 million in 1950 to around 940 million today. To this phenomenon must be added that of awareness about rights, which means that people who are out traveling and have a problem increasingly demand that consuls should help them. There are expatriates, and even locals, who phone the British consular service to have the recipe for Christmas pudding. But then there are those in serious trouble: people who have had spouses crossing borders with their common offspring, people who have been arrested and do not understand either the legal situation they have landed in or the language in which it is being conducted, journalists who are being abducted by armed groups. In Norway's case, for example, a number of Norwegian newspapers carried front-page stories in 2010 and 2011 about two Norwegians jailed and eventually sentenced to death in the Democratic Republic of the Congo. Such cases invariably lead to media attention; the premise of a countryman in trouble abroad can fuel nationalism and certainly sells newspapers. A number of northern European services were awakened to the enormity of this task during Christmas 2004, when tsunamis hit areas of mass tourism in, among other places, Thailand and Indonesia. The ensuing deaths and chaos quickly proved consular capacity inadequate. More than 2,000 tourists perished, with Sweden and Germany losing more than 500 each. More important, a much higher number of people were initially reported missing, and even higher numbers were left completely stranded. The Scandinavian countries alone had an estimated 30,000 to 40,000 tourists in the affected area. As the crisis subsided, various public inquiries asked the question of what it meant to run a consular service under conditions of globalization. What may a traveler reasonably expect in terms of services, and what should be left to other social institutions, such as insurance companies, travel operators, and police forces? Such debates are about to transform the face of the world's consul services yet again.

between consular and diplomatic tasks (Okano-Heijmans 2011a). This boundary is also blurred by the persistence of consulates carrying out activities that come close to traditional diplomacy, for instance, in capitals of autonomous regions.

The changes in functions are mirrored by a change in personnel. A century ago, the honorary consul would typically be a merchant or a shipowner, someone with a special knowledge of the commercial world. Today, lawyers would seem to be as common as businesspeople. This change may be read as an indication of the growing importance of law in postmodern society, but also of the maturity and complexity of the global economy. In earlier times, one primarily needed consuls who knew how to have goods physically moved from one place to another, whereas the current economy primarily rewards people who know the legalities of transfer. The change also reflects the changing patterns of interaction described earlier, where the focus has shifted from the mobility of goods to the mobility of people. Although both sending and receiving states have only approximate numbers and data, the number of honorary consuls seems to be on the increase (cf. Stringer 2011).

A focus on the challenges of dealing with ordinary citizens traveling abroad and providing them with assistance has the potential to increase the domestic standing of diplomats and consuls alike (see box 9-4). However, as expectations have been rising, foreign services are also vulnerable to the charge of not doing enough to help compatriots abroad. Ministries of foreign affairs thus find themselves in the unenviable position of having to engage in a careful balancing act of public affairs, educating the public about the dangers of going abroad and the limits to the assistance that can be expected, while not insulting foreign governments or giving the citizens the impression that they are on their own (cf. Maley 2011). Furthermore, the sheer amount of consular work presents a serious drain on the resources of foreign services. One solution, clearly visible in the consular affairs of countries of the European Union, is to cooperate on consular tasks (Fernández 2011; Wesseling and Boniface 2011).

The possibility of damaging bilateral relations, through negative travel advisories or engagement in thorny criminal cases, as well as the increasing general workload of consuls, has led to suggestions that everyone would be better off if consular services or part of them were outsourced. Several countries have already outsourced all or part of their visa-related activities in foreign countries. While the case can certainly be made for outsourcing both visa work and travel advice (cf. Maley 2011), it should also be noted that honorary consuls represent a long-standing form of outsourcing, and a cheap one at that.

BOX 9-4

The View of the British Foreign and Commonwealth Office

" 'Consular work is our principal shop-front to the British public. The media care far more about a British citizen overseas than about diplomatic relations and treaties.' (Foresight Report, Foreign Office, January 2000)" (quoted in Dickie 2008: xi).

KEY POINTS

- With increasing global mobility, there is a shift of emphasis in consular work from the mercantile to the legal.
- Consequently, more and more consuls have some legal expertise.
- Taking care of citizens abroad increases the domestic standing not only of a state's consular service but of its diplomats, too.
- The increased workload is beginning to lead to outsourcing, a trend that could eventually sever the consular service from the diplomatic one.

CONCLUSION

We have argued that what are today called consular functions stretch at least as far back as 4,000 years ago, when we find institutionalized attempts to promote and protect trade. The modern consular office began to evolve in the eastern Mediterranean during the High Middle Ages. Subsequently, beginning in the middle to late seventeenth century and culminating in the early nineteenth century, the principle of sovereignty associated with the territorial state system changed consular offices from focusing mainly on order within a community of merchants to focusing on representing the merchant's state of origin to the receiving state. This consular extraterritorial jurisdiction over compatriots could still be found in parts of Europe well into the nineteenth century, and consuls could still carry out political and diplomatic tasks. Because diplomats increasingly carried out these latter tasks, however, the consul became subordinate to the diplomat. Then, in the early twentieth century, states began to merge the two services—the diplomatic service and the consular service—with the home-based ministry of foreign affairs and a united foreign service. No matter how small a country's diplomatic representation abroad, a consul is almost always present.

Consuls may yet have their historical revenge on diplomats who, as we argued, have for so long regarded consuls as the poor cousins of the diplomatic world. Consuls or consul-like persons have conducted and will continue to conduct diplomatic tasks, in times of crisis and war, and outside of state capitals. In a world where a growing number of people are involved in transnational movement, diplomats, who specialize in representing polities, are worried about their role and relevance. Consuls, on the other hand, can rest assured that there will always be a need for people who can manage the practical tasks associated with movements that span more than one political unit.

QUESTIONS

1. Why have consul-like offices emerged?
2. What are the key differences between consuls and diplomats?
3. Why are consular tasks so much debated now, when previously academics largely ignored the subject and practitioners avoided consular postings abroad?

4. What are the implications of changes in consular affairs for the practical concept of consular diplomacy?
5. What are the roles of consuls in the contemporary era compared with the past?
6. What was and is the status of the consul in international law?
7. Why is the scope of foreign ministries' responsibilities to nationals abroad expanding at a time when sovereignty is said to be in decline?
8. Do recent trends suggest that foreign ministries are acquiring a domestic constituency within civil society?
9. What are the implications of the analysis in this chapter for your theoretical and practical understandings of contemporary diplomacy?

CHAPTER 10

Bilateral and Multilateral Diplomacy in Normal Times and in Crises

Thomas Wright

CHAPTER CONTENTS

- Introduction
- Distinguishing bilateralism and multilateralism
- Distinguishing between forms of multilateralism
- Understanding the contemporary international order
- The challenge of a power transition
- Conclusion

READER'S GUIDE

This chapter discusses bilateral and multilateral diplomatic strategies in contemporary international relations. It explores the differences between bilateralism and multilateralism, outlines different types of multilateralism, shows how both feature in the international order, and looks at the effect of two ongoing crises on the future of diplomacy and global cooperation. Bilateralism and multilateralism will remain central features of international relations, although states are likely to gravitate toward smaller, minilateral groupings of the like-minded.

INTRODUCTION

One of the great recurring debates of American diplomacy has to do with the relative merits of multilateralism and unilateralism. Advocates of multilateralism stress this method's **legitimacy** and capacity to increase international cooperation. Its detractors argue that multilateralism constrains American power and reduces international action to the lowest common denominator, which can often result in ineffectiveness in the face of severe threats and challenges. Yet this formulation can obscure more than it explains. After all, unilateral diplomacy is something of an oxymoron, given that a state cannot conduct a foreign policy without dealing with others. States rarely have the option of solving problems and advancing their interests without negotiating and managing relations with other governments (see Zartman, chapter 6 in this volume). When thinking about the form that diplomacy can take, it is more useful to distinguish between bilateralism and multilateralism. Nominally, the difference between the two is managing relations with other states on an individual basis (bilateralism) or in groups of three or more (multilateralism). However, multilateralism also has a qualitative aspect whereby states agree to cooperate according to certain principles or norms.

Bilateral and multilateral diplomatic structures are deeply embedded in the contemporary international order, with most dating back to the early post–Second World War period. But there is mounting concern that these structures are inadequate to the challenges states face in the twenty-first century. International politics in Asia relies primarily upon bilateral structures, and the absence of advanced multilateral organizations is seen as an impediment to cooperation to tackle shared problems. At a global level there is no shortage of multilateral institutions, but there is concern that these forums are unable to deal with modern-day crises, are too inclusive of diverse sets of interests, and may result in gridlock if governments cannot agree on a path forward. In Europe, the process of European integration is facing its most severe challenge yet as the international financial crisis created solvency crises in a number of the member states of the Eurozone, opened up a rift between the core and the periphery, and raised existential questions about the future of the single currency (see Bátora and Hardacre, chapter 17 in this volume). There is also a long-term challenge—the rise of China and other powers may jeopardize the legitimacy of institutions that were built to reflect the balance of power in the late 1940s (see Ye and Zhang, chapter 16 in this volume). Despite all these problems in bilateral and multilateral diplomacy, the interdependent nature of world politics requires cooperation.

Consequently, there are two issues deserving of further analysis. The first is the need to explain the differences between the bilateral and multilateral methods of diplomacy, including the conditions under which each approach is best applied. The second is to understand the character and impact of the contemporary crisis of bilateral and multilateral structures, including how bilateral and multilateral diplomacy have fared in tackling transnational threats and challenges. This chapter addresses both issues and in doing so sheds light upon several important questions about diplomacy and the contemporary international order. For instance, does it make a significant difference if a government pursues a bilateral or multilateral approach to a particular problem or issue? Are there just two choices, or are there more than two? Is the international order primarily characterized by one type of diplomacy or another? And, how are these diplomatic methods likely to be used to reduce the spread of nuclear weapons, tackle climate change, and restore the global economy to good health?

The focus of this chapter is on state-to-state relations, although it is important to recognize that the past decade has seen the emergence of new actors that are beginning to change the face of traditional diplomacy. International networks of government officials, from public health to central banks, play an increasingly influential role in generating cooperation between states (Slaughter 2004). Non-state actors are also involved in world politics for good (for example, the Gates Foundation now has a greater budget than the World Health Organization [WHO]) and for ill (transnational terror networks). This has led to studies on new dimensions of diplomacy, characterized by Geoffrey Wiseman (2010) as "polylateral diplomacy."

KEY POINTS

- Bilateralism is the management of relations between two states. Multilateralism is the management of relations between three or more states according to a set of principles.
- The international order has bilateral and multilateral features, most of which date back at least to the early post–Second World War period.
- Bilateral and multilateral structures are facing a number of contemporary challenges, including the shifting distribution of power and the emergence of transnational threats.

DISTINGUISHING BILATERALISM AND MULTILATERALISM

The nominal difference between bilateralism and multilateralism is that bilateralism involves relations between two actors whereas multilateralism means relations between three or more. But the tally of allies and partners only scratches the surface of a multilayered policy question. As understood in the literature, there is a qualitative difference between bilateralism and multilateralism in addition to the numerical distinction, and in many ways it is the qualitative difference that is the more important of the two. Bilateralism is a value-free concept. It can include the 1939 Molotov-Ribbentrop Pact to divide up Poland as well as the post–Second World War US-Japan alliance to preserve the peace in northeast Asia. For the most part, the substance and output of bilateral diplomacy are likely to be driven by the relative power between the two parties and, by extension, by the interests of the stronger party.

Multilateralism, by contrast, organizes relations between three or more states along a set of basic principles that lay out certain expectations of behavior that all parties must agree to and abide by, including the strongest party. Discussing the post–Second World War period in which most universal institutions developed, Miles Kahler (1992: 681) notes:

> Smaller, weaker states were believed to be disadvantaged by bilateralism; nondiscrimination awarded them advantages that had been denied them in the world of the 1930s. In their formal institutional designs at least, most postwar multilateral institutions incorporated a larger role in decision making for states that were not great powers and could not aspire to be.

This qualitative aspect is the key distinction between bilateralism and multilateralism (see box 10-1). Thus multilateralism can be defined as the management of relations between three or more parties according to a set of principles and entailing some reduction in the autonomy of all the parties, including the more powerful states (Ikenberry 2003: 534).

BOX 10-1

John Ruggie on Multilateralism

The sufficient condition concerns the principles on the basis of which relations are organized among those parties. In its pure form, a multilateral order embodies rules of conduct that are commonly applicable to countries, as opposed to discriminating among them, based on situational exigencies or particularistic preferences. Therefore, such an order entails a greater degree of indivisibility among the declared interests of countries than its alternative forms, making it easier to pursue those interests through joint action. And it permits each country to calculate its gains and losses from international transactions in the aggregate, across a broad array of relations and partners, as opposed to requiring case-by-case reciprocity. (Ruggie 1994: 556)

To understand what this means in practice, consider the application of the bilateral and multilateral models to trade and security arrangements. In the case of trade, bilateralism is inherently discriminatory, which is to say that a state will try to cut the best deal it can with other states on an individual and ad hoc basis. At one end of the spectrum, an asymmetry in power can result in dramatic asymmetries in the benefits accrued from trade relations. In colonial relations, as Albert O. Hirschman (1945: 13) observed, "An initial power supremacy enables the imperial power to shape the direction and composition of the colony's trade, and the trade relations which are thus established in turn strengthen markedly the original power position held by the imperial power." More commonly in today's world, in bilateral trade relations between states, each state will make use of any leverage it has to get the best deal possible. If the trade agreement is between a large and a small state, the large state may take advantage of the fact that the small state is dependent on its markets to cut a better deal than it would seek with another state closer to its size. By contrast, multilateral trade agreements are nondiscriminatory in the sense that what is offered to one member of an agreement must be offered to all members. This is what is known as the **most favored nation** clause. The most favored nation clause is a key component of the WTO and before that the General Agreement on Tariffs and Trade (GATT). One of its effects is to prevent powerful states from exploiting their size and economic strength vis-à-vis smaller partners.

With respect to national security, bilateralism refers to traditional alliances that are designed with a named enemy state in mind. The purpose of this alliance can be *defensive* or *offensive*—for instance, it includes the defensive alliance between Great Britain and Belgium, as well as the offensive alliance between Germany and Italy of the interwar period (1919–39). By contrast, a multilateral security agreement is based on the concept of **collective security**, which seeks to defend against a threat from wherever it emanates. The concept of collective security underpins the United Nations (UN) but also the North Atlantic Treaty Organization (NATO), which survived the end of the Cold War and is perceived as a means of guaranteeing peace and security in Europe by dissuading any actor from attempting to aggressively revise the international order.

Collective security is not exclusive to the post–Second World War era. Perhaps the most celebrated example of collective security was the **Concert of Europe**, created after the Napoleonic Wars to maintain peace in Europe. In that case, Europe's five leading powers—Austria, France, Great Britain, Prussia, and Russia—came together to protect and preserve the postwar order. They agreed to moderate their behavior and ambition, not to seek to exploit the weakness of their allies or to vie for a temporary advantage, and not to use military force to advance their interests. The Concert of Europe was not as institutionalized as post–Second World War multilateral arrangements, but it stands apart as an example of cooperation between large states based on a set of principles and norms.

This gives rise to a puzzle. If there is a key qualitative difference between bilateralism and multilateralism, why would a major democracy seek a bilateral alliance or extensive bilateral ties with another state instead of cooperating with it in a multilateral setting? Part of the answer lies in the difficulty of negotiating a multilateral agreement. However, there is also a compelling incentive for bilateral arrangements— it can offer the stronger state a means to control and shape the development of the weaker state. As Victor Cha (2009/10: 158) has put it, a bilateral alliance allows the larger state to execute a "powerplay" over its smaller ally, which Cha defines as "the construction of an asymmetric alliance designed to exert maximum control over the smaller ally's actions." An asymmetric bilateral alliance enables the larger state to ensure that the smaller state is economically, politically, and militarily dependent upon it, which can serve as a risk control measure.

Dependency can have two functions. First, it can be used to transform the weaker ally in accordance with the interests and wishes of the larger state, as in the transformation of postwar Japan into a democracy (for example, Berger 2003). In the aftermath of the 1945 American victory in the Pacific, the United States needed a strong partner in East Asia, but there was much concern over the potentially destabilizing effects of a revitalized Japan. Securely binding Japan to the United States mitigated this risk. Second, dependency enables the stronger state to constrain the weaker state from undesirable external actions, such as belligerent behavior that may result in a conflict with its neighbors. The degree of control in a bilateral alliance is much stronger than in a multilateral setting, where the power and influence of the dominant state are diluted by the presence of other allies and rules that deliberately lessen its coercive power. The case of the post–Second World War US alliances in Asia is a relatively benign example of bilateralism in action (for example, Tow 1991). It can also take a more coercive and zero-sum character, whether in the form of imperialism or with a totalitarian hegemonic power such as Nazi Germany or Soviet Russia.

In contemporary international politics, the greatest strength of bilateral arrangements is their propensity toward **risk reduction**. They offer stricter control over the actions of prospective partners and greater probability for reciprocal benefits. But, in dampening risk—cutting the probabilities of significantly damaging contingencies—the state forgoes potential higher-order gains that could be achieved through multilateral mechanisms. Bilateral organizations do not offer the same potential for **trust- and confidence-building** between disparate groups. The European Union (EU) is an example of a multilateral institution that enabled its members to trust each other over time, through repeated interactions and transparency along with the security guarantee offered by the United States through NATO. Reliance on bilateral mechanisms, as has been the case in Asia, means that a framework to build trust and cooperation regionally is only slowly emerging.

KEY POINTS

- Bilateral relations reflect the distribution of power between the parties whereas multilateral relations operate according to a set of principles or norms.
- More so than in multilateral arrangements, bilateralism can offer the stronger state a means to controlling and shaping the development of the weaker state.
- Multilateral trade agreements include the most favored nation clause that guarantees the same benefits to all parties to the agreement.
- Multilateral security agreements generally take the form of collective security whereas bilateral alliances are designed with a particular opponent in mind.
- Sometimes multilateral security agreements have a named opponent, but they are also much more likely to include additional collective security features.

DISTINGUISHING BETWEEN FORMS OF MULTILATERALISM

Even with characteristics identified in the previous section, multilateralism remains an amorphous concept, covering everything from the UN to the smaller groups of nations seeking to address specific problems, for example, the Proliferation Security Initiative, which is a grouping of like-minded nations seeking to disrupt trade in materials for nuclear proliferation. Today, decision makers do not just choose between bilateralism and multilateralism; they also choose between different forms of multilateralism. This section distinguishes between four types of multilateral structures: universal multilateralism, regional multilateralism, values-based multilateralism, and minilateralism.

Universal Multilateralism

Universal multilateralism refers to organizations and institutions that are open to all states regardless of geographic locale, size, or regime type. They can have conditions for membership, which vary in degree from organization to organization, but the barriers to entry are relatively low. The United Nations, for instance, accepts all recognized states that are willing to sign the UN Charter. Organizations such as the WTO require compliance with a set of policies and practices pertaining to international trade, but, as a matter of principle, membership is open to any state that complies with these conditions. Universal institutions are perceived to enjoy high levels of legitimacy because they include the vast majority of states, if not all of them.

The best known of the world's universal multilateral institutions is the UN, established in 1945 to provide collective security for the post–Second World War world (see Wiseman and Basu, chapter 18 in this volume). While the UN is a universal organization, not all member states are treated equally. In an effort to overcome the shortcomings of its predecessor organization, the League of Nations, President Franklin D. Roosevelt proposed that the United Nations include a Security Council entrusted to preserve peace and security. Therefore, the Security Council has five permanent members (Britain, China, France, Soviet Union/Russia, and the United States, each of which wield a veto), and ten non-veto-holding members elected for two-year terms. However, because it includes five veto players, the UN's critics argue that it is frequently rendered ineffective due to gridlock, and that its legitimacy is hampered because it treats dictatorships and democracies as equals.

A number of universal organizations and institutions operate under the UN umbrella. This includes organizations such as the UN Children's Fund and the World Food Program, but also more negotiating frameworks and formal treaties such as the Nuclear Non-Proliferation Treaty (NPT), the Montreal Protocol on Substances That Deplete the Ozone Layer, the Law of the Sea Treaty, and the UN Framework Convention on Climate Change. In addition to those associated with the United Nations, there are independent international institutions that are universal in their reach. Prominent examples include the International Monetary Fund (IMF), the World Bank, and the WTO, previously GATT.

Institutionalist scholars argue that universal institutions can help increase and improve cooperation between states if their core interests are aligned (Keohane 1984). For instance, the NPT or the WTO provides member states with the capacity to verify that other states are abiding by their commitments. Sometimes, as in the case of the WTO, it provides for redress if it is established that a state is breaking its commitments. Neorealist scholars argue that institutions reflect the interests of the most powerful states (for example, Mearsheimer 1994/95). When these institutions are universal, the potential for a collision of interests between the major powers is high, so the prospect for effective action in response to major international threats and challenges is low.

Regional Multilateralism

Regional multilateral institutions and organizations focus on policy coordination and cooperation among states in a specific geographic region. Although regional multilateralism can provide a way of managing security relations, it is more frequently used to manage economic relations between states. The most advanced regional multilateral organizations and institutions are in Europe and the Atlantic area. The European Economic Community (EEC, later called the EU) was created to promote economic integration between France and Germany in an effort to end Franco-German rivalry. NATO was the tool by which the United States sought to contain communism. After the Cold War, both the EU and NATO used the prospect of membership as an incentive to consolidate democracy in many of the former members of the Soviet bloc. Economic regionalism has also grown rapidly outside of Europe since the end of the Cold War, with the most prominent examples being the North American Free Trade Agreement, Mercosur (a customs union consisting of Argentina, Brazil, Paraguay, and Uruguay), and the Asia-Pacific Economic Cooperation grouping (see Bátora and Hardacre, chapter 17 in this volume).

Regional economic blocs are sometimes perceived as threatening universal efforts to promote free trade globally. After all, if members of a regional economic bloc agree to give each other preferential trade status, then countries that fall outside that bloc are disadvantaged. However, some experts argue that regional economic integration could actually serve as a spur for universal efforts. For instance, a healthy EU may be in a position to make concessions in WTO negotiations.

Values-Based Multilateralism

Multilateral initiatives need not be organized around strictly material criteria alone. The prominence of shared democratic values within bilateral and multilateral institutions has deep roots in both American and European foreign policy traditions, and it cuts across the various methods of multilateralism described earlier. There is plenty of reason to believe that democracies are capable of deeper and more far-reaching cooperation than nondemocracies. Democracies are more transparent, are more capable of making binding contractual commitments, and appear less threatening to each other (Lipson 2005). These attributes are visible in many of the diplomatic arrangements advanced by the United States and Western European governments, such as European integration and NATO. It may also explain why some regions with important authoritarian actors, such as Asia and the Middle East, have less multilateral cooperation.

NATO and the EU stand out as two examples of multilateral institutions heavily influenced by values. Both are regional organizations. NATO is committed to providing security in the Atlantic area, and the EU is primarily dedicated to political and economic matters, but both also play a crucial role in strengthening and sustaining an international liberal order. Both have made democracy a key condition of membership and have acted internationally to promote human rights. Cooperation between the member states of each of these institutions is emblematic of a wide range of shared interests and values that are not explained by narrow definitions of the national interest.

Minilateralism

Universal, regional, and values-based multilateralism all share a common characteristic—there is a unifying principle that determines whether or not a state can participate in the forum. However, these methods can be inflexible and result in a relatively large number of participants that could compromise the effectiveness of the effort. Minilateralism can provide a solution. As Moises Naim (2009: 135) puts it, minilateralism brings "to the table the smallest possible number of countries needed to have the largest possible impact on solving a particular problem." Minilateralism allows a powerful state or a small group of states to convene a select group that is capable of acting in a timely manner and in a way that is proportionate to the challenge at hand. By definition, the number of states involved in minilateral diplomacy will vary from issue to issue (see box 10-2).

The **Group of Twenty (G20)** leaders forum, which was created in the fall of 2008 to tackle the international financial crisis, is a prominent contemporary example of minilateralism. Membership in the G20 is somewhat arbitrary, reflecting the view of the great powers rather than being guided by objective criteria. Saudi

---

BOX 10-2

Moises Naim on Finding the Magic Number

Same with climate change…the magic number is about 20: The world's 20 top polluters account for 75 percent of the planet's greenhouse gas emissions. The number for nuclear proliferation is 21—enough to include both recognized and de facto nuclear countries, and several other powers who care about them. African poverty? About a dozen, including all the major donor countries and the sub-Saharan countries most in need. As for HIV/AIDS, 19 countries account for nearly two thirds of the world's AIDS-related deaths. (Naim 2009: 135)

Arabia (the world's twenty-third-largest economy), Argentina (thirtieth), and South Africa (thirty-second) are formal members, whereas Spain (ninth), the Netherlands (sixteenth), Poland (eighteenth), and Belgium (twentieth) are not.

Minilateralism's great advantage is the flexibility it provides to like-minded states that may otherwise become bogged down in more inclusive organizations where bureaucratic rules or the presence of states with different interests can act as an impediment to coordinated action. However, there is also a risk that minilateral organizations could be a veil for coalitions of the willing that allow strong states to circumvent the obligation and commitments that they would be bound by in other multilateral organizations.

KEY POINTS

- At least four types of multilateral structures are available to policy makers: universal multilateralism, regional multilateralism, values-based multilateralism, and minilateralism.
- These types of multilateralism can overlap. For instance, a regional organization such as NATO can also be heavily influenced and shaped by values-based multilateralism.

UNDERSTANDING THE CONTEMPORARY INTERNATIONAL ORDER

To understand the practice of bilateralism and multilateralism, it is important to analyze the changing international order over the last sixty-five or so years. In the immediate aftermath of the Second World War, the old order lay torn asunder, with Germany and Japan completely defeated and France and Britain victorious but exhausted, depleted, and lacking in influence. In their stead were two Allied powers—the Soviet Union, which suffered tremendous losses but occupied more than half of the European continent, and the United States, which emerged from the war relatively unscathed but yet to decide on the type of role it would play in the world. The structure of the postwar order quickly came into focus as attempts to forge a concert of powers built on Soviet-US cooperation failed amid mutual suspicion and clashing interests. The United States would take responsibility for the lands where its armies stood, and the Soviet Union would do the same in its **sphere of influence**. Each would balance the other, competing vociferously to gain an advantage—whether territorially, technologically, or psychologically—and reacting to prevent gains by the other side.

This **bipolar structure** defined international cooperation in the post–Second World War period. The United States was one of two powers on the global stage, but in its own sphere it enjoyed unrivaled hegemony. The Western order, as it became known, was based on American leadership. The United States provided the **public goods** necessary to create and sustain it. One such public good took the form of security guarantees to countries within its sphere, to protect them both from the Soviet Union and from each other by removing the need for defensively minded arms races that could trigger a **security dilemma** whereby actions taken by one state for defensive purposes is perceived as threatening by another state, leading to arms races. Another public good was provided when the United States created or supported the creation of international institutions to promote cooperation, transparency, interdependence, and trust-building between nations. It also built an open liberal Western economy that promoted trade and interdependence between nations to avoid a repeat of the 1930s, when protectionism was perceived to have contributed to the Great Depression and the rise of totalitarianism.

This was the overarching postwar plan of the United States, but there was considerable variance within the order. At a global level, the United States had placed great emphasis on the importance of the United Nations, which Americans hoped would serve not just as a universal forum for all nations but also as a means of building a concert of powers that would include the Soviet Union. It quickly became apparent that the Soviet Union would not be a cooperative partner of the United States, so the United Nations receded in importance as a forum to shape US policy (although it was still used by the United States to lay out its case in the court of global opinion). Other universal institutions, such as GATT, the IMF, and the World Bank, had more staying power but only because the Soviet Union and its satellites refused to take part.

The real distinction in US policy was between Europe and Asia. In Europe, the United States built a multilateral order by creating NATO and by later supporting the creation of the EEC. The existence of NATO, in particular, meant that there was no stand-alone bilateral alliance between the United States and Germany; instead, the United States, Germany, Great Britain, and many other nations were all part of the same multilateral alliance. The United States was able to influence the future direction of European states, but European states were also able to use the multilateral forum to consult with each other and work collectively to influence US policy (Risse-Kappen 1995). Over time, the EEC was able to take advantage of the security guarantees offered by the United States to facilitate a process of building trust to build a **security community** where war between Germany and France was not only unlikely but also unthinkable and unplanned for.

In Asia, the United States built a regional order, known as the "San Francisco System," based on bilateral relations with key allies. The reasons that US policy makers did not pursue a multilateral structure are contested. Some scholars argue that

Washington considered pursuing a multilateral strategy in Asia, but the outbreak of the Korean War exacerbated a number of practical difficulties that resulted in a second-best solution (for example, Ruggie 1997). Others argue that unresolved differences and disputes—related to territory, distrust, and hatred bred by war and ethnicity—served as a brake on reconciliation between Japan and its neighbors (for example, Hemmer and Katzenstein 2002). Whatever the reason, the San Francisco System, which took its name from the venue of the treaty signing with Japan in September 1951, has proved to be remarkably durable and influential (Tow 1991).

The San Francisco System had four elements that were developed in the first half of the 1950s (Calder 2008: 19). These were formal bilateral security alliances, including treaty alliances between the United States, Australia and New Zealand (September 1951), the Philippines (August 1951), Japan (September 1951), South Korea (November 1954), and the Republic of China/Taiwan (December 1954); US military bases throughout the Asia-Pacific region, as first conceptualized by the Joint Chiefs of Staff toward the end of the Second World War; some reconstruction aid (albeit much more limited than in Western Europe); and gradual integration of allies' economies on preferential terms into the bilateralist internationalist trade and financial order fostered by the United States.

The bilateral system succeeded in containing the Soviet Union, advancing regional peace and stability, contributed to economic growth, and helped a number of regimes build and consolidate democratic systems of government. However, much has changed. The Cold War is long over. Asia is in the midst of a historic power transition and appears to be trending toward multipolarity. Several critically important countries were not in the "hub and spokes" system, including China, India, Indonesia, and Malaysia. Economic integration has brought nations closer together. Meanwhile, there are also other trends in the opposite direction—rising nationalism stoked by unresolved historical grievances; concerns about the credibility of American power and the prospect that nations may have to fend for themselves; the risk that a reversal of economic fortune may force the Chinese Communist Party to turn to belligerent nationalism to legitimize its hold on power; the introduction of advanced new conventional military capabilities to the region; the innate danger of a collapse of Pakistan or North Korea; the continuing competition for scarce resources such as food, water, and energy; and the emergence of transnational threats such as terrorism, climate change, and global pandemics.

Many of these trends and challenges require multilateral cooperation between countries. It is no surprise, therefore, that Asia has seen greater multilateral security cooperation in recent years: the Association of Southeast Asian Nations (ASEAN) plus (China, Japan, and South Korea), the ASEAN Regional Forum, the now defunct Korean Peninsula Energy Development Organization, and the Six-Party Talks on North Korea are all examples of this dynamic. Some include the United States while others do not. However, most of these organizations remain underdeveloped and are relatively weak or limited in scope.

The bilateral system will continue to play a crucial role in regional order in Asia (see box 10-3). In the 2000s, China played a leading role in the construction of multilateral structures in Asia, which raised concerns in Washington that Beijing was using soft power to marginalize the United States. However, following the 2008

BOX 10-3

Kent Calder and Francis Fukuyama on the Limitations of Bilateralism in Asia

The lack of multilateral structures, the so called organization gap,

> complicates East Asian efforts to address common problems, increasing intra-regional security tensions and threatening the possibility of financial chaos in the absence of stabilizing outside interventions....Whatever utility East Asian divisions once had in sustaining American Cold War influence in the region is now outweighed by the geopolitical dangers and the senseless obstacles to economic progress that rampant nationalistic rivalries have created. (Calder and Fukuyama 2008: 2)

---

financial crisis, China was perceived to become much more assertive in its foreign policy, which had the effect of worrying China's neighbors and reminding them of the value of bilateral relations with the United States. Thus, starting in 2010 the United States was not only deepening its bilateral ties with traditional allies such as South Korea but also seeking to build new bilateral partnerships, including with India, Indonesia, and Vietnam.

KEY POINTS

- The Western liberal order was created after the Second World War in the US sphere of influence—Western Europe and parts of East Asia—with the hegemonic power (the United States) providing the public goods to create and sustain it.
- The Atlantic area was organized multilaterally while East Asia was organized bilaterally, with the United States at the center of a hub-and-spokes system.
- Recent years have seen increasing interest in creating new multilateral structures to foster greater cooperation to address transnational challenges, but these will likely complement rather than replace bilateral structures.

THE CHALLENGE OF A POWER TRANSITION

As argued earlier, the contemporary international order has its foundations in the 1940s. Today, a group of fast-growing developing countries—led by China and India—are rising and in the next several decades will have economies that will rival those of the United States and Europe. For the first time in the modern era, economic growth is bringing non-Western developing countries into the top ranks of the world system. This dramatic observation was made in a 2001 Goldman Sachs study, which noted that, if present economic trends continue, by 2040, Brazil, Russia, India, and China (the BRICs) could have economies that together would be larger than the old Group of Six (G6) advanced countries—France, Germany, Great Britain, Italy, Japan, and the United States (Wilson and Purushothaman 2003). Indeed, Goldman Sachs revised its analysis in light of the international financial crisis to predict that the BRICs will now overtake the G6 by 2031 (O'Neill and Stupnytska 2009).

This power transition poses a number of extremely important questions for existing bilateral and multilateral structures, including institutions and alliances. Will they seek to integrate and operate within existing institutions, or seek to transform or work around them? To what extent will these institutions need to be reformed so as to accommodate these rising developing countries? Will existing alliances be given a new lease on life as rising powers challenge the status quo, or will countries separate themselves from the United States and **bandwagon** with rapidly growing countries like China? What are the implications for the political direction and issue agendas of global institutions such as the United Nations and the Bretton Woods institutions (the IMF and the World Bank)?

The existing international order faces two sets of crises. The first is a long-term crisis of legitimacy and effectiveness resulting from the shifting distribution of power in the international system. The second set results from a failure to address long-term transnational threats that pose significant dangers to the international community. Both of these crises have the effect of pushing states away from more inclusive forms of multilateral diplomacy and toward smaller multilateral groupings and bilateral diplomacy. In the long run, the durability and robustness of the international order is contingent upon its capacity to reform and update its multilateral institutions so they can effectively cope with these crises.

Crises of Legitimacy and Effectiveness

The contemporary international order reflects the distribution of power at the moment of creation in the mid-1940s. As the distribution of power shifts, countries such as Brazil, China, India, Indonesia, Japan, Nigeria, South Africa, and to a lesser extent Germany and Japan are all more or less underrepresented or excluded from the governance structures of the international order. Consider, for instance, the voting weights in international financial institutions. The IMF and World Bank were created as part of the Bretton Woods agreement in 1944, dominated by the United Kingdom and the United States. As such, both institutions are dominated today by the United States and Western Europe. An American always heads the World Bank, while the top position at the IMF always goes to a European. The EU either appoints or has a major say in appointing ten members of the IMF's twenty-four-seat board. Changes, however, are being made. For some time, India, China, and other non-western states were greatly underrepresented. For example, in 2009, Belgium had a larger share of the votes than India despite being only 42% the size of its domestic product. In response to demands for reform, a significant reweighting was approved in 2011 and further changes are pending. However, the convention where the head of the IMF is always a European remains.

The situation is not much different in the realm of geopolitics and international security. Western countries dominate institutions and organizations that act as a steering committee for world affairs. The UN Security Council has two Western European states as permanent members and continues to be resistant to attempts to reform it despite major diplomatic efforts inside and outside of the UN. The **Group**

of Eight (G8) consists of Canada, France, Germany, Italy, Japan, Russia, the United Kingdom, and the United States but excludes China, India, and Brazil, as well as all other nations, even though it acted as a steering committee for world affairs until September 2008. NATO, a Cold War alliance, has taken on an increasingly important role in military interventions outside of its geographic area as it adjusts to a changing strategic environment.

A number of scholars have argued that the solution to this "legitimacy crisis" is to create new types of organizations and reform existing ones so that the new challenges are met and the voices and interests of the most populous and powerful states are heard and taken into account (Ikenberry and Slaughter 2006). Particular solutions include an enlarged Security Council, replacing the G8 with the G20, increased representation for Asia at the IMF, and a new East Asia security forum. Advocates of these reforms argue that they would modernize the international order, increase its legitimacy, and equip it with the legitimacy to tackle the shared threats and challenges of the coming decades.

However, there is reason to believe that the cure may exacerbate parts of the long-term crisis. Addressing the **legitimacy deficit** by including rising powers in the governance structures of the international order assumes that these states generally share the same interests and geopolitical outlook as existing members of the steering committee. The assumption of shared interests is important because if the interests dramatically diverge, inclusive multilateral forums are likely to lead to gridlock as the member states fail to agree on a path forward. Indeed, in international relations theory, shared interests are one of the key assumptions made by Robert Keohane (1984), the leading scholar of institutionalism. However, it is increasingly apparent that in today's world, there are growing divergences in preferences and perceived interests. While the world's major powers may share problems, they do not necessarily share the same assessment of the severity of the problem or how to tackle it. For instance, after an initial period of cooperation after the triggering of the global financial crisis in September 2008, international negotiations are now characterized by disagreements and deadlock. China now clashes with much of the rest of the world, including the United States and the EU, over the valuation of its currency. The EU and the United States have their own differences over the benefits of austerity versus an economic stimulus. With respect to international security, China has grown more assertive in the wake of the financial crisis and is now challenging the United States and the West more generally across a wide range of issues, such as maritime security.

A pattern is emerging. In the Western order of the Cold War, the closest economic partners of the United States were also its political allies in a shared struggle against a common foe. These allies not only shared the same problems but also had a broadly similar view about how to tackle the problem. In today's global order, however, the United States needs the support of countries with which it disagrees (see Henrikson, chapter 15 in this volume).

If this long-term crisis continues and worsens, the effect will be threefold. First, the major powers, particularly the United States, will have incentives to work through smaller, more exclusive multilateral forums that consist of states that see international politics in similar ways, that is, "coalitions of the like-minded." This could include minilateral or values-based multilateral forums. Second, there will be a competition for influence inside universal multilateral institutions as the United States and emerging powers seek to set the rules and agenda of organizations like the IMF, World Bank, and United Nations. Third, bilateral relations will become more important, particularly the US-China relationship. Indeed, strong bilateral relations between the major powers may be a necessary condition for strong multilateral relations.

Transnational Crises

The second set of crises confronting the contemporary international order has to do with transnational threats and challenges that affect many, if not all, states through-out the world. These crises are difficult for multilateral institutions to solve because they raise painful choices about who should bear the brunt of the burden to address complex problems. A contemporary example is the impact of the international financial crisis upon European integration.

The international financial crisis, triggered by the collapse of the financial firm Lehman Brothers in September 2008, has tested the capacity and effective-ness of some of the world's most important multilateral institutions. An immediate consequence was the creation of a G20 leaders' forum and the bypassing of the G8. The G20 had some success in the early stages of the crisis but subsequently became bogged down in disagreements between the key member states. However, the greatest casualty may turn out to be European monetary integration, one of the world's most important multilateral endeavors. In 2010, 2011, and thus far in 2012, the international financial crisis threatened the solvency of several members of the Eurozone, including Greece, Ireland, and Portugal. Although the immediate cause of the solvency crisis varied from country to country, each illuminated the short-comings of the Eurozone's legal structures, which made no provision for a bailout or for a default by a member state.

This is but one example. There are many others. Climate change poses a threat to all states, but the major carbon emitters have found it exceedingly difficult to agree who should bear the cost that any solution would entail. Likewise, all nuclear powers recognized by the NPT have an interest in preventing nuclear proliferation, but spe-cific cases affect the geopolitical calculus in different ways. Think of the reaction of China and the United States to Iran's nuclear program. What lessons can be learned? Significant international agreements that compel states to take costly actions to tackle shared challenges are extremely difficult to achieve. States will disagree about who should bear the brunt of the burden. Even if governments can agree, they may find it difficult to bring their people along and to get the agreements ratified through the domestic political process. The sheer number of states involved in regional or universal diplomatic processes raises considerable barriers, both substantive and procedural. Occasionally, multilateral treaties can be detrimentally impacted by bilateral agreements (for example, the United States made bilateral agreements with a number of states that were perceived as undermining the International Criminal Court). Compromise, which is generally seen as a necessary component of large-scale multilateral endeavors, may not produce the levels of cooperation required to effectively address the challenge.

These difficulties are causing governments to become more skeptical of inclusive multilateral agreements. In the future, they are likely to turn to smaller and more flexible forums. However, bilateral and minilateral diplomacy are not without their own drawbacks. For one, these processes will exclude a large number of states that have a stake in the issue. For another, it is often the major powers that disagree on how to tackle a transnational challenge or on how to share the burden.

KEY POINTS

- The existing international order faces two sets of crises. The first is a long-term crisis of legitimacy and effectiveness resulting from the shifting distribution of power in the international system. The second set results from a failure to address long-term transnational threats that pose significant dangers to the international community.
- Addressing the first set of crises by giving rising powers a greater stake in the governance structures of the international order could have the side effect of making international institutions less effective if the interests of the major stakeholders diverge. This is particularly problematic because unlike the member states of the old Western order, some of the rising powers are not allies of the United States.
- The second set of crises is difficult for multilateral institutions to solve because they raise painful choices about who should bear the brunt of the burden to address complex problems. Prominent examples include the Euro crisis of 2010–11 and international climate change negotiations.
- Both of these sets of crises have the effect of pushing states away from more inclusive forms of multilateral diplomacy and toward smaller multilateral groupings and bilateral diplomacy.

CONCLUSION

Bilateralism and multilateralism are important components of the contemporary international order. Each has a distinct logic and set of characteristics. Bilateralism means that interstate relations will unfold in line with the distribution of power, with the outcome reflecting the interest of the stronger party. It enables the stronger party to enjoy a greater level of control and influence than with multilateral arrangements. Multilateralism, on the other hand, is the management of relations between three or more states according to a set of agreed-upon principles that are binding on all parties. Multilateralism is more formal and less flexible than bilateralism, but it does allow for the building of trust and a deepening of cooperation.

Bilateral and multilateral structures are under pressure from two sources—the changing distribution of power in favor of states that were previously outside of the Western order, and the emergence of transnational challenges. A global environment that is increasingly fragmented, networked, and digitized enables these challenges. Neither dynamic lends itself to easy solutions. States will seek out smaller, minilateral groupings, but in so doing they must learn how to increase the net levels of international cooperation, engaging all the key actors, while advancing their interests.

QUESTIONS

1. Compare the advantages and disadvantages of bilateral and multilateral agreements.

2. Is there ever a case when a smaller state should prefer a bilateral alliance over a multilateral alliance?

3. Write a two-page memo to the UN secretary-general explaining how world leaders perceive the relative advantages and disadvantages of universal multilateralism.

4. The US national security adviser is considering making "minilateral diplomacy" the centerpiece of the administration's new national security strategy. Write him or her a memo assessing the advantages and disadvantages of such a policy. Include your own recommendation.

5. Does China's rise make values-based multilateralism more or less relevant?

6. Why are states in Asia struggling to create new multilateral institutions?

7. Should NATO intervene "out of area"? What are the risks associated with multilateral military interventions?

8. Are international institutions illegitimate?

9. What are the implications for European integration if the Eurozone breaks apart?

10. What are the implications of the analysis in this chapter for your theoretical and practical understandings of contemporary diplomacy?

CHAPTER 11

Public Diplomacy

Jan Melissen

CHAPTER CONTENTS

- Introduction: the rise of a practice and a field of study
- The epiphenomenal nature of public diplomacy
- Official and nongovernmental public diplomacy
- Beyond the new public diplomacy: evolving concepts
- Public diplomacy outside the West
- Conclusion

READER'S GUIDE

This chapter discusses the concept of public diplomacy—that is, diplomatic engagement with people—in contemporary diplomatic practice. Public diplomacy is a multidisciplinary area of scholarship, which is now receiving more attention by scholars than any other aspect of diplomacy. It is analyzed here as part of the evolution of contemporary diplomatic practice. This chapter is therefore not a guide explaining how public diplomacy should be undertaken. Besides states, many different actors are involved in public diplomacy, and fascination with this aspect of diplomatic practice is by no means limited to the West. The academic debate about public diplomacy only emerged after the turn of the twenty-first century, which still leaves important conceptual and theoretical issues to be determined. Public diplomacy has many advocates but is not without its critics, and the concept underlines how diplomatic practice is constantly changing.

INTRODUCTION: THE RISE OF A PRACTICE AND A FIELD OF STUDY

The concept and practice of public diplomacy have attracted much attention in academia over the last decade, and a great deal of scholarship is under way. If a review of articles in the *Hague Journal of Diplomacy* over the last six years is used as a guide, more academic work is now in progress on public diplomacy than on any other single theme on the diplomatic studies research agenda. The literature on public diplomacy has been flooded with contributions from other disciplines, including political science, international relations, history, communication studies, public relations, and marketing. According to Eytan Gilboa (2008: 56), the study of public diplomacy is "probably one of the most multidisciplinary areas in modern scholarship." Yet despite a cacophony of opinions on what the concept means, little exists in the way of theory-building. One study refers to a review of 150 definitional statements of public diplomacy, which can be grouped into six intellectual and practical categories (Fitzpatrick 2010: 89). Many students of diplomacy have a discernible sense of being overwhelmed by these developments. At the same time, most of these scholars want to be involved in the debate about what has become commonly known as the "new public diplomacy" (Melissen 2005). Gregory (2011: 353) deliberately steps aside from discussions about "traditional" and "new" and defines public diplomacy as "an instrument used by states, associations of states, and some sub-state and non-state actors to understand cultures, attitudes, and behavior; build and manage relationships; and influence thoughts and mobilize actions to advance their interests and values."

The remarkable academic vitality in public diplomacy studies reflects the upswing of attention on public diplomacy among practitioners across the world. A sense clearly now exists within many foreign ministries that it is essential to catch up with fast-moving developments in global communications, or risk being left behind in a field crowded with many other agile actors who practice public diplomacy. No government seems to be immune to the "public diplomacy fever." Few are at ease with their country's image or reputation, even though this quality is hard to measure (Pahlavi 2007). Even countries with consistently high scores in global popularity rankings, such as Finland, are often concerned about their image projection in foreign countries.

Many of the world's leading powers—for example, the United States after the Second World War, Japan from the 1970s onward, and China today—have all in their own way discovered that their rise in power can lead to greater vulnerability in terms of external reputation (Lee and Melissen 2011). These countries have financially invested quite substantially in public diplomacy, although, as critics correctly point out, such expenditure is dwarfed by military spending. In 2007, US secretary of defense Robert Gates endorsed the importance of combining both **soft power**, of which public diplomacy is an element (see later discussion), and **hard power**, comprising economic power as well as military force. Gates's statement that "based on my experience with seven presidents, as a former Director of the CIA and now as Secretary of Defense, I am here to make the case for strengthening our capacity to use 'soft power' and for better integrating it with 'hard' power" (*New York Times*, 27 November 2007) was both a tribute to public diplomacy and a plea to allocate more funds for it in the US State Department's budget. His comments also reflected the defense establishment's quiet, long-standing, and usually well-financed interest in **strategic communication**, the security community's variant of public diplomacy. According to Taylor (2010: 24), the **information operations** conducted by national defense departments and international organizations like the North Atlantic Treaty Organization (NATO) act as a support tool "to lubricate the business of military activity, rather like the role of public diplomacy in lubricating foreign policy."

The term "public diplomacy" has American heritage. It was coined in 1965 by Edmund Gullion, dean of the Fletcher School of Law and Diplomacy at Tufts University and founder of the Edward R. Murrow Center of Public Diplomacy. It took approximately forty years, however, for the term to enter US public discourse, cross the Atlantic, and become a neologism in multiple languages around the world. Academics' interest in public diplomacy soared in the 1990s, and it was only well into the first decade of the twenty-first century that textbooks on diplomacy started to cover it in more than a cursory fashion. Today, public diplomacy and related information activities that aim to influence foreign opinion are seen as too important to be left to diplomats and foreign ministries. In many countries other executive agencies—such as ministries of economic affairs, development cooperation, culture, and even agriculture—have their own stake in public diplomacy, economic branding, and related practices for promoting their portfolios. Ideally, such activities across government are **joined-up** or are coordinated across the **whole-of-government**. In reality, however, despite neat governmental organizational charts, bureaucratic life presents obstacles to streamlined activity and overall coherence.

Directly or indirectly, the dramatic terrorist attacks of 11 September 2001 highlighted the US and global debates on public diplomacy. It is important to stress, however, that the activities underlying this concept are not new. The practice of international reputation management can be traced back to the pre-Westphalian world, before the rise of the state, and even to the earliest written evidence about diplomacy in the ancient world. Diplomacy has never been able to neglect public opinion, although its importance was minuscule when information was still largely controlled by those in power. Still, more than 200 years ago, during classical diplomacy's finest hour, the Austrian statesman and diplomat Klemens von Metternich observed that "public opinion is the most important medium of all. Like religion it penetrates into the darkest corners" (Bátora 2010b). The early twentieth century, made conspicuous by sharply rising nationalism and widespread destruction during the First World War, marked the beginning of professional image cultivation. In 1917, US president Woodrow Wilson and Vladimir Lenin, the new Soviet Union's political leader, inaugurated an era in international politics when they presented the world with sharply contrasting ideological alternatives (Mayer 1959). After 1945, no citizen of the countries involved in the Cold War between East and West could escape from **propaganda**, for lack of a better term. In an increasingly interdependent and integrated Western Europe, practices such as Germany's *politische Öffentlichkeitsarbeit* and France's *politique d'influence*—synonyms for public diplomacy before they were substituted by it—were vital policy tools in managing relationships between former enemies.

The United States Information Agency (USIA), a special agency that existed in the United States from 1953 to 1999, became responsible for educating various generations of public diplomacy professionals, even though many saw this "information work," which was done outside the State Department, as a sundry activity at the periphery of diplomacy. The USIA was important in projecting US ideas and images to the public in different parts of the world. Edward R. Murrow, USIA's director during the John F. Kennedy and Lyndon B. Johnson administrations, is still known for his commonsense remarks about what works in public diplomacy and what does not (see box 11-1). With hindsight, crucial USIA wisdom and expertise were lost when the United States Information Service (USIS) was established after the end of the Cold War and integrated with the State Department. Arguably, subsequent US public diplomacy at the beginning of the twenty-first century, with its emphasis on "selling Uncle Sam" through product marketing, advertising techniques, and one-way messaging, could have benefited from learning the lessons of past approaches. Students of public diplomacy today can also learn from historical analysis of public diplomacy (Cull 2008, 2009; Osgood and Etheridge 2010) and from comparisons of the past with the present.

KEY POINTS

- Public diplomacy is a young field of study in which a cacophony of opinions still exists on what public diplomacy means, so far with only limited theory-building.
- Foreign ministries are aware that they need to catch up with developments in global communications or risk being left behind in an international arena where many others are practicing public diplomacy.
- Diplomacy has never been able to neglect public opinion, although its importance was minuscule when information was still largely controlled by those in power, which is no longer the case.

THE EPIPHENOMENAL NATURE OF PUBLIC DIPLOMACY

Because there are so many unanswered questions about public diplomacy and many disciplines with different perspectives to offer, the topic attracts a lot of debate. When delving into literature on the subject, a student of diplomacy can feel like a

---

BOX 11-1

Edward R. Murrow's Long Shadow in US Public Diplomacy

One of the most emblematic figures in the history of US public diplomacy was Edward R. Murrow, the CBS celebrity journalist who became director of the United States Information Agency in 1961. He testified to the US Congress that "American traditions and the American ethic require us to be truthful, but the most important reason is that truth is the best propaganda and lies are the worst. To be persuasive we must be believable; to be believable we must be credible; to be credible we must be truthful. It is as simple as that" (Public Diplomacy Alumni Association 2008). The verdict on Murrow is overwhelmingly positive, although some of his former colleagues at Voice of America aired their disappointment: "It seemed that Murrow cared less about the substance of truth, but rather focused on its appearance" (Cull 2003: 23–24).

pedestrian crossing a busy junction with all sorts of traffic approaching from different directions, but with little overview. Contributions from disciplines far from the mainstream study of diplomacy—such as marketing, media studies, public opinion research, rhetoric, or psychology—are very valuable but normally do not give priority to assessing public diplomacy from a wider diplomatic perspective.

From a diplomatic studies viewpoint, public diplomacy is not a freestanding activity. Rather, it has an "epiphenomenal" nature—that is, it accompanies wider developments in contemporary diplomatic practice. The most salient transformational development in diplomatic practice today is that a level diplomatic playing field, mainly consisting of state actors, can no longer be taken for granted. Geoffrey Wiseman's (2010) concept of **polylateralism** neatly captures the mutations or changing nature of contemporary diplomacy. Although it may now be common wisdom that a variety of non-state actors have joined the fray, a closer look at the societal dimension of diplomacy helps us to understand that a fundamental change is occurring in diplomatic practice and in traditional diplomatic actors' priorities.

To understand the societal nature of contemporary diplomacy (see Sharp, chapter 3; Pigman, chapter 4; and Badie, chapter 5, in this volume), we need to note that in the modern era states in the international system managed to absorb various forms of diplomatic innovation relatively easily.[1] In the midst of change there was always the basic comfort—for participants in the diplomatic process—of generally accepted rules of the game, a set of fundamental norms and working practices, and agreed protocol and ceremony. In the world of diplomats, elegantly depicted and admired by Harold Nicolson (1954), there was little sympathy for openness and democracy in diplomatic affairs and for society to play a meaningful role. By comparison, diplomacy today is becoming societized or, as Kelley (2010: 289) argues, is "becoming enmeshed within the public domain." Issues affecting citizens' daily lives that are far removed from classical diplomacy have moved upward on the agenda of foreign ministries and their diplomats. As practitioners have also come to realize, it no longer makes sense to distinguish between diplomacy and public diplomacy. In this broader contemporary context of diplomacy, public diplomacy has a distinct quality, in that it helps to entice diplomats out of their narrow domain of officially **accredited representatives**, ruling elites, and others orbiting around government. For diplomacy and individual official diplomats, this opening of their previously privileged habitat is not a superficial concession to a new era. Rather, it is an important historical development.

Not only is it difficult to distinguish between diplomacy and public diplomacy, but it is becoming clear that old and new diplomatic practices are merging into something new. As in the cinema technique of morphing, one image blends into another, and the two are transformed into something else. Foreign ministries are increasingly aware of the transnational dimension of external policies, as well as issues in domestic society. Public diplomacy can therefore no longer be approached as a separate consideration from governmental aspects of policy making and foreign relations. This is most clearly visible in the more integrated parts of the world, with multiple connections between societies of countries in the same international neighborhood. For instance, it is a given in the European Union (EU) that member states take public diplomacy considerations into account on all sorts of issues at different stages of the political debate and policy-making process, and also during international negotiations. It is unimaginable for governments today to live under the illusion that domestic policies and debates on internationally controversial issues stop at the porous borders with other countries, and they should therefore act accordingly. This view differs from the more conventional argument that postulates that the "old" and "new"—that is, traditional diplomacy and public diplomacy—coexist as practices that have a different diplomatic logic. It remains convenient and functional to continue to refer to public diplomacy under a separate heading, but it is important to remember that it should not be separated from diplomacy at large.

This argument clashes with the traditionalist view of public diplomacy, which does not deny that public diplomacy is now perhaps the most important duty for ambassadors (Berridge 2010: 190), but considers this development an unfortunate distraction from ambassadors' core diplomatic duties. Today's traditionalist scholars consider public diplomacy a euphemism for propaganda (Berridge and James 2001), while most classical scholars writing on diplomacy saw it as either a harmful development (Nicolson 1963) or simply something peripheral to diplomacy (Bull 1977; Watson 1982). Like many old-school practitioners today, traditionalist scholars do not accept that public diplomacy could be anything other than a form of political advertising (Berridge and James 2001: 197). They therefore reject the argument that the rise of public diplomacy is important to study. From the traditionalists' point of view, the patterns of interaction between the states that diplomats represent and the societies where they represent their states are of limited interest. The circle that traditionalists need to square, however, is that the same foreign ministries that are at the heart of their conception of diplomacy see public diplomacy as a concern affecting more and more of their day-to-day activities.

Despite acknowledging the importance of public diplomacy, foreign ministries find it difficult to dedicate sufficient financial and human resources to their public diplomacy activities. Governments always have pressing policy objectives, vested domestic interests, and important foreign policy agendas. Yet in spite of all these pressures, public diplomacy has moved center stage. The underlying reason is that public diplomacy is symptomatic of the changing balance between traditional diplomatic functions and other foreign ministry tasks that have recently come to the fore (see Hocking, chapter 7 in this volume). It is important for those practicing or studying diplomacy to emphasize this trend because it is not likely to be noticed by observers whose attention is still focused on classical policy areas and high-politics issues on the international politics agenda. This type of oversight by scholars and practitioners is not unique to public diplomacy. Consular affairs is another area of spectacular growth for ministries of foreign affairs, and—like public diplomacy—is based on connections with society (see Leira and Neumann, chapter 9 in this volume). Both public diplomacy and consular diplomacy can hence be understood as epiphenomena, acting as prisms for understanding significant changes in the conduct of international relations.

KEY POINTS

- Public diplomacy is accompanying wider developments in contemporary diplomatic practice, including the rise of a variety of diplomatic actors involved in it.

- The rise of public diplomacy is symptomatic of the recent changing balance between traditional diplomatic functions and foreign ministry tasks.
- From a conceptual point of view, public diplomacy is part of diplomacy at large, but it is more practical to continue to refer to it separately and to remember that it should not be considered in isolation.
- Traditionalist students of diplomacy consider public diplomacy as political advertising or a euphemism for propaganda.

OFFICIAL AND NONGOVERNMENTAL PUBLIC DIPLOMACY

From a historical, theoretical, or empirical point of view, it is hard to sustain the argument that diplomacy as a *practice* is limited to the state or any other particular actor. It follows that the same applies to public diplomacy. According to one scholar-diplomat (see box 11-2), public diplomacy for national governments has become part of the central diplomatic task of projecting one's country into the host nation by means of bridging the gap between the home and the host's government and society (Heine 2008: 279). States, however, are no longer on their own. A variety of inter-governmental organizations, including the World Trade Organization (WTO) and NATO, and regional organizations such as the EU, keep strengthening their institutional capacity and have, as a result, become more interested in nurturing their international reputation. Even international bodies where the constituent members' national interests loom particularly large, such as the Association of Southeast Asian Nations (ASEAN), worry about their collective image. NATO's Public Diplomacy Division, for instance, has extensive (and controversial) information programs aimed at out-of-area civil-military theaters, while it is simultaneously engaged in outreach activities in NATO's twenty-eight member states. Similarly, one aim of the EU's new diplomatic body, the European External Action Service, is to project a positive image of the "union of twenty-seven." With a declining power base, the EU needs to project this message to ensure that great powers and their populations are more likely to take the EU global norm entrepreneurship seriously. Instead of being involved in image competitions among states, some international organizations hence project themselves as actors in the cause of spreading democratic norms, values, and governance practices. It is hard to generalize about the public diplomacy of such a large and heterogeneous group of intergovernmental bodies, but it is important to note that their public diplomacy, including its purposes and messages, is distinct from the nation-states that they comprise. Finally, it is worth remembering that many international organizations are relatively new to the business of public diplomacy, and that their activities in this field are usually more about straightforward communication and information efforts than about engaging with people.

Below, or in parallel to, the state level, substate regions' public diplomacy is more visibly self-interested. Regions with legal muscle in foreign affairs, such as Flanders in Belgium, Catalonia in Spain, or Québec in Canada, employ public diplomacy both to raise international awareness of their distinct identity and interests and as a domestic nation-building instrument. With their sometimes long-standing experience and activist dedication to their cause, such actors occasionally outsmart

---

BOX 11-2

Scholar-Diplomats and the Study of Diplomacy

A great deal of the literature mentioned throughout this book refers to the writings of scholar-diplomats. They make an interesting contribution to the study of diplomacy. Their academic reflections on their own professional activity benefit from their personal practical experience, including a familiarity with the diplomatic customs that offers more to their writings than a mere "reality check." The list of such authors includes distinguished names like Harold Nicolson, George Kennan, Henry Kissinger, and Adam Watson. There are, however, many lesser-known contemporary authors who have contributed books (Robert Cooper, Daryl Copeland, Kishan Rana, Shaun Riordan, and Carne Ross) or small gems of articles with critical reflections and reminiscences to diplomatic studies.

---

the states of which they are constitutionally a component. For example, Catalonia came late to public diplomacy but has given it high priority in its external relations. In comparison with federal governments' more complex narrative, assertive regions generally have a more straightforward story to tell.

In comparison with official state-based public diplomacy, which is structurally constrained by governmental red tape and a professional culture that inclines toward risk avoidance, the campaign-oriented activities of nongovernmental organizations (NGOs) are usually quick-moving and supple. NGOs include actors of all sizes, from large organizations to individuals. Global celebrities such as Bono, Bob Geldof, or Angelina Jolie (Cooper 2008a, 2008b; Dieter and Kumar 2008; Thrall 2008) and bloggers such as the US-based and respected MountainRunner seem to have emerged from nowhere (www.MountainRunner.us). The public diplomacy activism of influential NGOs such as Greenpeace, Amnesty International, or Human Rights Watch is focused on timely activism, long-term relationship-building, and immediate political results. In their global operations, these NGOs see public diplomacy as a tool to mobilize individual public support and forge coalitions with a variety of actors, including states exploiting the idea of a normative **niche diplomacy**. One early and well-known example of such coordination was the 1990s campaigns resulting in the Convention on the Prohibition of the Use, Stockpiling, Production and Transfer of Anti-Personnel Mines and on Their Destruction, better known as the Ottawa or Anti-Personnel Mine Ban Treaty (Williams, Goose, and Wareham 2008).

Some smaller national NGOs dealing with issues such as dialogue across civilizations and religions see public diplomacy as an opportunity to strengthen their role as facilitating transnational relations among social actors, for instance, in supporting improved relations between the Islamic world and the West. However, although some NGOs declare their autonomy from state-based officialdom, they are often connected to governments in various ways, for instance, in an advisory role, or as bodies running politically sensitive government-funded projects. The question of autonomy can become an issue for so-called arm's length public diplomacy and government-funded cultural relations bodies, as the British Council found in

2008, when the Russian government closed the council's offices in St. Petersburg and Yekaterinburg and accused it of having violated Russian law. Quasi-nongovernmental organizations (quangos)—or nondepartmental public bodies to which government has devolved powers—are an example of structural connections between NGOs and governments. In other words, NGOs come in many shapes and sizes, are not always as independent as they appear, and are not free from criticism. Their role in diplomacy and international negotiations is, however, undisputed, and their modus operandi appears to fit public diplomacy's current networking milieu better than do the practices of states and international organizations.

Official public diplomacy can also learn from the corporate sector, which is spending ever-larger sums of money on its international reputation. Consumer-oriented disciplines, such as marketing and public relations, have a lot of useful practical knowledge to offer states.

Processes adopted by the commercial sector have also given birth to the largely quasi-academic study on **nation-branding** (Fitzpatrick 2010: 129–51), an approach that focuses on nation-states and other territorially defined actors in terms of their competition with each other. However, the nation-branding approach is considered to be dated, if not "old-fashioned," in much of the Western world, although ministries of economic affairs and the tourist sector are generally wedded to developing their nation's economic brand (Murphy 2008: 10). Nation-branding has consequently been able to profit from the conceptual and semantic confusion surrounding public diplomacy.

By contrast, and more generally, international business studies and approaches have a lot to offer. Best practices in the commercial sector can teach government officials a great deal. Multinational corporations like Microsoft and British Petroleum (BP) take their corporate understanding of public diplomacy very seriously. BP's historic 2010 oil spill in the Gulf of Mexico is an example of corporate public diplomacy aimed at protecting commercial interests and cultivating BP's corporate social profile. Even before the current debates about public diplomacy, consultancy firms were advising governments on their communication strategy (Manheim 1994). Small states, and great and emerging powers (including Kosovo, China, and Brazil), attempt to boost their image by hiring Western companies to conduct multimedia offensives.

Governments nowadays form coalitions with businesses, so-called public-private partnerships (Pigman 2010: 124–29), to promote themselves and underpin their economic and commercial diplomacy (see Kerr and Taylor, chapter 13 in this volume). The 2008 global economic crisis increased this type of activity. Private sector initiatives, such as Business for Diplomatic Action in the United States between 2004 and 2010, can be categorized under the heading of **citizen diplomacy**, a concept that, in the words of one American practitioner, is based on the idea that "in a vibrant democracy, the individual citizen has the right—even the responsibility—to shape foreign relations" (Mueller 2009: 47). The important underlying premise here is that governments and citizens are, broadly speaking, in agreement about their country's direction, but that greater formal coordination between the two sectors is required.

This description of activities conducted by different public diplomacy actors can often be understood collectively as overlapping networks, significantly "not only around institutional mechanisms and procedures of political representation but in public debates in the global public sphere" (Castells 2008: 90). Those who aim to enhance their power through public diplomacy have to take advantage of these complex networks, make a good assessment of their own position in such networks, and interact effectively with other actors (Fisher 2010). This chapter's representation of public diplomacy's evolution is linked to international actors and their relationships. A contrasting view is offered by Castells (2008: 91), who regards public diplomacy as the **diplomacy of the public**. He argues that the "project behind the idea of public diplomacy is not to assert the power of a state or of a social actor in the form of 'soft power.' It is, instead, to harness the dialogue between different social collectives and their cultures in the hope of sharing meaning and understanding." From Castell's perspective, public diplomacy seeks to build a public sphere intended "to induce a communication space in which a new, common language could emerge as a precondition for diplomacy" (91). A growing number of governments are indeed showing awareness that they require a nimble public diplomacy, not merely for narrow national interest, and are embracing normative themes such as global justice, human security, and issues related to the new international security agenda. The argument is that a more broad-minded public diplomacy, ultimately in states' own interests, should focus less on exclusively national goals but deliver more on common and global problems (Murphy 2008).

In sum, it is clear that public diplomacy is no longer the preserve of states, and that states can actually learn a great deal from those who feel equally or even more at ease in a transnational network environment. This is particularly true with the use of new technologies that facilitate social networking (see Kurbalija, chapter 8 in this volume). Social media are increasingly utilized not only by individual government ministers and practitioners on sites like Facebook and Twitter but also as strategic organizing tools that create communities of interest and offer opportunities for joint problem solving, for instance, by means of **crowdsourcing**. Strategists realize that public diplomacy should go where people are found, where debates that matter are taking place, and before such debates reach conventional media outlets. The inherently democratic social media are no miracle cures but have enormous potential for public diplomacy. They enable a single public diplomacy officer at an embassy to reach hundreds, thousands, or even hundreds of thousands of people. Diplomatic establishments are nevertheless adapting slowly. Most embassies around the world still have static websites with no appeal to users of modern electronic media, but the number of diplomatic missions with fingers on the pulse of the times is growing. Foreign ministries will have to get used to the fact that building networks through public diplomacy is a continuous activity, and that this requires collaborative diplomacy and working with an increasing number of partners outside government (Hanson 2011).

KEY POINTS

- The public diplomacy of the heterogeneous group of intergovernmental organizations is characterized by procedures, purposes, and messages that are different from those of individual states.

- NGOs often collaborate with governments, but their modus operandi fits the international networking environment better than states' public diplomacy does.
- The corporate sector spends large sums of money on international reputation management and has much useful knowledge to offer governments.
- Governments increasingly require a public diplomacy that is more broad-minded and not solely focused on the national interest but also on transnational and global problems.

BEYOND THE NEW PUBLIC DIPLOMACY:
EVOLVING CONCEPTS

During the last decade, many books and articles have attempted to define and update the concept of public diplomacy, for example, when new insights emerged or best practices were rediscovered from Cold War experience (Cull 2008; Gilboa 2008; Gregory 2008a; Melissen 2005; E. H. Potter 2009; Snow and Taylor 2009). During this process many propositions about public diplomacy were found to be "old," such as the idea that public diplomacy is limited to foreign ministries' one-way communication *to* foreign publics. New propositions about public diplomacy aimed to make it a better fit for our time. For example, the dialogical or two-way-street exchange of listening and receiving was stressed. More emphasis was placed on long-term relationship-building (instead of largely defensive and policy-driven initiatives) and on collaborative activities with social actors, who were seen as more credible interpreters and receivers than state representatives (Melissen 2005). Between 2005 and 2010, the academic debate—involving many new arrivals' contributions—showed that the learning process from earlier discussions of public diplomacy had been somewhat fragmented and incoherent. As Fitzpatrick (2010: 88) rightly concludes, "To some degree, discussions of 'old' and 'new' public diplomacy have interfered with efforts to bring conceptual clarity."

Recent discussions on public diplomacy reflect a growing consciousness inside foreign ministries that public diplomacy is often conditional upon the cultivation of extragovernmental networks and satisfactory collaboration with domestic civil society actors. The assumption is that this "hidden-hand" public diplomacy approach is not handicapped by the lack of legitimacy that is often associated with official representatives. On politically or culturally sensitive issues, as well as matters involving religion, nondiplomats or unofficial diplomats often have more credibility in the eyes of individuals in foreign societies than the foreign government's accredited representatives, and their views are therefore more easily accepted as "right." Conceptual and theoretical issues remain with this approach, however, which have been insufficiently explored, and two of these deserve mention here.

First, and briefly, most literature has failed to consider the engagement of domestic publics in the concept of public diplomacy (Bátora 2006; Huijgh 2010; E. H. Potter 2009). An interesting analogy can be made here. Just as generations of diplomacy students have largely overlooked consular affairs and indeed public diplomacy as an element of overall diplomacy, many scholars today regard public diplomacy's domestic dimension as alien territory or even impossible by definition. Scholars generally examine state-level practices directed toward foreign publics but resist analyzing the role of domestic publics in foreign policy formation, for instance, in foreign policy dialogues, policy e-discussions, or, as in the Dutch "Rent an Ambassador" initiative (see box 11-3). Arguments for including domestic publics in conceptualizing public diplomacy have to be understood within broader changes in global society. The democratization of foreign policy making emphasizes the need for participation by domestic constituencies because globalization and worldwide communications blur the boundaries between domestic and international publics and policy environments. Interestingly, the idea that the two variants of public diplomacy are two sides of the same coin has, from the start, received a particularly favorable reception in Asia (see Ye and Zhang, chapter 16 in this volume). Like the concept of citizen diplomacy, the domestic dimension of public diplomacy nevertheless remains a teaser for many academics wondering where the analytical boundaries lie between diplomacy and cross-cultural internationalism, or between diplomatic practice and domestic affairs.

A second issue that deserves further scrutiny is the concept of soft power, or **attractive power**, and the way soft power works and how it relates to public diplomacy. The term "soft power" has entered popular discourse, especially in North America, Europe, and Asia, and has been directly translated into several languages. Politicians often refer to its importance. Sometimes, however, the exchanges between international relations scholars and students of public diplomacy appear like a dialogue of the deaf. Theorizing about soft power takes place mainly among international relations scholars and foreign policy analysts, who often turn a blind eye to diplomacy, and consequently to public diplomacy (for literature on China's soft power, see Gill and Huang 2006; Kurlantzick 2007; Suzuki 2009). Public diplomacy scholars, meanwhile, have been inclined to use the notion rather loosely (Melissen 2005). The concept of soft power was developed by a practitioner-scholar, Joseph S. Nye (1990: 32), who—as early as 1990—referred to the importance of "intangible power

---

BOX 11-3

Rent a Dutch Ambassador

As well as houses, cars, and movies, Dutch citizens have, since 2008, also rented ambassadors. On the Dutch Ministry of Foreign Affairs' website, Dutch business, student, or even sporting organizations can indicate which Dutch ambassador they would like to meet. When the designated ambassador returns to, or visits, the Netherlands, the ministry will try to arrange a meeting with the interested group or organization. In the ministry's words, "'Rent an Ambassador' puts ambassadors in direct contact with Dutch nationals," and ambassadors "give lectures, answer questions and provide information on their country or their work as diplomats" (Dutch Ministry of Foreign Affairs 2008a). But what is in it for the Dutch Ministry of Foreign Affairs? The Netherlands ministry calculates that "effective foreign policy requires coalitions of different actors—the public, civil society organizations, the private sector, governments," and that "public support for foreign policy and a better understanding of how we get results are indispensable in today's interdependent world" (Dutch Ministry of Foreign Affairs 2008b).

resources, such as culture, ideology and institutions." Nye (2008b: 94) later defined soft power as "the ability to affect others to obtain the outcomes one wants through attraction rather than coercion or payment." What Nye (2004) did not sufficiently emphasize in his work in the 1990s and the early 2000s, however, is that states and other international actors, such as nongovernmental and international organizations and regions, use public diplomacy to enhance their soft power. Nye's concept nevertheless has the potential to bring thinking on the nature of power in international relations closer to diplomacy, and the soft power concept has an intellectual pedigree that is, inter alia, based on accumulated wisdom in diplomatic practice. Nye built on the insights of such diverse predecessors as French statesman and diplomat Charles-Maurice de Talleyrand, who emphasized the importance of a nation's *réputation*, and the passionate realist theorist Edward Hallett Carr (1939), whose book *The Twenty Years' Crisis* pays substantial attention to "power over opinion."

Of particular interest to students of diplomacy is the criticism that Nye and his followers have paid too little attention to the question of how soft power actually works through processes of transnational socialization, in spite of their early appreciation of societal and cultural factors of power (Nye 2002: 9). Nye recently met some of the critics of his soft power concept halfway, by placing more emphasis on the fact that soft power cannot simply be wielded by an actor possessing and projecting it, but that "the subjects matter as much as the agents" and that attraction is "codetermined and persuasion is socially constructed" (Nye 2008a: x; see also Nye 2010: 219–21). After two decades Nye (2011) synthesized his thinking on soft power, various other dimensions of power, and public diplomacy. Some of the latest theoretical critiques, however, point out that the way soft power works may not always be clear in diffuse processes of social relations, and that an agent-focused approach risks neglecting the crucial socialization process that connects soft power and the mechanism of persuasion (Y. W. Lee 2011). Recognition that power is encapsulated in a complex pattern of reciprocal relationships may result in a more expanded power concept with roots in the discipline of sociology (B. Barnes 1988).

In the international sphere, the idea of **social power** presents itself as a challenger of soft power. It builds on a more contextual understanding of power and examines "the capacity to establish norms and rules around which actors' actions converge" (van Ham 2010: 8). The concepts of soft power and social power encapsulate the practice of public diplomacy. Diplomacy students' engagement in this scholarly debate may therefore encourage understanding of the relationship between public diplomacy and power, and strengthen the link between their academic field and the study of international relations.

KEY POINTS

- Official public diplomacy often depends upon collaboration with civil society actors, who possess greater credibility and whose views are more easily accepted as "right."
- Paradoxically, domestic outreach expands a country's engagement with foreign publics, as well as challenging conventional wisdom about what public diplomacy is, and what it is not.

- Debate about the concepts of soft power and social power, which incorporate public diplomacy, potentially strengthens dialogue between the study of diplomacy and international relations.

PUBLIC DIPLOMACY OUTSIDE THE WEST

In comparison with other aspects of diplomacy, exchange of research findings and best practices on public diplomacy exists among think tanks, academia, and government (Wilton Park 2010). Much recent learning about public diplomacy has taken place within the confines of the West. However, public diplomacy is not a solely occidental affair. The non-Western world's experiences are evidence that **culture** helps to shape and define public diplomacy, and that one can learn a great deal from public diplomacy as it unfolds in different settings.

Several states outside North America and Europe have developed the idea of public diplomacy, but soft power and public diplomacy have become particularly fashionable in East Asia. In comparison with the West, the larger role of the state is a striking feature of the Asian flavor of public diplomacy, as is the case in other areas of international politics, and hence the smaller potential of civil society to play a meaningful role in public diplomacy. Important drivers behind East Asian governments' soft power strategies are concerns about their perceived national identity and long-standing, unstable regional relationships. The most obvious challenge for China, Japan, and South Korea—the region's three leading economic powers—is that their soft power has a tendency not to keep pace with economic growth. Many people admire China's dazzling economic rise, but that admiration has not made China a more attractive country in the eyes of foreign publics (Page and Xie 2011). To their dismay, Tokyo and Beijing have experienced that global public opinion can be confusingly fickle and inconstant, as the Chinese government famously found out in the glare of media attention during the 2008 Olympic Games (see box 11-4).

Asians have learned from the accumulated public diplomacy experience in the United States and Europe, but the West can learn from Asian experiences too. The importance of culture in public diplomacy has often been underestimated by the United States and European countries. Widely reported flaws in recent US public diplomacy are that it is too often crisis-driven and policy-oriented, suffers from a short-term perspective, is prone to one-way messaging, and is patronizing in relations with other parts of the world (Seib 2009). For years the dominant US approach boiled down to exerting soft power in the hope of attracting others, instead of trying to cultivate long-term relationships and understand how foreign publics actually perceived the United States.

As well as taking notice of culture, Western public diplomacy should take account of relations across civilizations and religious divides. For a variety of reasons, Western public diplomacy in the Middle East—one of the world's least democratic and impenetrable regions—is simply more difficult than anywhere else. Recent turbulence in the Middle East and North Africa has not made things easier for Western public diplomacy strategists. Against the backdrop of a history of Western intervention and with today's terrorist threat permanently shadowing relations, public diplomacy aimed at the Middle East has produced more failures

---

BOX 11-4

China's Olympic Games

The 2008 Olympic Games provided China with an opportunity to display itself as a great power on the rise. There was no public diplomacy master plan for Beijing's communication with the world, and the slogan "People's Olympics" in a sense showed that most official attention was on China's own population. Officials also hoped that the games would help the world to "better understand China." However, foreign publics took a critical interest in what was going on within China's borders, in regions like Tibet and Xinjiang, and in issues such as human rights and the rule of law. The Chinese government learned several lessons from the 2008 games: that international cultural barriers can distort what is heard by those with another worldview; that the positive effect of sporting events on a country's image overseas is overrated; and that a patriotic overreaction to foreign criticism is likely to be counterproductive (Brownell 2009; Manzenreiter 2010; Wang 2009).

---

than successes. Western military operations in Afghanistan and Iraq, and US and European policies toward Iran and the Israeli-Palestinian conflicts, have contributed to turning the Middle East into the ultimate testing ground for public diplomacy. From a more clinical point of view, public diplomacy failures and successes in this complex theater have shed light on the requirements for effective strategies under adverse circumstances. State-of-the-art Western public diplomacy in the Middle East may even give a glimpse of future conditions for success. In terms of policy learning, and following insights from academia, it has led to explicit differentiation between government-initiated public diplomacy and non-state actor public diplomacy. The latter activity is continuing in multiple transnational networks; civil society organizations and people from the Arab and Islamic world are active public diplomacy participants at the center of events (van Doeveren 2011). Nimble governments recognize their lack of legitimacy in such transnational networks, in which an actor's power is increasingly defined by "who is connected to whom and for what purposes" (Slaughter 2009: 112). Most governments today, however, are slow to adapt to such new realities, and in fact are "still lacking a strategy on how to incorporate these new actors to grasp the opportunities they seem to hold" (van Doeveren 2011: 27).

KEY POINTS

- The experiences of the non-Western world demonstrate that one can learn a great deal from public diplomacy as it unfolds in different settings.
- In East Asian public diplomacy, the role of the state is still larger, and civil society's potential to have an effect on public diplomacy is smaller, than in the West.
- Recent experience has led to differentiation between government-initiated and non-state actor public diplomacy in transnational networks.

CONCLUSION

A variety of complex public diplomacy puzzles reveals what some countries have learned the hard way: public diplomacy offers no easy answers or quick solutions. It is hard to establish the kind of causal links that would demonstrate the effectiveness of specific public diplomacy policy actions. Public diplomacy literature rarely questions public diplomacy's effectiveness in the way that diplomats do, looking at things from a purely practical viewpoint and confronted with public diplomacy's limitations on a daily basis. Whether or not public diplomacy "works" is a question that is also at the forefront of the minds of people who make decisions about allocating resources, but there is another fundamental reason underscoring the case for public diplomacy. Only governments that would settle for the unimaginable—that is, mastering the art of diplomacy as it was practiced yesterday—could theoretically opt out of the game. Conversely, public diplomacy can only be properly understood if it is analyzed in the context of change in diplomacy at large. One consequence of this evolutionary process is that it will be more difficult to distinguish between diplomacy and public diplomacy, as the two practices are in the process of morphing into a more inclusive mode of diplomacy.

Future public diplomacy is likely to be more culturally sensitive. It will build to a greater extent on the legitimacy of nongovernmental actors, as well as the efficacy of extragovernmental networks and partnerships. Yet the future of public diplomacy is not free from paradoxes. Governments are adjusting to public diplomacy's "newness" and will probably aim to develop a more forward-looking public diplomacy in the wider context of overall foreign policy strategy. Simultaneously, however, the credibility of official public diplomacy, looking for clear deliverables, depends on the involvement of sometimes fickle civil society actors that are reluctant to give up their autonomy.

Furthermore, the required coherence of public diplomacy narratives will compel states, and other official actors, to reflect on identity issues and their specific aspirations in unfolding global controversies. The flip side is that such debates will take the same actors out of their comfort zone of relative control, and into a democratic arena where issues are being politicized and argued. Authoritarian states are confronted with the limits of state influence and the challenge of moving the needle of foreign perceptions in a world that is progressively transnational and empowers individuals more than ever before. There is no alternative to public diplomacy modernization, but influencing foreign publics will not become any easier.

QUESTIONS

1. How is public diplomacy part of broader changes in diplomatic practice?
2. What are the obstacles in measuring public diplomacy's effectiveness?
3. What can be learned from comparing best practices and failures in public diplomacy?
4. What are the constraints and possibilities for public diplomacy in the new global communications environment?

5. What are the arguments for and against a conceptual distinction and separate approach for "foreign" and "domestic" activities in public diplomacy?

6. Compare and contrast the public diplomacy of substate actors with the same activity by nation-states.

7. How are the concepts of public diplomacy and citizen diplomacy related?

8. Does the West provide a model of public diplomacy that can be usefully emulated by non-Western countries?

9. How can Western states' public diplomacy with the Arab and Islamic world serve their national interest without compromising their legitimacy?

10. Are China's lack of democracy and human rights record obstacles to the development of a successful public diplomacy?

11. Do you agree that public diplomacy's importance is overstated by governments, international organizations, and scholars?

12. Can countries enhance their soft power without resorting to public diplomacy?

13. What are the implications of the analysis in this chapter for your theoretical and practical understandings of contemporary diplomacy?

NOTE

1. The modern period stretches from the establishment of the resident embassy in Renaissance Italy to the rise of summitry after the Second World War and diplomacy's multilateralization in the last quarter of the twentieth century.

CHAPTER 12

Economic Diplomacy

Stephen Woolcock

CHAPTER CONTENTS

READER'S GUIDE

This chapter suggests we should adopt a definition of economic diplomacy that is selectively broad and takes account of how process shapes outcomes. We should understand economic diplomacy as a process of decision making and negotiation in international economic relations focused on core issues such as trade, investment, and finance. Economic diplomacy applies to both the negotiation of the framework within which international economic relations exist—in other words, rules, regimes, and norms as reflected in binding or voluntary agreements—as well as discrete negotiations that affect the creation and distribution of international economic activity. From this perspective we can argue that economic diplomacy in a globalizing world is becoming increasingly important, and, interestingly, it may well differ from general diplomacy, or traditional understandings of contemporary diplomacy.

INTRODUCTION

This chapter discusses what we should understand by the term economic diplomacy. It first defines the term, stressing that it should be understood as decision making and negotiation in core issues of international economic relations (see Zartman, chapter 6 in this volume). Second, it sets out reasons that economic diplomacy has become more important. While this is largely uncontentious if one assumes there are no major reversals in the level of **interdependence** of national economies in the world today, a more challenging question is whether there is something distinctive about economic diplomacy as opposed to general diplomacy—that is, the traditional understanding of diplomacy as an institution centered on the ministry of foreign affairs and professional diplomats who, inter alia, negotiate and implement states' political and security foreign policies. This is an important claim in the context of the current volume on diplomacy. Third, ways in which economic diplomacy could be seen to differ from general diplomacy are considered. As in the treatment of the topic of economic diplomacy as a whole, the focus is more on the process of decision making and negotiation rather than the relative importance of economics in international relations. Rather than presenting only a definition of what economic diplomacy is, the chapter seeks to illustrate the main arguments with reference to examples.

The chapter argues that economic diplomacy as defined here has become more important for a number of reasons. First, in the prevailing **liberal international economic order**, domestic economic objectives now rely more than ever on international cooperation. Second, this cooperation can no longer be achieved through the use of economic hegemony or thanks to the leadership or combined normative power of the "Western capitalist" economies grouped in the Organisation for Economic Co-operation and Development (OECD) "club model" that shaped much of international economic relations until the turn of the twenty-first century. The international (or global) economy today is multipolar, more so than the international system. The cooperation required to sustain a stable, open international economic system therefore requires a more active economic diplomacy—either to negotiate outcomes among states with rather more varied interests and normative views or to form more fluid coalitions of states than was the case in the OECD-dominated order. Finally, the chapter suggests that what distinguishes economic diplomacy from general diplomacy is the relatively greater number of actors involved, the fact that markets are endogenous to economic diplomacy, and that binding **regimes** and liberal concepts of mutual gains tend to be relatively more important.

KEY POINTS

- Economic diplomacy should be understood as decision making and negotiation in core issues of international economic relations.
- As defined, it has become more important to foster cooperation in our globalizing and multipolar world.
- Economic diplomacy could be seen to differ from general diplomacy.

WHAT IS ECONOMIC DIPLOMACY?

The definition of economic diplomacy used here is decision making and negotiation in international economic relations in core issues such as trade, investment, and finance. Also included are topics, such as the environment and development, that have considerable economic implications for policies in these areas. In other words, economic diplomacy is made up of subfields such as **trade, financial,** and

environmental diplomacy (Okano-Heijmans 2011b). A distinction between these subfields is useful because decision making and negotiation differs between them in subtle but important ways. For example, trade and especially environmental diplomacy have become topics of wide public interest in which there are a large number of interests involved. National decision making therefore tends to be fairly political and public, with agents in negotiations subject to quite tight domestic constraints and influences. In comparison, financial diplomacy, at least until the 2007–8 financial crisis, has been conducted by a relatively small policy community of experts in ministries of finance or central banks. Agents therefore tend to have rather more autonomy and make decisions and negotiate internationally under conditions that are less transparent than in trade or environment. This was also the case with **investment diplomacy** until the end of the 1980s when the wider civil society nongovernmental organization (NGO) community latched onto the negotiations on the Multilateral Agreement on Investment (MAI) within the OECD.

Economic diplomacy as used here applies both to the negotiation of the framework within which international economic relations exist—in other words, rules, regimes, and norms as reflected in binding or voluntary agreements—and to discrete negotiations that affect the creation and distribution of international economic activity. The tendency with some definitions of economic diplomacy is to exclude negotiation of such regimes and to limit the concept to more day-to-day interaction between states (Berridge 2002). The wider definition to include regimes is important because the negotiation of these forms an important part of international economic negotiations. For example, to exclude negotiations of multilateral, regional, or bilateral trade or investment agreements from economic diplomacy would be to exclude negotiations that have an enduring effect on international economic relations.

This is a broad definition by any measure, but it is possible to narrow down the field of interest a little by stating what is not included under economic diplomacy. First, **economic sanctions** or the use of economic leverage in the pursuit of foreign policy or political or security policy objectives are excluded. With sanctions the focus is very much on the use of economic relations as a means of pursuing foreign policy interests, so decision-making procedures tend to be centralized in foreign ministries, which, as noted later, is seldom the case in economic diplomacy.[1] Second, economic diplomacy as defined here differs from the concept of "economic statecraft." Economic statecraft, as defined by David Baldwin (1985) and used in primarily US literature, is also close to the security end of the spectrum. Again, it tends to relate to the use of economic leverage as part of a broader, more strategic approach. This broad approach means that the focus of research is not on the detailed negotiation of mainstream economic issues but on how these can further a broader, one might even say grand, strategy. Third, the definition suggested here would not include "commercial diplomacy," which best describes the actions of governments or other actors in promoting investment or seeking contracts or orders for companies based in the home state. Economic diplomacy facilitates trade and investment by negotiating market access, rules, or agreed norms and standards, but does not extend to "looking for business." The latter activity continues to be undertaken by many countries, such as through trade delegations led by a head of state or minister.

BOX 12-1

Process Shapes International Economic Relations

The current Doha Development Agenda (DDA) of the WTO offers welfare gains for all participants, so an economic analysis would suggest there should be agreement. The nature of the negotiation—a largely conventional market access negotiation covering nonagricultural market access, agriculture, and perhaps services—is more straightforward than the previous Uruguay Round. But it has not been possible to conclude the DDA whereas the Uruguay Round was successfully concluded. While there are many factors at work here, it is clear that the way in which the parties have gone about the negotiation and national decision-making procedures have clearly been one fairly important factor in the DDA outcome.

The definition used here also relates to the process of decision making and negotiation in international economic relations rather than the substance, which would fall under trade or financial policy (Okano-Heijmans 2011b: 15). An analysis of economic diplomacy therefore implies a study of how the process shapes outcomes. Typically, research would compare negotiations in which the structure of power and interests are essentially the same, but the outcomes are different. One example would be a comparison of the Cancún World Trade Organization (WTO) ministerial meeting in September 2003, which collapsed, and the negotiations on the so-called Framework for the Doha Development Agenda (DDA) negotiations in Geneva in July 2004, which had a far more positive outcome. As the nature of interests changed little, process must have had an impact on the different outcomes. The rationale for such an approach is that process matters. A case can clearly be made that process issues rather than the structure of interests are factors in shaping international economic relations. Again, trade negotiations can be used as an example here (see box 12-1). This definition of economic diplomacy clearly locates it in the nexus of international political economy and international institutions.

KEY POINTS

- Economic diplomacy is made up of subfields—such as trade, financial, and environmental diplomacy—and decision making and negotiation differs between them in subtle but important ways.
- It is important to note what is *not* included in economic diplomacy.
- An analysis of economic diplomacy implies a study of how the process shapes outcomes and comparisons of negotiations in which the structure of power and interests are essentially the same, but the outcomes are different.

WHAT MAKES ECONOMIC DIPLOMACY IMPORTANT?

There are a number of reasons for arguing that economic diplomacy has become more important and therefore deserving of some distinctive treatment. This section summarizes a number of reasons for making this argument.

The Need to Reconcile Domestic and International Policy

All international relations and therefore all diplomacy require international policy to be reconciled with domestic policies. In the case of economic diplomacy, the need is arguably greater because, with the progression in international interdependence toward globalization, the ability to deliver in key areas of domestic policy has become dependent on international policies. Economic growth, jobs, investment, financial stability, and environmental aims depend on cooperation and thus on the outcome of economic diplomacy. This tends to make the interface more immediate. In foreign policy, a country's negotiating position or policy may be constrained by domestic policy considerations, and at the extreme, governments may stand or fall as a result of a foreign policy. But with globalization, the achievement of domestic policies has come to depend more and more on economic diplomacy.

Solutions to Challenges Facing National Governments Require International Cooperation

A related point to that made earlier is that in certain key policy areas, it is no longer possible to find responses to challenges purely through domestic policy. Financial stability and global warming provide the most obvious examples of this, but they are by no means the only ones. Given the degree of interdependence of financial markets, no country, not even the United States or the European Union (EU), was in a position to reestablish stability in financial markets following the 2007–8 financial crisis. Nor was it possible to deal with the effects on the real economy without international cooperation. Future financial crises will also only be avoided, or their impact diminished, through cooperation in establishing regulatory standards for the financial sector.

The environment provides another example of how domestic policies are no adequate response to challenges such as global warming. Reductions of climate change emissions in the EU, even if substantial, will have no impact on global warming if other countries fail to act. Perhaps less obvious, but equally important, is that the maintenance of a stable and open international trade and investment regime is now arguably a prerequisite for wealth creation and jobs. Although all states can theoretically close markets and withdraw from international markets, states can also decide on more or less liberal policies for investment and trade. But withdrawing from the international economy is only possible at considerable cost. Even the largest economies, including the United States, China, and the EU as a single market, now depend on companies engaged in global supply chains for their growth and employment.

Increased Need for Negotiated Solutions

Economic diplomacy is now relatively more important because of the greater need for negotiated solutions to challenges of international economic relations. In the multipolar international economy of the twenty-first century, coercion or even dominance by a group of key economies, such as the OECD, is no longer a viable approach. In the past it was possible for a hegemon to coerce or provide the international **public goods** required to maintain a stable international economy. The pros and cons of **hegemonic stability theory** or leadership can be discussed, but there seems little doubt that the United States largely shaped the Western capitalist international economic order in the immediate postwar years. As US hegemony waned, it was replaced by the US-led club model as exemplified by the OECD, the **Quad** and the **Group of Seven (G7)**. Although of somewhat different compositions, these clubs or coalitions of relatively like-minded countries were then able to shape international economic relations (see box 12-2).

In the field of financial diplomacy, the G7 constituted the club model approach to cooperation (albeit not always sufficiently) to manage the world economy after the floating of exchange rates from 1973. There was a strong transatlantic bias in trade, investment, and financial diplomacy, with policy cooperation between the United States and European members of General Agreement on Tariffs and Trade (GATT), the OECD, the International Monetary Fund (IMF), and G7 tending to dominate. Japan was of course a member of the club but not proactive in seeking to shape outcomes. This transatlantic-based system continued well into the 1990s in trade, with the United States and the EU in particular shaping the Uruguay Round. In financial diplomacy it endured even longer, up until the financial crisis of 2007–8, when it became clear that solutions could not be found without wider participation.

Since the turn of the century, however, the transatlantic-based system has become progressively less viable. In the case of trade, the emergence of China and India and the activism of Brazil have meant that agreement in international trade now requires the support of these countries. For India and Brazil, the desire to have a greater role is not new. They have always sought more influence, but until their economic growth enhanced their market power, they had little impact. Today, the **Group of Twenty (G20)**, established in mid-2003, now has both market and moral weight.[2]

The result of these structural changes in international economic relations is that outcomes now need to be negotiated. It is no longer possible for a hegemon to shape through leadership, or coerce other parties to cooperate. Nor is it possible

---

BOX 12-2

The OECD in International Economic Relations

The OECD developed (largely voluntary) norms and standards for cooperation that were then subsequently applied in more binding international rules. The OECD's work in the 1970s on technical barriers to trade and government procurement was transferred to the General Agreement on Tariffs and Trade (GATT) during the Tokyo Round. The OECD work on agriculture, services, and investment in the 1980s shaped GATT negotiations during the Uruguay Round. In terms of investment norms developed in the OECD during the 1960s, the Abs-Shawcross Draft Convention on Investments Abroad was used as the basis for bilateral investment agreements negotiated by the European states in the following decades. Later work in the OECD formed the basis for the approach to investment provisions in free trade agreements and negotiations on the Multilateral Agreement on Investment (MAI).

for the OECD club to shape the norms for others to follow. Outcomes now need to be negotiated because solutions are no longer possible without the "buy-in" from other major emerging or developing countries. There was of course negotiation in the OECD club. Indeed, OECD codes or norms often only emerged after many years of dialogue and debate among the members. But the OECD/Western club consisted of more or less like-minded countries. In the international economy of today, one cannot assume that all the major players have like minds. Negotiations have therefore also become more complex.

Shaping the Nature of the International Economic Order

Economic diplomacy is also important because it has an impact on the shape and nature of the international economic order, whether liberal or **mercantilist**, rules- or power-based, cooperative or anarchic. The general trends in the international economy order, such as from the **embedded liberalism** of the immediate post–Second World War systems, to the liberal paradigm of the 1980s and 1990s, are clearly shaped by many factors captured by international political economy. But insofar as the process of negotiations shapes outcomes, so too does economic diplomacy.

The End of High and Low Politics

Economic diplomacy has also become more important with the end of the distinction between "high politics" and "low politics" that prevailed during the Cold War. During much of the 1950s and especially the 1960s, when the Cold War was at its deepest, policy makers and analysts distinguished between the high politics of national security and foreign policy, and the low politics of international economic relations.

The end of the Cold War finally brought an end to this distinction. New security threats were identified, such as international crime, terrorism, and, more recently, global warming. There has been a "securitization of international economic relations," meaning that aspects of international economic relations are defined in terms of their impact on security. For example, the stability of the international financial system, or rather the lack of it, is seen as a threat to the security of the Western capitalist system and thus to **nation-states** that rely on this system for their wealth and prosperity. The concept of "collective security" has been used in the context of the effects of economic underdevelopment. For example, economic underdevelopment is seen as one cause of political instability in developing or middle-income countries that can, in turn, lead to destabilizing outward migration or terrorism.

But such securitization of international economic relations and development can distort the debate. By definition, such a securitization is concerned with a treatment of economic relations that is near the security end of the spectrum. Economic diplomacy as defined here is more concerned with wealth creation and its distribution, which requires proper consideration of economic means and objectives and should therefore be placed in the center of the spectrum. A simpler way of putting it is to say that international economic relations have become relatively more important since the end of the Cold War and the deepening of economic interdependence and globalization.

KEY POINTS

- Economic diplomacy is increasing in importance for several reasons.
- With globalization, the achievement of domestic policies has come to depend more and more on economic diplomacy.
- It is no longer possible to find responses to challenges purely through domestic policy.
- There is a greater need for negotiated solutions to challenges of international economic relations.
- Economic diplomacy has an important impact on the shape and nature of the international economic order.
- Since the end of the Cold War and the deepening of economic interdependence or globalization, international economic relations have become high politics.

IS ECONOMIC DIPLOMACY DISTINCTIVE?

Can economic diplomacy be seen as distinctive, as a separate field of analysis or study, or is it simply part and parcel of diplomacy? In many respects the differences between economic diplomacy and general diplomacy have been addressed earlier in this chapter. Diplomacy tends to be associated with general political relations, with the more or less formal relations between states, and with the reconciliation of the political aims and objectives of nation-states. Economic diplomacy is concerned with reconciling domestic and international economic policies, as well as reconciling states' foreign economic policies. A more difficult question is, then, whether there is a distinction between economic diplomacy and "foreign economic policy." While there appears to be no clear definition of the term "foreign economic policy," it is generally concerned with the content of policy rather then the process of decision making and negotiation. It has also tended to be used in the context of the foreign policies of specific states, so also tends to cover similar ground to that of economic statecraft and thus appears to be more toward the security/foreign policy end of the spectrum discussed earlier (Bergsten 2004; Smith 2004). Where foreign economic policy focuses on how decisions are taken or the factors shaping foreign economic policy, there would be little difference between it and what we have called economic diplomacy.

While a distinction can be made between the more substantive nature of foreign economic policy or foreign policy, on the one hand, and the more process nature of economic diplomacy, on the other, similar approaches are used to analyze the two. For example, it is normal to use rationalist, realist, domestic/institutional, **constructivist,** or **two-level game** approaches for both. The study of economic diplomacy may also use **regime theory** or international institutions theory to assess how these shape, and are shaped by, economic negotiations (Woolcock 2011). But these various analytical approaches have been adapted and applied to look at the process of negotiation (Sebenius 1983; Odell 2000). Negotiation analysis has also been used to some effect in analyzing economic diplomacy. First developed for business negotiations, there is now a growing literature on the application of negotiation analysis to international economic negotiations (Devereaux, Lawrence, and Watkins 2006). In more recent times, there has also been work in Europe on the issue of the EU (Dür and Elsig 2011; Woolcock 2012).

More Actors Involved

Economic diplomacy is distinctive in the sense that it tends to involve more actors than general diplomacy. There is of course a trend toward a greater number of actors in all forms of diplomacy, but it could be argued that this is especially true for economic diplomacy. In general diplomacy, the ministry of foreign affairs is still central to any analysis. This is not the case for economic diplomacy. Foreign ministries are seldom in control of economic diplomacy and often struggle to retain a role or even an overview of what is going on.

This is not to say that ministries of foreign affairs are not involved at all. For example, in **economic summitry,** ministries of foreign affairs often fulfill important coordinating functions, such as through the political **sous-sherpas** of the **Group of Eight (G8)** or in the G20 summits. Note that even here, overall coordination is generally undertaken by the main sherpas, who are in many cases located in the offices of the head of state or government, such as in the Cabinet Office in the UK, or the White House in the United States, or the Kanzleramt in Germany. When economic issues are discussed alongside broader foreign policy issues, such as in the G8, ministries of foreign affairs have a greater coordinating role. The G7 and G8 process has quite often linked economic and political or foreign policy issues, although the agenda has passed through various cycles. Originally the G7 was about economic relations. During the 1980s, there was more emphasis on foreign and security policy issues as the United States under President Ronald Reagan and the United Kingdom under Prime Minister Margaret Thatcher stressed that the main way of addressing international economic challenges was to put one's own house in order. The end of the Cold War brought economic issues back in with support for countries undergoing transition. The 2000s saw a shift toward concern about those countries that had not benefited from globalization. These were mostly in sub-Saharan Africa, hence the various initiatives aimed at supporting African development. With the response to the financial crisis, the cycle has come back to international finance in the G20 (Bayne 2011).

It is also important to recognize that in the normal course of events political-level negotiations follow more technical work. Typically, negotiations will start with a technical working group to explore the scope of future negotiations and the prospects of a mutually beneficial agreement. This stage in any negotiation is important as the issues are framed and the agenda is influenced. But the work is generally carried out by technical experts. When negotiations proper begin, they are often broken into various negotiating groups with officials taking the lead. Only at a later stage when there is a need to strike deals or make trade-offs between different issues will ministers become more involved in the detail of negotiations.

It is also helpful to consider the differences between countries. Some have significant institutional or administrative capacity, and some, such as least developed countries, have very little. In the smaller developing or least developed countries, a lot of the heavy lifting in terms of economic negotiations tends to be done by the foreign service because there is limited international expertise in other ministries, or because of limited resources for officials to participate in international negotiations. Thus **ambassadors** from developing or least developed countries are often involved in WTO negotiations in Geneva. As ambassadors will tend to be generalist or experts in general diplomacy, they will not be the best placed to deal with technical issues and will find themselves sitting across from expert officials from the larger or more developed countries. This raises important questions for developing country economic diplomacy, such as how to make best use of limited capacity, or how to adapt "classical" forms of foreign service to deal with technical, specialist economic negotiations. Given that "the devil is in the detail" in much economic diplomacy, failure to address this issue can put least developed countries at a disadvantage.

General diplomatic skills are not enough when it comes to negotiating detailed provisions in trade or other agreements. Often the more mundane issues, such as rules of origin in trade agreements, can have a major impact on trade. A lack of technical background or limited knowledge of the costs and benefits of any economic negotiation can also influence the negotiating positions adopted by agents. All negotiators must operate under conditions of "bounded rationality," that is, limited or at least incomplete knowledge of the economic implications of any agreement. But this will tend to be more the case for developing country negotiators with a classical diplomatic training, and little if any research capacity to draw on. When unsure about the costs and benefits of any agreement, the prudent negotiator will adopt defensive positions, prefer to defer or block new initiatives, and keep the debate on more political or ideological issues that require less technical expertise. Such defensive positions then put a break on negotiations (for two different standpoints, see Rana 2011; Soobramanien 2011).

Leaving aside these qualifications, the main point made here is that economic diplomacy is distinctive in that it generally involves and is often led by ministries other than the ministry of foreign affairs. These economic diplomacy negotiations are undertaken with their opposite numbers in other countries or in **multilateral**, regional, or bilateral negotiations with the aim of reconciling domestic and international policy objectives, and therefore constitute diplomacy, although not general diplomacy (see Wright, chapter 10 in this volume).

The picture varies from policy area to policy area as intimated earlier. In the case of trade, negotiations are either led by a specialist trade ministry or in some cases by a merged ministry of foreign affairs and trade. Some countries have recognized the growing importance of economic issues by merging trade and foreign affairs. This is more often the case among smaller countries, but not always. Canada, for example, has long had a combined ministry of trade and foreign affairs. There appears to be something of a trend toward such mergers, with more developing countries moving to merge trade or external economic relations and foreign policy. Kenya with its new constitution is an example. In the ministries that lead on trade, there will also be a distinction between technical- and political-level negotiations. As noted earlier, the real substance of trade diplomacy generally concerns detailed issues, such as schedules on market access or rules on how to discipline national regulatory policies. Negotiations of this type are, for the most part, conducted by specialist officials. Only in the critical stages of trade negotiations, when cross-issue bargains need to be struck, will ministers engage in detailed negotiations. For example, substantive negotiations for the twenty-seven member states of the EU are frequently conducted by officials at the level of heads of units, which is three levels down from the political level of European Commissioner.[3]

Ministries of finance have, if anything, more autonomy in conducting financial diplomacy than is the case in trade diplomacy. The shift to the G20 as the principle forum for financial diplomacy has tended to consolidate the role of ministries of finance in the sense that they have been leading on G20 issues since the original G20 finance ministers forum was established in 1999. The G20 summits, which also include the central banks of the countries concerned, work on the basis of detailed economic analysis, for which ministries of foreign affairs have no competence.

International environmental diplomacy is also conducted, for the most part, by specialist ministries. Again, as for the case of trade, much of negotiation concerns detailed technical issues and is conducted by expert officials. On issues such as climate change, it is the technical specialists in the ministries of environment (or specialist climate change departments) who have the institutional memory and negotiating capacity. Much of the early or preparatory negotiation on issues such as climate change is conducted in technical working groups that can last weeks at a time. Ministers will get involved in political-level negotiations in which consolidated texts or agreements are produced. Given the high political salience of some issues, heads of state and government may then get involved as in the case of the Copenhagen Conference of the Parties on the United Nations Framework Convention on Climate Change in December 2009. This can create coordination problems between the three levels (technical, ministerial, and heads of government) (Christiansen 2011).

In the case of economic diplomacy, therefore, the institutional memory and negotiating capacity are dispersed throughout government. This need not mean decentralized decision making, and there would generally be interministerial or departmental coordination to ensure that the views of all the relevant ministries are fed into the negotiations. But it means that economic diplomacy requires probably a greater degree of such coordination than in the case of foreign policy diplomacy.

In addition to negotiations being led and conducted by various ministries within government, there are also agents outside of government that engage in economic diplomacy. These can take the form of public—or quasi-public—agencies, or private, nongovernmental actors. An example of the former would be independent central banks or financial regulators. Central banks are engaged in economic diplomacy in a more or less structured form. Central banks have engaged in financial diplomacy for decades in the Bank for International Settlements, and they play a key role alongside ministries of finance in bodies such as the Financial Stability Board, which has the task of coordinating financial market regulation in the wake of the 2007–8 financial crisis. Independent regulatory agencies are also actively engaged in economic diplomacy in the field of international finance in organizations such as the Basel Committee on Banking Supervision, the International Organization of Securities Commissions, and the International Association of Insurance Supervisors. These bodies are key, developing and implementing regulatory standards for financial markets. When it comes to international accounting standards, it is a private organization, the International Accounting Standards Board, that plays a leading role in economic diplomacy. Adjustments to accounting standards were one of the important responses to the 2007–8 financial crisis: because the accounting standards used at the time of the crisis measured the value of assets on the market, the financial crisis resulted in a lower valuation of bank assets, which had a pro-cyclical effect. In other words, as the market value of assets fell during the crisis, the financial institutions had to either sell assets or retain existing capital in order to maintain a sufficient level of capital adequacy. This in turn exacerbated the credit crunch for the financial institutions. Another example, of purely private, market operators playing an important role in policy, can be found in the credit rating agencies; although it would be a stretch to say that these engage in economic diplomacy, their decisions can have profound implications on financial markets.

In other sectors of the economy, quasi-public bodies such as standards bodies are engaged in negotiating international standards in organizations such as the International Organization for Standardization or the International Electrotechnical Commission. These standards influence national regulatory policies on safety and environmental standards that facilitate production operations in different countries by providing, for example, common quality standards. Similarly, standards developed in the Codex Alimentarius Commission of the World Health Organization are important in setting standards for food and animal health, and provide a vital input into policy debates on issues such as the use of genetically modified crops, national sanitary and phytosanitary controls, and the uses of biotechnology.

The private sector and civil society NGOs are, of course, also engaged as actors in economic diplomacy (see box 12-3). In most cases, this is through lobbying or seeking to influence governments or international organizations. But in some cases, there is coordination and policy making within the private sector, as in the case of international accounting standards mentioned earlier.

Markets Endogenous to Policy

Another distinctive feature of economic diplomacy is that markets are endogenous. In other words, economic diplomacy is shaped by and shapes developments in markets to such a degree that markets become "actors" in the policy process. In a predominantly liberal order of global markets, this impact of markets has become arguably more pronounced. Again, the financial sector is a very clear illustration of

---

BOX 12-3

The Kimberley Process

The Kimberley process—which involved the regulation and control of the trade in diamonds in order to ensure that "blood diamonds" produced to fund insurgencies in various sub-Saharan African countries did not find their way onto international markets—was essentially negotiated by the main diamond trading companies in response to pressure from civil society NGOs.

---

how markets are endogenous to international financial diplomacy. The response to the 2007–8 and other financial crises shows how decision making and negotiation are geared to influence markets but at the same time are driven by markets. On occasions, financial diplomacy has had to be conducted over the weekend before financial markets open on the following Monday in an effort to stabilize markets and thus minimize the risks of bank failures, or the ultimate costs to the taxpayer in terms of bailing out troubled financial institutions or states in the case of sovereign debt negotiations.

Markets play a similar role in trade and investment diplomacy but with somewhat longer-term effects. For example, in a global economy in which nation-states compete less in exporting products and more in attracting foreign investment and thus economic activity and jobs, investment negotiations can have an important impact. Although the effect of investment agreements has probably been overstated in much of the policy debate, governments have been, in part, motivated to negotiate bilateral investment agreements, or to include investment in preferential trade agreements, by a desire to attract inward investment. The real or perceived threat of companies moving elsewhere is also a factor in a wide range of regulatory policies, from social and environmental policies to the protection of intellectual property rights. The financial services sector is again a recent example of this effect. Efforts to strengthen the regulation of financial markets and reduce the risk of a further international financial crisis have led governments to seek tighter regulation of the financial sector. But tighter regulation in one market can be perceived or presented as driving market activity to other financial centers that have lower regulatory standards or enforce regulation less rigorously. Governments then seek international cooperation to ensure that the regulatory standards are more or less equivalent in all the major markets because of market pressure. In other words, there is a desire to ensure that international financial market regulation is compatible with domestic policies. Here is a clear example of the need in economic diplomacy to reconcile domestic and international policy.

The endogenous nature of markets in economic diplomacy can also be illustrated in the field of environmental diplomacy, through the effects of what is termed "carbon leakage." Carbon leakage occurs when investment and thus production in carbon-intensive processes move from a jurisdiction in which greenhouse gases are relatively tightly regulated or taxed to a location of less control or lower taxation. In this case, markets are endogenous to decision making and negotiation of international environmental policies, because in the absence of an international agreement on climate change, market forces will result in increased costs for countries introducing policies aimed at reducing greenhouse gas emissions. Indeed, it is the economic costs of environmental policy that justify including environmental diplomacy under the general heading of economic diplomacy.

More Focus on Value Creation?

Another possible distinguishing feature of economic diplomacy is that it tends to be more concerned with value creation than value-claiming. This is less clear-cut, since economic diplomacy can also be driven by mercantilist objectives concerned with relative gains. But in a predominantly liberal international economic order, wealth creation through increased trade and investment is a central motivating factor in international negotiations. The growth of national economies in an interdependent or global economy depends on international efforts to cooperate. Economic growth, through increased trade and investment, requires cooperation in international trade or investment policies that increase mutually beneficial trade and are therefore value-creating. Economic diplomacy always involves elements of value-claiming as well as value-creating. For example, virtually all international economic negotiations have **reciprocity** as an explicit or implicit objective. Trade negotiations are based on reciprocal market openings, even if the position of developing countries is recognized by expecting less than full reciprocity from them. Climate change negotiations are based on common but differentiated commitments from all countries. In negotiations on how to reduce macroeconomic imbalances in the world economy, there is an expectation that both surplus and deficit countries will contribute. But the pursuit of excessive value-claiming would not be compatible with a predominantly liberal economic order.

Clearly any distinction between a predominantly value-creating economic diplomacy and a more value-claiming diplomacy is only relative and depends on the continuation of a predominant liberal economic order, compared with a more realist, balance-of-power based view of foreign and security policy.

Regimes Play a Bigger Role

Another potentially distinguishing feature of economic diplomacy is that it is more concerned with negotiating regimes. As discussed earlier, in some fields of economic diplomacy, regimes have become more binding on national governments. The Uruguay Round of trade negotiations, for example, resulted in trade rules that were both binding on national governments and enforceable through the equally binding WTO dispute settlement procedures. Subsequently, there has been a significant increase in preferential or free trade agreements that are equally binding on national governments and clearly impose real limits on national policy autonomy. Bilateral investment treaties, of which there are now around 3,000, also impose binding obligations on governments that are enforceable by international arbitration panels. Failure to provide adequate protection for foreign investors can result in states being required to pay substantial financial compensation to the companies concerned.

In the field of finance, regimes have been less binding, although again in the wake of financial crises there have been efforts to strengthen the various codes or standards. In environmental policy, the picture is mixed, with a trend toward binding agreements in some fields, such as the Montreal Protocol on Substances That Deplete the Ozone Layer, but less in other areas. In the crucial area of climate change, efforts to achieve binding international regimes have been only partially successful. Compared with international relations in general, however, international economics appears to have a denser network of relatively binding regimes. In foreign policy, national states have been much more reluctant to commit to binding regimes.

Where binding international regimes have been negotiated, this creates a clear obligation to bring domestic policy and legislation in line with international obligations. Thus economic diplomacy implies a more immediate link between domestic and international policies. Foreign policy or diplomacy is clearly also related to domestic politics (for example, domestic support for a particular policy or action), but the domestic pressures concerned are more often political (and thus no less important to a government) and less based on legislation.

A Greater Focus on Plurilateral or Multilateral Diplomacy?

Another possible distinctive feature of economic diplomacy is a greater use of multilateral or **plurilateral negotiations**. In all diplomacy, bilateral links and activity tend to predominate. But the emergence of a global economic order and more binding international regimes means that economic diplomacy makes greater use of all levels of negotiation, whereas foreign policy diplomacy remains relatively more based on bilateral relations. As with the other possibly distinguishing features of economic diplomacy, one is concerned with the relative importance of multilateral diplomacy. On this and other aspects of this section, more work would be needed to test the various suggested distinctions.

KEY POINTS

- Economic diplomacy is distinctive for a number of reasons: it involves more actors than general diplomacy; it is often led by ministries other than the ministry of foreign affairs; negotiations are often conducted by specialist officials; because many actors are involved it requires greater coordination than foreign policy diplomacy; there are many agents outside of governments involved in economic diplomacy; it is shaped by, and shapes, markets; it is more concerned with value creation than value-claiming; it is more focused on negotiating regimes than are foreign policy negotiations; it makes greater use of multilateral or plurilateral negotiations compared with the greater use of bilateralism in political and security foreign policy diplomacy.
- In these ways, economic diplomacy is different from general or traditional diplomacy.

CONCLUSION

Economic diplomacy is concerned with decision making and negotiation of core issues in international economic relations. Such a definition enables us to focus on the activities of governments and other actors that seek to promote stable, sustainable, economic growth in a predominantly liberal global economy. In such a global economy, national economic objectives cannot be achieved without international cooperation, hence the focus of economic diplomacy on reconciling domestic policies and international policies and obligations. Given the inevitable linkages between economic and political relations, it is helpful to focus on the use of economic instruments for economic ends and exclude the use of economic instruments or leverage for immediate political or foreign policy objectives. Political or foreign policy considerations will still be a factor in all economic diplomacy, such as when the promotion of stronger economic relations is seen as a means of promoting stability in a country or region or consolidating political relations with a strategic partner. Equally, it is suggested that the business end of the spectrum, what has been referred to here as commercial diplomacy, is excluded from the definition.

Economic diplomacy has become more important as a result of globalization, because domestic economic objectives rely more than ever on international cooperation, thus requiring governments to reconcile the two. It has also been argued that economic diplomacy has become more important because of the emergence of a multipolar international economic order in which negotiation has had to replace hegemonic leadership, or the OECD-club model. With a more heterogeneous economic order, there is a need for more negotiation between states that are less like-minded than those of the OECD. Alternatively, more active economic diplomacy is needed to form coalitions of states that can shape outcomes.

It is harder to identify factors that distinguish economic diplomacy from other forms of diplomacy. In this chapter, it has been suggested that there tend to be more actors engaged in economic diplomacy, that markets are of such immediate importance that they are endogenous to decision making, and that the negotiation of binding international regimes is relatively more important in economic diplomacy than in general diplomacy.

QUESTIONS

1. Compare and contrast the definitions of economic diplomacy in this chapter as well as those in Bayne and Woolcock (2011) and Okano-Heijmans (2011b).

2. What are advantages and disadvantages of the definition offered in this chapter?

3. How would you distinguish between process and structure? Why is it important to analyze process when explaining the nature of economic diplomacy?

4. Discuss the examples of process given in this chapter, research other examples, and then explain why the focus on process informs explanations of the outcomes.

5. Do you agree with the claim that economic diplomacy is increasing in importance?

6. What is the understanding of diplomacy that substantiates the claim that economic diplomacy has distinctive features?

7. Which actors have influence in economic diplomacy? What does this imply for the role of foreign ministries?

8. What are the disadvantages that least developed states confront in conducting economic diplomacy? How might such problems be addressed?

9. How have trade, financial, investment, and environmental diplomacy evolved over the last decade?

10. What are the implications of the analysis in this chapter for your theoretical and practical understandings of contemporary diplomacy?

NOTES

1. Maaike Okano-Heijmans refers to a spectrum reaching from the more political/strategic elements of economic diplomacy, such as sanctions, through core issues in economic relations as discussed here, to the business end of the spectrum in the shape of commercial diplomacy. Okano-Heijmanns also distinguishes between commercial diplomacy, trade and financial diplomacy, and inducements (all three of which would be seen as economic diplomacy here) and sanctions. Generally speaking, she has a similar understanding of economic diplomacy to that of the author, with the exception of appearing to exclude the negotiation of international rules governing economic relations. For a further discussion of definitions, see Okano-Heijmanns (2011b: 20).

2. This is the trade G20 consisting of Brazil, China, India, and other developing and emerging countries and should not be confused with the G20 meeting of finance ministers now extended to heads of state and government, which includes all major economies, that is, the developed OECD countries.

3. In the EU, the Foreign Affairs Council signs off on trade agreements, but it does so in most cases after the substance of any agreement has been approved at the level of senior trade officials in the Trade Policy Committee.

CHAPTER 13

Track-Two Diplomacy in East Asia

Pauline Kerr and Brendan Taylor

CHAPTER CONTENTS

- Introduction: debates about diplomacy and track-two diplomacy
- An analytical framework and methodology for investigating track-two diplomacy
- The practice of track-two diplomacy in East Asia: environmental, security, and economic issues
- Explaining track-two diplomacy in East Asia
- Conclusion

READER'S GUIDE

Studies of track-two diplomacy, that is, analyses of non-state actors (individuals or organizations) involved in diplomacy, are problematic for students.[1] There are different claims about the purpose and functions of track-two actors and their relationships with track-one, or state, actors. More research is needed to clarify the nature of track-two diplomacy before it can be understood from the perspectives of the traditional state-based or "new" multiactor models that offer contrasting explanations of contemporary diplomacy. This chapter is a response to this challenge. It argues that research based on three comparative studies of track-two diplomacy around environmental, security, and economic issues in East Asia reveal interesting findings. Rather than supporting the new multiactor diplomacy models, which elevate the importance of non-state actors and their role in track-two diplomacy, it appears that in this region, the traditional state-based model better explains track-two diplomacy. Contemporary diplomacy is changing, but the traditional model still retains explanatory power, at least in East Asia.

INTRODUCTION: DEBATES ABOUT DIPLOMACY AND TRACK-TWO DIPLOMACY

Studies of **globalization** highlighting new international issues and actors are changing the way many observers think about the nature of diplomacy. Indeed, there is now a debate about whether the traditional understandings of diplomacy—as a process of **communication, representation**, and **reporting** of states' interests by diplomats to and from foreign ministries by a network of **embassies** and **consulates**—remains a valid explanation of modern diplomacy. One development that has led to questions being raised about the traditional model is the increased role of **non-state actors** in both globalization and diplomacy. There are claims that non-state actors are now "nonofficial diplomats" and "new diplomats" and that their activities are evidence of a "new diplomacy," an alternative multiactor model that, it is claimed, better explains modern diplomacy than does the traditional model (Kelley 2010; Riordan 2003). A related claim is that some non-state actors conduct track-two diplomacy, a concept that is used to differentiate these actors from track-one diplomats serving as foreign service officers under the guidance of a foreign ministry in their country's capital.

The literature on track-two diplomacy is particularly challenging for students. There are different definitions of non-state actor diplomacy: for example, it is also called "citizen diplomacy," "parallel diplomacy," "unofficial diplomacy," and "private diplomacy." More important, there are different claims about the purpose and functions of track-two actors and their relationships with track-one state actors. Several examples illustrate the point. One of the key purposes of the US-based Carter Center, established in 1982 by former president Jimmy Carter and his wife, Rosalynn, is to conduct citizen diplomacy to further international peace between conflicting parties through dialogue and negotiation (Carter Center n.d.). However, the particular objectives of the center have at times been at odds with official US foreign policy, as when Carter met Fidel Castro in 2002. Carter's citizen diplomacy angered President Bill Clinton, who instructed his vice president, Al Gore, to tell Carter not to interfere in Cuban policy and US foreign policy (Leguey-Feilleux 2009: 333). It is not always clear in some accounts if the purpose of track-two diplomacy is to support a state's or government's view of its national interests, or not.

For some scholars the state's national interests are being overtaken by the transnational interests of non-state actors. John Kelley (2010: 302) argues that "non-state actors present a formidable challenge to state primacy in the diplomatic world" because they take on "issues 'no longer conterminous' with national interests" and they are "orientated towards transnational issue areas." Kelley's theoretical proposition challenges the traditional state-centric notion of diplomacy. Yet, against this idea that track-two actors challenge state primacy is the argument, found in the literature that analyzes track-two diplomacy in East Asia, that track-two diplomacy involves serving state officials who attend track-two meetings in "their 'unofficial' or 'private' capacities" often to "test" a potential state policy (P. M. Evans 1994: 125).

Another issue is that many studies of track-two diplomacy emphasize that its functions and processes are different than those of track-one diplomacy. If so, then that raises questions about its scope, conceptually and in practice. For example, Joseph Montville (1998), who coined the term "track-two" in 1982, argues that its processes operate outside those adopted by track-one officials and "[begin] with a few select participants who have unofficial and informal interactions with their opposite numbers." The differences between track-two and track-one diplomacy are highlighted strongly by Louise Arbour, president of International Crisis Group, a well-known nongovernmental organization (NGO). She argues that track-two diplomacy is "unofficial diplomacy" and that its agents "play multiple roles that go beyond traditional diplomacy" (Arbour 2009: 5). If, as both Arbour and Montville suggest, track-two diplomacy is different than track-one diplomacy, then its boundaries need to be clarified. This review shows that the existing literature offers different understandings about the nature of track-two diplomacy. It suggests that more research is needed to help students of diplomacy understand the concept and its boundaries.

This study is a partial response to this research challenge. It seeks to answer the following questions from an East Asian perspective: What is the nature of track-two diplomacy? What is the power relationship between track-two and track-one? Is track-two diplomacy explained by the two competing models of modern diplomacy? To answer these questions, all of which cast light on the nature of contemporary diplomacy, the chapter takes the following steps. First, it outlines an analytical framework for examining the purpose, functions, and relationships of track-two organizations that are indigenous to East Asia.[2] East Asia is chosen to examine track-two diplomacy not just because it is the most dynamic political and economic region in world politics but also because state-centric principles appear stronger in this region than they do in Europe and North America, where much of the literature on the role of nonstate actors has it origins. The framework is applied to a comparative study of three case studies of track-two diplomacy concerned with environmental, security, and economic issues.[3] A comparative methodology is adopted: there are few, if any, such studies on track-two diplomacy, including across these issue areas. Second, the chapter analyzes the comparative findings from the case studies and compares them with the dominant theories of modern diplomacy—the traditional and "new" multiactor diplomacy models. Judgments are made about which of the models best explains track-two diplomacy, and what that implies for the debate about the nature of contemporary diplomacy. Finally, the implications of the findings for future research on diplomacy are briefly discussed.

KEY POINTS

- Studies of track-two diplomacy present challenges for students of diplomacy. There is little clarity about the purpose, functions, and processes of track-two diplomacy and its relationship with track-one.
- Explaining track-two diplomacy from the perspective of the two models that are offered to explain contemporary diplomacy is thus difficult.
- In response to these challenges, this chapter offers some preliminary findings from comparative research on track-two diplomacy in East Asia.

AN ANALYTICAL FRAMEWORK AND METHODOLOGY FOR INVESTIGATING TRACK-TWO DIPLOMACY

The framework depicted in table 13.1 identifies the variables that are used to examine the three case studies of track-two diplomacy in East Asia. It builds on a framework developed by Karin Bäckstrand (2008) for examining the nature of "public-private partnerships," involving government and intergovernmental officials and non-state actors, focused on climate change issues. The framework developed in this chapter aims to establish the nature of track-two diplomacy by analyzing the following key variables: the purpose, function/processes, relationship with track-one, and the surrounding conditions or context of track-two diplomacy. To that end it suggests additional subvariables that operationalize, or provide indicators that substantiate the key variables. For example, the second column in table 13.1 highlights the main functions and processes that private actors can potentially perform: prevention, education, advocacy, rule and standard setting, mangement, and rule implementation through service delivery. Collectively these variables help to analyze the nature of track-two diplomacy and also provide the basis for assessing which model of diplomacy—the traditional or the new—best explains track-two diplomacy in East Asia. The methodology is comparative: it traces the variables across the three case studies and then compares the findings to the tenets of the two main theories of diplomacy.

Table 13.1 An Analytical Framework for Examining Track-Two Diplomacy

THE PURPOSE OF TRACK-TWO DIPLOMACY	FUNCTIONS AND PROCESSES	RELATIONSHIPS WITH TRACK-ONE DIPLOMACY
• State-centric interests • International public interest • Global governance objectives • Transnational policy networks • Other	• Prevention: via provision of services, e.g., mediation, confidence-building • Education: via academic and public information • Advocacy: via, e.g., political campaigns, lobbying officials • Rule and standard setting: via, e.g., active participation in decision making, negotiations • Management through service delivery: via goods (e.g., food for humanitarian relief) and facilitation of mediation and negotiation and socialization • Rule implementation: via, e.g., monitoring compliance • Other	• Hierarchical relations • Autonomy from the state • Equal partnership • Other **Conditions** • Internal and external sovereignty • Interdependence

KEY POINTS

- Table 13.1 provides an analytical framework that emphasizes key variables and several subvariables for understanding the nature of track-two diplomacy in East Asia.
- The framework supports a comparative methodology for answering the questions posed in this study.

THE PRACTICE OF TRACK-TWO DIPLOMACY IN EAST ASIA: ENVIRONMENTAL, SECURITY, AND ECONOMIC ISSUES

This section applies the framework depicted in table 13.1 to three case studies. Some preliminary comments about the selection of case studies and the East Asian context are useful at this point. The case study on the environmental issue of climate change has the potential to show the nature of track-two diplomacy on a matter that is reasonably new and, at this moment, low politics yet sensitive. The case studies on security and economic issues have the potential to show track-two diplomacy around traditional, high-politics matters. Locating the case studies in East Asia ensures that track-two diplomacy is examined in a region that is widely regarded as a hard state-centric context and is therefore an appropriate test.

Environmental (Climate Change) Track-Two Diplomacy

Much of the literature on environmental issues, including climate change, refers to the significant role that non-state actors play in globalization, global governance, and environmental diplomacy. Two examples of non-state activity confirm the point. In the 2009 Conference of the Parties (COP) to the United Nations Framework Convention on Climate Change in Copenhagen, some countries, such as Australia, invited climate change NGOs to be members of their official delegation (Callick 2010). The second example concerns the NGO TRAFFIC, a wildlife trade-monitoring network. TRAFFIC sets regulatory standards that many states adopt and which TRAFFIC monitors (www.traffic.org/overview). These two observations, showing the significance of non-state actors in particular contexts, obviously need to be placed in a broader body of research before generalizations about environmental non-state actors and their role in track-two diplomacy can be offered.

Bäckstrand (2008) provides some theoretical generalizations about the activities of climate change non-state actors. In her research on "transnational climate partnerships" between, on the one hand, governments and intergovernmental organizations (referred to in her study as public actors) and, on the other hand, corporate and civil society (referred to as private actors), she suggests some theoretical insights about the purpose, functions, and processes of non-state actors and the relationship between track-two and track-one actors. Bäckstrand's (2008: 84) findings indicate that, despite the growing number of climate partnerships, this development does not, contrary to popular perceptions, diminish the authority of the sovereign state because "much of private authority is exercised in the 'shadow of hierarchy' where the state and public actors exercise authoritative decision-making." Public actors maintain leadership over the processes of interstate bargaining and negotiation (Bäckstrand 2008: 99; Andonova 2010: 26). Non-state climate organizations certainly play key roles in advocacy, rule implementation, and service provision. But again these roles are usually delegated by the state or at least are not contested by the state (as evidenced by Australia inviting NGOs to the 2009 COP in Copenhagen).

When this general picture of climate governance and track-two diplomacy is compared with that in East Asia, there is evidence that there are further restrictions on the role of non-state actors. First, private environmental/climate actors remain in short supply, despite an increase in their numbers over the last decade or so (Yoon 2003: 49). The environmental NGOs (ENGOs) that have been established are a response to widespread public concern about the environmental degradation in East Asia. In northeast Asia acid rain, and marine and dust pollution are among the main problems, and in Southeast Asia forest degradation, and air and water pollution are prominent issues. Like the rest of the globe, both regions suffer from, and contribute to, climate change. China, for example, has the unenviable status of being the major regional emitter of human-produced carbon dioxide, mainly from coal-fire combustion and vehicle emissions.

Second, in northeast Asia, track-two diplomacy is restricted not just because there are a limited number of formal ENGOs but also because the formulation of climate and environmental policy is usually dominated by the states in that region. Most arrangements are bilateral or trilateral intergovernmental ones. For example, the Tripartite Environmental Ministers' Meeting (TEMM) launched in 1999 involves South Korea, Japan, and China. TEMM's objective is to promote sustainable development through environmental cooperation among officials of the environmental administrations of the three countries. An example of a **multilateral** meeting that includes and goes beyond northeast Asian countries is the East Asia Summit (EAS) Environment Ministers Meetings. It involves countries from the Asia-Pacific attending the EAS, most recently in 2011 the United States and Russia (see International Environmental Cooperation Toward Sustainable Development 2010).

A climate change arrangement that does involve state and non-state actors is the Asia-Pacific Partnership on Clean Development and Climate (APP), established in August 2005. Membership of the APP includes Australia, China, India, Japan, South Korea, and the United States. The arrangement is between the states and business groups, and the objective is to develop climate-friendly technologies for renewable energy and energy efficiency. However, Bäckstrand (2008: 86, 91) argues that this arrangement is an example of "cooptation of private actors by public actors" and that it functions primarily as an implementation network. That is, governments are partnered with private actors in this case not for their advocacy, rule-setting, or service delivery capabilities but rather for the implementation of a state-centric interest that also suits business interests.

Third, as just suggested, the purpose of climate change track-two diplomacy is confined to supporting state-centric interests. The main interests of the public actors tend to be self-interested state-centrism rather than "enlightened self-interest" that serves both state interests and a global good. Many powerful states can maintain control over their interests not only by co-opting private actors but also by establishing new agreements or forums that cause fragmentation and therefore weaken the potential for a robust global climate regime. The APP may well be an example of this tactic (Biermann et al. 2009: 23). A central interest of states, especially the many developing states in East Asia, is to have a strong economy. China, while sensitive to climate change and reducing coal-fire emissions and other climate change–inducing factors, in the final analysis puts economic growth before resolving environmental degradation.

Fourth, the state and public actors have almost complete authority over the range of functions and processes that private actors involved in public-private partnerships can potentially perform: prevention, education, advocacy, rule- and standard-setting, implementation, and service delivery. The processes adopted by those private actors who are *outside* of public-private partnerships in northeast Asia are primarily aimed at generating interaction between these groupings. For example, the processes of the Atmosphere Action Network Northeast Asia, a regional network comprising ENGOs, are confined to sharing resources and to educating the general public about environmental problems. Beyond supporting public protests on specific environmental problems and lobbying officials, ENGOs have few options for influencing track-one environmental diplomacy. ENGOs are constrained by public actors' domination of the environmental agenda, through government coercion and co-optation. Regional governments have little interest in private actors playing a significant role in regional environmental politics (Yoon 2003: 51).

Environmental track-two organizations in southeast Asia have a similar profile to those in northeast Asia. There are intergovernmental regional arrangements, such as the Association of Southeast Asian Nations (ASEAN) and the Mekong River Commission, which focus on environmental and climate change issues. However, these have structural limitations, such as the noninterference diplomatic code of the "ASEAN way" (see Bátora and Hardacre, chapter 17 in this volume), which undermine their effectiveness. Moreover, despite the growing number of civil society groups within Southeast Asia concerned with the region's numerous environmental problems as well as the introduction of several mechanisms that ostensibly allow for track-two organizations to interact with track-one organizations, there are constraints. Antonio Contreras (2008: 169) argues that non-state actor organizations (both local and transnational) are most often perceived by the state as eroding national sovereignty, and as a result there is "lukewarm state support, if not direct hostility and suspicion of multi-stakeholder and transnational efforts and partnerships." Moreover, the relationship between some non-state actors and the state is uncomfortably close. In the arena of non-state governance through forest certification for sustainable forest management, governments' relationships with logging corporations are often self-serving. Lars Gulbrandsen (2004: 90–91) cites a study by Peter Dauvergne of corporate forestry practices in the Asia-Pacific region, including Southeast Asia's tropical wood industry, which found that the "informal and political nature of state-business relations in the region represents a considerable barrier to change in logging practices on the ground."

Fifth, overall in East Asia the conditions that limit the development and the functions of non-state actors and their relationship with track-one actors include the following: deeply held perceptions and practices of internal and external sovereignty; the dominance of short-term economic interests over long-term environment interests; the supremacy in many countries of authoritarian governments over liberal democratic values and civil society; and, at the international level, geopolitical distrust and a preference for bilateral relationships over multilateralism.

In sum, the findings from this case study of environmental track-two diplomacy focused on climate change indicate that in East Asia this process is largely driven by state-centric interests and its functions mainly concern low-level and indirect advocacy by the relatively few ENGOs in the region. Rule- and standard-setting are not usually performed by non-state actors. The APP is a possible example of public-private partnership implementation, although business groups appear to be relegated to that task by the state. Similarly, there is little evidence of active service delivery in climate governance or by track-two actors beyond indirect advocacy. The conditions that appear to set the context for this situation are explained earlier in this chapter.

KEY POINTS

- The dominance of the state in East Asia sets the context of track-two diplomacy around environmental issues.
- There are relatively few environmental track-two actors.
- The purpose of the business non-state actors involved in environmental public-private partnerships with the state is largely to implement state-centric interests that coincide with business objectives.
- Beyond these relatively few public-private partnerships (compared with intergovernmental arrangements), the purpose of other track-two diplomacy efforts is to conduct low-level indirect advocacy to the state. The main function is building coalitions of civil society groups, which is done mostly through processes of resource-sharing.
- Although less so than in the past, the conditions that explain this situation are steadfast adherence by states to the principles of external and internal sovereignty and, as a result, limited expansion of civil society.

Security Track-Two Diplomacy

Track-two diplomacy is a relatively new phenomenon in Asian security politics. Prior to the 1990s there was a dearth of multilateral dialogue in the security sphere—at both the track-one and track-two levels—and the prospects for developing such channels appeared bleak. A lack of trust driven by deep-seated historical animosities, the region's relatively backward economic conditions, and the ideological discipline imposed by the superpower stalemate between the United States and the Soviet Union each played a part in dampening enthusiasm for regional security dialogue and cooperation. However, with the end of Cold War, there were dramatic changes in the economic and strategic dynamics of the Asian region, which have played an integral role in reversing this state of affairs. As this case study will demonstrate, the catalytic role played by track-two organizations should not be underestimated.

A survey of Asia's emerging institutional "architecture" highlights just how far security dialogue in this region has come in a relatively short period. This is nowhere more evident than at the track-two level, where, according to one reputable estimate, hundreds of such arrangements dedicated to the discussion of Asia-Pacific security matters are now operating in the region (Japan Center for International Exchange 2009). At one end of the spectrum are relatively long-standing track-two organizations, such as the ASEAN Institutes of Strategic and International Studies (ASEAN-ISIS) and the Council for Security Cooperation in the Asia-Pacific (CSCAP), typified by a high level of institutionalization. At the other are a number of smaller and arguably more nimble arrangements (for example, bilateral dialogues organized by regional institutes and think tanks such as the Shanghai Institute of International

Studies and the Australian Strategic Policy Institute). The track-two security organizations listed are similar to the track-two environmental arrangements in East Asia in that they have very limited roles in governance.

The purpose of track-two diplomacy in the Asia-Pacific is overwhelmingly one of supporting state-centric interests (see box 13-1). Indeed, it is not uncommon for security (and economic) track-two organizations to establish a formal relationship with a designated track-one counterpart wherein the track-two organization is formally designated as an "analogue" to a track-one counterpart body. ASEAN-ISIS and CSCAP, for instance, are track-two analogues to ASEAN and the **ASEAN Regional Forum (ARF)**, respectively. An interesting facet of these arrangements is the lack of cooperation between track-two bodies themselves. Consistent with the state-centric focus of both the track-one and track-two approach to diplomacy, there is also little evidence in the security sector to suggest that track-two organizations are designed to serve global governance or transnational interests. Even the nontraditional security agenda, involving such issues as human security, health security, and climate change, that are a feature of both track-two and track-one arrangements, is dominated by state interests or by transnational interests that complement those of the state.

In terms of functions and processes, the security contributions of track-two are concentrated in the service provision area. Track-two organizations such as CSCAP are intended to provide a reservoir of expertise that can serve as a source of advice, particularly with respect to issues of a longer-term nature where governments may not have sufficient expertise or time to contemplate these in depth. Governments will sometimes use track-two processes to float "trial balloons"—ideas that may simply be too sensitive to introduce immediately at the track-one level—to see how they are received. Track-two processes in the security sector can periodically provide an alternative diplomatic route when progress at the track-one level either stalls or is nonexistent. Two such examples are the South China Sea workshops and

---

BOX 13-1

An Example of Track-Two Support for State-Centric Interests

An oft-cited example of a track-two process explicitly supporting state-centric interests occurred during the late 1990s when the ARF called upon CSCAP to develop a working definition of **preventive diplomacy**. While agreeing on the importance of preventive diplomacy, ARF ministers were at that time unable to realize its implementation due to their inability to agree upon preventive diplomacy definitions and principles. This task was devolved to CSCAP on the grounds that track-two participants were better positioned to transcend national perspectives to arrive at a shared definition and set of principles governing the application of preventive diplomacy. In practice, however, it was precisely because of the familiarity of CSCAP participants with government thinking and the involvement of officials in the drafting of the CSCAP statement that their recommendations were taken seriously by policy makers and ultimately adopted by the ARF.

the Northeast Asian Cooperation Dialogue, which provided a venue for discussion and confidence-building on South China Sea and Korean peninsula security issues at a time when few mechanisms for addressing these at the track-one level were available.

Track-two organizations are also increasingly being viewed as a useful conduit for bringing together a range of state and non-state actors. The London-based International Institute for Strategic Studies has been able, through its annual Shangri-La Dialogue in Singapore, to bring together more than 200 Asian defense ministers, civilian and military officials, journalists, academics, and think tankers in the relaxed setting of an academic conference. Track-two processes are also seen as performing useful "socialization" functions, such as in the case of CSCAP "working group" meetings that allow Chinese and Taiwanese participants, for example, to exchange views in both formal and informal settings, when otherwise they may not have the opportunity to do so.

Of the other functions included in the framework guiding this chapter only *advocacy* is typically performed by track-two security organizations in the Asia-Pacific. So-called track-two elites—a descriptor employed by Brian Job (2003: 253) with reference to key individuals who have been influential in initiating and advancing track-two processes, such as CSCAP—frequently publish their writings on the pages of leading regional and international newspapers championing the merits of track-two activities or advocating a particular policy line that is consistent with the ethos of their affiliate track-two organization. Track-two organizations sometimes even find themselves having to lobby for the attention of their track-one counterpart.

Beyond this function, however, track-two organizations are rarely if ever involved in rule implementation, or rule- and standard-setting. As David Capie (2010: 292) observes, this reflects the prevailing conditions in East Asia, namely, "the continuing importance of narrow notions of sovereignty and a marked reluctance on the part of states to share policy making in the domestic context or to delegate decision making powers to regional institutions." In those rare instances where states are willing to devolve rule implementation, or rule- and standard-setting functions to regional institutions, increasingly governments are delegating this authority to track-one groupings, as opposed to their track-two counterparts. For example, where during the 1990s the development of technical cooperation and confidence-building measures relating to the South China Sea disputes largely remained the purview of the South China Sea workshops, increasingly that role has been elevated to the track-one level, leaving track-two actors out of the picture, as evidenced by the establishment in November 2002 of a code of conduct between ASEAN and China calling specifically for the exploration and undertaking of a range of cooperative activites not dissimilar to those previously being addressed through the workshop process.

The nature of track-two and track-one power relationships in the security sector is thus decidedly hierarchical. In at least three key respects, this has been to the detriment of track-two organizations in the Asia-Pacific. First, the system of establishing track-two analogues to service track-one institutions means that the fortunes of a number of leading track-two bodies are determined by the performance of their track-one counterparts. In recent years, for instance, perceptions of CSCAP's continued utility have been challenged by similar questions regarding the performance and relevance of the ARF. Second, given the catalytic role that track-two groupings played in spurring regional security dialogue during the 1990s, they have essentially become victims of their own success to the extent that a burgeoning of track-one institutions has diminished the perceived need for the additional capacity that track-two organizations were at that time seen as providing.

Finally, the symbiotic nature of the relationship between track-two and track-one arrangements has also generated what Herman Kraft (2000) terms an "autonomy dilemma" wherein track-two organizations are seen as having become too closely aligned with their track-one counterparts, thus inhibiting their capacity for independent and innovative thinking. The extent of this perceived problem differs from country to country. In some instances, such as in the Chinese and North Korean cases, the demarcation between track-one and track-two is virtually indistinguishable. In others, the strength and proximity of the relationship between track-one and track-two is much less intimate, and track-two groupings enjoy more autonomy from the state than perhaps they would prefer. This, in turn, suggests that it may be appropriate to think in terms of differing national "cultures" of track-two diplomacy in the Asia-Pacific security sector and thus be cautious about generalizations.

KEY POINTS

- In the security sector, the primary purpose of track-two groupings is to support state-centric interests. Relations between track-one and track-two processes are often institutionalized: for example, the track-two organization CSCAP is formally designated as an "analogue" to the track-one counterpart body, the ARF.
- Track-two organizations in the security sector provide services that typically include expertise on issues of a longer-term nature; floating of "trial balloons" pertaining to sensitive diplomatic issues; alternative diplomatic routes when official paths have stalled or are nonexistent; providing a conduit between state and non-state actors; and socialization functions.
- The relationship between track-two and track-one differs from country to country. In general, the relationship is hierarchical and sometimes detrimental to the track-two component due to issues of autonomy and the conditioning impact that success (or the lack thereof) of the track-one counterpart exacts.
- The conditions that restrict track-two activities include regional states' support for internal and external sovereignty and control over what constitutes national interests and a reluctance to share decision making.

Economic Track-Two Diplomacy

Multilateralism in the Asia-Pacific arguably owes much to the pioneering efforts of two important track-two initiatives in the economic sector—the Pacific Basin Economic Council (PBEC) and the Pacific Trade and Development (PAFTAD) conference. PBEC and PAFTAD were established in 1967 and 1968, respectively, at a time when little else in the way of regionwide multilateralism existed. To be sure, ASEAN was also emerging at that time, but its initial economic focus and mandate were very much at the subregional, Southeast Asian level. While treated as distinct case studies for the purposes of this chapter, it is also significant that track-two processes in the economic sector have directly inspired the shape of track-two organizations in the security sector. Many of the participants engaged in economic track-two processes—such as PAFTAD and the Pacific Economic Cooperation Council (PECC)—were also directly involved in the formation of CSCAP. Indeed, as Desmond Ball (2010: 11) notes, "CSCAP was loosely modelled on the PECC experience and practice."

PBEC and PAFTAD were forerunners to PECC, which, from the time of its emergence in 1980, gradually began to overshadow them as "arguably the most important track-two policy network in the Asia-Pacific region" (Komori 2009: 328). Unlike PBEC and PAFTAD—whose membership bases are composed predominantly of businesspersons and academics, respectively—PECC adopted a tripartite membership structure that included representatives from academia, business, and industry, plus government officials participating in their private capacities. As Charles Morrison (2004: 557) has observed, "This formula allowed PECC to acquire significant resources from government and government-related institutes as well as from business." Over recent years, however, PECC's largely unrivaled capacity to secure such support has been challenged by the appearance of new track-two actors in the economic sector. These include the Network of East Asian Think Tanks (NEAT), which is a track-two grouping established in 2003 and developed out of ASEAN plus (China, Japan, and South Korea); the Council on East Asian Community, which is a Japanese track-two initiative launched in May 2004; and the Economic Research Institute for ASEAN and East Asia (ERIA), which is also a Japanese initiative that was established in 2008 through the EAS. In addition to these organizations, prominent industry groups such as the **Asia-Pacific Economic Cooperation (APEC)** Business Advisory Council (ABAC), which was established in 1995 and is made up of three politically appointed business representatives from each APEC member economy, and the East Asian Business Council (EABC), which was inaugurated in 2004 and comprises three private sector representatives from each of the ASEAN plus economies, have also emerged.

As in the security and environmental sectors, supporting state-centric interests constitutes the primary function of these groupings. In most cases, a formal institutional tie has been established between each of the aforementioned track-two processes and a track-one counterpart. PECC is the track-two analogue for APEC, for example, while NEAT is officially recognized by ASEAN plus, and ERIA by the EAS. In the case of groups such as PBEC, ABAC, and EABC, supporting business and industry interests is also an important rationale for their existence. Indeed, when PBEC was first established, it was focused primarily upon facilitating dialogue and providing commercial opportunities between regional business leaders. Although gradually becoming more interested in policy issues through the 1970s, it was not until the establishment of APEC in 1989 that PBEC members actively sought to influence policy makers (Morrison 2004: 555).

A feature of track-two groupings in the economic sector that differentiates them from those in the security sphere is the extent to which many of the same individuals belong to a number of different track-two bodies. As Stuart Harris (1994: 384) observes:

The individuals involved are often close participants in one or more of the other organizations, and in Southeast Asia, many are also involved in ASEAN activities. These personal networks among the elites reinforce the influence of elite membership groupings, facilitate cross-cultural cooperation, and help develop a convergence of ideas and understandings.

Consistent with their mandate of serving state-centric and/or business and industry interests, the functions and processes of most Asian track-two processes are concentrated in the area of service provision. These services can be categorized into two broad categories—*ideational* and *practical*. As noted at the outset of this case study, many of the *ideas* developed in economic track-two settings have contributed directly to Asia's burgeoning multilateralism at the official and nonofficial levels. The formation of PECC, for example, has been partly attributed to a study produced by two PAFTAD members, Peter Drysdale and Hugh Patrick, which was initially commissioned by the US Senate to examine the feasibility of a Pacific regional trade organization (Harris 1994: 383). When APEC was formed in 1989, it subsequently borrowed directly from PECC's institutional model by identifying "economies" rather than "states" as the primary criterion for membership.

Over subsequent decades, APEC has sought out more *practical* contributions from PECC, asking its track-two analogue to gather information or to undertake studies in areas where it does not possess sufficient research capacities and/or expertise. An oft-cited example is the assistance that APEC officials requested from PECC to document existing trade barriers after they arrived at the so-called Bogor Goals for achieving free and open investment in the Asia-Pacific in November 1994.

Applying our analytical framework, advocacy is the other major function performed by track-two processes operating in the economic sector. A primary function of NEAT, for instance, is to advocate practical policy recommendations that are initially developed through designated working groups, finalized at the annual NEAT conference and formally tabled at subsequent ASEAN plus gatherings. In theory at least, this advocacy function ought to be facilitated in the case of many economic track-two organizations given that they formally participate in track-one meetings. Representatives from ABAC and PECC, for example, are able to attend APEC meetings. In practice, however, despite the privileged access of such track-two processes, their relationship with the track-one level is decidedly subservient. As Yasumasa Komori (2009: 328) suggests in his study of regional economic track-two diplomacy, "The relationships between track-one and track-two are more hierarchical than horizontal in the sense that states remain the primary actors in shaping the Asia-Pacific regional governance mechanism." The relationship is one of subservience not only because the first track essentially regulates the extent to which economic track-two processes are able to influence its decisions and the subsequent implementation thereof—track-two organizations in the economic sector rarely if ever perform standard-setting or rule implementation—but also because governments typically provide the funding upon which many track-two organizations in the economic sector depend for their survival.

While it is true that private sector organizations sometimes offer an alternative source of finance that can assist in circumventing this funding-dependence dilemma, the burgeoning economic track-two diplomatic activity that has taken place in Asia over recent decades has generated a heightened sense of competition for these still relatively scarce private sector resources. In this regard, some economic track-two organizations—such as PBEC—have arguably become victims of their own success by stimulating a growth in multilateral processes that has increasingly called into question their utility and undermined their financial viability.

KEY POINTS

- The primary function of most track-two bodies in the economic sector is to support state-centric interests. Some organizations also provide support to business and industry interests as a secondary function, although this function is becoming less prevalent.
- The services provided to track-one organizations by their track-two counterparts in the economic sector can broadly be characterized as being either *ideational* or *practical*.
- The relationship between track-one and track-two processes in the economic sector is hierarchical. The influence of track-two processes is heavily regulated by their track-one counterparts, which essentially also control the relatively scarce funding that these bodies have at their disposal and are increasingly competing for.
- Among the conditions that restrict track-two processes are a growing level of comfort with regional track-one arrangements in the economic sector, along with a concomitant burgeoning in track-two processes, which has led to an intensification of competition for governmental attention among these organizations.

EXPLAINING TRACK-TWO DIPLOMACY IN EAST ASIA

Having examined track-two activities across three issue areas in East Asia, we are in a better position to answer the questions that orientate this study: What is the nature of track-two diplomacy? What is the power relationship between track-two and track-one? Is track-two diplomacy explained by the two competing models of modern diplomacy? What does the answer to this question tell us about contemporary diplomacy?

It is useful at this point to briefly recall the main feature of the models, some of which were mentioned in the introduction. In addition, box 13-2 highlights the features of the new multiactor diplomacy model, while table 13.2 elaborates the traditional model.

Several findings support the relevance of the traditional model for explaining track-two diplomacy in East Asia (see table 13.2). First, the purpose of the three sets of track-two actors in the final analysis is to support, or at least not overly undermine, the state's environmental, security, or economic interests. If non-state organizations adopted another purpose, it would put them at risk of becoming irrelevant in policy circles. Some organizations may well believe that their governments should improve their policies, for example, that they ought to give more support to regional multilateral institutions, such as developing the ARF's agenda

---

BOX 13-2

The New Model of Diplomacy: Its Purpose, Function and Processes, and Relationships with Other Actors

Purpose: highly variable and overspecified (for example, ranging from supporting state-centric interests to supporting global interests, international public interests, or the interests of transnational policy networks that may or may not involve state interests).

Function and processes: the functions are highly varied and overspecified (for example, ranging from traditional functions to unlimited measures adopted by non-state actors and NGOs, such as delivering humanitarian assistance). The processes are also variable (for example, mediation, negotiation), but the power relations that pertain to these processes are underspecified.

Relationships with other actors: very variable (for example, includes traditional state-to-state, state/non-state, and non-state to non-state relationships). Again the power relationships around different issues is underspecified, although the inference is that state/non-state partnerships are based on near equal power-sharing.

---

and institutional structure, but the principle of state-centric interests appears to take precedence over the principle of purely transnational or global governance interests. Track-two actors support state interests or at least the perpetuation of the state system in East Asia.

Second, the functions and processes of track-two organizations across the three issue areas are very similar. Most track-two organizations are confined to service delivery of different types (for example, academic research on environmental, security, and economic trends that is policy relevant) to track-one actors. Two other functions of non-state actors included in the framework—rule-setting and rule implementation—are not routinely conducted across the issue areas.

Third, the relationship between track-two and track-one actors is one of hierarchy, with track-one actors dominating either directly or indirectly the role and possible influence of track-two actors. The conditions that correlate with these findings are both macro (states' support for the principles of internal and external sovereignty and underdeveloped civil societies) and micro (insufficient governmental ideational or material support for track-two organizations).

For these reasons the traditional model, rather than the new diplomacy model, better explains the nature of track-two diplomacy in East Asia. The traditional model emphasizes that officials, leaders, and diplomats interact with non-state actors over some of the government's policy issues, and that officials have more power to make final policy decisions. The empirical findings show that despite a globalizing context and degrees of interdependence, around economic development, for example, governments in the region continue to uphold principles of internal and external sovereignty and put state interests before transnational or global interests.

Table 13.2 Track-Two Diplomacy Compared with the Traditional Model of Modern Diplomacy

TRADITIONAL MODEL	TRACK-TWO DIPLOMACY ENVIRONMENTAL/CLIMATE ISSUE	TRACK-TWO DIPLOMACY SECURITY ISSUE	TRACK-TWO DIPLOMACY ECONOMIC ISSUE
Purpose: • State-centric policy interests **Function and processes:** • Representation, communication, reporting by foreign ministry officials via processes of persuasion (through argumentation, both noncoercive and coercive, short of the wholesale use of force) and political power **Relationships with other actors:** • State-to-state • Non-state actors and track-two actors: hierarchical with state actors dominating important high-politics issue agendas **Conditions:** • A mostly state-centric context	**Purpose:** • Primarily support for state-centric interests **Function and processes:** • Limited number of ENGOs in East Asia • Some but limited functions with the state, e.g., via service delivery such as climate change technologies and research • Primary function is facilitating collaboration between ENGOs **Relationships with track-one:** • Hierarchical with track-one dominance **Conditions:** • Constraints on civil society in many states • Background context of internal and external sovereignty in most states	**Purpose:** • Unequivocally state-centric interests **Function and processes:** • Service provision: expertise on long-term issues; policy trial-balloons; diplomatic assistance in situations where track-one relations are stalled or nonexistent; providing conduits between tracks one and two; socialization and learning between officials **Relationships with track-one:** • Hierarchical with track-one dominance **Conditions:** • The hierarchical relationship restricts the success of track-two to influence state positions and interests. Thus the contribution of track-two is questioned by both track-one and track-two • Background context of internal and external sovereignty in most states	**Purpose:** • Primarily support of state-centric interests **Function and processes:** • Service delivery: ideational and practical via the research and expertise of non-state individuals and organizations **Relationships with track-one:** • Hierarchical with track-one dominance • Track-one regulation of track-two via control of funding for sustaining track-two organizations **Conditions:** • Internal and external sovereignty • Interdependence

Some Caveats

Several qualifications need to accompany the preceding arguments. First, the claim that the traditional model explains track-two diplomacy needs to acknowledge that it, as well as the new model of diplomacy, has flaws. For example, the extent to which the traditional model incorporates officials outside of foreign ministries and explains the power relationships between different ministries is still unfolding. It is difficult, therefore, to generalize about this aspect of the traditional model. The shortcomings of the new diplomacy model are considerable. The main one is that its boundaries are unclear. As can be seen from box 13.2, the types of actors, their purpose, functions and processes, and relationships with track-one actors are over-specified in some instances and underspecified in others. In light of the flaws in both models, the argument that track-two actors in East Asia conduct track-two diplomacy is necessarily qualified.

The second qualification concerns the extent to which the findings can be generalized. There are two issues here. One is that it may well be the case that within the three issue areas there will be subissues, or niches, that are exceptions. For example, as mentioned earlier, in the environmental arena, TRAFFIC sets and monitors rules on endangered species that states adhere to. The important point to note is that the findings best explain high-politics issues—security and economics—or sensitive areas such as the environment, rather than low-politics issues, such as trafficking in wildlife. The other point is that while this study does generalize about track-two diplomacy around high politics and sensitive issues in East Asia, it does not compare track-two diplomacy in East Asia with that in other regions. It gives partial, not comprehensive, answers to the questions posed. The study's contribution is to provide an analytical framework and hypotheses for further research and generalizations on track-two diplomacy.

KEY POINTS

- The nature of track-two diplomacy in East Asia is largely dominated by state-centric interests and providing services to governments under conditions of internal and external sovereignty.
- When these findings are compared with the tenets of the two competing models of contemporary diplomacy, they appear to be better explained by the traditional model rather than the "new" multiactor model.
- There are several caveats about the generalizability of the findings.

CONCLUSION

This chapter was prompted by several questions about the nature of track-two diplomacy that are problematic for students of diplomacy. Both the study's analytical framework and its findings will hopefully contribute toward more comprehensive research that will provide generalizations for developing theories about the nature of track-two diplomacy. More broadly, the study shows that the East Asian experience of recent decades suggests that, in the most economically and politically dynamic region of a globalizing world, states are adapting to ensure that sovereignty and state interests are alive and well. Our understanding of contemporary diplomacy will need to take account of that fact.

QUESTIONS

1. Some conceptual issues:
   - Is track-two diplomacy necessarily state-centric? If not, why not?
   - How should track-two diplomacy be conceptualized?
   - What should be the criteria for deciding whether or not track-two diplomacy can be understood as diplomacy?
2. Some empirical issues:
   - How do governments in East Asia keep control over track-two activities concerned with environmental, security, and economic issues?
   - What are the prospects for non-state actors exerting more influence over governments? What is the evidence for your argument?
   - Are track-two organizations inevitably the victims of their own success?
   - In East Asia, how might the rise of China impact on the nature of track-two actors within China?
3. What are the implications of the analysis in this chapter for your theoretical and practical understandings of contemporary diplomacy?

NOTES

1. Although individuals may act independently of any organization, they are not the focus of this chapter. Furthermore, the chapter concentrates on the contemporary period and not earlier periods of history before the consolidation of the state system.

2. Because the aim of this study is to assess track-two diplomacy by non-state actors within East Asia, it does not focus on track-two organizations located outside of East Asia, such as the Centre for Humanitarian Dialogue, which played a mediating role in the 15 August 2005 Memorandum of Understanding between the Government of the Republic of Indonesia and the Free Aceh Movement.

3. The particular environmental issue that is the focus of this study is climate change.

CHAPTER 14

Diplomacy and Intelligence

Jennifer E. Sims

CHAPTER CONTENTS

- Introduction: exploring the "dark arts" in international politics and diplomacy
- Defining intelligence, deception, and covert action
- Ethical issues: how dark are the dark arts?
- Looking to the future
- Conclusion

READER'S GUIDE

This chapter discusses the role of intelligence, deception, and covert action in the practice of diplomacy. Intelligence is defined as the collection, analysis, and dissemination of information for competitive decision making. With superior assessments of the conflicts in which they are engaged, decision makers can gain competitive advantages over adversaries in both peacetime and war. Intelligence thus affects the distribution of power in the international system while making that distribution more or less transparent to states, depending on its quality. Done well, intelligence provides critical support to diplomacy, including strategies of coercion, confidence-building, and deterrence that depend for their success on a thorough understanding of the target state's reactions, vulnerabilities, and intentions. It also enables secret policies, such as covert action, surprise attack, and strategic deception. Given that successful diplomacy involves deft use of hard and soft power in appropriate mixes and at the right time, and that this success sometimes requires secrecy, deception, and the breaking of laws overseas, the techniques employed by the "dark arts" raise ethical questions, especially for democracies.

INTRODUCTION: EXPLORING THE "DARK ARTS" IN INTERNATIONAL POLITICS AND DIPLOMACY

The power to hurt is bargaining power. To exploit it is diplomacy—vicious diplomacy, but diplomacy. (Schelling 1966: 2)

States often attempt to coerce in peacetime or persuade with force (A. L. George 1991). In 2003, for example, the US government demanded that Iraq's leader, Saddam Hussein, give up his weapons of mass destruction (WMD) or suffer invasion. Although secrecy shrouded Iraq's weapons facilities, US policy makers and intelligence officials were convinced WMD programs were active. Saddam refused to comply, so the United States invaded. **Intelligence services**, using secrecy, **counterintelligence**, and **espionage**, played critical roles as both governments appraised threats and tailored strategies. Yet both services also failed: Saddam underestimated US resolve, and the United States misjudged Iraq's WMD.

The ability to manage force for diplomatic or military ends depends to a large extent on **intelligence capabilities**. Winners often master them; losers frequently do not. Intelligence worked, for example, when Israel planned and conducted its surprise attack on Syria's nuclear reactor in 2007. The reactor was revealed by an Iranian defector, described by Israeli intelligence agents and technical sensors, and eventually destroyed by Israeli bombers. After a brief period of confusion in Damascus, the incident was over without triggering war. The rather obvious connections the Iraqi and Syrian cases reveal between the powers to know and deceive and the powers to fight and coerce raise interesting questions: How are secrecy, intelligence, **covert action**, and the use of force entwined in the making and implementation of foreign and defense policy? As states seek to preserve their security during times of peace and war, how are the secret tools of **deception** and espionage employed? Although the specialized literature on the history of intelligence and certain memoirs that cover the practice of diplomacy and war touch on these important questions, little systematic theoretical work has been done on the synergies involved in threatening, influencing, and persuading. With a few exceptions, scholarship seems to skirt a great, dark void: the relationship of intelligence to politics and diplomacy.

This gap in the scholarly literature is striking because the issues that intelligence raises for organized societies are so profound. For example, should democracies seek political successes in secret? Certainly deception, covert action, and espionage—what we might call the dark arts of international politics—have mattered for centuries of **warfighting**, blackmail, **coercive diplomacy**, and **peacemaking**. Indeed, history suggests that the tendency to separate tools of **statecraft** into force, commerce, intelligence, and diplomacy obscures the utility of mixing them. Information advantages gained by deceit or timely collection have been conflict's silent partners: Greeks hid soldiers inside the gift of a large wooden horse to gain entry into Troy; Caesar sent spies into Britain before invading (Caesar 1982); and, while King Philip of Spain dithered, Elizabeth I's spymaster, Sir Francis Walsingham, collected secret information that helped his queen defeat the Spanish Armada (Budiansky 2005; Hutchinson 2007). Such capacities for deception and clandestine gathering of information, although offensive to democratic principles of openness, seem almost as necessary for the survival of states as are the machines of war.

Even friendly powers have used such techniques against each other to bolster their security (Sims 2006). Before US entry into the First World War, Sir William Wiseman provided intimate and informal advice to the US president. Although Woodrow Wilson reportedly considered him almost a son, Wiseman was actually a British spy and an agent of influence determined to lure the United States into the war on Britain's side (Jeffery 2010: 109–20). In contrast to Germany's witless pursuit of unrestricted submarine warfare and sabotage, which were offenses to US neutrality, Britain's clever use of Wiseman gained Wilson's sympathy through superior information, timely threats, stealth, and tricks. A little more than two decades later, another British agent, William Stephenson, fancied himself Wiseman's equal (Andrew 1995: 101). He passed intelligence, some of it false, to President Franklin D. Roosevelt for the purpose of nudging the United States into the Second World War (Jeffery 2010: 438–51). Although some historians now speculate that Stephenson was as instrumental to Roosevelt's goals as he was to Prime Minister Winston Churchill's, few would deny that he, like Wiseman before him, served as an instrument of state power—power exercised by a democracy against a friendly, though neutral, state.[1]

Indeed, London's successful influence campaigns prior to the world wars suggest that it had, by the early twentieth century, captured a special form of power that augmented the **hard power** of coercion and the **soft power** of attraction. The tools Britain used in these instances might be called the "smart" elements of state power because they offered refined options for decision makers pursuing the needs and interests of the state (see box 14-1).

Yet these ostensibly clever instruments, often secret and sometimes deceitful, hold an attraction that can also lead to folly, not least because they sometimes promise more than they can deliver. Although intelligence enables options less violent and bloody than war, it can also misdirect naive users and trigger policy failures. The dark arts also pose ethical dilemmas. The idea that well-placed spies and agents of influence can achieve powerful results inspires and perpetuates the development and use of them in the expectation that the ends (the absence or lessening of war, violence, and bloodshed) will justify the means (clandestine operations, effective coercion, or deceit). Policy makers and intelligence professionals often argue that the goal of advancing the interests of the state, and particularly a just, democratic polity, legitimize threats of violence and breaking foreign or international laws. Others disagree, believing that the tools themselves undermine such polities, rendering them less just and less democratic.

The growth of the Internet makes such issues more pressing than ever before (see Kurbalija, chapter 8 in this volume). For good or ill, intelligence capabilities are proliferating, allowing private organizations to image and map targets, share information rapidly, and track individuals in real time. Many of the tools of **smart power** formerly monopolized by states are now available not just to terrorists and internationally organized criminals but also to the couch potato. They can also be used in **cyberspace**, where **worms, bots, Trojan horses**, and viruses can do Wiseman's and Stephenson's kind of work as artfully and in much less time. In 2010, Iran suffered an attack of the Stuxnet worm, which apparently damaged its computer systems in key

---

BOX 14-1

Why Are the "Dark Arts" So Hard to Understand and to Appreciate in Practice and How Do They Relate to State Power?

Intelligence, including the capacity for deception and covert action, lends agility, precision, and timeliness to more traditional instruments of national security—often described as "hard" or "soft" power. Done well, intelligence makes power "smart" by helping diplomats and soldiers adjust force and persuasion for greatest effect at least cost. In this way, it supplies them with "decision advantages" over competitors.

The instruments of **smart power** are difficult to identify or measure because those involved in intelligence and the forms of policy it enables sometimes act out of uniform, causing confusion and tensions among national security agencies in the governments employing them. Intelligence officials sometimes fight wars or conduct diplomacy; diplomats sometimes behave covertly; and heads of state sometimes become their own intelligence officers. Former director of the Central Intelligence Agency (CIA) George Tenet served simultaneously as head of the US intelligence community and as Bill Clinton's behind-the-scenes power broker in the Middle East peace process. In Afghanistan, the CIA station chief became an important offstage negotiator who rivaled a sitting ambassador, Karl Ikenberry (Gorman 2010). By bartering guns, information, or money for intelligence, intelligence managers often become trusted interlocutors for foreign leaders. But these roles also raise issues of oversight, accountability, and the potential for politicized intelligence. Such mixed roles and methods have existed throughout the underside of history—a side often undisclosed until many years after events, if even then.

---

industrial and military sectors, including the Bushehr nuclear power plant. Stuxnet, which Tehran claimed to be under external control, perhaps demonstrated what smart power will look like in coming decades.[2]

This chapter aims not so much to fill the gap in the scholarly literature described earlier as set the groundwork for that task by exploring some of the conceptual, practical, and ethical aspects of intelligence support for diplomacy. It will argue three basic points: first, intelligence is a crucial element of effective policy making that all those engaged in national security policy should recognize and understand how to use. As a tool, intelligence is ethically neutral; its theoretical purpose is to improve knowledge of the capabilities and intentions of competitors. In fact, to the extent that it is used to increase transparency, intelligence can reduce the likelihood of war. To gain these advantages and avoid the inherent dangers of its use, decision makers must oversee their intelligence services. Second, certain strategies are particularly dependent on intelligence, such as those involving either surprise or the signaling of intent, such as deterrence, blackmail, and coercive diplomacy. Failures may appear most obvious in these domains. In any case, the risks that inhere in the symbiotic relationship between the tools of smart power and the nuanced strategies they support make assigning blame for failures very difficult. Third, the information revolution and **globalization** have, somewhat ironically, increased the importance of intelligence to statecraft. The growing importance of these tools heralds the reinvigoration of the secret state and the inherent **anarchy** of the state system.

In making these arguments, and to begin the process of making sense of this daunting subject more generally, this chapter explores the most important tools of smart power, including intelligence analysis, espionage, and technical collection, and their relationship to deception and covert action. The chapter then canvasses the ethical issues, particularly for democracies, of adopting these instruments of statecraft. Finally, it considers the role of intelligence in twenty-first-century diplomacy.

KEY POINTS

- Good intelligence can help states use hard and soft power to target their adversaries; bad intelligence can cripple states, causing the otherwise powerful to fail.
- Intelligence poses particularly difficult challenges for democracies because gaining and keeping advantages in information often entails secrecy and deception.
- The dark arts hold an allure that may tempt naive users to misuse them.
- The growth of the Internet poses new challenges for the conduct of intelligence and counterintelligence operations. For this and other reasons, the normative landscape for intelligence and its support for diplomacy may be changing.

DEFINING INTELLIGENCE, DECEPTION, AND COVERT ACTION

When we speak of the "dark arts," many images come to mind. We think of secrecy, illicit actions, and perhaps unethical behavior. But do the tools of intelligence, deception, and covert action always imply these attributes? Are these tools distinct, or do they overlap in important ways?

Intelligence

Intelligence can be defined in many ways, depending on what one wishes to explain. Here we wish to explain how states gather and use information to gain advantages over each other. For this reason, it would seem best to define national intelligence as the collection, analysis, and dissemination of information for national security decision makers. More generally, it is the mechanism by which states learn as they compete to secure their interests in the international system. The better their intelligence capabilities, the more transparent the distribution of power in the international system and the more states will fluidly adjust to changes in its structure (Sims 2009a).

Some readers may object to this definition because their purposes differ. Congressional overseers tend to define "intelligence" as anything intelligence agencies do but not, for example, Foreign Service reporting, which, according to the definition supplied earlier, would certainly constitute intelligence for policy making. In some countries, "intelligence" is a word synonymous with suppressing democratic movements, torturing dissenters, or executing domestic opponents. These kinds of activities, while sometimes performed by intelligence agencies, are policies for which other words are more precise: "counterrevolution" or "repression," for example. Intelligence agencies sometimes execute these kinds of policies because they are capable of acting in secret and have the capabilities to integrate information-gathering with secret action. But we are interested here in how states learn for the purposes of diplomacy and war. In this sense, "intelligence" is a value-neutral term; it serves policies ranging from genocide to the defeat of tyrants and can be discussed quite separately from repression, assassination, or covert action. These latter activities may rely on good intelligence even more than overt policy does, but they are not "intelligence" in the sense we will be using here.

Others might argue that this definition of intelligence is inadequate in other ways (Sims 2009a). For example, the lack of any mention of secrecy would seem to make the definition too broad. Some intelligence theorists, such as Peter Gill and Abram Shulsky, have argued that intelligence necessarily deals in secrets—stealing, protecting, and creating them—and that this attribute distinguishes it from most other information-related activities of governments (Gill 2009; also see the exchange between Sims 1995 and Shulsky 1995). An excessive focus on secrets, however, can make intelligence too narrow and thus lead to intelligence failure. If intelligence-gatherers were to seek only information that competitors keep secret, they might miss opportunities to exploit an enemy's ignorance, be manipulated by opposing security services, and thus be made vulnerable to surprise. The terrorists who struck the United States on 9/11 did not need to steal US secrets; they gathered intelligence for their mission by finding freely available airline schedules and unclassified pilot training programs. During operations such as the 1983 US invasion of Grenada, unclassified information, such as good maps, proved as important to military operations as materials deliberately hidden by the other side. Of course, a capacity for secrecy is necessary for sustained information superiority; but speed or information swamping are other plausible techniques for securing those same advantages without its use. Secrecy cannot, therefore, be considered a defining attribute of intelligence without rendering irrelevant some of the most important intelligence successes and failures in history. In fact, the US government has invested a significant amount of resources in open source intelligence (OSINT) and has created a center within the office of the director of national intelligence dedicated to this mission.

Besides a capacity for collecting open or unclassified sources and applying secrecy when needed, there are several other ingredients of good intelligence, such as robust collection capabilities and timely delivery of intelligence products to those who need them. A good intelligence service will collect information using a variety of techniques, such as the recruitment of agents (human intelligence, or HUMINT), and the gathering of technical data (TECHINT). The latter category includes signals intelligence (SIGINT), which in turn includes electronic data (ELINT) or communications (COMINT). Measurement and signature intelligence (MASINT) uses sensors to gather data and then employs specialized analytical methods to find patterns in them, such as the sonar signature of a particular kind of submarine or the biological signature of a certain dangerous pathogen (Johnson and Wirtz 2007). Intelligence services may employ overseas stations for gathering such information.

Chiefs of station generally support **ambassadors**, represent all intelligence agencies, and are accountable for all operations under way in the country. Ambassadors have the legal responsibility for approving these operations. For these reasons, the diplomatic and intelligence services are intimately related in the field, leading to great opportunities for fruitful diplomacy and, at times, deep friction. For this reason, the US State Department has assigned to the Bureau of Intelligence and Research the responsibility for helping ambassadors and the secretary coordinate intelligence policy with intelligence agencies.

Although collection is the raw material of intelligence, analysis is important too, because none of what is gathered matters if it cannot be made relevant to decision making (R. George and Bruce 2009). Analysis is needed at the point of collection to discern the most useful information and translate it into meaningful products. Sometimes this information can be provided directly to decision makers, as when a chief of station briefs an ambassador on an intercepted phone call as she negotiates the release of hostages, or the operators of drones locate terrorists and send the images directly to shooters. At other times decision makers need new intelligence to be combined so that a complete picture can be generated. Such all-source products put all the bits and pieces into context. While collectors within a good, healthy intelligence service evaluate what they gain and expedite its delivery to decision makers, all-source analysts integrate all collection available on a topic to ensure that intelligence is not duplicative, distracting, or misleading. Decision makers must strike a balance between their desire for speed of delivery and a comprehensive view; failure can come from getting this balance wrong.

The danger is that **all-source intelligence**, because it involves more cross-checking, analysis, and handling, can become too slow or too detached from the needs of decision makers. General H. Norman Schwartzkopf, commander of US troops during the first Gulf War (1990–91), said that national intelligence agencies provided highly accurate and objective intelligence, but that it was not always helpful. For example, reports of a bridge 82 percent destroyed may be the result of objective, comprehensive, and accurate intelligence but may not help a decision maker who needs to know whether the structure can still function as a bridge. Imprecise but relevant analysis may be more important than comprehensive, detailed analysis that fails to provide decisive advantages over an adversary. In this regard, proximity to policy makers matters. When, in the mid-1990s, the US intelligence community sent the ambassador to Bosnia his own field-based analytic team, his satisfaction with intelligence products improved, as did the productivity of the analysts sent to support him.

For these reasons, objectivity with respect to sources and policies is good, objectivity with respect to outcomes is not. Intelligence must be unabashedly on the side of the decision makers it supports if it is going to be trusted, have access to policy, and thus have a shot at being relevant and meaningful—that is, able to deliver information advantages. Since winning, not omniscience, is the goal, all-source processes must sometimes deliver timely advantages at the expense of perfect or complete information (Sims 2009b). Decision makers then need to protect intelligence services from charges that they got things wrong in retrospect when the press of policy forced intelligence to deliver the best it could, not total transparency.

This last point about the intelligence-policy partnership raises the issue of trust; intelligence services must be trusted to be effective. If diplomats believe that intelligence providers are working against them, or if intelligence officers do not believe that diplomats will protect them or the sources of their information, the relationship collapses and the advantages of information superiority will likely be lost. This is why intelligence oversight is critically important to effective and lasting information superiority (Snider 2005). Good oversight is necessary even in totalitarian states that are often assumed to have less constrained and therefore generally more aggressive and successful intelligence services. It is instructive to remember that Joseph Stalin repeatedly purged his intelligence services because he had poor oversight and did not trust them, losing much accumulated knowledge and expertise in the process (Andrew and Mitrokhin 1999).

Of course, advantages in competitive information can be obtained not just by improving intelligence for one's own side but by denying it to adversaries. Methods of denial include locks, safes, vaults, and classification systems. Countering hostile intelligence services can also involve ruining, distorting, or manipulating the information the other side collects. **Defensive counterintelligence** protects one's own assets from an adversary's intelligence service; **offensive counterintelligence** twists, distorts, and corrupts the intelligence processes of opposing services.

All the foregoing attributes make intelligence very different from newspaper reporting, which seeks information about events of concern to the polity in general; fortune-telling, which tries to predict the future; or religion and science, which aim to characterize "truth" in some fashion. The essence of intelligence is the acquisition of reliable, winning information in the rough-and-tumble context of political joust, business conflicts, horse races, or war. It helps diplomats and other decision makers to decide what to do next by reducing uncertainty, not eliminating it.

Deception

Careful readers will recognize the slippery nature of one particular intelligence tool: offensive counterintelligence. After all, twisting the mind of opponents in order to deflect their intelligence-gathering from sensitive areas will likely encourage them to gather intelligence on something else instead. In fact, as a result of offensive counterintelligence, their behavior could change the competition in unexpected and perhaps even undesirable ways. Manipulating an adversary's beliefs thus borders on policy making. Deception straddles two worlds—those of policy and intelligence—and therefore heightens both risk and potential gain.

To understand how this might be so, consider the case described in the book *The Man Who Never Was* (Montagu 2001). During the Second World War, clever British operatives dressed a corpse in the uniform of a major in the Royal Marines, planted false identity papers in his pockets, and tied to his wrist a briefcase with fake plans for an Allied invasion of Europe through Sardinia. Hoping to convince the Nazis that he went down in an aircraft, they set him adrift in the Mediterranean. The plotters expected that the body would be found and the credible but false plans delivered to Hitler. They were right. The body was found, the false intelligence did get to Berlin, and Hitler was deceived.

This story of successful British deception underscores most of the essential features of a well-constructed stratagem: plausibility, enhanced by the incorporation of half-truths; believability, accomplished by leveraging the prejudices of the opponent; induced trust, achieved by delivering the deceit through the opponent's intelligence and liaison services; stringent secrecy; and strategic fit. The last element was especially important. Allied forces were obviously gathering in North Africa. Under these circumstances, to have attempted to deceive Hitler into believing the attack would be coming in the eastern Mediterranean would have been difficult. He likely believed the attack would be farther west. But the proximity of Sardinia to the true route of invasion, Sicily, made the deceit both believable and dangerous. Employing the stratagem could have complicated the strategic planning of Allied forces by confirming Hitler's expectation of attack and the general area in which it would occur. Moreover, if the deception failed, it would have likely made Hitler more certain than he otherwise would have been that the attack was coming through Sicily (Montagu 2001).

In these ways, deception can raise risks even as it offers gains, and it must always be reconciled with policy because it directly influences an opponent's behavior. In this case, the plotters did confer with a select number of military commanders who initially raised grave doubts but ultimately agreed to the plan. The plotters' access to decrypted Nazi communications, including those of the German high command, allowed those involved to check and recheck whether the bait was not only swallowed but also digested in useful ways (Holt 2004; Kahn 1967). The successful prosecution of this stratagem arguably saved lives, enhancing the military capabilities of the Allies. But it required careful and intricate cooperation among the plotters, the commanders, and the key diplomats responsible for overall strategy and the conduct of wartime operations. Indeed, popular accounts of the wartime deception, known as Operation Mincemeat, may underplay the role of secret diplomacy in carrying it out. Civilian authorities may be involved in finding and evaluating planted evidence, particularly in neutral countries, and are thus crucial to successful deception operations (Burns 2009).

In any case, the requirement for intimate and secret coordination makes deception particularly difficult in peacetime. Unlike in war, in peacetime, diplomacy is often only loosely associated with the instruments of force; strategic decision making may be spread across governing institutions, making coordination and secrecy problematic. For a deceit to work, it must provide a clear signal of false intent to the opponent that can nonetheless be validated by the opponent's intelligence collection. This is relatively easy in wartime, when the disposition of forces and the signaling of intent can be readily controlled and thus conveyed. In peacetime, the noise of international politics makes signaling arguably more difficult. It is, however, still possible. In the 1980s, Saddam deceived the United States about his nuclear weapons programs by masking Iraq's nuclear weapons facilities and creating false end-user certificates for sensitive imports. He understood how US intelligence worked and created schemes of camouflage and cover that played to US biases. At the end of the first Gulf War, coalition forces were astonished to find how close he had come to creating a nuclear device, using technology the US intelligence experts had discounted as obsolete (Kay 1995).[3]

In some cases, peacetime deception is hard to distinguish from coercive diplomacy. In both cases, the intent is to change the target's behavior: deception does so by miscue; coercive diplomacy does so by threat (see box 14-2). Methods differ. The former conveys a lie wrapped in truth; coercion conveys a true demand that may threaten a lie—that is, a punishment the coercer may have no intention of delivering. In practice, the two nonetheless seem similar. Some have argued, for example, that the Ronald Reagan administration's heated rhetoric and declaration of intent to build up US forces in the 1980s—including the deployment of medium-range nuclear-tipped missiles in Europe, the development of strategic ballistic missile defenses, and plans for a 600-ship navy—were part of a deliberate peacetime deception designed to convince the USSR that the United States was preparing for war when it was not. In this way the US government was arguably forcing an economically weakened Soviet Union to overspend and exhaust itself or recognize the ultimatum and give up.

Whether President Reagan's buildup was a case of deception, coercive diplomacy, or neither is hard to disentangle from what is currently in the public record. In any case, the policy, if intentional, arguably worked. It did so, however, by making Moscow dangerously jumpy. According to Oleg Gordievsky, a former member of the KGB (Soviet intelligence) who defected to Britain in the mid-1980s, Moscow was not only intimidated but also convinced both superpowers were on the verge of nuclear war (ABC 2010). This could hardly have been the American administration's intent. In 1983, when the North Atlantic Treaty Organization (NATO) conducted Able Archer, an exercise of military mobilization culminating in simulated nuclear

---

BOX 14-2

Intelligence and Coercive Diplomacy

Coercive diplomatic and military strategies work best when intelligence is rich and decision making attentive to it. After 9/11, diplomatic entreaties and threats did not dislodge the Taliban or compel Osama Bin Laden to leave; military force combined with targeted intelligence strategies eventually did. Granular knowledge derived from years of working closely with local warlords enabled just 400 CIA-led US operatives to drive them out of Afghanistan (Crumpton 2005: 162–79). Compelling or deterring terrorists is demanding because they seem unmoved by threats of punishment. Learning what non-state actors fear is difficult and idiosyncratic. More generally, scholars such as Alexander George (1991) and Robert Art and Patrick Cronin (2003) suggest that effective coercive diplomacy involves clarity in objective and in terms of settlement; relative strength of motivation (high for the coercer as compared with the target); a recognized sense of urgency for both parties; domestic and international support; and the coercer's capacity to instill fear in the target. Even if these conditions are met, however, the target must know it is threatened and believe its situation to be urgent. Both intelligence services must therefore perform well for coercion to work. After 9/11, the Taliban literally did not know what hit them.

strikes, the Soviets were nearly certain that the United States was using the exercise as a cover for an actual first strike. While war was avoided in this case, perhaps because of the diligence of midlevel intelligence analysts working for Moscow, the crisis may have convinced the Soviets that they could not keep up with the new American call to arms. The Soviet Union collapsed just a few years later (ABC 2010).

Covert Action

Covert action is both a special form of deception and something very much more. Unlike deception its purpose is not just information superiority but masked control of events. In this respect, it is more akin to policy than to intelligence. Covert action involves the manipulation of military, economic, or political situations while hiding the perpetrator's hand. Done well, it incorporates excellent intelligence collection, analysis, and selective secrecy, but its aims are less to twist the minds of adversaries than to beat them outright. In this sense, it is a peacetime tool comparable to the use of force. Of course, intelligence often creates, through its trappings of secret communications, platforms for intelligence-gathering, and human sources, the critical infrastructure necessary for covert action to be successful. Covert action both employs intelligence and uses it up. Thus the decision to execute covert action can put a state's intelligence infrastructure at risk. Asking intelligence agencies to execute policy can easily reduce their capacity to deliver information advantages for statesmen. For these reasons intelligence and covert action are related, but also distinctly different and even competitive endeavors.

It seems prudent to assume that covert action sometimes works and sometimes does not, but that it always entails great risks, especially for democracies (Godson 2001). These include the risk that events may spin out of control, that sponsorship will be revealed and embarrass or endanger the perpetrator, or that the covert action will succeed but entail unanticipated blowback that distorts information available to policy makers, analysts not "in the know," or even the electorate at large. Nonetheless, the lure of this form of power—unattributed political influence and coercion enabled by intelligence operations—has proved enticing to decision makers throughout history. By making power plays plausibly deniable, covert action puts unaccountability and, therefore, plausible invulnerability within tempting reach. After experiencing some of the dangers covert action poses, however, the United States passed laws in the 1970s to ensure that this instrument would not be used domestically and that presidents would formally authorize each new effort and report it to Congress. In other countries, however, there are fewer constraints. Indeed, in some countries, governors secretly sponsor covert operations against their domestic opponents, using the power of the state to perpetuate their own rule.

How intelligence entails deception or is used for covert action depends very much on context. Deception can serve the attacker by facilitating surprise or the victim by helping him or her dodge a blow, but in either case, it will almost certainly fail if the policy maker forgets that deception depends as much on positive intelligence as it does on the ability to lie. Covert action can gain the ends of war without instigating it, or serve peacemakers once war has begun. But in either case it will almost certainly fail if intelligence managers assume objective analysis can be easily sustained in its support or if policy makers—in taking a hands-off attitude once an operation is launched—delegate difficult political decisions to intelligence officers who fear they may be left holding the bag.

When design and execution are married, however, covert action can bring good results. There is, therefore, a tendency for operations that look like covert action but are not legally considered such to thrive in the gray areas between policy and intelligence. The traditional operations of secret diplomacy or clandestine preparation of battlefields are instruments exempted from US legal definitions of covert action (see box 14-3). Thus, in recent years, the US Defense Department and State Department have conducted what are arguably forms of covert action tangential to battlefields in Bosnia, Iraq, and Afghanistan. They may not require "Findings"[4] under US law because they amount to "traditional" diplomatic and military activities, yet it is significant that the question of what activities are exempted is not finally resolved between the US Congress and the executive branch, or even among US national security agencies.

For example, when the US government wanted to bring the Serbs, Bosnians, and Croatians to the peace table in the 1990s, the Bill Clinton administration secretly allowed the Bosnians to violate an international embargo on the import of munitions. US officials believed that doing so, which violated overt US policy, would enhance Bosnian military power prior to the talks and therefore increase the chances for a solution to the conflict. Despite interagency squabbling over whether the diplomats had engaged in unauthorized covert action or traditional albeit secret diplomacy, the strategy arguably worked by helping set the stage for the Dayton Peace Accords. The US government had used secret power—intelligence-driven diplomacy—to achieve military effects that were, according to some experts, theoretically indistinguishable from "covert action."

KEY POINTS

- Intelligence is the collection, analysis, and dissemination of information for decision makers in competition. It helps them win. Good intelligence can help to target and focus policy so that it is more effective than it would otherwise be.

BOX 14-3

US Legal Definition of Covert Action: A Loophole?

Section 503(e) of the National Security Act of 1947 defines "covert action" as "an activity or activities of the United States Government to influence political, economic, or military conditions abroad, where it is intended that the role of the United States Government will not be apparent or acknowledged publicly" (National Security Act of 1947). Certain activities are exempted from the definition, including "traditional diplomatic or military activities." The term "traditional diplomatic" activities, however, is not clearly defined in the National Security Act, and ambiguity habitually surrounds secret diplomatic initiatives (United States Senate Select Committee on Intelligence 1996).

- Deception is the art of delivering misleading information to foreign officials, often through their intelligence services, in order to gain competitive advantage.
- Covert action is secret policy that depends on good intelligence to work, often "spending down" sensitive assets. Whether or not it succeeds depends as much on the underlying policy as on intelligence.

ETHICAL ISSUES: HOW DARK ARE THE DARK ARTS?

Clearly, intelligence operations, including deception and support for covert action, are ethically challenging. They involve lying, distortion, and secretiveness. In fact, these attributes would seem to undermine the founding pillars of true democracies, which rely on accountability, transparency, and rule of law to function well. So, if these dark arts offer states a nuanced ability to affect outcomes in the international system, including the resolution of crises short of war, are they tools that democratic states should nonetheless eschew on moral grounds?

Although an extended discussion of ethics is beyond the scope of this chapter, it makes sense to consider a few counterpoints to the intuitively logical assertion that these secretive instruments should be regarded as tools of last resort by governments and particularly democracies. First, it is important to remember that intelligence and covert action are *not* the same tools. Each raises very different moral and ethical questions. Intelligence, which often employs secrecy to get its job done, generally works to make governments smarter and adversaries less so. Deception is used to mislead, lie, and confound the adversary. The tools of intelligence and deception are linked, however, because the capacity to deceive depends on the capacity to know what the adversary is looking for, what will confuse it, and whether, in fact, it has been confused. Intelligence agencies engage in both knowledge-building and strategic deception, depending on the needs of the policy makers they support. Since, however, deception fails unless it is supported by excellent positive intelligence capabilities, the overall capacity for successful stratagems within a single intelligence service or within the international system at large will almost never be greater than the capacity for true knowledge-building. It follows that states possessing more capacity for positive intelligence-gathering than their opponents will tend to defeat the less endowed, regardless of the deceptions attempted by others.

Stated normatively, good intelligence systems should therefore aim more toward gathering information than engineering deceit, since the latter depends on the former to succeed. Strategic deceit is a tool governments can use as much to avoid war as to cause it and one they must understand if they are to recognize it when it is wielded by others. Paradoxically, good intelligence both *reduces* misperception, which has been at the root of many wars, and *enables* deception as an alternative to needless war and bloodshed (Jervis 1976, 2010; Tuchman 1985).

The caveat here is the quality of work: states would seem to be morally justified in developing intelligence services, so long as these services are dedicated to illuminating the choices policy makers may consider, not obscuring or twisting them for political purposes. Intelligence systems are morally compelled to get their business right or they may make decision making worse than it would otherwise be. Telling policy makers what they want to hear instead of what they need to hear, conducting unauthorized or illegal activities, neglecting good oversight, and even simply under-valuing the training of intelligence analysts are pathologies that not only lead to policy failures but also compromise the moral standing of the intelligence agencies themselves (Betts 2009).

Second, the philosophy of **just war** makes the case that violence and deception can and indeed should be employed when defending a just and accountable state against aggression by an unjust one (Gerber 2005). Thus, the Allies' theft of secrets and fabrication of deceits during the Second World War can be defended by pointing to the terror, genocide, and territorial aggression carried out by the Nazis. Defeating Hitler became, according to this logic, a moral imperative that justified the means employed. Similarly, a covert action that would have toppled Saddam during the 1990s—provided it was duly authorized and had a good chance of bringing about positive change at reasonable cost—might have been morally preferable to the 2003 Iraq War that had the same purpose but led to widespread death, destruction, and economic loss for both Iraq and the US coalition.

Third, since the international system remains arguably anarchic, states are compelled to secure their safety largely through **self-help**. In doing so, they develop weapons that can do great damage to others in order to avoid ever having to use them. A similar rationale exists for the development of the tools of intelligence and covert action. The moral questions concern when and how these tools should be used. Democracies, by developing legal and policy oversight, craft a delicate bal-ance that often makes the use of them both more difficult and morally tolerable. Reviewing this balance is, in itself, a moral imperative for democracies, lest their desire to curtail these dark arts makes it more likely that opponents will get away with using them unopposed and thus win. Indeed, it would seem morally irrespon-sible not to study these tools and become intimately familiar with them in order to gain the most advantage and avoid the most serious pitfalls that attend their use. And advantages there certainly are.

KEY POINTS

- Good intelligence can reduce the likelihood of wars of misperception.
- Just polities are arguably on solid moral ground when using ethically ques-tionable means to defend themselves against unjust polities.

LOOKING TO THE FUTURE

So what of the dark arts in the twenty-first century? Conflict is growing increasingly complex as new information technologies both expand the capacity for intelligence-driven strategies and deliver smart power into the hands of the individual, not just the state. Interstate war in Afghanistan and Iraq has involved population-centric strategies for which detailed knowledge of communities, tribes, and individuals has mattered as much as knowledge of munitions.

That intelligence is in the forefront of power ought not be surprising; rapid technological change usually increases both state power and collective uncertainty, permitting intelligence to deliver stunning advantages or to fail disastrously. A modern version of this dynamic is occurring in the cyber domain. In April 2007, hackers in Russia, perhaps with official support, conducted distributed denial of service attacks against Estonian websites to protest the move of a Soviet era statue, the *Bronze Soldier of Tallinn* (Vamosi 2007). Although some experts began referring to this incident as the first cyberwar, others called it a cyber-riot, since no effort was made to coerce the Estonian government. Yet the opportunities for coercion were evident and, in the subsequent Russo-Georgian skirmishing over South Ossetia in 2008, Russian hackers launched denial of service attacks that disrupted Georgian government websites, leading other European governments to lend alternative sites to Georgia and help reroute service. The privately conducted cyber attacks during these incidents demonstrated the difficulties of anticipating or terminating conflict in the cyber age. States are likely to have increasing difficulty in their efforts to control the boundary between war and peace at home and abroad. Non-state actors, adopting intelligence-driven strategies such as negotiated restraint, and confidence-building, on the one hand, or networked agitation and coercion, on the other, will intervene more often and with greater effect than in the past. As the United States has sought to counter a growing number of penetrations of its public and private sector networks, it has looked to federal law enforcement and homeland security agencies to take the lead in arresting this trend.

In fact, largely in response to the threats posed by transnational actors equipped with Internet-enabled intelligence, states are expanding their militaries, reorganizing and enlarging their own intelligence capabilities, and shoring up their national security institutions. In the process, what were once the dark tools of statecraft are now coming to light. Shortly after US reporters Dana Priest and William Arkin located the sixteen US intelligence agencies on a nationwide map in the *Washington Post*, someone used Google Maps to post the locations of 176 other intelligence agencies worldwide (World Intelligence HQ's). Priest and Arkin (2010) reported that in the United States alone, there are about 1,271 governmental organizations and 1,931 private companies involved in national security programs for counterterrorism, homeland security, and intelligence. Terrorists, international criminals, and corporate thieves are no less prolific in the world of cloak-and-dagger operations. Nongovernmental actors, such as Wikileaks, are exploiting the digitalization of secrets and the windfalls that digital sharing provides to disgruntled insiders. Such developments suggest that the equivalent to an arms race is under way in the intelligence domain.

States may have a good chance of prevailing in such a digital race. After all, they have confronted and opposed transnational threats before by ramping up resources for intelligence and counterintelligence capabilities in peacetime (Sims 2007). They certainly appear to be doing so again, as the Priest and Arkin article reveals. Yet, in an era of resource scarcity, there is reason for concern. The Achilles' heel may be the tendency of states, and particularly the United States, to mismanage their classification and declassification systems even as the gains for public diplomacy of a capacity for rapid public release become evident (see Melissen, chapter 11 in this volume). Although the 2011 raid on Osama Bin Laden's compound in Pakistan was an operational success, the release of information about its execution, so critical for the diplomatic challenge of managing its aftershocks, seemed haphazard at best.

Agility in the unfolding information age requires not only successful classification of sensitive operations but also their timely declassification. Thanks to decades of a bipolar standoff, states are generally talented at the former but not the latter. The US government now creates within one intelligence agency alone one petabyte of classified, digital data every eighteen months. According to the staff of the National Archives, it would take 2 million full-time professionals a year to review one petabyte and 20 million professionals a year to review the tens of petabytes of classified records being created across the US government annually (NARA 2011). On a cost basis alone, without considering the problems for policy that poorly managed secrecy entails, agile adversaries have an important edge in influencing public perceptions during crises. This is the widely overlooked lesson of the Wikileaks disaster: the United States is getting better at compartmenting and sharing digital secrets but is losing its mastery over the production and disposition of them.

Regardless of who the ultimate winner may be in the harnessing of secret power, something of a paradox results from the expansion of power to non-state actors. On the one hand, to fight transnational bad actors, states are promoting law enforcement, tightening their borders, and shoring up failed states. On the other hand, to win against these same adversaries, states are also engaging in unbounded information warfare, penetrating borders to conduct espionage, and undermining laws so that they can gather good intelligence. As already discussed, the paradox is ethical as well. To preserve sovereignty, peace, and the rule of law, modern democracies are wielding tools that threaten their own institutions. To achieve human security, the original rationale for the state and the predicate for representative government, states and international organizations are empowering themselves to hunt individuals. Are governments, in their insistence on transparency, developing a case against privacy that, at the international level, will ultimately undermine sovereignty itself in the name of peace and security?

KEY POINTS

- The international system is probably going through the greatest expansion of power since the advent of the nuclear age, and it is a form of intelligence power: expansion of the Internet, telecommunications, and digital packaging of vast quantities of data.
- The twenty-first century will, therefore, be a potentially unstable time in which states will assert new rights of access and control, sovereignty and personal privacy will be at risk, and the opportunities for winning will be greatest for those best able to manage secrets and secure decision advantage through intelligence.

CONCLUSION

It seems likely that the burden for diplomacy in the twenty-first century will be the sophisticated management of the dark arts, including in the newest and often darkest corners of all: failing states and cyber domains. Luckily, governments have new potential partners in international and nongovernmental organizations that are well positioned to help provide greater transparency themselves, through their access to good information on what is happening around the world, including inside closed or chaotic states where information is at a premium and access is often difficult. Such partnerships, although risky for all involved, hold out the prospect of a more transparent world and, therefore, perhaps a more stable one (Goodhand 2006). Getting there—to a world of greater transparency, less miscalculation, and more nuanced use of power short of war—would seem to require, somewhat ironically, collective mastery of the dark arts.

QUESTIONS

1. How would you conceptualize "smart power"? What practical and organization measures would you suggest to ensure the effective execution of smart power?
2. Why is the definition of intelligence controversial? Do you believe secrecy is essential to intelligence? Why or why not?
3. What are the advantages and disadvantages of all-source intelligence for diplomats and other decision makers?
4. If diplomatic negotiations aimed at win-win outcomes are based on trust between interlocutors, then should diplomats be part of the intelligence system that might undermine that trust through tactical deception and the pursuit of unilateral advantage?
5. If "coercive diplomacy works best against targets for which intelligence is rich," what priority would you give to developing the intelligence capabilities discussed in this chapter, bearing in mind the ethical dilemmas suggested?
6. Do non-state actors, such as terrorists, use intelligence, and if so, what might be their advantages in doing so?
7. Is Wikileaks a threat to international security?
8. Are governments, in their insistence on transparency, developing a case against privacy that, at the international level, will ultimately undermine sovereignty itself in the name of peace and security?
9. What are the implications of the analysis in this chapter for your theoretical and practical understandings of contemporary diplomacy?

NOTES

1. Keith Jeffery, the official historian of MI6, has said that Roosevelt almost certainly used Stephenson's "intelligence" to help make his case for war (lecture, 4 October 2010, Georgetown University, Washington, DC). See also Andrew (1995: 93–104). Stephenson's biography by William Stevenson (no relation) romanticizes and in some ways exaggerates his role (see Stevenson 1976). Roosevelt was, in any case, intent on arousing Americans to support entry into the Second World War on the Allied side well before the Japanese attacked Pearl Harbor.
2. There is no evidence at this time, however, that Stuxnet represents a deliberate attack by the West against Iran's nuclear establishment. In fact, the worm has struck elsewhere. See Dareini (2010).

3. Later, Saddam tried to deceive others that he had nuclear weapons when he did not, leading the United States to fall prey to a deception its own intelligence could not penetrate. In this case, Saddam's deception partially succeeded but also had unintended consequences.

4. These laws include the Hughes-Ryan amendment to the Foreign Assistance Act of 1974, which requires that the president sign a "Finding" that the proposed covert action is in the interest of national security. Shortly thereafter, the Congress created intelligence oversight committees in the House and Senate to monitor intelligence activities, including covert action.

PART IV

҂ᕁ

National, Regional, and International Diplomatic Practices

This part explores contemporary diplomatic practice from three different levels of analysis—the national, regional, and international.

Our *first* aim is for you to consider how a selection of players at these levels—the world's two major state actors (the United States and China), several major regional institutions (such as the European Union and the African Union), and the most important international organization (the United Nations)—practice contemporary diplomacy. A consensus view is that the United States provided the foundations for a liberal international order since the end of the Second World War in 1945. But China is now challenging that order, producing a robust debate as to whether "China's rise" will be peaceful or belligerent. In both the American and Chinese cases, the diplomacy practiced by both will need to change. As the European Union faces economic problems like everybody else, it remains the case that the Union provides something of a "model" for other regional institutions experimenting with new diplomatic practices. And the United Nations not only retains its status as the key organization of global governance but also—for our purposes—mirrors to some extent diplomacy's three evolving distinct, yet linked, forms (bilateral, multilateral, and polylateral).

Our *second* aim is for you to not only understand these national, regional, and international practices as important subjects in their own right but also, more challengingly, to invite readers to think about them and about the extent to which they are interconnected elements of a wider diplomatic culture. For example, we urge you to consider that individual European Union countries have a particular national diplomatic style that differentiates one from another, that this style is modified to some extent when European Union member states agree on joint initiatives and to shared diplomatic representation in regions such as Africa under the Union banner, and that Union member states increasingly take joint positions at the United Nations. These interconnections underscore the multilayered and complex nature of contemporary diplomacy.

CHAPTER 15

United States Contemporary Diplomacy

Implementing a Foreign Policy of "Engagement"

Alan K. Henrikson

CHAPTER CONTENTS

- Introduction: foreign policy as diplomatic process
- Containment: negotiating (only) from a position of strength
- Transformation: putting (others') domestic affairs at the center of foreign policy
- Engagement: talking with enemies as well as (just) with friends
- Conclusion: diplomacy now the primary means, but not the end of policy

READER'S GUIDE

This chapter traces and assesses the conceptual foundations and progression of American diplomacy from the Cold War period to the present day through the lenses of three major US policy ideas—containment, transformation, and engagement. It suggests that there has been a shift in the way US foreign policy is originated substantively, not just in the way it is implemented. US diplomats in the field increasingly "engage with" others—with adversaries as well as with allies and friends—in two-way, interactive relationships. The chapter questions the adequacy of dynamic "engagement"— essentially a process, rather than a program or purpose—as foreign policy itself.

INTRODUCTION: FOREIGN POLICY AS DIPLOMATIC PROCESS

Diplomacy has become a central theme of American foreign policy. Indeed, it is becoming almost a policy itself—that of "engagement." During the Cold War, military, economic, and political "containment" was the main strategic concept of the United States. The dominant motif of US foreign policy today is the need to establish and maintain firm contact, efficient communication, and, if possible, friendly relationships with the leadership elites, wider political structures, and even populations of all countries, especially those that are or might become adversarial or could otherwise, through maladministration or impotence, pose threats to world order. "Engagement" is the term used, officially and popularly, to describe the new emphasis on diplomatic outreach in American foreign policy.

The transition from containment to engagement—as both the superpower nuclear rivalry and the ideological battle between communist East and democratic West diminished—required reflection and intellectual adjustment. There needed to be accommodation of foreign policy, and also of diplomatic procedure, to the new global situation. The 1989 fall of the Berlin Wall and 1991 collapse of the Soviet Union left a "post–Cold War" conceptual void. The new globalizing economy further exposed the lack of a compelling political purpose.

The Al Qaeda attacks on the World Trade Center and the Pentagon in the United States on 11 September 2001 filled this void with anger. The event, like the Japanese attack on Pearl Harbor on 7 December 1941, marked a fundamental change in American orientation. After launching a war on terror abroad and securing the country with the Patriot Act at home, the US government under President George W. Bush during his second administration embarked upon a new nominal course in diplomacy called "transformational diplomacy." Elevating the struggle against terrorism, it espoused a new higher purpose—to "end tyranny" in the world. It also entailed a major shift of diplomatic resources and focus: from the capitals of Europe to the dynamic new economic centers and other regions of the developing world, from which future challenges to American security and welfare might come.

With Barack Obama's election as US president in November 2008, the "engagement" policy concept took hold. While the term had been used earlier (see box 15-1), it was given new status and formal recognition as well as complexity, meaning, and comprehensiveness. Without an overarching ideological view, comparable to the Cold War or the global war on terror, American foreign policy became, expressly, more diplomatic. Indeed, diplomacy—the engagement process—became virtually policy itself, as distinct from being policy precursor or the instrument of policy. Implicitly, to "engage" was to be present, active, and committed. But it does not say exactly how, where, or why—to what larger end.

The engagement idea is often presented as an alternative, and antidote, to "isolationism." It also has been offered, however, in contrast to the other extreme, "interventionism," particularly military intervention. The term "engagement" has a strong military resonance. It conjures an image of opposing armies, not merely arrayed against each other but engaged in combat. The term's policy origin may in fact be military—an intragovernmental transposition from US Army handbooks and Department of Defense thinking. The significance of this point is that "engagement" has a coercive connotation. The threat of coercion can be explicit, as when "consequences" are hinted at if cooperation is not forthcoming. Engagement, as actually being implemented, is well described by *New York Times* reporter David Sanger (2010) as "a complicated mixture of openness to negotiation, constantly escalating

---

BOX 15-1

US Engagement with India

On 11 May 1998, Strobe Talbott, US deputy secretary of state, received word that India had exploded a nuclear device. What follows, he writes, is the story of the "negotiation—or, as we agreed to call it, the dialogue"—that he had with "the Indian statesman Jaswant Singh" (Talbott 2004: 3). Over the next two and half years, they met fourteen times at ten locations in seven countries on three continents. Talbott also held parallel meetings with various Pakistani officials.

> Those encounters added up to the most intense and prolonged set of exchanges ever between American and Indian officials at a level higher than ambassadors.... In a successful dialogue, the two parties do more than just talk to each other. Each makes an effort to understand what the other has said and to incorporate that understanding into a reply. A dialogue does not, however, necessarily mean that the participants change each other's minds. Hence the other term that figured prominently in the way Jaswant Singh and I defined our task: engagement. That word can connote eye-to-eye contact, a firm hand-shake, a pledge, or a long-term commitment. But engagement can also mean the crossing of swords, a clash of armies or warships or wills. Both elements, conciliation and contest, were present in what went on between Jaswant Singh and me. (Talbott 2004: 4)

---

pressure and a series of deadlines, some explicit, some vague." For the "engaged" party, such a forward approach can appear to be "interference" and if it penetrates deeply into the recipient country's domestic affairs it is seen as a violation of its sovereignty, as recognized by the United Nations Charter and the terms of the Vienna Convention on Diplomatic Relations (1961).

While premised on physical strength and a forward military presence overseas, the essential meaning of engagement today is *diplomatic*. There remain basic commonalities, however. Diplomatic contact, like military engagement, gives the involved parties an awareness of the other side's capabilities and intentions. To *test* the other party's intentions can be a major purpose of diplomatic engagement. Like wrestlers, those in direct contact can better anticipate the other's moves, and maybe the direction if not the exact degree of the other's possible thrusts. Engagement is inherently interactive and, optimally, also intercommunicative.

The diplomatic engagement concept encompasses not only "traditional diplomacy"—representation by resident ambassadors at foreign capitals—but also "special representatives" and "special envoys" to manage particular problems and to "engage" foreign leaders. Moreover, it covers multifaceted involvement with other countries' nongovernmental elites and populations. Engagement diplomacy thus is not only, although it is mainly, a state-to-state relationship. It is also a state-to-society mode of interaction. It can embrace, as some theorists of "citizen diplomacy" suggest, a society-to-society interchange, especially if the flow of ideas is internally directed within a country and is politically purposeful (see Badie, chapter 5, and Melissen, chapter 11 in this volume).

At all levels, the engagement idea suggests a deliberate meshing of gears with, and within, the country that is engaged. Such contact, as noted, occurs on different planes: at the national level—at summit meetings or during diplomats' visits to foreign ministries, for example—but also in purposeful encounters at the provincial or district level and even at the city, town, or village level. The methods of engagement diplomacy are widening. Its practitioners use not only traditional methods, for example, formal delivery of **démarches** in person, but also nontraditional means, such as the devices of information and communication technology (ICT). Engagement diplomacy has many points of potential contact, virtual as well as real. Its geography is extensive, ranging from chancelleries to conference centers, where informal talks by negotiators are possible, to Internet "chat rooms."

The United States, which emerged as a global power following the Second World War and which exerts a planetary influence, now is diplomatically "engaged" almost everywhere. How does it exert this influence? How does the US government implement "engagement," a process-as-policy? Can diplomatic process substitute for foreign policy—for actual strategy aimed at well-targeted objectives? Or must the goals of policy be well identified for engagement diplomacy to succeed? The latter would be a logical presumption. Engagement per se, however, might create political opportunities and, through the exercise of it, increase capacities to think and act strategically, and thereby contribute to the maintenance of US "leadership."

KEY POINTS

- The Cold War's end left a conceptual void in American foreign policy, as the "containment" of Russia and communism no longer seemed necessary and globalization made foreign policy seem less relevant.
- The 2001 Al Qaeda attacks redirected US foreign policy, which, through "transformational diplomacy" as well as the military and political war on terror, sought to "end tyranny."
- "Engagement," both military and diplomatic, emerged as a middle course between isolationism and interventionism.
- Engagement diplomacy, conducted through a variety of methods and levels, sometimes alongside US military operations, mixes coercion with outreach in a complex and shifting pattern of intended persuasiveness.

CONTAINMENT: NEGOTIATING (ONLY) FROM A POSITION OF STRENGTH

A strategic basis for engagement was laid in the early Cold War period by the American diplomat and policy planner George F. Kennan—recognized as the father of "containment" in his famous July 1947 "X" article in *Foreign Affairs*. In this article, Kennan (X 1947: 576) proposed, "Soviet pressure against the free institutions of the western world [was] something that [could] be contained by the adroit and vigilant application of counter-force at a series of constantly shifting geographical and political points, corresponding to the shifts and manoeuvres of Soviet policy." Such pressure could not, however, be "charmed or talked out of existence" (576). His idea of coun-terpressure thus was not an active diplomatic strategy (Gaddis 2005: 24–52).

Kennan, who served briefly as US ambassador to the Soviet Union (1951–52), did not consider the Russian dictator Joseph Stalin a trustworthy or otherwise suit-able partner for the United States. However, following Stalin's death on 5 March 1953, Kennan came to believe that a negotiated East-West understanding might be achievable. In his 1957 BBC Reith Lectures, he proposed the mutual "disengage-ment" of military forces—those of the North Atlantic Treaty Organization (NATO) as well as the Warsaw Pact—from a zone in central Europe, to include the Federal Republic of Germany (Kennan 1958).

The prevailing view, however, was that of former US secretary of state Dean Acheson, who advocated "negotiation from strength" (Bell 1963). Western superior-ity, arguably, had been established with the formation of NATO, which the Federal Republic of Germany under Chancellor Konrad Adenauer had joined in 1955. The demonstration of Soviet technological prowess with the launching in October 1957 of the orbital satellite *Sputnik* suggested, however, that the United States and the Western powers had lost the scientific and technological high ground. From this perspective, Kennan's idea of negotiating with the Soviet Union to achieve military disengagement was an "illusion," as Acheson (1958) declared it. Nonetheless, others, such as the influential columnist Walter Lippmann, considered Kennan's approach to be "the only alternative which has some promise of leading to the reunifica-tion of Germany and to the national independence of the East European states." Nonetheless, even he believed that it was "too soon" to adopt a program of action, for "the re-orientation of our thinking" had still further to go (Lippmann 1958).

John F. Kennedy's election as US president advanced that thinking, to a serious consideration of breaking the East-West impasse through diplomacy. In his January 1961 inaugural address, Kennedy said: "We dare not tempt them with weakness," referring to those nations that would make themselves America's adversary. "For only when our arms are sufficient beyond doubt can we be certain beyond doubt that they will never be employed." Yet the mounting costs and the steady spread of atomic weaponry, with two great groups of nations "racing to alter that uncertain balance of terror that stays the hand of mankind's final war," offered less and less comfort. "So let us begin anew—remembering on both sides that civility is not a sign of weakness, and sincerity is always subject to proof." He then memorably declared: "Let us never negotiate out of fear. But let us never fear to negotiate" (J. F. Kennedy 1962: 2).

The October 1962 Cuban missile crisis and its resolution, through the cautious exercise of power and brilliant diplomatic improvisation in bilateral contacts with Soviet diplomats and others as well as at the United Nations, demonstrated the need for a better connection to Moscow (R. F. Kennedy 1971; May and Zelikow 1997). Crisis management had worked, and it established a new paradigm for decision making and diplomacy (Allison and Zelikow 1999). But it was ad hoc and unreliable. Following the crisis, a **hotline** was set up between Moscow and Washington, and the Partial Test Ban Treaty was negotiated, thereby establishing direct and continuous contact between the Kremlin and White House and beginning a systemic process of arms control. Tension between the Soviet Union and the United States thereby was considerably reduced, even though both sides continued their military programs.

President Richard M. Nixon proclaimed **détente** as US policy and sought to move from an "era of confrontation" to an "era of negotiation." Hoping to gain negotiating space for ending the Vietnam war by exploiting Sino-Soviet rivalry, national security adviser Henry Kissinger and President Nixon traveled to the People's Republic of China (PRC) (Kissinger 1979: 684–787, 1049–96; MacMillan 2007). The opening to China was followed by a less spectacular but more substantive meeting in Moscow in 1972. The results of these initiatives included the Shanghai Communiqué with the PRC and, with the Soviet Union, the Anti-Ballistic Missile Treaty and the Strategic Arms Limitation Treaty.

President Nixon's successor, Gerald Ford, and President Jimmy Carter also engaged in summit meetings with the Soviet leadership, although without significant results. President Ronald Reagan, initially reluctant to deal with leaders of what he viewed as an "evil empire," and convinced that only "peace through strength" worked, was at the same time unwilling to accept the logic of "mutual assured destruction" (MAD). In September 1983 he therefore dramatically proposed an alternative to strategic deterrence, the Strategic Defense Initiative (SDI), or "Star Wars." He even offered the Soviet Union coparticipation in the project, which implied a major American technological advance. A meeting in Reykjavík, Iceland, in August 1986 between President Reagan and the new Soviet leader, Mikhail Gorbachev—considered a failure at the time—began a process of nuclear arms reduction and military withdrawal. This process resulted ultimately, during the George H. W. Bush administration, in a free Europe and the Cold War's end. "Containment worked," said President Bush (2009: 34). It had to be supplemented, however, by diplomacy.

KEY POINTS

- "Containment," introduced by George F. Kennan, posited that the way to respond to Soviet expansionism under Stalin was through the vigilant, patient, and proportionate application of "counterforce" of various unspecified kinds.
- Containment was premised on the balance of power that for those such as Secretary of State Acheson (aware of the US military disadvantage in central Europe) meant no negotiation with the Soviet Union except from a position of clearly superior allied strength.
- President Kennedy, although also concerned about the Soviet-American military balance, argued famously for direct negotiations.
- The 1962 Cuban missile crisis, including the possibility of a mutually devastating nuclear conflict, caused US presidential administrations, most notably those of Nixon and Reagan, to enter serious negotiations with Moscow for joint management of nuclear weaponry, although still premised on "peace through strength."

TRANSFORMATION: PUTTING (OTHERS') DOMESTIC AFFAIRS AT THE CENTER OF FOREIGN POLICY

A new approach to diplomacy occurred with the administration of President William J. Clinton in the context of a rapidly globalizing world economy. Born after the

Second World War and with no military experience, Clinton viewed foreign affairs and domestic affairs as not only inseparable but also equally amenable to presidential mediation. His handling of relations with Russia under Gorbachev's successor, President Boris Yeltsin, was adroit (Talbott 2002). It was also more institutionalized—a key factor in implementing a foreign policy of engagement. A commission cochaired by Vice President Al Gore Jr. and Soviet prime minister Viktor Chernomyrdin was established following a Canadian-arranged Clinton-Yeltsin meeting in Vancouver in April 1993 (B. Clinton 2004: 505–8). No less skillful was Clinton's personal intercession between the contending parties in Northern Ireland and also, although without ultimately achieving any result, in the Arab-Israeli dispute.

More consequential was President Clinton's and his administration's involvement in economic negotiations, which resulted in the conclusion of the North American Free Trade Agreement, formation of an Asia-Pacific Economic Cooperation grouping that included the PRC, and transformation of the General Agreement on Tariffs and Trade into the World Trade Organization. The Department of State under Warren Christopher set up an "America Desk" to strengthen the nexus of foreign and domestic affairs. Its purpose was to support US businesses and other American private interests that might be having difficulty overseas partly in the hope of creating a stronger domestic constituency for American foreign policy, and for the Department of State itself.

The 11 September 2001 Al Qaeda attacks on the World Trade Center and the Pentagon violently brought foreign policy "home" to Americans, and drew attention to the relevance of the internal conditions of other societies, notably Afghanistan, which Osama bin Laden had used as a sanctuary. President George W. Bush characterized the Al Qaeda hijacking of airplanes as an attack on the United States of America and its values of freedom and democracy. He outlined his administration's response: "This crusade, this war on terrorism is going to take a while" (G. W. Bush 2003b: 1116). In an address to Congress, he stated: "Our war on terror begins with Al Qaida, but it does not end there. It will not end until every terrorist group of global reach has been found, stopped, and defeated" (G. W. Bush 2003a: 1141). Official American diplomacy adhered to this message, although some diplomats dissented, and a few resigned (Kiesling 2006).

The reaction abroad to the 2003 US invasion of Iraq, following a failed effort by Secretary of State Colin Powell to secure a United Nations resolution explicitly authorizing the use of military force, was almost universally negative. It demonstrated the need to engage foreign publics as well as governments. US **public diplomacy** was severely challenged not only among Muslims but also among the populations of America's closest friends and allies. The appointment of an accomplished Madison Avenue advertising executive, Charlotte Beers, to the position of under secretary of state for public diplomacy and public affairs was unsuccessful. Her media campaign to win the hearts and minds of people in the Arab street by showing how well Muslims in the United States itself were doing did not work. It only deepened resentment. The difficulties encountered by Department of State personnel and the much larger numbers of Department of Defense and military personnel in the Middle East, following the invasion of Afghanistan and ensuing de facto occupation of Iraq, produced a partial change of outlook within the Bush administration itself.

Organizationally, significant steps were taken. Secretary of State Powell, a former soldier who had become chairman of the Joint Chiefs of Staff, saw major deficiencies in the Department of State's structures and systems. He sought to build its capacity, including, notably, modernization of its outdated ICT facilities. He also launched a Diplomatic Readiness Initiative to strengthen the Department of State's human resources—numbers of personnel as well as their managerial and other skills. The **Foreign Service** was expanded and better supported. Believing that career **Foreign Service Officers (FSOs)** had been underappreciated and underused, he abolished many of the existing special envoy positions. He preferred to work cooperatively within the international community, not only with NATO but also with the United Nations. This put him at odds with unilateralist-minded members of the Bush administration, including Vice President Richard Cheney. Powell's resignation after one term of service was accepted.

President Bush chose his close friend and national security adviser Condoleezza Rice to succeed General Powell as secretary of state. Appearing before the Committee on Foreign Relations preparatory to her Senate confirmation in January 2005, she declared: "The time for diplomacy is now" (Kessler 2005: A01). A year later, she outlined her transformational diplomacy concept. This corresponded ideologically with President Bush's declared objective in his second inaugural address of "ending tyranny in our world." Focusing on the internal governance of states rather than on their external behavior, she theorized: "The fundamental character of regimes now matters more than the international distribution of power." The peoples of other countries, on whom even authoritarian regimes ultimately depended for support, therefore appeared to be key instruments of change and international stability. The US government, accordingly, would "use America's diplomatic power to help foreign citizens better their own lives and to build their own nations and to transform their own futures." For that purpose, it would be necessary to "transform old diplomatic institutions to serve new diplomatic purposes" (Rice 2006).

Among the changes Secretary Rice proposed was "shifting existing resources"— FSOs themselves—out of the larger, comfortable US embassies in Europe, for example, to embassies in major developing countries such as Egypt, India, Indonesia, and Nigeria. Officers would even be assigned to run one-person "American Presence Posts" in noncapital cities. The "diplomatic posture" of the United States would be not only localized but also regionalized and made more thematic. For example, "small, agile transnational networks" of diplomats in rapid response teams would be formed to address the problem of disease, thus better to combat "the spread of pandemics across entire continents," she explained (Rice 2006). A broader transregional approach also would be taken in public diplomacy, better to counter the influence of Al Jazeera throughout the wider Middle East (Seib 2008).

The "newest and most cost effective way" of reaching people, Secretary Rice pointed out, was the "Virtual Presence Post"—an Internet site managed by computer-adept younger officers, based mostly in Washington, that would be focused on "key population centers" elsewhere. She had high hopes for the site: "This digital meeting room enables foreign citizens, young people most of all, to engage online with American diplomats who could be hundreds of miles away." Such communities could be affiliated by interest and identity rather than by geography or statehood—"network" communities.

Secretary Rice acknowledged that some officers would be sent to "hardship posts" in highly dangerous places. She foresaw that American diplomats would "serve in different kinds of conditions, like reconstruction and stabilization missions, where they must partner more directly with the military"—as in Afghanistan and Iraq. Steps already were being taken to achieve better "jointness" between American soldiers and civilians, including those from the Department of State. Increased field activity required greater local knowledge. Moreover, she said, "record numbers of people" must be trained "to master difficult languages" such as Arabic and Chinese. Regarding the Foreign Service's own composition, Rice (2006) advocated a diverse diplomatic service to match the world's diversity.

Within the US Foreign Service itself, the changes proposed by Rice met with resistance. New concerns compounded old grievances about inadequate resources and excessive political appointees. There had been little consultation within the Department of State before the secretary announced the changes, and many FSOs felt they would be assigned involuntarily to perilous duties without preparation or protection. "By demanding that FSOs take on the unprecedented, open-ended, and fundamentally impossible challenge of nation building under fire without adequate training or funding," wrote Ambassador J. Anthony Holmes, who was president of the American Foreign Service Association, "the White House was continuing a myopic tradition of shortchanging the civilian institutions of foreign policy while lavishing resources on the military. Furthermore," he added, "the Bush administration's general efforts to stifle dissent and to reward those serving in Iraq with promotions and choice assignments has led to the unmistakable politicization of the Foreign Service" (Holmes 2009: 148–49). American professional diplomacy awaited a new day, hoping it would be different.

KEY POINTS

- The Clinton administration concentrated on negotiating agreements to expand trade and promote American business involvement in the formerly closed economies of Russia and China.
- The 2001 Al Qaeda attacks, directed by a terrorist organization based in Afghanistan, brought "home" to Americans the problem of weak and failing states, and the danger posed by conditions inside them that could be exploited by violent extremist groups hostile to the United States.
- To meet the new challenge, President Bush launched a "crusade," vowing to defeat global terrorism, pursuing bin Laden in Afghanistan, and overthrowing Saddam Hussein in Iraq.
- Recognizing the high costs of forcible "regime change," and also the impossibility of winning the hearts and minds of local populations, especially in Muslim countries, by military means alone, the Bush administration learned the value of field-oriented diplomatic action, introducing "transformational diplomacy."

ENGAGEMENT: TALKING WITH ENEMIES
AS WELL AS (JUST) WITH FRIENDS

Since the final years of the Bush administration and especially since President Obama's inauguration, the American emphasis on "engaging with" others has continued, although with less ideological emphasis and adversarial political tone. It was also less unilateralist, and more open to working through international institutions. The term "engagement," although used by his predecessors, has become almost the name of Obama administration foreign policy. It has differed from that of the Bush administration most distinctively in its seeming proclivity for "talking with enemies"—as some of its critics characterized its new, more flexible approach.

A controversy arose during the 2008 presidential election campaign when then-senator Obama indicated his willingness to talk even "without preconditions" with the leaders of Iran, Syria, Venezuela, Cuba, and North Korea. At the time, America's major European allies—Britain, France, and Germany, known as the EU3—*were* talking with Iran, and the United States was in effect "outsourcing" its diplomacy and losing its position of international leadership. The United States under President Bush had refused to have any bilateral contact with the Iranian government stemming from the 1979 takeover of the US embassy in Tehran and Iran's refusal fully to report its nuclear activities, as it was legally obliged to do under the Nuclear Non-Proliferation Treaty and International Atomic Energy Agency safeguards system. The Bush administration seemed to prefer instead a loosely coordinated "good cop/ bad cop" approach, letting the Europeans entice the Iranians with carrots while the United States, and also Israel, brandished the sticks. There seemed to be no real unity of effort.

The Obama administration, abandoning this approach as unproductive, had difficulty defending itself against the charge that engagement was tantamount to "appeasement"—that is, weak, shortsighted, immoral, and dangerous compromise. Meeting and negotiating with aggressive dictators can indeed imply acquiescence, approval, and, worse, surrender of both principles and interests—including, importantly, the interests of others. However, just *talking*, as defenders of diplomacy insist, does not mean *agreeing*. Such encounters, even if begun at a low level and conducted by diplomats rather than by political leaders, can generate useful information, supplementing other sources of knowledge and intelligence (see Sims, chapter 14 in this volume). Shunning, from this perspective, is simply a form of self-denial. Moreover, "diplomatic sanctions" (that is, diplomatic disengagement) can actually reduce the leveraging effect of **economic sanctions**, which can continue even as adversaries talk (Maller 2010). Most important, nonengagement precludes the possibility of exerting influence through rational persuasion, which can be effective even with ostensibly irrational regimes, depending on how they view and calculate their own interests. Their appreciation of their situations can be influenced by direct interchange, especially with representatives of powerful countries and also international organizations, with military and other resources to bring to bear.

US diplomacy has been prominently conducted by President Obama himself. He has had frequent encounters with foreign leaders at the summit level. He personally has led detailed, substantive discussions of major issues, notably the danger of nuclear proliferation. Even more characteristic of his personal engagement with the world has been his public delivery of thematic addresses on important policy questions— nuclear issues in Prague, relations with Islam and the Muslim world in Cairo, and the future of the African continent in Accra. His eloquence carried over from his campaigning for the presidency into the international realm. The Norwegian Nobel Committee awarded him the 2009 Nobel Peace Prize, observing that "Obama has as President created a new climate in international politics" (Norwegian Nobel Committee 2009). He has capitalized as well, in his trips abroad, on his own personal, international background. There is an implicit strategy behind his overseas travel. Closer involvement, through visits and speeches, with other countries' populations becomes an intermediate end in itself—a way of directly shaping world public opinion, and an indirect way of influencing leaders at the top to make them more amenable, willing to engage in productive discussion, and even cooperating as partners.

In the Obama administration's 2010 "National Security Strategy" (NSS), "engagement" is defined broadly, in a positive way, as "the active participation of the United States in relationships beyond our borders." Negatively defined, it was, "quite simply, the opposite of a self-imposed isolation that denies us the ability to shape outcomes." The NSS stated: "Engagement begins with our closest friends and allies"—that is, those countries with which the United States shares a common history as well as values and commitments to norms. It mentioned in particular as "active partners" the United Kingdom, France, and Germany. It next emphasized the deepening of cooperation with "other 21st century centers of influence"—including China, India, and Russia. It proceeded then to espouse the diplomacy and development that supports "new and successful partners" from the Americas to Africa, from the Middle East to South Asia—including emerging-market countries. On the issue of relations with "adversarial governments," the NSS offered "a clear choice: abide by international norms, and achieve the political and economic benefits that come with greater integration with the international community; or refuse to accept this pathway, and bear the consequences of that decision, including greater isolation" ("National Security Strategy" 2010: 11). Here the NSS implicitly defended the Obama administration's rationale for engaging diplomatically with dictatorial regimes. "Through engagement," the document stated, "we can create opportunities to resolve differences, strengthen the international community's support for our actions, learn about the intentions and nature of closed regimes, and plainly demonstrate to the publics within those nations that their governments are to blame for their isolation" (11). Rather than being a gesture of appeasement, therefore, engagement conceivably could bring regime change.

In his pursuit of "comprehensive engagement," President Obama has taken advantage of his relative popularity abroad to attempt to reknit frayed ties. In the span of three weeks in late 2010, Obama, together with Secretary of State Hillary Clinton, participated in five European summits—the NATO Summit; the summit of nations participating in the International Security Assistance Force (ISAF) in Afghanistan; the NATO-Russia Council Summit; the US–European Union Summit (all of which were held in Lisbon); and the Astana Summit of the Organization for Security and Co-operation in Europe (OSCE). Philip Gordon, the US assistant secretary of state for European and Eurasian affairs, saw this "extraordinary period of summits" as "an unprecedented opportunity for engagement with our partners in Europe and Eurasia." Indeed, some partnerships—notably that of NATO, which endorsed a new strategic concept, and the US-EU tandem, which was pulling together in the economic and regulatory fields—were solidified. ISAF and US-Russia relations were less consensual, and the OSCE summit in Kazakhstan even less so. The American delegation did not consent to a proposed action plan at Astana because the plan did not "adequately reflect our longstanding position on unresolved conflicts," including those in Georgia and its two breakaway regions, South Ossetia and Abkhazia, Moldova's Transdniestr region, and Nagorno-Karabakh, as Assistant Secretary Gordon explained. "We took a principled stand on the issue of sovereignty and territorial integrity and host nation consent" (Kellerhals 2010). As this illustrates, diplomatic engagement does not automatically entail political agreement or compromise.

At a time of economic uncertainty and with the high cost of involvement in war and peace-building in Afghanistan and Iraq, the resources available for US diplomacy are woefully inadequate in relation to American ambition "to lead once more," as President Obama hopefully declared ("National Security Strategy" 2010: cover letter). Partly, the problem was one of internal resource allocation. Significantly, the strongest advocate for increasing the US government's international affairs budget, in order to strengthen the "civilian" capacity of the United States abroad, was Secretary of Defense Robert Gates, an experienced holdover from the Bush administration. Strikingly, Gates contrasted the annual appropriation for the Department of Defense, not counting funds for the wars in Iraq and Afghanistan, of nearly $500 billion with the Department of State's budget of just $36 billion. He noted that, even with newly hired personnel, the size of the Foreign Service—some 6,600 career diplomats—was "less than the manning for one aircraft carrier strike group" (Barnes 2007). Others, including the American Foreign Service Association (2007), observed pointedly that the Department of Defense had more people in its military bands than the Department of State had diplomats.

Under the combined influence of Secretary Gates and Secretary Clinton, there was a new emphasis on the coordinated application of all the instruments of American power—a "whole-of-government" approach—to influence, optimally without resort to military force, foreign governments and populations. Secretary Clinton envisioned "a global civilian service of the same caliber and flexibility as the US military" (H. Rodham Clinton 2010: 16). The Department of State would try to lead the way. Following the example of the Department of Defense, in 2009 she launched the first Quadrennial Diplomacy and Development Review to create better long-term synergy between the Foreign Service and the US Agency for International Development (USAID), both under her supervision.

The scope of Clinton's proposal, however, was even broader. She advocated bringing together in the name of "civilian power" relevant resources, including personnel posted overseas, of other US government agencies, such as the Millennium Challenge Corporation and the Peace Corps. How could "leading through civilian power" be achieved? At the managerial level, heavy reliance would be placed on the interagency process. Secretary Clinton emphasized that "the US foreign policy apparatus must reward teamwork, promote collaboration, and support interagency rotations" (H. Rodham Clinton 2010: 16).

At posts abroad, there already had been coordination, if not yet systemic exchange of personnel or amalgamation of them into a practical "civilian service." To illustrate her case for the creation of such a broad-based body, Clinton cited the example of the US embassy in Islamabad, noting that the American mission there included 800 staff members, about 450 of whom were diplomats and civil servants from the Department of State and 100 from USAID. "A large portion of the work there consists of traditional diplomacy—Foreign Service officers helping Americans travelling or doing business in the region, issuing visas, and engaging with their Pakistani civilian and military counterparts," as she characterized it. However, she pointed out that the US ambassador "also leads civilians from 11 other federal agencies." These included disaster relief and reconstruction experts helping to rebuild the country following the historic 2010 floods, as well as specialists in health, energy, communications, finance, agriculture, and justice. Finally, there were numerous military personnel working with their Pakistani counterparts (H. Rodham Clinton 2010: 15).

The diverse tools of the Obama administration's integrated **smart power** approach included economic development assistance, reconstruction and stabilization support, trade and investment promotion, cultural and educational exchange, and also, in the communications sphere, the use of social media as well as expanded radio and television broadcasting in local languages. Engagement diplomacy, however, meant not just reaching people but also *relating* with them in multiple ways. As Judith McHale, under secretary of state for public diplomacy and public affairs, explained: "So it's not public diplomacy, it's not messaging, it's not just a marketing message. It's really fostering an environment where you can strengthen relationships between people" (A. Johnson 2010).

Even "military diplomacy," conducted particularly with other militaries, would foster new relationships, not just operational liaisons but also bonds of effective collaboration and genuine community with host societies. Particularly in Iraq and Afghanistan, American diplomats working in "Provincial Reconstruction Teams" sought to engender long-lasting links using an array of methods. Their efforts, sometimes referred to as "expeditionary diplomacy," recall an older, days-of-empire style of interacting with local officials and chieftains.

"Partnerships" at every level—with leading countries, with international organizations, and even with influential private groups at home and abroad—are being pursued. The development of a stable US relationship with the PRC carries particular urgency because of China's inherent weight and because of the many geographic and functional areas in which its influence is felt, either positively or negatively. China's rise is clearly a preoccupation within US government circles. The contradictory strategic thoughts of American officials as to how to deal with a rising China have been termed "congagement"—a hybrid of "containment" and "engagement." It reflects deep wariness, a serious political-ideological strategic concern about China's exercise of power, including its naval deployments, and its refusal to let its currency float to reduce its huge trade surplus with the United States. "Engagement," *New York Times* correspondent David Sanger (2010) notes with regard to China particularly, "has its limits. Here in Beijing, a once-promising effort to engage the world's greatest rising power has gone badly off track. Chinese officials welcomed Mr. Obama's outreach in 2009. But increasingly, they are determined to show that they will not be pushed around by a country they view as a fading superpower." Engagement, like containment, seems to require strength, but even more so, perhaps, evidence of dynamism and drive—and of leadership.

The principal framework that the United States uses for engaging the PRC is the Strategic and Economic Dialogue, a bilateral forum that combines the separate dialogues—Strategic Dialogue and Economic Dialogue—inherited from the Bush administration. Another, more specific diplomatic mechanism, focused on a regional security problem, is the Six-Party Talks, which include the Pyongyang regime, concerning the North Korean nuclear weapons program. That was dealt with directly by the Obama administration through the use of a presidential special representative, Ambassador Stephen Bosworth, a veteran US diplomat described by the Department of State as "the senior official handling all aspects of North Korea policy and the senior emissary for engagement with North Korea" (H. Rodham Clinton 2009a).

Other special envoys also have tried to manage difficult regional problems. The late Richard Holbrooke, a bold and iconic figure in American diplomatic history owing to his stewardship of the Dayton Peace Accords that ended the war in Bosnia-Herzegovina, was assigned the herculean task of stabilizing the Afghanistan-Pakistan frontier (Packer 2009). A no less intractable difficulty—that of moving the Israeli-Palestinian peace process toward completion—was given to former senator George Mitchell, who earlier had helped to achieve peace in Northern Ireland. Critics have noted that handing over these major foreign policy challenges to special emissaries, giving the appearance of "subcontracting," seriously complicates the implementation of policy (Ignatius 2010). It can blur lines of authority, duplicate channels of communication, and confuse areas of responsibility, bewildering US central administrators and host government officials alike.

These various examples of engagement suggest that it may now be diplomacy, rather than policy, that is the key to political success. Is that truly the case, however? With regard to the Middle East in particular, it frequently is observed that no amount of diplomacy, whether quiet or public, can compensate for a US policy that is perceived by many in the Arab world as biased in favor of the state of Israel. Can diplomats themselves make policy, even if not formally charged with responsibility for doing so? The 2010 public revelation by WikiLeaks of a trove of US embassy cables sent by American diplomats posted around the world caused Secretary of State Clinton to deny the documents' significance as indications of policy. "I want to make clear," she said, "that our official foreign policy is not set through these messages, but here in Washington. Our policy is a matter of public record, as reflected in our statements and our actions around the world" (US Department of State 2010). While it may be true that the *setting* of policy is done in Washington, by the president and other elected officials, along with cabinet officers and other top presidential appointees, American diplomats and other representatives in the field may provide much of the actual substance of the US policy as it is *implemented* (Stearns 1996: xiii). Especially in remote places and turbulent situations, they are the ones who know best what the conditions are and what policy responses are needed to address them. Furthermore, as Secretary Clinton herself noted, it is not only "our statements," made in Washington, that reflect US policy. It is also "our actions around the world" that do so. First and foremost, professional diplomats are the ones who take those actions.

KEY POINTS

- "Engagement," although a very broad term covering military interaction as well as active civilian involvement abroad, has primarily a diplomatic meaning, specifically implying a willingness to talk directly with those with whom it may not be possible, or even desirable, to agree.
- The Obama administration initially made its willingness to "engage with" others—those that may be considered to be enemies, as well as allies and friends—and to do so "without preconditions" (if nevertheless with careful preparation) a hallmark of its approach to diplomacy.
- To shun relations with adversaries, such as the leaders or other representatives of Iran with regard to its nuclear program, can lead to the "outsourcing" of American diplomacy.
- President Obama himself has engaged actively in international relations, not only at the popular level by giving highly publicized speeches abroad but also at the summit level with his political counterparts, in shared leadership. Secretaries Clinton and Gates sought to coordinate all the instruments of American power—a "whole-of-government" approach, sometimes referred to as "smart power"—to maximize America's persuasive influence abroad.
- The United States' engagement diplomacy has its limits, especially in dealing with large, powerful, and distinctly un-like-minded states.

CONCLUSION: DIPLOMACY NOW THE PRIMARY MEANS, BUT NOT THE END OF POLICY

The overarching idea in the preceding analysis of the cumulative progression of concepts—from containment through transformation to engagement—is the increasing need for, and the increasing actual centrality of, *diplomacy* in US foreign policy, which now consists of official responses to a wide variety of regional and functional "problems" that cannot be subsumed under broad, declaratory statements of *policy*, set in Washington. Diplomacy, for that reason, turns out to be perhaps more important than foreign policy as such. This is in marked contrast with the Cold War era. It is also very different from the more recent "global war on terror" period. While there are basic principles, values, and interests that must govern American official action taken abroad, that action itself often is now taken in response to reports and advice from diplomatic missions around the world.

The term "engagement," as suggested earlier, has become almost a policy in itself. This is true not only for the United States but also for its allies, whose rhetoric is profoundly affected by, and sometimes emulates and reinforces, American diplomatic terminology. Thus, for example, the British Foreign and Commonwealth Office (2008) commissioned the report *Engagement: Public Diplomacy in a Globalised World*. The

Group of Experts chaired by former secretary of state Madeleine Albright that advised NATO in revising its strategic concept proposed, under the heading "Engaging with Russia," that "NATO should pursue a policy of engagement with Russia while reassuring all Allies that their security and interests will be defended" (NATO 2010b). The new NATO strategic concept that was adopted by the NATO heads of state and government in Lisbon in November 2010 is titled "Active Engagement, Modern Defense." The document, among its other provisions, "offers our partners around the globe more political engagement with the Alliance, and a substantial role in shaping NATO-led operations to which they contribute" (NATO 2010a).

While *almost* a policy itself, "engagement" is essentially only a process no matter how formally structured. It cannot be a substitute for policy. Principles, values, and interests must be included. These need to be structured in coherent form and united by strategic purpose. President Obama has said of the US government's efforts to "build new and deeper partnerships in every region, and strengthen international standards and institutions": "This engagement is no end in itself." Its purpose is to achieve an "international order" that "can resolve challenges of our times" ("National Security Strategy" 2010: cover letter). Contemporary American diplomacy needs, however, more specific, intermediate-level guidance, so that influence can be brought to bear in the right amounts in the right places. When commenting on the WikiLeaks revelations, Richard Haass, president of the Council on Foreign Relations and a former US Department of State director of policy planning, observed that President Obama's team seemed to understand from the start that "engagement isn't an on-off switch, it's a rheostat, and they knew how to turn it up quickly." However, he noted that "what the cables don't tell you is how far he's willing to keep turning it up, especially in hard cases like Iran" (quoted in Sanger 2010). The calibration of power should be governed by the regulation of policy. Yet events like the waves of protests of the 2011 Arab uprising demonstrate the continuing need for pure diplomatic reaction—differentiated, definite, and decisive. The implementation of American diplomacy depends not only on the instrument—the Department of State, its administrative officials, its diplomats abroad—but also on its control, its higher ideological and political direction. Diplomacy is ultimately a means rather than an end. Yet it is the primary means today, one less of coercion than of persuasion, through which the United States achieves s its international goals.

QUESTIONS

1. Can we practically distinguish between large foreign policy concepts like "containment," "transformation," and "engagement," and the diplomacy that is conducted in accordance with them?
2. Should diplomatic engagement be regarded as an end in itself, or as a basis for achieving other ends?
3. At what point does diplomatic "engagement" turn into unacceptable, perhaps even illegal, "interference" in another country's domestic affairs?
4. Should diplomatic negotiation always be from a "position of strength"?
5. Is "transformation" of other societies an appropriate, and realistic, goal for American diplomats?

6. Can good diplomacy, and skillful diplomats, ever compensate for faulty, indeed even immoral policy? What are the limits of professional obedience? Is dissent by diplomats realistic?

7. Is the word "power," as in the expression "smart power," an appropriate term to use in diplomacy, or does the terminology of power have no place in formal diplomatic discourse?

8. Do American diplomats today share in the "making" of policy? Or is it "set" entirely in Washington?

9. What are the implications of the analysis in this chapter for your theoretical and practical understandings of contemporary diplomacy?

CHAPTER 16

China's Contemporary Diplomacy

Ye Zicheng and Zhang Qingmin

CHAPTER CONTENTS

READER'S GUIDE

This chapter discusses some important trends and developments in China's diplomacy after the end of the Cold War. The major changes include China's proactive multilateral diplomacy and engagement with international society, a restructured omnidirectional Chinese diplomatic structure, increasingly broad diplomatic practices, and expanded channels of external diplomatic involvement. These changes have not only made China an important player on the world stage but also shaped China's strategic thinking and diplomatic practice. These trends will continue as China rises.

INTRODUCTION

In his speech at the founding ceremony of China's Foreign Ministry on 8 November 1949, Premier and Foreign Minister Zhou Enlai said, "We have accumulated some experiences in external struggle in the past more than ten years since the war against aggression, but the work to sort out and make them a scientific and systematic discipline has not started yet" (Zhou 1990: 1). He also said that "we should

282

sinify diplomacy science [*waijiaoxue zhongguo hua*], but we are unable to do it now" (Zhou 1990: 1). Ever since then, Chinese scholars of diplomacy have wanted to sinify diplomatic theory, that is, develop a systematic Chinese theory of China's diplomacy (Lu et al. 1997). However, China's diplomatic isolation from 1949 to 1979 made that desire difficult to fulfill. After Deng Xiaoping's opening-up and reform polices in 1978, China became increasingly integrated with the international community, and its diplomacy became more active and sophisticated. It is, therefore, the right time to think about whether the late premier's desire has been successfully realized, and whether it can be realized.

This chapter begins by setting the international and domestic context of China's diplomacy in the post–Cold War era. It then analyzes the major developments in China's contemporary diplomacy, including its diplomatic strategies and thoughts, its attitudes toward the international system and norms, its restructured omnidirectional bilateral relations, its expanded diplomatic arenas, and the pluralization of diplomatic actors within China. The conclusion briefly reflects on the implications of these new developments for China's future diplomacy.

KEY POINT

- Since 1979, China's diplomacy has continued to evolve from isolationism toward a more pragmatic and sophisticated engagement with the international community.

THE CONTEXT OF CHINA'S CONTEMPORARY DIPLOMACY

Diplomacy, according to Sir Ernest Satow (1979: 1), "is the application of intelligence and tact to the conduct of relations between the governments of independent states, extending sometimes also to their relations with vassal states; or, more briefly still, the conduct of adjustment and management of interstate relations." Diplomacy is not a static but a very dynamic social phenomenon; it is the natural consequence of constant changes in the international environment and rapidly transforming internal social changes. The rapid process of globalization after the end of the Cold War, which is a comprehensive and multilevel process, has fundamentally changed the context of states' diplomacy. In the economic field, international trade and global investment have expanded at an unprecedented speed in both geographic distribution and scale, making the world an intertwined global market. New high technology has not only increased communications between countries and regions but also provided the material foundation for the globalization of production, markets, and information (see Kurbalija, chapter 8 in this volume). Meanwhile, the extensive employment of modern transportation has quickened long-distance travel, and cross-border migration of people has been on the rise day by day. The world we live in has become a global village.

Globalization is changing the context of contemporary diplomacy by blurring the boundary between domestic and international issues and making countries intimately connected and interdependent. International cooperation and coordination is an imperative for all countries. Diplomatic agendas are becoming increasingly pluralized: expanding from the conventional political and security realm to that of economy and culture; and the actors of diplomacy have expanded from sovereign state actors to international organizations and transnational corporations, as well as to political parties, parliaments, and nongovernmental organizations (NGOs). At the same time, the means and channels, and even the content and concept of diplomacy, are undergoing unprecedented transformation.

Not only has the international context within which contemporary China conducts its diplomacy changed, but so too has the domestic context. The social and economic changes that have taken place in China since 1979 have created a different China. China has made a historical great leap forward in almost every aspect of social life: with a record of sustained economic growth rate of 9.9 percent since 1978, China's gross domestic product (GDP) in 2010 surpassed that of all major powers except the United States. The impact that the world has on China and China's influence on the world are both unprecedented. China's diplomacy is becoming ever more dynamic and sophisticated in both its relations with the world and its ideas on these relations. China realizes that it cannot develop without the world and the world cannot become prosperous without China.

KEY POINTS

- Globalization has fundamentally changed the context of states' diplomacy.
- The social and economic changes that have taken place in China since 1979 have created a different China.
- The changing international and domestic context has given China's diplomatic practice some new features.

EVOLVING DIPLOMATIC STRATEGIES AND THINKING

Since the early 1980s, the foreign policy strategy and guiding principle of the People's Republic of China (PRC) has been one of independence and nonalignment. The Chinese government reiterated after the end of the Cold War that this strategy—which emphasizes avoidance of formal alignment with or against major power blocs, solidarity with developing countries, and developing good relations with all countries according to the five principles of peaceful coexistence (mutual respect for each other's sovereignty and territorial integrity, mutual nonaggression, mutual noninterference in each other's internal affairs, equality and mutual benefit, and peaceful coexistence)—will not change. But it followed a more reactive and expedient strategy to address the catalytic changes of the post–Cold War period, which is known as *taoguang yanghui, yousuo zuowei* (keep a low profile and bide our time in order to accomplish something) (see box 16-1). Such a strategy has guided China out of the great waves caused by the disintegration of the Soviet Union and the collapse of other socialist countries in Eastern Europe.

The Chinese communists learned precious lessons from their former Soviet comrades, not only how to survive the demise of the Soviet Union but also how

---

BOX 16-1

Keeping a Low Profile

After the disintegration of the Soviet Union and collapse of Eastern European socialist countries, Chinese leader Deng Xiaoping proposed a strategy of keeping a low profile. This strategy has different interpretations and translations, but its content can be substantiated as *sibu* and *liangge chaotuo* (four "nots" and two "surpasses"). The four "nots" are "do not claim to be the standard bearer of socialism, do not assume the leadership of developing countries, do not engage in confrontation with Western powers, and do not make enemies with former socialist countries who have changed political system." The two "surpasses" are "go beyond ideological consideration and detach from concrete issues that do not concern China's national interests" (Qu 1994: 18–19).

---

to sustain a high economic growth rate and defy the prediction that China would follow in the Soviets' footsteps and collapse or disintegrate. China's success led to the replacement of the prediction that China would collapse with the prediction that China would be a threat. Different interpretations of the China threat thesis became the main theme of discourse on China in the late 1990s. To repel such concerns, Chinese elites as well as Chinese leaders proposed a road of "peaceful rise," a very different path to that proposed by international relations realist thinkers who predicted China would be a threat (Hu 2003; Wen 2003; Zheng 2007: 467). But this concept was differently interpreted abroad and resulted in unexpected international repercussions about China's rise. The new term was short-lived and gave way to "peaceful development" (see box 16-2) (Suettinger 2004).

The 2008–9 financial crisis affected countries around the world differently. While China was not immune, the crisis landed China in a comparatively advantageous position. By the second quarter of 2010, China's GDP surpassed that of Japan's, and the difference between China's economic power and that of the United States had narrowed remarkably, making China the second-largest economy in the world. In response to the appeal from the international community for China to shoulder a bigger responsibility, the Chinese government kept a cool head, saying that it was still a developing country and would remain so as to eschew a responsibility beyond its capability (Wen 2010).

With China's pronounced diplomatic strategies undergoing constant changes in response to international public and official commentary about it an unprecedented debate emerged in China as to whether it should keep to the strategy of maintaining a low profile or should change its diplomatic course to pursue a big-power strategy. While the mainstream view in China continues to follow the official line that keeping a low-profile strategy should be a long-term national strategy, others, including one of the authors of this chapter, propose the inevitability of China pursuing a big power strategy as it rises (Ye 2003).

In tandem with its changing strategy, since the end of the Cold War, China has changed its diplomatic pronouncements. In 1988, Deng (1993: 281–83) proposed

---

BOX 16-2

From Peaceful Rise to Peaceful Development

China's rapid development has attracted worldwide attention in recent years. The implications of various aspects of China's rise became a heated topic of debate in the international community as well as within China. Former vice principal of the Central Party School, Zheng Bijian, proposed in late 2003 that the rise of a new power in the past often resulted in drastic changes to global political structures, and even war, whereas the PRC should instead develop peaceably, and in turn help to maintain a peaceful international environment. Zheng's concept of peaceful rise was then reiterated by Premier Wen Jiabao and President Hu Jintao. However, the term proved controversial among the Chinese leadership, and China's peaceful rise was replaced by peaceful development.

---

that a new world order be built on the basis of the five principles of peaceful coexistence. This proposal has remained a lofty diplomatic goal for China since then. But another former leader, President Jiang Zemin, wanted to make his own mark on China's diplomacy when he became the core of the third generation of Chinese leadership. From the early 1990s to the turn of the century, he successively put forward such diplomatic ideals as multipolarization and the democratization of international relations and **multilateralism**.

The leadership of President Hu Jintao does not disregard the ideals of past leaders from Deng to Jiang, but Hu has his own diplomatic concepts. In his speech to the Asia-Africa Summit in Jakarta in April 2005, Hu proposed that Asian and African countries should work together to construct a "harmonious world" that featured friendly coexistence among different civilizations, dialogue on an equal footing, and development and prosperity (J. Hu 2005). In his speech to the United Nations (UN) in September of the same year, he further elaborated the ideas of "building a harmonious world of sustained peace and common prosperity," revealing the new perspective on world affairs with Hu's characteristics (J. Hu 2009). The substance of a harmonious world, a utopian notion, can be summarized as follows: it should be democratic, friendly, fair, and tolerant; uphold democracy and equality to achieve coordination and cooperation; uphold harmony and mutual trust to realize common security; uphold fairness and mutual benefit to achieve common development; and uphold tolerance and opening dialogue among citizens (Q. Zhang 2010: 8–10).

KEY POINTS

- China's diplomatic strategic thinking has evolved from nonaligned independence, to keeping a low profile, to peaceful development.
- China's diplomatic ideals have evolved from establishing a new world order, to proposing multipolarization and democratization of international relations, and calling for multilateralism and a harmonious world.

PROACTIVE MULTILATERAL DIPLOMACY

The most important feature of China's contemporary diplomacy has been its proactive multilateral diplomacy and its associated changing attitude toward international regimes and norms. This change from a passive response to active participation is especially significant from a historical perspective. The process that brought China into the international system after its traditional tribute system was defeated in the nineteenth century was one of humiliation for China (see Zhao, chapter 2 in this volume). China gained its independence from foreign invaders after bitter struggles and revolution. Upon China's founding in 1949, its policy toward international regimes was clearly shown by its bombastic language toward the UN during the Cold War. After its legitimate rights in the UN were restored in 1971, and in other international organizations in the 1980s, China's relations with the international system have been characterized as an evolutionary process: from a system transformer, to a system reformer, to a system maintainer (Kim 1994).

The requirement in an age of globalization for the international community to reinforce coordination gave new momentum to the process of China's integration with the international system. China regards globalization neither as "a panacea for all development problems" nor "a scourge inevitably leading to disaster." Instead, globalization is considered as an objective trend in world economic development independent of humankind's will and one that no country can avoid. Making full use of the beneficial conditions and opportunities of economic globalization, China has energetically expanded its multilateral diplomacy, making it more integrated into the international community and with remarkable accomplishments. By 2008, China had joined more than 130 intergovernmental organizations at the global, regional, and transregional level, including the UN, the World Trade Organization (WTO), the Shanghai Cooperation Organisation (SCO), the Association of Southeast Asian Nations (ASEAN) plus (China, Japan, and South Korea), the Asia-Europe Meeting, the Asia-Pacific Economic Cooperation (APEC) grouping, and the China-Africa Cooperation Forum. By 2008, Chinese NGOs were associated with thousands of nongovernmental international organizations and had signed or acceded to more than 300 multilateral international treaties, conventions, agreements, and protocols covering such fields as politics, security, the economy, and culture (Q. Zhang 2010: 53).

China's proactive multilateral diplomacy is best exemplified by its role in the UN. Before the end of the Cold War, Chinese leaders seldom participated in the annual meetings of the UN General Assembly. After the end of the Cold War, not only have Chinese presidents and premiers participated in these meetings, but Chinese leaders continually reiterate in these forums and on other important occasions that China strongly supports the UN and its Security Council.

One of the ways China supports the UN is through participation in its peacekeeping operations. China's contribution started in 1988, toward the end of the Cold War, when it became a member of the UN Special Committee on Peacekeeping Operations. By June 2008, China had sent more than 10,000 person-times (includes persons deployed twice) of military personnel and police to twenty-four UN peacekeeping operations, making it the leading contributor out of the five permanent members of the Security Council. As China's economic power increased, its contribution to the UN's regular and peacekeeping budget also increased, reaching US$80 million and US$220 million, respectively, and accounting for 3.189 percent and 3.939 percent of the two budgets, during the term starting from 2010 (*People's Daily Online* 2009).

China's proactive multilateral diplomacy is not just confined to the UN and its Security Council but covers many other multilateral arenas. For instance, China has acceded to all international treaties on nonproliferation and joined the relevant arms control and disarmament international organizations. China has participated in international cooperation on human rights within the framework of the UN and joined twenty-two international human rights conventions. China has also joined ten and signed one of the twelve international antiterror conventions. Finally, China has acceded to more than fifty international treaties or conventions on environmental protection.

During the process of joining the international community, China has changed from passive and reactive diplomacy to proactive diplomacy. For example, China spearheaded the SCO and, since 2003, took initiatives to orchestrate and host the Six-Party Talks on the North Korean nuclear issue. China also learned from this process that it cannot exert influence on the world unless it changes itself (B. Zhang 2002). It changed its strategies from challenging the existing international arrangement to being a "responsible stakeholder," which seeks "maximum opportunities for its development from within the existing order" (Q. Zhao 1996: 14). China moved away from tedious political propaganda and polemics to effectively employing international law, rules, and practices to advance its policy goals. A good example has been China's success at the UN Human Rights Commission, since 1990, in provoking a procedural motion of "no action" on resolutions that target China's human rights situation. By China blocking these resolutions, the human rights conference has never been able to discuss China's human rights situation.

China's rise and integration with the international community have several consequences. Internationally, it has raised both expectations for China to shoulder more responsibility and concerns about the "China threat." Domestically, it has inflated nationalism and calls for a more assertive foreign policy. The Chinese government tries to walk a fine line—to reconcile expectations and concerns abroad and to maintain stability at home—so as not to derail its economic development. At the same time, as a country with the dual characteristics of both a developing country and a developed country, China tries to accommodate the big powers so as to maintain its involvement in multilateral negotiations, on the one hand, while coordinating closely with developing countries, on the other hand. China proposes open multilateralism and tries to play the role of a bridge builder between the developed and developing countries: for example, China's policies in the global negotiation on climate change and the North-South dialogue between the **Group of Eight (G8)** dialogue meeting with developing countries, and its polices on reform of the International Monetary Fund and the World Bank.

KEY POINTS

- China's relations with multilateral organizations have changed from a passive response to them to active participation in them.

- China's proactive multilateral diplomacy is represented by, but not limited to, its strong support of and active involvement with the UN and the UN Security Council.
- With its proactive multilateral diplomacy, China's attitude toward international regimes and norms is also changing from negative to positive.

AN OMNIDIRECTIONAL DIPLOMATIC STRUCTURE

Integrating with the international community is not the only change in China's contemporary diplomacy. Equally impressive is the reshuffling of its diplomatic relations with different countries, to the point where China now has an omnidirectional diplomatic structure with some 171 countries. This development contrasts with China's diplomacy in earlier periods. After its founding in 1949, the PRC faced threats from one or another great power, and as a result directed its struggle against the country that posed the gravest threat. The fact that the countries China opposed were, without exception, the most powerful ones in the world at the time was one of the remarkable features of China's period of "revolutionary diplomacy" in the 1960s and 1970s. Its strong opposition to the superpowers (first the United States and then the Soviet Union) made China associate closely with the poor and developing countries as the cornerstone of its overall foreign relations, a relationship that remains very important today.

As China's economic power increased, the overall framework of its diplomatic relations also changed. This change formally took shape in the political report to the sixteenth Chinese Communist Party (CCP) Congress in 2002 and remained unchanged in a similar document to the seventeenth CCP Congress in 2007. The new framework has been widely interpreted as acknowledging four important points: "Relations with the great powers are the key, those with the surrounding countries are priority, and those with the developing countries are the foundation, while multilateral diplomacy is a new arena" (Q. Zhang 2009: 38–39).

This new diplomatic framework demonstrates a change in China's identity from a revolutionary country to a developing country, and then from an unequivocal developing country to a country with dual characteristics of both developed and developing countries. Giving relations with developed countries the top priority reveals the overall pragmatic nature of China's foreign relations, and it gives full expression to the aim of having diplomacy serve the interests of domestic economic development. The sustained and rapid growth of China's economy over the past thirty years is largely attributed to the reforms and opening up introduced by Deng in 1978. In terms of promoting foreign trade, attracting foreign investment, and introducing advanced technology, the developed big powers have been China's major trade partners and sources of capital and technology. China's relations with neighboring countries were, for the first time, given second place in the rankings, indicating both the state of relations between China and its surrounding countries, and China's status and identity as an important regional power. That these relations with other developing countries are the foundation for Chinese foreign relations is a historical fact. However, in terms of serving the interests of China's economic development as the central domestic task, the position of developing countries is undeniably in decline.

China maintains diplomatic relations with 171 countries, forming a good foreign relations structure of omnidirection. With a shift in China's diplomatic framework, the nature of its foreign relations has substantially changed. China is developing new kinds of partnerships—characterized as nonalliance, nonconfrontational, and non-targeting of any third party—with major countries in the world. By the turn of the century, Chinese leaders were able to claim that China's relations with neighboring countries were the best in history, and the government began to call the first twenty years of the twenty-first century the strategic opportunity for China (Jiang 2002a).

KEY POINTS

- China has formed an omnidirectional foreign diplomatic structure.
- China's diplomacy with developed countries is the key.
- China's diplomacy with neighboring countries is the priority.
- China's diplomacy with other developing countries is the foundation.

THE BROADENING OF DIPLOMATIC ARENAS

Globalization has altered contemporary diplomacy worldwide. Globalization has expanded the main themes of diplomacy: from traditional security and political issues, such as sovereignty, security, and territorial integrity, to nontraditional issues, concerned with economic, cultural, terrorism, environmental, and migration problems, among others. To cope with such an expanded diplomatic agenda, the Chinese government introduced the concept of *dawaijiao* (grand or big diplomacy), or *zongti waijiao* (comprehensive diplomacy) to foreign affairs and proceeded to conduct multidimensional diplomacy, which highlighted economic diplomacy, public diplomacy, cultural diplomacy, consular diplomacy, and military diplomacy (Tang 2004).

Economic Diplomacy

The significance of economic diplomacy was revealed when the Chinese government decided in 1978 to shift the focus of domestic policy to economic construction. The goal of China's diplomacy therefore switched to creating a sound international and neighboring environment for domestic economic development. This remains China's diplomatic objective. Great efforts have been made to promote foreign trade, expand international cooperation, and participate in global economic cooperation. One of the most significant and remarkable efforts was China's fifteen-year-long endeavor (from 1986 to 2001) to restore its contracting status in the General Agreement on Tariffs and Trade and to accede to the WTO. During the process, China sped up domestic economic reforms and at the same time insisted on the principle of balancing rights and obligations that served its economic development in its negotiation with the WTO China Group. After its accession to the WTO in 2001, China adopted further measures within the WTO framework to open up to the outside world. For example, it pursued further reductions of tariff and nontariff barriers, promoted liberalization, facilitated trade and investment, strengthened openness in service trade, enhanced transparency in trade, protected intellectual property rights, and deepened reform in the exchange rate formation mechanism to strengthen the elasticity of the renminbi exchange rate.

China has also actively joined other regional and bilateral trade arrangements as complements to create a favorable external environment for sustained and rapid growth of its economy. An example is the China-ASEAN Free Trade Zone, which came into effect in 2010. China is negotiating similar arrangements with more countries and regions. Furthermore, since its initial participation in the G8 dialogue meeting with the major developing countries in 2003, China has kept in close touch with G8 members and has been an active participant in the fast-evolving **Group of Twenty (G20)** forum. Within all these economic forums, China continues to stress that economic development is its main concern. Economic diplomacy has become the primary means for cementing China's ties with the major developed countries, and it is the basis of China's relations with other developing countries. China's relations with developing countries, which previously were focused on shared histories of anticolonialism and safeguarding national independence, are today based on mutually beneficial economic cooperation.

The achievement of China's economic diplomacy is evidenced by its skyrocketing foreign trade, which increased from US$20.6 billion in 1978 to US$2.2 trillion in 2009 (Ministry of Commerce, People's Republic of China 2004, 2010). China's export-oriented economy has made it today both stronger and more vulnerable. China has reiterated unambiguously that its economy cannot sustain fast development without the development and prosperity of the world economy. At the same time, economic diplomacy has also changed the content of its relations with different countries. For instance, China's demand for market access in the developed countries and resources and materials in developing countries—both indispensable for China's economic growth—has changed the nature and main themes of its relations with these countries. In its relations with developed countries, China is under pressure, for example, to open its markets, protect its intellectual property rights, and reevaluate its currency. In its relations with developing countries, it faces criticism for its close association with failed or irresponsible states, for its disregard for human rights in these countries, and even for being a new colonialist. To fend off these pressures and criticism, China has tried to neutralize the incompatibility between its economic interests and the principle of noninterference, on the one hand, and Western appeals for it to intervene in such areas as Darfur/Sudan to support long-term stability, on the other hand.

Public Diplomacy

Public diplomacy is a new notion but not a new practice in China. There are many definitions of public diplomacy (see Melissen, chapter 11 in this volume). One recent definition refers to it as "a process by which direct relations with people in a country are pursued to advance the interests and extend the values of those being represented" (Sharp 2005: 106). By comparison, the Chinese definition is more state-centric, and public diplomacy

> is usually led by the government, which uses various means of publicity and communications to present to foreign audiences its basic national conditions and policies, and to inform its own citizens of its foreign policy and related measures.

The purpose is to win the understanding, recognition and support of the public both in the country and abroad (Yang 2011: 43).

This is a very reactive and expedient tactical approach, and it is the result of the domestic and international political situation after the end of the Cold War, which has rendered an image of China that is detrimental to its diplomatic goal of creating a long-lasting favorable international environment for its domestic economic construction. As Chinese foreign minister Yang Jiechi wrote, "Prejudices, misunderstandings and misgivings about China still exist due to different ideologies and values, hangover from the Cold War or failure to adjust to China's rapid development" (Yang 2011: 43). So China feels it imperative to engage in public diplomacy to encourage an objective and comprehensive view and better understanding of China.

There are two differences between Chinese public diplomacy and that in many other countries. First, in China, public diplomacy is a new brand name given to old practices. The main substance of China's public diplomacy is not new. For instance, cultural diplomacy and civil diplomacy (see later discussion), which are two major forms of public diplomacy in other countries, have a long history and are very dynamic in China. This chapter discusses these two forms of diplomacy separately because they are not subordinate to public diplomacy conceptually and institutionally. Rather, they occupy equal if not more important positions in China's overall diplomatic strategy.

Second, China's public diplomacy has two fronts: the international and the domestic. Internationally, the Chinese government has been trying to effectively use the tools of public diplomacy to project a positive image of China to the world. For instance, the CCP has changed the translation of Xuan chuan bu from Department of Propaganda to Department of Publicity of the CCP Central Committee and established the State Council Information Office. As Zhao Qizheng has warned, the term "propaganda" has a very negative meaning in foreign languages while in Chinese it does not. The responsibility of the Information Office, according to its website, is not to propagandize China but rather to explain China to the world (State Council Information Office of the People's Republic of China 2010). Following the Ministry of Foreign Affairs (MOFA), all ministries of the central government and governments at different levels have now appointed spokespeople to explain the government's policies to domestic and international publics. The Information Office holds regular press conferences, invites relevant ministry leaders to brief the public on topics of common concern, and publishes white papers in different languages on topics of global concern. Externally, the Chinese government has developed a remarkable array of public diplomacy measures over the last two decades, including establishing Confucius Institutes abroad; increasing student exchanges; improving the efficiency of Chinese media; making good use of foreign media, Internet, and foreign-language publications; making use of important events such as the Beijing Olympic Games and Shanghai Expo to showcase China and its history and culture; and providing economic aid and conducting business deals to project a positive image of China to the world (d'Hooghe 2007: 29–35).

Public diplomacy on the domestic front in China is the equivalent of what is known as "public affairs" in other countries, and its main purpose is to shorten the distance between Chinese diplomats and ordinary people by informing domestic audiences about China's foreign affairs and diplomacy. The Chinese MOFA established the Public Diplomacy Division under the Department of Information in March 2004, and it was elevated to the Office of Public Diplomacy in 2009. The office has been active in organizing conferences and Internet discussions between foreign ministry officials and the general public, and inviting citizens from all walks of life to visit the foreign ministry. Leaders from the Chinese MOFA said these diplomatic activities are to implement the notion of *zhizheng weimin* (governing for the people) in the diplomatic realm. Such an inward expansion of China's diplomacy has extended diplomacy toward domestic politics.

The efficacy of China's public diplomacy is mixed. It appeared to help improve China's international image, although it is difficult to measure exactly how much or to what extent it has contributed to that goal (d'Hooghe 2007: 35–36). Problems exist in China's public diplomacy: it is a new form of diplomacy that is unfamiliar to many officials, it lacks bureaucratic coordination, and it suffers from the inertia of the old propaganda tradition. What is evident is that public diplomacy will continue to rise in China's contemporary diplomacy as manifested by the remarkable array of public diplomacy activities over the past two decades and its endorsement by Chinese leaders (Wen 2007).

Cultural Diplomacy

Cultural diplomacy is conventionally regarded as a strand of public diplomacy in other countries, but it occupies a more important position in the diplomatic work of China, which has abundant cultural capital. Cultural diversification is emphasized in China, along with democratization of international relations and other modes of social development, and it is considered as important as political diplomacy and economic diplomacy in the twenty-first century (Jiang 2000). To enrich the foundation of China's cultural diplomacy, the Chinese government has taken measures to preserve Chinese traditional culture, or to promote cultural innovation by absorbing the fine achievements of other cultures through drawing on their strengths and virtues. Domestic cultural preservation and revitalization pave the way for the promotion of cultural diplomacy externally.

Chinese traditional culture, not communist ideology, has become the main source of the ideas and policies of China's contemporary diplomacy. The harmonious world concept is one such example. Great efforts have been made for China to be understood by the rest of the world by carrying out a series of colorful cultural brand names, such as the activities of "Spring Festival," "National Day," and "Feel the Charms of Chinese Culture." In addition, China has cooperated with many countries in holding culture weeks, culture tours, culture festivals, and culture years on reciprocal terms—to demonstrate the charm of Chinese culture, on the one hand, and to understand other cultures, on the other hand. Government-sponsored Confucius Institutes have been the most visible means of Chinese cultural diplomacy. Between 2004 and 2008, China funded 256 Confucius Institutes and fifty-eight Confucius Classrooms in eighty-one countries (Confucius Institute Online 2010). Having promoted exchanges and mutual understanding between the Chinese people and other peoples, these activities have become new ways to enhance friendship between China and relevant countries.

Consular Diplomacy

Protecting the lawful interests and rights of its nationals abroad is the responsibility of a country's diplomatic services and is professionally known as consular diplomacy (see Leira and Neumann, chapter 9 in this volume). The significance of this dimension of Chinese diplomacy is growing as the number of Chinese traveling abroad increases. Some 12 million Chinese people travel overseas, while 24 million foreigners visit China every year (Q. Zhao 2009). The protection of Chinese nationals and corporations overseas is the legal responsibility of China's diplomacy, and the protection of Chinese people abroad is the touchstone for the Chinese public to judge the work of the MOFA bureaucracies. The Chinese government adheres to international law that states that a person's nationality entitles them to be provided consular protection from their state. In accordance with the principle of "putting prevention first and giving equal importance to prevention and the management of emergencies," the Chinese MOFA makes use of modern technology to disseminate early warnings in consular protection (see box 16-3). Information such as "Consular News" and "Notes on Traveling to Certain Countries and Cities" is updated on the official website of the MOFA to report recent cases of consular protection. Along with issuing documents, such as the "Guide of Proper Behavior for Chinese Citizens in Outbound Travel" and "Guide of Chinese Overseas Consular Protection and Service," the website has updated travel advice and notes and tips for traveling to specific countries and regions, including warnings to people who are traveling to some unsafe areas (MOFA, People's Republic of China 2010).

To ensure the smooth undertaking of consular protection, the Chinese government has upgraded and expanded its consular protection instruments. More resources and staff have been put into consular work. Among the more than 240 overseas foreign service institutions, 70 or so specialize in consular affairs, with the protection of the interests of overseas Chinese citizens as their main task. In addition to upgrading the Consular Protection Division of the Department of Consular Affairs to Consular Protection Center in 2007, China's MOFA departments have also set up cross-sector coordination and emergency response mechanisms. For China, consular work represents "conducting diplomacy for the people."

Military Diplomacy

Traditionally, it is claimed that diplomacy starts when the war ends, indicating that military and diplomatic activities do not lie in one sack. But in practice, military

---

BOX 16-3

Chinese Consular Protection

Of the more than 30,000 consular protection cases that the Chinese MOFA handles every year, a few examples are the mass evacuation of Chinese from Kuwait after it was invaded by Iraq in 1990, the evacuation of overseas Chinese from Indonesia during the Asian financial crisis (1997–98), and the evacuation of Chinese citizens from Chad during the civil war in 2008.

activities are always associated with diplomacy, and exchanges of armed forces are a major means of enhancing mutual confidence and maintaining peace. The white paper on China's national defense, issued by the Chinese government in 1998, revised the term "foreign military contacts" to "military diplomacy" and put forward the policy of developing omnidirectional and multilevel military diplomacy (State Council Information Office of the People's Republic of China 1998) (see box 16-4).

By 2008, China had established military ties with more than 150 countries and had military attaché offices in 109 countries. A total of 98 countries have had military attaché offices in China. China has had twenty-eight major joint military exercises with the armed forces of different countries. China's International Search and Rescue Team, composed mainly of Chinese servicemen, has assisted in fifteen emergency disaster relief operations, for example, to victims of the 2004 Indian Ocean tsunami, the 2005 Katrina hurricane in the United States, the 2005 South Asian earthquakes, and the 2006 mudslides in the Philippines. China used to demonstrate its peaceful foreign policy by emphasizing that it did not have one soldier on the territory of any foreign country. As noted earlier, China leads its fellow permanent members of the UN Security Council in dispatching peacekeepers abroad (L. Zhao 2010: 542).

China's diplomatic activities are not limited to the arenas discussed here. Diplomacy today is related to all walks of life in China. The expansion of diplomatic arenas accelerated the professionalization of China's diplomats that started with the founding of the PRC (X. Liu 2001). Today, "professionalism, specialization,

---

BOX 16-4

Examples of China's Military Diplomacy Activities

China's major military diplomatic activities include the following:

- institutionalization of the mechanism of military communications and connections with other countries;
- developing high-level military exchanges;
- conducting military cooperation and exchanges in personnel development;
- establishing mechanisms for different types of security cooperative dialogue;
- conducting defense consultations and security dialogues with countries concerned;
- promoting and participating in regional security cooperation;
- promoting gradual military transparency;
- holding joint military exercises with other countries;
- taking full and active participation in international peacekeeping operations and international relief and rescue activities; and
- participating in international convoys on the high seas in the Gulf of Aden since 2008.

and bureaucratic differentiation" are among the important characteristics of Chinese diplomacy (Lampton 2001: 10). These changes contribute to a large extent to the "erosion in the roles of the 'preeminent leaders,'" or "fractured diplomatic authority" at the top of the political leadership (Lampton 2001: 10). As a result, the paramount leaders in China today are becoming less powerful strategic diplomatic players and more like consultative technocrats. The Chinese diplomatic corps is less a group of "soldiers in civilian clothes," as Zhou Enlai said in the 1950s. Rather, it comprises professionals who are better trained, speak foreign languages fluently, and are encouraged to engage more with foreign societies and interact with the foreign media.

KEY POINTS

- Globalization has expanded the themes of diplomacy to nontraditional issues.
- The Chinese government introduced the concept of *zongti waijiao* (comprehensive diplomacy) to foreign affairs and conducted multidimensional diplomacy.
- Economic diplomacy is the priority of China's comprehensive diplomacy.
- Public diplomacy is a new and most active form of China's contemporary diplomacy.
- Cultural diplomacy has the strongest Chinese characteristics.
- Consular diplomacy and military diplomacy are becoming increasingly important.
- The role of the Chinese diplomatic corps is changing.

MULTILEVEL FOREIGN RELATIONS AND DIPLOMACY

The expansion of China's diplomatic areas demands professionalism, expertise, and "cooperative pluralization" in foreign affairs bureaucracies (see Hocking, chapter 7 in this volume). This process in turn brings about decentralization of diplomatic power away from MOFA to other ministries of the central government, and away from central government to localities, and even incorporates private sectors such as enterprises, research institutions, and individual citizens and the community of Chinese foreign policy actors (Yakobson and Knox 2010: 24–46). The fracturing of diplomatic actors and the decentralization of diplomatic power are leading to a multichannel or multitrack diplomacy in China's external relations. Summit diplomacy, party diplomacy, parliamentary diplomacy, and civil diplomacy are now the most important channels in China today.

Summit Diplomacy

Summit diplomacy refers to the diplomatic activities conducted by the heads of state or government. It involves such activities as visits by heads of state or government, summit meetings, correspondence and phone calls between heads of state or government, dispatching of envoys or personal representatives of leaders abroad, and delivering foreign policy pronouncements in person (Lu et al. 1997: 159–63; Plischke 1990: 17). The need to increase global cooperation and the convenience of modern transportation and communications have brought a coming of age of summit diplomacy (Melissen 2006). Summit diplomacy was not a central component of China's diplomatic history, but today it has become a popular and active diplomatic activity in China. For example, hotlines are frequently used for communications between Chinese heads of government and state with their counterparts, bilateral and multilateral summit conferences are common, and so too are envoy visits and attendance of the many summits held in countries around the world (Q. Zhang and Liu 2008).

The enhanced role of summit diplomacy in China's foreign affairs was confirmed in the second session of the tenth National People's Congress (NPC) in 2002. Article 81 of the constitution was amended to read: "The President of the People's Republic of China *engages in activities of State Affairs* and receives foreign diplomatic representatives on behalf of the People's Republic of China" (Constitution of the People's Republic of China, emphasis added). The president's engagement in "activities of State Affairs" is therefore a relatively new function that provides the president with a constitutional basis to conduct more active international diplomacy. Active summit diplomacy, however, has undermined the function and authority of foreign affairs bureaucracies. As one Chinese ambassador joked in a private conversation, ambassadors are now not ambassador extraordinary and plenipotentiary but ambassador extraordinary and no-power.

Party Diplomacy

As the ruling party of China, the CCP plays an important role in China's overall foreign relations. No party in any other country has a similar role. The CCP's diplomacy used to take precedence over state-to-state relations or state diplomacy when the PRC's diplomacy was limited to a few socialist countries during the 1950s. The twelfth CCP National Congress in 1982 decided to separate party-to-party relations from those of interstate relations, and it put forward the principles of "independence, complete equality, mutual respect, and noninterference in each other's internal affairs" for developing relations with foreign parties (Han 1987: 457). Thereafter, the CCP began extensive contacts and exchanges with different foreign, including nonsocialist, parties. In conforming to the more open situation after the end of the Cold War, the CCP established relations with more foreign parties: the level, content, and areas of exchanges increased substantially. By 2008, the CCP had established and maintained friendly relations with 528 parties and political organizations in 166 countries and regions in the world. The CCP conducts dozens of exchange visits with its foreign counterparts every year and has become an important strand of China's foreign relations.

Parliamentary Diplomacy

Parliamentary diplomacy consists of the diplomatic activities conducted by the parliament, the legislative branch of the state. The external relations of the legislative body are a significant component of China's overall foreign relations. The Chinese NPC is more than the legislative branch of the state; it is the most powerful government organ according to China's constitution. In China, it occupies an important position in the country's social life and in its politics. Exchanges of visits between the

Chinese NPC with its foreign counterparts have increased significantly. China's NPC has established quite a few mechanisms of exchanges with foreign parliaments and has cooperated with, and participated in, the multilateral affairs of regional or global interparliamentary organizations. China's NPC is a member of twelve international parliamentary organizations. The chairman of the standing committee of the NPC, Wu Bangguo, made ten foreign visits, and members of the standing committee have made fifty-eight foreign visits to five continents between 2003 and 2008 (Q. Zhang 2010: 118).

Civil Diplomacy

Civil diplomacy is different from the diplomacy conducted by governments; it is the diplomacy of making friends, which is also referred to as people-to-people diplomacy in the Chinese context. Civil diplomacy focuses on enhancing trust and understanding between peoples, and it emphasizes establishing friendships that go beyond concrete political and economic interests. This type of diplomacy has played a significant role in the normalization of Sino-Japanese diplomatic relations and Sino-US rapprochement. China has a special institution of civil diplomacy, the Chinese People's Association for Friendship with Foreign Countries. In conducting civil diplomacy, it follows such guidelines as making civil cooperative relations with great powers a priority, focusing on developing countries, conducting multilateral civil diplomacy with NGOs, and developing civil relations with countries that have not yet established diplomatic relations with China. These guidelines, which coincide with China's foreign relations structure, show that civil diplomacy in China is an important supplement to government diplomacy.

In sum, the number of actors that participate in diplomatic processes varies according to the issues involved. The MOFA today is merely one actor, and not necessarily the most important one. However, many of the other actors have narrow perceptions of China's national interest and even rival motives, often as a result of the focus on their domestic portfolios and their limited international outreach. The consequence is a mixed blessing. On the one hand, it "enhance[s] system legitimacy" and "increases the chances that decision-makers will have heard a greater number of…considerations" (Lampton 2001: 12). On the other hand, building consensus among these different actors lengthens the decision-making process and makes coordination an imperative for Chinese foreign policy and diplomacy: "The need to solicit, digest, bargain, and balance a greater number of views slows down the policy formulation process" (Lampton 2001: 13).

KEY POINTS

- Professionalism brings about decentralization of diplomatic power in China.
- The fracturing of diplomatic actors leads to a multichannel or multitrack diplomacy.
- The enhanced role of summit diplomacy in China's diplomacy was confirmed by an amendment to China's constitution.
- Party diplomacy, parliamentary diplomacy, and civil diplomacy are becoming important channels in China's contemporary diplomacy.

CONCLUSION

The changes analyzed in this chapter are only a few of the many new developments in China's contemporary diplomacy. What is equally important, but not discussed, is that the ideas of the Chinese elite on almost every aspect of China's diplomacy have changed in the process. As China becomes more active on the global stage, the trends this chapter has discussed will undoubtedly continue to evolve. As a result, China's gradual integration with the international system has made the country more cooperative and constructive, and more willing to accept and follow international law and norms that originated in the Western world. China's diplomatic practice during this process is becoming more similar to, rather than different from, that of other members of the international community, and the Chinese characteristics are become less and less salient. In this sense, we do not see that Zhou Enlai's call for a theory that would distinguish China's diplomacy from that of other countries in this contemporary world has been answered, and we do not see it likely to be realized in the near future.

QUESTIONS

1. Critically evaluate China's contemporary diplomatic thoughts and strategies.
2. How has China's attitude toward international society changed? What are the driving forces behind such changes?
3. Critically evaluate China's diplomatic structure.
4. What are the differences between Chinese and Western understandings of public diplomacy (refer to Melissen, chapter 11 in this volume)?
5. Why does China put so much emphasis on cultural diplomacy?
6. How does globalization change China's diplomatic behavior?
7. Do you think it likely that a distinctive Chinese diplomatic theory will be developed?
8. Compare the Chinese diplomatic features with those of other countries.
9. What are the implications of the analysis in this chapter for your theoretical and practical understandings of contemporary diplomacy?

CHAPTER 17

Regional Institutional Diplomacies
Europe, Asia, Africa, South America, and Other Regions

Jozef Bátora and Alan Hardacre

READER'S GUIDE

This chapter reviews the diplomatic structures and processes within regional institutions that are emerging around the globe. Anchored in a conceptualization of diplomacy as an institution, the European Union (EU) model of pooling resources toward the creation of a regional diplomatic system, including a set of dedicated institutional structures for performing diplomacy, is analyzed first. The chapter then addresses how similar processes are at work in Asia, Africa, and South America and in a number of other regional integration schemes. The chapter argues that there is a global trend toward increased regional diplomatic institutions and processes, inspired and catalyzed by developments in the EU, while not necessarily completely copying the European "model."

INTRODUCTION

The post–Second World War international environment is characterized by a proliferation of regional integration processes in various world regions, and this has important implications for the formation of regional diplomatic systems. The EU has been at the forefront of these developments. Bilateral diplomacy, multilateral diplomacy, consular diplomacy, economic diplomacy, and public diplomacy all appear to have changed significantly within the EU. The most profound changes relate to the Lisbon Treaty that came into force in December 2009, initiating a major evolution of the EU's external affairs administration including a new High Representative post and the **European External Action Service** (EEAS) (see box 17-1). However, as regional integration processes are not unique to the EU, it is important to assess similar change dynamics in other regions of the world. Through this analysis, the chapter assesses the nature of the diplomatic systems within other regional organizations and evaluates the extent to which they are similar and different. This assessment will entail looking at the particular diplomatic structures and processes that characterize regional organizations in Asia, Africa, and South America. After presenting the key diplomatic structures and processes of the EU as a comparative baseline, the chapter will use them to examine other regional organizations, concluding with a table to highlight our comparative findings.

The chapter starts by introducing the concept of diplomacy as an institution of international order. Anchored in new institutionalist approaches in political science, this conceptualization sets the analytical structure for understanding the systemic challenge that the formation of regional institutional diplomacies represents. The chapter then assesses the features of regional institutional diplomacies and a number of other regional integrationist schemes. We conclude that there are significant

---

BOX 17-1

Main Institutions of the European Union

Council of the European Union: also known as "Council of Ministers" or "Council," the Council of the European Union is the Union's main decision-making body. It represents member state interests in the EU. Member state ministers attend its meetings. The Council meets in ten different sectoral configurations to decide member state positions and take decisions. Each country of the EU presides over the Council for six months, by rotation.

European Commission: comprises twenty-seven commissioners and a permanent staff of some 37,000 European civil servants. Its main function is to propose EU legislation to the Council of the EU and the European Parliament. Also tasked with implementing EU legislation and the EU budget and acting in the general interest of the Union with complete independence from national governments.

European Council: comprises the heads of state or government of the member states and the president of the European Commission. It elects its president for a two-and-a-half-year period, and it meets at least four times a year. Its primary function is to provide general political impetus and guidelines for the EU.

European External Action Service: the diplomatic service of the EU. Established in 2010 based on articles in the Lisbon Treaty and composed of officials formerly attached to the European Commission, Council of the EU, and EU member states.

developments in regional diplomatic systems around the globe as a number of regions look toward developing regional integration schemes. There are, however, disparities in both the levels of development and the characteristics of regional diplomatic systems.

DIPLOMACY AS AN INSTITUTION AND THE CHALLENGE OF REGIONAL INSTITUTIONAL DIPLOMATIC SYSTEMS

Diplomacy as a process of mediation of relations has existed ever since the first human collectives started to communicate. Various historical periods featured different kinds of more or less sophisticated diplomatic systems (Satow 1922; Nicolson 1939; Numelin 1950; Der Derian 1987; Hamilton and Langhorne 1995; also see Cohen, chapter 1 in this volume). The way diplomacy is organized today as a set of standardized processes regulating relations between states via ministries of foreign affairs and permanent embassies is a relatively new phenomenon with origins in Europe. Well into the seventeenth century, diplomacy in Europe was organized around a reasonably open and multifaceted set of structures, processes, and actors (Mattingly 1955; Queller 1967). It was only with the rise of **sovereign** states and their increasing dominance as a key paradigm of political organization that the conduct of diplomacy was gradually associated exclusively with sovereign states (Anderson 1993). In what is often referred to as the "Westphalian state order," diplomacy emerged as one of the key institutions (Bull 1977; Watson 1982; Wight 1979). Diplomats from different sovereign states share a set of norms, principles, unwritten codes, and rules that they all adhere to. Building upon the definition of institutions by James March and Johan Olsen (1989), diplomacy as an "institution" can be defined as a set of rules and routines that define appropriate actions of states in the international environment (Bátora 2005: 48). In this sense, diplomacy may be considered an expression of a particular **logic of appropriateness**, informing appropriate actions and interactions of states, providing meanings to situations and actions, and indicating who might be deemed legitimate actors and what might be deemed legitimate situations (see box 17-2).

Explaining the maintenance and endurance of this interstate social structure in an international environment without any overarching hierarchy is a conceptual challenge. If international relations theory is less useful here, organization theory provides a pertinent conceptual toolbox. Thus, diplomacy may be seen as a global **organizational field** (see box 17-2) in which the standards of diplomatic organization, including ministries of foreign affairs and embassies, are maintained through peer pressure and mutual adaptation. Legitimate entry and operation within the global organizational diplomacy field are conditioned by subscribing to particular standards and expectations of how a diplomatic apparatus is to be organized, what it is to do, and how it is to do it. When new states are founded, ministries of foreign affairs are among the first governmental agencies to be created, and this is done by copying structures and processes of established foreign ministries. This is not necessarily due to the presumed organizational efficiency of this kind of a governmental agency—as numerous reorganization efforts in foreign ministries around the globe indicate, more often than not, these agencies are highly inefficient

=============== **BOX 17-2** ===============

Some Terms Associated with Regional Institutional Diplomacy

Logic of appropriateness: conceptualizes habitual behavior and institutionalized action where actors fulfill obligations and expectations related to a specific role in a specific situation. It constitutes an alternative to the **logic of consequences**, that is, instrumentally, rational action-driven strategic calculations, and expectations of specific outcomes (March and Olsen 1989, 2006).

Organizational field: may be defined as a collection of organizations "that in the aggregate, constitute a recognized area of institutional life: key suppliers, resource and product consumers, regulatory agencies, and other organizations that produce similar services and products" (DiMaggio and Powell 1991: 64–65).

Regional integration: generally refers to the process of proliferation of linkages and joint policy making across state borders in a given region and the development of regional supranational governance—the capacity to make binding rules in given policy areas (see Stone Sweet and Sandholtz 1998: 1). The classic writings of regional integration theory by Karl Deutsch (1957) and Ernest Haas (1958) and their followers provide varying interpretations of what characterizes regional integration processes (for an analytical review of different approaches, see Caporaso 1998).

(Hocking 1999b). Yet foreign ministries are extremely important as symbols of sovereignty and statehood and as expressions of social existence in the interstate order.

The systemic challenge brought about by **regional integration** (see box 17-2) and by the formation of regional diplomatic systems around the world is twofold. First, these processes challenge the primacy of the state as the dominant diplomatic actor—regional integrationist entities such as the EU are not states, but they do establish diplomatic structures similar to states, including central foreign affairs administrations, embassies, and foreign services. As we elaborate later, the EU may have gone furthest, but the Association of Southeast Asian Nations (ASEAN) Secretariat based in Jakarta has also done its share (Reiterer 2006). Second, these processes also challenge the unity and homogeneity of the standards and expectations established within the global organizational diplomacy field. As regional integration progresses at different speeds and with different effects in various world regions, there is increasing pressure toward fragmentation of the globally shared set of rules, routines, and norms that represent diplomacy as an institution of the interstate order. The solution may be either to limit the depth and breadth in the formation of regional institutional diplomatic systems or to adapt the global diplomatic order gradually so as to allow non-state regional diplomatic systems a seat at the diplomatic table.

The EU has been a leader in the formation of a regionally integrated institutional diplomatic system. This leadership has had implications for the foreign affairs administrations of its member states and for the patterns of interaction with "third countries" (that is, countries outside the EU) and other regionally integrated entities.

KEY POINTS

- Diplomacy is an institution of the modern state order, that is, it provides a framework of norms and rules regularizing interactions among sovereign states as key actors in world politics.
- Regional integration processes and the formation of regional diplomacies challenge established standards of diplomacy as an institution.

EU REGIONAL INSTITUTIONAL DIPLOMACY

The origins and the political evolution of what is the EU today are sufficiently well known. What is important is that two underlying processes have driven the structural development of the EU's regional institutional diplomacy. The first was the creation of the single market accompanied by standardization and mutual technical-functional adjustments in the "low politics" (socioeconomic) realm, producing "spillover" effects leading to further integration in other areas and to strengthening of **supranational** institutions (Haas 1958). The second integration process, in the field of "high politics" (foreign affairs and diplomacy), has been framed and defined by **intergovernmental** frameworks centered on the **Council of the European Union** (also known as the **Council of Ministers**) (see box 17-1). It is around these two processes of integration (supranational and intergovernmental) that the structures of regional institutional diplomacy have been developed in the EU.

The *supranational structures* for managing the external affairs of the European Communities (EC), as the EU's predecessor was once known, grew out of technical aid programs to the countries of Africa, the Caribbean, and the Pacific in the 1960s. Because the EC was not a sovereign state, the diplomatic status of officials representing the EC was ambiguous in the early years. Gradually, the EC **delegations** and their staff gained formal recognition as diplomatic agents from the authorities of host countries. This kind of recognition was stretching established concepts of whom or what is to be considered a standard diplomatic actor. As Véronique Dimier and Mike McGeever (2006: 496) observe, the "argument was that the EC was a 'partial' state. The Japanese were first to accept that somewhat revolutionary thesis." Since the mid-1980s, the EC had a well-functioning network of diplomatic representation featuring delegation offices around the world, a dedicated External Service, and an external affairs administration in Brussels built around several Directorates General in the sphere of trade, aid, and later external relations and enlargement. Since the entry into force of the Maastricht Treaty in 1993, EC delegations have been conducting more standard diplomatic functions, including political and security-related reporting. Training has been aimed at introducing standard elements of diplomatic service culture. Training has also been strengthened by exchange schemes for officers from member states' diplomatic services. On the ground in third countries, the heads of EC delegations have been charged with coordinating the activities of member states' embassies aiming for coherent EU action (see Maastricht Treaty 1992: Article 20). Also, the delegations have been charged with managing the financial portfolios from the EU's aid budget, which means they have been responsible for some key instruments in the EU's foreign policy. Nevertheless, the diplomatic status of the heads of EC delegations as ambassadors on par with ambassadors of sovereign states has been somewhat ambiguous as they represent a non-state entity with no head of state (Bruter 1999).[1]

If the **European Commission** (see box 17-1), responsible for the external service and the network of worldwide delegations, has been a foreign policy actor "by stealth" (see Keukeleire and MacNaughtan 2008: 84), EU foreign policy making has been centered on the intergovernmental framework of the Council of the EU. It is here that foreign policy actions of the EU are negotiated and decided by **consensus** by the foreign ministers of member states. Coordination is performed by the permanent EU presidency and the EEAS, and negotiation is performed primarily in the Committee of Permanent Representatives as well as in the Political and Security Committee. Since the Amsterdam Treaty (1999), the EU was represented externally by the High Representative for Common Foreign and Security Policy. The Council of the EU negotiations and the work of the High Representative were supported by the General Secretariat of the Council (known as the Council Secretariat). The origins of the latter go back to the loose foreign policy coordination mechanism known as "European Political Cooperation," initiated in 1970. While the Council Secretariat was created in the 1970s as a bureaucratic support body, in the first decade of the twenty-first century, it was playing the role of an embryonic "foreign ministry" of the EU.

As crises in Bosnia-Herzegovina and Kosovo unfolded in the 1990s, numerous coordination problems among the EU actors were exposed. In particular, coordinating the political decisions made in the Council of the EU with the flows of financial and technical assistance controlled by the European Commission and managed by heads of EC delegations in countries outside the EU often proved to be a severe challenge, undermining the EU's effectiveness in its foreign policy efforts (Knaus and Martin 2003). A series of similar problems along with the multiplicity of diplomatic representation of the EU were among the key motivations behind the change proposals contained in the 2009 Lisbon Treaty.

The Lisbon Treaty introduced a number of innovations in terms of institutional structures, legal status of diplomatic representatives, and in leading principles of the EU's external action. The key institutional innovations include the post of the High Representative of the Union for Foreign Affairs and Security Policy and the EEAS—the "diplomatic service" of the EU. The current High Representative, Catherine Ashton is in charge of coordinating the EU's external action and representing the EU to the outside. She is also vice president of the European Commission responsible for coordinating the commission's external relations portfolio. For the first time, an element of hierarchy was introduced in the so-called **College of Commissioners**, where the High Representative coordinates the work of the commissioners responsible for enlargement, trade, and developmental aid.

The EEAS was established in 2010. It is neither a supranational nor an intergovernmental institution, but a separate element in the institutional architecture of the EU. Its status is being described as a sui generis institution. Organizationally, it is based on selected units and staff from the European Commission's external affairs directorates, from the Council Secretariat, and from the EU member states. The staff is a multinational diplomatic service enjoying full **immunities and privileges** on a par with diplomatic services of states. The idea behind its creation was to achieve better coordination in Brussels and in third countries, linking political decisions with financial aid and other foreign policy instruments at the disposal of the European Commission.

Among the key legal changes introduced with the entry into force of the Lisbon Treaty was that the EC delegations abroad changed their status to delegations of the EU. This has raised the issue of who, and in what situations, represents member states in those third states where member states have their own national embassies.

A further challenge concerns the question of ensuring democratic legitimacy and accountability in the EEAS (Bátora 2010a). This relates to the fact that the EEAS is a new element in the architecture of the EU separate from both the European Commission and the **European Council** (see box 17-1), which means that specific procedures need to be set up to ensure political control and democratic accountability. This is particularly pertinent in light of the fact that the EEAS now manages the considerable budget for supporting the EU's external relations portfolio. In addition, it can also set the parameters for the EU's political decisions via the High Representative's role in presiding over the Foreign Affairs Council of the EU (which is where the foreign ministers of the twenty-seven member states meet to discuss and decide upon the EU's actions in the realm of the Common Foreign and Security Policy). Finally, the Lisbon Treaty has also introduced a transformative agenda concerning the content of the EU's external relations, for example, when it states that the EU is to spread the principles that it itself is built upon to other parts of the world (Lisbon Treaty 2009). This implies, among other things, supporting regional integration processes in other world regions.

In sum, multiple features have characterized the EU model of regional institutional diplomacy. First, it is a combination of supranational and intergovernmental institutional structures. This enables integrating processes of political decision making with financial aid, technical and legal expertise, and other instruments of the EU's external affairs toolbox. Second, it is a multinational diplomatic service. In this, the EU has departed from the standard model of national foreign services, restricted to one's own nationals. A parallel to the EU here can be found in what have perhaps been two systemic oddities, or medieval relics, within the modern diplomatic order—the foreign service of the Holy See and the foreign service of the Sovereign Military Order of Malta. Third, the structural development of EU diplomacy continues in parallel with the maintenance and adaptation of structures of member states' national diplomacy. Most of the governments of the EU-27 maintain their embassies around the world, even though some have decided to shift personnel and resources to areas with a high priority while relying upon the EU delegations in places of lower importance for them. Fourth, the combination of the rise and strengthening of diplomatic structures at the EU level with the maintenance and adaptation of structures at the member state level means that the EU now has a multilayered network of diplomatic representation with multiple channels and decision-making centers. While this has been the case at least since the entry into force of the 1993 Maastricht Treaty, the current setup has decreased the institutional fragmentation among the Brussels-based institutions and EU-level foreign affairs administration. Of key importance in further development of an esprit de corps in the EEAS will be the establishment of some form of shared diplomatic training, focusing on the functions and tasks performed by the service. No specific institution has been set up with this purpose in mind, however. The approach being considered is to select a number of diplomatic training institutions in the EU member states to provide training on a rotating basis to EU diplomats.

KEY POINTS

- European integration has led to the formation of both intergovernmental and supranational decision-making capacities at the EU level.
- External relations in the intergovernmental pillar of the EU (Common Foreign and Security Policy, European Security and Defense Policy) have been centered on the Council of the EU.
- External relations in the supranational pillar of the EU (single market, external trade, aid policies, and enlargement) have been centered on the European Commission.
- The Lisbon Treaty includes the following arrangements for conducting EU diplomacy: an integrated set of supranational tools and intergovernmental decision-making structures for foreign policy decision making; a multinational diplomatic service; parallel structures of diplomatic representation with member states; and a legal personality.

The following sections of the chapter review the formation of regional diplomacies in Asia, Africa, South America, and within other major regional groups in the world. The focus is on the key political and organizational developments, as well as on the role of local integration approaches, that provide the ideational underpinning to the formation of regional diplomatic systems. These sections also address to what extent these regions learn from, and emulate, the EU, and how these processes and institutions are modified and appropriated to local circumstances and political experience.

REGIONAL DIPLOMACY IN ASIA

Regional integration in Asia has followed a very different path than that taken by the EU. There are a number of regional entities in Asia (see figure 17.1). This section will concentrate on the two main ones: ASEAN and the South Asian Association for Regional Cooperation (SAARC).

ASEAN has a population of about 600 million people and is the largest and most important Asian regional integration initiative. It was established in 1967 between Indonesia, Malaysia, the Philippines, Singapore, and Thailand, and although its initial objectives were concerned with regional peace and harmony, it has focused more recently on political and economic integration in order to compete more effectively in an increasingly globalized world. Integration has progressed according to the "ASEAN way," a diplomatic code of conduct built on consensual and flexible decision making, limited institutionalization, informality, and mutual noninterference. This incremental approach to integration is characterized by high levels of head of government/state networking and decision taking combined with a reluctance to use

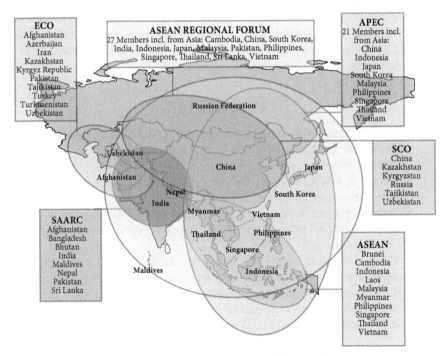

ECO
Afghanistan
Azerbaijan
Iran
Kazakhstan
Kyrgyz Republic
Pakistan
Tajikistan
Turkey
Turkmenistan
Uzbekistan

ASEAN REGIONAL FORUM
27 Members incl. from Asia: Cambodia, China, South Korea,
India, Indonesia, Japan, Malaysia, Pakistan, Philippines,
Singapore, Thailand, Sri Lanka, Vietnam

APEC
21 Members incl.
from Asia:
China
Indonesia
Japan
South Korea
Malaysia
Philippines
Singapore
Thailand
Vietnam

SCO
China
Kazakhstan
Kyrgyzstan
Russia
Tajikistan
Uzbekistan

SAARC
Afghanistan
Bangladesh
Bhutan
India
Maldives
Nepal
Pakistan
Sri Lanka

ASEAN
Brunei
Cambodia
Indonesia
Laos
Malaysia
Myanmar
Philippines
Singapore
Thailand
Vietnam

Figure 17.1 Overlapping membership in Asian regional integration.

binding institutions or legal instruments. Through this approach, which is substantially different than the EU supranational approach (Rüland 2001), ASEAN hopes to achieve its aim of becoming a full ASEAN Community by 2015. This community will be based on a Security Community, an Economic Community, and a Socio-Cultural Community—although there is some debate as to whether these three will be realized on time, or at all.

The ASEAN way—a state-centric approach—pervades the institutions, processes, and procedures of regional integration, as well as regional diplomacy. The ASEAN Secretariat in Jakarta coordinates and implements projects and activities, but it is not—and does not aspire to become—supranational with binding powers like the EU model. Instead, the ASEAN Secretariat's vision is to become the "nerve center," which means a central organizing and information function. The ASEAN institutional structure contains dispute settlement mechanisms, a development fund, and arrangements for a high level of cooperation with the business sector. Two further important structural elements of ASEAN are the rotating chairmanship and the Jakarta-based Committee of Permanent Representatives, alongside the Secretariat, to help merge national positions into ASEAN positions. The ability to coordinate ASEAN diplomacy is based on a willingness to merge national positions and to vote and act as a region—a major challenge in the creation of any regional diplomacy. ASEAN very rarely votes as a group in multilateral forums, although it consistently votes, as a group, against United Nations (UN) resolutions condemning Burma.

ASEAN has extensive external relations, notably in the security and economic fields. It has free trade agreements (FTAs) with countries such as Australia, India, Japan, and New Zealand and an important FTA with China that came into effect in January 2010. External negotiations and relations are always conducted, or endorsed, on an intergovernmental basis, usually by the foreign ministers under the ASEAN umbrella, as the foreign ministers did for the ASEAN-China FTA. In addition to these external trade relations, ASEAN has had a diplomatic relationship with the United States for more than thirty years. Arguably, the ASEAN way is even more important as a diplomatic code of conduct that guides external negotiations and discussions. It is based on respect for sovereignty, a nonconfrontational and low-key style that is different from Western diplomacy, which is more comfortable with sanctions, threats, and warnings. This emergent regional diplomatic culture has also spread to other regional arrangements, for example, the **ASEAN Regional Forum**. Interestingly, there is a debate about the limits of the ASEAN way and the extent to which ASEAN actually follows it (Yuzawa 2006).

While ASEAN clearly does not replicate the regional integration or, by extension, the diplomatic structures and processes of the EU, developments in the region indicate some elements of "learning" from the EU experience, or at least some similarities with the path the EU has taken. ASEAN now has third countries accredited to its Secretariat, in recognition of the nerve center role that it aspires to play. ASEAN also currently has twenty-one committees abroad, all staffed by local member state ambassadors under rotating chairmanships, such as in Geneva, Beijing, Washington, Paris, Brussels, and New York. The role of these committees is to help coordinate the external activities of ASEAN in their respective locations.

SAARC, the second major regional initiative in Asia, was created in 1985 by Bangladesh, Bhutan, India, the Maldives, Nepal, Pakistan, and Sri Lanka. SAARC applies a diplomatic code of conduct similar but not identical to the ASEAN way to its decision-making methods and its integration philosophy. It is therefore also a summit-driven process with the Council of Ministers as a second level of institutional architecture—again supported by a nonsupranational Secretariat. SAARC is much less active on the international scene than ASEAN and has shown a smaller appetite for a regional diplomatic presence. Unlike ASEAN, SAARC does not have third-country representations to its Secretariat, or nascent committees to coordinate and cooperate abroad, which is a reflection of its limited integration objectives.

The extent to which these two regional vehicles—ASEAN and SAARC—display regional diplomatic tendencies differs quite markedly. While neither of them has the explicit objectives of creating a centralized diplomatic machinery, harmonized positions, and a joint outlook, ASEAN is clearly developing institutions and techniques that reveal a nascent regional diplomacy that is a logical consequence of its regional integration process. ASEAN is an increasingly active player on the regional and global stage, and its activities require structures and processes to find positions and negotiate mandates. In spite of the ASEAN way, the countries of ASEAN appear to be replicating a number of structural elements of EU regional diplomacy. For example, ASEAN seeks to develop and engage in both low and high politics, and the Secretariat is developing into a key actor assisted by a committee of permanent representatives and by third-country representations. The objectives of these structures are to harmonize national positions and allow ASEAN to act as one. In addition, ASEAN has a number of coordinating committees around the world in key economic and political locations, as a further embryonic attempt to harmonize its activities. Where ASEAN and SAARC remain reluctant to follow the EU diplomatic integration model is in the adoption of supranational arrangements, binding regional positions, and the creation of formal regional representations (Acharya 2004).

KEY POINTS

- The nature of regional diplomacy in South and Southeast Asia is driven by the level (and objectives) of regional integration and the structures for interaction with third countries and organizations.
- Regional diplomacy in these regions is characterized by a strong degree of intergovernmentalism.

REGIONAL DIPLOMACY IN AFRICA

Africa is home to more regional integration initiatives than any other continent in the world, and also to the oldest integration scheme—the Southern African Customs Union of 1910. Despite this, Africa has an extremely mixed record in regional integration and subsequently in regional diplomacy.

The African Union (AU), the successor to the Organization of African Unity, is the only pan-African regional organization with fifty-three of the fifty-four African states as members (Morocco is the only country not a member due to a political conflict with other AU members over the membership of Western Sahara, which has a special status allowing it access to functions and negotiations). The AU is formally, and explicitly, modeled on the EU, which it is striving to replicate. The AU has an Assembly of the Union made up of heads of state as the primary decision-taking body, along with the Executive Council, Pan-African Parliament, Court of Justice, Committee of Permanent Representatives, and Commission. All major countries in the world have diplomatic representation to the AU housed in Addis Ababa. The AU is an umbrella organization, covering the plethora of regional integration schemes that coexist in Africa—with the long-term intention of subsuming them all into one body. Currently, it is an important African political body and is assuming new diplomatic significance as well. For example, the AU has special diplomatic relations with both the United States and the EU and is a permanent observer at the UN General Assembly.

The indicative list of regional integration schemes in Africa shows that, aside from the AU, the twelve other integration projects involving the fifty-four states of Africa have a combined 138 members. Thus, there is significant quantitative overlap in African regional integration (see figure 17.2).

The issue of overlapping membership is an important one to consider when thinking about the formation of regional diplomacies because it helps to assess whether the region is a coherent and unified entity. In addition, as we have argued, the formation of a regional diplomatic system depends to a significant extent on the

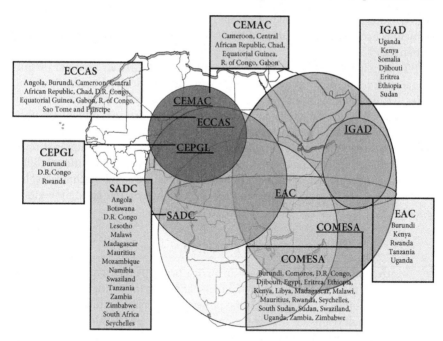

Figure 17.2 Overlapping membership in African regional integration.
NOTE: This figure does not depict all of Africa's regional integration schemes. It also does not take account of the qualitative nature of integration of each project.

objectives and goals of the regional integration scheme. For example, the focus of the Intergovernmental Authority on Development (IGAD) on drought control and development initiatives has an impact on its structure and diplomatic aspirations. Almost all the other regional groupings identified have strong and explicit economic integration motivations and objectives—thus they are more concerned with low-politics issues, as described earlier. The most direct implication of this is that in the majority of African countries, diplomacy is concentrated in the area of trade negotiations, with the bulk of political and security diplomacy being handled by the AU and other international organizations.

African regional integration is closely fashioned on the EU "model," in terms of institutional structure and objectives. Consequently, there are some clear, although at times competing, emerging regional diplomatic tendencies. Many of the African regional groups are striving toward economic and political integration, with the direct consequence that structures and institutions for creating and delivering regional diplomacy are being actively sought and built. The majority of the regional groups have turned to the EU as a blueprint for how to create the right structures for regional diplomacy, so closer analysis of the African schemes, such as EAC, often reveals almost identical institutional architectures, goals, objectives, and processes to develop diplomatic positions, One final important aspect of African regional integration is regional peacekeeping and cooperation with the UN, notably numerous Economic Community of West African States (ECOWAS) peacekeeping initiatives.

To conclude, there are two related caveats about African regional institutional diplomatic development. First, having almost identical institutions and objectives does not in any way guarantee an ability to develop and deliver regional diplomacy. Second, the ability to develop and deliver regional diplomatic positions on international issues is very difficult without deep respect for regional law that ensures agreements are adhered to and a commitment to supranationality that would supersede national interests. African regional institutional diplomacy is well developed in terms of objectives, structures, and mechanisms, but it will take more time to solidify and represent coherent and strongly regional positions.

KEY POINT

- Advancing regional diplomacy in Africa has depended on several factors, among them the cohesion of the regional group; the strength and depth of regional integration schemes; the presence of strong institutions and structures to develop and deliver regional diplomacy; and resources for building regional capacity.

REGIONAL DIPLOMACY IN SOUTH AMERICA

In South America, a number of regional integration developments have come to the fore in the 1990s; some are new, and some are rejuvenated vehicles from the 1960s. South America, more than any other continent, has embraced regional integration as a reaction to global changes and developments, using it to gain influence and assert itself on the global stage. In addition, regional integration in South America has to contend with US hegemony—meaning that many regional groups have an element of identity and independence that regional groups in other parts of the world do not have. This has given rise to a small number of coherent regional groups.

The most important regional group in South America is Mercosur, the world's third-largest regional grouping. Mercosur was created in 1991 by Argentina, Brazil, Paraguay, and Uruguay with the signing of the Treaty of Asunción. It had an ambitious initial program, borne of political desire, that included the creation of a free trade area, a customs union, and eventually a common market—all closely modeled on the EU's history. While Mercosur has not achieved the status of a complete common market, it has made significant progress over its short life span, such that it represents an advanced regional integration body with political, economic, and security interests (Doctor 2007; Malamud 2003, 2005; Peña 2005).

Mercosur was built on the EU blueprint, sharing Europe's objectives and institutional architecture but without any form of supranationalism (Malamud 2005). It has presidential summits to drive the agenda forward, backed up by the Common Market Council, the Joint Parliamentary Committee, the Economic and Social

Consultative Forum, the Committee of Permanent Representatives, and an administrative secretariat based in Montevideo that has extensive third-country representation. Mercosur is active in regional and global diplomacy and has an expressed objective to be a key actor across trade, security, and political issues. It is a globally recognized regional entity. Mercosur has already negotiated a number of FTAs, engaged in a number of current negotiations, such as with the EU, and seeks to play an active political role in the Americas and beyond. Unlike many other regional groups, Mercosur actively seeks to construct a regional diplomatic role beyond trade. Thus, Mercosur has developed a very strong regional diplomatic presence in international forums. This presence, however, continues to be based on "presidential initiatives" between member state leaders, notably Brazil, a practice that is not based on the EU model of common positions delivered by supranational civil servants.

The Andean Community (CAN) is the most institutionalized regional project in South America, with internal free trade applied to all products in all sectors, supranational institutions, and developed external links and relationships. The current CAN stems mostly from major internal changes made in the 1990s that created stronger, more flexible institutions, based on the EU integration model. The current institutional architecture is the most ambitious regional project after the EU itself. CAN's architectural schema includes the Andean Presidential Council, the Andean Council of Ministers of External Affairs, the Andean Community Commission, the Tribunal of Justice, and the Andean Parliament. The most distinguishing feature of CAN is its supranationality, something no other South American regional initiative is even close to attaining. Its supranationality comes through "direct applicability," which means regulations do not need to be ratified at the national level once officially published. This aspect of regional integration has important potential consequences for the development of regional diplomacy because it would allow CAN to mirror developments in the EU more closely than regional groups relying on presidential initiative and guidance.

The Central American Common Market (CACM) is the oldest regional initiative in South America, created by the General Treaty on Central American Economic Integration in 1960. The Central American Integration System (SICA) supplemented this in 1993 as a renewed attempt to integrate a region that, despite close linguistic, geographic, cultural, and historical ties, had failed to integrate successfully. The EU model has heavily influenced CACM, like the other South American regional groups; hence its institutional architecture is headed by presidential summits. The implementation of these meetings is assured by the Council of Ministers. In addition, there is a Central American Parliament, as well as a Central American Court of Justice, which is a permanent institution that guarantees the judicial security of the integration process. The daily task of running the integration system falls to the General Secretariat of SICA.

In sum, these three regional integration bodies in South America are different from many of their counterparts elsewhere in their level of development and their ambitions. Additionally, they do not have overlapping membership (compared with groups in Africa and Asia that do have overlapping membership), and they are explicitly modeled on the EU (in the same way groups in Africa are modeled on the EU), with similar objectives and institutions. Because they are relatively advanced in regional integration, they have all developed numerous external relations and, through this, distinct diplomatic structures and identities. This is most notable in the case of Mercosur, which is active in the regional and global political and trade realms. In the case of Mercosur, there are regional diplomatic structures such as a committee of permanent representatives with third-country representation, but its regional diplomacy is strongly based on presidential summits and networking. Mercosur is intergovernmental and is represented by its heads of state—making it unlikely that Mercosur would follow recent developments in the EU's diplomatic model. The only regional group in South America likely to closely pursue the EU model is CAN, due to its commitment to supranationalism.

KEY POINT

- Advancing regional diplomacy in South America is dependent upon such measures as a combination of trade negotiations and political/security discussions; supranational institutions that deliver more consistent regional diplomacy than presidential-driven integration; and further replication of the EU model to decrease presidential-driven diplomacy.

OTHER REGIONAL DIPLOMATIC SYSTEMS

Having reviewed developing regional diplomacies in Europe, Asia, Africa, and South America, we complete the picture by outlining some other emerging regional diplomatic entities.

Both North American Free Trade Agreement (NAFTA) and Free Trade Area of the Americas (FTAA) are trading arrangements with no current intention, or structures, to develop and deliver nontrade regional diplomacy. To a certain extent, the same can be said for the three European regional groupings, which, despite having wider objectives, remits, and intentions, are still focused on fostering interaction and in maintaining peace and stability. Here, we will assess two regional groups: the Gulf Cooperation Council (GCC) and the Caribbean Community (CARICOM).

The GCC was created in 1981, bringing together Bahrain, Kuwait, Oman, Qatar, Saudi Arabia, and the United Arab Emirates, with the objective of creating an economic and political union. Like many regional groups, the GCC is driven by a presidential summit, called the Supreme Council, with the Ministerial Council and Consultative Commission implementing the decisions of the presidents. It also has a commission for dispute settlement and an administrative secretariat. The GCC actively discusses economic, political, and security issues concerning the Middle East and beyond and, consequently, has had to create structures and mechanisms to find common diplomatic positions and ways to deliver them. The GCC has advanced to the stage of a common market and has initiated a program to develop a common currency highlighting its ability to deliver on integration promises through coordination and joint action. The GCC has acted in unison in trade negotiations with the EU, the United States, and Japan. In political and security relations in the Middle East, the GCC has evolved into a coherent and strong regional diplomatic actor. In sum, the GCC is actively developing as a region and also developing and delivering its own regional diplomacy based on presidential leadership. The GCC also has a delegation office in Brussels to interact with the EU. The GCC has progressed in a similar way to Asian regional integration in that it has not explicitly copied the EU "model"—something that remains unlikely in the coming years as it is so bound to the presidential nature of the process.

CARICOM was created in 1973 with four signatories (Barbados, Jamaica, Guyana, and Trinidad and Tobago). It grew quickly to encompass the current fifteen members and is, like its South American and African counterparts, heavily influenced by the EU model of integration. Among the objectives of CARICOM are economic integration to generate greater trade bargaining power and the coordination of foreign policy issues of mutual interest. To do this, CARICOM's institutional architecture is led by the Conference of Heads of Government and the Community Council of Ministers, which are both supported by an administrative secretariat based in Georgetown, Guyana. CARICOM initiated extended discussions in 2010 to create a committee of permanent representatives to help solidify the work of the regional group and to speed up its processes.

CARICOM, much like the GCC, is a regional integration project for smaller countries with a great deal of shared history and ambition. CARICOM has developed a wide variety of internal projects and external relations on the same basis of presidential drive and will. It has, for example, completed an FTA with the EU in 2009—a process that drained substantial regional resources from CARICOM. For cost-saving and other related reasons, CARICOM proposed the creation of additional structures to deal with the formation of regional diplomatic positions on issues such as trade and climate change, and within multilateral forums such as the UN—namely, a committee of permanent representatives. CARICOM chairman, and prime minister of Jamaica, Bruce Golding explained that this development occurred because "domestic political structures cannot respond with that kind of 'automaticity'" (Richards 2010). The process of developing additional institutional regional diplomacy will not be easy because fourteen sovereign states will have to make important political changes to bring about this new regional structure. This underscores the importance of a strong regional institutional architecture to support the formation and delivery of regional diplomacy, and also the difficulties that there can be in setting up such architecture (for more information on CARICOM regional diplomacy, see Cooper and Shaw 2009).

KEY POINTS

- Some regional bodies in other parts of the world do not strive to develop regional diplomacy. NAFTA, for example, is driven by economic imperatives rather than integration.
- Small states, such as those in CARICOM and GCC, benefit from regional projects and diplomacy because such efforts aim to pool their resources and increase their visibility and presence.
- Regional diplomacy relies on institutions that harmonize national positions.

CONCLUSION

As the chapter has shown, there are pervasive processes of regional integration in virtually all parts of the world. These processes generate an extra layer of regional diplomatic activities, forums, and codes, which deepen and complicate the structure of relations within the global organizational field of diplomacy. However, the nature of regional institutional diplomacies varies considerably (see table 17.1).

The main findings of this chapter are as follows: first, most of the processes remain strongly intergovernmental. An institutional architecture to develop and deliver regional diplomacy is vital. The copying of the EU template has also been shown to be no guarantee of the emergence of regional diplomacy. What seems to set some of the regional integration processes apart is the existence of supranational structures, defined at the beginning of this chapter.

Second, regions with supranational integration dynamics seem to create the most advanced diplomatic structural arrangements. The EU has been in the vanguard here, while CAN in Latin America has followed suit. These two regions have been most active in serving as integrated regional entities in relation to third parties

Table 17.1 Comparative Regional Diplomatic Structure and Processes

STRUCTURES AND PROCESSES	EU	ASEAN	SAARC	AU	EAC	MERCOSUR	CAN	CARICOM
Intergovernmental structures of foreign policy decision making	Yes	Yes	Yes	Yes	Yes	Yes	Yes	Yes
Supranational tools of foreign policy making	Yes	No	No	No	No	No	Yes	No
Acting as host to diplomatic missions of third countries	Yes	Yes	No	Yes	Yes	Yes	Yes	Yes
Represented by own separate missions to other regional integrationist entities	Yes	No	No	No	No	No	No	No
Multinational diplomatic service	Yes	No	No	No	No	No	No	No
Delegations (embassies)	Yes	No	No	No	No	No	No	No
High Representative ("foreign minister")	Yes	No	No	No	No	No	No	No
Diplomatic academy	No	No	No	No	No	No	No	No
Legal personality	Yes	Yes	Yes	Yes	Yes	Yes	Yes	Yes
Seat at the UN	No	No	No	No	No	No	No	No
Parallel structures of diplomatic representation at the regional and member state levels	Yes	No	No	No	No	No	No	No

and in seeking recognition as such. The EU has served as an explicit integration model for regional integration in Africa and Latin America.

Third, many regional institutions mimic, to varying degrees, such organizational structures as the Committee of Permanent Representatives and various codes of conduct supporting cooperation and coordination, notably the ASEAN way, which parallels, while not copying, codes found in the EU. Such structures are essential to devise and deliver regional diplomacy. Finally, regions with strong regional integration and ambitious political objectives tend to be more active in creating and developing regional diplomatic structures.

From these main points it can be seen that both the supranational and the intergovernmental structures of EU diplomacy have served as a source of reference, even if not inspiration, for other world regions. So far, there is no other world region that appears close to constructing a regional institutional diplomacy along the lines of the EU, in the sense of not only featuring intergovernmental and supranational structures but also integrating those structures into one external affairs framework as the EU has been attempting to do since the Lisbon Treaty.

If other world regions go about establishing direct regional-level diplomatic links with EU-level diplomacy and eventually follow suit in their own integration processes in order to establish regional diplomatic structures compatible with that of Europe, then the EU model of regionally integrated diplomacy (outlined in table 17.1) may become a more accepted standard.

It is no surprise that the EU has sought to maintain its character as an international entity that is different from states, notably by providing extensive assistance for integration in other world regions. This, in part, explains why so many regions around the world at least look to the EU regional template. The EU's regional integration support has spilled over and will continue to impact diplomatic structures at the regional level. Although driven by a quest for its own legitimacy, the EU may be doing the UN's work in promoting regional integration processes around the globe (Wiseman 2011b: 11). Finally, in a fast-changing, globalizing world, a key challenge to regionalism around the world is whether, and how, major players, such as China, Russia, Brazil, India, and the United States, will be incorporated into, and actively recognize and engage with, this evolving system of regional diplomacies.

QUESTIONS

1. What are the main features of the EU diplomatic model?
2. What role do institutions play in regional diplomacy?
3. What aspects of the EU model have been most successfully replicated around the world?
4. What are the prerequisites for other world regions to develop their own regional diplomacy?
5. Compare and contrast the regional diplomacy of at least two world regions.
6. How important are international and interregional negotiations for the formation of regional diplomacy?
7. What is the relationship between regional integration and regional diplomacy?

8. What do you think are the main difficulties for the replication of the EU model?
9. What are the implications of the analysis in this chapter for your theoretical and practical understandings of contemporary diplomacy?

NOTE

1. They have even been the object of some ridicule. For instance, Jack Straw, in his role as the British foreign minister, had famously referred to EC diplomats as "all sorts of odd bods running these sorts of odd offices." See Watt (2004).

ACKNOWLEDGMENT

Jozef Bátora's work on the chapter was supported by the Slovak Research and Development Agency under the contract No. APVV-0484-10.

CHAPTER 18

The United Nations

Geoffrey Wiseman and Soumita Basu

CHAPTER CONTENTS

- Introduction
- Historical origins and emergence
- Main UN organs
- Evolution of diplomatic practices
- The diplomatic community
- Conclusion

READER'S GUIDE

This chapter examines diplomacy at the United Nations (UN). Set up after the Second World War, the UN emerged as a central stage (and actor) for mitigating international conflict and managing international cooperation, thus facilitating diplomatic efforts in multiple ways. Widely regarded as the main twentieth-century experiment in "multilateral diplomacy," it continues to evolve as both an intergovernmental organization and a key component of contemporary global governance. Yet the diplomatic underpinnings of its political processes have been mostly neglected by the literature on the UN, including international relations scholarship. The chapter traces the evolution of diplomatic activities and the "diplomatic community" at the UN from its founding in 1945 and assesses such developments as the use of World Conferences and the significance of nongovernmental organizations (NGOs). The tensions between national interests and shared international values are apparent in both major policy making and everyday practices at the UN. In this context, the chapter examines whether the norms of the UN diplomatic community can transcend national interests to secure more broadly conceived goals of international peace and progress.

INTRODUCTION

Opinions are divided on the UN's value in world politics. However, some of the most highly skilled diplomats in the world represent their countries at UN headquarters in New York. Indeed, a posting to the UN is among the most coveted in the profession. For scholars of international relations, the UN is seen in different ways. Michael Barnett and Martha Finnemore (2008) identify five different images of the UN: a tool of the great powers, a facilitator of interstate competition, a governor of the society of states, a constructor of the social world, and a framework legitimizing specific decisions and principles governing international order—and their list is not exhaustive. But irrespective of the many images of the UN, students of diplomacy appreciate both the political efforts behind "getting things done" at a practical level and the organization's inefficiencies and inertia (Wiseman 2011b).

The UN's institutional context stands apart from all others, because of both the many actors involved and the range of issues under its purview. As in **bilateral** contexts, there is diversity in the size of national diplomatic representations at the UN. In a moderate to large diplomatic mission, an individual diplomat is assigned to "cover" one or more of the main UN organs, such as the Security Council and the six main committees of the General Assembly.[1] In addition, diplomats liaise with the Executive Office of the Secretary-General, UN programs, funds, and agencies, and the ever-growing number of NGOs working in and around the UN. Other UN diplomats in New York may focus on special bilateral diplomacy with certain member state representatives or engage in negotiating drafts of UN resolutions. In all such activities, they carefully keep an eye on the international media accredited to the UN in order to communicate their government's position on any given issue. The outcome is an array of diplomatic processes and, in some cases, the achievement of seemingly contradictory goals relating to an intriguing tension underlying everything that happens at the UN: the competing impulses of promoting national interests and advancing international norms of cooperation.

This chapter traces the evolution of UN diplomatic practices and assesses recent important developments, such as the increasing use of "public diplomacy," or outreach to global publics, and the growing political significance of NGOs. It examines the UN's emergence as the primary multilateral organization in world politics and the relevance of the main UN organs from a diplomatic perspective, discusses the multiple diplomatic avenues at the UN and identifies changes in the institutional context and practices over time, and considers the evolution of the traditional UN diplomatic corps into an emerging UN "diplomatic community." Finally, it discusses prospects for UN diplomacy's future evolution.

HISTORICAL ORIGINS AND EMERGENCE

The UN's pre-twentieth-century origins can be traced a long way back. For example, multilateral diplomacy, the essence of UN diplomacy, was evident in the negotiations during the Congress of Westphalia from 1644 to 1648, the 1815 Congress of Vienna, and the congresses convened under the so-called Concert of Europe from 1815 to 1914 (see Cohen, chapter 1 in this volume). Many important technical conferences, such as the Universal Postal Union, were established during the later part of the nineteenth century (Berridge 2005: 151–56; Hamilton and Langhorne 2011: 94–102). Thus, while multilateral diplomacy predates the UN, the intergovernmental organization represents a major step toward "institutionalized multilateralism" of contemporary world politics (Thakur 2002: 283). As such, it provides a conceptual step in the direction of forms of **global governance** beyond **multilateralism** (also see Badie, chapter 5 in this volume)

Broadly speaking, there are three ways to explain why the UN was created in 1945: a realist great power view; a liberal internationalist view; and a Western imperial dominance view.

The Great Power View

In the aftermath of the First World War, US president Woodrow Wilson, along with several European leaders, promoted the idea of the League of Nations, a new international organization created by the Paris Peace Conference in 1919 attended by some twenty-five state participants. The league was designed to prevent future wars, but the new organization, established in Geneva, was weakened by the absence of some of the day's major powers—notably, the United States and the Soviet Union— for extended periods. The Soviet Union's absence was not surprising, given the 1917 Bolshevik revolution. However, the United States' absence was, given that Wilson had championed the league (notably to the US Congress in his famous Fourteen Points of January 1919). As it turned out, the league's fate appeared to be sealed with its inability to deal inter alia with Japan's 1931 occupation of Manchuria, Italy's 1936 occupation of Abyssinia (Ethiopia), and Hitler's 1938 annexation of Austria. With the outbreak of the Second World War in 1939, the league was regarded as a failure.

Against this background of the league's failure to respond to outright military aggression sits the traditional explanation for the UN's creation at the end the Second World War: that it was established by the victorious great powers (the United States, the Soviet Union, the United Kingdom, France, and China), all determined to ensure a system that would prevent the kind of territorial aggression that had led to war in the first place. This time, all major powers would be members, and they would create mechanisms to ensure that their interests were secured.

The Liberal Internationalist View

A second explanation, reflecting the legacy of Wilsonian liberal values about national self-determination, democracy, and what became known as "collective security," is that the UN was created under the United States' diplomatic leadership. In this view, the United States managed the founding of the new body, determined to avoid the league's mistakes. Thus, when the UN was created at the 1945 San Francisco Conference (hosted, significantly, by the United States), its structure reflected both the prevailing power relations of the time and the aspirations of people everywhere for a return to peace (Patrick 2009; Schlesinger 2003). The UN began with fifty-one member states, more than double the number of states at the 1919 Paris Peace Conference.

A Western Imperial Dominance View

The two previous explanations have been challenged by world-order historian Mark Mazower (2009), who argues that the UN was founded to perpetuate British and American global dominance while accommodating the unwelcome emergence of the Soviet Union. High-minded talk of national self-determination and human rights, Mazower further argues, served only to conceal this reality. As fears of an emerging Cold War surfaced at that time, Soviet suspicions of Western motives also reflected the Western imperialism explanation.

As is so often the case, wars—whose outbreak implies the failure of diplomacy—produce new thinking about diplomacy in their termination or aftermath. In the twentieth century, this was indeed the case after the two world wars. Therefore, it is unremarkable that the multilateral institutions emerging from those wars were intended to prevent devastating armed conflicts ("high politics"). However, it is noteworthy that the UN recognized, as hinted at in its wide-ranging institutional design, that wars are caused not just by dictators invading other countries but by socioeconomic factors, such as poverty and resource scarcity ("low politics"). Still, the scholarly consensus is that the UN's design reflected a world of great powers as the primary means to keep the peace, even if there is disagreement about the motives of those powers.

Consisting of nineteen chapters divided into 111 articles, the UN Charter opened its preamble with the striking phrase "We the peoples of the United Nations." The charter's key principles, however, are less about people and more about the sovereign states that would make up the membership. The core principles were the "sovereign equality of states," "non-intervention" in the affairs of other member states, the "peaceful settlement of disputes," and the "non-use of force." These principles are reflected in many of the charter's articles, but under various articles in chapter 7, "Action with Respect to Threats to the Peace, Breaches of the Peace, and Acts of Aggression," the UN Security Council was authorized to act on any measures necessary to maintain international peace and security. By allowing the use of force under this provision, the charter's framers left no doubt that the UN's main role was to prevent future wars. Moreover, the Security Council was intended to be the most important UN organ, managed by the great powers, whose own interests would be protected by their **veto** powers.

KEY POINTS

- Multilateral diplomacy has a long, pre-1945 history, but the creation of the UN's permanent headquarters, offices, and networks across the world heralded the arrival of institutionalized multilateralism in international relations.
- The UN was born of the great powers and focused primarily on peace and security (high politics).
- The UN's institutional design opened the door for consideration of socioeconomic issues (low politics) and for the rise of new diplomatic actors.

MAIN UN ORGANS

Under the charter, six principal organs were created to carry out the organization's work—the General Assembly, Security Council, Economic and Social Council (ECOSOC), Trusteeship Council, International Court of Justice (ICJ), and the Secretariat led by the Secretary-General.

Loosely endorsing the idea that the UN would represent all the world's "peoples," the *General Assembly* was created under the charter's Article 9 to consist of all member states; and, reflecting the sovereign equality principle mentioned earlier, each member state would have one vote. Even though General Assembly resolutions are nonbinding, the one-country, one-vote principle created a parliamentary environment in which diplomats (rather than making private representations to a foreign ministry official as they do in a bilateral capital) sponsor public resolutions, lobby over their provisions, and wheel and deal in circumstances not unlike politicians in national parliaments. In the UN's early years, Western countries and their friends and allies dominated the General Assembly to such a point that they "circumvented deadlocks within the Council" by transforming "the Assembly's recommendations into actions," the best example being the passage of the US-sponsored "Uniting for Peace" resolution of 1950, which authorized a multinational force to be sent to Korea under the UN flag (Hamilton and Langhorne 2011: 198). However, a powerful hint of changes to come to this "Western" profile of the General Assembly was India's admission as a member in 1947. This newly independent member state staked strong declaratory claims against apartheid in South Africa, in particular, and colonialism, in general. In short, the General Assembly provided a parliamentary platform for new state diplomats to challenge Western dominance of the UN, compelling diplomats to speak more often and more openly in "public" (see box 18-1).

Article 24 of the UN Charter conferred on the *Security Council* executive responsibility for maintaining international peace and security. At the time of its founding, the council comprised five permanent members (P5)—China, the Soviet Union, France, the United Kingdom, and the United States—and six nonpermanent members elected for two-year terms (in 1967, elected members increased to ten). Decision making in the Security Council was generally done behind closed doors, and council decisions were binding in nature. Due to the council's significance, member states generally sent their most senior diplomats to represent them at this forum.

BOX 18-1

The Public Face of UN Diplomats

The UN diplomat plays a uniquely performative role on the world stage. Unlike most bilateral diplomacy, UN diplomats are often "performing" in plenary and in committees, for each other and for wider world publics through television coverage, the press corps, and even visitors in the public gallery. This role as performer is a feature of the General Assembly's annual general debate, a notable historical case being Soviet leader Nikita Khrushchev's 1960 shoe-banging on a desk to protest what he believed were the West's and Secretary-General Dag Hammarskjöld's anti-Soviet policies (Meisler 1995: 116, 121, 360). Also in this vein were Venezuelan president Hugo Chavez's ad hominem remarks about US president George W. Bush during the 2006 annual general debate; and, Libya's Muammar Qaddafi's 2009 General Assembly speech in which he, inter alia, proposed the dismemberment of Switzerland.

The council's role as the most powerful UN organ, reinforced by the P5's veto rights, is encapsulated in the title of David Bosco's book *Five to Rule Them All* (2009). The five most powerful members therefore dominated diplomacy within the Security Council (see also Luck 2006; Ross 2007). However, with the rise of such new powers as Brazil, Germany, India, Japan, and South Africa, the role of the ten nonpermanent members, elected for two-year periods, is attracting increasing attention.

The *Economic and Social Council* was established to promote human rights and economic and social cooperation between member states, reflecting in part the recognition that the high politics of security and war could often be explained by underlying socioeconomic factors, such as poverty and human suffering, or the low politics of human rights and human security. Organizationally, ECOSOC was to be the umbrella organ for important and often powerful specialized agencies, such as the UN High Commissioner for Refugees (UNHCR). ECOSOC provided a forum for debates about socioeconomic justice for the world's poor and disempowered. From a diplomatic perspective, it opened the UN to public participation in 1947 through the creation of an innovative process allowing for "accredited," or formally registered, NGOs to participate in certain aspects of ECOSOC's work (Rosenthal 2008).

The *Trusteeship Council* was established to oversee aspects of the "decolonization" process, a revolt against Western colonial power from the 1950s to the 1970s on a scale not envisaged in 1945 (Bull and Watson 1984). While the work of the Trusteeship Council, managed by the P5, mirrored the power configurations of the mid-twentieth century, the outcome of the council's efforts—attainment of self-governance or independence by erstwhile colonies—reinforced the UN's expanding membership and signaled the rising influence of new states. While the new states embraced many of the UN's diplomatic practices, they also added a North-South (rich versus poor) dimension to world politics hitherto defined by the East-West dynamics of the Cold War. With the formal decolonization process deemed complete, the Trusteeship Council suspended its operations in 1994 (Wilde 2008).

The *International Court of Justice* was created as the UN's court. Also referred to as the World Court, the ICJ, which is based in The Hague in the Netherlands, consists of fifteen judges. Because the court does not have compulsory jurisdiction over states (thus reinforcing the primacy of the sovereignty norm), its impact on diplomatic practice has not been as significant as that of the General Assembly and the Security Council. However, the General Assembly or the Security Council may request that the ICJ give an advisory opinion on any legal matter, including such controversial issues as the legality of the threat or use of nuclear weapons (Crawford and Grant 2008). In addition, states have in certain circumstances agreed to submit their dispute to the ICJ for a decision (Crawford and Grant 2008: 195–97). In 2002, the International Criminal Court (ICC) was established with the necessary ratification of the 1998 Rome Statute. It is independent of the UN, but the Security Council may initiate proceedings. Also based in The Hague, the ICC can prosecute individuals, thus representing an expansion in the diplomatic and legal activities of the UN beyond sovereign states.

Under Article 97, the *secretary-general* was to be appointed—by the General Assembly on the Security Council's recommendation—as the UN's chief administrative officer, at the helm of the *Secretariat* set up to provide staff support for the organization (Jonah 2008). In practice, the P5 determine the candidate for the post of secretary-general, with the General Assembly approving their recommendation. Proposals to formalize the selection process have been made but generally ignored (Urquhart 1995). The secretary-general's role as a potentially powerful diplomatic actor emerged after Dag Hammarskjöld's tenure (1953–61), following which it became clear that a strong secretary-general could in certain circumstances be "more general than secretary" (Chesterman 2007; Peterson 2006; Traub 1998, 2006). These circumstances could range from a divided P5 to an amenable international context (for a full list of secretaries-general, see box 18-2). In the overall conduct of diplomacy at the UN, the Secretariat has become much more of a player behind the secretary-general and less of a faceless, bureaucratic staff unit for member states.

KEY POINTS

- Diplomatic practices in the Security Council have reinforced realism's great power assumptions.
- A proto-parliamentary system at the General Assembly, combined with decolonization, opened the door to non–great powers voicing their views in novel ways.
- ECOSOC's accreditation process recognized certain NGOs as having some standing in the world body, providing opportunities for non-state involvement.
- The secretary-general, supported by the Secretariat, is a potentially powerful diplomatic actor.

BOX 18-2

United Nations Secretaries-General

Trygve Lie	Norway	1946–52
Dag Hammarskjöld	Sweden	1953–61
U Thant	Myanmar	1961–71
Kurt Waldheim	Austria	1972–81
Javier Perez de Cuellar	Peru	1982–91
Boutros Boutros-Ghali	Egypt	1992–96
Kofi A. Annan	Ghana	1997–2006
Ban Ki-Moon	South Korea	2007–present

EVOLUTION OF DIPLOMATIC PRACTICES

As described earlier, the UN was generally seen early on as primarily concerned with international peace and security. However, the charter's preamble lays out the organization's commitment "to establish[ing] conditions under which justice and respect for the obligations arising from treaties and other sources of international law can be maintained." Preambular references to conflict prevention, human rights, and social and economic advancement provide a window into the UN's procedural significance in international politics.

The UN offers governments a vital platform for promoting their *individual* foreign policy interests, but under the umbrella of the *universal* goals espoused in the UN Charter. Diplomats appointed to the UN have had to struggle with the oft-times contradictory pull of these two—national interests and shared international values. Manifestations of this tension depend on the subject and aims of deliberation (for example, gender mainstreaming), the kind of UN platform used (for example, the General Assembly), and the range of actors involved (governments, UN agencies, and/or NGOs). These factors are significant in tracing the evolution of diplomatic norms and practices at the UN since 1945.

"Preventive diplomacy," a founding premise of the UN, has been emphasized by virtually every UN "administration" (see Claude 1971: 312–33; Ramcharan 2008). In the 1950s, Secretary-General Hammarskjöld described preventive diplomacy as involving UN efforts to alleviate cases of localized disputes and wars that might provoke wider confrontation between the two Cold War superpowers (Urquhart 1984: 256, 257, 265). Most famously, in *An Agenda for Peace*, Boutros Boutros-Ghali (1992: 11) defined it as "action to prevent disputes from arising between parties, to prevent existing disputes from escalating into conflicts and to limit the spread of the latter when they occur." Formally, the UN provides a multilateral setting for peaceful settlement of disputes, but entrepreneurial secretaries-general can use the moral power of the office to push such concepts as preventive diplomacy.

Even at times of intense conflict, the symbolically neutral grounds of the UN headquarters can keep open channels of communication between conflicting states. As Jean Krasno (2004: 4) writes, "The UN is the only place where all Member States have permanent representatives as ambassadors throughout the year, so that when a crisis or issue arises, formal or informal conversations can take place conveniently and in a timely manner" (see also Karns and Mingst 2004: 97). The UN's dispute resolution mechanisms, including international agreements and the presence of external actors for mediation and negotiation, also facilitate this process. Further, particularly in recent years, the Security Council and **Special Representatives** of the secretary-general have engaged parties to a conflict directly, in New York as well as through short-term visiting missions to conflict areas (Hulton 2004: 241).

While international attention on the UN tends to be devoted to political maneuverings around resolution of armed conflicts (high politics) and responses to major humanitarian crises, the amalgam of UN diplomatic actors has been important in developing a vibrant socioeconomic agenda (low politics). Issues relating to education, health, environment, social change, and economic development became more pertinent with increasing participation of countries from Asia and Africa, especially during and after the 1950s. As discussed later, the priorities of these newly independent member states were different from those of the P5, who controlled the Security Council's agenda.

The UN allows country representatives the opportunity to collectively build international policies and legislation in the form of resolutions on human welfare and well-being. The General Assembly's six committees and ECOSOC's committees and commissions provide the institutional space for such deliberations. The UN's significance as an enabler in this respect is a strong counterpoint to the dominant view that it was paralyzed during the Cold War because of deep ideological schisms between the Eastern and Western blocs. Its role may well have been curtailed on certain high-politics issues, but not on low politics, where the UN flourished, making major contributions to debates about such matters as human development (Jolly, Emmerij, and Weiss 2009).

In the crowded UN meetings, groups of member states often present a collective stand on an issue. This partnership may be based on regional positions (Leigh-Phippard 1999), a shared agenda, or indeed any mutually beneficial interest. For instance, the **Non-Aligned Movement** founded in 1961 by leaders from Egypt, India, Indonesia, and (former) Yugoslavia proved to be an influential force in the General Assembly. It became a united front for countries choosing not to align with either the Eastern or the Western bloc during the Cold War. This paved the way for the Group of 77 (G77) countries to dominate in the General Assembly in later years, promoting economic development.

National representatives also come together to deliberate on particular themes. This is best demonstrated in the formation of "Groups of Friends" (also known as "Friends of the Secretary-General") at the UN. These groups have played notable roles in preventive diplomacy and have sought to push forward specific thematic agendas at the UN (Prantl and Krasno 2004). Regional alliances outside the UN framework are also used strategically in this multilateral setting. For example, the European Union (EU) usually offers its own statement—beyond those of participating EU member states—at the open sessions of the Security Council and in the General Assembly. In these ways, the UN context fosters relations between smaller collectives of states.

Furthermore, national representatives find an avenue for expression at the UN World Conferences. These conferences, which have a long history (for example, the First World Conference on Women took place in 1975 in Mexico City), provide diplomats additional avenues for participating in international policy making on particular themes. In the 1990s alone, there was a wide range of themes—for example, environment (Rio de Janeiro, 1992), population (Cairo, 1994), human settlements (Istanbul, 1996), and establishment of the ICC (Rome, 1998).

UN conferences gained greater popularity following the Cold War in spite of criticism about their being another extravagant UN spectacle where government representatives negotiate and commit to international agreements not subsequently honored at home. The significance of these events is evident in attempts made by governments to renegotiate the agreements at later conferences. This has been a concern in relation to women's issues, and a major reason why gender advocates at the UN have not organized a Fifth World Conference on Women since the fourth one took place in Beijing in 1995. According to Berridge (2010: 144–45), the UN conferences provide two further opportunities for diplomacy: "public diplomacy," since these conferences are open to the media and have an international audience, and "behind-the-scenes bilateral diplomacy" (see also Fomerand 1996).

In the 1980s and 1990s, the changing nature of threats to international peace and security—such as the increasing number of intrastate armed conflicts and acute humanitarian crises—forced the UN, especially the Security Council, to reassess its agenda (Wallensteen and Johansson 2004). The entrepreneurship of such diplomats as Jeremy Greenstock (United Kingdom) and Anwarul K. Chowdhury (Bangladesh) was decisive in adapting the council's role to the changing international political context at the century's end. As a collective decision-making entity, the Security Council has actively responded to these developments by passing resolutions and mobilizing UN **peacekeeping** forces toward more **coercive diplomacy**. This activism is also reflected in the emergence of international norms such as the "Responsibility to Protect" (ICISS 2001; see box 18-3).

These changes in diplomatic practices at the UN raise the issue of how to conceptualize such practices. The basic distinction to bear in mind is that "diplomatic

---

BOX 18-3

The UN's Role in the Emergence of the Responsibility to Protect (R2P) Norm

Nonintervention in states' domestic affairs is one of the UN's core founding principles. In the 1990s, however, the UN was increasingly confronted with state failure and/or complicity in violent armed conflicts leading to widespread humanitarian crises. Following Secretary-General Kofi Annan's call to the international community for collective action in circumstances such as the mass civilian fatalities in Rwanda and Srebenica (Bosnia), the Canadian government established the International Commission on Intervention and State Sovereignty (ICISS) in 2000. Chaired by former Australian foreign minister Gareth Evans and senior Algerian diplomat Mohamed Sahnoun, the ICISS formally submitted the report *The Responsibility to Protect* to Annan in December 2001. The report identified circumstances in which it is appropriate for states, and the international community more broadly, to take military action against those states that fail to protect their citizens from grave danger or suffering. It thus proposed the "responsibility to protect" people from such threats as ethnic cleansing and genocide (ICISS 2001; G. Evans and Sahnoun 2002). The international community has been reluctant to make this conceptual shift and to shoulder this humanitarian responsibility. Asian states in particular have warned against the challenge to sovereignty posed by the report's recommendations. However, with support from Annan and diplomatic lobbying for the recommendations, the principle of R2P—albeit a somewhat diluted version—was included in the outcome document of the 2005 World Summit, as well as in a Security Council resolution on the Protection of Civilians in Armed Conflict in 2006 (Thakur 2008: 398; Welsh 2008: 557). In 2011, the UN Security Council–sanctioned and NATO-led air campaign against Qaddafi's Libya was couched, amid some controversy, in terms of the need to protect innocent civilians.

relations" are generally understood to be between representatives of two states ("bilateral") or between three or more states at ad hoc or permanent conferences ("multilateral") (see Wright, chapter 10 in this volume). As this chapter demonstrates, the fundamental form of diplomacy practiced at the UN is multilateral (Ruggie 1993). However, under that broad multilateral umbrella, a significant amount of traditional, bilateral diplomacy is conducted (Berridge 2010). Increasingly, however, a third form, "polylateral diplomacy," which is between state and non-state representatives, has emerged at the UN and is now attracting wider scholarly interest (Wiseman 2004, 2007, 2010). As noted earlier, NGOs working at the UN are formally accredited with ECOSOC and hold formal consultative status under Article 71 of the charter, and an increasing and impressive number of NGOs are using this mechanism. In addition to their participation in the UN's socioeconomic and human rights agenda, NGOs have facilitated the engagement of Security Council members with civil society organizations and individuals through "Arria Formula" meetings, critically on high-politics issues, such as the conflict in Sudan (see box 18-4).

While our focus so far has been on the UN as a *platform*, it is necessary also to recognize its increasing role as an *actor* in international politics. Even though there are no UN ambassadors (in the traditional conception associated with national representatives), we can identify at least three ways in which the UN represents itself to the world and seeks to engage elites and wider publics via public diplomacy, or public information, strategies. First, the secretary-general and the UN Department of Public Information (DPI) communicate the organization's purpose and work to the wider world (see box 18-5); second, the secretary-general appoints a significant number of Special Representatives to handle especially daunting problems (Peck 2004); and third, the secretary-general appoints a small number of "Messengers of Peace" (for example, George Clooney, Jane Goodall, and Wangari Mathai), and most UN agencies have increasingly used UN "goodwill ambassadors" to help promote UN goals in their specified areas (UNHCR ambassadors include Giorgio Armani and Angelina Jolie). All these "celebrity diplomats" (Cooper 2008b) agree to use their celebrity status to communicate UN agenda issues to an international audience.

BOX 18-4

Civil Society and High Politics: The Arria Formula

The Arria Formula is

> an extremely informal procedure of the UN Security Council enabling its members to engage in discussion with non-members, including non-state parties. Under this formula meetings are held in private, away from the Council chamber, usually under the chairmanship of a Council member other than the current Council president, and without the attendance of officials or the keeping of any official records. The formula takes its name from Diego Arria, the Venezuelan ambassador who presided over the first meeting of this nature during his country's tenure of a seat on the Security Council during the period 1992–93. (Berridge and James 2003: 14)

BOX 18-5

The UN Department of Public Information: "The Public Voice of the United Nations"

The UN DPI describes its role as promoting "global awareness and greater under-standing of the work of the United Nations, using various communication tools." The department was established in 1946 by General Assembly Resolution 13(1). Information is disseminated through the UN website, UN News Center, UN Radio, and UN publications, as well as through such innovative multimedia platforms as Unifeed which involves extensive webcasting of UN activities. The department works closely with a global network of more than sixty UN Information Centres located around the world (adapted from UNIC 2008).

Beyond these three high-profile areas of public diplomacy, the UN is also seeking to expand and enhance its public outreach program through the use of the Internet and new social media.[2]

In these different ways, the UN—as platform and actor—has not only mirrored enhanced traditional diplomatic norms based on state interests (such as continuous dialogue) but also made a vital contribution to the evolution of more expansive diplomatic practices in contemporary international politics. Through a diplomatic lens, the intensely political nature of the UN platform is evidence of the richness of this institutional context and the multiple ways in which it can facilitate diplomatic relations.

KEY POINTS

- International norms, such as preventive diplomacy, are important at the UN.
- From the mid-twentieth century, decolonization challenged the dominance of powerful states at the UN. Among other developments, this led to an expanded socioeconomic agenda.
- Region-based groupings are now an enduring component of UN diplomacy.
- UN World Conferences have gained wider attention since the 1990s and, in the process, have opened the door to greater nongovernmental participation in international policy-making debates.
- The UN has experimented with new kinds of less formal "ambassadors," such as the secretary-general's Special Representatives, Messengers of Peace, and Goodwill Ambassadors.

THE DIPLOMATIC COMMUNITY

The UN's near universality brings diplomats from 193 member states to its New York headquarters. Clearly, states value UN membership, not least because it legitimizes them as members of the wider international **society of states**, a role once performed through the international legal and diplomatic norms of recognition and the exchange of embassies in bilateral capitals. As shown above, this was especially true for the new states of the post-Second World War era (see Roberts and Kingsbury 1993).

The perceived importance of the UN "diplomatic corps" (consisting of member state diplomats accredited to the UN) is underlined by the charter provision permitting missions to have up to five national representatives and allowing some (for example, the US mission) to have five senior diplomats at the ambassadorial level. For average-sized missions, the custom is to have two ambassadorial-level representatives, the Permanent Representative—the formal term for the UN ambassador—and the Deputy Permanent Representative. The quantitative dimension is representative of power configurations at the UN—for example, whereas some small member states are represented by a handful of diplomats, the United States has more than 100.

Beyond the vast expansion of UN membership (from 51 member states in 1945 to 193 in 2011) is the proliferation of numerous non-state actors who participate actively—formally and informally—in the UN diplomatic process. As described in other chapters of this book, traditional diplomacy focuses on the diplomatic corps, the "body of diplomats of all states... who are resident at one post" (Berridge and James 2003: 72). However, because varied actors are involved, it is more appropriate to refer to the UN "diplomatic community" (Sharp and Wiseman 2007: 267) rather than the "diplomatic corps." Thus, UN diplomacy is now tied to a larger and more complex diplomatic community of diplomats *and* non-state actors. Our focus is on the community in the UN headquarters in New York.[3] Four trends support this claim of a shift from corps to community.

First, UN diplomats have an image and reputation of being highly skilled. Member states are widely thought to send their best diplomats to the UN, and not only to serve as permanent representatives. The sense of having high-quality colleagues produces a community self-image of diplomatic professionalism and political clout back home. This is especially true for ambassadors representing the P5. Two prominent examples are the former Russian foreign minister Sergei Lavrov, who had previously served as Russia's UN ambassador, and former French prime minister Dominique de Villepin, who had played a visibly public role as France's ambassador to the UN during the lead-up to the 2003 Iraq War.

Second, the image of high-quality UN diplomats is reinforced by a high degree of "cross-fertilization"—that is, the mixing of diplomats from at least two different diplomatic corps at any given moment—which is now a systematic practice at the UN. For example, diplomats and UN officials based in Geneva routinely participate in New York meetings on such subjects as disarmament.

Third, a relatively high number of diplomats at the UN are "recycled"—that is, reassigned, at a higher level, to a diplomatic post they held earlier in their careers. This practice provides missions with needed expertise and experience. The recycling concept can be expanded to include diplomats who join the Secretariat following a posting to the UN. Recycling likely enhances an already strong professional "epistemic sensibility" at the UN and strengthens the cooperation—the Habermasian "feelings for others"—widely assumed to arise from direct personal contact (see also Johnston 2008). Further, the physical presence of the UN and diplomatic missions and residents in the Turtle Bay/midtown area of Manhattan increases informal social contact between diplomats (see box 18-6 for more on the UN and New York).

Fourth, the preceding networks are also linked and reinforced by the work of civil society actors. These include influential New York–based philanthropic

---

BOX 18-6

New York, New York

Venue is important as a diplomatic consideration, and the esteem granted to UN diplomats is also enhanced by having the UN headquarters in New York, a major US city. Being in New York and in the United States produces a social and political dynamic arguably more complex than that of any comparable multilateral capital, such as Vienna or Geneva, where host countries unreservedly welcome the UN's presence. Politically, the US-UN relationship has been mixed since 1945, complicated by the United States, as host country, being both the biggest financial contributor to the world body and often its biggest critic (Fasulo 2004: 33–38; Luck 1999). The political sensitivity of the United States' role as host country is reflected in New York City's role as host city. Secretaries-general reinforce the UN–New York City relationship in public appearances, and New York City mayors officially welcome the UN presence but occasionally criticize it for its views on Israel. Moreover, UN diplomats are highly aware of the powerful constraining presence of Washington, DC, and of US society and its general antipathy to the UN.

---

foundations, major university centers, key NGOs, UN associations, think tanks, institutes, and prominent individuals, all following UN affairs closely and actively seeking the participation of UN diplomats in their programs and activities.

The result is that a UN diplomatic community appears to have emerged in New York, one that links both state and non-state representatives in an elaborate and complex network. This networked diplomatic community is yet to be fully elaborated by scholars to discuss, for example, any epistemic or diplomatic norms shared by its participants, the informal hierarchies and power dynamics that exist and are developing within it, and, importantly, possible influences on resolutions and related UN policy outcomes. However, the idea of a diplomatic community is clearly less formal and far more nebulous than that of a traditional diplomatic corps. Although the impact of the many simultaneous diplomatic activities may be difficult to grasp, it is possible to identify a new "hybrid" **diplomatic culture** from the interactions of the transnational civil society with the prevailing state-based diplomatic culture (Sharp and Wiseman 2007: 266–67; Wiseman 2010: 39).

Interactions between the UN, state, and non-state representatives in New York—characteristic of the UN diplomatic community—are demonstrated by the extraordinarily high number of NGOs accredited to the UN. Such exchanges are perhaps more prevalent at the UN than in most **bilateral capitals** and, with the possible exception of Brussels, in **multilateral capitals**. The formal accreditation with ECOSOC is interesting from a diplomatic perspective, and the number of accredited NGOs with consultative status at the US has grown manifold in the past six decades (from 40 in 1948 to 3,413 in 2010). In addition, the DPI's NGO section liaises with approximately 1,500 NGOs that are associated with it, while the UN's Non-Governmental Liaison Service facilitates UN engagement with more than 9,000 NGOs (Wapner 2008; Willetts 2000).

BOX 18-7

Passage of Security Council Resolution 1325 (2000) on Women and Peace and Security

On 31 October 2000, the Security Council unanimously adopted resolution 1325 on Women and Peace and Security. This was the first time the council recognized the gendered nature of armed conflicts and made recommendations inter alia for protection of women and for increasing their participation in conflict resolution and postconflict reconstruction. The Security Council had no significant record of deliberating on such issues, and the role of gender advocates inside and outside the UN was significant in bringing together policy making on "women" (low politics) and "peace and security" (high politics) that had previously occupied separate places at the organization. The leadership of such international NGOs as the Women's International League for Peace and Freedom, International Alert, and Amnesty International, which came together to form the NGO Working Group on Women, Peace and Security, was particularly influential (Adrian-Paul et al. 2004; Cockburn 2007; Cohn, Kinsella, and Gibbings 2004). Since 2000, four follow-up Security Council resolutions on women and armed conflicts have been adopted— resolutions 1820 (2008), 1888 (2009), 1889 (2009), and 1960 (2010). While the council is yet to incorporate the resolutions effectively into its work, the "women, peace and security" network at the UN—which includes advocates from NGOs, the UN, and member states—has kept the resolution 1325 agenda alive (Basu 2010).

An additional noteworthy aspect of these working relationships is the now commonplace use—by missions and the Secretariat—of not only NGOs but also other members of the UN diplomatic community (universities, think tanks, and foundations) to convene meetings outside the formal UN rules and structures. Further, since the late 1990s, the UN has reached out to the private sector, notably through the innovative Global Compact on corporate responsibility (McIntosh, Waddock, and Kell 2004).

The UN Secretariat and diplomats are perhaps more open (to varying degrees among departments) than are foreign ministries to nongovernmental, academic, and other public contacts, especially concerning low-politics policy matters. However, the degree of engagement tends to depend on the issue (see Box 18-7). Member states are less inclined toward nongovernmental involvement in matters of international peace and security. Richard Jolly, Louis Emmerij, and Thomas Weiss (2009: 33) argue that NGOs have been active in environmental negotiations but tend to be shut out of disarmament deliberations. Difficult as it may be, NGOs have made inroads into the Security Council as well. In 1997, Pierre Sane of Amnesty International became the first NGO representative to address the council. In 2006, film actor George Clooney met with council members to discuss Darfur.

KEY POINTS

- The image of high-quality UN diplomats is reinforced by a relatively high degree of cross-fertilization and recycling.

- The location of UN Headquarters in New York elevates the UN's image but is also a factor in its complicated relationship with the United States.
- The increasing role of UN officials and NGOs in UN diplomacy has led the UN "diplomatic corps" to evolve into the UN "diplomatic community."

CONCLUSION

Consistent with transformations at the UN since 1945, marked particularly by such major historical shifts as decolonization and the end of the Cold War, diplomacy at the UN has evolved over the decades. The rising influence and activism of newer member states, expansion of the issue areas under purview, use of thematic World Conferences, and the growing significance of UN officials and NGOs in diplomacy are some developments that have been accompanied by changing diplomatic practices at the UN. Indeed, diversity of issues and actors has led to a hybrid diplomatic culture at the UN.

Despite innovations in UN diplomatic practices, however, the UN's basic structure has not evolved with the changing international political climate and configurations. Most obviously, the P5 member states' privileged status has skewed the relations between government representatives who otherwise hold equal legal status in the international state system. Formal charter reform has been rare, and the oft-discussed potential reform and enlargement of the Security Council seems more unlikely than ever in the current political climate. As a diplomatic venue, the UN represents a dynamic fusion of traditional structure with nontraditional actors and daunting global issues for deliberation.

In conclusion, we highlight three key elements that help predict diplomacy's evolution at the UN. First, the UN will likely continue to be generally recognized as the "centerpiece of global governance" (Karns and Mingst 2004: 97). Despite the UN's finite resources, the range of issues brought under its purview has increased manifold. Diplomats are forced to deliberate not only on issues of national interests but also, in partnership with other actors, on matters of international peace and progress. While the UN has been criticized for "more talk" and "less action," diplomats are set to deepen their engagement on a growing number of concerns and contribute to further development of international norms through "talking." Second, the public nature of much of UN diplomacy will further strengthen state-non-state diplomacy (what Geoffrey Wiseman calls polylateralism), signifying greater engagement with NGOs and the increasing—albeit discreet—influence of many UN officials who, among their other official roles, are an important conduit between member states and non-state actors. Third, significant formal UN reform has been rare, and its absence poses a major challenge to the UN's perceived effectiveness and legitimacy on a wide range of issues. However, the changing configuration of actors and the diversity of issues are leading to transformations in and around the UN, including in UN diplomacy. The UN diplomatic community, as a collective identity, is ever expanding, reinforcing, and even reconstituting the scope of diplomatic practices, carrying important lessons for multilateralism and global governance.

QUESTIONS

1. Identify and contrast the diplomatic underpinnings of the three explanations for the birth of the UN.
2. In what order of importance would you rank the six major UN organs? Explain the criteria you would use in your ranking.
3. Why is national representation at the UN important for governments?
4. What are the key components of the UN's public diplomacy efforts?
5. Discuss the role of the Secretariat and the secretary-general in facilitating the work of the UN diplomatic community.
6. Why and how have NGOs gained significance at the UN since the 1990s?
7. In what ways does the location of the permanent UN Headquarters in New York impact the work of the organization?
8. Critically evaluate the role of the five permanent members of the Security Council.
9. In view of the fast-paced institutionalization of multilateralism in the twentieth century, what is the relative significance of the UN in contemporary international politics?
10. Discuss the argument that a hybrid diplomatic community is replacing the diplomatic corps (as traditionally understood) at the UN.
11. What are the implications of the analysis in this chapter for your theoretical and practical understandings of contemporary diplomacy?

NOTES

1. The General Assembly's six main committees include delegations of the *whole* membership, primarily because there is no party system or alternative method to divide the assembly into mutually exclusive groups (Peterson 2006: 59-60). Each committee specializes as follows: First Committee—Disarmament and International Security; Second Committee—Economic and Financial; Third Committee—Social, Humanitarian, and Cultural; Fourth Committee—Special Political and Decolonization; Fifth Committee—Administrative and Budgetary; and Sixth Committee—Legal.
2. A notable supporter of such new media efforts, and of the UN's public outreach in general, is the UN Foundation, created in 1998 with a major donation from CNN founder, Ted Turner.
3. Other major UN centers are Geneva, Vienna, Nairobi, Addis Ababa, Bangkok, Beirut, and Santiago. Arguably, there are only a few truly multilateral cities (for example, Geneva and Vienna), as distinct from cities, some of which are capitals, that host major international organizations but generally are not identified as multilateral cities (for example, Washington, DC; Rome; and Nairobi).

Conclusion

Geoffrey Wiseman and Pauline Kerr

CHAPTER CONTENTS

- Introduction
- How is diplomacy changing?
- Why is diplomacy changing?
- Implications for future theories and practices
- Complex diplomacy

INTRODUCTION

"There has never been a better time for studying diplomacy." So wrote one of our contributors, Paul Sharp (2011: 695–96), who went on to observe: "The United States is rediscovering it. The European Union is reinventing it. The Chinese are inscribing it with their own characteristics. Even the Taliban are thinking about it.... Diplomacy, the institutions and processes by which states and, increasingly others, represent themselves and their interests to one another in international and world societies, is back on center stage." In addition to the abundant evidence provided in this book, there are plenty of current, empirical examples to support the claim that now is indeed a good time to be studying and researching what diplomats do and what purposes diplomacy serves in today's world. The following accounts of reports published during September 2011 (the tenth anniversary of the 11 September 2011 terrorist attacks on New York City) make the point:

- Two US citizens were released from prison in Iran, where they were being held on charges of spying for the United States. While the men were imprisoned, the Swiss embassy in Tehran provided them with consular protection because the United States does not have formal diplomatic relations with Iran. Additionally, Iran chose to announce the Americans' release on the eve of the annual United Nations (UN) General Assembly meeting, possibly to garner favorable attention before appearing on the world stage.
- At the UN, the president of the Palestinian Authority submitted an application for Palestine to become a full UN member, even though the United States had announced that it would veto the application in the Security Council. Although the United States argued that direct negotiations were the

genuine path to Palestinian statehood, the Palestinian Authority continued its campaign to win international recognition at the UN.

- Republican senators delayed confirmation of Robert Ford as President Barack Obama's ambassador to Syria. Although President Obama gave Ford a one-year "recess appointment" as ambassador, congressional approval is needed for a full-term appointment. Republican senators could continue to block the nomination on the grounds that sending an ambassador legitimized Bashar Assad's regime. Ford attracted attention because of his travels across Syria to meet with opposition leaders and speak forcefully against Assad's repression.

- In contrast to the peaceful protests in Cairo's Tahrir Square that galvanized the 2011 Arab uprising, a violent mob of protesters recently attacked the Israeli embassy in Cairo and the Egyptian Interior Ministry after Israeli officials failed to issue an apology for the accidental killing of Egyptian citizens. Although the attack raised concerns about the future of Egyptian-Israeli relations, Israeli diplomats returned to Cairo ten days after the embassy's evacuation. Moreover, the Egyptian government reiterated its commitment to peaceful relations with Israel and vowed to take a tougher stance against protesters.

- Taliban insurgents wearing suicide vests and armed with rocket-propelled grenades launched a highly coordinated attack on the US embassy and the North Atlantic Treaty Organization headquarters in Kabul. Although no American embassy personnel or Afghan security officials were killed, this attack (which was the most direct one on the American embassy since it opened in 2001) demonstrated the Taliban's willingness to continue challenging the Afghan forces that took official control of security in Kabul in July.

Now that you have read this book, or parts of it, we believe you can better see diplomacy's central place in these events with sharpened—in terms of history, theory, and policy—analytical lenses. Indeed, the book is based on the premise that a comparative and comprehensive understanding of diplomacy facilitates a better appreciation of world politics. That is why we framed the book's key purpose in a way we thought would contribute to such an understanding.

This book's primary purpose was to answer, in the context of a globalizing world, three interconnected and puzzling questions: Exactly how is diplomacy changing? Why is it changing? And what implications do our answers to these questions have for future diplomatic theories and practices?

HOW IS DIPLOMACY CHANGING?

There is little doubt from the evidence presented in this book that diplomacy has a very long history, with origins that can be traced back some 4,500 years to the city-state diplomacy of Southern Mesopotamia, now modern Iraq. The basic expressions of ancient diplomacy—sovereigns sending accredited envoys to represent them to other sovereigns, and an emphasis on relationships, communications, reporting, negotiations, and protocol—are all recognizable in today's modern diplomatic culture.

At the same time, diplomacy as an "institution" has changed greatly and, in our view, continues to do so. We get the sense of an institution capable of reinventing itself to keep pace with the times—from the introduction of the resident mission in the fifteenth century to the establishment of the foreign ministry as a central bureaucracy for managing diplomats serving in other countries in the seventeenth century, and from the establishment of the League of Nations as a form of institutionalized multilateral diplomacy after the First World War to the embassy premises shared by certain like-minded countries at the beginning of the twenty-first century.

Yet so many of our conclusions depend on a difficult question: What exactly do we mean by diplomacy? Today—although it must be stressed that there are many definitions of the term—*diplomacy* is conventionally understood as "the processes and institutions by which [a] country represents itself and its interests to the rest of the world" (Sharp and Wiseman 2012: 223). However, readers will note that many of the authors in this book think that diplomacy as a state-based concept is changing, evolving to include non-state actors, and to encompass more than just states mutually recognizing each other and conducting formal relations in a *bilateral* and, increasingly in the twentieth century, *multilateral* setting. In addition, there is the definitional issue of distinguishing between foreign policy and diplomacy. Many of this book's contributors have tended to draw, or assume, the foreign policy–diplomacy distinction made most famously by Ernest Satow and Harold Nicolson.

And then there are the effects of globalization to consider in trying to solve the diplomacy puzzle. We see little evidence for the claim that globalization spells the death of diplomacy. Indeed, we see evidence that diplomacy, redefined, is everywhere: public diplomacy, citizens diplomacy, sports diplomacy, city diplomacy. These empirical conclusions about diplomacy's current standing in world politics are reflected in the way scholars think about or theorize diplomacy, a topic to which we return later.

The book's chapters tell much about how diplomacy has changed over time:

- how countries with a long history, such as China, have adapted to diplomacy in good times and bad;
- how scholars have brought contending disciplinary frameworks to diplomacy;
- how diplomacy has generated debates;
- how negotiators use diplomacy to prevent and mediate conflicts;
- how foreign ministries have seen their gatekeeping role fluctuate;
- how diplomacy is both threatened and emancipated by modern information and communication technologies;
- how consular officials have returned to prominence as citizens demand services and protection when they travel and do business abroad;
- how multilateral diplomacy became institutionalized and, arguably, superseded bilateral diplomacy as the preferred diplomatic method;
- how public diplomacy has emerged as a dynamic field of study;
- how economic diplomacy became more important as the world economy became increasingly multipolar;

- how track-two (unofficial) diplomats provide new services but struggle to find a place at the table with the state in East Asia;
- how intelligence-gathering raises the prospect of a return to more secretive times;
- how the United States has wrestled with the terms of its diplomatic engagement with the rest of the world;
- how China's modern embrace of diplomatic methods has helped its rise, providing a plausible argument for the country's peaceful intentions;
- how the world is moving toward increased regional diplomatic institutions and processes; and
- how the UN has shifted from its original state-based culture to one that is more open to non-state participation.

In sum, whether we think of diplomacy in the "traditional" state-centric way or a "beyond-the-sovereign-state" multiple actor way, it has changed significantly over time. However, as a set of state and social practices, it remains recognizably similar to what it was many centuries ago.

WHY IS DIPLOMACY CHANGING?

It is not possible here to explain why all the changes in diplomatic practices chronicled in this book have taken place. We can, however, classify the main explanations in terms of international context, domestic-national context, and institutional context.

In the international context, four explanatory factors recur in several of the book's chapters. The first is the *end of the Cold War*, including the dissolution of the former Soviet Union. This event had an almost immediate impact, creating several new democracies in Eastern and Central Europe, such as Hungary and Poland. Moreover, the Soviet Union's breakup created fifteen "new" states, including very large ones, such as Russia, and very small ones, such as Georgia. Similarly, the breakup of the former Yugoslavia eventually created seven new states. In virtually all these cases, the new states were keen to establish a diplomatic profile on the international stage. Foreign ministries were reinvigorated, and new embassies and consulates established or restaffed to better represent redefined interests and identities to other recognized polities. In short, the Cold War's end produced more states, all of which turned to diplomatic culture for support in an uncertain world.

The second factor, one that in fact transcends the term *international* itself and is central to this book, is *globalization*, including the associated communications and information revolutions of the past two decades. In one view, globalization seemed at first to work against the traditional conduct of diplomacy via foreign ministries and embassies. Governments could gather all the information they needed from multiple news sources and the Internet without having diplomats in costly embassies and consulates abroad. Also in this view, governments, especially their foreign ministries and networks of embassies and consulates, were becoming less important in solving global problems. Yet what seems to have happened over time is that foreign ministries adapted, admittedly some more than others, to the new hyperconnected world.

UN corridors are full of diplomats with laptops searching for information that may once have required a cable back home. Diplomats involved in bilateral and multilateral negotiations are using their cell phones to check instructions with superiors at headquarters. And foreign ministers are regularly texting each other on important issues. On the whole, diplomats have embraced new forms of communications and in some sense have become comanagers of the globalization process, rather than its hapless victims.

Whereas globalization is generally, but by no means conclusively, seen as changing or diminishing the state's role in world politics, the third international factor is a perceived dramatic post–Cold War *shift in the traditional balance of world power*. Key to this development has been the rise of the so-called BRIC countries—Brazil, Russia, India, and China—but especially China. Other rising or important powers include such countries as Germany, Japan, and South Africa. At the same time, many see the United States entering a new era of relative decline (Quinn 2011) and the beginnings of the post-American world (Zakaria 2011). Whatever conclusion one draws about these power shifts, foreign ministries and diplomats are now being asked to respond flexibly in order to manage the new power relationships. Diplomats are needed by both rising and declining powers. One good example illustrating the complexity of these new power relationships is how the five permanent members of the UN Security Council now have to manage the elected ten members much more judiciously than ever before (Romita, Chowdhury Fink, and Papenfuss 2011). In short, we are seeing a double power shift: a changing balance of power between state and non-state actors (globalization) and between the main state actors in the system (traditional power balancing). This double shift helps explain changes in diplomatic culture.

The fourth international factor emerging from this book that helps explain why diplomacy has changed is *regionalization*. While attention has focused mainly on the three factors just described—the Cold War's end, globalization, and the rise of new power centers—a quieter change has taken place in the form of region-building, or the regionalizing of world politics. We have seen the European Union (EU) push forward with impressive changes to its many diplomatic practices that suggest that "supranational diplomacy" is now conceivable. Other regional bodies around the world do not emulate the EU, but the evidence suggests that they look to it and draw lessons from it. As track-two (nonofficial) actors in East Asia well know, one lesson that official diplomats in their region appear to have drawn from the EU is that East Asian regionalism will continue to be better guided by national rather than supranational interests. Officials may see the EU's 2011–12 currency problems as supporting evidence for their view.

The second way in which we can classify the main explanations given in this book for changes in diplomatic practices is in terms of domestic-national context. Our own experience here is that more and more countries have shifted from neglecting or deriding their diplomats to expecting more of them. President Obama's secretary of state, Hillary Clinton, made it perfectly clear in 2009, early in her tenure, that US foreign policy would focus on the three Ds: "defense, diplomacy and development" (H. Rodham Clinton 2009b). And to support these objectives, the US Department of State budget requests for 2011 and 2012 would "represent 4.2 per cent and 1.6 per cent increases over the 2010 actuals" (Oliver and Shearer 2011: 25).

The Australian foreign minister, Kevin Rudd (2010), stated adamantly in 2010 that "in an increasingly globalised order, on what might be called the age of globalisation of everything, [the] Australian foreign service will become more important to the prosecution of our national interests, not less." However, the irony is that while governments have elevated the role of foreign ministries and increased the policy objectives of diplomats, many have not provided sufficient financial support to sustain a commensurate international policy infrastructure.

The third way to classify the explanations is in terms of institutional context. There is evidence that many foreign ministries and the diplomats themselves are responding positively to the challenges facing contemporary diplomacy (outlined in the introduction to this volume) and to governments' expectations, despite increased workloads and insufficient financial and human resources. A number of governments, from Argentina to Sweden, have merged their foreign ministries with trade departments. Furthermore, many foreign ministries have undergone reforms to introduce modern management practices and more diverse recruitment policies that promise to alter the traditional images of ambassadors and envoys (Rana 2005).

In sum, contributions to this book reveal a long history of continuity in diplomatic practices matched by a quite impressive history of change. This change arguably sped up in the twentieth century and, we suggest, has become even speedier over the past two decades as a result of the factors just described.

IMPLICATIONS FOR FUTURE THEORIES AND PRACTICES

What do our answers to the preceding "how" and "why" questions imply for future theorizing about diplomacy and for its future conduct, the final element of the diplomacy puzzle? Not surprisingly, different theorists give different answers depending on their worldview. We can expect at least three responses: one based on a realist view, one based on what we call a "new diplomacy" view, and one based on a "traditional diplomacy" view.

In the influential structural realist view of international relations (Waltz 1979), diplomacy and diplomats are generally overlooked. More important for these theorists are hard power, military force, and coercion; less important are soft power, diplomacy, and persuasion (Kerr 2010). Moreover, realists, as is true of many kinds of international relations theorists, tend to focus on macro decisions. This neglect in structural realism, and indeed in the American International Relations discipline (Wiseman 2011a), seems greatly out of place given the evidence of diplomacy's relevance amassed in this book.

The last decade or more has seen the rise of what we call "new diplomacy" theorists, who are quite distinct from realists. In addition to authors in this book who might identify with this group, other scholars representing a range of perspectives might be included, such as postmodernists (Constantinou 1996; Der Derian 1987), historians and globalization scholars (Hamilton and Langhorne 2011; Langhorne 1997), anthropologists and international political sociologists (Neumann 2010; Pouliot 2011), semiotic-reflectivists (Götz 2011), social constructivists (Løse 2001), and public diplomacy theorists (Gregory 2008b). This eclectic group of new diplomacy theorists shares several assumptions: analytically, the sovereign state is losing its grip on international relations in the face of globalizing forces that are irreversible; normatively, new non-state actors are justly demanding a greater role in international policy making; and, methodologically, the focus must be not only on macro foreign policy decisions but equally on micro, everyday diplomatic practices. New diplomacy theorists ask, who are the diplomats now (Langhorne 1997)? For them, the new diplomats are not only state diplomats but also global civil society actors, such as nongovernmental organizations, individual philanthropists, Hollywood celebrities, and company executives. Some new diplomacy theorists are beginning to take this "cosmopolitan" conception of diplomacy to what might be called a "universal" conception, in which millions of human beings armed with a small computer can theoretically be diplomats. Accordingly, diplomacy is a more universal social phenomenon than a territorial, state-based one.

In contrast to realism's neglect of diplomacy and new diplomacy's expansive view of diplomacy's potential stands the traditional diplomacy view. G. R. Berridge (2011: 15) has argued that the study and researching of traditional diplomacy are making a remarkable recovery: "In the decades since the 1960s a counter-revolution has occurred in diplomatic practice which, as a general tendency if not in its discrete parts, has gone almost completely unnoticed." This "diplomatic counter-revolution," Berridge concludes, is demonstrated by the return of secret negotiations as standard diplomatic practice in place of more open parliamentary forms, the recovery of the resident mission, the reemergence of the foreign ministry, and the use of serial summitry as a complement to one of diplomacy's core ideas, continuous dialogue.

All three approaches have advantages and disadvantages, of course, and this book reflects all three views to differing degrees. What is fascinating and suggestive of diplomacy's bright future is that some scholars are describing changes in traditional diplomacy at the same time as others are describing and theorizing the emergence of new diplomatic practices.

If it is true that now is a good time to be *studying* diplomacy, it is at least equally true that now is a good time to be *researching* diplomacy. Indeed, there is strong evidence of a research renaissance in the field of diplomatic studies (Hall 2010; Murray 2008). In recent years, a number of books on diplomacy have included such subjects as American negotiating behavior (Solomon and Quinney 2010); sustainable diplomacies (Constantinou and Der Derian 2010); new diplomacy (Ross 2007); public diplomacy (Seib 2009); global governance and diplomacy (Cooper, Hocking, and Maley 2008); the diplomatic corps (Sharp and Wiseman 2007); a diplomatic theory of international relations (Sharp 2009); representation and communication (Pigman 2010); celebrity diplomacy (Cooper 2008b); guerrilla diplomacy (Copeland 2009); diplomatic networks (Davis Cross 2007); economic diplomacy (Bayne and Woolcock 2011); and humanitarian diplomacy (Acuto forthcoming).

As editors, we have tried to synthesize the timeliness of diplomatic study with this emerging research literature in a book organized around the idea of *research-based teaching*. Like all social theory, diplomacy is dynamic, not static, so the latest research must be part of any approach to teaching.

COMPLEX DIPLOMACY

Whether one takes the narrower, traditional, state-based view or the broader, new diplomacy view, we are in little doubt that now is indeed a good time to be studying diplomacy, both its theories and its practices. Diplomacy is now clearly relevant in world politics, and it may in fact be becoming more so. In addition, diplomacy is more complex today than it has ever been. What emerges inductively from the combined efforts of the books' authors is a new idea: "complex diplomacy." As a result of several factors described throughout the book and in this chapter—including, notably, globalization and instantly available information—diplomacy has taken on a complexity never before seen. Consequently, those who study diplomacy will in the future need to consider its trans-Westphalian character, its ancient rituals that remain oddly recognizable in an interdependent and connected world, its flexibility and innovative capacities, its main accepted forms (bilateral and multilateral), its secretive impulses and stated aspirations to openness, its many new practitioners, its micro as well as macro practices, and its inherent limitations. But most of all, they will have to consider its potential to contribute to a less conflict-prone, more cooperation-based world diplomatic system, facing unprecedented policy challenges.

Glossary

Note: Definitions can be controversial, and scholars and practitioners alike hotly debate many. We encourage you to use these definitions as a starting point only for your inquiry and not as the last word on the subject at hand.

Accredited representative Term describing a diplomatic agent or head of mission who has been furnished with letters of credence signed by the agent's own head of state and addressed to the host country's head of state.

Agency The ability of persons or political entities to make free and rational decisions on their own behalf. Agency is often linked to rationality and forms an integral part of many conceptions of human subjectivity.

Alliance A formal coalition of two or more states that agree to collaborate on mutual security interests, usually codified through a treaty.

All-source intelligence Finished intelligence products based on all intelligence collection methods, including human intelligence, imagery and geospatial intelligence, measurement and signature intelligence, signals intelligence, and open source data.

Ambassador A diplomatic representative ranked at the highest level, accredited to a foreign state and bearing the full title "Ambassador Extraordinary and Plenipotentiary."

Anarchy *See* international anarchy.

ASEAN Regional Forum (ARF) A formal multilateral security dialogue established in 1994 comprising twenty-seven countries in the Asia-Pacific region and the European Union.

Asia-Pacific Economic Cooperation (APEC) Intergovernmental group with twenty-one member states established in 1989 to promote economic growth in the Asia-Pacific region; based on nonbinding commitments, open dialogue, and mutual respect for all participants.

Attractive power A synonym for soft power, which is based on actors' capacity to shape the preferences of others by means of attraction.

Balance of power The existing distribution of power in the international system (often categorized as unipolar, bipolar, or multipolar); also a doctrine associated with Realist theory suggesting that the power of one state (or group of states) is checked by the countervailing power of other states to maintain an equilibrium.

Bandwagon In balance of power politics, when a weak state joins with a more powerful state rather than opposes it.

Bargaining Method of achieving a mutual agreement or compromise by introducing concessions, conditional offers, threats, and incentives.

Bilateral/bilateralism Interaction involving two parties. Often refers to relations in general or to trade agreements or military treaties between two states.

Bilateral capitals A term used by diplomats to refer to the capital cities of two countries conducting diplomacy, dialogue, or negotiation.

Bilateral mission A diplomatic entity, usually an embassy, responsible for formal relations between two states, generally in each other's capital city. Members of one or both of these missions do not always reside in the receiving state. Generally regarded as the quintessential, traditional, diplomatic institution.

Bipolar structure/bipolarity Term describing an international order in which two states dominate all others. Often used to describe the Cold War era in which the international system was organized around two superpowers—the United States and the Soviet Union.

Blogosphere The digital community of all web-based journals, called blogs, where writers can self-publish their opinions, comment on other blogs, and develop social commentary. Often organized around specific issues, such as climate change policy or migration.

Bots Generally, any software that runs automated tasks over the Internet; however, the term is often associated with malware (damaging software), which can perform a variety of tasks including, but certainly not limited to, sending spam email from infected servers; conducting Distributed Denial of Service (DDoS) attacks; and automated collection of user information.

Bureaucratic politics The interactions among individuals within a government and the bargaining that occurs between them. Policy decisions are linked to the hierarchy between these actors and the agency to which they belong, including the idea that "'where they stand depends on where they sit'" (Allison and Halperin 1972: 73).

Citizen diplomacy The engagement of individual citizens in private sector programs and activities that increase cross-cultural understanding and knowledge between people from different countries, leading to greater mutual understanding and respect, and contributing to international relationships between countries.

Civil society groups/organizations Nongovernmental groups/organizations that are private, not for profit, and frequently have specific political and/or societal goals. Many maintain an international presence and aim to monitor and influence the actions of states.

Clausewitzian The idea associated with Carl von Clausewitz that war is the continuation of politics by other means. Clausewitz (1780–1831) was a Prussian military thinker and the author of *On War*, a major work of strategy, emphasizing war's role in shaping competition among states.

Coercive diplomacy The practice of employing threats or limited use of force to persuade an opponent to avoid, call off, or reverse a particular course of action. Some scholars use the term to refer exclusively to "compellence" and not "deterrence." The former threatens force unless an action is stopped; the latter threatens retaliation for an action not yet taken.

Collective security An arrangement in which member states of an international organization are jointly responsible for the security of one and all members; an alternative solution to the security dilemma, one that promotes institution-building and communal action rather than traditional alliances and reliance on the balance of power. Generally associated with the League of Nations and the United Nations Charter, but alliances also present themselves as a form of collective security.

College of Commissioners The twenty-seven members of the European Commission. Although each commissioner is nominated by his or her national government, the commissioners do not specifically represent their own state but instead represent the interests of the European Union as a whole.

Colocation Placing several different entities or institutions within the same location. Often a single building that houses embassies from several states or a variety of government offices from a single state.

Commercial diplomacy The use of foreign services or other branches of government to promote trade or investment.

Communicate/communication The exchange of information or ideas between two or more parties, most commonly through written or verbal means. Communication and representation are defining features of diplomacy. For examples of particular methods of diplomatic communication, such as a note (*see* note), see I. Roberts (2011: 48–59).

Concert of Europe An informal security arrangement, or "regime," composed of five great powers (Austria, Britain, France, Prussia, and Russia) that established basic, if informal, principles to manage and regulate conflict in the nineteenth century. The system was widely thought to have kept the peace in Europe from 1815 to the outbreak of the First World War in 1914.

Conflict trap A cyclical effect that often results from intrastate conflict, suggesting that a country with a history of conflict is more likely to have conflict in the future. The cycle is difficult to break because internal conflict has a tendency to weaken the economy, breed social distrust, and bring violence-prone leaders to power.

Consensus Achieving the agreement of all participants without calling for a vote. Allows for a proposal to be endorsed, even though at least one participant might have reservations about it.

Constructivists Theorists that emphasize the norms and the social, political, and economic structures that influence and shape actors' interests and interactions; also examines efforts to reform or transform those structures.

Consulate A diplomatic office, subordinate to an embassy, established in an important city of another state, usually other than the capital city. A consulate's primary purpose is to provide services to its citizens traveling or residing there and to promote bilateral trade between the two states. A consulate-general is the term used in a larger city. Headed by a consul or a consul-general, respectively.

Continuous dialogue A key diplomatic norm, which asserts that states, even adversaries, should maintain regular communication and interaction, usually through mutual recognition and representation.

Counterintelligence The identification, neutralization, and exploitation of the intelligence activities of adversaries (Godson 2001).

Covert action Influencing political, military, or economic conditions overseas while hiding the actual sponsor. Covert action may include propaganda, political action, and paramilitary operations.

Crisis management Using diplomacy to de-escalate an acute conflict that has a significant risk of leading to war; concept introduced by the US secretary of defense, Robert McNamara, following the 1962 Cuban missile crisis.

Crowdsourcing Outsourcing tasks, traditionally performed by an employee or contractor, to an undefined, large group of people or community, through an open invitation to participate in the task.

Culture Knowledge and behavior learned and shared through processes of socialization that identifies and distinguishes groups from one another and results in different ways of perceiving and dealing with social reality.

Cybercrime Crime committed using computers and the Internet, including unauthorized access to computer systems, damage to computer data or programs, computer sabotage, unauthorized interception of data, computer-related fraud, spreading child pornography, and other related activities. Enforced internationally through the Council of Europe Convention on Cybercrime, which entered into force on 1 July 2004; additional signatories include Canada, Japan, South Africa, and the United States.

Cybersecurity Maintaining the integrity of cyber infrastructure through the protection of data and systems in networks that are connected to the Internet; includes protection from cyberwar, terrorist attack, and cybercrime.

Cyberspace The electronic medium of computer networks, in which online communication takes place.

Deception Misleading an enemy by manipulating perceptions, often through intelligence operations involving double agents.

Defensive counterintelligence Efforts to protect intelligence information by securing it or by blocking the intelligence operations of an opponent.

Delegation A party sent to represent a state or other large entity at an international conference or gathering.

Démarche A formal message delivered in either oral or written form by a diplomat to host country officials, usually involving a protest of some kind.

Desecuritization Reframing an issue to reduce its stigma as a "security concern," in order to move away from the idea that the use of force is an ever-present possibility in all international relations.

Détente French word for relaxation, used to describe a relaxation of tension in previously strained relations between states by embracing negotiation rather than confrontation. Most commonly associated with the warming of relations between the United States and the Soviet Union led by Richard Nixon's administration in the early 1960s and 1970s. During the Cold War, détente was implemented through increased diplomatic exchanges, nuclear arms control agreements, and summit meetings. Critics argued that détente weakens a state's security by providing the opponent with an opportunity to gain advantage.

Diaspora Peoples who have moved permanently from their homeland but still identify with it in terms of cultural, ethnic, and linguistic traditions.

Digital divide The economic and social inequalities caused by a gap in the availability of technology—including computers, Internet access, and software capabilities. Commonly used to describe the technological differences between developed and developing countries; however, the concept also includes divisions between young and old, urban and rural, male and female, and between various professions.

Diplomacy of the public A form of collective dialogue aimed at the creation of a global communication space that is meant to result in a common language underpinning diplomatic efforts.

Diplomatic cable A message, usually classified according to its security importance, giving instruction to a mission or reporting results back to a capital.

Diplomatic culture "The accumulated communicative and representational norms, rules, and institutions devised to improve relations and avoid war between interacting and mutually recognizing political entities" (Wiseman 2005: 409–10).

Diplomatic immunity Privileged legal status accorded to diplomatic representatives by the states that receive them. According to this status, diplomatic officials (1) are inviolable, meaning they cannot be arrested or detained, and their offices cannot be entered or tampered with; (2) are immune from criminal jurisdiction, and often from civil and administrative jurisdiction as well; and (3) are exempt from taxes, inspections, and customs duties.

Diplomatic mission *See* diplomatic post/mission.

Diplomatic passport An official travel document issued by a state to the members of its diplomatic service and their families permitting expedited treatment by customs officials and border police of other countries.

Diplomatic post/mission A diplomatic or consular establishment or presence in a given city or state.

Diplomatic reporting *See* report/reporting.

Diplomatic representation *See* represent/representation.

Diplomatic signaling All acts, verbal or nonverbal, intentional or unintentional, that communicate a message from a diplomat to a foreign government or audience; signals often involve ambiguity.

Doha Development Round The multilateral trade negotiation round conducted under the auspices of the World Trade Organization, initiated in 2001. Doha's objectives are to lower trade barriers around the world, increase international trade, and promote global economic development.

Economic sanctions Using economic capabilities in a manipulative manner to achieve policy goals; a state imposing sanctions seeks to coerce the receiving state into behaving more compliantly. Often includes freeing banking assets, cutting financial aid, or banning trade.

Economic summitry Form of economic diplomacy that has as its aim coordination of international economic relations at the level of ministers or more normally the head of government.

Embassy Building accommodating offices, and sometimes a residence, for a diplomatic mission headed by an ambassador.

Embedded liberalism Term used to describe the economic structure that emerged after the Second World War in which capitalist countries reconciled market efficiency with sociocultural values. A quasi-grand social bargain whereby all sectors of society agreed to open markets, which in some cases had become heavily administered if not autarchic in the 1930s. Included agreement to contain and share the social adjustment costs that open markets inevitably produce (Ruggie 1982).

Emissary Diplomatic representative sent on a mission to another country.

Environmental diplomacy Negotiations aimed at addressing environmental challenges (whether cross-border or global) such as global warming, sustainable development, and biodiversity.

Envoy Originally a diplomat of less than ambassadorial rank, now used for an ambassador or special emissary between two heads of state.

Epistemological Claims about knowledge. To state that something is the case is to make such a claim. Epistemology is a branch of philosophy concerned with the nature of truth and knowledge and with how we know what we know.

Espionage Intelligence activity directed toward the acquisition of information through clandestine means and proscribed by the laws of the country against which it is committed; most often associated with clandestine human intelligence (HUMINT).

Estrangement The condition of being estranged, separated, withdrawn, and/or alienated from something or someone. Typically, estranged entities were previously closer and more cooperative.

European Commission Comprises twenty-seven commissioners and a permanent staff of some 37,000 European civil servants. Main function is to propose EU legislation to the Council of the EU and the European Parliament. Also tasked with implementing EU legislation and the EU budget and acting in the general interest of the Union with complete independence from national governments.

European Council Comprises the heads of state or government of the member states and the president of the European Commission. It elects its president for a two-and-a-half-year period, and it meets at least four times a year. Its primary function is to provide general political impetus and guidelines for the EU.

Extraterritorial rights/jurisdiction The exercise of legal jurisdiction by one state in the territory of another, related to diplomatic immunity in that the diplomat remains under the legal jurisdiction of the home, or sending, state and not that of the host, or receiving, state.

Extraterritoriality *See* extraterritorial rights/jurisdiction.

Financial diplomacy Negotiations conducted by a relatively small policy community of experts in ministries of finance or central banks concerned with managing the world economy and stabilizing markets.

Foreign service A term used to describe the bureaucratic organization of professional diplomatic and consular officials. A foreign service is part of a country's ministry of foreign affairs. The US Foreign Service is part of the Department of State.

Foreign Service Officer (FSO) A commissioned member of the US Foreign Service; a diplomatic official responsible for implementing US foreign policy.

Functionalism A theoretical approach that suggests that international conflict can be avoided and eventually ended by increasing international cooperation in economic and social issues. Functionalism argues that such cooperation will eventually be adopted by areas and states torn by political violence.

Global civil society Term used to describe the loose community of non-state and nongovernmental actors—individuals, organizations, networks, and coalitions—that conduct political, economic, and social activity across national borders and outside of governmental and corporate structures. Different from *transnational* civil society, which has less global coverage.

Global governance "The totality of institutions, policies, rules, practices, norms, procedures, and initiatives by which states and their citizens try to bring order and predictability to their responses to such universal problems as warfare, poverty, and environmental degradation" (Weiss 2009: 222).

Global North Term nowadays describing economically developed countries, used in place of the "First World" from the Cold War. Not all countries within this category are located in the Northern Hemisphere (for example, Australia and New Zealand); rather, it is a loose geographic metaphor.

Global public Composed of the citizens of the countries of the world who actively keep abreast of international social and political issues.

Global South Term describing countries with lower levels of economic development, used in place of the Cold War's "Third World," although there is a large variation in level of development between countries within the Global South.

Globalization A *process* involving increased political, social, economic, and cultural interconnectedness across regions and continents, linking formerly distant communities and transforming the traditional parameters of power. Also seen as the *outcome* of this process, whereby the international system experiences a decrease in state-based agencies in relation to global ones, rather than merely intergovernmental, operations. Commonly associated with the fall of communism at the end of the 1980s and the subsequent expansion of the free market economy. Also accompanied by the rapid evolution of global transportation and communication systems.

Globalized state A state that responds positively to globalization by welcoming its transformative force for the state's own gain. Instead of retreating in the face of globalization pressures, the globalized state adapts its behavior accordingly.

Group of Seven/Group of Eight (G7/G8) An informal intergovernmental grouping of the world's leading industrialized democracies. Established in 1975 as the G5 (France, Germany, Japan, the United Kingdom, and the United States) and subsequently growing to include Canada (1976), Italy (1977), and finally the Russian Federation (1998). Originally designed to promote collaboration and problem solving on economic issues, primarily through annual summit meetings between heads of state/government, the G8 agenda has since expanded to address political issues as well.

Group of Twenty (G20) An international coalition of finance ministers and central bank governors from both industrialized and developing economies. Established in 1999 as a forum to address critical issues in the global economy through open and constructive discussion. Made up of representatives from Argentina, Australia, Brazil, Canada, China, the EU, France, Germany, India, Indonesia, Italy, Japan, Mexico, Russia, Saudi Arabia, South Africa, South Korea, Turkey, the United Kingdom, and the United States of America.

Hard law Precise, legally binding obligations that delegate an authority for interpreting and enforcing the law.

Hard power A form of political power derived from military strength, economic influence, or diplomatic pressure that influences the behavior of others (Campbell and O'Hanlon 2006).

Hegemonic stability theory Theory suggesting that the international political economy is more stable when a dominant power can establish norms and rules, while using its power to encourage other states to comply.

Hegemony A system in which a single dominant leader, such as a superpower, exercises power and control (political and/or economic and even social) over other states; this dominant state is said to be the hegemon.

Hotline A secure and private method of direct communication maintained between world powers. Hotlines are often employed by heads of state, government officials, and diplomats in order to allow communication between opposed parties in times of crisis and/or uncertainty.

Human security Freedom from fear and freedom from want; an all-encompassing definition of security that considers physical safety, economic and social well-being, and respect for human dignity and human rights.

Immunities and privileges *See* diplomatic immunity.

Information operations The military use of electronic warfare, computer networks, psychological operations, and deception aimed at influencing an adversary's perceptions and decision making.

Intelligence capabilities The collective authorizations, organization, equipment, personnel, training, and resources to conduct intelligence activities.

Intelligence services The organizations or entities that collect, analyze, and disseminate information for decision makers in competition.

Interdependence Condition in which decisions made by states (or peoples) will necessarily affect other actors in the international system as well. Interdependence can be symmetric, where both sets of actors are affected equally, or asymmetric, where the impact varies between actors.

Intergovernmental Integration led by state governments, rather than by supranational institutions, that have a mission transcending the state.

International anarchy Notion that there is no common power or central governing authority within the international system.

International system (or system of states) "Formed when two or more states have sufficient contact between them, and have sufficient impact on one another's decisions, to cause them to behave—at least in some measure—as parts of a whole" (Bull 2002: 9).

Internet governance The development and application of shared principles, norms, rules, decision-making procedures, and programs that shape the evolution and use of the Internet.

Intersubjective Shared meanings constructed by people in their interactions with each other. Intersubjectivity stresses the shared and communal status of language and meaning.

Investment diplomacy Negotiations concerning access for foreign investment or the protection of foreign investment in host states.

Joined-up Term referring to improved government based on different departments working together, or enhanced forms of collaboration cutting across hierarchies, different levels of government, or connecting the public and private sectors.

Just war Ethical principles used to define the justice of war. Divided into two main categories: *jus ad bellum*, or the justice of the war's causes, which determines whether the use of force is permissible (for example, self-defense); and *jus in bello*, or justice in the war's conduct, which determines whether actual actions in warfare are permissible.

Knowledge society A society in which access to and control of knowledge are defining factors of social and economic success.

Legate Historic term used for a person sent on diplomatic business; also used in the twentieth century to refer to a papal emissary of the Holy See, now called a nuncio.

Legitimacy A legitimate authority is one that is respected or recognized both domestically and internationally. In diplomacy, linked to the concept of diplomatic, or international, recognition.

Legitimacy deficit Governing regimes that lack some form of legitimacy, either popular support or international recognition; efforts to govern are met with resistance or noncompliance.

Letter of accreditation A formal letter presenting the credentials of a newly appointed ambassador, announcing the diplomat's authority to act on behalf of the sending head of state or government.

Liberal international economic order The economic order established in the West in which markets are the predominant means of shaping investment, production, and trade.

Mandates Territories placed under the oversight of the League of Nations after the powers that previously controlled these territories were defeated in the First World War.

Mercantilist Economic ideology emphasizing state interest. Aims to maintain a positive balance of trade by increasing exports and decreasing imports, expanding markets, and, at times, implementing protectionist policies.

Ministry of foreign affairs (MFA) The government department responsible for conducting a state's foreign policy and coordinating its international activity, including any diplomatic activity.

Mission *See* diplomatic post/mission.

Mission diplomacy Conducting formal relations between sovereign states through the use of permanent embassies or legations in a receiving state, although some members of the mission may reside in a different country. Also refers to delegations sent to another country to conduct targeted and temporary diplomatic negotiations.

Mobile diplomats An officer who resides in a single post but travels frequently to serve other cities or regions, also known as "circuit riders."

Most favored nation (MFN) A fundamental principle of international trade that establishes equality and nondiscrimination among trading states—each trading state must be treated as if it were the most favored nation; an essential principle of free trade agreements.

Multilateral capitals Capital cities that host, and are widely identified as hosting, major international organizations, such as Geneva and Vienna. Distinct from cities, some of which are capitals, that host international organizations but generally are not identified as multilateral cities, such as Washington, DC; Rome; and Nairobi.

Multilateral mission A diplomatic entity accredited to an international, or multilateral, organization, such as the United Nations; often referred to as a "permanent" or "special" mission.

Multilateral negotiations Negotiations between three or more states.

Multilateral/multilateralism The process by which three or more countries cooperate to address a common issue rather than acting on a unilateral or bilateral basis.

Multiple accreditation When an ambassador, or head of mission, lives in one country but is accredited to and represents the sending government in one or more other countries or international organizations. A common practice for smaller states.

Nation-branding The application of corporate marketing concepts and techniques to countries, in the interests of enhancing their reputation in international relations.

Nation-state A sovereign political entity in which all members of the state also share a single national identity. The nation-state is the dominant political entity in modern international relations.

Neoliberal institutionalism Social theory that emphasizes the interdependence between autonomous social and political institutions.

Neoliberalism A theoretical approach to domestic and international economic and social policy that stresses the importance of privatization and open markets. Neoliberalism seeks to privatize national control of industries and economies and frequently pursues international cooperation to further its goals.

Neorealism A theoretical approach to international relations that assumes relations between states and territories are prone to conflict and war. Neorealism takes survival to be the primary motivating factor behind states' behavior and regards any peace agreements between nations with skepticism. For a state sympathetic to neorealism, security will be of the greatest importance.

New diplomacy Term describing the latest methods of diplomacy. Used to describe resident missions in the late fifteenth century, the parliamentary style of diplomacy developed under the League of Nations after the First World War, and currently nontraditional actors who assume diplomatic roles in global affairs.

Niche diplomacy Diplomacy based on clear foreign policy priorities so as to concentrate resources in specific areas with the expectation that they will generate more returns. Mostly associated with states having limited power and therefore no capacity to be active in all sectors.

Non-Aligned Movement Founded in 1961 and consisting overwhelmingly of Third World states that wanted to remain unaffiliated with either Cold War superpower and beyond the influence of the former colonial powers. Today, with some 120 members, its primary aim is to promote security and Third World development.

Nonresident ambassador Ambassador who does not reside in the state to which he or she is accredited but makes periodic visits.

Non-state actor Any entity that attempts to have an influence on international politics that does not possess the sovereign authority of a territorial state; an all-encompassing term that includes international organizations, nongovernmental organizations, multinational corporations, armed domestic militias, or transnational terrorist organizations. For some theorists, an individual may also qualify as a non-state actor.

Norm A general standard that specifies right or proper conduct.

Note A formal written communication between an embassy and a ministry of foreign affairs.

Nuncio An ambassadorial-level representative of the Holy See.

Offensive counterintelligence Efforts to manipulate the perceptions of another intelligence service through camouflage or deception in order to protect one's own competitive advantage.

Overseas posts A diplomatic or consular presence in a given city or state.

Papacy The office of the pope, whose jurisdiction is formally called the Holy See physically located in the Vatican, a small enclave in Rome.

Peacekeeping Impartial, nonthreatening third-party missions that help to resolve a conflict at the request of the disputing parties. The United Nations' traditional principles of peacekeeping include consent of the parties, impartiality, and the nonuse of force except in self-defense or defense of the mandate.

Peacemaking The process of conflict resolution through pacific settlement, includes any process used to create cooperation, compromise, and social institutions that contribute to building a sustainable peace.

Personality of laws Laws concerning the condition, state, or capacity of persons, as opposed to the *reality of laws*, which are laws that concern property or things.

Plurilateral negotiations Negotiations between a group of limited and normally like-minded governments.

Policy network A group of varied actors, both public and private, who have an active interest and expertise in a given policy sector. Sometimes seen as a specific type of governance in which policy is crafted by utilizing a variety of political resources in both the public and private sphere.

Polity An organized society within a specific territory that corresponds to a particular governing authority.

Polylateralism "The conduct of relations between official entities (such as a state, several states acting together, or a state-based international organization) and at least one unofficial, nonstate entity in which there is a reasonable expectation of systematic relationships, involving some form of reporting, communication, negotiation, and representation, but not involving mutual recognition as sovereign, equivalent entities" (Wiseman 2010: 24).

Positivist Theory claiming that only knowledge based on sense experience and quantitative analytical methods yields authentic, objective knowledge. Positivism relies upon direct observation and often avoids abstract theory.

Postpositivist A critique of positivism claiming that human knowledge rests not on a solid, unquestioned foundation but on human conjectures, warranted traditions, and cultural norms. Postpositivism questions knowledge assumed to be objectively true and suggests that such knowledge rests upon contingent foundations.

Preventive diplomacy Diplomatic activity intended to minimize conflict or prevent escalation of disagreements into violence—includes confidence-building measures, fact-finding, and deployment of UN-authorized peacekeeping forces before conflict erupts.

Procurator A Roman legal officer sent to serve in a country under Roman civil law.

Propaganda The attempt to influence opinions of an audience by means of a pattern of communication that is one-directional and excluding meaningful dialogue as a means of persuasion, as is the case with recent views of public diplomacy.

Protocol Rules of diplomatic procedure used to regulate the proper treatment of accredited state officials and diplomatic officers. Can also refer to an annex to a more formal document, such as a treaty.

Public diplomacy Traditionally seen as "the transparent means by which a sovereign country communicates with publics in other countries aimed at informing and influencing audiences overseas for the purpose of promoting the national interest and advancing its foreign policy goals" (USC Annenberg Center on Public Diplomacy 2011).

Public goods A good or service that is *nonrival*, meaning that multiple individuals can consume the same good without diminishing its value, and *nonexcludable*, meaning that an individual cannot be prevented from consuming the good whether or not he or she pays for it.

Quad The name used at the World Trade Organization to describe the four major industrialized country markets: Canada, the European Union, Japan, and the United States.

Rationalist Term used by economists to describe decision making that ranks preferences by their ability to maximize gains and minimize losses, and then selects the option that achieves the greatest overall gains. Term used by English school theorists to suggest that people, and states, share a commitment to the application of reason and restraint to human relations.

Realist Theoretical approach to international relations in which the sovereign state is the primary actor. The international system is seen as anarchic, and states' action is driven by the pursuit of power and fulfillment of the national interest. Conflict is seen as inevitable.

Reciprocity Principle in which state action is contingent on the previous action of other states, in a "tit-for-tat" manner—good is returned for good, and bad for bad. Often applied to international law in which states will cooperate only if others are likely to do so as well.

Regimes An implicit or explicit framework of rules, norms, principles, and procedures that governs a specific regional or global policy area, more simply defined as an international governing arrangement.

Regime theory A theory of international relations suggesting that strong and widely supported international regimes can provide governance within the anarchic international system.

Regional integration Growing political and/or economic interdependence between actors, mostly states, in a particular geographic region, for example, the European Union, the Organization of American States, the Association of Southeast Asian Nations, and the African Union.

Report/reporting Closed system of communication between members of a diplomatic mission and their home government (usually the ministry of foreign affairs); includes both routine and confidential information.

Represent/representation Diplomatic mission representing one state in another. Since the Second World War, almost all representations take place though the exchange of ambassadors, although the size and importance of embassies vary considerably. Although states are not obliged to exchange diplomatic representation, refusing to do so could be seen as a hostile act.

Resident ambassador The head of a diplomatic mission who resides in the receiving state.

Resident embassy The building that houses a permanent diplomatic presence in a receiving state.

Risk reduction Implementing strategies that minimize vulnerability to unforeseen hazards, conflicts, or disasters that have significant potential to cause damage.

Satrap Historically, a Persian provincial governor. Nowadays, term used with negative connotations to mean a subordinate official.

Security community A form of international cooperation that leads to integration. Connotes a community of sovereign states with such deeply shared political ideals that cooperation in many fields is unusually high and war is unimaginable, for example, the European Union (Deutsch 1957).

Security dilemma In an anarchic international system, a condition whereby a state's own defensive security measures are seen as offensive and threatening by other states, leading to mutual distrust and spiraling arms races.

Self-help Term used in Realist theory suggesting that each state must take care of itself and cannot rely on any other state, even an ally, to come to its defense.

Smart power Targeted influence that combines the timely and directed use of hard and soft power to achieve a state's objectives in the international system.

Social media Refers to Internet-based applications that facilitate the expression and exchange of social communication. They are built upon Web 2.0 technology concepts but deal explicitly with social intercourse. These applications are increasingly accessible, mobile, and immediate. Examples are Internet forums, weblogs, social blogs, and wikis. The term is used interchangeably with "Web 2.0." *See* Web 2.0.

Social power Notion challenging the soft power paradigm, building on a relationship-based and contextual understanding of power that examines "the capacity to establish norms and rules around which actors' actions converge" (van Ham 2010: 8).

Society of states Used interchangeably with "international society" in English school theory to describe "a group of states, conscious of certain common interests and common values, form a society in the sense that they conceive themselves to be bound by a common set of rules in their relations with one another, and share in the working of common institutions" (Bull 2002: 13).

Sociologist Scholar who studies the development, structure, and function of human social interaction.

Soft law Nonbinding legal arrangements or codes of conduct that are interpreted and "enforced" by their normative power rather than by a traditional sovereign authority.

Soft power Influence through attraction instead of coercion, pressure, or force (Nye 1990).

Sous-sherpa An official below the sherpa who is concerned with the preparatory work for economic summits. The term was used in G7/G8 economic summits but has now found wider use.

Sovereign An entity that possesses sovereignty.

Sovereign state A body of territory that possesses sovereignty, usually recognized through membership of the United Nations.

Sovereignty The condition whereby a state claims ultimate legal authority over defined territory and the right to represent the people of that territory in the international community. It is the extent to which a polity is under no external pressure from other political entities regarding any aspect of its behavior or decision making.

Special Representative Official appointed to head a particular diplomatic or peacekeeping mission; often used by the United Nations secretary-general and the European Union.

Sphere of influence A geopolitical region within which a powerful state claims exclusive rights of influence and intervention.

Statecraft The development and use of instruments of the state, including diplomacy, intelligence, force, economic leverage, and the law, to secure the state's interests in the international system.

Strategic communication An activity by defense departments or international security organizations, involving horizontal and vertical coordination of a variety of information activities aimed at supporting political and military objectives in foreign operations.

Summitry Diplomatic meetings between heads of state or heads of government; can be either ad hoc or regularly occurring.

Supranational Laws or institutions that supersede, or transcend, the authority of the sovereign state.

Suzerain A feudal lord to whom vassals pay tribute; most commonly refers to the Ottoman Empire.

Trade diplomacy Negotiations concerned with barriers to market access (tariffs and nontariff barriers), as well as regulatory policies that affect the exchange of goods and services between countries.

Transnational Operating across national boundaries.

Treaty A formal, mutually binding contract or agreement between two or more states.

Trojan horse The technique by which malware is surreptitiously introduced into a system by disguising itself as a normal piece of software or file.

Trust- and confidence-building Joint activities to reduce tension between two parties in dispute; demonstrates the advantages of cooperation and diplomacy to begin the process of conflict resolution.

Trust territories Territories under the oversight of the United Nations. Many were once mandate territories before the dissolution of the League of Nations.

Two-level game Theory suggesting that a state's ability to negotiate at the international level is often influenced and/or hindered by the state's simultaneous bargaining at the domestic level.

Unreflexively To act without consciously evaluating the status or implications of the action. An unreflexive action is one that is performed unconsciously, often out of habit or ritual.

Vassal A landholder, subject to the rule of a feudal ruler or lord, who must follow certain obligations in order to maintain possession of the land.

Veto A vote that has the authority to forbid any proposal, thus preventing its implementation. Often refers to the five permanent members of the UN Security Council (China, France, Great Britain, Russia, and the United States) that hold the power to prevent the adoption of any substantive council resolution.

Vienna Convention on Consular Relations Code of international law on consular posts and officers, particularly regarding facilities, immunities, and privileges. Established through a 1963 conference in Vienna.

Vienna Convention on Diplomatic Relations Code of international law regarding diplomatic actors and diplomatic missions, particularly addressing immunities and privileges. Established in 1961 through a conference in Vienna attended by eighty-one states.

Warfighting Active engagement in a war or an armed conflict.

Web 2.0 Refers to a shift in the design of browser-based software applications as well as an attendant shift in the way people engage with information on the Web. Rather than the noninteractive static screens of data that characterized the early years of the Web (the "brochure" phase), Web 2.0 applications are dynamic, interactive, and collaborative. Users engaging with these applications move from simply "consuming" information to creating, modifying, and exchanging it. The term is often used interchangeably with "social media." *See* social media.

Whole-of-government A way of organizing government work in an integrated fashion, based on horizontal linkages and coordination, thus counterbalancing government activities in separate functional silos.

Wireless technology The transfer of digital data without physical connection. Includes radio communication and cellular telephones but predominantly involves Wi-Fi, which is revolutionizing the use of computers by enabling portable computing devices to wirelessly connect to the Internet.

World Trade Organization (WTO) Founded in 1995 and based in Geneva, the WTO is the multilateral institution created to administer the General Agreement on Tariffs and Trade. The WTO is not part of the United Nations but often cooperates with it and participates in its initiatives.

Worm Self-replicating computer program, often malware, that uses computer networks to forward copies of itself to other nodes on the network. This is most often achieved without any user intervention.

References

ABC (Australian Broadcasting Corporation) 2010. "Torn Curtain: The Secret History of the Cold War." ABC Radio National. www.abc.net.au/rn/history/hindsight/features/torn/episode5.htm (accessed 8 December 2010).

Acharya, A. 2004. "How Ideas Spread: Whose Norms Matter? Norm Localization and Institutional Change in Asian Regionalism." *International Organization* 58 (2): 239–75.

Acheson, D. 1958. "The Illusion of Disengagement." *Foreign Affairs* 36 (3): 371–82.

Acuto, M., ed. Forthcoming. *Negotiating Relief: The Dialectics of Humanitarian Space.* New York: Columbia University Press.

Adcock, F., and D. J. Mosley. 1975. *Diplomacy in Ancient Greece.* London: Thames and Hudson.

Adrian-Paul, A., K. Clements, E. P. Lopez, and N. Johnston. 2004. "Legitimizing the Role of Women in Peacebuilding at the United Nations: A Campaign Approach." In M. Fitzduff and C. Church, eds., *NGOs at the Table: Strategies for Influencing Policies in Areas of Conflict,* 95–112. Lanham, MD: Rowman & Littlefield.

Aggestam, K., and M. Jerneck, eds. 2009. *Diplomacy in Theory and Practice: Essays in Honor of Christer Jönsson.* Malmö: Liber.

Albright, M., and W. Cohen, eds. 2008. *Preventing Genocide: A Blueprint for US Policymakers.* Washington, DC: United States Holocaust Memorial Museum, American Academy of Diplomacy, and United States Institute of Peace.

Allison, G. T., and M. H. Halperin. 1972. "Bureaucratic Politics: A Paradigm and Some Policy Implications." *World Politics* 24 (Spring): 40–79.

Allison, G. T., and P. D. Zelikow. 1999. *Essence of Decision: Explaining the Cuban Missile Crisis.* 2nd ed. New York: Longman.

Altman, A. 2004. "Tracing the Earliest Recorded Concepts of International Law: The Early Dynastic Period in Southern Mesopotamia." *Journal of the History of International Law* 6 (2): 153–72.

———. 2005. "Tracing the Earliest Recorded Concepts of International Law. The Old Akkadian and Ur III Periods in Mesopotamia." *Journal of the History of International Law* 7 (2): 115–36.

American Foreign Service Association. 2007. "Telling Our Story." AFSAnet, 17 October, updated 26 November.

Anderson, M. S. 1993. *The Rise of Modern Diplomacy, 1450–1919*. London: Longman.

Anderson, S. P. 1989. *An English Consul in Turkey: Paul Rycaut at Smyrna, 1667–1678*. Oxford: Clarendon Press.

Andonova, L. B. 2010. "Public–Private Partnerships for the Earth: Politics and Patterns of Hybrid Authority in the Multilateral System." *Global Environmental Politics* 10 (2): 25–53.

Andrew, C. 1995. *For the President's Eyes Only: Secret Intelligence and the American Presidency from Washington to Bush*. New York: HarperPerennial.

Andrew, C., and V. Mitrokhin. 1999. *The Sword and the Shield: The Mitrokhin Archive and the Secret History of the KGB*. New York: Basic Books.

Annan, K. 1998. "Intervention." Ditchley Foundation Lecture XXXV, Ditchley House, Oxfordshire, 26 June.

Arbour, L. 2009. "Civil Society and Public Interest Diplomacy." Address at Georgetown University, Washington, DC, 30 September. www.crisisgroup.org/en/publication-type/speeches/2009/civil-society-and-public-interest-diplomacy.aspx (accessed 7 September 2011).

Argyros, G., M. Grossman, and F. G. Rohatyn. 2007. "The Embassy of the Future." Washington, DC: Center for Strategic and International Studies.

Aron, R. 1966. *Peace and War: A Theory of International Relations*. London: Weidenfeld and Nicolson.

Art, R., and P. Cronin, P. eds. 2003. *The United States and Coercive Diplomacy*. Washington, DC: United States Institute of Peace Press.

Art, R., and K. N. Waltz, eds. 1971. *The Use of Force: International Politics and Foreign Policy*. Boston: Little, Brown.

Ashley, R. 1989. "Living on Border Lines: Man, Poststructuralism, and War." In J. Der Derian and M. J. Shapiro, eds., *International/Intertextual Relations: Postmodern Readings of World Politics*, 259–321. Lexington, MA: Lexington Books.

Bäckstrand, K. 2008. "Accountability of Networked Climate Change Governance: The Rise of Transnational Partnerships." *Global Environmental Politics* 8 (3): 74–102.

Badie, B. 2001. "Realism under Praise, or a Requiem? The Paradigmatic Debate in International Relations." *International Political Science Review* 22 (3): 253–60.

———. 2008. *Le diplomate et l'intrus*. Paris: Fayard.

———. 2011. "French Power-Seeking and Overachievement." In T. J. Volgy, R. Corbetta, K. A. Grant, and R. G. Baird, eds., *Major Powers and the Quest for Status in International Politics: Global and Regional Perspectives*, pp. 97–113. New York: Palgrave Macmillan.

Baldwin, D. A. 1985. *Economic Statecraft*. Princeton, NJ: Princeton University Press.

Ball, D. 2010. "CSCAP's Foundation and Achievements." In D. Ball and K. C. Guan, eds., *Assessing Track 2 Diplomacy in the Asia-Pacific Region: A CSCAP Reader*, 9–61. Canberra: Strategic and Defence Studies Centre; Singapore: S. Rajaratnam School of International Studies.

Ball, G. W. 1982. *The Past Has Another Pattern: Memoirs*. New York: Norton.

Ban, K. M. 2009. "Implementing the Responsibility to Protect." Report of the Secretary-General, A/63/677. New York: United Nations, 12 January.

Barker, A. 2010. "Trade Becomes the Business of Diplomacy." *Financial Times* (London), 4 August.

Barnes, B. 1988. *The Nature of Power*. London: Polity Press.

Barnes, J. E. 2007. "Defense Chief Urges Bigger Budget for State Department." *Los Angeles Times*, 27 November.

Barnett, M., and M. Finnemore. 2008. "Political Approaches." In T. G. Weiss and S. Daws, eds., *The Oxford Handbook on the United Nations*, 41–57. Oxford: Oxford University Press.

Basu, S. 2010. "Security Council Resolution 1325: Toward Gender Equality in Peace and Security Policy Making." In B. A. Reardon and A. Hans, eds., *The Gender Imperative: Human Security vs State Security*, 287–316. New Delhi and Abingdon: Routledge.

Bátora, J. 2005. "Does the European Union Transform the Institution of Diplomacy?" *Journal of European Public Policy* 12 (1): 44–66.

———. 2006. "Public Diplomacy between Home and Abroad: Norway and Canada." *Hague Journal of Diplomacy* 1 (1): 53–80.

———. 2008. *Foreign Ministries and the Information Revolution: Going Virtual?* Leiden: Martinus Nijhoff.

———. 2010a. "A Democratically Accountable External Action Service: Three Scenarios." *European Integration online Papers (EIoP)* 14 (special issue 1): 1–20, eiop.or.at/eiop/texte/2010-013a.htm (accessed 13 December 2010).

———. 2010b. "Diplomacy and People." In R. A. Denemark, ed., *International Studies Encyclopaedia Online*. Blackwell Publishing (accessed 18 March 2010).

Bátora, J., and B. Hocking. 2009. "EU-Oriented Bilateralism: Evaluating the Role of Member State Embassies in the European Union." *Cambridge Review of International Affairs* 22 (1): 163–82.

Bayne, N. 2011. "The Decline of the G8 Summit and Lessons for the G20." In N. Bayne and S. Woolcock, eds., *The New Economic Diplomacy: Decision-Making and Negotiation in International Economic Relations*, 249–62. 3rd ed. Burlington, VT: Ashgate.

Bayne, N., and S. Woolcock, eds. 2011. *The New Economic Diplomacy: Decision-Making and Negotiation in International Economic Relations*. 3rd ed. Burlington, VT: Ashgate.

Bell, C. 1963. *Negotiation from Strength: A Study in the Politics of Power*. New York: Alfred A. Knopf.

Berger, T. U. 2003. *Cultures of Antimilitarism: National Security in Germany and Japan*. Baltimore, MD: Johns Hopkins University Press.

Bergsten, C. F. 2004. "A New Foreign Policy for the United States." Washington, DC: Peterson Institute for International Economics.

Berridge, G. R. 1995. *Diplomacy: Theory and Practice*. London: Macmillan.

———. 2002. *Diplomacy: Theory and Practice*. 2nd ed. Basingstoke: Palgrave Macmillan.

———. 2005. *Diplomacy: Theory and Practice*. 3rd ed. Basingstoke: Palgrave Macmillan.

———. 2010. *Diplomacy: Theory and Practice*, 4th ed. Basingstoke: Palgrave Macmillan.

———. 2011. *The Counter-revolution in Diplomacy and Other Essays*. Basingstoke: Palgrave Macmillan.

Berridge, G. R., and A. James. 2001. *A Dictionary of Diplomacy*. Basingstoke: Palgrave.

———. 2003. *A Dictionary of Diplomacy*. 2nd ed. Basingstoke: Palgrave Macmillan.

Betts, R. K. 2009. *Enemies of Intelligence: Knowledge and Power in American National Security*. New York: Columbia University Press.

Biermann, F., P. Pattberg, H. van Asselt, and F. Zelli. 2009. "The Fragmentation of Global Governance Architectures: A Framework for Analysis." *Global Environmental Politics* 9 (4): 14–40.

Bisley, N. 2007. *Rethinking Globalization*. Basingstoke: Palgrave Macmillan.

Björkdahl, A. 2000. "Developing a Toolbox for Conflict Prevention." In *Preventing Violent Conflict: The Search for Political Will, Strategies and Effective Tools*, 17–22. Report of the Krusenberg Seminar, 19–20 June. Stockholm: Swedish International Peace Research Institute.

Blockley, R. C. 1985. *The History of Menander the Guardsman: Introductory Essay, Text, Translation and Historigraphical Notes*. Liverpool: F. Cairns.

Boak, A. E. R. 1924. *The Master of the Offices in the Later Roman and Byzantine Empires*. New York: Macmillan.

Bollier, D. 2003. "The Rise of Netpolitik: How the Internet Is Changing International Politics and Diplomacy." Washington, DC: Aspen Institute.

Borger, J. 2008. "Foreign Office to Court Youth on YouTube." *Guardian*, 15 January.

Bosco, D. L. 2009. *Five to Rule Them All: The UN Security Council and the Making of the Modern World*. Oxford: Oxford University Press.

Boutros-Ghali, B. 1992. *An Agenda for Peace: Preventive Diplomacy, Peacemaking and Peace-keeping*. Report of the Secretary-General Pursuant to the Statement Adopted by the Summit Meeting of the Security Council on 31 January. New York: United Nations.

———. 1995. *An Agenda for Peace*. 2nd ed. New York: United Nations.

Brams, S. J. 1985. *Superpower Games: Applying Game Theory to Superpower Conflict*. New Haven, CT: Yale University Press.

British Foreign and Commonwealth Office. 2008. *Engagement: Public Diplomacy in a Globalised World*. London: Foreign and Commonwealth Office.

———. 2010. "Digital Diplomacy." digitaldiplomacy.fco.gov.uk/en/about/ (accessed 23 November 2010).

Brooks, S. P. 2008. "Enforcing a Turning Point and Imposing a Deal: An Analysis of the Darfur Abuja Negotiations of 2006." *International Negotiation* 13 (3): 413–40.

Brownell, S. 2009. "The Impact of the Olympics." 27 March. china.usc.edu/ShowArticle.asp x?articleID=1397&AspxAutoDetectCookieSupport=1 (accessed 10 October 2010).

Bruter, M. 1999. "Diplomacy without a State: The External Delegations of the European Commission." *Journal of European Public Policy* 6 (2): 183–205.

Budiansky, S. 2005. *Her Majesty's Spymaster: Elizabeth I, Sir Francis Walsingham, and the Birth of Modern Espionage*. New York: Plume.

Bueno de Mesquita, B. 2003. *Principles of International Politics*. 2nd ed. Washington, DC: CQ Press.

Builder, C. H., 1993. "Is It a Transition or a Revolution?" *Futures* 25 (2): 155–68.

Bull, H. 1966. "International Theory: The Case for a Classical Approach." *World Politics* 18 (3): 361–77.

———. 1977. *The Anarchical Society: A Study of Order in World Politics*. London: Macmillan.

———. 2002. *The Anarchical Society: A Study of Order in World Politics*. 3rd ed. New York: Columbia University Press.

Bull, H., and A. Watson, eds. 1984. *The Expansion of International Society*. Oxford: Clarendon Press.

Burns, J. 2009. *Papa Spy: Love, Faith and Betrayal in Wartime Spain*. New York: Walker.

Bush, G. H. W. 2009. "Remarks at the Texas A&M University Commencement Ceremony." College Station, Texas, 12 May 1989. In G. H. W. Bush, *Speaking of Freedom: The Collected Speeches*, 33–38. New York: Scribner.

Bush, G. W. 2003a. "Address Before a Joint Session of the Congress of the United States: Response to the Terrorists Attacks of September 11, September 2001." *Public Papers of the Presidents of the United States, George W. Bush: 2001*, Book II, 1140–44. Washington, DC: United States Government Printing Office.

———. 2003b. "Remarks on Arrival at the White House and an Exchange with Reporters, September 16, 2001." *Public Papers of the Presidents of the United States, George W. Bush: 2001*, Book II, 1114–17. Washington, DC: United States Government Printing Office.

Buzan, B., O. Wæver, and J. de Wilde. 1998. *Security: A New Framework for Analysis.* Boulder, CO: Lynne Rienner.

Caesar, J. 1982. *The Conquest of Gaul*, trans. S. A. Hanford. Harmondsworth: Penguin.

Calder, K. E. 2008. "Critical Junctures and the Contours of Northeast Asian Regionalism." In K. E. Calder and F. Fukuyama, eds., *East Asian Multilateralism: Prospects for Regional Stability*, 15–39. Baltimore, MD: Johns Hopkins University Press.

Calder, K. E., and F. Fukuyama. 2008. "Introduction." In K. E. Calder and F. Fukuyama, eds., *East Asian Multilateralism: Prospects for Regional Stability*, 1–12. Baltimore, MD: Johns Hopkins University Press.

Callick, R. 2010. "Movement for Progress Gets Stuck in the Lobby." *Australian*, 2 January.

Campbell, B. 2001. "Diplomacy in the Roman World (c.500 BC–AD 235)." *Diplomacy & Statecraft* 12 (1): 1–22.

Campbell, K. M., and M. E. O'Hanlon. 2006. *Hard Power: The New Politics of National Security.* New York: Basic Books.

Capie, D. 2010. "When Does Track Two Matter? Structure, Agency and Asian Regionalism." *Review of International Political Economy* 17 (2): 291–318.

Caporaso, J. A. 1998. "Regional Integration Theory: Understanding Our Past and Anticipating Our Future." In W. Sandholtz and A. Stone Sweet, eds., *European Integration and Supranational Governance*, 334–52. Oxford: Oxford University Press.

———. 2000. "Changes in the Westphalian Order: Territory, Public Authority, and Sovereignty." *International Studies Review* 2 (2): 1–28.

Carr, E. H. 1939. *The Twenty Years' Crisis, 1919–1939: An Introduction to the Study of International Relations.* London: Macmillan.

Carter Center. N.d. "North Korea." www.cartercenter.org/countries/north_korea.html (accessed 7 September 2011).

Castells, M. 2008. "The New Public Sphere: Global Civil Society, Communication Networks, and Global Governance." *Annals of the American Academy of Political and Social Science* 616 (March): 78–93.

Cha, V. D. 2009/10. "Powerplay: Origins of the US Alliance System in Asia." *International Security* 34 (3): 158–96.

Charillon, F., ed. 2002. *Politique étrangère: Nouveaux regards.* Paris: Presses de Sciences Po.

Charter of the United Nations. 1945. www.un.org/en/documents/charter/index.shtml (accessed 22 September 2011).

Chesterman, S., ed. 2007. *Secretary or General? The UN Secretary-General in World Politics.* Cambridge: Cambridge University Press.

Christensen, J., and N. Petersen. 2005. "Managing Foreign Affairs: A Comparative Perspective." DIIS Report 2005: 15. Copenhagen: Danish Institute for International Studies.

Christensen, T. J. 2006. "Fostering Stability or Creating a Monster? The Rise of China and US Policy toward East Asia." *International Security* 31 (1): 81–126.

Christiansen, T. 2011. "Governments and Climate Change: The UN Process." In N. Bayne and S. Woolcock, eds., *The New Economic Diplomacy: Decision-Making and Negotiation in International Economic Relations*, 303–22. 3rd ed. Burlington, VT: Ashgate.

Clark, I. 2008. "Globalization and the Post-Cold War Order." In J. Baylis, S. Smith, and P. Owens, eds., *The Globalization of World Politics: An Introduction to International Relations*, 560–75. Oxford: Oxford University Press.

Claude, I. L., Jr. 1971. *Swords into Plowshares: The Problems and Progress of International Organization*, 4th ed. New York: Random House.

Clinton, B. 2004. *My Life*. New York: Alfred A. Knopf.

Clinton, D. 2011. "The Distinction between Foreign Policy and Diplomacy in American International Thought and Practice." *Hague Journal of Diplomacy* 6 (3–4): 261–76.

Clinton, H. R. 2009a. "Appointment of Ambassador Stephen Bosworth as Special Representative for North Korea Policy." Press Statement, 20 February. www.state.gov/secretary/rm/2009a/02/119421.htm (accessed 23 September 2011).

———. 2009b. "Opening Remarks on the President's FY 2009 War Supplemental Request." Testimony before the Senate Appropriations Committee, Washington, DC, 30 April. www.state.gov/secretary/rm/2009a/04/122463.htm (accessed 18 October 2011).

———. 2010. "Leading through Civilian Power: Redefining American Diplomacy and Development." *Foreign Affairs* 89 (6): 13–24.

Cockburn, C. 2007. *From Where We Stand: War, Women's Activism and Feminist Analysis*. London: Zed.

Cohen, R. 1996. "On Diplomacy in the Ancient Near East: The Amarna Letters." *Diplomacy & Statecraft* 7 (2): 245–70.

———. 2002. *Negotiating across Cultures: Communication Obstacles in International Diplomacy*. Washington, DC: United States Institute of Peace.

Cohn, C., H. Kinsella, and S. Gibbings. 2004. "Women, Peace and Security: Resolution 1325." *International Feminist Journal of Politics* 6 (1): 130–40.

Colegrove, K. 1919. "Diplomatic Procedure Preliminary to the Congress of Westphalia." *American Journal of International Law* 13 (3): 450–82.

Collier, P., L. Elliott, H. Hegre, A. Hoeffler, M. Reynal-Querol, and N. Sambanis. 2003. *Breaking the Conflict Trap: Civil War and Development Policy*. Washington, DC: World Bank.

Confucius Institute Online. 2010. "Confucius Institutes Worldwide." college.chinese.cn/node_1941.htm (accessed 13 December 2010).

Connolly, J. 1915. "Diplomacy." *Workers' Republic*, 6 November. www.marxists.org/archive/connolly/1915/11/diplmacy.htm (accessed 14 September 2011).

Conrad, J. 1907. *The Secret Agent*. London: Methuen.

Constantinou, C. 1996. *On the Way to Diplomacy*. Minneapolis, MN: University of Minnesota Press.

Constantinou, C. M., and J. Der Derian, eds. 2010. *Sustainable Diplomacies*. Basingstoke: Palgrave Macmillan.

Constitution of the People's Republic of China. www.gov.cn/ziliao/flfg/2005-06/14/content_6310_6.htm (accessed 1 September 2011).

Contreras, A. P. 2008. "Transboundary Environmental Governance in Southeast Asia." In A. Pandya and E. Laipson, eds., *Transnational Trends: Middle Eastern and Asian Views*, 155–70. Washington, DC: The Henry L. Stimson Center.

Cooper, A. F. 2008a. "Beyond One Image Fits All: Bono and the Complexity of Celebrity Diplomacy." *Global Governance* 14 (3): 265–72.

———. 2008b. *Celebrity Diplomacy*. Boulder, CO: Paradigm.

Cooper, A. F., and T. M. Shaw, eds. 2009. *The Diplomacies of Small States: Between Vulnerability and Resilience*. Basingstoke: Palgrave Macmillan.

Cooper, A. F., B. Hocking, and W. Maley, eds. 2008. *Global Governance and Diplomacy: Worlds Apart?* Basingstoke: Palgrave Macmillan.

Copeland, D. 2009. *Guerrilla Diplomacy: Rethinking International Relations*. Boulder, CO: Lynne Rienner.

Cox, R. 1987. *Power, Production, and World Order: Social Forces in the Making of History.* New York: Columbia University Press.

Crawford, J., and T. Grant. 2008. "International Court of Justice." In T. G. Weiss and S. Daws, eds., *The Oxford Handbook on the United Nations,* 193–213. Oxford: Oxford University Press.

Crocker, C. A. 1992. *High Noon in Southern Africa: Making Peace in a Rough Neighorbood.* New York: W. W. Norton.

Croxton, D. 1999. "The Peace of Westphalia of 1648 and the Origins of Sovereignty." *International History Review* 21 (3): 569–91.

Crump, L., and I. W. Zartman, eds. 2003. "Multilateral Negotiation and Complexity." *International Negotiation* 8 (1) special issue: 1–186.

Crumpton, H. A. 2005. "Intelligence and War: Afghanistan 2001–2002." In J. E. Sims and B. Gerber, eds., *Transforming US Intelligence,* 162–79. Washington, DC: Georgetown University Press.

Cull, N. J. 2003. "'The Man Who Invented Truth': The Tenure of Edward R. Murrow as Director of the United States Information Agency During the Kennedy Years." *Cold War History* 4 (1): 23–48.

———. 2008. "Public Diplomacy: Taxonomies and Histories." *Annals of the American Academy of Political and Social Science* 616 (March): 31–54.

———. 2009. "Public Diplomacy: Lessons from the Past." CPD Perspectives on Public Diplomacy. Los Angeles: Figueroa Press.

Dallin, D. J. 1944. *The Real Soviet Russia.* New Haven, CT: Yale University Press.

Dareini, A. A. 2010. "Iran Claims Computer Worm Is Western Plot." *Washington Post,* 5 October.

Davis Cross, M. K. 2007. *The European Diplomatic Corps: Diplomats and International Cooperation from Westphalia to Maastricht.* Basingstoke: Palgrave Macmillan.

de Callières, F. 1716/2000. *On the Manner of Negotiating with Princes: From Sovereigns to CEOs, Envoys to Executives—Classic Principles of Diplomacy for Success in Today's Business World.* New York: Houghton Mifflin.

de Felice, F. B. 1778/1976. "Negotiations, or the Art of Negotiating. " In I. W. Zartman, trans. and ed., *The 50% Solution: How to Bargain Successfully with Hijackers, Strikers, Bosses, Oil Magnates, Arabs, Russians, and Other Worthy Opponents in this Modern World,* 47–65. Garden City, NY: Anchor Press.

Deng, F. M., S. Kimaro, T. Lyons, D. Rothchild, and I. W. Zartman. 1996. *Sovereignty as Responsibility: Conflict Management in Africa.* Washington, DC: Brookings Institution.

Deng, X. 1993. *Deng Xiaoping Wenxuan* [Selected Works of Deng Xiaoping]. Vol. 3. Beijing: People's Press.

Der Derian, J. 1987. *On Diplomacy: A Genealogy of Western Estrangement.* Oxford: Blackwell.

———. 1996. "Hedley Bull and the Idea of Diplomatic Culture." In R. Fawn and J. Larkins, eds., *International Society after the Cold War: Anarchy and Order Reconsidered,* 84–100. New York: St. Martin's Press.

Deutsch, K. W. 1957. *Political Community and the North Atlantic Area: International Organization in the Light of Historical Experience.* Princeton, NJ: Princeton University Press.

Deveraux, C., R. Z. Lawrence, and M. D. Watkins. 2006. *Case Studies in US Trade Negotiations.* Vol. 1. Washington, DC: Institute for International Economics.

Devin, G. 2002. "Les diplomaties de la politique étrangère." In F. Charillon, ed., *Politique étrangère: Nouveaux Regards*, 215–45. Paris: Presses de Sciences Po.

d'Hooghe, I. 2007. "The Rise of China's Public Diplomacy." Clingendael: Netherlands Institute of International Relations.

Dickie, J. 2008. *The British Consul: Heir to a Great Tradition*. New York: Columbia University Press.

Dieter, H., and R. Kumar. 2008. "The Downside of Celebrity Diplomacy: The Neglected Complexity of Development." *Global Governance* 14 (3): 259–64.

DiMaggio, P. J., and W. W. Powell. 1991. "The Iron Cage Revisited: Institutional Isomorphism and Collective Rationality in Organizational Fields." In W. W. Powell and P. J. DiMaggio, eds., *The New Institutionalism in Organizational Analysis*, 63–82. Chicago: University of Chicago Press.

Dimier, V., and M. McGeever. 2006. "Diplomats without a Flag: The Institutionalization of the Delegations of the Commission in African, Caribbean and Pacific Countries." *Journal of Common Market Studies* 44 (3): 483–505.

Doctor, M. 2007. "Why Bother with Inter-regionalism? Negotiations for a European Union-Mercosur Agreement." *Journal of Common Market Studies* 45 (2): 281–314.

Drucker, P. F. 1989. *The New Realities: In Government and Politics, in Economics and Business, in Society and World View*. New York: Harper & Row.

Druckman, D. 2007. "Negotiating in the International Context." In I. W. Zartman, ed., *Peacemaking in International Conflict: Methods and Techniques*, 111–62. Rev. ed. Washington, DC: United States Institute of Peace.

Dür, A., and M. Elsig. 2011. *The European Union's Foreign Economic Policies: A Principal-Agent Perspective*. Abingdon: Routledge.

Dutch Ministry of Foreign Affairs. 2008a. "Verhagen Launches 'Rent-an-Ambassador' Programme." Newsflash, 21 May. www.minbuza.nl/en/News/Newsflashes/2008/05/ Verhagen_launches_Rent_an_Ambassador_programme (accessed 11 November 2010).

———. 2008b. "Speech by Verhagen at the Opening of the Joint Training of Palestinian and Israeli Diplomats." Clingendael, The Hague, 11 November. www.minbuza.nl/en/ News/Speeches_and_Articles/2008/11/Speech_by_Verhagen_at_the_opening_of_ the_joint_training_of_Palestinian_and_Israeli_diplomats (accessed 11 November 2010).

Elgavish, D. 2000. "Did Diplomatic Immunity Exist in the Ancient Near East?" *Journal of the History of International Law* 2 (1): 73–90.

Emerson, R. 1960. *From Empire to Nation: The Rise to Self-Assertion of Asian and African Peoples*. Cambridge, MA: Harvard University Press.

Evans, A., and D. Steven. 2008. "Towards a Theory of Influence for Twenty-First-Century Foreign Policy: Public Diplomacy in a Globalised World." In J. Welsh and D. Fearn, eds., *Engagement: Public Diplomacy in a Globalised World*, 44–61. London: Foreign and Commonwealth Office.

Evans, G., and M. Sahnoun. 2002. "The Responsibility to Protect." *Foreign Affairs* 81 (6): 99–110.

Evans, P. M. 1994. "Building Security: The Council for Security Cooperation in the Asia Pacific (CSCAP)." *Pacific Review* 7 (2): 125–39.

Fagot Aviel, J. 2011. "The Role of Nonstate Actors." In J. P. Muldoon Jr., J. Fagot Aviel, R. Reitano, and E. Sullivan, eds., *The New Dynamics of Multilateralism: Diplomacy,*

International Organizations, and Global Governance, 297–315. Boulder, CO: Westview Press.

Fasulo, L. 2004. *An Insider's Guide to the UN*. New Haven, CT: Yale University Press.

Fernández, A. M. 2011. "Consular Affairs in an Integrated Europe." In J. Melissen and A. M. Fernández, eds., *Consular Affairs and Diplomacy*, 97–114. Leiden: Martinus Nijhoff.

Fisher, A. 2010. "Mapping the Great Beyond: Identifying Meaningful Networks in Public Diplomacy." CPD Perspectives on Public Diplomacy, Paper 2. Los Angeles: Figueroa Press.

Fitzpatrick, K. R. 2010. *The Future of US Public Diplomacy: An Uncertain Fate*. Leiden: Martinus Nijhoff.

Fomerand, J. 1996. "UN Conferences: Media Events or Genuine Diplomacy?" *Global Governance* 2 (3): 361–75.

Fortna, V. P. 2004. *Peace Time: Cease-Fire Agreements and the Durability of Peace*. Princeton, NJ: Princeton University Press.

Foster, M. K. 1985. "Another Look at the Function of Wampum in Iroquois–White Councils." In F. Jennings, W. N. Fenton, M. A. Druke, and D. R. Miller, eds., *The History and Culture of Iroquois Diplomacy: An Interdisciplinary Guide to the Treaties of the Six Nations and Their League*, 99–114. Syracuse, NY: Syracuse University Press.

Freeman, C. 1997. *The Diplomat's Dictionary*. Washington DC: United States Institute of Peace Press.

Friedman, T. L. 2007. *The World Is Flat: A Brief History of the Twenty-First Century*. New York: Picador.

Future of Diplomacy Project. 2010. "Harvard Kennedy School Launches the Future of Diplomacy Project, a New Initiative on Diplomacy, Negotiations and Statecraft." 29 November. http://belfercenter.ksg.harvard.edu/files/uploads/futureofdiplomacy/fodp-launch-release.html (accessed 11 October 2011).

Gaddis, J. L. 2005. *Strategies of Containment: A Critical Appraisal of Postwar American National Security Policy during the Cold War*. New York: Oxford University Press.

Gartner, S. S., and M. M. Melin. 2009. "Assessing Outcomes: Conflict Management and the Durability of Peace." In J. Bercovitch, V. Kremenyuk, and I. W. Zartman, eds., *The SAGE Handbook of Conflict Resolution*, 564–79. London: Sage.

Garver, J. W. 1993. *Foreign Relations of the People's Republic of China*. Englewood Cliffs, NJ: Prentice Hall.

George, A. L. 1991. *Forceful Persuasion: Coercive Diplomacy as an Alternative to War*. Washington, DC: United States Institute of Peace Press.

George, R., and J. Bruce,eds. 2009. *Analyzing Intelligence: Origins, Obstacles, and Innovations*. Washington, DC: Georgetown University Press.

Gerber, B. 2005. "Managing HUMINT: The Need for a New Approach." In J. E. Sims and B. Gerber, eds., *Transforming US Intelligence*, 180–97. Washington, DC: Georgetown University Press.

German Federal Foreign Office. N.d. "The German Missions Abroad." www.auswaertiges-amt.de/EN/AAmt/Auslandsvertretungen/Uebersicht_node.html (accessed 26 June 2011).

Giddens, A. 1990. *The Consequences of Modernity*. Stanford, CA: Stanford University Press.

Gilboa, E. 2008. "Searching for a Theory of Public Diplomacy." *Annals of the American Academy of Political and Social Science* 616 (March): 55–77.

Gill, B., and Y. Huang. 2006. "Sources and Limits of Chinese 'Soft Power.'" *Survival* 48 (2): 17–35.

Gill, P. 2009. "Theories of Intelligence: Where Are We, Where Should We Go and How Might We Proceed?" In P. Gill, S. Marrin, and M. Pythian, eds., *Intelligence Theory: Key Questions and Debates*, 208–26. New York: Routledge.

Godson, R. 2001. *Dirty Tricks or Trump Cards: US Covert Action and Counterintelligence*. New Brunswick, NJ: Transaction Publishers.

Goldstein, J. S. 2010. "Chicken Dilemmas: Crossing the Road to Cooperation." In I. W. Zartman and S. Touval, eds., *International Cooperation: The Extents and Limits of Multilateralism*, 135–60. Cambridge: Cambridge University Press.

Goodhand, J. 2006. *Aiding Peace? The Role of NGOs in Armed Conflict*. Boulder, CO: Lynne Rienner.

Gordon, D. C. 1971. *Self-Determination and History in the Third World*. Princeton, NJ: Princeton University Press.

Gorman, S. 2010. "CIA Man Is Key to US Relations with Karzai." *Wall Street Journal*, 24 August.

Götz, N. 2011. *Deliberative Diplomacy: The Nordic Approach to Global Governance and Societal Representation at the United Nations*. Dordrecht: Republic of Letters Publishing.

Graffy, C. 2009. "The Rise of Public Diplomacy 2.0." *Journal of International Security Affairs* 17 (Fall). www.ciaonet.org/journals/jisa/v0i17/08.html (accessed 23 March 2012).

Gregory, B. 2008a. "Public Diplomacy and Governance: Challenges for Scholars and Practitioners." In A. F. Cooper, B. Hocking, and W. Maley, eds., *Global Governance and Diplomacy: Worlds Apart?*, 241–56. Basingstoke: Palgrave Macmillan.

———. 2008b. "Public Diplomacy: Sunrise of an Academic Field." In G. Cowan and N. J. Cull, eds., *Public Diplomacy in a Changing World, The Annals*, 274–90. Thousand Oaks, CA: Sage.

———. 2011. "American Public Diplomacy: Enduring Characteristics, Elusive Transformation." *Hague Journal of Diplomacy* 6 (3–4): 351–72.

Gross, L. 1948. "The Peace of Westphalia, 1648–1948." *American Journal of International Law* 42 (1): 20–41.

Gruen, E. S. 2004. "Rome and the Greek World." In H. I. Flower, ed., *The Cambridge Companion to the Roman Republic*, 242–67. Cambridge, MA: Cambridge University Press.

Guardian. 2011. "Arab Spring: Google's Wael Ghonim on the Fall of Mubarak." 18 May.

Gulbrandsen, L. H. 2004. "Overlapping Public and Private Governance: Can Forest Certification Fill the Gaps in the Global Forest Regime?" *Global Environmental Politics* 4 (2): 75–99.

Güterbock, H. G. 1983. "The Hittites and the Aegean World: Part 1. The Ahhiyawa Problem Reconsidered." *American Journal of Archaeology* 87 (2): 133–38.

Gyngell, A., and M. Wesley. 2003. *Making Australian Foreign Policy*. Cambridge: Cambridge University Press.

Haas, E. B. 1958. *The Uniting of Europe: Political, Social, and Economic Forces, 1950–1957*. Stanford, CA: Stanford University Press.

Hall, I. 2010. "The Transformation of Diplomacy: Mysteries, Insurgencies and Public Relations." *International Affairs* 86 (1): 247–56.

Hamburg, D. A. 2008. *Preventing Genocide: Practical Steps toward Early Detection and Effective Action*. Boulder, CO: Paradigm.

Hamilton, K. A., and R. Langhorne. 1995. *The Practice of Diplomacy: Its Evolution, Theory, and Administration.* London: Routledge.

———. 2011. *The Practice of Diplomacy: Its Evolution, Theory, and Administration.* 2nd ed. London: Routledge.

Hampson, F. O., with J. Daudelin, J. B. Hay, T. Martin, and H. Reid. 2002. *Madness in the Multitude: Human Security and World Disorder.* Don Mills, ON: Oxford University Press.

Hampson, F. O., with M. Hart. 1995. *Multilateral Negotiations: Lessons from Arms Control, Trade, and the Environment.* Baltimore, MD: Johns Hopkins University Press.

Han, N., ed. 1987. *Dangdai Zhongguo Waijiao* [Diplomacy of Contemporary China]. Beijing: China's Social Science Press.

Hanson, F. 2011. "The New Public Diplomacy." In M. Conley Tyler, ed., *ICT4IR: International Relations in the Digital Age,* 35–41. Deakin, ACT: Australian Institute of International Affairs.

Hara, F. 1999. "Burundi: A Case of Parallel Diplomacy." In C. Crocker, F. O. Hampson, and P. Aall, eds., *Herding Cats: Multiparty Mediation in a Complex World,* 135–58. Washington, DC: United States Institute of Peace.

Harding, H. 1988. *China and Northeast Asia: The Political Dimension.* Lanham, MD: University Press of America.

———. 1992. *A Fragile Relationship: The United States and China since 1972.* Washington, DC: Brookings Institution.

Harris, P., and P. Gallagher. 2011. "Terry Jones Defiant Despite Murders in Afghanistan Over Qur'an Burning." *Guardian,* 2 April.

Harris, S. 1994. "Policy Networks and Economic Cooperation: Policy Coordination in the Asia-Pacific Region." *Pacific Review* 7 (4): 381–95.

Hasenclever, A., P. Mayer, and V. Rittberger. 1997. *Theories of International Regimes.* Cambridge: Cambridge University Press.

Headrick, D. R. 1991. *The Invisible Weapon: Telecommunications and International Politics, 1851–1945.* New York: Oxford University Press.

Heine, J. 2008. "On the Manner of Practising the New Diplomacy." In A. F. Cooper, B. Hocking, and W. Maley, eds., *Global Governance and Diplomacy: Worlds Apart?,* 271–87. Basingstoke: Palgrave Macmillan.

Hemmer, C., and P. Katzenstein. 2002. "Why Is There No NATO in Asia? Collective Identity, Regionalism, and the Origins of Multilateralism." *International Organization* 56 (3): 575–607.

Herodotus. 1925. *The Persian Wars,* transl. A. D. Godley, Vols I–IV, Loeb Classical Library. Cambridge, MA: Harvard University Press.

Herz, M., and J. P. Nogueira. 2002. *Ecuador vs Peru: Peacemaking Amid Rivalry.* Boulder, CO: Lynne Rienner.

Hill, C. 2005. "The Beijing Accord and the Future of the Six Party Talks." Briefing at United States Institute of Peace, Washington, DC, 28 September.

Hirschman, A. O. 1945. *National Power and the Structure of Foreign Trade,* 1980 expanded ed. Berkeley: University of California Press.

Hocking, B. 1999a. "Catalytic Diplomacy: Beyond 'Newness' and 'Decline.'" In J. Melissen, ed., *Innovation in Diplomatic Practice,* 21–42. Basingstoke: Palgrave.

———. ed. 1999b. *Foreign Ministries: Change and Adaptation.* Basingstoke: Macmillan.

———. 2008. "Reconfiguring Public Diplomacy: From Competition to Collaboration." In J. Welsh and D. Fearn, eds., *Engagement: Public Diplomacy in a Globalised World,* 62–75. London: Foreign and Commonwealth Office.

Hocking, B., and D. Spence, eds. 2005. *Foreign Ministries in the European Union: Integrating Diplomats*. Rev. ed. Basingstoke: Palgrave.

Holmes, J. A. 2009. "Where Are the Civilians? How to Rebuild the US Foreign Service." *Foreign Affairs* 88 (1): 148–60.

Holt, T. 2004. *The Deceivers: Allied Military Deception in the Second World War*. New York: Scribner.

Homans, G. C. 1961. *Social Behavior: Its Elementary Forms*. New York: Harcourt, Brace and World.

Hopmann, P. T. 1996. *The Negotiation Process and the Resolution of International Conflicts*. Columbia: University of South Carolina Press.

———. 2001. "Disintegrating States: Separating without Violence." In I. W. Zartman, ed., *Preventive Negotiation: Avoiding Conflict Escalation*, 113–64. Lanham, MD: Rowman & Littlefield.

Hopmann, P. T., and I. W. Zartman, eds. 2010. "Negotiating the Nagorno–Karabakh Conflict." *International Negotiation* 15 (1) special issue: 1–152.

HSRP (Human Security Report Project). 2008. *miniAtlas of Human Security*. Vancouver: Human Security Research Group and World Bank. www.hsrgroup.org/our-work/publications/miniatlas.aspx (accessed 16 December 2010).

Hu, J. 2003. "Hu Jintao zai jinian maozedong danchen 110 zhounian jinianhui shang de jianghua" [Hu Jintao's Speech at the Ceremony in Memory of Mao Zedong's 110 Birthday]. *People's Daily*, 27 December.

———. 2005. "Yushi jujin, jiwang kailai, gouzhuy yafei xinxing zhanlue guanxi" [Seize the Opportunity for All-round Cooperation and Common Development]. *People's Daily*, 22 April.

———. 2009. "Tongzhougongji, gongchaungweilai" [Building a Harmonious World of Sustained Peace and Common Prosperity]. *People's Daily*, 25 September.

Hu, Y. 1982. "Create a New Situation in All Fields of Socialist Modernization." In *The Twelfth National Congress of the CPC, September 1982*, 59. Beijing: Foreign Language Press.

Huan, G.-C. 1986. "Sino-Soviet Relations to the Year 2000: Implications for US Interests." Washington, DC: Atlantic Council of the United States.

Hudson, V. M., M. Caprioli, B. Ballif-Spanvill, R. McDermott, and C. F. Emmett. 2008. "The Heart of the Matter: The Security of Women and the Security of States." *International Security* 33 (3): 7–45.

Huijgh, E. 2010. "The Public Diplomacy of Federated Entities: Examining the Quebec Model." *Hague Journal of Diplomacy* 5 (1–2): 125–50.

Hulton, S. C. 2004. "Council Working Methods and Procedure." In D. M. Malone, ed., *The UN Security Council: From the Cold War to the 21st Century*, 237–51. Boulder, CO: Lynne Rienner.

Hurewitz, J. C. 1961. "Ottoman Diplomacy and the European State System." *Middle East Journal* 15 (2): 141–52.

Hutchinson, R. 2007. *Elizabeth's Spymaster: Francis Walsingham and the Secret War That Saved England*. London: Phoenix.

Hyman, G. 2010. "Foreign Policy and Development: Structure, Process, Policy, and the Drip-by-Drip Erosion of USAID." Washington, DC: Center for Strategic and International Studies.

ICISS (International Commission on Intervention and State Sovereignty). 2001. *The Responsibility to Protect: Report of the International Commission on Intervention and State Sovereignty*. Ottawa, ON: International Development Research Centre.

Ignatius, D. 2010. "Obama's Foreign Policy: Big Ideas, Little Implementation." *Washington Post*, 17 October.

Ikenberry, G. J. 2001. *After Victory: Institutions, Strategic Restraint, and the Rebuilding of Order after Major Wars*. Princeton, NJ: Princeton University Press.

——. 2003. "Is American Multilateralism in Decline?" *Perspectives on Politics* 1 (3): 533–50.

Ikenberry, G. J., and A.-M. Slaughter. 2006. "Forging a World of Liberty Under Law: US National Security in the 21st Century." Final Report of the Princeton Project on National Security. Princeton, NJ: Princeton Project on National Security.

Iklé, F. C. 1964. *How Nations Negotiate*. New York: Harper & Row.

IMF (International Monetary Fund). 2009. "World Economic Outlook Database." April. www.imf.org/external/pubs/ft/weo/2009/01/weodata/weoselgr.aspx (accessed 19 September 2011).

International Environmental Cooperation toward Sustainable Development. 2010. "East Asia Summit Environment Minters [sic] Meeting (EAS EMM)." www.env.go.jp/earth/coop/coop/english/dialogue/easemm.html (accessed 13 December 2010).

ISIS (International Security and Information Service). 1999. "Restructuring for Conflict Prevention and Management: EU Restructuring Conference Report and Comments." Brussels: ISIS, Europe.

Italian Ministry of Foreign Affairs. 2010. "Foreign Ministry Reform, Present Responses for Future Governance." www.esteri.it/MAE/EN/Sala_Stampa/ArchivioNotizie/Approfondimenti/2010/06/20100604_Riforma_Farnesina.htm (accessed 23 November 2010).

Jackson, R. H. 2007. *Sovereignty: Evolution of an Idea*. Cambridge: Polity Press.

Jakobson, L., and D. Knox. 2010. "New Foreign Policy Actors in China." SIPRI Policy Paper No 26. Stockholm: Stockholm International Peace Research Institute.

Japan Center for International Exchange. 2009. "Dialogue and Research Monitor 2008: Overview." Vol. 8 (January–December). Tokyo: Japan Center for International Exchange.

Jeffery, K. 2010. *MI6: The History of the Secret Intelligence Service 1909–1949*. London: Bloomsbury.

Jentleson, B. W., ed. 2000. *Opportunities Missed, Opportunities Seized: Preventive Diplomacy in the Post–Cold War World*. Lanham, MD: Rowman & Littlefield.

Jervis, R. 1976. *Perception and Misperception in International Politics*. Princeton, NJ: Princeton University Press.

——. 2010. *Why Intelligence Fails: Lessons from the Iranian Revolution and the Iraq War*. Ithaca, NY: Cornell University Press.

Jiang, Z. 2000. "Jiang zemin zai lianheguo qiannian shounao huiyishang fabiao jianghua" [Jiang Zemin Addresses the UN Millennium Summit]. *People's Daily*, 7 September.

——. 2002a. "Build a Well-Off Society in an All-Round Way and Create a New Situation in Building Socialism with Chinese Characteristics." 8 November. news.xinhuanet.com/english/2002-11/18/content_632532.htm (accessed 24 August 2011).

——. 2002b. "Jiang zemin zongshuji zai zhongyang dangxiao fabiao zhongyao jianghua" [Secretary General Jiang Zemin Delivers Important Talks at the Central Party School]. *People's Daily*, 31 May.

Job, B. 2003. "Track-Two Diplomacy: Ideational Contribution to the Evolving Asian Security Order." In M. Alagappa, ed., *Asian Security Order: Instrumental and Normative Features*, 241–79. Stanford, CA: Stanford University Press.

Johnson, A. 2010. "Public Diplomacy Critical in Information Age." gulfnews.com, 11 November, gulfnews.com/news/world/usa/public-diplomacy-critical-in-information-age-1.710512 (accessed 2 June 2011).

Johnson, L., and J. Wirtz, eds. 2007. *Strategic Intelligence: Windows into a Secret World: An Anthology*. 2nd ed. Los Angeles: Roxbury Publishing.

Johnston, A. I. 2008. *Social States: China in International Institutions, 1980–2000*. Princeton, NJ: Princeton University Press.

Jolly, R., L. Emmerij, and T. G. Weiss. 2009. *UN Ideas That Changed the World*. Bloomington: Indiana University Press.

Jonah, J. O. C. 2008. "Secretariat: Independence and Reform." In T. G. Weiss and S. Daws, eds., *The Oxford Handbook on the United Nations*, 160–74. Oxford: Oxford University Press.

Jones, P., and S. Kevill, comps. 1985. *China and the Soviet Union, 1949–84*. New York: Facts on File Publications.

Jönsson, C., and M. Hall. 2003. "Communication: An Essential Aspect of Diplomacy." *International Studies Perspectives* 4 (2): 195–210.

———. 2005. *Essence of Diplomacy*. Basingstoke: Palgrave Macmillan.

Kahler, M. 1992. "Multilateralism with Small and Large Numbers." *International Organization* 46 (3): 681–708.

Kahn, D. 1967. *The Codebreakers: The Story of Secret Writing*. New York: Macmillan.

Karns, M. P., and K. A. Mingst. 2004. *International Organizations: The Politics and Processes of Global Governance*. Boulder, CO: Lynne Rienner.

Kassim, H., B.G. Peters, and V. Wright, eds. 2000. *The National Co-ordination of EU Policy: The Domestic Level*. Oxford: Oxford University Press.

Kay, D. 1995. "Denial and Deception: The Lessons of Iraq." In R. Godson, E. R. May, and G. Schmitt, eds., *US Intelligence at the Crossroads: Agendas for Reform*, 109–27. Washington, DC: Brassey's.

Keens Soper, M. 1974. "The Liberal Pedigree of Diplomacy." Unpublished Paper. Cambridge: Butterfield Collection, Box 332, University Library.

Kellerhals, M. D., Jr. 2010. "United States Expanded Engagement at Five European Summits." Embassy of the United States, Brussels, Belgium, 9 December. www.uspolicy.be/headline/united-states-expanded-engagement-five-european-summits (accessed 2 June 2011).

Kelley, J. R. 2010. "The New Diplomacy: Evolution of a Revolution." *Diplomacy & Statecraft* 21 (2): 286–305.

Kennan, G. F. 1958. *Russia, the Atom and the West*. New York: Harper.

Kennedy, J. F. 1962. "Inaugural Address, January 20, 1961." *Public Papers of the Presidents of the United States, John F. Kennedy, Containing the Public Messages, Speeches, and Statements of the President, January 20 to December 31, 1961*, 1–3. Washington, DC: United States Government Printing Office.

Kennedy, R. F. 1971. *Thirteen Days: A Memoir of the Cuban Missile Crisis*. New York: W. W. Norton.

Keohane, R. O. 1984. *After Hegemony: Cooperation and Discord in the World Political Economy*. Princeton, NJ: Princeton University Press.

Keohane, R. O., and J. S. Nye, Jr. 1972. *Transnational Relations and World Politics*. Cambridge, MA: Harvard University Press.

———. 2002. "Governance in a Globalizing World." In R. O. Keohane, *Power and Governance in a Partially Globalized World*, 193–218. New York: Routledge.

Kerr, P. 2010. "Diplomatic Persuasion: An Under-investigated Process." *Hague Journal of Diplomacy* 5 (3): 235–61.

Kessler, G. 2005. "Rice Stays Close to Bush Policies in Hearing." *Washington Post,* 19 January.

Keukeleire, S., and J. MacNaughtan. 2008. *The Foreign Policy of the European Union.* Basingstoke: Palgrave Macmillan.

Khrushchev, N. 1970. *Khrushchev Remembers.* Boston: Little, Brown.

Kiesling, J. B. 2006. *Diplomacy Lessons: Realism for an Unloved Superpower.* Washington, DC: Potomac Books.

Kim, S. 1994. "China's International Organizational Behavior." In T. Robinson and D. Shambaugh, eds., *Chinese Foreign Policy: Theory and Practice,* 401–34. Oxford: Clarendon Press.

Kissinger, H. 1979. *White House Years.* Boston: Little, Brown.

———. 1994. *Diplomacy.* New York: Simon & Schuster.

Kjellén, B. 2008. *A New Diplomacy for Sustainable Development: The Challenge of Global Change.* New York: Routledge.

Klare, M. T., and D. C. Thomas, eds. 1994. *World Security: Challenges for a New Century.* 2nd ed. New York: St. Martin's Press.

Knaus, G., and F. Martin. 2003. "Travails of the European Raj." *Journal of Democracy* 14 (3): 60–74.

Knight, W. A. 2000. *A Changing UN: Multilateral Evolution and the Quest for Global Governance.* New York: Palgrave.

Komori, Y. 2009. "Regional Governance in East Asia and the Asia-Pacific." *East Asia: An International Quarterly* 26 (4): 321–41.

Kraft, H. J. S. 2000. "The Autonomy Dilemma of Track Two Diplomacy in Southeast Asia." *Security Dialogue* 31 (3): 343–56.

Krasno, J. E. 2004. "The UN Landscape: An Overview." In J. E. Krasno, ed., *The United Nations: Confronting the Challenges of a Global Society,* 3–18. Boulder, CO: Lynne Rienner.

Kurbalija, J. 2010. *An Introduction to Internet Governance.* 4th ed. Malta and Geneva: DiploFoundation. igbook.diplomacy.edu/ (accessed 4 February 2010).

Kurlantzick, J. 2007. *Charm Offensive: How China's Soft Power Is Transforming the World.* New Haven, CT: Yale University Press.

Lafont, B. 2001. "International Relations in the Ancient Near East: The Birth of a Complete Diplomatic System." *Diplomacy & Statecraft* 12 (1): 39–60.

Lagon, M. P. 1996. "Are 'Influentials' Less Influential? US Foreign Policy Elites in a Post–Cold War Information Age." *World Affairs* 158 (3): 124–35.

Lampton, D. 2001. "China's Foreign and National Security Policy-Making Process: Is It Changing, and Does It Matter?" in D. Lampton, ed., *The Making of China's Foreign and Security Policy Making in the Era of Reform,* 1–36. Stanford, CA: University of California Press.

Langhorne, R. 1996. "Who Are the Diplomats Now? Current Developments in Diplomatic Services." Wilton Park Papers 117. London: HMSO.

———. 1997. "Current Developments in Diplomacy: Who Are the Diplomats Now?" *Diplomacy & Statecraft* 8 (2): 1–15.

———. 2004a. *Diplomacy and Governance.* Moscow: M. Mgimo University.

———. 2004b. "The Regulation of Diplomatic Practice: The Beginnings to the Vienna Convention on Diplomatic Practice, 1961." In C. Jönsson and R. Langhorne, eds., *Diplomacy.* Vol. 2, *History of Diplomacy,* 315–33. London: Sage.

Lauren, P. G., ed. 1979. *Diplomacy: New Approaches in History, Theory, and Policy*. New York: Free Press.

Lee, A. D. 1991. "The Role of Hostages in Roman Diplomacy with Sasanian Persia." *Historia: Zeitschrift für Alte Geschichte* 40 (3): 366–74.

Lee, D., and D. Hudson. 2004. "The Old and New Significance of Political Economy in Diplomacy." *Review of International Studies* 30 (3): 343–60.

Lee, D., and N. Smith. 2008. "The Political Economy of Small African States in the WTO." *The Round Table* 97 (395): 259–71.

Lee, S. J., and J. Melissen, eds. 2011. *Public Diplomacy and Soft Power in East Asia*. Basingstoke: Palgrave Macmillan.

Lee, Y. W. 2011. "Soft Power as Productive Power." In S. J. Lee and J. Melissen,eds., *Public Diplomacy and Soft Power in East Asia*, 33–49. Basingstoke: Palgrave Macmillan.

Leguey-Feilleux, J.-R. 2009. *The Dynamics of Diplomacy*. Boulder, CO: Lynne Rienner.

Leigh-Phippard, H. 1999. "The Influence of Informal Groups in Multilateral Diplomacy." In J. Melissen, ed., *Innovation in Diplomatic Practice*, 94–110. Basingstoke: Palgrave.

Leira, H., and I. B. Neumann. 2006. "Fremmede konsuler i Norge ca. 1660–2005." *Historisk Tidsskrift* 106 (2): 449–87.

Lesaffer, R. 2000. "The Medieval Canon Law of Contract and Early Modern Treaty Law." *Journal of the History of International Law* 2 (2): 178–98.

Li, Z. 1994. *The Private Life of Chairman Mao: Memoirs of Mao's Personal Physician*. New York: Random House.

Lichtenstein, J. 2010. "Digital Diplomacy." *New York Times Magazine*, 16 July.

Lieberthal, K. 1984. "Domestic Politics and Foreign Policy." In H. Harding, ed., *China's Foreign Relations in the 1980s*, 43–70. New Haven, CT: Yale University Press.

Lippmann, W. 1958. "Mr. Kennan and Reappraisal in Europe." *Atlantic Monthly* 201 (4): 33–37. www.theatlantic.com/past/docs/issues/96jan/nato/lipp.htm (accessed 28 September 2011).

Lipson, C. 2005. *Reliable Partners: How Democracies Have Made a Separate Peace*. Princeton, NJ: Princeton University Press.

Lisbon Treaty. 2009. www.lisbon-treaty.org/wcm/the-lisbon-treaty.html (accessed 13 December 2010).

Litwak, R. 2000. *Rogue States and US Foreign Policy: Containment after the Cold War*. Washington, DC: Woodrow Wilson Center Press.

Liu, S. S. 1925. *Extraterritoriality: Its Rise and Its Decline*. New York: Columbia University.

Liu, X. 2001. *Chinese Ambassador: The Rise of Diplomatic Professionalism since 1949*. Hong Kong: Hong Kong University Press.

Lloyd, T. H. 1991. *England and the German Hanse, 1157–1611: A Study of Their Trade and Commercial Diplomacy*. Cambridge: Cambridge University Press.

Lobell, S. E., N. M. Ripsman, and J. W. Taliaferro, eds. 2009. *Neoclassical Realism, the State, and Foreign Policy*. Cambridge: Cambridge University Press.

Løse, L. G. 2001. "Communicative Action and the World of Diplomacy." In K. M. Fierke and K. E. Jørgensen, eds., *Constructing International Relations: The Next Generation*, 179–200. Armonk, NY: M. E. Sharpe.

Lu Y., J. Huang, D. Wang, Q. Zhou, C. Yang, and P. Xie, eds. 1997. *Waijiaoxue gailun* [Introduction to Diplomacy]. Beijing: World Affairs Press.

Luck, E. C. 1999. *Mixed Messages: American Politics and International Organization, 1919–1999*. Washington, DC: Brookings Institution Press.

———. 2006. *UN Security Council: Practice and Promise*. London: Routledge.

Lund, M. S. 1996. *Preventing Violent Conflicts: A Strategy for Preventive Diplomacy.* Washington, DC: United States Institute of Peace Press.

Lute, J. H., ed. 1997. *Preventing Deadly Conflict: Final Report.* Washington, DC: Carnegie Commission on Preventing Deadly Conflict.

Lyman, P. N. 2002. *Partner to History: The US Role in South Africa's Transition to Democracy.* Washington, DC: United States Institute of Peace Press.

Maastricht Treaty. 1992. www.eurotreaties.com/maastrichtec.pdf (accessed 13 December 2010).

MacMillan, M. 2007. *Nixon and Mao: The Week That Changed the World.* New York: Random House.

Maitland, A. 2010. "Job Sharing Diplomats Are a Model of Leadership." *Financial Times* (London), 27 September.

Malamud, A. 2003. "Presidentialism and Mercosur: A Hidden Cause for a Successful Experience." In F. Laursen, ed., *Comparative Regional Integration: Theoretical Perspectives*, 53–73. Aldershot: Ashgate.

———. 2005. "Presidential Diplomacy and the Institutional Underpinnings of Mercosur: An Empirical Examination." *Latin American Research Review* 40 (1): 138–64.

Maley, W. 2011. "Risk, Populism and the Evolution of Consular Responsibilities." In J. Melissen and A. M. Fernández, eds., *Consular Affairs and Diplomacy*, 43–62. Leiden: Martinus Nijhoff.

Maller, T. 2010. "Diplomacy Derailed: The Consequences of Diplomatic Sanctions." *Washington Quarterly* 33 (3): 61–79.

Mallett, M. 2001. "Italian Renaissance Diplomacy." *Diplomacy & Statecraft* 12 (1): 61–70.

Manheim, J. B. 1994. *Strategic Public Diplomacy and American Foreign Policy: The Evolution of Influence.* New York: Oxford University Press.

Manzenreiter, W. 2010. "The Beijing Games in the Western Imagination of China: The Weak Power of Soft Power." *Journal of Sport and Social Issues* 34 (1): 29–48.

Mao, Z. 1969. "On the People's Democratic Dictatorship." In *Selected Works of Mao Tse-tung.* Vol. 4. Beijing: Foreign Language Press.

MAR (Minorities at Risk Project). 2010. University of Maryland. www.cidcm.umd.edu/mar/ (accessed 16 December 2010).

March, J. G., and J. P. Olsen. 1989. *Rediscovering Institutions: The Organizational Basis of Politics.* New York: The Free Press.

———. 2006. "The Logic of Appropriateness." In M. Moran, M. Rein, and R. E. Goodin, eds., *The Oxford Handbook of Public Policy*, 689–708. Oxford: Oxford University Press.

Markey, D. 2009. "Developing India's Foreign Policy 'Software.'" *Asia Policy* 8 (1): 73–96.

Mattingly, G. 1955. *Renaissance Diplomacy.* London: Jonathan Cape.

Maundi, M. O., I. W. Zartman, G. M. Khadiagala, and K. Nuamah. 2006. *Getting In: Mediators' Entry into the Settlement of African Conflicts.* Washington, DC: United States Institute of Peace Press.

May, E. R., and P. D. Zelikow, eds. 1997. *The Kennedy Tapes: Inside the White House during the Cuban Missile Crisis.* Cambridge, MA: Belknap Press of Harvard University Press.

Mayer, A. J. 1959. *Political Origins of the New Diplomacy, 1917–1918.* New Haven, CT: Yale University Press.

Mazower, M. 2009. *No Enchanted Palace: The End of Empire and the Ideological Origins of the United Nations.* Princeton, NJ: Princeton University Press.

McGrew, A. 2008. "Globalization and Global Politics." In J. Baylis, S. Smith, and P. Owens, eds., *The Globalization of World Politics: An Introduction to International Relations*, 4th ed., 14–33. Oxford: Oxford University Press.

McIntosh, M., S. Waddock, and G. Kell, eds. 2004. *Learning to Talk: Corporate Citizenship and the Development of the UN Global Compact*. Sheffield: Greenleaf Publishing.

Mearsheimer, J. J. 1994/95. "The False Promise of International Institutions." *International Security* 19 (3): 5–49.

Meisler, S. 1995. *United Nations: The First Fifty Years*. New York: Atlantic Monthly Press.

Melissen, J., ed. 2005. *The New Public Diplomacy: Soft Power in International Relations*. Basingstoke: Palgrave Macmillan.

———. 2006. "Summit Diplomacy Coming of Age." Discussion Paper in Diplomacy. Clingendael: Netherlands Institute of International Relations.

Metzl, J. F. 2001. "Network Diplomacy." *Georgetown Journal of International Affairs* 2 (1): 77–87.

Millar, F. 1988. "Government and Diplomacy in the Roman Empire during the First Three Centuries." *International History Review* 10 (3): 345–77.

Ministry of Commerce, People's Republic of China. 2004. "Import and Export Volume since 1978," 10 March, zhs.mofcom.gov.cn/aarticle/Nocategory/200405/20040500218163. html (accessed 1 September 2011).

———. 2010. "December 2009 Summary of Import and Export," 15 January, zhs.mofcom. gov.cn/aarticle/Nocategory/201001/20100106747574.html (accessed 1 September 2011).

Mitrany, D. 1966. *A Working Peace System*. Chicago: Quadrangle Books.

MOFA (Ministry of Foreign Affairs), People's Republic of China. 2010. www.fmprc.gov.cn/chn/gxh/cgb/ (accessed 13 December 2010).

Montagu, E. 2001. *The Man Who Never Was: World War II's Boldest Counterintelligence Operation*. Annapolis, MD: Naval Institute Press.

Montalbano, E. 2010. "State Department Building Facebook Style Site." *Information Week Government*, 8 April. www.informationweek.com/news/government/enterprise-apps/showArticle.jhtml?articleID=224202306 (accessed 7 December 2010).

Montville, J. V. 1998. "Neve Shalom: A Model of Arab-Israeli Coexistence?" *Middle East Quarterly* 5 (4): 21–28. www.meforum.org/133/neve-shalom-a-model-of-arab-israeli-coexistence (accessed 21 March 2012).

———. ed. 1990. *Conflict and Peacemaking in Multiethnic Societies*. Lexington, MA: Lexington Books.

Mooradian, M., and D. Druckman. 1999. "Hurting Stalemate or Mediation? The Conflict Over Nagorno–Karabakh, 1990–95." *Journal of Peace Research* 36 (6): 709–27.

Morgenthau, H. J. 1948. *Politics among Nations: The Struggle for Power and Peace*. New York: Alfred A. Knopf.

Morrison, C. E. 2004. "Track 1/Track 2 Symbiosis in Asia-Pacific Regionalism." *Pacific Review* 17 (4): 547–65.

Mueller, S. L. 2009. "A Half Century of Citizen Diplomacy: A Unique Public–Private Sector Partnership." *Ambassadors Review*, (Fall): 46–50. www.ciaonet.org/journals/ambrev/ambrev627/f_0017770_15221.pdf (accessed 23 March 2012).

Müller, L. 2004. *Consuls, Corsairs, and Commerce: The Swedish Consular Service and Long-Distance Shipping, 1720–1815*. Uppsala: Studia Historica Upsaliensia.

Murphy, J. 2008. "Engagement." In J. Welsh and D. Fearn, eds., *Engagement: Public Diplomacy in a Globalised World*, 6–15. London: Foreign and Commonwealth Office.

Murray, S. 2008. "Consolidating the Gains Made in Diplomacy Studies: A Taxonomy." *International Studies Perspectives* 9 (1): 22–39.

Mutwol, J. 2009. *Peace Agreements and Civil Wars in Africa: Insurgent Motivations, State Responses, and Third-Party Peacemaking in Liberia, Rwanda, and Sierra Leone.* Amherst, NY: Cambria Press.

Naim, M. 2009. "Minilateralism: The Magic Number to Get Real International Action." *Foreign Policy* 173 (July/August): 136, 135.

NARA (National Archives and Records Administration). 2011. "Briefing Sheet on Electronic Records." Unclassified document. Washington, DC: Information Security and Oversight Office.

Nardin, T. 2009. "International Political Theory." In S. Burchill, A. Linklater, R. Devetak, J. Donnelly, T. Nardin, M. Paterson, C. Reus-Smit, and J. True, *Theories of International Relations*, 4th ed., 284–310. Basingstoke: Palgrave Macmillan.

Nathan, L. 2001. "Undue Pressure." In L. Reychler and T. Paffenholz, eds., *Peacebuilding: A Field Guide*, 184–98. Boulder, CO: Lynne Rienner.

National Security Act of 1947 [As Amended through PL 110–53, Enacted August 3, 2007]. intelligence.senate.gov/nsaact1947.pdf (accessed 8 December 2010).

"National Security Strategy." 2010. May. www.whitehouse.gov/sites/default/files/rss_viewer/national_security_strategy.pdf (accessed 23 September 2011).

NATO (North Atlantic Treaty Organization). 2010a. "NATO Adopts New Strategic Concept." Lisbon, 19 November. www.nato.int/strategic-concept/index.html (accessed 2 June 2011).

———. 2010b. "Presentation of the Recommendations of the Group of Experts on NATO's New Strategic Concept." Brussels, 17 May. www.nato.int/cps/en/natolive/events_63395.htm (accessed 2 June 2011).

Nelson, M. F. 1945. *Korea and the Old Orders in Eastern Asia.* Baton Rouge: Louisiana State University Press.

Neumann, I. B. 2003. "The English School on Diplomacy: Scholarly Promise Unfulfilled." *International Relations* 17 (3): 341–69.

———. 2005. "To Be a Diplomat." *International Studies Perspectives* 6 (1): 72–93.

———. 2010. "Sustainability and Transformation in Diplomatic Culture: The Case of Eurocentrism." In C. M. Constantinou and J. Der Derian, eds., *Sustainable Diplomacies*, 128–47. Basingstoke: Palgrave Macmillan.

Newsom, D. D. 1989. "The New Diplomatic Agenda: Are Governments Ready?" *International Affairs* 65 (1): 29–41.

Nicol, D. M. 1988. *Byzantium and Venice: A Study in Diplomatic and Cultural Relations.* Cambridge: Cambridge University Press.

Nicolson, H. 1939. *Diplomacy.* London: Thornton Butterworth.

———. 1946. *The Congress of Vienna: A Study in Allied Unity, 1812–1822.* London: Constable.

———. 1954. *The Evolution of Diplomatic Method.* Oxford: Oxford University Press.

———. 1963. *Diplomacy.* 3rd ed. London: Oxford University Press.

Norwegian Nobel Committee. 2009. "The Nobel Peace Prize 2009." Press Release, Nobelprize.org, 9 October, nobelprize.org/nobel_prizes/peace/laureates/2009/press.html (accessed 2 June 2011).

Numelin, R. J. 1950. *The Beginnings of Diplomacy: A Sociological Study of Intertribal and International Relations.* London: Oxford University Press.

Nye, J. S., Jr. 1990. *Bound to Lead: The Changing Nature of American Power.* New York: Basic Books.

——. 2002. *The Paradox of American Power: Why the World's Superpower Can't Go It Alone*. Oxford: Oxford University Press.

——. 2004. *Soft Power: The Means to Success in World Politics*. New York: PublicAffairs.

——. 2008a. "Foreword." In Y. Watanabe and D. L. McConnell, eds., *Soft Power Superpowers: Cultural and National Assets of Japan and the United States*, ix–xiv. Armonk, NY: M. E. Sharpe.

——. 2008b. "Public Diplomacy and Soft Power." *Annals of the American Academy of Social and Political Science* 616 (March): 94–109.

——. 2010. "Responding to My Critics and Concluding Thoughts." In I. Parmar and M. Cox, eds., *Soft Power and US Foreign Policy: Theoretical, Historical and Contemporary Perspectives*, 215–27. New York: Routledge.

——. 2011. *The Future of Power*. New York: PublicAffairs.

Obolensky, D. 1963. "The Principles and Methods of Byzantine Diplomacy." *Actes Du XIIe Congrès International d'Études Byzantines*, 1:45–61. Belgrade: Comité Yougoslave des Études Byzantines.

O'Brien, P. K., and G. A. Pigman. 1992. "Free Trade, British Hegemony and the International Economic Order in the Nineteenth Century." *Review of International Studies* 18 (2): 89–113.

O'Brien, R., A. M. Goetz, J. A. Scholte, and M. Williams, eds. 2000. *Contesting Global Governance: Multilateral Economic Institutions and Global Social Movements*. Cambridge: Cambridge University Press.

Odell, J. 2000. *Negotiating the World Economy*. Ithaca, NY: Cornell University Press.

Okano-Heijmans, M. 2011a. "Changes in Consular Assistance and the Emergence of Consular Diplomacy." In J. Melissen and A. M. Fernández, eds., *Consular Affairs and Diplomacy*, 21–41. Leiden: Martinus Nijhoff.

——. 2011b. "Conceptualizing Economic Diplomacy." In P. A. G. van Bergeijk, M. Okano-Heijmans, and J. Melissen, eds., *Economic Diplomacy: Economic and Political Perspectives*, 7–36. Leiden: Martinus Nijhoff.

Oksenberg, M. 1980. "China Policy for the 1980s." *Foreign Affairs* 59 (2): 304–22.

——. 1982. "A Decade of Sino-American Relations." *Foreign Affairs* 61 (1): 175–95.

Oliver, A. and A. Shearer. 2011. "Diplomatic Disrepair: Rebuilding Australia's International Policy Infrastructure." Sydney: Lowy Institute for International Policy, August.

O'Neill, J., and A. Stupnytska. 2009. "The Long-Term Outlook for the BRICs and N-11 Post Crisis." Global Economics Paper 192. London: Goldman Sachs Group.

Osborne, R. 2008. *The World of Athens: An Introduction to Classical Athenian Culture*. 2nd ed. Cambridge: Cambridge University Press.

Osgood, K. A., and B. C. Etheridge, eds. 2010. *The United States and Public Diplomacy: New Directions in Cultural and International History*. Leiden: Martinus Nijhoff.

Oxford English Dictionary. 1933. Oxford: Clarendon Press.

Packer, G. 2009. "The Last Mission: Richard Holbrooke's Plan to Avoid the Mistakes of Vietnam in Afghanistan." *New Yorker*, 28 September, 38–55.

Page, B. I., and T. Xie. 2011. "The Complexities of Economic Soft Power: The US–China Case." In S. J. Lee and J. Melissen, eds., *Public Diplomacy and Soft Power in East Asia*, 223–46. New York: Palgrave Macmillan.

Pahlavi, P. C. 2007. "Evaluating Public Diplomacy Programmes." *Hague Journal of Diplomacy* 2 (3): 255–81.

Patrick, S. 2009. *The Best Laid Plans: The Origins of American Multilateralism and the Dawn of the Cold War*. Lanham, MD: Rowman & Littlefield.

Peck, C. 2004. "Special Representatives of the Secretary-General." In D. M. Malone, ed., *The UN Security Council: From the Cold War to the 21st Century*, 325–39. Boulder, CO: Lynne Rienner.

Peña, F. 2005. "Understanding Mercosur and Its Future." Jean Monnet/Robert Schuman Paper Series 5(14). Coral Gables, FL: Miami European Union Center, University of Miami.

People's Daily Online. 2009. "China to See Large Rise of Contributions to UN Budget in New Year." 30 December, english.peopledaily.com.cn/90001/90776/90883/6855482.html (accessed 9 December 2010).

Peterson, M. J. 2006. *The UN General Assembly.* London: Routledge.

Pigman, G. A. 1997. "Hegemony and Trade Liberalization Policy: Britain and the Brussels Sugar Convention of 1902." *Review of International Studies* 23 (2): 185–210.

———. 2010. *Contemporary Diplomacy: Representation and Communication in a Globalized World.* Cambridge: Polity Press.

Platt, D. C. M. 1971. *The Cinderella Service: British Consuls since 1825.* London: Longman.

———. 1972. *Finance, Trade and Politics in British Foreign Policy, 1815–1914.* Oxford: Clarendon Press.

Plischke, E. 1990. *Diplomat in Chief,* Chinese ed. Beijing: World Affairs Press.

Potter, E. H. 2009. *Branding Canada: Projecting Canada's Soft Power through Public Diplomacy.* Montreal: McGill-Queen's University Press.

Potter, P. B. 1926. "The Future of the Consular Office." *American Political Science Review* 20 (2): 284–98.

Pouliot, V. 2011. "Multilateralism as an End in Itself." *International Studies Perspectives* 12 (1): 18–26.

Powell, R. 1991. "Absolute and Relative Gains in International Relations Theory." *American Political Science Review* 85 (4): 1303–20.

Prantl, J., and J. E. Krasno. 2004. "Informal Groups of Member States." In J. E. Krasno, ed., *The United Nations: Confronting the Challenges of a Global Society*, 311–57. Boulder, CO: Lynne Rienner.

Priest, D., and W. Arkin. 2010. "A Hidden World, Growing Beyond Control." *Washington Post*, 19 July.

Public Diplomacy Alumni Association. 2008. "What Is Public Diplomacy?" www.publicdiplomacy.org/1.htm (accessed 24 September 2010).

Putnam, R. D. 1988. "Diplomacy and Domestic Politics: The Logic of Two-Level Games." *International Organization* 42 (3): 427–60.

Qu, X. 1994. "Shilun dong'ou jubian he sulian jieti hou de zhongguo duiwai zhengce" [Chinese Foreign Policy after the Catalytic Changes in East Europe and the Disintegration of the Soviet Union]. *Waijiao xueyuan xuebao* [Journal of Foreign Affairs College], 4: 16–22.

Queller, D. E. 1967. *The Office of Ambassador in the Middle Ages.* Princeton, NJ: Princeton University Press.

Quinn, A. 2011. "The Art of Declining Politely: Obama's Prudent Presidency and the Waning of American Power." *International Affairs* 87 (4): 803–24.

Ralston, J. H. 1929. *International Arbitration, from Athens to Locarno.* Stanford, CA: Stanford University Press.

Ramcharan, B. G. 2008. *Preventive Diplomacy at the UN.* Bloomington: Indiana University Press.

Rana, K. 2011. "Serving the Private Sector: India's Experience in Context." In N. Bayne and S. Woolcock, eds., *The New Economic Diplomacy: Decision-Making and Negotiation in International Economic Relations*, 93–112. 3rd ed. Burlington, VT: Ashgate.

Rana, K. S. 2002. *Inside Diplomacy*. New Delhi: Manas Publications.

———. 2005. *The 21st Century Ambassador: Plenipotentiary to Chief Executive*. New Delhi: Oxford University Press.

———. 2007a. *Asian Diplomacy: The Foreign Ministries of China, India, Japan, Singapore and Thailand*. Malta and Geneva: DiploFoundation.

———. 2007b. "MFA Reform: Global Trends." In K. S. Rana and J. Kurbalija, eds., *Foreign Ministries: Managing Diplomatic Networks and Optimizing Value*, 20–43. Malta and Geneva: DiploFoundation.

Rathus, J. 2010. "Japan's Foreign Ministry Reforms: Shifting Priorities?" *East Asia Forum*, 4 September.

Reiterer, M. 2006. "Interregionalism as a New Diplomatic Tool: The EU and East Asia." *European Foreign Affairs Review* 11 (2): 223–43.

Rice, C. 2006. "Remarks at Georgetown School of Foreign Service." Georgetown University, Washington, DC, 18 January. www.unc.edu/depts/diplomat/item/2006/0103/rice/rice_georgetown.html (accessed 2 June 2011).

Richards, P. 2010. "Caribbean Leaders Inch Forward on Regional Integration." CARIBARENA Dominica, 9 July. www.caribarena.com/dominica/caribbean/regional/7371-caribbean-leaders-inch-forward-on-regional-integration.html (accessed 22 September 2011).

Richardson, L. 2006. *What Terrorists Want: Understanding the Terrorist Threat*. London: John Murray.

Riordan, S. 2003. *The New Diplomacy*. Cambridge: Polity Press.

Risse-Kappen, T. 1995. *Cooperation among Democracies: The European Influence on US Foreign Policy*. Princeton, NJ: Princeton University Press.

Roberts, A., and B. Kingsbury, eds. 1993. *United Nations, Divided World: The UN's Roles in International Relations*. 2nd ed. Oxford: Clarendon Press.

Roberts, I., ed. 2011. *Satow's Diplomatic Practice*, 6th ed. Oxford: Oxford University Press.

Robinson, M. 2008. "Hybrid States: Globalisation and the Politics of State Capacity." *Political Studies* 56 (3): 566–83.

Romita, P., N. Chowdhury Fink, and T. Papenfuss. 2011. "What Impact? The E10 and the 2011 Security Council." International Peace Institute Issue Brief. New York: International Peace Institute, March.

Rosen, E. 2010. "Taking Collaborative Risk at the State Department." The Culture of Collaboration blog, 14 September, collaborationblog.typepad.com/collaboration/government (accessed 6 December 2010).

Rosenau, J. N. 1990. *Turbulence in World Politics: A Theory of Change and Continuity*. Princeton, NJ: Princeton University Press.

Rosenau, J. N., and E.-O. Czempiel, eds. 1992. *Governance without Government: Order and Change in World Politics*. Cambridge: Cambridge University Press.

Rosenthal, G. 2008. "Economic and Social Council." In T. G. Weiss and S. Daws, eds., *The Oxford Handbook on the United Nations*, 136–48. Oxford: Oxford University Press.

Ross, C. 2007. *Independent Diplomat: Dispatches from an Unaccountable Elite*. Ithaca, NY: Cornell University Press.

Rubin, J. Z., ed. 1981. *Dynamics of Third Party Intervention: Kissinger in the Middle East*. New York: Praeger.

Rudd, K. 2010. "The Future of the Australian Foreign Service." Canberra, 18 November. www.foreignminister.gov.au/speeches/2010/kr_sp_101118.html (accessed 14 October 2011).

Ruggie, J. G. 1982. "International Regimes, Transactions, and Change: Embedded Liberalism in the Postwar Economic Order." *International Organization* 36 (2): 379–415.

———. ed. 1993. *Multilateralism Matters: The Theory and Praxis of an Institutional Form.* New York: Columbia University Press.

———. 1994. "Third Try at World Order? America and Multilateralism after the Cold War." *Political Science Quarterly* 109 (3): 553–70.

———. 1997. "The Past as Prologue? Interests, Identity, and American Foreign Policy." *International Security* 21 (4): 89–125.

Rüland, J. 2001. "ASEAN and the European Union: A Bumpy Interregional Relationship." ZEI Discussion Paper C95. Bonn: Centre for European Integration Studies, University of Bonn. aei.pitt.edu/archive/00000197/ (accessed 13 December 2010).

Rumbold, H. 1902. *Recollections of a Diplomatist.* London: E. Arnold.

Sanger, D. E. 2010. "Cables Depict Range of Obama Diplomacy." *New York Times,* 4 December.

Satow, E. 1922. *A Guide to Diplomatic Practice.* London: Longmans, Green.

———. 1979. *Satow's Guide to Diplomatic Practice.* Edited by Lord Gore Booth. 5th ed. London: Longman.

Saunders, H. H. 1999. *A Public Peace Process: Sustained Dialogue to Transform Racial and Ethnic Conflicts.* New York: St. Martin's Press.

Schelling, T. C. 1966. *Arms and Influence.* New Haven, CT: Yale University Press.

Schlesinger, S. C. 2003. *Act of Creation: The Founding of the United Nations: A Story of Superpowers, Secret Agents, Wartime Allies and Enemies, and Their Quest for a Peaceful World.* Boulder, CO: Westview Press.

Sebenius, J. K. 1983. "Negotiation Arithmetic: Adding and Subtracting Issues and Parties." *International Organization* 37 (2): 281–316.

———. 1984. *Negotiating the Law of the Sea.* Cambridge, MA: Harvard University Press.

Seib, P. 2008. *The Al Jazeera Effect: How the New Global Media Are Reshaping World Politics.* Washington, DC: Potomac Books.

———. ed. 2009. *Toward a New Public Diplomacy: Redirecting US Foreign Policy.* New York: Palgrave Macmillan.

Sharlach, T. M. 2005. "Diplomacy and the Rituals of Politics at the Ur III Court." *Journal of Cuneiform Studies* 57: 17–29.

Sharp, P. 1999. "For Diplomacy: Representation and the Study of International Relations." *International Studies Review* 1 (1): 35–57.

———. 2005. "Revolutionary States, Outlaw Regimes and the Techniques of Public Diplomacy." In J. Melissen, ed., *The New Public Diplomacy: Soft Power in International Relations,* 106–23. Basingstoke: Palgrave Macmillan.

———. 2009. *Diplomatic Theory of International Relations.* Cambridge: Cambridge University Press.

———. 2011. "Diplomats, Diplomacy, Diplomatic Studies, and the Future of International Relations and International Studies." *International Studies Review* 13 (4): 695–98.

Sharp, P., and G. Wiseman. 2007. "Conclusion: The Diplomatic Corps' Role in Constituting International Society." In P. Sharp and G. Wiseman, eds., *The Diplomatic Corps as an Institution of International Society,* 265–77. Basingstoke: Palgrave Macmillan.

———. 2012. "Conclusion." In P. Sharp and G. Wiseman, eds., *American Diplomacy,* 223–28. Leiden: Martinus Nijhoff Publishers.

Shehadi, K. S. 1993. "Ethnic Self-Determination and the Break-up of States." Adelphi Paper 283. London: Brassey's for International Institute for Strategic Studies.

Shulsky, A. 1995. "What Is Intelligence? Secrets and Competition among States." In R. Godson, E. R. May, and G. Schmitt, eds., *US Intelligence at the Crossroads: Agendas for Reform*, 17–27. Washington, DC: Brassey's.

Simmons, B. A. 1999. "Territorial Disputes and Their Resolution: The Case of Ecuador and Peru." Peaceworks 27. Washington, DC: United States Institute of Peace.

Sims, J. E. 1995. "What Is Intelligence? Information for Decision Makers." In R. Godson, E. R. May, and G. Schmitt, eds., *US Intelligence at the Crossroads: Agendas for Reform*, 3–16. Washington, DC: Brassey's.

———. 2006. "Foreign Intelligence Liaison: Devils, Deals, and Details." *International Journal of Intelligence and Counterintelligence* 19 (2): 195–217.

———. 2007. "Intelligence to Counter Terror: The Importance of All-Source Fusion." In L. K. Johnson, ed., *Strategic Intelligence*. Vol. 4, *Counterintelligence and Counterterrorism: Defending the Nation against Hostile Forces*, 139–56. Westport, CT: Praeger Security International.

———. 2009a. "Defending Adaptive Realism: Intelligence Theory Comes of Age." In P. Gill, S. Marrin, and M. Pythian, eds., *Intelligence Theory: Key Questions and Debates*, 151–65. New York: Routledge.

———. 2009b. "A Theory of Intelligence and International Politics." In G. F. Treverton and W. Agrell, eds., *National Intelligence Systems: Current Research and Future Prospects*, 58–92. New York: Cambridge University Press.

Singer, J. D. 1961. "The Level-of-Analysis Problem in International Relations." *World Politics* 14 (1): 77–92.

Slaughter, A.-M. 2004. *A New World Order*. Princeton, NJ: Princeton University Press.

———. 2009. "America's Edge: Power in the Networked Century." *Foreign Affairs* 88 (1): 94–113.

Smith, M. 2004. "Foreign Economic Policy." In W. Carlsnaes, H. Sjursen, and B. White, eds., *Contemporary European Foreign Policy*, 75–90. London: Sage.

Smythe, E., and P. J. Smith. 2002. "New Technologies and Networks of Resistance." In E. H. Potter, ed., *Cyber-Diplomacy: Managing Foreign Policy in the Twenty-First Century*, 48–82. Montreal: McGill-Queen's University Press.

Snider, L. B. 2005. "Congressional Oversight of Intelligence after September 11." In J. E. Sims and B. Gerber, eds., *Transforming US Intelligence*, 239–58. Washington, DC: Georgetown University Press.

Snow, N., and P. M. Taylor. 2009. *Routledge Handbook of Public Diplomacy*. New York: Routledge.

Snyder, G. H., and P. Diesing. 1977. *Conflict among Nations: Bargaining, Decision Making, and System Structure in International Crises*. Princeton, NJ: Princeton University Press.

So, A. Y., and S. W. K. Chiu. 1995. *East Asia and the World Economy*. Thousand Oaks, CA: Sage.

Solomon, R. H. 1981. "The China Factor in America's Foreign Relations: Perceptions and Policy Choices." In R. H. Solomon, ed., *The China Factor: Sino-American Relations and the Global Scene*, 1–47. Englewood Cliffs, NJ: Prentice-Hall.

Solomon, R. H., and N. Quinney, eds. 2010. *American Negotiating Behavior: Wheeler-Dealers, Legal Eagles, Bullies, and Preachers*. Washington, DC: United States Institute of Peace.

Soobramanien, T. 2011. "Economic Diplomacy for Small and Low Income Countries." In N. Bayne and S. Woolcock, eds., *The New Economic Diplomacy: Decision-Making and Negotiation in International Economic Relations*, 187–204. 3rd ed. Burlington, VT: Ashgate.

Spector, B. I., and I. W. Zartman, eds. 2003. *Getting It Done: Postagreement Negotiation and International Regimes*. Washington, DC: United States Institute of Peace Press.

Starovoitova, G. 1997. "National Self-Determination: Approaches and Case Studies." Occasional Paper 27. Providence, RI: Watson Institute of International Affairs, Brown University.

State Council Information Office of the People's Republic of China. 1998. *China National Defense, 1998*. www.scio.gov.cn/zfbps/gfbps/1998/200905/t308295.htm (accessed 13 December 2010).

———. 2010. www.scio.gov.cn/xwbjs/xwbjs/200905/t306817.htm (accessed 13 December 2010).

Stearns, M. 1996. *Talking to Strangers: Improving American Diplomacy at Home and Abroad*. Princeton, NJ: Princeton University Press.

Steiger, H. 2001. "From the International Law of Christianity to the International Law of the World Citizen: Reflections on the Formation of the Epochs of the History of International Law." *Journal of the History of International Law* 3 (2): 180–93.

Steiner, Z., ed. 1982. *The Times Survey of Foreign Ministries of the World*. London: Times Books.

Stevenson, W. 1976. *A Man Called Intrepid: The Secret War*. London: Macmillan.

Stone Sweet, A., and W. Sandholtz. 1998. "Integration, Supranational Governance, and the Institutionalization of the European Polity." In W. Sandholtz and A. Stone Sweet, eds., *European Integration and Supranational Governance*, 1–26. Oxford: Oxford University Press.

Strange, S. 1994. *States and Markets*. 2nd ed. London: Pinter Publishers.

Stringer, K. D. 2011. "Honorary Consuls in an Era of Globalization, Trade and Investment." In J. Melissen and A. M. Fernández, eds., *Consular Affairs and Diplomacy*, 63–96. Leiden: Martinus Nijhoff.

Su, C. 1989. "Sino-Soviet Relations of the 1980s: From Confrontation to Conciliation." In S. Kim, ed., *China and the World: New Directions in Chinese Foreign Relations*, 148–78. 2nd ed. Boulder, CO: Westview Press.

Suettinger, R. L. 2004. "The Rise and Descent of 'Peaceful Rise.'" *China Leadership Monitor* 12 (Fall): 1–12.

Suzuki, S. 2009. "Chinese Soft Power, Insecurity Studies, Myopia and Fantasy." *Third World Quarterly* 30 (4): 779–93.

Swedish Foreign Ministry. 1997. "Strategi för konfliktförebyggande og konflikthantering." Ds 1997:18. Stockholm: Swedish Foreign Ministry.

———. 1999. "Preventing Violent Conflict: A Swedish Action Plan." Ds 1999:24. Stockholm: Swedish Foreign Ministry.

Talbott, S. 2002. *The Russia Hand: A Memoir of Presidential Diplomacy*. New York: Random House.

———. 2004. *Engaging India: Diplomacy, Democracy, and the Bomb*. Washington, DC: Brookings Institution Press.

Tang, J. 2004. "Buduan tigao yingdui guojijueshi he chuli guoji shiwu de nengli" [Increasing Upgrade Our Capability in Coping with International Situation and Managing International Affairs]. *Seeking Truth* 23: 43–46.

Tarrow, S. G. 2005. *The New Transnational Activism*. Cambridge: Cambridge University Press.

Taylor, P. M. 2010. "Public Diplomacy on Trial?" in A. Fisher and S. Lucas, eds., *The Trials of Engagement: The Future of US Public Diplomacy*, 19–31. Leiden: Martinus Nijhoff.

Thakur, R. 2002. "Security in the New Millennium." In A. F. Cooper, J. English, and R. Thakur, eds., *Enhancing Global Governance: Towards a New Diplomacy?*, 268–86. Tokyo: United Nations University Press.

——. 2008. "Humanitarian Intervention." In T. G. Weiss and S. Daws, eds., *The Oxford Handbook on the United Nations*, 387–403. Oxford: Oxford University Press.

Thompson, W. S., and I. W. Zartman. 1975. "The Development of Norms in the African System." In Y. El-Ayouty, ed., *The Organization of African Unity after Ten Years: Comparative Perspectives*, 3–24. New York: Praeger.

Thrall, A. T., J. Lollio-Fakhreddine, J. Berent, L. Donnelly, W. Herrin, Z. Paquette, R. Wenglinski, and A. Wyatt. 2008. "Star Power: Celebrity Advocacy and the Evolution of the Public Sphere." *International Journal of Press/Politics* 13 (4): 362–85.

Tilley, J., and S. Gaselee. 1933. *The Foreign Office*. London: G. P. Putnam's Sons.

Toft, M. D. 2010. *Securing the Peace: The Durable Settlement of Civil Wars*. Princeton, NJ: Princeton University Press.

Touval, S. 1982. *The Peace Brokers: Mediators in the Arab-Israeli Conflict, 1948–1979*. Princeton, NJ: Princeton University Press.

Tow, W. T. 1991. *Encountering the Dominant Player: US Extended Deterrence Strategy in the Asia-Pacific*. New York: Columbia University Press.

Traub, J. 1998. "Kofi Annan's Next Test." *New York Times Magazine*, 29 March.

——. 2006. *The Best Intentions: Kofi Annan and the UN in the Era of American World Power*. New York: Farrar, Straus and Giroux.

Trotsky, L. 1930. *My Life*. www.marxists.org/archive/trotsky/1930/mylife/ch29.htm (accessed 14 September 2011).

Tuchman, B. 1985. *The March of Folly: From Troy to Vietnam*. New York: Ballantine Books.

UCDP (Uppsala Conflict Data Project). 2010. Uppsala University. www.pcr.uu.se/research/UCDP (accessed 16 December 2010).

Ulbert, J. 2006. "Introduction: La function consulaire à l'epoque moderne: definition, état des connaissances et perspectives de recherche." In J. Ulbert and G. Le Bouëdec, eds., *La fonction consulaire à l'époque moderne: L'Affirmation d'une institution économique et politique (1500–1800)*, 9–20. Rennes: Presses Universitaires de Rennes.

UNDP (United Nations Development Programme). 1994. *Human Development Report 1994*. Oxford: Oxford University Press.

UNIC (United Nations Information Centres). 2008. unic.un.org/aroundworld/unics/en/index.asp (accessed 22 September 2011).

United Nations. 2005. "Vienna Convention on Consular Relations, 1963." untreaty.un.org/ilc/texts/instruments/english/conventions/9_2_1963.pdf (accessed 30 November 2010).

——. 2006. "Delivering as One." Report of the Secretary-General's High-Level Panel. New York: United Nations, November.

United States Senate Select Committee on Intelligence. 1996. "US Actions Regarding Iranian and Other Arms Transfers to the Bosnian Army, 1994–1995." Report of the Select Committee on Intelligence, United States Senate, together with additional views. November. www.fas.org/irp/congress/1996_rpt/bosnia.htm (accessed 8 December 2010).

Urquhart, B. 1984. *Hammarskjold*. New York: Harper and Row.

——. 1995. "Selecting the World's CEO: Remembering the Secretaries-General." *Foreign Affairs* 74 (3): 21–26.

USC Annenberg Center on Public Diplomacy. 2011. "What Is Public Diplomacy?" uscpublicdiplomacy.org/index.php/about/what_is_pd/ (accessed 13 October 2011).

US Department of State. 2010. "Secretary Clinton Delivers Remarks to the Press on the Release of Confidential Documents." DipNote: US Department of State Official Blog, 29 November, blogs.state.gov/index.php/site/entry/clinton_statement_2010_11_29 (accessed 2 June 2011).

US Department of State/US Agency for International Development. 2010. *Leading through Civilian Power: The First Quadrennial Diplomacy and Development Review.* www.state.gov/s/dmr/qddr/ (accessed 25 June 2011).

Vamosi, R. 2007. "Newsmaker: Cyberattack in Estonia—What It Really Means." 29 May, news.cnet.com/2008-7349_3-6186751.html (accessed 30 August 2010).

van Doeveren, R. 2011. "Customizing the New Public Diplomacy." Paper presented at the workshop "European Public Diplomacy: Soft Power at Work," 23–24 June, Netherlands Institute of International Relations "Clingendael," The Hague.

van Ham, P. 2010. *Social Power in International Politics.* New York: Routledge.

Viotti, P. R., and M. V. Kauppi. 1998. *International Relations Theory: Realism, Pluralism, Globalism.* Upper Saddle River, NJ: Prentice Hall.

Waijiaobu Yanjiushi [Research Office of Chinese Ministry of Foreign Affairs]. 1960. *Zhongmei Guanxi Wenjian Huibian* [Collected Documents on Sino-US Relations]. Beijing: Shejie Zhishi Chuban She.

Wallensteen, P., and P. Johansson. 2004. "Security Council Decisions in Perspective." In D. M. Malone, ed., *The UN Security Council: From the Cold War to the 21st Century,* 17–33. Boulder, CO: Lynne Rienner.

Walter, B. F. 2002. *Committing to Peace: The Successful Settlement of Civil Wars.* Princeton, NJ: Princeton University Press.

Waltz, K. N. 1979. *Theory of International Politics.* Reading, MA: Addison Wesley.

Wang, J. 2009. "Through the 2008 Olympics Looking Glass: What Beijing Taught the Chinese People about Themselves." *Public Diplomacy Magazine* 1 (Winter): 73–75.

Wapner, P. 2008. "Civil Society." In T. G. Weiss and S. Daws, eds., *The Oxford Handbook on the United Nations,* 254–63. Oxford: Oxford University Press.

Watson, A. 1982. *Diplomacy: The Dialogue between States.* London: Eyre Methuen.

Watt, N. 2004. "Straw Pokes Fun at EU 'Odd Bods.'" *Guardian,* 26 May.

Wei, S. 1994. "Ni kesong zhongtong fanghua" [The Visit to China by President Nixon]. In Waijiaobu Waijiaoshi Yanjiushi [Diplomatic History Research Office, the Ministry of Foreign Affairs], ed., *Xinzhongguo waijiao fengyun: Zhongguo waijiaoguan huiyilu* [Diplomatic Winds and Clouds of New China: Memoirs of the Chinese Diplomats], 77–93. Beijing: Shijie Zhishi Chuban She.

Weinfeld, M. 1973. "Covenant Terminology in the Ancient Near East and Its Influence on the West." *Journal of the American Oriental Society* 93 (2): 190–99.

Weiss, T. G. 2009. *What's Wrong with the United Nations and How to Fix It.* Cambridge: Polity Press.

Wellman, D. J. 2004. *Sustainable Diplomacy: Ecology, Religion and Ethics in Muslim–Christian Relations.* New York: Palgrave Macmillan.

Welsh, J. M. 2008. "The Security Council and Humanitarian Intervention." In V. Lowe, A. Roberts, J. Welsh, and D. Zaum, eds., *The United Nations Security Council and War: The Evolution of Thought and Practice since 1945,* 535–62. New York: Oxford University Press.

Wen, J. 2003. "Ba muguang touxiang zhongguo" [Turn Your Attention to China]. *People's Daily*, 11 December.

———. 2007. "Shehui zhuyi chuji jieduan women de lishi renwu he ruogan zhongguo wai-jiao zhengce de wenti" [Our Historical Tasks in the Primary Stage of Socialism and Several Issues Concerning China's Foreign Policy]. *People's Daily*, 27 February.

———. 2010. "Renshi yige zhenshi de zhongguo" [Getting to Know a True China]. *People's Daily*, 25 September.

Wendt, A. 1999. *Social Theory of International Politics*. Cambridge: Cambridge University Press.

Wesseling, M., and J. Boniface. 2011. "New Trends in European Consular Services: Visa Policy in the EU Neighbourhood." In J. Melissen and A. M. Fernández, eds., *Consular Affairs and Diplomacy*, 115–42. Leiden: Martinus Nijhoff.

White, H. 2010. "Power Shift: Australia's Future between Washington and Beijing." *Quarterly Essay* 39: 1–74.

Wight, M. 1979. *Power Politics*. Harmondsworth: Penguin.

———. 1991. *International Theory: The Three Traditions*. Edited by G. Wight and B. Porter. Leicester: Leicester University Press for the Royal Institute of International Affairs.

Wilde, R. 2008. "Trusteeship Council." In T. G. Weiss and S. Daws, eds., *The Oxford Handbook on the United Nations*, 149–59. Oxford: Oxford University Press.

Willetts, P. 2000. "From 'Consultative Arrangements' to 'Partnership': The Changing Status of NGOs in Diplomacy at the UN." *Global Governance* 6 (2): 191–212.

Williams, J., S. D. Goose, and M. Wareham, eds. 2008. *Banning Landmines: Disarmament, Citizen Diplomacy, and Human Security*. Lanham, MD: Rowman & Littlefield.

Wilson, D., and R. Purushothaman. 2003. "Dreaming with BRICS: The Path to 2050." Global Economics Paper 99. London: Goldman Sachs Group.

Wilton Park. 2010. "Public Diplomacy: Moving from Policy to Practice." 7–9 June. www.wiltonpark.org.uk/en/reports/?view=Report&id=22859434 (accessed 10 October 2010).

Wiseman, G. 1999. "'Polylateralism' and New Modes of Global Dialogue." Discussion Paper 59. Leicester: Diplomatic Studies Programme, November.

———. 2004. "'Polylateralism' and New Modes of Global Dialogue." In C. Jönsson and R. Langhorne, eds., *Diplomacy*. Vol. 3, *Problems and Issues in Contemporary Diplomacy*, 36–57. London: Sage.

———. 2005. "Pax Americana: Bumping into Diplomatic Culture." *International Studies Perspectives* 6 (4): 409–30.

———. 2007. "Esprit de Corps: Sketches of Diplomatic Life in Stockholm, Hanoi, and New York." In P. Sharp and G. Wiseman, eds., *The Diplomatic Corps as an Institution of International Society*, 246–64. Basingstoke: Palgrave Macmillan.

———. 2010. "'Polylateralism': Diplomacy's Third Dimension." *Public Diplomacy Magazine* 4 (Summer): 24–39.

———. 2011a. "Bringing Diplomacy Back In: Time for Theory to Catch Up with Practice." *International Studies Review* 13 (4): 689–92.

———. 2011b. "Norms and Diplomacy: The Diplomatic Underpinnings of Multilateralism." In J. P. Muldoon Jr., J. Fagot Aviel, R. Reitano, and E. Sullivan, eds., *The New Dynamics of Multilateralism: Diplomacy, International Organizations, and Global Governance*, 5–22. Boulder, CO: Westview Press.

Wiseman, G., and P. Sharp. 2012. "Diplomacy." In R. Devetak, A. Burke, and J. George, eds., *An Introduction to International Relations*, 256–67. 2nd ed. Cambridge: Cambridge University Press.

Woolcock, S. 2011. "Factors Shaping Economic Diplomacy: An Analytical Toolkit." In N. Bayne and S. Woolcock, eds., *The New Economic Diplomacy: Decision-Making and Negotiation in International Economic Relations*, 17–40. 3rd ed. Burlington, VT: Ashgate.

———. 2012. *European Union Economic Diplomacy: The Role of the EU in External Economic Relations*. Farnham: Ashgate.

World Intelligence HQ's, Google Maps. maps.google.pt/maps/ms?hl=pt-PT&ie=UTF8&msa=0&msid=102228811394544621996.0004821371c35c91cbd39&t=h&ll=51.897219,-2.12537&spn=101.222511,226.054688&z=2 (accessed 24 August 2010).

X. 1947. "The Sources of Soviet Conduct." *Foreign Affairs* 25 (4): 566–82.

Yakobson, L., and D. Knox. 2010. "New Foreign Policy Actors in China." SIPRI Policy Paper 26. Stockholm: Stockholm International Peace Research Institute, September.

Yang J. 2011. "Nuli kaichuang you zhongguo tese gonggong waijiao xin jumian" [Endeavor to Open a New Horizon of Public Diplomacy with Chinese Characteristics]. *Seeking Truth*, February: 43–46.

Ye, Z. 2003. *Zhongguo da zhanlue* [China's Grand Strategy]. Beijing: China Social Science Press.

Yoon, E. 2003. "The Growth of Environmental Cooperation in Northeast Asia: The Potential Roles of Civil Society." *Good Society* 12 (1): 46–51.

Yu, Y. S. 1967. *Trade and Expansion in Han China: A Study in the Structure of Sino-Barbarian Economic Relations*. Berkeley: University of California Press.

Yu, Z. 1994. "Yici buxunchang de shiming: Yi zhou zongli zuihou yici fangwen sulian" [An Unusual Mission: Premier Zhou's Last Visit to the Soviet Union]. In Waijiaobu Waijiaoshi Yanjiushi [Diplomatic History Research Office, the Ministry of Foreign Affairs], ed., *Xinzhongguo waijiao fengyun: Zhongguo waijiaoguan huiyilu* [Diplomatic Winds and Clouds of New China: Memoirs of the Chinese Diplomats], 10–25. Beijing: Shijie Zhishi Chuban She.

Yuzawa, T. 2006. "The Evolution of Preventive Diplomacy in the ASEAN Regional Forum: Problems and Prospects." *Asian Survey* 46 (5): 785–804.

Zakaria, F. 2011. *The Post-American World: Release 2.0*. New York: W. W. Norton.

Zartman, I. W. 1989. *Ripe for Resolution: Conflict and Intervention in Africa*, updated ed. New York: Oxford University Press.

———, ed. 1994. *International Multilateral Negotiation: Approaches to the Management of Complexity*. San Francisco: Jossey-Bass.

———, ed. 1995. *Elusive Peace: Negotiating an End to Civil Wars*. Washington, DC: Brookings Institution.

———. 1998. "An Apology Needs a Pledge." *New York Times*, 1 April.

———. 2000. "Ripeness: The Hurting Stalemate and Beyond." In P. C. Stern and D. Druckman, eds., *International Conflict Resolution after the Cold War*, 225–50. Washington, DC: National Academy Press.

———, ed. 2001. *Preventive Negotiation: Avoiding Conflict Escalation*. Lanham, MD: Rowman & Littlefield.

———. 2005. *Cowardly Lions: Missed Opportunities to Prevent Deadly Conflict and State Collapse*. Boulder, CO: Lynne Rienner.

———, ed. 2009. *Imbalance of Power: US Hegemony and International Order*. Boulder, CO: Lynne Rienner.

———. 2010. "Preventing Identity Conflicts Leading to Genocide and Mass Killings." New York: International Peace Institute. November.

Zartman, I. W., and T. Alfredson. 2010. "Negotiating with Terrorists and the Tactical Question." In R. Reuveny and W. R. Thompson, eds., *Coping with Terrorism: Origins,*

Escalation, Counterstrategies, and Responses, 247–86. Albany: State University of New York Press.

Zartman, I. W., M. Anstey, and P. Meerts, eds. 2011. *The Slippery Slope to Genocide: Reducing Identity Conflicts and Preventing Mass Murder*. New York: Oxford University Press.

Zartman, I. W., and G. O. Faure, eds. 2005. *Escalation and Negotiation in International Conflicts*. Cambridge: Cambridge University Press.

Zartman, I. W., and V. Kremenyuk, eds. 2005. *Peace versus Justice: Negotiating Forward- and Backward-Looking Outcomes*. Lanham, MD: Rowman & Littlefield.

Zartman, I. W., and S. Touval. 2007. "International Mediation." In C. A. Crocker, F. O. Hampson, and P. Aall, eds., *Leashing the Dogs of War: Conflict Management in a Divided World*, 437–54. Washington, DC: United States Institute of Peace.

Zhang, B. 2002. "Gaibian ziji, yingxiang shijie: Ershi shijie zhongguo waijiao jiben xiansuo zouyi" [Change Ourselves, Influence the World: An Outline of China's Diplomacy During the 20th Century]. *China Social Science* 1: 4–19.

Zhang, Q. 2009. "Liushi nianlai zhongguo waijiao buju de fazhan" [Sixty Years of Evolution in the Overall Arrangement of New China's Diplomacy]. *Foreign Affairs Review* 4: 33–43.

———. 2010. *China's Diplomacy*. Beijing: China International Press.

Zhang, Q., and Liu B. 2008. "Shounao chufang yu zhongguo waijiao" [Leadership Travel Abroad and China's Diplomacy]. *Guoji Zhengzhi Yanjiu* [International Politics Research] 2: 1–20.

Zhao, L. 2010. *Goujian hexie shijie de zhongyao shijian: Zhongguo canyu lianheguo weichi heping xingdong yanjiu* [Significant Practice of Building a Harmonious World: Research on China's Participation in UN Peace-Keeping Operations]. Beijing: CCP Central Party School Press.

Zhao, Q, 1996. *Interpreting Chinese Foreign Policy: The Micro-Macro Linkage Approach*. Oxford: Oxford University Press.

———. 2009. "Cong minjian waijiao dao gonggong waijiao" [From Civil Diplomacy to Public Diplomacy]. *People's Daily* (overseas edition), 9 October.

Zheng, B. 2007. *Zhengbijian zixuanji* [Zheng Bijian's Self Selected Works]. Beijing: Studies Press.

Zhou, E. 1990. *Zhou enlai waijiao wenxuan* [Selected Works of Zhou Enlai on Diplomacy]. Beijing: CCP Document Press.

Zourek, J. 1957. "Consular Intercourse and Immunities: Report by Jaroslav Zourek, Special Rapporteur." UN Document A/CN.4/108, *Yearbook of the International Law Commission 1957*, 2: 71–103. New York: United Nations.

———. 1960. "Consular Intercourse and Immunities: Second Report by Jaroslav Zourek, Special Rapporteur." UN Document A/CN.4/131, *Yearbook of the International Law Commission 1960*, 2: 2–32. New York: United Nations.

Index